THIS
INCOMPERABLE
LANDE

THIS
INCOMPERABLE
LANDE

❦

A Book of American
Nature Writing

Edited and with a history by
THOMAS J. LYON

HOUGHTON MIFFLIN COMPANY

BOSTON   1989

For information about permission to reproduce selections from
this book, write to Permissions, Houghton Mifflin Company,
2 Park Street, Boston, Massachusetts 02108.

Library of Congress Cataloging-in-Publication Data

This incomperable lande : a book of American nature writing / edited
and with a history by Thomas J. Lyon.
p.   cm.
Bibliography: p.
Includes index.
ISBN 0-395-48312-3
1. Nature.   2. Natural history—United States.   I. Lyon, Thomas
J. (Thomas Jefferson), date.
QH81.T355   1989   88-13451
508.73— dc19   CIP

Printed in the United States of America

V 10 9 8 7 6 5 4 3 2 1

"Of the Beasts That Live on the Land," "Beasts Living in the Water,"
and "Of the Birds and Fowls Both of Land and Water," by William Wood.
First published in *New England's Prospect* (1634). Reprinted from *New
England's Prospect*, ed. by Alden T. Vaughan (Amherst: University of
Massachusetts Press, 1977), by permission of the publisher. Copyright ©
1977 by The University of Massachusetts Press.

"Introduction" to the *Travels*, by William Bartram. First published in
the *Travels through North and South Carolina, Georgia, East and West Florida,
the Cherokee Country, the Extensive Territories of the Muscogulges, or Creek
Confederacy, and the Country of the Choctaws* (1791). Reprinted from *The
Travels of William Bartram*, ed. by Francis Harper (New Haven: Yale
University Press, 1958), by permission of the publisher. Copyright ©
1958 by Yale University Press.

"Wood Thrush," by Alexander Wilson. First published in *American
Ornithology* (Philadelphia: Bradford & Inskeep, 1808–1814).

"No. IX," from *Rambles of a Naturalist*, by John D. Godman. First
published in *The Friend* (1828). Reprinted from vol. 2 of *American Natural
History* (Philadelphia: R. W. Pomeroy, 1842).

"The Wood Thrush" and "The Great Pine Swamp," by John James
Audubon. First published in *Ornithological Biography* (Edinburgh: Adam
Black, 1831).

"Introduction," by Thomas Nuttall. First published in *A Manual of the
Ornithology of the United States and Canada* (Boston: Hilliard and Brown,
1832).

"March, 1854," from vol. 6 of the *Journal*, by Henry David Thoreau.
First published in *The Writings of Henry David Thoreau* (Boston: Houghton
Mifflin, 1906).

"Walking," by Henry David Thoreau. First published in *The Atlantic
Monthly* (June, 1862).

"Renegotiating the Contracts," by Barry Lopez. First published in *Parabola* 8 (Spring, 1983). Copyright © 1983 by Barry Lopez. Reprinted by permission of Sterling Lord Literistic, Inc.

"Custodians of Space," by John Hay. First published in *The Immortal Wilderness* (New York: Norton, 1987). Copyright © 1987 by John Hay. Reprinted by permission of the publisher.

. . . A man need not know how to name all the oaks or the moths, or be able to recognize a synclinal fault, or tell time by the stars, in order to possess Nature. He may have his mind solely on growing larkspurs, or he may love a boat and a sail and a blue-eyed day at sea. He may have a bent for making paths or banding birds, or he may be only an inveterate and curious walker.

But I contend that such a fellow has the best out of life—he and the naturalists. You are ignorant of life if you do not love it or some portion of it, just as it is, a shaft of light from a nearby star, a flash of the blue salt water that curls around the five upthrust rocks of the continents, a net of green leaves spread to catch the light and use it, and you, walking under the trees. You, a handful of supple earth and long white stones, with seawater running in your veins.

DONALD CULROSS PEATTIE,
An Almanac for Moderns, 1935

Contents

Bibliography

Preface

Earlier this year, I had the opportunity to see the special exhibition of the wildlife art of Robert Bateman at the National Museum of Natural History in Washington, D.C. His images stay with me still. In particular, the rendering of a "Coyote in Winter Sage" brought me to a long stand in front of it, in the midst of the swirling throngs of schoolchildren. The expression, the winter light that filled the painting, the detail, the absolute fidelity — everything conspired to demonstrate what can only be called fealty. The work was luminous with Bateman's respect for his subjects. In my eyes, this was more than beautiful; the paintings were worthy of the best resources one could possibly bring to them.

But I suspect that "wildlife realism" (or so I imagine Bateman's art may be categorized) does not rank terribly high in the world of art criticism. It isn't very subtle, I suppose, much less sophisticated; what you see is what you get. *Ah, but what you see.*

Looking at Bateman's work helped me to understand nature writing better. I saw an essential connection, I thought, in attitude, mind, allegiance — something going on at the heart, something that might render cosmopolitan criticism trivial. I had been immersed in the American nature essay, preparing this book, and while searching in the standard academic fashion for secondary sources, I had gradually come to realize that this literature does not command much attention in critical circles. For example, I found that the compendious and authoritative *Literary History of the United States,* published in 1948, makes no mention at all of the nature essay. I learned that even some students of nature writing tend to apologize for it: Wayne Hanley, for instance, began his 1977 anthology *Natural History in America* with the words, "This is not a profound volume,"[1] and Philip M. Hicks, in one of the few literary-critical studies on the subject, *The Development of the Natural History Essay in American Literature,* published in 1924, stated simply, "Great prose is not to be expected in the natural history field."[2] The apparent academic skepticism regarding nature writing was further reinforced in my mind by David Robertson's caution (in the introduction to his excellent 1984 study, *West of Eden: A History of the Art and Literature of Yosemite*) that devoting years of research to such an unfashionable topic was "to some extent, professionally risky."[3] Even outside academia, I discovered that Edward Abbey, author of several highly interesting books describing wild areas of the West, has pointedly wished not to be known solely as a nature writer.[4]

In short, a student of the literature of nature soon faces the fact that its status is secondary at best. But why? Perhaps the subjects — rocks, animals, weather, the look of the landscape, and so forth — are simply too obvious or easy. Edgar Allan Poe, in a critique of James Fenimore Cooper written a century and a half ago, stated that when the subject is life in the wilderness, success is "expected as a matter of course," while "failure might be properly regarded as conclusive evidence of imbecility on the part of the author."[5] More recently, the novelist Joyce Carol Oates has described nature writing as exhibiting "a painfully limited set of responses," which she sets forth all in capital letters to emphasize, perhaps, the headline-like simplicity she sees: "REVERENCE, AWE, PIETY, MYSTICAL ONENESS."[6]

Giving such criticisms their due, and they seem more or less just, as far as they go, I have come to think that the humble standing of nature writing is simply the corollary of our culture's preference for literature that focuses on humans and their personal and social lives. Possibly, nothing less than an entire cultural critique would be required to analyze such a predilection; this book, I hasten to say, is not such a critique. But I hope it may provide some materials for a re-evaluation, at least: an interpretation of the development of nature writing in this country, along with a revisionist estimate of that literature's significance; a gathering of several interesting and, I believe, important American nature essays, which will speak for themselves; and finally, an annotated booklist for readers who may want to go further.

Most of these materials emphasize in one way or another what seems to me the crucial point about nature writing, the awakening of perception to an ecological way of seeing. "Ecological" here is meant to characterize the capacity to notice pattern in nature, and community, and to recognize that the patterns observed ultimately radiate outward to include the human observer. This latter dimension may be the key, for it enables an ethical response. The "pattern which connects," in philosopher of ecology Gregory Bateson's phrase, carries with it enormous implications, including of necessity a transcendence, to some degree, of the isolated consciousness of self. The perception of pattern has been the moving spirit of American nature writing almost from the beginning; this is why it is inherently concerned with ethical questions. It is not primarily or exclusively concerned with self or strictly human society. The guardians of high culture may not approve, but now, as the literature itself amply records, the perception of inclusive pattern and the perhaps disturbing implications of such perception have strong corroboration from science. It may be that this body of literature will one day soon be looked at in a new and more complete way.

Not all nature writing, of course, is philosophical. Some of it seems merely to record facts of nature; some, at the other extreme, appears to be founded on impression or sentiment alone. I would argue, though, that just the turning of our attention to the natural world tends to subvert our anthropocentric heritage. The nature essay may even be seen as reflecting a general human stirring over the past two or three centuries, a movement in thinking toward what may be a great watershed. We may be on some sort of a halting journey toward understanding the world, and ourselves within it, as one system. No one, to my knowledge, has spoken of the "death of the nature essay."

I have limited this book to essays on natural history and experiences in nature, believing that in fiction and poetry, though there are often beautiful descriptions of nature, other themes and intentions tend to predominate. There is, to be sure, a most interesting gray area here: some works classified as novels, such as the "Adventures" series of "David Grayson" (Ray Stannard Baker), may be nature essays in light disguise, and many nature essays use fictional techniques of narration and characterization. Perhaps it would be more accurate to say that I have arbitrarily confined this book to materials I consider nonfictional. The selection is similarly limited to writings by the European-American "white man," though in Native American mythic narrative there is a strong sense of the power of nature, particularly the dignity and the respectability, in the literal sense, of animals. Indians were here, of course, long before there was an "America" (the entity Henry David Thoreau said he wanted to get out of his head, some part of every day, by walking into the woods and fields), and they led, according to the evidence, nature-embedded lives. For the Indian, as has often been noted, there was no wilderness here, in the sense of a dichotomous term opposed to "civilization." The literature covered in this book reveals, perhaps, something convergent to that native outlook developing, on the part of at least some of the newcomers of recent centuries. One of the strengths of American nature writing is its depiction of a growing psychic at-homeness.

I am greatly indebted to Annemarie Dietzgen, of Berkeley; Mardy Murie, of Moose, Wyoming; Lyn and Robert Paton, of Kelly, Wyoming; and Gary and Masa Snyder, of Kitkitdizze, California, for hospitality, for the use of their personal libraries, and for the opportunity to talk about nature writing. These good friends opened their homes to me. I thank too my colleagues Glenn R. Wilde and Patricia Gardner, of Utah State University, Glenn for leading me to sources in the agrarian literature, and Pat, head of the English Department, for services, materials, and accommodations too numerous to detail. At the University of California, I have been grateful for the efficiency and helpfulness of the staffs of the Bancroft Library and the Biology Library, and for a sponsorship to the Faculty Club kindly provided by James D. Hart, Director of the Bancroft Library. Constance Hatch and Suzan McBride of the Reference and Interlibrary Loan Department of the Merrill Library, Utah State University, gave me very special assistance, for which I thank them heartily. I am much obliged to Emily Jordan of Colorado State University for aid on some particularly obscure research. Max Lyon gave me helpful criticism, and Ernest Duncan, a special boost at a crucial time; and Barbara R. Stratton of Houghton Mifflin Company clarified the manuscript at several points; and I thank them too. Jack Turner called many sources to my attention and gave me the benefit of his good judgment on a number of points. My wife Janis has walked, read, and thought with me during the whole time of this study.

THOMAS J. LYON

August, 1987   Logan, Utah

PART I

A History

A Taxonomy of Nature Writing

" . . . this incomperable lande"
JEAN RIBAUT, *The Whole & True Discouerye*
of Terra Florida (London, 1563)

IF WE FIRST DESCRIBE nature writing in quasi-taxonomic terms, that in a general way can help us see what is important about the genre and how its themes are developed. I must introduce a cautionary note, though, before laying out a proposed classification scheme of American nature literature: the types I have listed tend to intergrade, and with great frequency. This may be somewhat irritating to lovers of neatness who would like their categories to be immutable, but nature writing is not in truth a neat and orderly field. Nevertheless, we can make a few sound and, I hope, helpful generalizations. First and most fundamentally, the literature of nature has three main dimensions to it: natural history information, personal responses to nature, and philosophical interpretation of nature. The relative weight or interplay of these three aspects determines all the permutations and categories within the field. If conveying information is almost the whole intention, for example (see the left edge of the spectrum in the chart on p. 4), the writing in question is likely to be a professional paper or a field guide or handbook, most of which are only intermittently personal or philosophical and also, perhaps, literary only in spots. A good example is Roger Tory Peterson's *A Field Guide to Western Birds* (1961). The brief description of the canyon wren's song, among other little gems in the book, immediately suggests something more than just accuracy. "Voice: A gushing cadence of clear curved notes tripping down the scale."[1] That single line may evoke the entire ambience of a shaded, slickrock canyon somewhere in the Southwest on a June morning. But few people would expect a field guide to be a literary effort.

Writing About Nature: A Spectrum

Field Guides and Professional Papers	Natural History Essays	Rambles	Essays on Experiences in Nature			
			Solitude and Back-Country Living	Travel and Adventure	Farm Life	Man's Role in Nature
Clarence King, *Systematic Geology* (1878)	John Muir, *Studies in the Sierra* (1874–1875)	John D. Godman, *Rambles of a Naturalist* (1828)	Henry David Thoreau, *Walden* (1854)	William Bartram, *Travels* (1791)	Hector St. John de Crèvecoeur, *Letters from an American Farmer* (1782)	John Burroughs, *Accepting the Universe* (1920)
Olaus Murie, *A Field Guide to Animal Tracks* (1954)	Rachel Carson, *The Sea Around Us* (1950)	John Burroughs, *Wake-Robin* (1871)	Henry Beston, *The Outermost House* (1928)	Henry David Thoreau, *The Maine Woods* (1865)	Liberty Hyde Bailey, *The Harvest of the Year to the Tiller of the Soil* (1927)	Joseph Wood Krutch, *The Great Chain of Life* (1956)
Roger Tory Peterson, *A Field Guide to Western Birds* (1961)	Ann Zwinger and Beatrice Willard, *The Land Above the Trees* (1972)	John K. Terres, *From Laurel Hill to Siler's Bog* (1969)	Sigurd F. Olson, *Listening Point* (1958)	Charles Sheldon, *The Wilderness of the Upper Yukon* (1911)		John Hay, *In Defense of Nature* (1969)
	John Hay, *Spirit of Survival* (1974)	Annie Dillard, *Pilgrim at Tinker Creek* (1974)	Edward Abbey, *Desert Solitaire* (1968)	Edward Hoagland, *Notes from the Century Before* (1969)	Wendell Berry, *A Continuous Harmony* (1972)	
				Barry Lopez, *Arctic Dreams* (1986)		

When expository descriptions of nature, still the dominant aspect of a book, are fitted into a literary design, so that the facts then give rise to some sort of meaning or interpretation, then we have the basic conditions for the natural history essay. The themes that make natural history information into a coherent, literary whole may be stated by the author in the first person, as in John Hay's *Spirit of Survival* (1974), where Hay found in the life histories of terns wonderfully cogent statements of the beauty and vulnerability of life itself — the life we share with these birds; or they may emerge from the facts as related in a third-person, more or less objective fashion. This latter way was Rachel Carson's choice in *The Sea Around Us* (1950, 1961); she arranged the facts of oceanography and marine biology tellingly, so that the drama and interplay of forces pointed inescapably toward a holistic, ecological view of nature. William O. Pruitt used a similar artistic strategy in *Animals of the North* (1967). By concentrating upon the central fact of the cold of the Arctic and showing the myriad adaptations such a climate requires, he brought out the theme of relationship, which is perhaps the essence of ecology.

The defining characteristic of the natural history essay is that whatever the method chosen for presentation, the main burden of the writing is to convey pointed instruction in the facts of nature. As we move toward the right on the spectrum, the role and relative importance of the author loom a bit larger: experience in nature — the feel of being outdoors, the pleasure of looking closely, and the sense of revelation in small things closely attended to — takes an equal or almost equal place with the facts themselves. Where the natural history and the author's presence are more or less balanced, we have the "ramble." This is a classic American form. The author goes forth into nature, usually on a short excursion near home, and records the walk as observer-participant. Almost the entire work of John Burroughs, to take a prominent example, fits into the category of the ramble, from his earliest published bird walks in *Wake-Robin* (1871). Burroughs's own personality and way of responding to the natural scene were very much a part of his writing and were important to his popular success. His intense feeling for the woods and fields of his home ground — there may never have been such a homebody, in all of American literature, as Burroughs — is also a distinguishing mark of the "ramble" type of nature writing. Burroughs became identified with the patchwork of farms and woods in the vicinity of the Catskill Mountains in New York. The writer of rambles usually does not travel far, and seldom to wilderness; he or she is primarily interested in a loving study of the near, and often the pastoral. To say that the ramble is local, however, or that it often takes place on worked-over ground, is not to imply that it is in any way superficial. As Annie Dillard showed in *Pilgrim at Tinker Creek* (1974), deep familiarity with the most ordinary landscapes can blossom into immense themes.

Continuing rightward on the spectrum, we begin to move away from the primacy of natural history facts to a clear emphasis on the writer's experience. In essays of experience, the author's first-hand contact with nature is the frame for the writing: putting up a cabin in the wilderness (as Richard Proenneke did, in *One Man's Wilderness*, 1973), canoeing down a clear, wild river (John McPhee, *Coming into the Country*, 1977), walking the beach at night (Henry Beston, *The*

Outermost House, 1928), rebuilding the soil of a rundown farm (Louis Bromfield, *Malabar Farm,* 1948), or contemplating a desert sunset (Edward Abbey, *Desert Solitaire,* 1968). And much else. Instruction in natural history is often present in the "nature experience" essay, but it is not what structures the book. We are placed behind the writer's eyes here, looking out on this interesting and vital world and moving through it with the protagonist.

Within the broad category of the essay of experience in nature, there are three fairly well-defined subtypes, each with a distinctive avenue for philosophical reflection. Essays of solitude or escape from the city, as might be expected, work much with the contrast between conventional existence and the more intense, more wakeful life in contact with nature. This subtype, like the ramble, is a classic American form, but it tends to be much more critical and radical — compare Thoreau at Walden, anathematizing the false economy of society, and Abbey in the desert, waiting until the engineers drive away in their jeep, then pulling up and throwing away the stakes they had pounded into the ground to mark the location for a new, paved road.

Accounts of travel and adventure (which usually have a strong element of solitude in them) often present the same sort of contrast between the too-safe, habituated existence left behind and the vivid life of discovery. The travel and adventure writer often seems like a ramble writer gone wild; there is less emphasis on natural history and more on movement, solitude, and wildness. Often, the account is framed on the great mythic pattern of departure, initiation, and return,[2] and always the account gains meaning from the basic American circumstance that wilderness, where the traveler and adventurer usually go, has always in our history been considered a realm apart. It is true that some travelers, such as William Bartram, have been deeply interested in the natural history of the new territories they explored: for example, in the *Travels* (1791), Bartram made extensive lists of the species he encountered. Nonetheless, the exhilaration of release from civilization, the sense of self-contained and self-reliant movement, and above all, the thrill of the new, are the prominent qualities here.

The farm essay, with its rooted and consistent emphasis upon stewardship and work (rather than study, or solitude, or discovery), may seem at first to be unrelated to the nature essay. It might be argued, too, that since farming is "only" about ten thousand years old, whereas our connections with wilderness are unimaginably deeper, the entire sensibility may be different. The sublime, so important to the aesthetic of the traveler, and even to the rambler, seems somehow foreign to the farm. But we should be alert to blend-ings. In practice, American farm writers from Hector St. John de Crèvecoeur in the late eighteenth century to Wendell Berry in the present day have paid close attention to the wildlife on and around their places, and have conveyed the deep, poetic pull of nature on the spirit. Berry, for example, describes how observing some birds at his family's land in Kentucky became instrumental in his development of a "placed" point of view. Stewardship, so prominent in farm lit-erature, also has ecological ramifications; the common understanding of American farm writers is that fitting into natural patterns, rather than imposing some sort of abstract order upon them, is the farmer's proper role. In this ethical commitment, nature writers with an agrar-ian point of view join with the mainstream philosophy of American nature writing.

On the right-hand edge of the spectrum are the analytic and com-prehensive works on man and nature. In these works, interpretation predominates, and the natural history facts or the personal experi-ences are decidedly secondary. They are illustrations for the argu-ment. Here, philosophy is all. The actual points that are made, typ-ically, are not different from those made in natural history essays, or personal-experience essays, but the mode of presentation tends to be more abstract and scholarly.

I need to add here that the usual terminology covering all of the forms of nature writing tends to lump them. They have all, at one time or another, been called "natural history essays" or "nature es-says" interchangeably. I see no real problem in this state of affairs, and not much practical benefit in any attempt to promote an academ-ically rigorous classification. Nature writing itself, in any case, would not rest easily in any static system, prizing as it does vitality and variety, the virtues of its subject. The categories offered here are meant simply to show the breadth of the spectrum and to help indicate some of the special powers each type within the genre may possess.

Whatever the artistic means chosen, and whatever the type of essay we may choose to call a certain piece of nature writing, the funda-mental goal of the genre is to turn our attention outward to the activity of nature. This is so, across the spectrum. The literary record time and again displays the claim that there is a lifting and a clarifying of perception inherent in this refocusing, which opens up something like a new world. The sense of wonder conveyed is perhaps very much in the American grain; it may eventually be seen as a more important discovery beyond the finding of new lands.

An American Chronology

1492 Columbus makes landfall in the Bahamas. "All is so green that it is a pleasure to gaze upon it."

1524 Giovanni Verrazzano, cruising the eastern coast of North America, stops in southern New England for two weeks, in present-day Rhode Island; goes inland and sees "champaigns [great meadows] twenty-five to thirty leagues in extent, open and without any impediment of trees. . . ."

1528 Cabeza de Vaca begins a journey across much of the Southwest; in eight years and something over 2,000 miles of wandering, he is out of sight of Indians for only a few days.

1539 Hernando De Soto begins his expedition into the Southeast. Accompanying him are 600 troops, 213 horses, a pack of fighting hounds, and 13 pigs, to be bred along the way as a source of food.

1542 De Soto dies on the banks of the Mississippi River; his share of the swine herd is reckoned at 700 animals.

1562 Jean Ribaut coasts along Florida and South Carolina, looking for a site for a dissenters' colony. He responds with joy to the abundance of wildlife.

1585 Thomas Heriot, member of a voyage to Virginia sponsored by Sir Walter Raleigh, makes observations in his "briefe and true report of the new found land of Virginia," cataloguing some of the prominent trees and wildlife species.

1622 Thomas Morton arrives in New England and makes a survey of natural resources.

1624 The first cattle ("three Heifers and a Bull," according to John Josselyn) are brought to New England.

1629 William Wood begins a four-year residence in New England; he keeps notes on trees, soil, wildlife, and Indian methods of land use.

1632 Thomas Morton's *New English Canaan* is published.

1634 William Wood's *New England's Prospect* is published.

1638 John Josselyn makes his first voyage to New England.

1649 According to Josselyn's chronology (published in 1672), "This year a strange multitude of caterpillars in New England."

1672 Josselyn's *New England's Rarities Discovered* is published. It includes a list of twenty-two weeds introduced into the New World by the Europeans, including dandelion and plantain.

1678 John Banister ("America's first resident naturalist," according to his biographer) arrives in Virginia; he begins collecting plants and insects and sending them back to England.

1691 In England, John Ray publishes *The Wisdom of God Manifested in the Works of Creation*, signaling a new, higher status for scientific nature study and promoting a non-anthropocentric view.

1709 John Lawson, a surveyor, publishes *A New Voyage to Carolina*, which has been described as "the first major attempt at a natural history of the New World."

1712 Mark Catesby arrives in Virginia from England and begins a seven-year visit to the colonies.

1718 Massachusetts declares a three-year moratorium on deer hunting.

1722 Catesby begins a four-year study of the natural history of Carolina, Florida, and the Bahamas, including expeditions to areas uninhabited by Europeans.

1731 Catesby, having returned to England, begins serial publication of *The Natural History of Carolina, Florida, and the Bahama Islands*. The artistic quality is praised, and the natural history accounts are regarded as the most detailed and comprehensive attempted to date in the colonies.

1734 John Bartram of Pennsylvania (William Bartram's father — see p. 36) begins collecting plants for his English patron Peter Collinson.

1735 The Swedish naturalist Linnaeus publishes *Systema Naturae*, rationalizing the nomenclature of natural history and stimulating its study.

1743 Benjamin Franklin proposes the organization of the American Philosophical Society, saying that "the first drudgery of settling new colonies" is now "pretty well over," leaving leisure for the pursuit of knowledge.

1748 Peter Kalm, one of Linnaeus's best pupils, begins his travels in the colonies, making extensive natural history notes over the next two and a half years.

1749 Pennsylvania pays bounties on 640,000 gray squirrels.

1755 John Bartram proposes a geological map of the colonies. By systematic "borings" into the earth, he suggests, "we may compose a curious subterranean map."

1759 William Bartram (John's son) writes to the British ornithologist George Edwards that "many animals, which abounded formerly in settled parts, are now no more to be found, but retire to the unsettled border of the province; and that some birds, never known to early settlers, now appear in great numbers, and much annoy their corn-fields and plantations."

1773 William Bartram begins four years of travel into the wilds of the Southeast.

1782 Crèvecoeur publishes *Letters from an American Farmer* in London, an evocative appreciation of rural life, nature, and America.

1784 Thomas Jefferson's *Notes on the State of Virginia* is published in Paris. It includes natural history information and dismisses certain theories of the Comte de Buffon (see p. 36) on New World animals.

1790 The first United States Census records a population of 3,929,214.

1791 William Bartram's *Travels* is published to lukewarm reviews, but several British and European editions and translations follow.

1794 Samuel Williams, a Rutland minister, publishes *A Natural and Civil History of Vermont*.

1799 The last bison in the East is killed, in Pennsylvania.

1802 Alexander Wilson, who had arrived in America in 1794, begins his study of American birds.

1803 John James Audubon, eighteen, arrives in Pennsylvania.

1804 Lewis and Clark begin their expedition to the Pacific with thirty men; on the way, they will collect several hundred specimens of western flora and fauna.

1807 Cedar waxwings sell for twenty-five cents a dozen in Philadelphia meat markets.

1808 Thomas Nuttall arrives in Philadelphia; he begins botanizing the day after his arrival.
      William Maclure completes the first geological survey of the United States.
      Volume 1 of Alexander Wilson's *American Ornithology* is published; when complete in 1814, the study fills nine volumes and covers 260 species, in prose both precise and affecting.

1821 *A Journal of Travels into the Arkansa Territory, During the Year 1819,* by Thomas Nuttall, is published.

1825 The Erie Canal opens, facilitating midwestern and Great Lakes development.

1826 John D. Godman's *American Natural History*, a text with a progressive view of predation, is published.

1829 The first locomotive in America proves too heavy for the tracks during a trial run in Pennsylvania.

1831 John James Audubon commences publication of the *Ornithological Biography*, which includes essays on American scenes and citizens.

1832 Thomas Nuttall's *Manual of the Ornithology of the United States and Canada*, a handbook that will be in use throughout the nineteenth century, is published.

1834 Nuttall crosses the continent in company with a commercial expedition; the natural history studies he undertakes in California in 1835 are the first conducted there by an American. The last elk in the Adirondacks is killed.

1836 Ralph Waldo Emerson publishes his immensely influential *Nature*.

1841 The artist George Catlin, after a venture into the western wilderness, proposes a *"nation's Park."*

1845 On July 4, Henry David Thoreau moves into the "tight shingled and plastered" 10′ × 15′ house he had built at Walden Pond for $28.12½.

1849 The Gold Rush begins the rapid transformation of much of the accessible California landscape.
      John Muir's father brings his young family from Scotland to wild Wisconsin, and begins clearing land for a farm.

1851 Henry David Thoreau delivers his lecture on "The Wild" for the first time.

1854 Henry David Thoreau's *Walden* is published.

1859 In England, Charles Darwin publishes *The Origin of Species*.

1860 The population of the United States is 31,443,321.
      United States railroad tracks total 30,000 miles.

1862 Henry David Thoreau dies. His last words are " . . . moose . . . Indian."

1864 George Perkins Marsh publishes *Man and Nature*, a study of the decline of cultures following the abuse of their environment.

1867 Alaska is purchased.
      The last elk in Pennsylvania is killed.

1869 John Wesley Powell, with a crew of nine men in four boats, descends the Green and Colorado rivers. On his explorations of the West, Powell describes the Escalante and the Henry

Mountains (both in Utah Territory), the last river and mountain range to be discovered.

In this year of the "Golden Spike," American locomotives are estimated to have burned 19,000 cords of wood per day.

John Muir spends his first summer in the Sierra.

1871   John Burroughs' first book of nature essays, *Wake-Robin,* is published.

1872   Yellowstone National Park, the first such reserve in the world, is established.

From this year to 1883, the last bison hunts are conducted, in something very like frenzy: "never before in all history were so many large wild animals of one species slain in so short a space of time" (Theodore Roosevelt).

1878   Barbed wire comes to Texas.

The last Labrador duck is killed on December 12, on Long Island.

1882   Clarence Dutton's *Tertiary History of the Grand Cañon District* is published.

1883   The gasoline engine is developed.

1890   The United States Census Bureau declares the frontier closed.

Yosemite National Park is created, drawn on boundaries suggested by John Muir.

The population of the United States is 62,947,714.

1893   Frederick Jackson Turner delivers his influential thesis, "The Significance of the Frontier in American History."

1894   The last pair of wild whooping cranes to have nested in the United States is seen at a marsh near Eagle Lake, Iowa.

John Muir's first book, *The Mountains of California,* is published.

1900   On March 24, the last passenger pigeon to be seen in the wild is killed at Sargents, Ohio.

1901   John C. Van Dyke's *The Desert* is published.

1903   The "nature-fakers" controversy (see p. 66) begins with an article by John Burroughs attacking anthropomorphism.

The nation's first federal wildlife refuge is created, in Florida.

Mary Austin's first book, *The Land of Little Rain,* is published.

1904   The last Carolina parakeet is seen in the wild.

The American chestnut blight breaks out in the Brooklyn Botanical Garden following an importation of Oriental plants, and quickly spreads.

1906   *The Writings of Henry David Thoreau* are published, in twenty volumes.

The United States Forest Service is established.

1911   Enos Mills' *The Spell of the Rockies,* one of the comparatively small number of natural history books from that region, is published.

1914   The last passenger pigeon dies in the Cincinnati Zoo.

1915   Liberty Hyde Bailey publishes *The Holy Earth,* a radical agrarian text.

1916   The National Park Service is established.

1920   John Burroughs' *Accepting the Universe* is published.
Rockwell Kent's *Wilderness* is published.

1921   John Burroughs dies on a train somewhere in Ohio. His last words are "How far are we from home?"

1924   The first wilderness reserve within a National Forest is established in New Mexico, in part due to the efforts of Aldo Leopold.

1925   The last cougar in Yellowstone to be killed in the Park Service's "control" program is dispatched.

1928   Henry Beston's *The Outermost House* is published.

1930   The population of the United States is 122,775,046.

1932   The last heath hen is seen on Martha's Vineyard, Massachusetts.

1934   Hawk Mountain, Pennsylvania, a ridge on a noted raptor migration route, is leased by conservationists, and two wardens are hired.
Over this year and the next, predator control within Yellowstone National Park comes to an end.

1935   Donald Culross Peattie's *Almanac for Moderns* is published.

1938   Hawk Mountain, Pennsylvania, is purchased by conservationists and becomes the world's first sanctuary for birds of prey.

1939   In Mount McKinley National Park, Adolph Murie begins the first scientific study of wolf behavior in the wild.

1944   Sally Carrighar's *One Day on Beetle Rock* is published.
Adolph Murie's *The Wolves of Mount McKinley* is published.

1948   Fairfield Osborn's *Our Plundered Planet,* one of the first post-World War II environmental alarm calls, is published.

1949   Aldo Leopold's *Sand County Almanac* is published.
J. Frank Dobie's *The Voice of the Coyote* is published.

1951   *The Sea Around Us,* by Rachel Carson, is published; the book becomes a major best seller.
Edwin Way Teale's *North with the Spring,* the first of the "American Seasons" series, is published.

1954   *The Voice of the Desert,* by Joseph Wood Krutch, is published.

1956   Robert Marshall's *Arctic Wilderness* is published.

1959   Peter Matthiessen's *Wildlife in America,* a comprehensive history of extinctions and protective measures, is published.

1960   John Graves' *Goodbye to a River* is published.

1962   Rachel Carson's *Silent Spring* is published; the book inaugurates a new era of environmental concern.

Margaret Murie's *Two in the Far North* is published; the final section directs attention to Alaskan wilderness concerns.

1964   The Wilderness Act, establishing a National Wilderness Preservation System, becomes law after eight years of legislative struggle. By 1986, 3.78 percent of the United States is under protection as legal wilderness, with more than half of that located in Alaska.

1967   Roderick Nash's *Wilderness and the American Mind* is published, helping to establish wilderness as a field for historical scholarship.

1968   Edward Abbey's *Desert Solitaire* is published.

The National Wild and Scenic Rivers System is created. By 1986, 72 rivers or parts of rivers are included, totaling somewhat more than 7,000 miles of flowing water, out of 356,000 possible within the United States.

1969   A notable year for the literature of nature: Wendell Berry's *The Long-Legged House,* John Hay's *In Defense of Nature,* Edward Hoagland's *Notes from the Century Before,* Josephine Johnson's *The Inland Island,* Gary Snyder's *Earth House Hold,* and John and Mildred Teal's *Life and Death of the Salt Marsh* are published.

1970   On January 1 the National Environmental Policy Act of 1969 becomes law, mandating consideration of the environment before any major federal action is taken.

The first "Earth Day" is celebrated, heightening public awareness of environmental issues.

The Clean Air Act of 1970 establishes nondegradation of existing clean air as a principle, and for the first time requires the states to attain air quality of specified standards within a specified time.

1972   The Federal Water Pollution Control Act of 1972 becomes law, establishing regulatory programs.

1973   The Endangered Species Act becomes law, requiring both protection of listed species and recovery programs.

1974   Annie Dillard's *Pilgrim at Tinker Creek* is published.

1977   Wendell Berry's *The Unsettling of America* is published.

1978   *Of Wolves and Men,* by Barry Lopez, is published.

Peter Matthiessen's *The Snow Leopard* is published.

1980   Paul Brooks publishes *Speaking for Nature*.
        The Alaska National Interest Lands Conservation Act be-
        comes law, increasing by nearly four times the size of the
        National Wilderness Preservation System and more than dou-
        bling the size of the National Park and National Wildlife Ref-
        uge systems.
        The population of the United States is 226,504,825.
1982   Paul Shepard's *Nature and Madness* is published.
1984   The National Academy of Sciences reports that approximately
        53,500 synthetic chemicals are in use in the United States.
        Fourteen percent of these have been tested sufficiently to
        allow a partial hazard assessment.
1985   In *An Environmental Agenda for the Future,* the chief executive
        officers of the ten largest American environmental organiza-
        tions write, "Continued economic growth is essential."
1986   *Arctic Dreams,* by Barry Lopez, is published.
1987   As part of a captive breeding program, the last wild California
        condor is captured and taken to the San Diego Zoo.
        John Hay's *The Immortal Wilderness* is published.

❧ 3 ❧

The American Setting

THE FIRST AND GREATEST INFLUENCE on nature writing, of course, is the land itself. The major temperate ecosystems are represented beautifully in America, and the sheer variety is staggering. Just to name a few of the places that have inspired excellent nature writing is to get the sense of an amazing range of possibilities for experience: Cape Cod, that spare and vivid arm of land crooking out into the North Atlantic; the richly mulched eastern deciduous forest, pealing with the songs of thrushes; the bright green of the Florida peninsula, where William Bartram derived a vision of paradise unspoiled; the plains and prairies, over which massed and rumbled one of the world's primary symbols of wild abundance, the bison; the wide, still deserts of the Southwest, with their daunting and exhilarating space; sublime, sacred Yosemite; and the Grand Canyon, of which so much has been written, although almost every writer at last has declared in despair the inadequacy of words.

What seems to have made the deepest — indeed, indelible — impression, on both explorers and settlers in the beginning, was simply the morning freshness of the continent. The New World, as they called it, was ecologically intact, and exuded the beauty of health. We did not come to an abused land. We can now see that the fact that a continent which had been occupied for many thousands of years appeared, to European eyes, as the quintessence of virgin nature is a tribute of the highest order to America's native inhabitants, but the point, for our literature and perhaps indeed for our whole American sense of the world, was that wild freshness. What it offered to us was a chance for renewal.

The French Huguenot sailor Jean Ribaut, looking over coastal South Carolina in 1562 with a colony for dissenters in mind, responded to the unspoiled landscape so strongly that his account, written almost a year afterward and not in his native tongue, still sings:

. . . on the other side, [we] enterd and veued the cuntry therabowte, which is the fairest, frutefullest and plesantest of all the worlde, habonding in honney, veneson, wildfoule, forrests, woodes of all sortes, palme trees, cipers, ceders, bayes, the hiest, greatest and fairest vynes in all the wourld with grapes accordingly, which naturally and without mans helpe and tryining growe to the top of the okes and other trees that be of a wonderfull greatnes and height. And the sight of the faire medowes is a pleasure not able to be expressed with tonge, full of herons, corleux, bitters, mallardes, egertes, woodkockes, and of all other kinde of smale birdes with hartes, hyndes, buckes, wild swyne, and sondery other wild beastes as we perceved well bothe then by there foteing there and also afterwardes in other places by ther crye and brayeng which we herde in the night tyme. Also there be cunys, hares, guynia cockes in mervelus numbre, a great dele fairer and better then be oures, silke wormes, and to be shorte it is a thinge inspeakable, the comodities that be sene there and shal be founde more and more in this incomperable lande, never as yet broken with plowe irons, bringing fourthe all thinges according to his first nature, whereof the eternall God endued yt.[1]

The discoverer's note of rejuvenation sounds again and again in American nature literature, even to the present day when the official wilderness area is a remnant that has to stand for the world in its once and former wholeness. Coming upon an abundance of wild animals or birds, or a sweep of rugged country with not a mark of diminishment on it — experiences described in the works of Robert Marshall and Barry Lopez, to name just two representative figures from recent times — may bring a shock of recognition, a sense of re-entering a world greater and older than anything dominated by humans. The mind, as if suddenly given back its accustomed scope, becomes alert to the moment.

But the history we have created here as a culture quite obviously does not reflect this inner, new life as anything more than a minority response. We have not, in the main, been so alive to the country. No doubt there are many reasons for our comparative numbness; in what follows I propose just one speculation, attempting to focus on what it might be that distances and dulls perception so pervasively that in order to see the world as new and living we have to be hit over the head, as it were, with pure wilderness.

The great traditions of Western civilization that stand behind our history, identified succinctly by Matthew Arnold as "Hebraism" and "Hellenism," are traditions of a powerfully dualistic cast, both philosophically and psychologically, tending to enforce the separation of mind from matter, self from surroundings, and man from nature.

Both the Christian and rationalist influences deriving from Hebraism and Hellenism promote a centralized, isolated sense of identity for the individual and for man in general. The Christian concept of man as a special creation and the Aristotelian concept of reason as the best and distinguishing part of man alike foster egoism and its collective form, anthropocentrism. This is not to "blame" Christianity and the Greek inheritance; they no doubt merely embody human predispositions of much earlier origin. The sense of self as a separate and distinct entity, that sense which seems to place nature at a distance, may indeed trace all the way back to one of the innate features of human consciousness, the ability to perceive objects in one-at-a-time, sequential fashion. This ability may give rise to a certain logic: if there is a world of separate and distinct objects out there, then in here, behind these eyes, there must be a likewise distinct entity — a subject. Every moment of perception on the one-at-a-time basis generates anew the consciousness of "I" or "ego." The other givens of human consciousness, especially the sense of the world that Freud referred to (rather scornfully) as the "oceanic," seem to decline in use before the persuasiveness of the egoistic vision. Again, to state the obvious, there should be no particular fault or blame declared here — clearly, the universe grew the human ego just as naturally as it grew columbines and wood thrushes.

It seems equally clear from the historical record, however, that the Mediterranean and European culture known to the world as Western civilization has put a sharp point, in effect, on the egoistic sense of life. The perceived distinctiveness of the individual self, and man's separateness from the rest of the world, were given what amounted to cosmic sanction in Christianity's theology of special creation. As success reinforced the Western mentality, particularly during the great period of European expansion from the sixteenth through the nineteenth centuries, a certain heedlessness also became characteristic.

There are two consequences of the dominant Western view of the world that have had particular impact on the American context, both on the land itself and on the intellectual and moral climate of this country. One is that egoism tends to inspire the expansionist behavior associated with "the frontier": the logic in this case seems to be that from a perceived position of isolation, the ego, or identity, needs to secure itself, but that each success at creating security only enlarges the zone needing security. The other consequence is that the one-at-a-time mind does not see context and relation very well, and thus tends not to notice the "side" effects of its activities, overlooking information that could urge self-restraint. The "frontier" mind does not perceive things as an ecological whole. Working from the commanding need to secure itself, a task that has a strong, innate tendency to grow and keep growing, the frontier mind becomes preoccupied with use. From this narrowed outlook, nature consists merely of "natural resources." The focus on utility not only seems to hinder perception of basic, practical relations — between forest clearing and the drying up of springs, for example — but also to limit the possibility of empathy. In America, the cutting and burning of the largest deciduous forest on earth proceeded rapidly and without notable hindrance on either practical or ethical grounds. The expropriation and indeed extirpation of the native inhabitants over much of their territory was accomplished with few serious objections; the extermination of the most magnificent assemblage of birds, the passenger pigeons, and the near extinction of the most astounding assemblage of large herbivores, the bison, were, so the records seem to show, largely matters to which most Americans were indifferent, on an ethical level. What happened, in essence, was that a people with a strong tradition of righteousness carried off an invasion of "the frontier" with remarkable success and little apparent reflection.

Within such a history, naturalists and nature writers make up a distinctly nonconforming, even heretical minority. The principal cultural heresy expressed in American nature writing is the refocusing of vision outward from the self, individually, and from the corporate self, our species. A radical proposal follows on the widened vision: that the environment, nature, is the ground of a positive and sufficient human joy. Nature writers and naturalists do not appear to have conceptualized America as "a vast body of wealth without proprietors," in the phrase of one student of the frontier period;[2] on the contrary, they very often recognized the priority of the Indians' claims and sympathized with them. John Lawson (who, ironically, was killed by Indians), William Bartram, Henry David Thoreau, Mary Austin, and Bob Marshall are a few of those who shared this concern. Though some naturalists, to be sure, pursued the morally anomalous practice of "collecting," that is, killing animals for specimens, well into the twentieth century, no one in this group took part in the casual slaughter of wildlife.

It is probably not coincidental that the nature essay developed as a distinct genre only toward the close of the eighteenth century, after the Romantic movement in philosophy and literature had helped give the individual experience of nature, in all its intuitive and emotional vagueness yet penetrating insight, some credibility and standing. Many of the values seen in nature writing are shared with Romanticism: affirmation of the world as congenial to man, in essence; skepticism toward purely rationalistic (that is, logical and sequential, as opposed to intuitive) thought; scorn for materialism; love for what is spontaneous, fecund, and life-giving; and a predilection for the simple and primitive.

But nature writing is not simply Romantic; it also owes much to science, both in its use of the empirical findings of scientists and in its incorporation, over more than two hundred years, of scientific theories. Edgar Allan Poe, who perhaps is representative of many Romantic thinkers, complained of science's demystification of the world, but Henry David Thoreau stated clearly the accommodating attitude of most nature essayists: "Let us not underrate the value of a fact," he wrote; "it will one day flower in a truth."[3] Nature writers have been inveterate and important synthesizers, indeed, from the time of the early "Argument from Design" (the proof of God's wisdom and beneficence as shown by the intricate workings of nature) through the Darwinian revolution, seeking always to express the possible meanings and implications of new data. John Muir, for example, working in the very early years of the science of glaciology, made painstaking studies of moraines and striations and "erratic" boulders in the Sierra Nevada, discovered sixty-odd small, active glaciers high in the range, placed stakes in some of them to measure their movement, and organized all of his findings into a narrative of the mountains' glacial history. Then he went the crucial step further and described the work of the glaciers as only one element in a grand evolutionary process, a process that, for Muir, expressed the divine activity. For Muir, there was no conflict between science and religion in the highest, nonsectarian sense; any new scientific finding simply filled in the sacred pattern a little more completely.

Muir's synthesis may be instructive. It happens that some of the most important scientific discoveries of the last two centuries, the evidence for ecological relationship and evolutionary change (as opposed to the old theories of immutable entities — species — walking across stagelike settings) are remarkably consonant with the intuitive and experiential theory of holism espoused by many Romantics and transcendentalists. The Romantic listens to the heart and hears that it beats in profound cooperation with all else; the follower of the scientific method sees in nature undeniable evidence of relationships and symbioses, patterns strongly suggesting the inadequacy of any theory based upon separate entities. There is a true convergence here. But of course not all nature writers share John Muir's ultimate confidence in the divine pattern, or even see pattern as necessarily divine. The important point demonstrated in the literature of nature since late in the eighteenth century is that the experience and detailed study of nature may both lead toward an ecological understanding of the world.

In the eighteenth century and through much of the nineteenth, the enlarged scope of scientific attention retained a theistic or deistic premise. What science was building then, as many thought, was a conclusive Argument from Design; indeed, it was on just such a basis that science had entered mainstream Christian culture, showing that the marvels of nature — the circulation of the blood, the movements of the planets, the incredibly intricate lives of social insects, for example — were further evidence of the omniscience of the Deity, making Him, in our awakening eyes, all the more worthy of awe and worship. William Bartram's view was typical of this period: "Perhaps there is not any part of creation, within the reach of our observations, which exhibits a more glorious display of the Almighty hand, than the vegetable world. . . . The animal creation also, excites our admiration, and equally manifests the almighty power, wisdom and beneficence of the Supreme Creator and Sovereign Lord of the universe. . . . "[4]

The ability to see pattern, and thus, for many, to see the "Almighty hand" as William Bartram did, was considerably enhanced in the eighteenth century by the development of a logical system of classification for the world's flora and fauna. The major figure in this endeavor was the Swedish systematist Linnaeus, whose arrangement of class, order, genus, and species, with the species itself to be known by just two Latin names, not only made a disciplined approach to nature study possible (and possible even for the layman, an important point), but also focused attention upon likenesses and thus upon pattern in nature. Plants and animals began to sort out into recognizable groupings and possible lines of descent — though the mechanism for any such descent was as yet undiscovered. The logical categorization of nature increased the likelihood of seeing relationships of all kinds, and it is no exaggeration to say that Darwin, and indeed all subsequent investigators into evolution, stood on the shoulders of Linnaeus. The debt remained even though Linnaeus's particular arrangement was later supplanted.

With the Darwinian revolution in the mid- and late nineteenth century, the theistic or deistic premise of science began to be replaced by a naturalistic approach. John Muir, who can be seen as a transitional figure, is instructive. Writing in the late nineteenth and early twentieth centuries, Muir used the term "God" freely, but with a more diffuse reference, apparently, than William Bartram intended when he spoke of his "Supreme Creator." Muir accepted much of the theory of evolution and natural selection, though he balked at the "struggle for existence," as he said. He preferred to see the elements of the world as a partnership, with God representing more of a divine principle synonymous with the whole than a separate, transcendent Creator.

Most nature writers in the twentieth century have been rather quiet on the subject of deity, according well with the temper of the time, perhaps, but they have without exception maintained a reverential attitude toward nature. Oneness with nature, awe, and the spiritually potent deepening of consciousness beyond the egoistic level brought about by intimacy with an environment remain prominent. So strong are these elements, and so closely linked with the emotion of joy, that nature writing, unlike other genres, did not decline into pessimism or determinism with the so-called "death of God," nor with the ominous development of the modern urban-industrial state. Instead, nature writers have simply become more militant critics of urbanization and industrialization, while maintaining, in the great majority, a consistently affirmative vision.

Besides incorporating great intellectual currents, nature writing in America has also responded to actual historical conditions, in particular the decline of environmental quality, as the country was settled and relentlessly developed. The nation's fall from pristine wholeness burned itself into the mind of nature writers, so resplendent had been the original sightings and reports. John Josselyn, an early student of natural history, noted that between 1638 and 1663, wild turkeys, formerly abundant, had been virtually eliminated from seaboard Massachusetts, and the Swedish visitor Peter Kalm, in the mid-eighteenth century, was alarmed at the profligacy with which Americans treated valuable woodlands. A century later, Henry David Thoreau lamented that the environment he and his generation had been bequeathed was like a book with pages missing, and Wilson Flagg, a near-contemporary of Thoreau's, looked with sorrow upon the importation of modern, citified tastes and modern farming methods into the rural landscape of New England; he made a plea for a modified kind of wilderness preservation as at least a partial corrective to the rush of progress. In the twentieth century, as an already large American population continues to grow and make use of an extraordinary energy subsidy from fossil fuels, to the detriment of the environment, contemporary nature writers continue to take pained note of losses, and more than a few have expressed denunciation. From about the time of World War II, nature writers have mounted detailed critiques and proposed specific corrective measures for environmental outrages: John Graves's portion of *The Water Hustlers* (1971), Edward Abbey's fiery "The Second Rape of the West" in *The Journey Home* (1977), and Barry Lopez's somber account of the American campaigns against wolves in *Of Wolves and Men* (1978) are good examples. Perhaps the most effective critique in the modern era has been Rachel Carson's *Silent Spring* (1962), a supremely careful, even understated thesis against the careless and excessive use of chemical pesticides and herbicides. This book declared, as Paul Brooks has written in *Speaking for Nature* (1980), "the basic responsibility of an industrialized, technological society toward the natural world";[5] its influence on the environmental awakening of the 1960s and 1970s, and upon public policy to some degree, is unquestioned.

In almost every practical aspect, we in the late twentieth century live in a world that would certainly amaze and perhaps dishearten someone as close to us in time as Henry David Thoreau. We have lost a great deal, in just the time since he compared the natural America he inherited to a damaged volume: many rivers, formerly free-flowing; many valuable wetlands;[6] many old-growth forests; and much plain open space and possibility. And we have set in motion trains of cause and effect — notably those arising from the broad-scale use of toxic chemicals and the burning of coal and oil — whose consequences may be enormous and are almost certain to be negative. In addition to having wrought deep changes in our natural surroundings, we have used our mechanical advantage to construct, in the century or so of the oil-powered industrial age, a radically more insulated life than was possible in Thoreau's time. It is highly interesting, a mark perhaps of the true complexity of the American character, that natural history study, and nature writing, persist and perhaps even gain in influence.

Our literature of nature owes a great deal of its content and development, and its currency now, to the major contributions of Romanticism and science. And it has always been morally alive to the circumstances of its environmental moment. But in the end, the deepest influence, the inner life of the nature essay, is still the writer's response to the land itself. In the face of all that has happened, in a modern nation where pavement is now said to occupy as much territory as protected wilderness, the setting that F. Scott Fitzgerald described so memorably as the "fresh green breast of the new world" continues in mythic potency to generate profound allegiance and durable affirmation.

❦ 4 ❧

Beginnings

THE MODERN PERSONAL ESSAY began with Michel de Montaigne's *Essais* in 1580, but more than two centuries would pass before the *nature* essay emerged as a literary form. When the two great eighteenth-century revolutions in natural philosophy had progressed far enough that both the response of an individual to nature and the role of nature in revealing God were legitimized, the preconditions for nature writing were in place. There also had to be sufficient knowledge of natural history, of course, and this was being provided by the tremendous growth in field observation taking place during the Enlightenment period. In England, as the first sign that the times were ripe for nature writing, we have the Reverend Gilbert White's *A Natural History of Selborne* (1789), a text much read in America; and in this country, writings by Thomas Jefferson and Hector St. John de Crèvecoeur in the 1780s. When William Bartram published his *Travels* in 1791, he became the first American nature essayist.

But though there were no formally or philosophically realized essays before the late Revolutionary period, there were attempts at cataloguing American nature, and frequent responses to its pristine beauty; these remain interesting in their own right and often presage a great deal. Early travelers to the New World and some colonists had the incomparable fortune to see America in its aboriginal state. Their accounts, naive and sometimes relatively innocent of scientific knowledge as they may be, and even at times looking over the shoulder of the country, as it were, toward some other goal, have the undeniable strength of priority.

The earliest visitors to North America, by and large, were preoccupied with gold-seeking or market-seeking or European power politics, or simply survival, but they often made interesting observations, and some of these have proved useful to later ecological historians. Giovanni Verrazzano's description of Rhode Island in 1524, for example, mentions "champaigns [meadows] twenty-five to thirty leagues [seventy-five to ninety miles] in extent . . . without any . . . trees," and this has helped to challenge the image of the tangled eastern forest.[1] Even explorers who were caught up in more pressing concerns made appreciative remarks. Christopher Columbus, for example, wrote in his journal for October 15, 1492, "These islands are very green and fertile and the breezes are very soft, and it is possible that there are in them many things, of which I do not know, because I did not wish to delay in finding gold, by discovering and going about many islands." Six days later the commander wrote wistfully, "The singing of little birds is such that it seems that a man could never wish to leave this place."[2] (Leave he did, though.)

In the sixteenth century, we have Jacques Cartier's pleased amazement at the multitudes of seabirds frequenting the islands in the Gulf of St. Lawrence (1534); Alvar Nuñez Cabeza de Vaca's rather vague account of bison, seen during his eight-year struggle to cross the Southwest (1528–1536), which was the first description of this animal to reach Europe; and Coronado's sighting of huge herds of bison in 1540, probably somewhere in modern Kansas. Often in the early accounts, the authentic note of freshness is heard — for instance, the innocent vagueness in Thomas Heriot's description of the wildlife of the outer banks and near shore of North Carolina. Though Heriot was known as a man of wide learning in natural history, a "scientist" in the terms of his time, his report of 1585 is revealingly brief and poised at the very moment of discovery: "I have the names of eight and twenty severall sorts of beasts, which I have heard of to be here and there dispersed in the countrey, especially in the maine: of which there are only twelve kinds that we have yet discovered; and of those that be good meat we know only them before mentioned."[3]

The first extended descriptions of North American nature come out of New England in the 1630s. The two most valuable early accounts, Thomas Morton's *New English Canaan* (1632) and William Wood's *New England's Prospect* (1634), showed a lively interest in wildlife, the environment in general, and Indians. (It seemed natural for Europeans, at one time, to describe Indians under the heading of natural history.) In the case of Morton, whom we remember now for "Merrymount," the interest in wildlife seems to have been mainly gustatory. With an apparent pleasure reminiscent of the Elizabethan tone, he was sure to note in his lists of birds and animals which ones tasted best: "Teales, there are of two sorts greene winged and blew winged: but a dainty bird. I have bin much delighted with a rost of these for a second course. . . ."[4] The wild turkeys likewise pleased this gentleman's palate, being "by mainy degrees sweeter than the tame Turkies of England, feede them how you can."[5] The word "commodity" appears regularly in Morton's account (it seems to have been the seventeenth-century equivalent of our term "resources"), but he also took an aesthetic satisfaction in much of what he saw. Sparrow hawks (kestrels), for example, were beautiful to him, "the fairest, and best, shaped birds that I have ever beheld of that kinde. . . ."[6]

William Wood was much more thorough than Morton, perhaps because he was not inclined to notice the Puritans, much less to castigate them for page after page, as Morton did. The focus in Wood's *Prospect* falls much more steadily on the natural world. There are apt and reliable descriptions in this book. Henry David Thoreau, reading Wood's account in 1855, liked it for its gusto, and wrote that Wood was "not to be caught napping by the wonders of Nature in a new country."[7] Wood wrote a clear, concrete prose that supports his claim of purely "experimentall" (experience-derived) description. He declared that the aim of his stay in New England (from 1629 to 1633) had been observation pure and simple, which is certainly unusual, if not unique, among the first waves of Europeans coming to these shores. His description of a flight of passenger pigeons, one of the earliest such on record (see p. 103), is a good example of Wood's engaging and image-filled style. His natural history catalog, as might be expected and forgiven, is incomplete — he lists only two species of owl, for instance, apparently the screech owl and the great horned owl — but his obvious feeling for animals and his care in description mark him as having something of the poetic-scientific temperament of many later, more accomplished nature writers. He notes the migration of birds and the hibernation of snakes with accuracy, something that not every observer of his time was able to do. He does say that wolves have no joints in their bodies, an odd blunder that Thoreau later noted, and worse, he falls into the ancient and common error of supposing predation by wolves to be an unmitigated evil for nature — "the greatest inconveniency the country hath."[8] It is less easy to fault Wood for this particular opinion if we remember that it was well into the twentieth century before a better understanding of predation, and particularly predation by wolves, became widespread.

What develops out of such early accounts as Morton's and Wood's is a valuable picture of New England before European activity had drastically modified it. As William Cronon has shown in his ecological history of New England, *Changes in the Land* (1983), a remarkable diversity in vegetation patterns flourished at the beginning of the settlement period, with much open meadow land, particularly in the southern portions of the region. There was a great deal of "edge," the fruitful zone where different types of natural communities meet. Edges have more niches, and this is why New England's "mosaic of tree stands with widely varying compositions,"[9] in Cronon's words, supported a superlative abundance of wildlife. As Cronon also points out, the diversity was in part created and maintained by the Indians' twice-yearly burnings of undergrowth, so that over large areas of New England, the image of the "forest primeval" as a dark tangle had little basis in fact. It was to a degree a managed landscape, but the nature of the management was subtle enough, or (more likely) different enough from patterns the Europeans were accustomed to, that most of the settlers perceived the country as unmanaged, that is, as a wilderness. This image had a practical effect, helping to justify the expropriation of land and conversion of it to European patterns of ownership and use. The result of settlement, overall, was a simplification of plant and animal communities. The fur trade, lumbering, road building, and especially grazing and plowing had a major impact on ecosystems. Overgrazing became a problem even in Governor William Bradford's time, in the first generation of colonists; so rapid was the transformation of the land and the accompanying decimation of wildlife that as early as 1718, Massachusetts was forced to declare a three-year moratorium on deer hunting.[10]

One of the earliest observers to note the importation of new forms (weeds, specifically) and the decline in native wildlife was John Josselyn, who made two extended trips to New England, the first in 1638 and the second in 1663. Josselyn has been described as "the first Englishman to write of the New England flora with any degree of scientific interest."[11] His *New England's Rarities Discovered* (1672) includes as one of its major divisions of the flora "Such plants as have sprung up since the English planted and kept cattle in New England,"[12] and describes under the heading twenty-two weeds; two years later, in his second book, *An Account of Two Voyages to New-England, Made During the Years 1638, 1663* (1674), he points out that the first cattle in New England had been brought to New Plymouth in 1624, some fourteen years before his own first arrival, so his weed list must have involved a certain amount of reconstruction and inference on his part, and an historian's motivation. Indeed, he appears to have been quite conscious of his role as a recorder of momentous things, for a chronology that he appends to *Two Voyages* runs from 265 B.C. to 1674! Apparently no great friend of the Puritan rule of Massachusetts,[13] and thus no apologist for the changes that were befalling the country, Josselyn was forthright in noting the precipitous decline of turkeys, once one of the distinctively abundant birds of the Bay

Colony area. In *Rarities,* after describing how he had once seen "three-score broods of young turkies on the side of a marsh, sunning of themselves in a morning betimes," he quickly adds, "But this was thirty years since; the English and the Indians having now destroyed the breed, so that 'tis very rare to meet with a wild turkie in the woods."[14] (Josselyn makes no further remark on the subject of Indian complicity, but other evidence shows that the Indians were rather quickly absorbed into the European style of resource extraction, and contributed to the decline of wildlife as their dependence on the new economy of the land deepened.[15])

Besides making an early statement of loss, Josselyn's writings anticipate other aspects of later nature literature. He wrote in a rather quirky, jumpy manner, never staying with an idea long enough to develop it into a finished essay, but he did venture both nature-experience narratives and philosophical commentaries based on natural history. In *Two Voyages,* he describes tracking and shooting at a wolf that had taken one of his brother's goats, on a farm in the "Province of Main," and he also presents a lively account of an Indian moose hunt, presumably in the same region. When the hunters have run the moose down, and lanced him, "the poor Creature groans, and walks on heavily, for a space, then sinks and falls down like a ruined building. . . ."[16] Upon certain other occasions in *Two Voyages,* Josselyn departs from narrative to make interpretive comments on the ways of nature. One of these is a capsule statement of the Argument from Design, but one attributing more to the Design than mere mechanical ingenuity. Josselyn's Design has heart. "There are certain transcendentia in every Creature, which are the indelible Characters of God, and which discover God. . . ."[17] Shortly after this apparent ascription of soul to animals, Josselyn makes what is probably the first interpretive ecological statement in American literature. Describing the moose, he suddenly inserts an italicized passage:

> *Some particular living Creatures cannot live in every particular place or region, especially with the same joy or felicity as it did where it was first bred, for the certain agreement of nature that is between the place and the thing bred in that place: As appeareth by* Elephants, *which being translated and brought out of the Second or Third Climate, though they may live, yet will they never ingender or bring forth young.* So for plants, Birds, &c.[18]

This wide-ranging author also appreciated Indians rather unbiasedly. "I have seen half a hundred of their *Wigwams* together in a piece of ground and they shew prettily. . . ."[19]

What we see in Josselyn's interesting work is many of the materials
of the American nature essay assembling loosely, in effect, ahead of
their time. Those materials would begin to jell as parts of a recognized
view of the world, and as a literary possibility, about a century after
Josselyn. In that period, both in Europe and America, there grew up
widespread acceptance of the idea that studying nature in detail,
even as a life work, and caring deeply for animals and plants, were
appropriate things for a member of Christian society to do. A movement toward such a new attitude began to be evident in England in
the seventeenth century, and gained momentum in the early decades
of the eighteenth, partly as a result of the immensely popular work
of John Ray, who was both a clergyman and a naturalist. Ray's major
work, *The Wisdom of God Manifested in the Works of the Creation* (1691),
summarized the Argument from Design with authority. Just as significantly, it drew from the Design a major inference, the disen-
thronement of man from his accustomed, self-described position as
the centerpiece of creation. Ray was quite clear on this point:

> . . . it is a generally received Opinion, that all this visible World was
> created for Man; that Man is the End of the Creation; as if there were
> no other End of any Creature, but some way or other to be serviceable
> to Man.
> . . . But tho' this be vulgarly receiv'd, yet wise Men now-a-days think
> otherwise.
> . . . For my part, I cannot believe that all Things in the World were so
> made for Man, that they have no other Use.[20]

In this non-utilitarian view of nature, which grants spiritual standing to the "Things of the World," we see what one scholar of Ray's
period calls the beginnings of the "modern sensibility."[21] The effect
of the new doctrine was to give a great push forward to natural
history. In America, John Banister and John Lawson, two British
colonists in Virginia and Carolina, respectively, indicated some of the
scope of the new thinking, and the general interest in nature now in
the air, by their plans to write comprehensive natural histories of
their areas. Both men made important botanical collections, and
Lawson actually completed a valuable book (*A New Voyage to Carolina*,
published in 1709) deriving from a 550-mile, two-month surveying
trip into the interior of the colony. But both men were killed in the
wilderness, Banister in a hunting accident in 1692, and Lawson by
Indians in 1712, before bringing their natural history ambitions to
fruition. Drawing upon his 1700–1701 winter expedition into the
back country, Lawson had infused the "Natural History of Carolina"

section of *A New Voyage* with vivid details and personal responses to sights and sounds, giving indication that had he lived, he might have written truly significant nature literature. His writing shows not only a ready responsiveness to the scenes before him but also a certain flair, a recognition of some of the responsibilities of authorship to tell a story and present information in unified fashion. *A New Voyage* has some shape to it, in short, which was lacking in Josselyn's work, for instance. Banister, who first came to Virginia in 1678 and was probably, as his modern editors write, "America's first resident naturalist"[22] (or at least university-trained naturalist), also had a sharp eye. His drawings of plants are detailed and lifelike, and could only have been by someone passionately interested in what was before him. His writing, as Joseph Kastner notes in *A Species of Eternity* (1977), was bright with the delight he took in nature.[23]

The first attempt at a comprehensive natural history of the colonies to reach something like its hoped-for completeness was that of another Englishman, Mark Catesby. Catesby invested his life work, *The Natural History of Carolina, Florida, and the Bahama Islands* (two volumes, 1731–1743), with enough detail (some of it borrowed from Lawson, to be sure) and artistic skill that it lasted as an authority on its subject for close to a century. Supported by a modest inheritance from his father's estate, Catesby was able to make two extended visits to America, the first from 1712 to 1719 and apparently consisting mainly of leisurely stays at plantations in the South (including William Byrd's Westover in Virginia), and the second from 1722 to 1726, when he got down to the serious business of compiling a full-scale natural history. Although he did not, apparently, have university training,[24] he seems to have been acquainted with John Ray and perhaps through Ray's influence to have been fired with a profound interest in the natural world. He dedicated his life to producing as complete a natural history of the Southeast as he could, and even taught himself engraving, so that his illustrations might reflect as accurately as possible what he had observed.

During his second stay in America, Catesby undertook long journeys on foot, collecting, taking extensive notes, and making drawings. Many of these drawings were from live specimens, a practice that, in the case of birds in particular, sets Catesby apart from the great majority of subsequent students and artists. After four intensive years he returned to England and began his book. He would put very nearly the rest of his life into it: the first volume, devoted to birds, was published in 1731; the second, covering fish, snakes, and plants, in 1743; and an Appendix was completed in 1747, two years before the author's death.

The stature of the work derives from its attempted exhaustiveness, its impressive detail and accuracy in many of the descriptions, and its 220 evocative plates. Catesby listed 113 species of birds, and his documentation of these was authoritative enough for so careful a student as Thomas Jefferson, whose own list of birds in *Notes on the State of Virginia* (1785) was basically Catesby's plus thirty-three of his own observation.[25] Catesby also tried to cover all of the snakes in authoritative fashion: "Of serpents, very few, I believe, have escaped me, for upon showing my designs of them to several of the most intelligent persons, many of them confessed that they had not seen them all, and none of them pretended to have seen any other kinds."[26] (One could hardly ask for a comment more revealing of this naturalist's pioneering position.)

Besides listing and describing species, Catesby also attempted a broad-gauge ecological overview by dividing Carolina into four main zones, each denoted by a dominant vegetation type: rice country, oak and hickory country, pine barrens, and scrub oak land. This is one of the earliest attempts to describe an ecotype by means of key species. Catesby's *Natural History* also makes a good guess, for its time, about bird migration: "the Place to which they retire is probably in the same Latitude of the southern Hemisphere, or where they may enjoy the like Temperature of Air, as in the Country from whence they came. . . ."[27]

Catesby could be fooled, as in his account of the "Hog-nose Snake," which he believed to be "of the venomous Tribe,"[28] and some of his plates and descriptions are not very precise (his "Little Thrush," for example, could be any one of several species in the thrush family), but on the whole his care shines through. He is not an essayist in the Montaigne-Bacon-Addison tradition — that is, he does not develop formed essays from a distinctive personal point of view — but many of his descriptions, if not literary in the traditional sense, are vivid and do suggest the experience of nature. The "Regulus Cristatus" (ruby-crowned kinglet), he wrote, can often be found with other winter species "ranging the woods together, from tree to tree, as if they were all of one brood, running up and down the bark of lofty oaks, from the crevices of which they collect their food, which are Insects lodged in their Winter-dormitories, in a torpid state."[29]

In the end, probably, it will be Catesby's art that ensures his being remembered. His rendering of the blue jay, to take an example of particular excellence, will stand well beside any subsequent representations of that bird. The vivacity and activity captured in that engraving show clearly that at this point in the mid-eighteenth century,

it was possible to look very closely at even "useless" wildlife, and to
see there the material of art.

The first European thoroughly trained in Enlightenment science
to come to America was the Swede Peter Kalm, who had been a
student of Linnaeus's at the University of Uppsala. Kalm arrived in
the colonies in the fall of 1748, sent by the Swedish Royal Academy
to look for useful plants that might do well in the cold climate of
Sweden. From his home base at the Swedish settlement of Raccoon
(now Swedesboro, New Jersey), Kalm traveled for two and a half
years in the middle Atlantic region and made journeys as far north
as Lake Champlain and Canada and as far west as Niagara Falls, all
the while keeping a remarkably detailed journal. This record, *Travels
in North America* (first published in English in 1770), is a kind of early,
undeveloped "de Tocqueville" on American habits, and also offers a
great deal of useful commentary on the state of the American environment in the mid-eighteenth century. It is a travel journal and thus
inevitably fragmentary, but it contains three of what would become
standard themes in later and more finished American nature writing:
the decline of abundance caused by carelessness and greed; the agrarian dream of life in a decentralized, rural situation; and the adventure
to the edges of the wilderness — the sublime.

Kalm's training in descriptive science appears to have helped make
him a judicious observer and interviewer. His account of the depre-
ciation of the American environment was necessarily second-hand.
"All the old Swedes and Englishmen born in America whom I ever
questioned asserted that there were not nearly so many edible birds
at present as there used to be when they were children, and that
their decrease was visible. They even said that they had heard the
same complaint from their fathers. . . ."[30] But he followed up this
sort of report with personal observations. Writing of the Philadelphia
area, he stated that "People are here (and in many other places) in
regard to wood, bent only upon their own present advantage, utterly
regardless of posterity. By these means many swamps are already
quite destitute of cedars. . . ."[31] Cedars were being used for shingles
in the growing city of Philadelphia, but no attempt was being made
to plant replacement trees. The same sort of disregard for the future
appeared in the exploitation of wildlife, and aroused Kalm to one of
his strongest comments on America. He wrote of the yearly assault
on vulnerable waterfowl, "In spring the people still steal eggs, moth-
ers and young indifferently, because no regulations are made to the
contrary. And if any had been made, the spirit of freedom which
prevails in the country would not suffer them to be obeyed."[32]

Kalm was attracted, however, to the agrarian life led by most Americans at this time. He criticized careless farming practices, particularly the widespread habit of letting livestock run loose over the land, but some of his accounts of the yeoman-farmer existence suggest a kind of paradise.

> As we went on in the forest we continually saw at moderate distances little fields which had been cleared of the wood. Each one of these was a farm. These farms were commonly very pretty, and a walk of trees frequently led from them to the highroad. The houses were all built of brick or of the stone which is found here everywhere. Every countryman, even the poorest peasant, had an orchard with apples, peaches, chestnuts, walnuts, cherries, quinces and such fruits, and sometimes we saw vines climbing in them. The valleys were frequently blessed with little brooks of crystal-clear water.[33]

At Niagara Falls, Kalm's placid prose took on some new life: "It is enough to make the hair stand on end of any observer who may be sitting or standing close by, and who attentively watches such a large amount of water falling vertically over a ledge from such a height. The effect is awful, tremendous!"[34] In the manner of the writer of adventures, Kalm dramatized his feelings by introducing into the narrative some "Indian lads" who "walked right out to the very edge of the cataract . . . and looked down. . . . I was chilled inside, when I saw it, and called to them; but they only smiled, and still stood a while on the outermost brink."[35] This depiction of Niagara is one of the early descriptions of American nature in the vein of the "sublime," an aesthetic category which would, in later times, elevate the literary respectability of wilderness considerably.

The first literarily coherent American works based in some significant portion on nature experience or natural history were Hector St. John de Crèvecoeur's *Letters from an American Farmer,* published in London in 1782, and Thomas Jefferson's *Notes on the State of Virginia,* published in Paris in 1785. The *Letters* of Crèvecoeur are much the more consciously literary work of the two. The ideas in the *Letters,* and in Crèvecoeur's *Sketches of Eighteenth Century America,* essays that were not published together until 1925 but were all written between 1770 and 1778, flow from the distinctive personality and responses of the narrator-participant. Crèvecoeur's sympathetic temperament and his very good eye for the telling detail give his work an identifiable tone, a literary personality. The very first paragraph of "A Snow Storm as It Affects the American Farmer," an essay that the author translated into French and included in the 1784 Paris edition of *Lettres d'un Cultivateur Américain,* evinces a command of theme and a strong emotional presence.

> No man of the least degree of sensibility can journey through any number of years in whatever climate without often being compelled to make many useful observations on the different phenomena of Nature which surround him; and without involuntarily being struck either with awe or admiration in beholding some of the elementary conflicts in the midst of which he lives. A great thunderstorm; an extensive flood; a desolating hurricane; a sudden and intense frost; an overwhelming snow-storm; a sultry day — each of these different scenes exhibits singular beauties even in spite of the damage they cause. Often whilst the heart laments the loss to the citizen, the enlightened mind, seeking for the natural causes, and astonished at the effects, awakes itself to surprise and wonder.[36]

Crèvecoeur then narrates a snowstorm, such as undoubtedly he experienced at "Pine Hill," his farm in Orange County, New York, sometime during his happy tenure there from 1769 to 1778. "The wind, which is a great regulator of the weather, shifts to the northeast; the air becomes bleak and then intensely cold; the light of the sun becomes dimmed as if an eclipse had happened; a general night seems coming on."[37] As the storm develops, Crèvecoeur describes in detail the preparations the careful farmer has made, and narrates the farm family's activity within the snug safety of their home. The American-agrarian point of view is explicit: "Finally they go to bed, not to that bed of slavery or sorrow as is the case in Europe with people of their class, but on the substantial collection of honest feathers picked and provided by the industrious wife."[38]

D. H. Lawrence may have had just such a sentimental passage in mind when he termed Crèvecoeur the emotional prototype of the American,[39] but it is not true that the "American farmer" was entirely swept up in agrarian dreaming. In "Reflections on the Manners of the Americans," another essay he translated into French for the 1784 *Lettres,* Crèvecoeur gave very particular details on the financial process of acquiring a farm (farms did not simply materialize as part of the boon of all Americans — by Crèvecoeur's time most of the good land on the eastern seaboard was indeed owned by someone), and he went further to show that economic realities may shape a farmer into something quite unlike the honest yeoman of agrarian mythology. He wrote that the farmer may become shrewd, litigious, even deceitful. "Fearful of fraud in all his dealings and transactions, he arms himself, therefore, with it. Strict integrity is not much wanted. . . ."[40] As further evidence of Crèvecoeur's realistic streak, he criticized the deforestation that could accompany the establishment of an agrarian society. In "Thoughts of an American Farmer on Various Rural Subjects," Crèvecoeur anticipated the work of George Perkins Marsh (*Man and Nature*, 1864) and other critics of watershed abuse:

> I could show you in this county the ruins of eleven grist-mills which twenty years ago had plenty of water, but now stand on the dry ground, with no other marks of running water about them than the ancient bed of the creek, on the shores of which they had been erected. This effect does not surprise me. Our ancient woods kept the earth moist and damp, and the sun could evaporate none of the waters contained within their shades. Who knows how far these effects may extend?[41]

This last sentence is a dark-side echo to Crèvecoeur's upbeat (and better-known) rhetorical question, "Who can tell how far it [North America] extends?" in the much-anthologized essay, "What Is an American?" This farmer, like the great majority of agrarian essayists to come after him, was well aware of the changes abroad in the land.

Crèvecoeur also paid close attention to the birds, wasps, bees, and other less obviously utile inhabitants of his farm. He did more than pay attention — he delighted in them and viewed them as co-inhabitants. In "On Snakes; And on the Humming Bird," one of his *Letters from an American Farmer*, he praised the ruby-throated hummingbird:

> On this little bird nature has profusely lavished her most splendid colors. . . . The richest pallet of the most luxuriant painter, could never invent any thing to be compared to the variegated tints, with which this insect bird is arrayed. . . . When fatigued, it has often perched within a few feet of me, and on such favourable opportunities I have surveyed it with the most minute attention. Its little eyes appear like diamonds, reflecting light on every side: most elegantly finished in all parts it is a miniature work of our great parent; who seems to have formed it the smallest, and at the same time the most beautiful of the winged species.[42]

Thomas Jefferson's *Notes on the State of Virginia* is noteworthy for its demonstration of the importance of nature to the just-forming American national identity. It catalogs various life forms, much in the fashion of earlier lists, and at one point makes use of dramatic personal narrative to convey the awesomeness of a local geological formation (the Virginia Natural Bridge), both techniques integral to much nature writing. But perhaps the *Notes'* American identity is most clearly manifested in its author's attack on a curious idea promoted by the French encyclopedist George Louis Leclerc, Comte de Buffon, that New World animals were smaller, weaker, degenerate versions of similar European species. This supposition had been put forth in Buffon's monumental *Histoire Naturelle, Générale, et Particulière* (1749–1788), where it was presented as simple truth. Using logic, citation of his own observations, and scholarly references to Catesby, Kalm, and the work of his Pennsylvania friend John Bartram (who was America's first native-born naturalist of stature), Jefferson proceeded to demolish the mythical comparison, proving that American animals were actually quite robust. He also defended the American Indian against Buffon's assertion that "the savage is feeble, and has small organs of generation . . . and no ardor whatever for his female," merely adding, "An afflicting picture indeed, which, for the honor of human nature, I am glad to believe has no original."[43]

John Bartram, a friend also of Crèvecoeur's, was a farmer whose land lay on the west bank of the Schuylkill River just a few miles from Philadelphia. Besides running a farm, he was a far-journeying collector of plants for his English sponsor, the London cloth merchant Peter Collinson, and a self-taught naturalist of real stature. No less an authority than Linnaeus himself described Bartram as "the greatest natural botanist in the world";[44] Crèvecoeur, who praised him in *Letters from an American Farmer,* saw the Pennsylvanian as proof of the goodness of the simple life — close to nature and at the same time rational. Beginning as a plant collector in 1734 at the age of thirty-five, in four decades Bartram increased the European catalog of New World plants by some 150 species, and in the process came to know in person or by correspondence most of the world's leading naturalists. He was not a writer, either by intention or accomplishment, but he did leave succinct journal accounts of some of his wilderness travels, in which a modern reader can learn, for example, that there were wolves in Florida in 1766, or that the Catskill Mountains held a remarkable diversity of rare trees and shrubs. Bartram's journals and letters also demonstrate the eighteenth-century opening of thought. His experience in nature convinced him that sentience was not limited to human beings. "I also am of the opinion that the creatures commonly called brutes possess higher qualifications, and more exalted ideas, than our traditional mystery-mongers are willing to allow them," he wrote.[45] He saw the hand of God in the natural world, a common enough view in his time, but when his deistical leanings brought him to deny the divinity of Jesus, he let his ideas be known, and there was a falling-out with his Quaker meeting. A man who during the course of his life had built four stone houses, provided for a large family, taught himself the new natural science, and traveled thousands of wilderness miles in search of plants, Bartram was unaffected by the meeting's show of disapproval, and continued on his own, independent way.

One of John Bartram's sons, William, grew up practically at the center of the American Enlightenment, and enjoyed some second-generation advantages. In contrast to his father, "Billy" had a very good education; he showed artistic inclinations quite early, as well as ability in natural history, and was encouraged in these areas. He accompanied his father on a collecting trip to the wild Catskills in 1753, at the age of fourteen, and was apparently introduced there to what became, so the evidence seems to show, the supreme pleasure of his life: a kind of wandering botanizing, done in an exploratory, discovering, goal-less frame of mind, so that the forest world, as he walked slowly through it, became a garden of delight and revelation. New plants, unusually large trees, the manner in which sandhill cranes take off and gain altitude, the elegance of fish seen swimming in clear springs, just about everything that he came upon in his life of travels except alligators and thunderstorms (and these moved him to awe, another sort of delight) touched William Bartram's aesthetic sense and brought him joy. His praise for others was framed in terms of their sensibility, to use his word, and it is clear that his own was high and refined. As a teenager he was apprenticed to a Philadelphia merchant, and he later tried business on his own, setting up a store at Cape Fear on the Carolina coast. But he did not take to business, and all his ventures failed. By the middle 1760s he was at loose enough ends that he could accompany his father on another botanizing trip, this one to Florida. He was again immersed in the beautiful wilderness and, it is fair to suppose, confirmed in his fundamental desires. In 1768, he received the sponsorship of a British physician and amateur botanist, John Fothergill. Five years later, bolstered by a salary of fifty pounds per year, he went back over the river routes through Florida that he and his father had taken in the previous decade, and then pressed on into new country farther inland. He spent the better part of the years 1773 through 1777 happily rambling through the back country of the Southeast, on a loose itinerary that may be surmised in passages like the following from his record of the trip: "On my return to the store on St. Juan's the trading schooner was there, but as she was not to return to Georgia until the autumn, I found I had time to pursue my travels in Florida, and might at leisure plan my excursions to collect seeds and roots in boxes, &c."[46]

Bartram's account of these four blithe years, published in 1791 under the title *Travels Through North and South Carolina, Georgia, East and West Florida, the Cherokee Country, the Extensive Territories of the Muscogulges, or Creek Confederacy, and the Country of the Choctaws,* and for good reason known usually as "Bartram's *Travels*," is rambling, diverse, florid, oddly put together in places, sketchy on dates and distances traveled, clogged in places with long lists of Latin names of plants, and probably more than a little repetitive, to most readers. But it is also the first fully developed nature essay in this country; it is a brilliant evocation of a mind and vision, and the land that inspired them. Perhaps the greatest single impression is of the author's receptivity, and of the fluid ease with which his mind followed the hints that nature provided. At one point in his journeying along the east coast of Florida, Bartram had gone out to botanize. While he was admiring some agaves and myrtles, he found his attention attracted to some butterflies, when suddenly he saw a large spider in the process of stalking a bumblebee. He described the spider in detail, drawing himself into the drama by noting that the predator kept an eye on him while conducting the attack. The scene is vivid, and reinforces the author's theme at this point in the narrative, which is that the animal creation "offers manifest examples of premeditation, perseverance, resolution, and consummate artifice," a theme that further illustrates the overall idea of the continuity of man and other forms of life. Bartram's ready impressionability to whatever he happened upon, and his mind's quickness to recognize not only relationships but also the possibility that he himself might be included in them in some fashion, create his ecological style. He saw a grand, systematic patterning, all revealing the "Almighty hand," as we have seen, so that whatever a man of sensibility and training looked upon, if he looked well, became meaningful. Simply walking through the woods, or catching an unexpected view of the ocean, could evoke from this sensitive man a spiritual excitement. "O thou Creator supreme, almighty! how infinite and incomprehensible thy works! most perfect, and every way astonishing!"[47]

Inevitably, both as a man of the Enlightenment who at home had doubtless heard many philosophical discussions and as one who had, on his own travels, many times crossed the meaningful border between civilization and the wilderness, Bartram reflected upon human nature and human society. Describing a camp in the wilderness of back-country Georgia, where he had ventured with a few companions, he wrote, "How supremely blessed were our hours at this time! Plenty of delicious and healthful food, our stomachs keen, with contented minds; under no control, but what reason and ordinate passions dictated, far removed from the seats of strife."[48] He continued interpretively, "Our situation was like that of the primitive state of man, peaceable, contented, and sociable. The simple and necessary calls of nature being satisfied, we were altogether as brethren of one family, strangers to envy, malice, and rapine."[49] That Bartram was not a primitivist, however, is shown by his admiration for well-kept plantations, and his musing at times upon the possible commercial advantages a particularly fruitful site, still in a wild state, might someday have. It was 1791, after all, and the horse-drawn nation's first census had just counted less than four million inhabitants. It would be another forty-odd years before there came a serious call for the preservation of large areas of American wilderness — a call embodying the suspicion, perhaps, that progress might in truth be insatiable.

Just three years after Bartram's *Travels* appeared, the Reverend Samuel Williams of Rutland, Vermont, published a most interesting survey of his state, *The Natural and Civil History of Vermont* (1794). Unlike Bartram's book, this book was not framed on personal experience, but on statistics and observations of a more dispassionate nature. Williams, a man of wide interests who had for eight years lectured at Harvard on mathematics and astronomy, was conscious that Vermont in his time was "rapidly changing from a vast tract of uncultivated wilderness, to numerous and extensive settlements."[50] Perhaps moved by this awareness, he recorded such facts as that there was still a good Atlantic salmon run in the Connecticut River, all the way to its highest branches, that there were still cougars in Vermont, and that the "most aged" white pine tree in the state was between 350 and 400 years old, with a diameter of 6 feet and a height of 247 feet.[51] *The Natural and Civil History of Vermont* used a straightforwardly encyclopedic style to describe exactly where the state stood, in space as well as time. Williams' organization would today be called "bioregional": the first six chapters are "Situation," "Mountains," "Rivers and Lakes," "Climate," "Vegetable Productions," and "Native Animals." Only then are the Indians discussed, and finally the white man's political history. Williams's promotion of a wider ethical outlook toward animals was also modern. While he described wolves as "noxious" (in common with most writers of his time and much later), he nevertheless criticized certain other manifestations of anthropocentric arrogance:

> To the tribes of reptiles and insects, we have affixed the idea of something, unpleasant, diminutive, or odious. The designs, the wisdom, and the power of the Creator, are not to be estimated by such feelings, fears, and prejudices.[52]

Just why wolves were excluded from the Creator's wise planning, Williams did not say. Here indeed was a species which provided a difficult "final examination" in ecological consciousness, not just for Williams but for many American naturalists down to very recent times.

Williams's book presented Vermont in transition, virginity gone. For a glimpse of the pristine, a modern reader can do no better than to consult the journals of the Lewis and Clark expedition, written a little more than a decade after the Vermont history. The record of the outward trek in particular is impressive in its evocation of the immensity and quiet of the country, and the spectacular abundance of wildlife. The high Plains region was perhaps the most vast wilderness of all — going westward from the Mandan villages in 1805, the expedition's members did not see even a single Indian for some four months. Meriwether Lewis, perhaps more than the rest, seemed to respond to the utter wildness:

> The whole face of the country was covered with herds of Buffaloe, Elk & Antelopes; deer are also abundant, but keep themselves more concealed in the woodland. The buffaloe Elk and Antelope are so gentle that we pass near them while feeding, without appearing to excite any alarm among them; and when we attract their attention, they frequently approach us more nearly to discover what we are, and in some instances pursue us a considerable distance apparently with that view.[53]

Lewis frequently went off by himself to contemplate long views, and he wrote quite often of the romantic appearance, to use his phrase, of scenes like the "Missouri Breaks." He had projected a three-volume history of the expedition in 1807, just a year after the company's return; the third volume would deal with natural history.[54] In this book, we might have seen Meriwether Lewis emerge as a significant American nature writer. Few men, literally, had seen more of the country, and there is no doubting his sensitivity to it, nor his natural history knowledge. But Lewis died in 1809, under mysterious circumstances; the journals of the expedition remain just that, in the literary sense — they were never shaped into the history Lewis had envisioned. Even so, they evoke the untamed dimension of the American wilderness as nothing else can. They give a sense of the original, by which all that followed can be measured.

William Bartram was invited to accompany Lewis and Clark, but declined on account of his age. From 1777 until his death forty-six years later, Bartram lived quietly in Philadelphia. His travels were confined mainly within the eight-acre botanical garden his father had established (the first such garden in North America, apparently). He kept records of bird migration, helped care for the garden, wrote his great book, maintained close contact with the American scientific community (which at that time was centered in Philadelphia, where both the American Philosophical Society and the Academy of Natural Sciences had their headquarters), and in the first decades of the nineteenth century found himself becoming a mentor to a new generation of naturalists. He was particularly helpful to two young immigrants who came to the garden, one from Scotland and one from England, both of whom became giants in American natural history. Alexander Wilson and Thomas Nuttall revered Bartram for his knowledge and generous spirit. Wilson, who had met the older naturalist in 1802, lived at the Bartram garden for a time. Nuttall, who first visited Bartram within weeks of his arrival in this country in 1808, also had a room reserved for him at Bartram's. Both Wilson and Nuttall profited greatly from Bartram's fund of knowledge won from the field, and from his position as elder statesman of natural history, for through him they were able to make contacts crucial to their own enterprises.

Wilson's is one of the most compelling stories from the early period of American nature study — a time not lacking in interesting characters. Born in Scotland in 1766, he had been "put" to a weaver as a bound apprentice in 1779, had achieved journeyman weaver status, and had eventually become a peddler, going on foot from village to village in the Scottish countryside, carrying a large pack of cloth goods. His journals and letters from these early days indicate a sensitive, aspiring man who suffered periods of despondency. Inspired by his countryman Robert Burns, Wilson wrote poetry, some of it quite good (one of his efforts, in fact, published anonymously, was widely believed to have been written by Burns), and when he had enough poems for a volume he peddled subscriptions to his book right along with his cloth. In 1794, after being accused of libel and in fact spending some time in jail for writing a radical poem in which he had satirized a local capitalist, Wilson emigrated to the United States, where he supported himself at first by weaving and later by teaching school. At some point during his first years in this country he became deeply interested in the birds of his adopted land, and after he met Bartram the interest became a passion. Within a year of their meeting he had declared, "I AM NOW ABOUT TO MAKE A COLLECTION OF ALL OUR FINEST BIRDS."[55]

Over the remaining ten years of Wilson's life, this "collection" would become *American Ornithology; or, the Natural History of the Birds of the United States* (published 1808–1814, in nine volumes), the first comprehensive description of American birds and thus a monument in science, and also a book whose clear, precise prose and heartfelt enthusiasm help make it a significant work in the literature of nature. To gather data for the descriptions, and to secure the birds themselves for his paintings which illustrated the text, and finally to sell subscriptions for the work, Wilson traveled some 15,000 miles in America, most of it on foot. He drew from life, he said, and furthermore scorned those he called "closet-naturalists and sedentary travellers."[56] ("Closet," as a term of utter derision, turns up again and again in the writings of the early American field naturalists.) Almost entirely self-taught both in science and art (though, clearly, he must have benefited from Bartram in both areas), Wilson seemed undaunted by the magnitude of his undertaking, and saw eight volumes through the press before his death from dysentery in 1813. The ninth and final volume was published the next year.

Wilson's love of field work, together with his poet's eye for the focal image, helped give his writing concreteness and a dramatic sense of behavior in context. Even the expository, non-narrative accounts of species — for example, Wilson's description of the ivory-billed woodpecker — are likely to convey the energy he felt in nature. The miles and years in the woods came most obviously to bear in narrative vignettes of behavior, as in this meeting with a nesting yellow-billed cuckoo:

> While the female is sitting the male is generally not far distant, and gives the alarm by his notes, when any person is approaching. The female sits so close that you may almost reach her with your hand, and then precipitates herself to the ground, feigning lameness to draw you away from the spot, fluttering, trailing her wings, and tumbling over, in the manner of the Partridge, Woodcock, and many other species.[57]

Wilson's efforts toward an emotionally resonant yet empirically accurate prose, a style that would in effect poeticize science, represent an improved synthesis over Bartram's style. Wilson's writing, in fact, is an improvement over that of every American naturalist who had gone before him on this central point of the linking of science and art, with full expression of both dimensions. Where Catesby had written of his "Little Thrush" that "It never sings, having only a single note,"[58] for example, Wilson made a very considerable advance by describing several species of the thrush family, carefully noting their various songs and calls, and then, in the descriptions of the birds' typical habitats, giving a strong sense of the ambience of these

places through poetically charged images and emotional responses
of his own. He seemed to realize that he was in fact engaged in a
great leap beyond what had gone before, and not only in literary and
scientific terms; this would be the first *national* bird book as well.
Wilson worked hard to find travelers' accounts so that his range
descriptions would be complete. He cited Meriwether Lewis, whom
he knew, Zebulon Pike, and others, looking always for the authentic
field man's word. There seemed to be almost the joy of possession in
his search, a looking with high expectancy to all the far reaches of
the land. He came to know his adopted country, and in the end, his
ten-year book amounted to a hymn of love to American nature. It
should be regarded as an important American document.

Thomas Nuttall, who also enjoyed the mentorship of William Bartram, had an aesthetic sense for natural history much resembling
Wilson's, and a similar dedication, but in the course of a long career
was able to amass far greater scientific knowledge. Indeed, he may
have been the most knowledgeable of the all-purpose naturalists of
the early period in this country. He was also a writer who conveyed
perhaps more adequately than anyone before him, that is, with more
scientific precision, the complexity of the relationships between species and their habitats. In its description of these tightly woven relationships, Nuttall's introduction to his *Manual of the Ornithology of the
United States and Canada* (1832; see pp. 143–171) is one of the important natural history essays of its time.

Nuttall came to America in 1808, specifically to study nature.
Within weeks of his arrival in Philadelphia he had been hired as a
field researcher for Benjamin Smith Barton, a botanist and professor
at the University of Pennsylvania. With his first excursions, botanical
errands for Barton into Delaware, Pennsylvania, and New York,
Nuttall began one of the most energetic field careers in American
science. He would spend a total of thirty-three years in this country,
a surprising proportion of that time in the field. He made several
extended journeys into the wilderness, often traveling solo. In 1810
he crossed the "Old Northwest," mostly on foot, and was with the
Astorians at the Mandan villages in 1811; after descending the Missouri and Mississippi to New Orleans and then waiting out the War
of 1812 in England, Nuttall came back to America and spent almost
two years botanizing in the Southeast; from 1818 to 1820 he was out
on the prairies, following the Arkansas River westward; in 1830,
doing research for his *Manual of Ornithology*, he walked some 1,200
miles in the southeastern states; in 1834, after resigning his curator-
ship at the Botanic Garden at Harvard (where he had also been a

lecturer since 1822), he journeyed overland to the Pacific with the Cambridge entrepreneur Nathaniel Wyeth, sailing on eventually to the Sandwich Islands and then, in 1835, back to the California coast where, thousands of miles from Massachusetts, he met up with the former Harvard student Richard Henry Dana, a meeting later described in *Two Years Before the Mast.* On the way back to Boston, Nuttall wanted to be put ashore at the stormy tip of South America to botanize, but the ship's captain demurred. Finally, following the proviso of a will that kept him in England for nine months of every year (he had inherited a small estate), he lived out the rest of his life rather placidly in the country of his birth, making a last visit to the United States in 1847–1848.[59]

Some of his remarkable life in the American outdoors found expression in Nuttall's written work. *The Genera of North American Plants* (1818), the *Manual of Ornithology* (1832), and the final two volumes of *The North American Sylva* (1841), covering western trees (the first three volumes were the work of François André Michaux), are his major contributions to science, with the latter two works having some literary interest as well. The two journals he kept of his expeditions ("travels" does not seem to be the right word in Nuttall's case), only one of which was published in his lifetime, are interesting for their presentation of the author's character, which was stoic about hardship, illness, and loneliness, and mostly ecstatic about nature. They also comment on frontier life in America with some acerbity. The daily diary of Nuttall's 1810 trip to Michilimackinac from Pennsylvania (not published until the mid-twentieth century) is not high-grade literary ore, although its understatement of the author's sufferings from malaria has a poignant quality.[60] By 1820 he had a more mature command of his materials, and the *Journal of Travels into the Arkansa Territory During the Year 1819* (first published in 1821) is framed more like an essay. Much of it describes intense experience, running the gamut from happy discovery to the alarm of a near-death situation, far in the wilderness. As he moved westward up the Arkansas River, Nuttall was energized by leaving behind the "umbrageous forest," as he called it, and setting forth on the open prairies of the West. He delighted in the sweep of grassland and the innumerable flowers, describing the Plains not as the "Great American Desert," as other explorers had termed it, but a "magnificent garden."

Nuttall's enthusiasm for nature contrasted with his apparent view of the run of humanity on the edges of the wilderness. He made quick, cutting comments about "sharpers" and other frontier characters, and spoke of the "mental darkness" in which he thought children of the frontier were being raised. Most of the time, however, he appears to have simply looked past society and man, and much of the *Journal* has the true American Eden flavor — pure wilderness and no people. Apparently a shy man (he was said to have had a secret door by which he could exit his Cambridge lodgings when an unwanted visitor loomed), Nuttall was nonetheless not above cultivating a certain authorial identity in his published journal. The persona was that of an obsessively dedicated student of nature, naturally enough — an image corroborated, by the way, both by Dana in *Two Years Before the Mast* and Washington Irving in *Astoria.*

> In the meanest garb of the working boat-man, and unattended by a single slave, I was no doubt considered . . . one of the canaille [the lowest class], and I neither claimed nor expected attention; my thoughts centered upon other objects, and all pride of appearance I willingly sacrificed to promote with frugality and industry the objects of my mission.[61]

Among lesser naturalists from the early decades of the nineteenth century, the English traveler John Bradbury and the Philadelphian John Kirk Townsend wrote some interesting travel literature that occasionally suggests some of the subject matter of the nature essay. Neither Bradbury's *Travels in the Interior of America in the Years 1809, 1810, and 1811* (1815) nor Townsend's *Narrative of a Journey Across the Rocky Mountains* (1839), however, gets very close to its subjects or develops sustained reflections. These accounts lack the passion for nature that gives meaning and life to Nuttall's journals, for example. For their depiction of "scenes" in the picturesque manner and as a record of the times, these journals do have some value, however. For example, Bradbury's account of the New Madrid earthquake of 1811, one of the strongest on this continent since it was settled by Europeans, and Townsend's picture of a "mountain-man" rendezvous, though drawn from both a literal and moral distance, are useful glimpses of history.

Both Bradbury and Townsend have been much reprinted. An unjustly neglected figure who, had he lived longer, might have contributed significantly to the emergence of the natural history essay as a literary form was Dr. John D. Godman of Philadelphia. Godman's major work, *American Natural History* (1826), is largely a catalog of American mammals, emphasizing anatomy, but it also contains some thoughtful essays on subjects like time and scientific truth. The intellectual concerns, and Godman's careful style of reasoning, indicate he probably would have been a capable participant in the great

debates over evolution at mid-century and after. He was a devout
Christian but exhibited a scientific turn of mind and was disposed to
cut through fable and anthropomorphic folly. After noting that a
good deal of folklore surrounds the life of bats, including a certain
sinister imputation, Godman cleared the air with an ecologically sophisticated statement based on scientific observation:

> The fact . . . is, that the Bat is one of a large number of animals whose
> structure is adapted for activity and usefulness only when the light is
> feeble, and food is to be obtained. However amusing it may be in
> poetry or apouloge to consider such creatures as choosing night for
> their appearance from a desire concealment, it is by no means allowable
> for students of natural history to forget that all beings must live in
> conformity to the laws of their organization, that the perfection of
> every species is relative to the situation in which it exists, and that our
> notions of beauty and deformity are neither true tests of the excellence
> nor importance of any inferior animal.[62]

Despite its emphasis on anatomy (Godman was an inveterate dissector
of animals), *American Natural History* is in good part a philosophical
text, and may be seen as an important American continuation of the
line established in England by John Ray. In Ray's view, science — the
study of nature — promotes an expansion and naturalizing of our
view of things, particularly our ethical sense. Writing of the wild cats,
and by extension, of predators in general, Godman held that

> We must not rashly contend that these animals are an evil unattended
> by any utility or good. They are designed by nature to occupy regions
> where animal life is most likely to increase in undue proportion, and
> it is their province to keep this increase from becoming excessive.[63]

Godman's other book, *Rambles of a Naturalist* (published in 1833),
first appeared serially in *The Friend,* a Philadelphia weekly, in 1828,
during a time when Godman was trying to support his family by
writing, and trying to stave off somehow the disease that was killing
him. Before his death from tuberculosis, Godman finished twelve
personal essays, most of them based on short walks close to home.
These are not the great, Nuttallian expeditions into the far wilderness, but they have in them a similar sense of discovery; we might
even say that Godman made as much, in literary terms, from an
afternoon stroll as Nuttall did from a month's trekking. Godman
writes, "One of my favourite walks was through Turner's-lane, near
Philadelphia, which is about a quarter of a mile long, and not much
wider than an ordinary street,"[64] and proceeds to describe mole tunnels, a small brook spangling in the sunshine, the dewdrops on a

spider's web, and other sights he found extraordinary. To Godman, anything in nature, seen with a contemplative eye, witnessed the "beneficence of the great Creator"; the trick then, as now, is to go slowly and to look carefully. The essays in Godman's *Rambles* are some of the earliest in the durable subgenre of the short, instructive nature walk. They reveal a mind awake to beauty as well as minute and interesting facts, and help confirm the suggestion that Godman's early death was a loss both to natural history and literature. He had something to say.

John James Audubon, whose period of active field study and creative work spans the time of Wilson and Nuttall, is of course known for his expressive and beautiful paintings. In their artistry they represent something like a quantum leap in the painting of natural history subjects. Alexander Wilson, among others, had supplemented his works with paintings, but had only accuracy for his aim. Although Audubon is much better known as a painter, he was also a writer, we may need to be reminded, and some of his prose is memorable. Like Wilson and Nuttall, Audubon had the passion; he was "fervently desirous of becoming acquainted with nature," as he wrote in his "Introductory Address" to the *Ornithological Biography* (1831–1839),[65] and, like the other two great students of birds, he demonstrated commitment by spending a great deal of time in the field. Audubon's bird biographies are often vivid with colors, shapes, and movement that could only be known first hand. Not every observer, for instance, can have seen enough snipes and goshawks to make the following statement: "It [the goshawk] is extremely expert at catching Snipes on the wing, and so well do these birds know their insecurity, that, on his approach, they prefer squatting."[66]

That brief example shows Audubon at his most direct and concrete; often, it must be said, his prose became extravagantly "literary":

> It was the month of October. The autumnal tints already decorated the shores of that queen of rivers, the Ohio. Every tree was hung with long and flowing festoons of different species of vines, many loaded with clustered fruits of varied brilliancy, their rich bronzed carmine mingling beautifully with the yellow foliage, which now predominated over the yet green leaves, reflecting more lively tints from the clear stream than ever landscape painter portrayed or poet imagined.[67]

This facile side of Audubon is usually found in the "sketches" of American life, which he interspersed with the more sober and scientific bird biographies. But even in the sketches, some objects occasionally captured Audubon's attention so fully that he could write strong, undecorated prose. His account of the exploitation of guillemot eggs on the Labrador nesting grounds, for example, hits hard.

Audubon was saddened by the erosion of wilderness that he saw almost everywhere he traveled. By the 1820s, clearing of the eastern forest had reached so far that swamps in remote areas offered him the best opportunities for wildlife observation (see pp. 136–142). He appeared to share, however, the characteristic ambivalence of many American citizens about the march of progress; although he was sensitive on some environmental matters, he could also quite willingly take part in the killing of a cougar at one point in his travels, and of a wolf at another, and he could praise the owner of a beautiful spring in Florida for having turned it into a source of power for a sugarcane mill. This apparent variation in Audubon's viewpoint finds a parallel in his prose expression, which could move quickly from an egoism that is uncomfortable to read to some of the clearest devotion to the subject that the ornithological literature affords, and from knowledgeable, focused anger to blithe superficiality. It could be argued that Audubon himself, whose personality is so prominent in the writing, gave his prose a certain unity and character, but the values expressed in that prose were not consistent enough to bring off the performance. A nature writing which would carry a strong sense of the author's mind, but at the same time not seem limited by too much self-concern, would have to wait for the next generation, the more contemplative generation of Henry David Thoreau.

The Age of Thoreau, Muir, and Burroughs

THE EARLY PURITANS, with their strongly dualistic world view, associated wilderness with the evil opponent to Christian civilization. Breaking the wild nature of New England and setting up the City of God were thus inevitably and naturally accompanied by a certain righteousness. Little more than a century after settlement, however, both the self-congratulation and the linkage of wilderness with Satan seemed to have weakened. The woods had been pushed back, and civilization had indeed been created, but somehow the purification desired so strongly a century before had not been achieved. Ministers from the late seventeenth century and on into the eighteenth called repeatedly for renewal of the faith. Among these was Jonathan Edwards of Northampton, Massachusetts, famous for fire and brimstone; but very interestingly, Edwards's view of the wilderness was quite different from that of the earlier generations. He saw it in a positive light, as the place where an individual's renewal might begin. Describing his inward life in his *Personal Narrative* (1743), Edwards wrote that he sometimes experienced "a calm, sweet abstraction of soul from all the concerns of this world; and sometimes a kind of vision, or fixed ideas and imaginations, of being alone in the mountains, or some solitary wilderness, far from all mankind, sweetly conversing with Christ, and wrapt and swallowed up in God."[1] The level of society that had been elaborated in America, in all its success, had apparently become no more than "this world" after all; for purity, one would have to look elsewhere. Unspoiled nature was beginning to appear as a spiritual haven, and would one day become popularly known as "God's country."

Also at this time, as we have seen, empirical investigation was steadily cutting into the old superstitious and anthropomorphic views of nature. By the end of the eighteenth century, science had so opened up the field of consciousness that another New England minister, Samuel Williams of Vermont, would as a scientist not only keep temperature records and measure trees, but would even question man's traditional, confident assignment of his own moral values to nature.

By the time Ralph Waldo Emerson took the pulpit of the Second Church of Boston in 1829, an intellectual climate that was amazingly liberal and open compared to that of two centuries before prevailed. The successes of the scientific method in revealing the workings of nature, the undeniable gains in standard of living, and the general psychology of a culture in a "boom" phase of growth and development all conspired to create a climate of optimism and experiment. In addition, over the preceding century, the political status of the individual had undergone changes that were literally revolutionary. Emerson, in a series of influential essays and many public lectures after leaving the ministry, spoke with great accuracy to this new state of man and a new sense of nature as knowable. Perhaps more persuasively than any other thinker of his time in America, Emerson made his audience feel truly modern — liberated, and able to conceptualize the universe not as mystery but as something they could experience. Man, Emerson believed, is at home in the universe. As for tradition and authority, they were simply obstacles to our expanded, rightful consciousness of the universe; each individual could have, must have, an original relation with nature.

Emerson framed this radical proposal in homely, local terms. "In the woods," he wrote in his first book, *Nature* (1836), "we return to reason and faith."[2] The folksy, American usage, "the woods," makes a grand philosophical concept immediately available.[3] The woods is where one can transcend the limited, habitual, conforming, social self. The experience, as Emerson described it, was expansive in the extreme (he spoke of becoming "part or parcel of God") and joyful. This was a new way of looking at the American woods.

At the same time while Emerson was entering upon the larger public scene in America, Henry David Thoreau had just been graduated from Harvard College and was looking for a suitable vocation. In the case of Thoreau, who was, as his later editor wrote, "constitutionally earnest,"[4] vocation meant a good deal more than the means of earning a living. Thoreau met Emerson in 1836, and probably heard Emerson's inspirational address, "The American Scholar," in August of 1837 at the Harvard commencement; if not, he certainly knew it as an essay. In the fall of 1837 Thoreau became something like a protégé to Emerson, who lived not far from Thoreau in Concord. On October 22, 1837, at Emerson's suggestion, Thoreau began keeping a journal, modeling it on Emerson's.[5] It was tempting, indeed, for many of their contemporaries to see Thoreau as an imitation Emerson (James Russell Lowell, for one, had this opinion), but it turned out that Thoreau had his own ideas and experiences, and in the end formed from them an outlook quite distinct from Emerson's. It is pertinent, perhaps, that the first entry in young Thoreau's journal, after a brief bow toward Emerson, is titled "Solitude." Although Emerson had mapped in a general way so much of the new philosophical territory of nature, and man's connection with nature, he was never in sympathy with the intensity of Thoreau's commitment to wildness. He was unencouraging, in particular, about three of Thoreau's early, nature-centered essays, "A Natural History of Massachusetts," "A Walk to Wachusett," and "A Winter Walk."[6] It is clear that quite early in his career, Thoreau adopted a naturalistic perspective that was more radical than Emerson was willing to espouse.

This passionate allegiance to nature empowered Thoreau as a distinctive and original thinker. The note of independence, not simply from Emerson but also from much of the rest of humanity, sounded in his first published nature essay, "A Natural History of Massachusetts" (1842):

> We fancy that this din of religion, literature, and philosophy, which is heard in pulpits, lyceums, and parlors, vibrates through the universe, and is as catholic a sound as the creaking of the earth's axle; but if a man sleep soundly, he will forget it all between sunset and dawn. It is the three-inch swing of a pendulum in a cupboard, which the great pulse of nature vibrates by and through each instant. When we lift our eyelids and open our ears, it disappears with smoke and rattle like the cars on a railroad.[7]

What Thoreau affirmed as absolutely instructive was his own experience of the particulars of nature:

> Men tire me when I am not constantly greeted and refreshed as by the flux of sparkling streams. Surely joy is the condition of life. Think of the young fry that leap in ponds, the myriad of insects ushered into being on a summer evening, the incessant note of the hyla with which the woods ring in spring, the nonchalance of the butterfly carrying accident and change painted in a thousand hues upon its wings, or the brook minnow stoutly stemming the current, the luster of whose scales, worn bright by the attrition, is reflected upon the bank![8]

Thoreau drew, to be sure, upon the trust in individual experience that Emerson had preached, a concept that in turn reflected the confidence of their era, and also upon the general awakening to natural history that had been in progress for a century and a half, but the extent to which Thoreau had taken nature as his standard, the unqualified standing he proposed for such creatures as minnows and frogs, and the sure tone in which he voiced his position are his own. At twenty-five, in this early essay, which began as a book review for the Transcendentalist magazine *The Dial,* Thoreau upheld natural history as philosophically potent, and argued that the intuitive experience of nature ("direct intercourse and sympathy," as he called it) could lead to wisdom of an authentic and practical kind. Thoreau placed science and fact as helpful tools within the transcending philosophical context of experience, and presented this view of the world in accomplished, even artistic prose. It is thus fair to say that the possibilities of the nature essay as a modern literary form were first outlined in Thoreau's first essay, published in July, 1842.

One of the central traditions of his culture from which Thoreau declared independence was that of philosophical dualism. He posited nature, most of the time, as a realm of clarity, freedom, and innocence that the dichotomous approach to life only obscured. As early as 1841, he had become aware of the limiting effect of the ethical dualism so strong in the New England heritage:

> *Aug. 1. Sunday.* I never met a man who cast a free and healthy glance over life, but the best live in a sort of Sabbath light, a Jewish gloom. The best thought is not only without sombreness, but even without morality. The universe lies outspread in floods of white light to it. The moral aspect of nature is a jaundice reflected from man. To the innocent there are no cherubim nor angels. Occasionally we rise above the necessity of virtue into an unchangeable morning light, in which we have not to choose in a dilemma between right and wrong, but simply to live right on and breathe the circumambient air. There is no name for this life unless it be the very vitality of *vita.* Silent is the preacher about this, and silent must ever be, for he who knows it will not preach.[9]

Thoreau did not keep to this naturalistic position with perfect consistency — see the "Higher Laws" chapter of *Walden,* for instance — but there is evidence that he was deeply engaged with the problem of dualism throughout his life. His repeated dreaming of what he called "the rough and the smooth" is perhaps evidence of such a preoccupation; his love of paradox (which irritated Emerson) shows a willingness to twit the usual habits of mind. More fundamentally, some of his statements, such as his surprising deathbed utterance that it was "just as good to have a poor time as a good time," suggest that he may have reached, at the end, a profound realization.[10] For all his life, Thoreau appears to have sought above all a pure and direct experience, that is, a nondual experience, which would transcend the usual distance between subject and object and grant participation in the wholeness of nature. The hope for this state drew forth some of his most impassioned writing:

> I heard a robin in the distance, the first I had heard for many a thousand years, methought, whose note I shall not forget for many a thousand more, — the same sweet and powerful song as of yore. O the evening robin, at the end of a New England summer day! If I could ever find the twig he sits upon! I mean *he;* I mean *the twig.*[11]

The song of the wood thrush, a common bird in the Concord area, touched Thoreau deeply, catalyzing the thought of enlightenment to nature. There are thirty-nine references to the wood thrush in his journal, almost as many as to Emerson (with those to the bird taking the honors for apparent depth of response, in any case), and it is possible to see in these references just what it was that Thoreau brought new to the American nature essay. Mark Catesby evidently did not hear the wood thrush sing, since he merely listed it as the "Little Thrush" (see p. 31) and was not particularly attuned to bird song in general. William Bartram does little more than list the bird. However, Wilson, Nuttall, and Audubon all testify to the beauty of its song and its power to lift the spirits, with Nuttall suggesting a mysterious, ethereal quality: "It is nearly impossible by words to convey any idea of the peculiar warble of this vocal hermit. . . ."[12] But it is from Thoreau that we learn to hear the thrush's song as the distillation of the woods itself, the essence of wildness, and thus the key to the opened self. This is an entirely new dimension.

> The wood thrush's is no opera music; it is not so much the composition as the strain, the tone, — cool bars of melody from the atmosphere of everlasting morning or evening. It is the quality of the song, not the sequence. In the peawai's note there is some sultriness, but in the thrush's, though heard at noon, there is the liquid coolness of things that are just drawn from the bottom of springs. The thrush alone declares the immortal wealth and vigor that is in the forest. Here is a bird in whose strain the story is told, though Nature waited for the science of aesthetics to discover it to man. Whenever a man hears it, he is young, and Nature is in her spring. Wherever he hears it, it is a new world and a free country, and the gates of heaven are not shut against him. Most other birds sing from the level of my ordinary cheerful hours — a carol; but this bird never fails to speak to me out of an ether purer than that I breathe, of immortal beauty and vigor. He deepens the significance of all things seen in the light of his strain. He sings to make men take higher and truer views of things.[13]

To describe the awakening of higher consciousness in such meta-phorical but not abstract terms — to root it in nature, that is — was one of the Thoreau's major accomplishments as a writer. Such description makes "the woods" more believable as a philosophical standpoint. From the woods, Thoreau looked at his times with a wild perspective that no one before him in American life had developed so concretely or thoroughly. He had gone beyond the Western mind's accustomed paths.

The essay "Walking," which began as a lecture more than a decade before Thoreau's death and which he revised in his last months, became his final word on the wild. He warned his readers in the opening paragraph that he would be standing apart from the "champions of civilization" in what he had to say, but the reflections that follow are not so much concerned with the differences between society and the wild as they are with the positive spark of wildness that remains and that might be redeeming. Here again, Thoreau used a familiar subject, the simple act of walking, as the base from which to develop profound metaphors of awakening and sacrality. "Walking" is an essay asserting the wildness within the civilized self: "When we walk, we naturally go to the fields and woods"; "I believe that there is a subtle magnetism in Nature, which, if we unconsciously yield to it, will direct us aright"; "In literature it is only the wild that attracts us."[14] Thus wildness is not limited to the distant wilderness but is something innate, something that might awaken one day. The non-dualistic theme of the essay is further demonstrated by its emphasis on walking as a continuing process. "It is a living way, / As the Christians say," Thoreau writes in the poem "The Old Marlborough Road" (see p. 199) and the final sentence of the essay states that "we saunter toward the Holy Land," that is, we do not arrive there as if it were a specific locale. To think that we might, if we were good enough walkers, arrive at a discrete state of enlightenment would be to commit the same dualistic error as believing wildness is only in the wilderness. Thoreau's summary of the thrust of the essay (". . . what I have been preparing to say. . .") is in this same vein: ". . .in Wildness is the preservation of the world."[15] Not wilderness, that is, the named and the mapped, but something more inner and involving. The meaning of "preservation" thus suggested is not saving apart, as under glass, but sustaining the creative power, that which keeps the world continually renewing. The wildness that preserves the world is the "eternal morning" that the wood thrush sings, and is what sends us out walking.

Throughout his work, Thoreau's images of nature have a palpable quality; he is not looking at scenery. Awakened consciousness, apparently, is not a separate state, a property of humans, but a partnership with real places.

> This is a delicious evening, when the whole body is one sense, and imbibes delight through every pore. I go and come with a strange liberty in Nature, a part of herself. As I walk along the stony shore of the pond in my shirt sleeves, though it is cool as well as cloudy and windy, and I see nothing special to attract me, all the elements are unusually congenial to me. The bullfrogs trump to usher in the night, and the note of the whippoorwill is borne on the rippling wind from over the water. Sympathy with the fluttering alder and poplar leaves almost takes away my breath; yet, like the lake, my serenity is rippled but not ruffled.[16]

This sense for process and involvement carried over into Thoreau's awareness of language; he once praised words like "delicious" and "avaricious" because in saying them one had to perform certain lip and jaw movements that reinforced the words' meanings. He was profoundly aware of the physical content of thought and language, conscious that even in the most cerebral human activities the wild played an essential part. It was indeed, as every evidence demonstrated to Thoreau, a "great pulse" preserving the world.

In contrast with the contributions made by Emerson, Thoreau, and other nineteenth-century writers to our understanding of nature, the environmental history of America in their time was marked by severe displacements and losses. Disruption of environmental patterns was nothing new, of course, having accompanied European settlement on the eastern seaboard from the earliest times. But now the new order spread rapidly across the country; with the opening of the Erie Canal in 1825, with steam navigation on the Great Lakes established by the late 1830s, and with the phenomenal increase in miles of railroad tracks beginning also in the 1830s, occupation of the interior and exploitation of its resources were greatly facilitated. In 1776, Daniel Boone had surveyed the Wilderness Road through the forests of the Cumberland Gap into the rich land of Kentucky, and the first trickle of settlers began to move across the Appalachian barrier; a mere century and a quarter later, the continental United States was trussed with a network of 197,000 miles of railroads. By the end of the nineteenth century, the herds of bison, which had in Boone's time ranged from the Great Basin to Pennsylvania and from Canada to Mexico, were virtually gone. The frontier which had beckoned Boone and others so compellingly had been declared closed in 1890. Throughout the nineteenth century, waves of immigrants, many from distressed European countries, added to the population and inevitably to its impact on the land. As the westward expansion pushed toward its conclusion, with the last "free" lands in sight, an atmosphere much like frenzy developed. "This restless, nervous, bustling, trivial Nineteenth Century," Thoreau had called it,[17] but he had seen nothing like what would happen after the Civil War.

The railroad network became intimately involved with the massive accumulation of capital that characterized the latter half of the century, thus facilitating the assault on the environment in two ways: mechanically, by transporting large quantities of resources that were the fruits of exploitation (crops, livestock, minerals, and lumber), and financially, by enabling the major industrial powers to become centralized. Large-scale monoculture became not only possible but profitable on land far from major markets. Centralized capital meant that environments could be affected by market forces and decisions made far from the scene; this tended to weaken any restraint, or even planning for the future, that might conceivably have operated under localized control. Worse yet, the arms of the railroad "octopus," as the novelist Frank Norris called it, were for several decades literally supported and fueled by wood, a fact that had significant negative impact on the size and composition of American forests. Even in Thoreau's time, during the 1850s, the railroads of the United States were using between 4 and 5 million cords of wood per year to generate steam in locomotive engines, and after the switch to coal, which itself had powerful environmental effects, the railroads still needed wood for ties. In 1910, one-fourth of the nation's total wood consumption was accounted for by this use.[18]

The factory system, and its enlargement of capacity to massive production in the decades following the Civil War, complemented the growth of the rail transportation network and the centralization of capital. There had been just one small factory in the United States in 1790, a mill in Pawtucket, Rhode Island, where cotton yarn was produced. By the dawn of the twentieth century, great factories were responsible for carrying on all of the major means of production, including the processing of agricultural products. This conclusive dominance of the economy by industry stimulated the rapid growth of large cities.

In the countryside, swamps and wet lowlands were drained and filled at almost every opportunity; both tallgrass and shortgrass prairies, which in their pristine state had supported a stunning variety and abundance of wildlife, were converted to monocultures of corn and wheat, or to pastures for domestic stock. In areas where forests were allowed to grow back, the composition of forests was often radically changed (according to a 1958 account, much of the new-growth woods in New England was "a sorry mixture of the most persistent weed trees and low-grade stump sprouts");[19] and perhaps the most striking of all changes, hardest not to notice, was the steep decline in wildlife countrywide. This included the bison and the passenger pigeon, of course, most prominently, but also the wolf, cougar, and caribou, all essentially gone from the eastern half of the country by the close of the nineteenth century; seals, sea otters, and whales were decimated along the Pacific Coast in the same time period, and populations of shorebirds and even many songbirds were seriously reduced by market hunting. In the Rockies, elk and bighorn sheep were forced onto small islands of mountain wilderness.[20] In one century, the United States was transformed from a smallish seaboard republic, mostly agrarian, where canals and mule-drawn barges were a key link in the economy, to an urban-industrial power of some 76 million citizens.

It is well to remember, on the other hand, that it was within this same America of unrestrained growth that the first modern voices for the preservation of nature were heard. As Paul Brooks has shown in his important study, *Speaking for Nature* (1980), writers like Henry David Thoreau, John Muir, and John Burroughs, along with a number of others, reached and moved the book-reading portion of the public. Their ideas came eventually to have an effect, perhaps a significant effect, on national policy. Speaking for the wild, one might say, they helped to moderate seemingly insatiable appetites for growth and consumption of resources.

John Muir experienced frontier America at first hand, as a child and teenager on his father's homestead in Wisconsin. The family had emigrated from Scotland in 1849, when Muir was eleven, and by the time he left home at twenty-two, they had built two farms where previously there had been a wilderness — that "glorious Wisconsin wilderness," Muir later wrote.[21] Muir spent his twenties studying at the recently established University of Wisconsin (where he was influenced deeply by both science and the philosophy of Emerson), botanizing in the countryside and working in small factories in Ontario and Indiana, walking from southern Indiana to Florida in 1867, and, in his inner life, coming slowly out from under the fundamentalist Calvinism that his father had enforced upon the family. He was thirty years old when he arrived in California in 1868, and in many ways just coming to maturity.

In his journal of the southern trip, Muir had criticized the anthropocentrism of his father's religion. The journals he kept during his first winter in California, when he lived in the foothills of the Sierra

Nevada, show him reaching further beyond philosophical dualism: "But out here in the free unplanted fields there is no rectilineal sectioning of times and seasons. All things *flow* here in indivisible, measureless currents."[22] In the next summer, the baptismal and glorious summer of 1869, Muir's experiences in the mountains gave body to these concepts, leading him to an intense feeling of continuity with the wild beauty around him, simply overwhelming "petty personal hope or experience," in his words.[23] In June, 1869, he had accompanied a band of some 2,000 sheep into the mountains, walking slowly upward through the heat-blasted foothills into the cooler, forested portion of the Sierra proper. Starting from the sheep camp there, he was free to take long, physically demanding rambles into the high country of glacial meadows and clean gray granite. Living on simple food and surrounded for several months by only natural forms and forces, Muir stretched himself physically, learning in particular the poise and balance needed for traveling on talus slopes, as this was his initial experience of alpine country. Most of all, Muir came alive to the mountains.

> Drinking this champagne water is pure pleasure, so is breathing the living air, and every movement of the limbs is pleasure, while the whole body seems to feel beauty when exposed to it as it feels a campfire or sunshine, entering not by the eyes alone, but equally through all one's flesh like radiant heat, making a passionate ecstatic pleasure-glow not explainable.[24]

After taking up residence in Yosemite Valley in the fall of 1869, Muir embarked on an investigation of the glacial history of the Sierra, making several extended study-journeys into the mountains over the next few years. He added to his physical and emotional "pleasure-glow" the discipline of daily practice in the scientific method. As the months and years progressed, and his knowledge of the range widened, there matured in Muir an outlook on the world that gave full scope to both the ecstatic perception of oneness with nature and the empirical discernment of its particulars. In an instructive journal entry, he outlined his own personal odyssey toward totalistic understanding:

> Grand North Womb of
> Mount Clark Glacier
> *October* 7 (?), 1871.

> In streams of ice, of water, of minerals, of plants, of animals, the tendency is to unification. We at once find ourselves among eternities,

infinitudes, and scarce know whether to be happy in the sublime simplicity of radical causes and origins or whether to be sorry on losing
the beautiful fragments which we thought perfect and primary absolute
units; but as we study and mingle with nature more, the pain caused
by the melting of all beauties into one First Beauty disappears, because,
after their first baptismal submergence in fountain God, they go again
washed and clean into their individualisms, more clearly defined than
ever, unified yet separate.[25]

One could hardly ask for a clearer account of the struggle to match
human consciousness to the complexity of nature, or of Muir's
scientific-poetic faith that all that is required, in order to transcend
the usual limitations of thought, is to "study and mingle with nature
more." The passage bears an uncanny resemblance to the traditional
Zen Buddhist account of the passage through the "gateless gate":
before one studied Zen (that is, meditated), mountains were simply
mountains; at a certain point, after the first flush of nondualistic
awakening, mountains are no longer mountains; now, at last, but in
fuller realization, mountains are again mountains.

In contrast with this journal entry, most of Muir's published writings, for most of his career as an author, did not focus on the inner
dimension. In fact, as his biographer Linnie Marsh Wolfe pointed
out, he "studied . . . to keep himself and his mystical interpretations
of nature in the background,"[26] apparently believing that such matters were beyond communicating. His emphasis in writing was on
what he called the "beautiful fragments": the morning light "stinging," as he put it, the topmost cliffs of the Grand Canyon at sunrise;
a sky full of towering, light-shot cumulus clouds building to an afternoon thunderstorm over the Sierra; the inevitably symmetrical
branching habit of the giant sequoia; and the chattering, electric
energy of the Douglas squirrel. These images were not static; Muir
always rendered these nouns of the world as alive and changing. His
ecological consciousness was folded into his expression of the scene
before him, helping to animate it. He was careful to describe nothing
in isolation. Flowering plants push up through the moist earth in
spring, grasses hang over stream banks and are moved by the running
water, and glaciers press their weight on the land, scouring, scraping,
and molding the mountains. Muir also tried to suggest, in the smooth,
fluent rhythms of his sentences, the flow that was, to his mind, the
primary fact of nature. His is one of the great efforts to make nature
come alive on the page, and he worked hard at his writing, tapping
out sentence-rhythms, for example, despite his stated belief that "no
amount of word-making will ever make a single soul to *know* these

mountains."[27] Eventually the effort had an impact on American life. Indeed, among American nature writers, Muir's effectiveness is one of the easiest to quantify, from his ideas for a watershed-encompassing boundary for Yosemite National Park, to his direct influence on President Theodore Roosevelt in the matter of forest and park preservation, and his role in inspiring the important Lacey Antiquities Act of 1906.

Muir's contribution to the developing American nature essay was threefold: he enlarged it to include wild-country adventures, while essentially continuing Thoreau's philosophy of wildness; deepened its evolutionary and ecological content with his emphasis on flow and harmony; and added a strong new note of militancy, in response to the dramatic environmental conditions of his time. As is often pointed out, Henry David Thoreau may have been at least momentarily disquieted when he scrambled alone onto the summit plateau of Mount Katahdin in 1846, only to find himself in the midst of blowing cloud. He described his state there in the wild elements as "more lone than you can imagine."[28] Muir, though, never admitted to being daunted, at least for long, whatever the circumstances — a free-solo climb of Mount Ritter in the Sierra; a forced bivouac in a storm, near the summit of Mount Shasta; or a dangerous traverse of a deeply crevassed glacier in Alaska. Any experience in the wilderness seemed to be proof for his theme that the mountains were "home." In Muir's view, the wild universe gave birth to us and was not to be feared. At the start of the Inyo earthquake of 1872, a shock that toppled hundreds of tons of rock from the cliffs of Yosemite and sent inhabitants of the valley fleeing out of the mountains, Muir emerged from his cabin calling out (so he wrote to the Boston Society of Natural History), "A noble earthquake!"[29] He described the earthquake, one of the strongest recorded in United States history, as "Mother Earth . . . trotting us on her knee. . . ."[30]

Muir's transmutation of the fear of death into a hymn of praise, a motif often repeated in his work, is closely related to his concept of wilderness as familiar. To Muir, wilderness was not any sort of "other," much less a threat, but simply the most obvious manifestation of the total patterning of things; not chaos but a complete, unified order that included humans. His best statement of this point was in "Wild Wool," an 1875 essay later reprinted in *Steep Trails* (1918), in which he held that all creatures are "killing and being killed, eating and being eaten," and that this constant predation results only in harmony and rightness: "And it is right that we should thus reciprocally make use of one another, rob, cook, and consume, to the utmost of our healthy abilities and desires."[31] All would be well in this naturalistic universe except that man, thinking himself special, has interfered with the evolutionary integrity of other beings in the pattern and bent them to his exclusive use. Taming apples, roses, and sheep, he proceeds to build up not only an economy but a mentality of separateness, and loses sight of the beautiful fitness of things.

> No dogma taught by the present civilization seems to form so insuperable an obstacle in the way of a right understanding of the relations which culture sustains to wildness, as that which declares that the world was made especially for the uses of men. Every animal, plant, and crystal controverts it in the plainest terms. Yet it is taught from century to century as something ever new and precious, and in the resulting darkness the enormous conceit is allowed to go unchallenged.[32]

The glacier study had awakened Muir's sense of both geologic time and the many subtle interweavings of causes and effects that had evolved into the present state of things. His sense of evolutionary time strengthened his interpretation of the world as congenial. Man, he wrote, had "flowed down" through other forms of life, incorporating parts of them and becoming in the process "most richly terrestrial."[33] "Terrestrial" for Muir meant "sacred," so in effect his evolutionary view kept spirituality, reverence, and other sacred matters alive, but rooted them in Darwinian realities.

Though he did not have the command of history and cultural reference of Thoreau, Muir could comment forcefully on his times, usually in the manner of the Old Testament prophets, by holding up the sordid or the grasping against the clear beauty of the wilderness. As might be expected, given his rearing, he had a strong feel for damnation and salvation, though his definitions of these states became roughly opposite those of his culture, and his vituperation of the thoughtless or selfish had thunder in it. When he described how herds of sheep had been driven into a once-beautiful Sierra meadow, it was in terms of Biblical desecration: "The money changers were in the temple."[34] In the great battle of his life, the struggle to save the Hetch Hetchy Valley of Yosemite from dam builders, Muir's outrage was again cast in language reflecting his religious upbringing: "Dam Hetch Hetchy! As well dam for water-tanks the people's cathedrals and churches, for no holier temple has ever been consecrated by the heart of man."[35] He also defended nature on scientific and practical terms, arguing consistently and as early as 1875 that forest preservation simply made good sense for watershed health,[36] but his major thrust was philosophical and moral. "The battle for conservation will go on endlessly," he once wrote. "It is part of the universal warfare between right and wrong."[37]

Muir's militant criticism of modern society may not have been as broad or as deep as Thoreau's, perhaps, but it was topically to the point, and it was pitched accurately to his times. His ideas, his rhetorical strategies, and his whole style as a man spoke effectively to an age in philosophical transition. He alerted people to the moral dimension of the attack on wild nature, and he demonstrated the qualities of heart and mind that would be needed for a post-frontier civilization to come into being. In his acceptance of evolution yet retention of an essentially religious view of the world, he demonstrated that "studying and mingling more" with nature could help a Christian culture enter the new philosophical era.

That new era, of course, centered on the work of Charles Darwin. Darwin himself, as is well known, had studied for the ministry and had begun the famous voyage on H.M.S. *Beagle* as a believer in Genesis. Five years of field work, another twenty or more of scholarly pondering, and Darwin had come to a different view. The world, in all its intricate relational complexity, was still wonderful, but it had got that way, and was continuing onward to who knows what state, through an entirely natural process that included, integrally and importantly, a good deal of accident. With the publication of *The Origin of Species* in November, 1859, the traditional and rather placid view of the world as divinely ordained began to come apart. The great work of natural philosophy since that time has been to explore the naturalistic universe, where relativity and change are the basic laws, and where chance is completely pervasive, to see if there might exist anything solid upon which to base the conduct of human life. In short, evolution and natural selection, coming out of somewhat obscure researches in natural history, have laid waste absolutist and revealed theories, and have thrown the philosophical door wide open.

Among naturalists and nature writers, however, the impact of Darwinism was not devastating or even, apparently, terribly shocking. Nature literature since Darwin does not reflect any sense of terror at being adrift in a blankly materialistic universe. As we have seen, American nature writers for some time had been criticizing anthropocentrism and anthropomorphism, and had been promoting wider views based upon empirical evidence. In a sense, Darwin merely took this same theme further. Evolution had been "in the air" for decades; his contribution was to explain its heretofore unseen mechanism. This was no small thing, for understanding the mechanism, natural selection, involved a revolution in Western thought; but the point is that Darwin's great work should be seen as part of an expansion of knowledge and perspective that had been underway among students of natural history for more than two centuries.

Henry David Thoreau read *The Origin of Species* a few weeks after its publication and took several pages of notes, but was not revolutionized. Perhaps one reason for his interested but mild reaction was that he was accustomed already to a relational view of the world. Mutable species did not seem to shock him. "Am I not partly leaves and vegetable mould myself?" he had asked in Walden,[38] having already found his own answer.

The most common stance in American nature literature, after Darwin had thrown open the great questions of existence and meaning, was to grant science the realm of the finite, preserving the divine as an infinite but at the same time indwelling mystery — a principle rather than anything anthropomorphically familiar. This was essentially the position of Muir and of John Burroughs, the two most important American nature writers in the time of the Darwinian controversy. This position stops short of pure mechanism — the view that all phenomena in nature can be explained in terms of mechanical principles and material causes — and leaves room for the mysterious, ecstatic feeling of intense connectedness with the world which is, for many nature writers, the root of and the justification for right conduct. Most of American nature literature since Darwin has simply incorporated evolution and natural selection into its perception of the web of life, without any particular hitch. Many writers have not emphasized these subjects at all. But there was a time, extending roughly from 1860 to about 1920, when the new theories and the resulting need for grand-scale philosophizing and interpretation of these views necessarily occupied center stage. In that time, John Burroughs was perhaps the most congenial and effective American interpreter of the new views.

An almost exact contemporary of Muir's, Burroughs was far less of a wilderness man. He was not an activist at all in conservation matters, and his prose had considerably less charge to it than Muir's. But he was extraordinarily popular, first as a writer of pleasant rambles, and later as nothing less than an American country sage, a man who could make the new universe seem an accessible, friendly place. He did this by telling and showing people how to look. Answering the philosophical challenge of mechanism, he set forth an approach to nature study that preserved both empirical accuracy and the sense of wonder and enjoyment. He recommended rigor in interpreting animal behavior, and was especially scornful of the tendency to anthropomorphize. He recognized that nature is ruled mostly by evolutionary patterning and instinct, and felt that we needed to be clear about this. But at the same time, there is an ineffable dimension to life — our own experience of deep agreement with nature, of being at home in it, and then the great and mysterious pattern of the whole — and this must simply remain ineffable. "We cannot find God by thinking," Burroughs wrote.[39]

From his earliest works, Burroughs had charmed his readers with relaxed, realistic accounts of fields and woods. Reading his books, the novelist and critic William Dean Howells said, was like taking a summer vacation. Typically, the author went on short walks out into the country, where he saw and heard everything with remarkable receptivity, and was refreshed and made reflective and appreciative by the experience. Burroughs was a companionable guide who spoke confidingly to his readers, instructing them genially in the ways of nature and providing a model for a reasonable and fitting emotional response. As a nature writer he was less testing than Thoreau and less heroic than Muir, but his middling way nevertheless presented nature in some experiential depth.

Much of the emotional resonance in Burroughs' descriptions derives from his powerful attachment to his home ground, the Catskill Mountains of New York and the surrounding farming country. He was born and raised on a farm there, came back to the area in adulthood as soon as he was financially able to settle there, and eventually purchased the old family property. His friend William Sloane Kennedy wrote in *The Real John Burroughs* (1924) that "the *idée fixe* of John o' the Catskills is that there is no place like his home locality, and there are no birds, anywhere in the world equal to those of his native hills."[40] It may even be true that Burroughs' often-expressed sense of the "home" quality of the universe at large, as in "the universe is good, and it is our rare good fortune to form a part of it,"[41] originated in those softly rolling hills and pleasingly varied rural landscapes.

Burroughs' mature idea of the scheme of things, in the large sense, probably owed much to the influence of the poet Walt Whitman. In 1863, at twenty-six, young Burroughs had gone to Washington, D.C., to seek employment. He had been thinking of himself as a writer for some time, and had published an essay of Emersonian tone in *The Atlantic Monthly*, but had been unable to support his wife of six years. At this crucial time he met Whitman, who was working as a government clerk while tending sick and wounded Civil War soldiers in Washington hospitals, and the poet heartened the younger man by the sheer force of his charismatic and nurturing personality. Burroughs, demonstrating the character he later described as "very yielding, and very quick to receive an impression,"[42] took on some of Whitman's cosmic confidence. He became a writer with more of his own voice now (though at first there were strong overtones of Whitman's in it, certainly), and, just as important, he began to develop a concept of nature that went beyond scenery-oriented Romanticism. In his first book, *Notes on Walt Whitman, As Poet and Person* (1867), Burroughs described the poet's idea of nature and said that he understood it:

> The word Nature, now, to most readers, suggests only some flower bank, or summer cloud, or pretty scene that appeals to the sentiments. None of this is in Walt Whitman. And it is because he corrects this false, artificial Nature, and shows me the real article, that I hail his appearance as the most important literary event of our time.[43]

Whitman remained a friend and an influence. Burroughs closed his literary career almost as he had begun it: the final chapter of *Accepting the Universe* (1920), which was the last book published during his lifetime, was entitled "The Poet of the Cosmos," and was a tribute to Whitman's scope and seriousness.

Burroughs' reaction to Darwin, whom he first read in 1883, was much like his response to Whitman. He saw the naturalist as the bringer of a whole new vision. "Everything about Darwin indicates the master. In reading him you breathe the air of the largest and most serene mind," Burroughs wrote in his journal. "[His theory] is as ample as the earth, and as deep as time."[44] To Burroughs, the largest minds saw beyond the usual categories of good and evil, predator and prey, life and death, and perceived that all terms that seemed to be polar opposites were essentially complementary, as was the great system that gave birth to them. This penetration is what "accepting the universe" means. Typically, Burroughs framed his exposition of this truth in very specific, natural history terms:

> The conflicting interests in Nature sooner or later adjust themselves; her checks and balances bring about her equilibrium. In vegetation rivalries and antagonisms bring about adaptations. The mosses and the ferns and the tender wood plants grow beneath the oaks and the pines and are favored by the shade and protection which the latter afford them. The farmer's seeding of grass and clover takes better under the shade of the oats than it would upon the naked ground. In Africa some species of flesh-eaters live upon the leavings of larger and

stronger species, and in the tropics certain birds become benefactors of the cattle by preying upon the insects that pester them. Fabre tells of certain insect hosts that blindly favor the parasites that destroy them. The scheme has worked itself out that way and Nature is satisfied. Victim or victor, host or parasite, it is all one to her. Life goes on, and all forms of it are hers.[45]

With this breadth of acceptance, Burroughs demonstrated that he had come a long philosophical way in the half-century since his first nature book, *Wake-Robin* (1871), in which he had written quite forthrightly of killing a black snake for the crime of eating a catbird, and of removing a baby cowbird from the nest of a Canada warbler and dropping the cowbird chick into a nearby creek.

Burroughs once described himself in comparison to Thoreau as "soft, flexible, and adaptive,"[46] but it is doubtful that the victims of his lash in the "nature-faker" controversy would have agreed. In the March, 1903, issue of *The Atlantic Monthly*, Burroughs attacked a school of nature writing (specifically, two popular writers, Ernest Thompson Seton and the Reverend William J. Long) for spicing their narratives of nature by attributing humanlike reason and emotion to animals, and for describing as perfectly factual certain improbable happenings. The article stung, and a sometimes rancorous exchange of open letters and articles ensued, drawing into the heated controversy even the president, Theodore Roosevelt (on Burroughs' side); the overall effect, however, was undoubtedly healthful for nature writing. Burroughs had reinforced in the public mind the scientific content of the genre, and helped to establish standards of credibility for the interpretation of animal behavior. The controversy also brought out nature writing's potential for insight into the human condition in nature, for in defining the minds of the other animals, one necessarily tries to deal with what might make humanity distinctive. Burroughs himself demonstrated some of the good effects of the discussion in a fair-minded and reflective book, *Ways of Nature* (1905). In this study, he carefully differentiated instinct from judgment, and the ability to communicate feeling from language. He found, in the end, that although "the line that divides man from the lower orders is not a straight line. It has many breaks and curves and deep indentations,"[47] it is a line nevertheless. He described sentimentality (excessive line-crossing) as simply anthropomorphism, a distraction hurtful to clear understanding.

But Burroughs did not want science to completely demystify or mechanize our response to nature. Experience, for him, always stood equal in importance with knowledge.

I have taken persons to hear the hermit thrush, and I have fancied that they were all the time saying to themselves, "Is that all?" But should one hear the bird in his walk, when the mind is attuned to simple things and is open and receptive, when expectation is not aroused and the song comes as a surprise out of the dusky silence of the woods, then one feels that it merits all the fine things that can be said of it.[48]

The genteel tradition, which helped set the tone for many literary works of the later nineteenth century, was well represented in the nature essay. Indeed, nature writing may seem made to order for gentility. On the surface at least, all is well and all is upright in the world of nature. It is pleasurable, harmless, and uplifting to walk out and hear the birds. But even in some of the most obviously genteel nature writers, deeper issues involving man and his relationship with the environment have a way of coming to the surface. The work of Wilson Flagg, who was an insurance agent and clerk at the Boston customs house as well as an inveterate walker, is illustrative.

When Thoreau read Flagg's *Studies in the Field and Forest* (1857), he wrote to a friend that Flagg "wants stirring up with a pole," and could gain a little vigor, which his sentences seemed to need, by "turning a series of somersets rapidly."[49] Flagg's own description of his purposes as a writer, set forth in 1872, was mild enough — he would try to "inspire [his] readers with a love of nature and a simplicity of life, confident that the great fallacy of the present age is that of mistaking the increase of national wealth for the advancement of civilization."[50] There was little energy, much less Muirian denunciation, in such a statement. But in his long walks on what he called "By-ways," the meandering roads and paths that had served the New England of an earlier day, Flagg came to a clear idea of what he thought was right for the land. When he considered the spread of "model farming," which, in the name of efficiency and order, was plowing every square rod of land, leaving no edge for wildlife, and creating an artificial landscape around farmhouses, he became aroused. He realized that he was witnessing the death of the old ways, with their pleasing variety, and the "model" of the new age disturbed him. "We may distinguish the possessions of these model farmers by observing, as we pass by, their singular blankness, such as you observe in the face of an overfed idiot."[51]

Flagg's ideal landscape was the old American middle ground, the pastoral zone, but he recognized that wilderness, rather near by, was fundamentally necessary to the existence of that favorite environment. "Woods and their undergrowth are indeed the only barriers against frequent and sudden inundations, and the only means in the economy of nature for preserving an equal fullness of streams during all seasons of the year"; furthermore, "civilization has never, in any country, long survived, the destruction of its forests."[52] Accordingly, he proposed what he called "Forest Conservatories." These would amount to "three or four square miles each, in the ratio of one such tract to every square degree of latitude and longitude." Within these special areas, there would be no hunting, trapping, or landscaping, and the walking paths would be only a few feet wide (thus barring carriages). There would be a little farming allowed, in places, but not for profit (Flagg thus implies a government entity overseeing the land, or a beneficent landlord, or philosophically minded farmers), because, as he thought, "rustic tillage would be needful for the subsistence of the birds and animals. . . ."[53] Flagg did not develop many of the possible implications of his proposal, nor did he ever describe the practical steps that would be needed to institute it, but the idea remains suggestive. (It is somewhat similar to Thoreau's better-known proposition that each village should have a wilderness woods adjacent to it.) Suggestion, indeed, was Flagg's method as a writer; he had a light touch. "Studies" were his chief mode:

> I never believe so much in the immortality of the soul as when, at sunset, I look through a long vista of luminous clouds, far down into that mystic region of light in which, we are fain to imagine, are deposited the secrets of the universe. I cannot believe that all this panorama of unimaginable loveliness, which is spread out over earth, sea, and sky, is without some moral signification. The blue heavens are the page whereon nature has revealed some pleasant intimations of the mysteries of a more spiritual existence; and no charming vision of heaven or immortality entered the human soul, but the Deity responded to it upon the firmament, in letters of gold, ruby, and sapphire.[54]

The undeveloped portions of the desert Southwest had special attractiveness for nature- and wilderness-minded people at the close of the frontier era, because here the freshness of unspoiled land persisted. There were great stretches of uninhabited country, along with silence and isolation, and where there was culture, it tended to have a native, authentic stamp of the country on it. Most of this is gone now, of course, as another kind of life blossoms in the Sun Belt, but less than a century ago the desert corner of this country was largely wilderness. Even as recently as the 1930s, the forester Robert Marshall found some 18 million acres of pristine land in Utah, in a survey of government holdings in that state. Wild country on a scale like that speaks, to some, of powerful and illuminative experience.

Thus the meanings that writers attached to the Southwest, from the late nineteenth century onward, have been consistently transcendental and spiritual. There is a strong mystique of place, even today. On a slightly less elevated level, the flora and fauna of the area, in their remarkable adaptations to the environment, fairly shout the lessons of ecology. So it is for substantial environmental reasons, at heart, that the desert has been predominant in the nature literature of the West, down to the present.

From the start, describers of this dry quarter have insisted that pastoral and Romantic conventions of scenery appreciation do not apply here; they frame perception, when what is needed is a wilder way of seeing, some way to open the mind to the bright light and the raw-looking, naked and rocky landscape. You cannot call the Grand Canyon "charming." The first appeal for a new perception was made by a United States Government surveyor, Clarence Dutton, who spent parts of several years doing geological surveys of northern Arizona and southern Utah. In his *Tertiary History of the Grand Cañon District* (1882), Dutton repeatedly urged the abandonment of tradition: "Forms so new to the culture of civilized races and so strongly contrasted with those which have been the ideals of thirty generations of white men cannot indeed be appreciated after the study of a single hour or day," he wrote, recommending lengthy immersion. He also recommended a respectful realism: "There is no need, as we look upon them [the Vermilion Cliffs], of fancy to heighten the picture, nor of metaphor to present it. The simple truth is quite enough."[55]

John Charles Van Dyke, a librarian and a professor of art history at Rutgers College who spent most of three years on long, difficult solo treks in the deserts of California and Arizona, and who wrote from that experience one of the most highly regarded xeric texts, *The Desert* (1901), must have felt the same aesthetic challenge keenly. Already well known as an expert on art before he entered the desert in 1898 for the first of his journeys, Van Dyke had been deeply influenced by the work of the British critic John Ruskin, and was particularly like Ruskin in his acute awareness of his own aesthetic responses. His perceptions in *The Desert* are given in painstaking, step-by-step fashion, with attention to form, color, perspective, and all other possible ingredients of a view. Perhaps the desert has had no better-trained pair of eyes look on it. Indeed, there may be no more detailed parsing-out of scenes anywhere in American nature writing.

But Van Dyke's attention was not fragmented. He had a moral passion for the desert, an overwhelming love that kept him traveling in it despite some serious health problems, and his perceptions unified around that master feeling. His consciousness of the land was fundamentally participative, not remote.

> The long line of dunes at the north are just as desolate, yet they are wonderfully beautiful. The desert sand is finer than snow, and its curves and arches, as it builds its succession of drifts out and over an arroyo, are as graceful as the lines of running water. The dunes are always rhythmical and flowing in their forms; and for color the desert has nothing that surpasses them. In the early morning, before the sun is up, they are air-blue, reflecting the sky overhead; at noon they are pale lines of dazzling orange-colored light, waving and undulating in the heated air; at sunset they are often flooded with a rose or mauve color; under a blue moonlight they shine white as icebergs in the northern seas.[56]

Passion unified Van Dyke's sensibility, and it also inspired him to want to tell only the truth about the desert and its wildlife. The truth of the struggle for life under hard conditions, the simple realism of it, existed beyond traditional, human categories of judgment. "Nature neither rejoices in the life nor sorrows in the death. She is neither good nor evil; she is only a great law of change that passeth understanding."[57]

Like Ruskin, Van Dyke scorned the utilitarian view of nature; the desert was not, he wrote, a "livable place," and it should never be reclaimed. Its virtue, a kind of partnership with a finer, liberated human awareness, was on an entirely higher plane. If we could only perceive nature with clarity, Van Dyke argued, we would know better than to turn the earth to account with blunt instruments. Seeing an appropriate human role on the earth is partly a matter of taste, one could judge from Van Dyke's writings, but not a taste that can be cultivated indoors. One needs to go out — way out, to where the earth is still wild enough to manifest its beautiful power clearly. "I was never over-fond of park and garden nature-study," Van Dyke wrote in his preface to The Desert. "If we would know the great truths we must seek them at the source."[58]

This sense of the power of experience beyond the fences is also prominent in the work of Mary Hunter Austin, who, like Van Dyke, saw wildness and all of its soul-stirring meanings come to their sharpest focus in the desert. She had come to southern California in 1888, at the age of twenty, accompanying her brother and her widowed mother to a homestead near Bakersfield. The difficult environment could hardly have been less like that of the family's home in Carlinville, Illinois, and during their first year in the West, Mary was undernourished and ill a good part of the time. But she had a strong curiosity, particularly about natural history (she had majored in science at Blackburn College in Illinois), and she walked and rode out into the hills as often as possible, attempting to learn something of the new land. During one of these rides, on an April morning as she was walking down an arroyo leading her horse, she suddenly and quite unexpectedly perceived the flame-colored poppies she was walking among with extraordinary intensity, and was moved to feel, as she wrote later, "the warm pervasive sweetness of ultimate reality."[59] The experience reaffirmed for Mary Hunter something she had been holding on to as a memory ever since a similar experience at age six — her identity as "I-Mary," a level of being much more profound and whole than the social self, or "Mary-by-herself."[60] I-Mary was alert to nature, highly intuitive, and able to see into the way entities that seem separate actually interpenetrate each other. This was Mary Hunter's mystical center, and when she became Mary Austin, it sustained her through a difficult marriage, gave her confidence in her ideas and in her writing, and, directly relevant to her study of nature, kept her awake to the relational aspect, the ecological patterning of the fabric of life. A sense for pattern became one of her strongest faculties.[61]

In the dry hills and mesas surrounding the Owens Valley in eastern California, where she went with her husband Stafford Austin in 1892, young Mary resumed her outdoor study. Emotionally abandoned by her husband, as she said, and then tried more deeply by the birth of her hopelessly retarded daughter, Austin was thrown back upon the resources of her deeper self. As often as she could, she walked out into the dramatic landscape of rocky canyons and sun-blasted foothills, looking and absorbing, waiting for the "transaction," as she later named it, between her "spirit and the spirit of the land."[62] In later years, after she had written many books, she spoke with great assurance of her ability to renew the connection:

> Let me loose in the desert with the necessity for discovering truth about any creative process of the human mind, and I can pick up the thread from the movement of quail, from the shards of a broken bottle in the grass, from anything of beauty which comes my way.[63]

But it is clear that the thirteen years she spent in the California deserts were a difficult and lonely apprenticeship. Though she was helped by some members of a local tribe of Indians, both practically and in her understanding of the "transaction" between herself and the land, and though she was aided toward publication by the southwestern-culture aficionado Charles Fletcher Lummis, she was on her own in the task of making a whole expression out of her observations.[64]

The sustained freshness and artistic unity of her first book, *The Land of Little Rain* (1903), are thus marks of a coming-through. Each of her sharp images in some way expressed the ecological coherence of the desert. Vultures perched themselves in a row on fenceposts, drooping in the heat and glare, and thirsty mules made "hideous, maimed noises";[65] where there *was* water, the aliveness of the favored place and its visitors seemed naturally expressed in metaphors of liquidity and flow:

> The crested quail that troop in the Ceriso are the happiest frequenters of the water trails. There is no furtiveness about their morning drink. About the time the burrowers and all that feed upon them are addressing themselves to sleep, great flocks pour down the trails with that peculiar melting motion of moving quail, twittering, shoving, and shouldering. They splatter into the shallows, drink daintily, shake out small showers over their perfect coats, and melt away again into the scrub, preening and pranking, with soft contented noises.[66]

The ecological sense of place is also strong in three other books by Mary Austin that can be considered under the "nature writing" heading: *The Flock* (1906), a tribute to outdoor folk life centered on sheep raising; *California, the Land of the Sun* (1914, reprinted in 1927 as *The Lands of the Sun*), which contains fairly specific instruction on how to come into deep and creative contact with a landscape; and *The Land of Journeys' Ending* (1924), an account of Austin's return to the Southwest from the literary world of New York. The last of these three books was also (as she called it) a "book of prophecy" about how the American desert lands could, and would, give rise to "the *next* great and fructifying world culture."[67] But as Austin gained wider acceptance in the cultural world, leaving Owens Valley for the Carmel artists' colony in 1905, and later moving on to New York and Europe, her literary treatment of the environment, understandably perhaps, tended to become less sharp. She began to favor broad, sweeping statements and appeared to enjoy the oracular persona she presented to the world: I-Mary of the desert. Thus the return she describes in *The Land of Journeys' Ending* is rather like that of a prodigal. Although the book makes enigmatic, grand-scale remarks about the power of the desert to shape history and the minds of men, the writing also presents, here and there, the illuminated detail that seems to have come with fresh experience — in a vivid description of the blooming and fruiting of the giant saguaro or a close-focus account of the way a common tree may suddenly strike an observer as a thing entirely new and alive. It appears that on Austin's motor trip across the Southwest, as she was doing field work for her projected book of homecoming, she went below the drama of the occasion and found the desert again, the place of her authentic inspiration. It was again a country where at any moment there could occur between writer and landscape the "flash of mutual awareness."[68]

Mary Austin's death in 1934 came at the close of a great transitional era. Only a century before, when Henry Thoreau was a seventeen-year-old college student, the railroads were in their infancy, little more than experimental, and to cross the continent, as Thomas Nuttall did in that year of 1834, was a serious expeditionary undertaking. Huge stretches of the country were still wild, and there were many Indian tribes in the West still living in the old way. Now, in 1934, the United States had consolidated as a modern technological state. The frontier had been closed for almost half a century, and the remaining wilderness, outside Alaska, had been reduced to fragments. Even in the early 1920s, Mary Austin in her homecoming had traveled over Arizona and New Mexico by automobile, rather comfortably. The wild bloom was gone, in fact, from a good deal of the desert, where the reclamation that John Van Dyke had said should never be imposed on what he called the "breathing-spaces" of the West was well under way. Hoover Dam (which Austin had opposed) had been completed in the early 1930s, inaugurating an intense, decades-long period of reservoir building that would alter the face of much of the western landscape. Most Americans' daily lives, indeed, took place within a built, managed environment. The overriding concern in the country, in the Depression year of 1934, was how to get the economic system back to the health it had enjoyed in the long boom. What room would there be, in an increasingly artificial, dollars-and-cents world, for nature and the "flash of mutual awareness"?

❧ 6 ❧

Modern Developments

THE AMERICAN LITERATURE OF NATURE may seem, on first acquaintance, to have undergone little development, as if it had somehow resisted, at the core, the realities of changing times. From the age of Bartram to the present, the main outlines of the genre — presentation of instructive natural history information, description of personal experience in nature, and commentary on man's relationship with the wild world — have not changed an iota. The great question "How shall we live?" is the same today as when William Bartram described his paradise of a wilderness campsite in Georgia, comparing it to the strife-filled civilization he had temporarily left behind.

But the twentieth century has required of nature writers a depth of response that is fundamentally new. In the brief survey that follows, I have chosen a few representative writers to illustrate how the capacities of nature literature have been stretched by modern conditions. First and most obviously, writers about nature have had to keep up with a tremendous increase in natural history knowledge. For example, it is probably fair to say that John McPhee (as shown in *Basin and Range,* 1980, and *Rising from the Plains,* 1986) has had to learn more geology than John Muir, who first made a reputation with a study of Sierran glacial history, ever knew, in order to describe landforms in their true depth. When Muir died in 1914, plate tectonics, a major reference for McPhee, was not yet even an hypothesis, though there had been intuitions about continental drift. It can be argued that Muir, with his limited factual knowledge, saw as deeply into the implications of geology as McPhee does, and thus made as much of his materials, however primitive. But to write precisely about nature now simply takes more study than it did a century ago. There have also been great advances in marine biology, so that if Rachel Carson were alive today to update once more *The Sea Around Us* (1950, revised in 1951 and 1961), she would be faced with an enormous new body of research data to incorporate. Equally far-reaching advances have been made in cellular biology, where Lewis Thomas has made a literary breakthrough, and in ethology, the study of animal behavior, out of which insights into our own lives leap regularly, as well as in evolutionary biology and ecology, which provide a literally endless array of evidence on the interdependence of life forms and their environments. The new knowledge has invigorated nature writing with a fresh infusion of subjects for wonder, and has also increased the importance of the genre's status as an interpretive literature, for today, in an age of specialization and overspecialization, it is commonly the nature essayist who ponders the human and cultural implications as new facts come to light.

Nonetheless, individuals probably continue to experience the environment in much the same way as in pre-industrial times; not enough time has passed in the impoverished, indoor situation for there to have been alterations in the ways of the brain and mind. Indeed, the essay of experience in nature continues to celebrate widened perception and the numinous moment of connection. But there have been sweeping changes in the human ecology of America that have to be taken into account. The brute fact is that urban industrialism is now pervasive and totally dominant. There are no more blank places on the map, those wild realms which Thoreau in the nineteenth century and Aldo Leopold in the twentieth, with many of their countrymen, thought to be a necessity of life. The Wilderness Act of 1964, an admirable piece of protective legislation, nevertheless could only safeguard remnants. Even in the most remote wilderness area, furthermore, the sights and sounds of the modern apparatus may prove inescapable; jet planes pass overhead, making noise and leaving trails across the sky, and at night the satellites (of which there are now several thousand) cross and recross — reminders, if we need reminding, that the environment is virtually saturated with message-bearing long waves, medium waves, short waves, and microwaves.

The specter of a tamed world has haunted many American nature essayists. In "Walking," Thoreau asked, "What would become of us, if we walked only in a garden or a mall?" (see p. 197), but in his day the question could only be conjectural. The situation had become more ominous by 1969, when John Hay wrote, "As we diminish our environment, both physically and in terms of our attitude toward it, so we diminish our range of attention. Half the beauties of the world are no longer seen. What will we be when left to nothing but our own devices!"[1] But as the truly wild places in the natural world have been cut back, many modern nature writers, while militantly decrying this process, have at the same time recognized their own membership in the dominant modern pattern. This is a crucial realization, granting authenticity to their observations and allowing the nature essay to reach toward a new psychological comprehensiveness. One *could* choose to write only of the "green" side of oneself, so to speak, but the insights would be unpenetrating. The best of the moderns reveal much more. In *The Undiscovered Country* (1981), a book that makes a strong argument for living settled in one place, John Hay begins with a statement of his own sense of dis-placement after World War II. Hay describes watching a sunset on Cape Cod, which is where he came to rest, "with no sense that having moved to this place I was really planted anywhere."[2] Edward Abbey, with his typical knowing sense of humor, declares his preference for refrigerated beer, even, or especially, in the hot desert, and describes himself driving a "safe and sane" eighty-five miles an hour down a two-lane road in Utah. Edward Hoagland demonstrates his membership in our mixed human scene by writing of wolves, bears, mountain lions (see p. 319), and wilderness with an ardent lover's tone and yet somehow with a city man's edge of realism, coolly assessing their chances for survival. Barry Lopez sees the ironies in being transported by airplane to the wild Arctic, and describes with evident fellow-feeling the oil-rig workers whose job, in effect, is to undo the wilderness he honors. These writers, and many others of today, respond to the national gestalt from a position both in and out of it. The vision they present seems unmistakably modern and more comprehending than the simple ambivalence that prevailed in the day of Audubon.

Modern nature writing has acquired another level of intellectual complexity from the discovery, in the past century, of a vast amount of new knowledge about man's past. We know a great deal more about our ragged course on earth than our eighteenth- and nineteenth-century counterparts could have. Through such disciplines as archeology, anthropology, paleontology, and paleobotany, we have learned, for example, that agriculture emerged only some ten or twelve thousand years ago, that the first cities are only half that age, and that the very establishment of agriculture, long regarded as integral to man's progress, may in fact have involved some serious, perhaps irreparable, negatives. A different perspective is latent in findings such as these, and we have become self-conscious as a species in much the same fashion as we have on the individual level. Not only do we know that we have become a major force on the earth, we know in fairly good detail how we got that way.

The writings of two influential twentieth-century nature essayists, Aldo Leopold and Joseph Wood Krutch, incorporate much of the modern perspective. Both these men had an acute interest, quite scholarly in Krutch's case, in Western man's eco-philosophical history, and both were conscious of having made, in their own lives, a significant intellectual turn. As they moved from the traditional, dualistic outlook on the world to an ecological view, each writer left a rather clearly marked trail of his journey, and in the process helped shape the great change in our outlook on the environment.

Aldo Leopold, a graduate of the School of Forestry at Yale University, went to the Southwest in 1909 as a ranger in the brand-new United States Forest Service. At that time, he apparently shared in the emphasis on production which has colored the philosophy of the Forest Service from its founding in 1906, and in addition joined with a will the Service's public relations campaign to gain favor with local stockmen. To that end, Leopold became a leader in the war on predators in Arizona and New Mexico. The idea behind this program of elimination was that fewer wolves and mountain lions would mean more deer for hunters and more safety for cattle and sheep. "In those days, we had never heard of passing up a chance to kill a wolf," Leopold later wrote.[3] From his official position, Leopold exhorted southwesterners to kill "varmints" and "vermin," in his words — that is, predatory animals. However, this crusade did not subsume all of Leopold's attitudes toward nature. He was also aesthetically sensitive to wild country, particularly the mountainous southwestern corner of New Mexico and the nearby ranges of eastern Arizona, and as a hunter enjoyed back-country pack trips greatly. He proposed to his superiors in the Forest Service the preservation of "representative portions of some forests" for recreation as the highest use.[1] As early as 1922, he argued for wilderness classification for over a million acres of land in the Gila Mountains of New Mexico, and in 1924 the Gila Primitive Area was created as the first such protected wilderness on Forest Service land.

Despite this signal accomplishment, Leopold's major emphasis during his southwestern years was on production-oriented resource management. He searched for the keys to the increase of trees, cattle, sheep, wild turkeys, and deer. Over the years, as his career took him to Wisconsin and specialization in game management, and as he found repeatedly that manipulations of the environment based upon linear cause-and-effect theory did not work as planned, Leopold gradually came to believe that nature was more complex, mystifyingly more complex, than the traditional, managerial outlook could understand. His ecological research into population fluctuations of white-tailed deer showed that deer numbers were more sensitive to habitat health and climatic factors than to hunting regulations; man,

Leopold found, could not turn on and turn off wildlife populations like so many faucets. More and more, he came to see productivity as a function of the overall health of the habitat.

In 1936, Leopold made a trip to the mountains of Chihuahua, Mexico, and there had an experience which seemed to focus his uneasiness with the simple, linear, "resource-management" outlook. It was in Chihuahua that he "first clearly realized that land is an organism, that all my life I had seen only sick land, whereas here was a biota still in perfect aboriginal health. The term 'unspoiled wilderness' took on a new meaning."[5] The frustratingly complicated world of game management, and then this sudden vision of wild integrity, together appeared to have catalyzed Leopold's philosophical awareness. Clearly, when man attempted to manage nature on simplistic lines (almost always for selfish reasons, to boot), he was acting out of both ignorance and arrogance. Ecology was showing an infinitely more complex world than had heretofore even been suspected, and man's ethical sense should somehow expand to match the new knowledge. In *A Sand County Almanac* (1949), Leopold brought his humbling scientific research, his illuminative experience of the Mexican wilderness, and an admission of his complicity in predator elimination together into a daring, elegantly phrased ethical formula:

> A thing is right when it tends to preserve the integrity, stability, and beauty of the biotic community. It is wrong when it tends otherwise.[6]

These two sentences have become a rallying point for biocentrist thinking in the decades since their publication. They represent perhaps the clearest statement we have that moral content may be found in the science of ecology and in the experience of wild beauty. The intellectual, aesthetic, and ethical understanding is here founded in biological reality, and that fusion may amount to one of the few genuinely new philosophical statements of the twentieth century.

Joseph Wood Krutch's intellectual journey was a bit different, since he had never been a forest ranger, nor killed a predator, but in essence it maps the same critical watershed of thought. As a professor of literature and a well-known drama critic living in New York City, Krutch in the 1920s and 1930s was in touch with the main intellectual currents of his time and place. In an influential book, *The Modern Temper* (1929), he expressed what seemed to him the thinking person's only logical response to the naturalistic universe that science had revealed: pessimism. But Krutch's pessimism had a heroic tinge: "Ours is a lost cause and there is no place for us in the natural universe, but we are not, for all that, sorry to be human. We should rather die as men than live like animals."[7] One could hardly ask for a neater, more ringing summary of the dualistic and specist view of life. Krutch's position here was similar to Sigmund Freud's, voiced in 1930 in *Civilization and Its Discontents,* especially in its concept of man and his tragic-heroic separateness. It may be taken as representative of a predominant theme in urban Western thought. "Humanism" and "Nature," Krutch declared, are "fundamentally antithetical."[8]

But Krutch was apparently not as dogmatic as his book's conclusion would indicate. Perhaps influenced by Thoreau, whom he first read in 1930 and about whom he wrote an insightful biography in 1948, and perhaps also influenced by the surroundings of his country home in Connecticut, he began sometime in the later 1930s to move away from the alienated position of *The Modern Temper.* By 1950, as demonstrated in his "Prologue" to *Great American Nature Writing,* Krutch had become doubtful that the assertion of human separateness was true to the facts. In that essay he leaned strongly toward the countertradition of empathy with nature. A sabbatical year in the Arizona desert seems to have been decisive in his philosophical turn, for in 1952 Krutch moved to Arizona and commenced an intensive, devoted study of the desert flora and fauna. In the next several years, he wrote some of the most important nature essays of the post-World War II era, essays whose great theme was human intelligence coming awake to its essential continuity with nature. This was, of course, his own story. In *The Voice of the Desert* (1954), he quietly rejected the dualistic model of human consciousness, a major step.

> Perhaps the mind is not merely a blank slate upon which anything may be written. Perhaps it reaches out spontaneously toward what can nourish either intelligence or imagination. Perhaps it is part of nature and, without being taught, shares nature's intentions.[9]

Living in the desert, studying its well-adapted life forms, opening up to what he wittily called the "xeric profundities" of the Southwest, Krutch seemed to come alive to nonseparatist possibilities. When birds sang, he wondered, why should they not be expressing joy, as well as marking their nesting territories? He scorned the Cartesian, mechanistic description of animals' lives, and looked for lines of connection between them and man. As he learned more about ecological patterns, and then experienced wilderness first-hand in the Grand Canyon and in Baja California, he began to consider the possibility of wildness as an overarching concept. His books became wilder and wilder. Perhaps, as Thoreau had said, wildness was the sustaining, creative principle of the world — its preservation. As such, it would of course be greater by far than our powers of intellect, and thus might suggest to us a wholeness beyond alienation. In one of his last essays, Krutch affirmed the possibility of a healing, spiritual allegiance to the wild:

> Faith in wildness, or in nature as a creative force, has the deeper, possibly the deepest, significance for our future. It is a philosophy, a faith; it is even, if you like, a religion. It puts our ultimate trust, not in human intelligence, but in whatever it is that created human intelligence and is, in the long run, more likely than we to solve our problems.[10]

However clearly writers like Leopold and Krutch were affirming this new view, actual practice in industrial America, through the 1940s and 1950s, continued virtually undisturbed by the implications of ecology. World War II accelerated the development of certain technologies like the bulldozer, airplane, and helicopter, and enlarged the arsenal of chemicals used against insects and weeds. In the economically prosperous 1950s, as the nation resumed the boom psychology it had not enjoyed for over twenty years, all of these instruments and more were used on the American environment, to great effect.

Not many questions were asked. When, finally, an editor and writer who had gained fame as an essayist on the sea, Rachel Carson, marshaled a body of evidence against the careless use of pesticides and herbicides in *Silent Spring* (1962), so outraged was the chemical establishment at this unaccustomed criticism that the author herself became a center of controversy and an object of attack from industrial and bureaucratic quarters. But Carson had earned her standing as an ecologist, and her work stood firm. Using a large number of case histories, she demonstrated that the chemical warfare against certain insects and weeds, which had begun only in the mid-1940s, had by 1962 already worked an incalculable negative effect on the biotic community and on man himself. It came as a shock to many readers of *Silent Spring* to learn that humanity's capacity for environmental mischief was now, with the new power to affect life on the cellular and genetic levels, much more serious than mere mischief. The very character of man's influence on the earth had changed, becoming both more penetrating and more universal. In this new situation, where over-the-counter consumer products were damaging biological communities hundreds and even thousands of miles distant, nothing less than an ecologically conscious public would be required.

Carson was well prepared for this challenge. The first female editor-in-chief for the United States Fish and Wildlife Service, she had also written three substantial and well-researched books on the ocean and the littoral zone: *Under the Sea-Wind* (1941); *The Sea Around Us* (1950), which became one of the best sellers of its time and which has subsequently been translated into some thirty-eight languages;[11] and *The Edge of the Sea* (1955), also much honored. In these books, in a deceptively simple style, Carson structured remarkable quantities of data, bringing the facts of oceanography and marine biology to life by stressing their interrelationships. She also conveyed the poetry and sublimity of her subjects, though keeping narrative accounts of her own responses to a minimum, by a precise combination of dramatic language, well-thought-out rhythms, and the concrete terminology of science. Thus, the sudden drop from the continental shelf to the abyssal plain shows, in her words, the "grandeur of slope topography." Combining aesthetic and scientific language in this manner allowed Carson to describe vast and complex natural systems with impressive economy: in *The Sea Around Us,* for example, her account of the formation of the planet, the possible origin of the moon, the gathering of the oceans, the establishment of continents, and the history of life on earth — in outline, to be sure — comes to only a little over twelve pages of text, yet is so well controlled in shape and pace, so vivid in its images and accurate in choice of verbs, and so careful and scholarly in its attributions, that it persuades conclusively. The key to the economy of her writing and her ability to evoke the full sense of life is her concentration on relationships. In *The Sea Around Us,* Carson describes each element in the complex food chains of the ocean, from the salts that have washed from the land to the herrings that swarm in certain good locations, making sure that her readers perceive the linkages that make abundance possible. The diverse wind patterns, the differences in salinity of the various oceans, even the varying sea levels all create different, immensely ramifying ecological conditions; thus each ecosystem has a unique complement of flora and fauna. Carson's genius was to portray relationship not as some sort of structural juxtaposition but as the living quick of things.

The fundamental responsibility to facts, and then the artistic control of a complex, interactive scene, are what give *Silent Spring* its authority. It was absolutely necessary to the book's success that its readers understand living relationships. Carson directed her strengths as a writer to that end. But that was not all, for after understanding there must come action. To the ecological lecture, she added sharp, plain-spoken criticism, designed to arouse her readers.

A careful description of the complexity and aliveness of soil, for example, is followed by "The plain truth is that this critically important subject of the ecology of the soil has been largely neglected even by scientists and almost completely ignored by control men."[12] A similarly detailed account of the fire ant, a recent import into the Southeast that has aroused great alarm in some quarters, is rounded out by a concise denunciation of the chemical campaign against it:

> Never has any pesticide program been so thoroughly and deservedly damned by practically everyone except the beneficiaries of this "sales bonanza." It is an outstanding example of an ill-conceived, badly executed, and thoroughly detrimental experiment in the mass control of insects, an experiment so expensive in dollars, in destruction of animal life, and in loss of public confidence in the Agriculture Department that it is incomprehensible that any funds should still be devoted to it.[13]

Silent Spring became a force in American life. There had been solid books about man's abuse of the environment well before its time, of course, notably George Perkins Marsh's pioneering *Man and Nature* (1864), and Fairfield Osborn's *Our Plundered Planet* (1948) in Carson's own day, but none had rested on so wide a knowledge of ecological processes, and none had aroused such a strong response. Carson's work has been a basic text for the ecological awakening of the past quarter-century because it told clearly what can happen when intricate natural systems are, in effect, bludgeoned. It brought right down to earth, to daily life, the need for ecological consciousness.

The expanding technosphere, some of whose consequences were described so cogently by Rachel Carson, has also had an inevitable effect upon the literature of solitude. In the modern era, being alone in nature may still refresh the spirit, but the literary record indicates there now may be, quite often, a certain shadowed quality to the experience. Henry Beston, for one, felt the historical moment keenly, as he makes clear in his poetic record of a year on the Great Beach of Cape Cod, *The Outermost House* (1928). He does not give his personal reasons for wanting to spend a year alone, facing out to the ocean not far from the pounding surf on the "forearm" of the Cape, but he does describe the insulation and malaise of modern man: "The world to-day is sick to its thin blood for lack of elemental things, for fire before the hands, for water welling from the earth, for air, for the dear earth itself underfoot."[14] Solitude, then, is a recovery, quite consciously undertaken. Beston's writing conveys a tactile sense of the sandy footing and the scouring, dune-shaping wind, a clear awareness of the stars at night and the look of the rocking waves offshore. These things bring a restoration of health. On the Great Beach, where the outlines of one's world are simpler than in most places, each element and each perception seem to register deeply. The world appears charged with meaning. A flock of shorebirds has wheeled in the bright air, their sudden changes of direction mysterious, absorbing: "Does some current flow through them and between them as they fly?"[15]

Good evidence for the healing effect of Beston's year on the beach may be indicated by his positive, natural-seeming attitude toward mankind. He describes his nearest neighbors, the young men of a Coast Guard station some miles up the beach, with interest and care, sharing a comradeship of night and storm with them on several occasions. The great natural context of the beach grants mankind here what Beston's contemporary, the poet Robinson Jeffers, called the "dignity of rareness." In an incident that occurs near the end of his record, and thus one carrying a certain summary emphasis perhaps, Beston comes upon a young man swimming in the surf. He sets forth a description of this swimmer with the same well-knit phrasing and clear imagery that he has used to express his reverence for birds, or deer seen playing on the beach, or the breaking surf itself.

> It was all a beautiful thing to see: the surf thundering across the great natural world, the beautiful and compact body in its naked strength and symmetry, the astounding plunge across the air, arms extended ahead, legs and feet together, the emerging stroke of the flat hands, and the alternate rhythms of the sunburned and powerful shoulders.[16]

The Outermost House closes with earnest exhortations, as if marking a far traveler's return to the world of men: "Whatever attitude to human existence you fashion for yourself, know that it is valid only if it be the shadow of an attitude to Nature. . . . Do no dishonour to the earth lest you dishonour the spirit of man. . . . Touch the earth, love the earth, honour the earth, her plains, her valleys, her hills, and her seas; rest your spirit in her solitary places."[17]

It was forty years before another talismanic book of solitude in American nature appeared. Those forty years included the Great Depression, World War II, the invention and use of the atomic bomb, the rise and flourishing of a sophisticated, existential outlook that deeply undercut our ability and willingness to make confident statements on the meanings of things, and, in the developed countries, perhaps especially the United States, the ascendancy of consumerism, which is to say, the tendency to trivialize all items by seeing them as commodities. The world that developed in those forty years inspired urgency by its hectic and worsening political and environmental conditions; but at the same time, the intellectual climate tended toward super-self-consciousness and thus a certain ironic attitude toward any human motivation. In this modern time it is difficult to be whole-hearted, even about nature; we have *that* orientation, after all, pigeonholed as "Romanticism."

By the time of the publication of *Desert Solitaire* in 1968, it seems apparent that Edward Abbey had digested the implications of this modern complexity, at least as they applied to writing about experience in nature. He had developed a style that spoke idiomatically to his audience — Americans, that is, who believed almost as a genetic article of faith that there was still a wilderness somewhere, where perhaps purification was still possible, but who also had purchased enough shoddy goods in their lifetimes to be profoundly skeptical people. In *Desert Solitaire* and other works, Abbey has reproduced this mixed consciousness perfectly, preserving the authenticity of his deepest commitment, which is to wilderness, honoring it in its essential mystery above all else, and yet at the same time speaking knowingly, with an edge of black humor, as a realist firmly in touch with his time.

The seriousness of *Desert Solitaire* is paradoxically well served by its bantering, self-deprecating, yet often hyperbolic prose. The style is loose, able to move about in the world, so to speak, not constricted too much by righteousness or self-importance. Using this style, Abbey is able to breathe life into some of the hoariest dilemmas of philosophy, such as the ancient conflict in epistemology between realism and idealism, and he is able to present his own search for meaning in the desert (a quest that must transcend that old perceptual dilemma, among other obstacles) in personal, accessible terms.

The scene of *Desert Solitaire* is the deeply dissected Colorado Plateau country of southern Utah, mainly the area in and around Arches National Monument (now Park), where Abbey was a seasonal ranger for some years. The "plot," loosely, is separation into solitude, attempted initiation, and return: classic. The central quest, although Abbey probably would not call it that, is to come into contact with the desert, to know the desert if possible, to learn there something about life in general — "what it had to teach," as Thoreau said in *Walden*.

> Noon is the crucial hour: the desert reveals itself nakedly and cruelly, with no meaning but its own existence.

My lone juniper stands half-alive, half-dead, the silvery wind-rubbed claw of wood projected stiffly at the sun. A single cloud floats in the sky to the northeast, motionless, a magical coalescence of vapor where a few minutes before there was nothing visible but the hot, deep, black-grained blueness of infinity.

Life has come to a standstill, at least for the hour. In this forgotten place the tree and I wait on the shore of time, temporarily free from the force of motion and process and the surge toward — what? Something called the *future*? I am free, I am compelled, to contemplate the world which underlies life, struggle, thought, ideas, the human labyrinth of hope and despair.[18]

Looking to know that world better in action, Abbey hikes into the Grand Canyon, climbs to the summit of a 13,000-foot mountain, and descends into "terra incognita," a maze of canyons, among other journeys, tests, and inquiries. In the end, what he reports back as real and undeniable are, in his word, "surfaces": "the sunlight on rock and leaves, the feel of music, the bark of a tree, the abrasion of granite and sand, the plunge of clear water into a pool, the face of the wind — what else is there? What else do we need?"[19]

Apparently, some of us believe we need much more, and in illustration of the society of surfeit Abbey presents "Industrial Tourism." The object of this consumerist mode of travel is to go to as many certified destinations as possible, as swiftly as possible, in maximum comfort. In Abbey's satiric but somewhat compassionate depiction, however, the industrial tourist, for all his possessions and seeming command of time and space, is a victim. He is forced to cover enormous mileages in his car, to endure fatigue, and to face heavy and dangerous traffic, in order to have only a quick look at a famous scene. What he ought to do, if the spark of revolution were to touch him, is escape the machine. "In the first place you can't see *anything* from a car; you've got to get out of the goddamned contraption and walk, better yet crawl on hands and knees, over the sandstone and through the thornbush and cactus."[20] But the victim remains immured, a poignant case, last seen making "the long drive home at night in a stream of racing cars against the lights of another stream racing in the opposite direction, passing now and then the obscure tangle, the shattered glass, the patrolman's lurid blinker light, of one more wreck."[21]

Like the journey into solitude, the theme of commitment to a piece of land as a steward derives from an old and honored American circumstance. In the twentieth century, though, in response to radically changed conditions, writing based on farm life has matured significantly, growing in its range of comment well beyond the emotional core of agrarianism. As we have seen, even Crèvecoeur in the late eighteenth century depicted the dark side of the farmer's existence, but it is doubtful that he could have imagined what would be demanded of a farm essayist in the age of agribusiness.

The prominent American attitude toward the small family farm, which might be termed the "Currier and Ives" view, remains alive in the urban-industrial era, but is rendered sentimental and more or less irrelevant by demographics: the number of people on farms, which amounted to nine-tenths of the United States population in 1800, had slipped to only slightly more than 30 percent by 1920. By 1950, only 15 percent of Americans lived on farms, and by 1982 the figure had eroded further to just 3 percent. In less than two hundred years, capitalism and industrialism had fully transformed American agriculture, consolidating farmland into the paying proposition of big-scale monoculture, a revolution greatly facilitated by the change in farming's energy base from human and animal labor to fossil fuels. The often-cited independence of the American farmer, a trait that to Thomas Jefferson had seemed a fundamental ingredient of democracy, had had its economic base severely undercut. The trend was evident early in the nineteenth century; by the time of *Walden* (1854), Thoreau lamented the "fall from the farmer to the operative" as a fact of New England life. Between 1820 and 1860, writes Jan Wojcik, a modern agricultural historian, American farming changed from "many self-sufficient enterprises to fewer commercial enterprises growing cheap food for good profits."[22] Centralization proceeded even during the homestead era, and continues at present.

What all this has meant for the writer is that the farm has become a battleground between two great value systems. Hamlin Garland, in fiction, depicted the takeover of land by the absentee power of capitalism; Liberty Hyde Bailey, one of the important essayists of farm life in the early twentieth century (see p. 247), saw the displacement of the farm population as the work of the city, which he described as a "parasite . . . running out its roots into the open country and draining it of its substance."[23] Wendell Berry, in our own time, sees the farm "problem" as essentially the moral and spiritual problem of our civilization at large — we want food and fiber, and much else, but we do not want to work or take responsibility for these things. We want our needs to be supplied by industrial magic.

These writers see the farm as emblematic. For Bailey, for example, agriculture was not a "problem" that could perhaps be solved, or at least tinkered with, in the way a positivist society approaches its difficulties. What was required for a healthy agriculture was no less than a revolution in a people's entire concept of the world. In *The Holy Earth* (1915), Bailey wrote that American agriculture could not be restored to health, and thus to its full, necessary role in civilization, by "instructing the young," or by "any movement merely to have gardens, or to own farms," nor would "rhapsodies on the beauties of nature" help much. A deep change, the adoption of what he called the "brotherhood relation," was needed, so that in our view of things, "The creation, and not man, is the norm."[24] Here, in this sample of what might be termed the "higher agrarianism" of the modern era, Bailey illustrated the essential continuity of the farm essay and the nature essay. He was proposing the same ecological and ethical outlook as John Burroughs, for example, or Aldo Leopold. Leopold, in fact, acknowledged Bailey as an influence.[25]

The emphasis on proportion and rightness which marks the moral essays of Wendell Berry appears to derive in large part from his working a small farm in Kentucky. This is a home place that had been in his family for generations, and to which he returned in the 1960s, having made a foray out into the national (which is to say, largely urban and not tied to any one place) literary world. The homecoming, as Berry described it in *The Long-Legged House* (1969), grew into a kind of revelation:

> . . . I began to think of myself as living within rather than upon the life of the place. I began to think of my life as one among many, and one kind among many kinds. I began to see how little of the beauty and the richness of the world is of human origin, and how superficial and crude and destructive — even self-destructive — is man's conception of himself as the owner of the land and the master of nature and the center of the universe.[26]

In the succeeding twenty-odd years, Berry's writing has elaborated upon that moral insight. He has farmed the ancestral acres, dealing with inherited problems of erosion and trying to build up the health of the soil; while doing this work, he has written, after *The Long-Legged House*, *A Continuous Harmony* (1972), *The Unsettling of America* (1977), and *The Gift of Good Land* (1981), and these books form an interesting progression. After the return and the dawning of commitment, *A Continuous Harmony* describes the work of restoration:

> At home the great delight is to see the clover and grass now growing on places that were bare when we came. These small healings of the ground are my model accomplishment — everything else I do must aspire to that. While I was at work the world gained with every move I made, and I harmed nothing.[27]

The Unsettling of America applies the lessons learned to the larger scale of American agribusiness. The crisis in industrial agriculture connects to the crisis in the environment in general, and to the physical diseases, social problems, and moral malaise that bedevil our time. "No longer does human life rise from the earth like a pyramid, broadly and considerately founded upon its sources. Now it scatters itself out in a reckless horizontal sprawl, like a disorderly city whose suburbs and pavements destroy the fields."[28] *The Gift of Good Land* continues at wide focus by examining traditional (small-scale, labor-intensive) farming in a couple of places where it still survives, and by looking again at the religious and philosophical roots of our culture to see if there might be a directive toward stewardship there, one that we could revive. The effect of juxtaposing the practical and philosophical inquiries is to imply a complete reconsideration of our way of life. Berry presents his heresy of humble stewardship with workaday calmness; all that is new in it is actually quite old, he implies, and well tested. The working base of the needed modern revolution, pointing toward the enlightened fitting together of man and nature, may turn out to be nothing more radical than "an excellent homestead." Berry describes a farm he visited:

> Everywhere you look you see the signs of care. You are in what appears to be a little cove, a wedge of flat land tucked in against a wooded hill. The natural character of the place has been respected, and yet it has been made to accommodate gracefully the various necessities of a family's life and work.[29]

The American nature essay based on travel obviously has a different bent from the agrarian essay; its charge of interest comes from the excitement of crossing the frontier between civilization and wilderness. In the modern time such a crossing is still potent, but now commonly involves a more complex awareness on the part of the traveler, who is a member of a world-dominant technological society and who is likely to realize that wilderness exists today only if human society wants it to exist. A certain balance has been tipped. Thus a modern traveler into the wild will be sensitive to his or her own perceptions and values, with regard to the wilderness, in ways that would not have been possible for someone of earlier times.

Two good examples of this present-day heightening of consciousness are furnished by the writings of Edward Hoagland and Barry Lopez (see pp. 319–333 and 381–388). Hoagland, who describes himself as living half the year in New York City and the other half in Vermont, unblinkingly registers the actual state of the environment (the very small amount of true wilderness in New England, for instance) while letting his heart go out to its fated beauty. He hears the wilderness singing, but it is, in his words, a "swan song." He gravitates toward old-timers and field men who can perhaps convey what it was like to touch the former world. In *Notes from the Century Before: A Journal from British Columbia* (1969), Hoagland's most fully developed travel essay, he describes a journey into a realm of health and variety and interest which may even now be as remote as any fictional Shangri-La. In the summer of 1966, Hoagland left New York and in a few days, traveling by airplane, train, and boat, reached the tiny hamlet of Telegraph Creek, on the Stikine River in northwestern British Columbia. "To me it [Telegraph Creek] was a crossroads . . . , where I could step back to the Snake River of 1885, hearing stories which hadn't worn threadbare with handling."[30] As the summer bloomed, he walked, boated, drove on primitive roads, and flew by bush plane over a magnificent wild area the size of two Ohios, as he says, reveling in the greenness. In the shadow of helicopters, almost literally, and just ahead of the bulldozers, he managed to interview some eighty people, from ancient Indians and holdover prospectors to the very young on their way up, growing up with the country, as the frontier phrase has it. He moved swiftly from one discovery to the next, exhilarated both by the country and the people. An undertone of elegy was provided by the trembling fragility of some of the old-timers and by the always ominous presence of helicopters — there had been a copper strike nearby. But Hoagland didn't snag on nostalgia; he was busy making a record.

The spirit of the summer was set with the author's first sight of Telegraph Creek. A young man, himself a newcomer and nervous about flying to Telegraph Creek for the first time, ferried the writer from lower on the Stikine in a two-seat Cessna floatplane:

> We fly over an old clearing, with its sole horse and its laborious log houses close enough to the bank for a fishing line to be run out the window. Telegraph Creek is a scatter of buildings, fantastic after coming so far. Both relieved, we land on the lake behind and unload the groceries. Nobody meets us except a curlew that does a curlew. I take it to be a good omen. The sky is clearing. The boy roars into the air, and I walk the two miles to town. The brush is full of birds cheeping and whistling. There's an elaborate system of flumes and trestles which carries spring water, and I follow them down. The town is wonderfully sprinkled out on a half dozen terraces, high levels and low. People wave and smile. I can scarcely remember ever being any happier.[31]

By the end of summer, Hoagland was tired from the sheer abundance of it, but he concluded his explorations ringingly, interviewing two of the old heroic surveyors, Frank Swannell in Victoria and

E. C. Lamarque in Vancouver. These men had made prodigious journeys into the wilderness in a time when the wild was not recreation ground. As Hoagland put it, referring to Swannell's case, "These walks were just about the last go-round — the last exploration of the continent by foot that we'll ever have."[32] Hoagland described one of Lamarque's treks in terms suggesting what his own experiences that summer had meant: "It was that airy, aerial moment in time when a man is in country which nobody has ever set eyes on before, feeling blithe and surrounded by the sublime, yet constantly moving, as though to stop would be to founder and fall like a trapeze artist."[33] In Vancouver and at the airport before flying back to New York, plunged suddenly back into the "relentless, metronome scurry around," Hoagland sensed the true significance of the flight ahead of him:

> It wasn't like coming home from one of the ancient cities of Europe or a month's isolation in one of the second-growth forests of Maine. This was a return to man himself from the previous existence, about to be sealed off and stoppered. I was alarmed by the crush.[34]

Barry Lopez has also gone north to see the remnant wilderness world, and has also witnessed the dismaying suddenness with which its ecosystems can be unraveled. In *Arctic Dreams* (1986) he has recorded his quests, and those of several others who preceded him, into the difficult and fragile Far North; and he has attempted to go beyond recording events and observations into an investigation of the mentality of seeking itself. *Arctic Dreams*, therefore, is a highly self-conscious book. But Lopez's consciousness of self and nature is meant to be representative, and what develops is an exposition of two paths, two ways of seeing. We can approach the wild world (which is to say, *the* world) with designs on it, projections and preconceptions; or we can try to simply perceive it, to let it be whatever it is. Lopez's exposition becomes then a contemporary statement, almost a précis, of what may be the major ethical motif in American nature literature, the choice between domination and democratic membership. The alternatives frame the great question of how we should live.

What helps make this question fresh, when asked in the Arctic, is that the environment there is strange to us. Its extremes of light, its simplicity of contour, and of course its climate, taken together make a perceptual field that people from the temperate zone are not accustomed to; and so it is, in some true sense, a "new world." For all our technological powers to make ourselves comfortable in the Arctic, and they are considerable, in the ways of the mind we have been placed again in a position somewhat like that of sixteenth-century Europeans confronting the lower latitudes of America. The Arctic has given us a chance to see the world anew. What most have done so far, as Lopez makes clear, is replay the heroic-tragic explorations (the search for the Northwest Passage, for example) and then the careless, gutting exploitation that has marked our settlement of the temperate zone. But there have been occasional quiet spirits who responded to the North on its own terms, not only not caring to convert it into something else but wanting positively to go to it as a student, in particular to learn the ways in which its native inhabitants lived, and possibly to see there some relevance for humanity in general. With a time lag of a century or two, and perhaps with a new historical awareness that opens up possibilities for ethical behavior, we have come again (very late, though, and with the world behind us pushing) to the wilderness in its innocence. The choice that defines us is before us once again. "Like other landscapes that initially appear barren, arctic tundra can open suddenly, like the corolla of a flower, when any intimacy with it is sought."[35]

In a brief magazine note, Barry Lopez has recently ventured the rather daring idea that nature writing "will not only one day produce a major and lasting body of American literature, but that it might also provide the foundation for a reorganization of American political thought."[36] In a sense, I think, this has already happened; the foundation is in place, if we understand political thought to mean fundamentally the understanding of relationships. William Bartram, Henry Thoreau, John Muir, John Burroughs, Aldo Leopold, Wendell Berry, and many others have set forth a vision of the world that is fully and authentically political, and democratic. Politics properly understood is not simply human affairs; it involves the standing of each and every element making up the one world, the biosphere we partake of. Democracy properly understood gives the vote to trees — they *should* have standing, as Justice William O. Douglas argued in a pathfinding dissent — and to hawks, worms, aquifers, coal seams, wolves, bats, and the life-sustaining atmosphere. Democracy as American nature literature has presented it widens and fulfills the American premise. It is not the portioning out of power strictly within human society, but a much deeper movement of mind and heart, an opening of the self in recognition and gratitude to an all-including greater self.

PART II

An Anthology of American Nature Writing

WILLIAM WOOD

(flourished 1629–1635)

🐎 Not much is known about William Wood in the strictly biographical sense, except that he spent the years from 1629 to 1633 in Massachusetts. But it is clear from his writing that his interest was mainly in the woods and meadows and the Indians; his guide to New England, in contrast with most seventeenth-century accounts, is entirely unconcerned with Providence or theological argument or the heroism of the settlers. His outward look has indeed supported speculation that he may not have been a "saint" but a "stranger." He looked with curiosity at trees, grapevines, moose, passenger pigeons, bears, the soil underfoot, and the abundant fish in the nearby rivers and sea, noting always commodity values but also responding aesthetically.

Of the Beasts That Live on the Land

HAVING RELATED UNTO YOU the pleasant situation of the country, the healthfulness of the climate, the nature of the soil, with his vegetatives and other commodities, it will not be amiss to inform you of such irrational creatures as are daily bred and continually nourished in this country, which do much conduce to the well-being of the inhabitants, affording not only meat for the belly but clothing for the back. The beasts be as followeth:

> The kingly lion and the strong-armed bear,
> The large-limbed mooses, with the tripping deer,
> Quill-darting porcupines, and raccoons be

From *New England's Prospect* (1634)

Castled in the hollow of an aged tree;
The skipping squirrel, rabbit, purblind hare,
Immured in the selfsame castle are,
Lest red-eyed ferrets, wily foxes should
Them undermine, if rampired but with mold.
The grim-faced ounce,[1] and ravenous, howling wolf,
Whose meagre paunch sucks like a swallowing gulf.
Black, glistering otters and rich-coated beaver,
The civet-scented musquash[2] smelling ever.

Concerning lions,[3] I will not say that I ever saw any myself, but some affirm that they have seen a lion at Cape Ann, which is not above six leagues from Boston. Some likewise being lost in woods have heard such terrible roarings as have made them much aghast, which must either be devils or lions, there being no other creatures which use to roar saving bears, which have not such a terrible kind of roaring. Besides, Plymouth men have traded for lions' skins in former times. But sure it is that there be lions on that continent, for the Virginians saw an old lion in their plantation, who having lost his jackal, which was wont to hunt his prey, was brought so poor that he could go no further.

For bears, they be common, being a great black kind of bear which be most fierce in strawberry time, at which time they have young ones. At this time likewise they will go upright like a man, and climb trees, and swim to the islands; which if the Indians see, there will be more sportful bear-baiting than Paris Garden can afford. For seeing the bears take water, an Indian will leap after him, where they go to water cuffs for bloody noses and scratched sides; in the end the man gets the victory, riding the bear over the watery plain till he can bear him no longer. In the winter they take themselves to the clefts of rocks and thick swamps to shelter them from the cold; and food being scant in those cold and hard times, they live only by sleeping and sucking their paws, which keepeth them as fat as they are in summer. There would be more of them if it were not for the wolves, which devour them. A kennel of those ravening runnagadoes [renegades] setting on a poor single bear will tear him as a dog will tear a kid.

It would be a good change if the country had for every wolf a bear, upon the condition all the wolves were banished; so should the

[1] The "wildcat" (see p. 99), or bobcat.
[2] The muskrat.
[3] The mountain lion, now extirpated over nearly all of the East.

inhabitants be not only rid of their greatest annoyance but furnished with more store of provisions, bears being accounted very good meat, esteemed of all men above venison. Again they never prey upon the English cattle, or offer to assault the person of any man, unless being vexed with a shot, and a man run upon them before they be dead, in which case they will stand in their own defence, as may appear by this instance. Two men going afowling, appointed at evening to meet at a certain pond side to share equally and to return home; one of these gunners having killed a seal or sea calf brought it to the pond where he was to meet his comrade, afterwards returning to the seaside for more gain; and having loaded himself with more geese and ducks, he repaired to the pond where he saw a great bear feeding on his seal, which caused him to throw down his load and give the bear a salute; which, though it was but with goose shot, yet tumbled him over and over, whereupon the man, supposing him to be in a manner dead, ran and beat him with the hand of his gun. The bear perceiving him to be such a coward to strike him when he was down, scrambled up, standing at defiance with him, scratching his legs, tearing his clothes and face, who stood it out till his six foot gun was broken in the middle. Then being deprived of his weapon, he ran up to the shoulders into the pond where he remained till the bear was gone and his mate come in, who accompanied him home.

The beast called a moose is not much unlike red deer. This beast is as big as an ox, slow of foot, headed like a buck, with a broad beam, some being two yards wide in the head. Their flesh is as good as beef, their hides good for clothing. The English have some thoughts of keeping them tame and to accustom them to the yoke, which will be a great commodity: first, because they are so fruitful, bringing forth three at a time, being likewise very uberous [supplying milk or nourishment in abundance]; secondly, because they will live in winter without fodder. There be not many of these in the Massachusetts Bay, but forty miles to the northeast there be great store of them. These poor beasts likewise are much devoured by the wolves.

The ordinary deer be much bigger than the deer of England, of a brighter color, more inclining to red, with spotted bellies. The most store of these be in winter, when the more northern parts of the country be cold for them. They desire to be near the sea, so that they may swim to the island when they are chased by the wolves. It is not to be thought into what great multitudes they would increase were it not for the common devourer, the wolf. They have generally three [calves] at a time, which they hide a mile one from another, giving them suck by turns. Thus they do, that if the wolf should find one he might miss the other. These deer be fat in the deep of winter. In summer it is hard catching of them with the best greyhounds that may be procured because they be swift of foot. Some credible persons have affirmed that they have seen a deer leap threescore feet at little or no forcement; besides, there be so many old trees, rotten stumps, and Indian barns, that a dog cannot well run without being shoulder-shot. Yet would I not dissuade any from carrying good dogs, for in the wintertime they be very useful, for when the snow is hard frozen, the deer being heavy sinks into the snow; the dogs being light run upon the top and overtake them and pull them down. Some by this means have gotten twenty bucks and does in a winter. The horns of these deer grow in a straight manner (overhanging their heads) that they cannot feed upon such things as grow low till they have cast their old horns. Of these deer there be a great many, and more in the Massachusetts Bay than in any other place, which is a great help and refreshment to those planters.

The porcupine is a small thing not much unlike a hedgehog, something bigger, who stands upon his guard and proclaims a *noli me tangere* ["Do not touch me"] to man and beast that shall approach too near him, darting his quills into their legs and hides. The raccoon is a deep-furred beast, not much unlike a badger, having a tail like a fox, as good meat as a lamb; there is one of them in the Tower [of London]. These beasts in the daytime sleep in hollow trees, in the moonshine night they go to feed on clams at a low tide by the seaside, where the English hunt them with their dogs.

The squirrels be of three sorts: first the great gray squirrel, which is almost as big as an English rabbit. Of these there be the greatest plenty; one may kill a dozen of them in an afternoon — about three of the clock they begin to walk. The second is a small squirrel, not unlike the English squirrel, which doth much trouble the planters of corn, so that they are constrained to set diverse traps and to carry their cats into the corn fields till their corn be three weeks old. The third kind is a flying squirrel which is not very big, slender of body, with a great deal of loose skin which she spreads when she flies, which the wind gets and so wafts her batlike body from place to place. It is a creature more for sight and wonderment than either pleasure and profit.

The rabbits be much like ours in England. The hares be some of them white and a yard long; these two harmless creatures are glad to shelter themselves from the harmful foxes in hollow trees having a hole at the entrance no bigger than they can creep in at. If they should make them holes in the ground, as our English rabbits do, the undermining renoilds [foxes] would rob them of their lives and extirpate their generation.

The beasts of offence be skunks, ferrets, foxes, whose impudence sometimes drives them to the goodwives' hen roost to fill their paunch. Some of these be black; their fur is of much esteem.

The ounce or the wildcat is as big as a mongrel dog. This creature is by nature fierce and more dangerous to be met withal than any other creature, not fearing either dog or man. He useth to kill deer, which he thus effecteth: knowing the deer's tracts, he will lie lurking in long weeds, the deer passing by he suddenly leaps upon his back, from thence gets to his neck and scratcheth out his throat. He hath likewise a device to get geese, for being much of the color of a goose he will place himself close by the water, holding up his bob tail, which is like a goose neck; the geese seeing this counterfeiting goose approach nigh to visit him, who with a sudden jerk apprehends his mistrustless prey. The English kill many of those, accounting them very good meat. Their skins be a very deep kind of fur, spotted white and black on the belly.

The wolves be in some respect different from them in other countries. It was never known yet that a wolf ever set upon a man or woman. Neither do they trouble horses or cows; but swine, goats, and red calves, which they take for deer, be often destroyed by them, so that a red calf is cheaper than a black one in that regard in some places. In the time of autumn and in the beginning of spring, these ravenous rangers do most frequent our English habitations, following the deer which come down at that time to those parts. They be made much like a mongrel, being big boned, lank paunched, deep breasted, having a thick neck and head, prick ears, and long snout, with dangerous teeth, long-staring hair, and a great bush tail. It is thought of many that our English mastiffs might be too hard for them; but it is no such matter, for they care no more for an ordinary mastiff than an ordinary mastiff cares for a cur. Many good dogs have been spoiled by them. Once a fair greyhound, hearing them at their howlings, run out to chide them, who was torn in pieces before he could be rescued. One of them makes no more bones to run away with a pig than a dog to run away with a marrow bone. It is observed that they have no joints from their head to the tail, which prevents them from leaping, or sudden turning, as may appear by what I shall show you.

A certain man having shot a wolf as he was feeding upon a swine, breaking his leg only, he knew not how to devise his death on a sudden. The wolf being a black one, he was loath to spoil his fur with a second shot, his skin being worth five or six pound sterling. Wherefore he resolved to get him by the tail and thrust him into a river that was hard by; which effected, the wolf being not able to turn his jointless body to bite him, was taken. That they cannot leap may appear by this wolf, whose mouth watering at a few poor impaled kids, would needs leap over a five-footed pale to be at them; but his foot slipping in the rise, he fell short of his desire, and being hung in the carpenters' stocks howled so loud that he frighted away the kids and called the English, who killed him.

These be killed daily in some place or other, either by the English or Indian, who have a certain rate for every head. Yet is there little hope of their utter destruction, the country being so spacious and they so numerous, travelling in the swamps by kennels. Sometimes ten or twelve are of a company. Late at night and early in the morning they set up their howlings and call their companies together — at night to hunt, at morning to sleep. In a word they be the greatest inconveniency the country hath, both for matter of damage to private men in particular, and the whole country in general.

Beasts Living in the Water

FOR ALL CREATURES that lived both by land and water, they be first otters, which be most of them black, whose fur is much used for muffs and are held almost as dear as beaver. The flesh of them is none of the best meat, but their oil is of rare use for many things. Secondly, martins, a good fur for their bigness. Thirdly, musquashes, which be much like a beaver for shape, but nothing near so big. The male hath two stones which smell as sweet as musk, and being killed in winter and the spring never lose their sweet smell. These skins are no bigger than a cony [rabbit] skin, yet are sold for five shillings apiece, being sent for tokens into England. One good skin will perfume a whole house full of clothes if it be right and good. Fourthly, the beaver, concerning whom, if I should at large discourse according to knowledge or information, I might take a volume.

The wisdom and understanding of this beast will almost conclude him a reasonable creature. His shape is thick and short, having likewise short legs, feet like a mole before and behind like a goose, a broad tail in form like a shoe sole, very tough and strong. His head is something like an otter's head, saving that his teeth before be placed like the teeth of a rabbit, two above and two beneath, sharp and broad, with which he cuts down trees as thick as a man's thigh, sometimes as big as a man's body, afterwards dividing them into lengths according to the use they are appointed for. If one beaver be too weak to carry the log, then another helps him; if they two be too weak, then *multorum manibus grande levatur onus* [loosely translated, "Many hands make light work"], four more adding their help, being placed three to three, which set their teeth in one another's tough tails, and laying the load on the two hindermost, they draw the log to the desired place, also tow it in the water, the strongest getting under, bearing it up that it may swim the lighter. That this may not seem altogether incredible, remember that the like almost may be seen in our ants, which will join sometimes seven or eight together in the carrying of a burthen.

These creatures build themselves houses of wood and clay close by the pond's side, and knowing the seasons build them answerable houses, having them three stories high so that as land-floods are raised by great rains, as the water arise they mount higher in their houses; as they assuage they descend lower again. These houses are so strong that no creature saving an industrious man with his penetrating tools can prejudice them, their ingress and egress being under water. These make likewise very good ponds, knowing whence a stream runs from between two rising hills they will there pitch down piles of wood, placing smaller rubbish before it with clay and sods, not leaving till by their art and industry they have made a firm and curious damhead which may draw admiration from wise, understanding men.

These creatures keep themselves to their own families, never parting so long as they are able to keep house together. And it is commonly said, if any beaver accidentally light into a strange place, he is made a drudge so long as he lives there, to carry at the greater end of the log, unless he creep away by stealth. Their wisdom secures them from the English who seldom or never kills any of them, being not patient to lay a long siege or to be so often deceived by their cunning evasions, so that all the beaver which the English have comes first from the Indians whose time and experience fits them for that employment.

Of the Birds and Fowls
Both of Land and Water

HAVING SHOWED YOU the most desirable, useful, and beneficial creatures, with the most offensive carrions that belong to our wilderness, it remains in the next place to show you such kinds of fowl as the country affords. They are many, and we have much variety both at sea and on land, and such as yield us much profit and honest pleasure, and are these that follow; as

> The princely eagle, and the soaring hawk,
> Whom in their unknown ways there's none can chalk:
> The humbird for some queen's rich cage more fit,
> Than in the vacant wilderness to sit.
> The swift-winged swallow sweeping to and fro,
> As swift as arrow from Tartarian bow.
> When as Aurora's infant day new springs,
> There the morning mounting lark her sweet lays sings.
> The harmonious thrush, swift pigeon, turtledove,
> Who to her mate doth ever constant prove.
> The turkey-pheasant, heathcock, partridge rare,
> The carrion-tearing crow, and hurtful stare,
> The long-lived raven, the ominous screech-owl,
> Who tells, as old wives say, disasters foul.
> The drowsy madge that leaves her day-loved nest,
> And loves to rove when day-birds be at rest;
> The eel-murthering hearn, and greedy cormorant,
> That near the creeks in moorish marshes haunt.
> The bellowing bittern, with the long-legged crane,
> Presaging winters hard, and dearth of grain.
> The silver swan that tunes her mournful breath,
> To sing the dirge of her approaching death.
> The tatling oldwives, and the cackling geese,
> The fearful gull that shuns the murthering piece.
> The strong winged mallard, with the nimble teal,
> And ill-shaped loon who his harsh notes doth squeal.
> There widgins, sheldrackes, and humilities,
> Snites, doppers, sea-larks, in whole millions flee.[4]

The eagles of the country be of two sorts, one like the eagles that be in England, the other is something bigger with a great white head and white tail. These be commonly called gripes; they prey upon

---

[4] Other seventeenth-century descriptions of birds mentioned by Wood may be found in the works of John Josselyn (see p. 428). Wood's "hurtful stare" was apparently a blackbird of some kind; his "madge" was the barn owl; his "sheldrackes" are shovelers; "humilities" and "snites" are varieties of shorebirds; "doppers" are buffleheads; and "sea-larks" are ringed plovers. See H. Kirke Swan, *A Dictionary of English and Folk-Names of British Birds* (London: Witherby, 1913), and Alfred Newton, *A Dictionary of Birds* (London: Adam and Charles Black, 1896). — ED.

ducks and geese and such fish as are cast upon the seashore. And although an eagle be counted king of that feathered regiment, yet is there a certain black hawk that beats him so that he is constrained to soar so high till heat expel his adversary. This hawk is much prized of the Indians, being accounted a sagamore's ransom.

To speak much of the hawks were to trespass upon my own judgment and bring upon myself a deserved censure for abusing the falconer's terms. But by relation from those that have more insight into them than myself, there be diverse kinds of hawks. Their aeries are easy to come by, being in the holes of rocks near the shore, so that any who are addicted to that sport — if he will be but at the charge of finding poultry for them — may have his desires. We could wish them well mewed in England, for they make havoc of hens, partridges, heathcocks, and ducks, often hindering the fowler of his long looked-for shoot.

The humbird is one of the wonders of the country, being no bigger than a hornet, yet hath all the dimensions of a bird, as bill and wings, with quills, spider-like legs, small claws. For color, she is as glorious as the rainbow. As she flies, she makes a little humming noise like a humblebee: wherefore she is called the humbird.

The pigeon of that country is something different from our dove-house pigeons in England, being more like turtles, of the same color. They have long tails like a magpie. And they seem not so big, because they carry not so many feathers on their backs as our English doves, yet are they as big in body. These birds come into the country to go to the north parts in the beginning of our spring, at which time (if I may be counted worthy to be believed in a thing that is not so strange as true) I have seen them fly as if the airy regiment had been pigeons, seeing neither beginning nor ending, length or breadth of these millions of millions. The shouting of people, the rattling of guns, and pelting of small shot could not drive them out of their course, but so they continued for four or five hours together. Yet it must not be concluded that it is thus often, for it is but at the beginning of the spring, and at Michaelmas when they return back to the southward; yet are there some all the year long, which are easily attained by such as look after them. Many of them build amongst the pine trees, thirty miles to the northeast of our plantations, joining nest to nest and tree to tree by their nests, so that the sun never sees the ground in that place, from whence the Indians fetch whole loads of them.

The turkey is a very large bird, of a black color yet white in flesh, much bigger than our English turkey. He hath the use of his long legs so ready that he can run as fast as a dog and fly as well as a

goose. Of these sometimes there will be forty, threescore, and an hundred of a flock, sometimes more and sometimes less. Their feeding is acorns, haws and berries; some of them get a haunt to frequent our English corn. In winter when the snow covers the ground, they resort to the seashore to look for shrimps and such small fishes at low tides. Such as love turkey hunting must follow it in winter after a new fallen snow, when he may follow them by their tracks. Some have killed ten or a dozen in half a day. If they can be found towards an evening and watched where they perch, if one come about ten or eleven of the clock, he may shoot as often as he will; they will sit unless they be slenderly wounded. These turkey remain all the year long. The price of a good turkey cock is four shillings, and he is well worth it, for he may be in weight forty pound, a hen two shillings.

Pheasants be very rare, but heathcocks and partridges be common. He that is a husband [farmer], and will be stirring betime, may kill half a dozen in a morning. The partridges be bigger than they be in England. The flesh of the heathcocks is red and the flesh of a partridge white; their price is four pence apiece.

The ravens and the crows be much like them of other countries. There are no magpies, jackdaws. cuckoos, jays, sparrows, etc. The stares be bigger than those in England, as black as crows, being the most troublesome and injurious bird of all others, pulling up the corns by the roots when it is young so that those who plant by reedy and seggy ["sedgy"] places, where they frequent, are much annoyed with them, they being so audacious that they fear not guns or their fellows hung upon poles. But the corn having a week or nine days growth is past their spoiling. The owls be of two sorts: the one being small, speckled like a partridge, with ears; the other being a great owl, almost as big as an eagle, his body being as good meat as a partridge.

Cormorants be as common as other fowls, which destroy abundance of small fish. These be not worth the shooting because they are the worst of fowls for meat, tasting rank and fishy. Again, one may shoot twenty times and miss, for seeing the fire in the pan, they dive under the water before the shot comes to the place where they were. They use[d] to roost upon the tops of trees and rocks, being a very heavy drowsy creature, so that the Indians will go in their canoes in the night and take them from the rocks as easily as women take a hen from roost. No ducking ponds can afford more delight than a lame cormorant and two or three lusty dogs.

The crane, although he be almost as tall as a man by reason of his long legs and neck, yet is his body rounder than other fowls, not much unlike the body of a turkey. I have seen many of these fowls, yet did I never see one that was fat — though very sleeky. I suppose it is contrary to their nature to grow fat. Of these there be many in summer but none in winter. Their price is two shillings. There be likewise many swans which frequent the fresh ponds and rivers, seldom consorting themselves with ducks and geese. These be very good meat; the price of one is six shillings.

The geese of the country be of three sorts: first a brant goose, which is a goose almost like the wild goose in England; the price of one of these is six pence. The second kind is a white goose, almost as big as an English tame goose. These come in great flocks about Michaelmas. Sometimes there will be two or three thousand in a flock; those continue six weeks and so fly to the southward, returning in March and staying six weeks more, returning again to the northward. The price of one of these is eight pence. The third kind of geese is a great gray goose with a black neck and a black and white head, strong of flight, and these be a great deal bigger than the ordinary geese of England, some very fat, and in the spring so full of feathers that the shot can scarce pierce them. Most of these geese remain with us from Michaelmas to April. They feed on the sea, upon grass in the bays at low water and gravel, and in the woods of acorns, having as other fowl have their pass and repass to the northward and southward. The accurate marksmen kill of these both flying and sitting; the price of a good gray goose is eighteen pence.

The ducks of the country be very large ones and in great abundance, so is there of teal likewise. The price of a duck is six pence, of a teal three pence. If I should tell you how some have killed a hundred geese in a week, fifty ducks at a shot, forty teals at another, it may be counted impossible though nothing more certain.

The oldwives be a foul that never leave tatling day or night, something bigger than a duck. The loon is an ill-shaped thing like a cormorant, but that he can neither go nor fly. He maketh a noise sometimes like a sow-gelder's horn. The humilities or simplicities (as I may rather call them) be of two sorts, the biggest being as big as a green plover, the other as big as birds that we call knots in England. Such is the simplicity of the smaller sorts of these birds that one may drive them on a heap like so many sheep, and seeing a fit time shoot them. The living seeing the dead, settle themselves on the same place again, amongst which the fowler discharges again. I myself have killed twelve score at two shoots. These birds are to be had upon sandy brakes at the latter end of summer before the geese come in.

Thus much have I showed you as I know to be true concerning the fowl of the country. But methinks I hear some say that this is very good if it could be caught, or likely to continue, and that much shooting will fright away the fowls. True it is that everyone's employment will not permit him to fowl: what then? Yet their employments furnish them with silver guns with which they may have it more easy. For the frighting of the fowl, true it is that many go blurting away their powder and shot that have no more skill to kill or win a goose than many in England that have rusty muskets in their houses knows what belongs to a soldier, yet are they not much affrighted. I have seen more living and dead the last year than I have done in former years.

WILLIAM BARTRAM

(*1739–1823*)

❧ The author was none too careful with dates and places in the record of his travels, but his memory for impression and inner experience was superb. There is, perhaps, something of the quality of the dream to the *Travels:* Bartram moves glidingly from beautiful sight to beautiful sight, responding with ready emotion, continually being surprised and delighted by what the next turn in the trail or bend in the river reveals. His book is an early, thus quintessential statement of immersion in the American wilderness; it was almost immediately taken up into the Romantic canon via Coleridge and Wordsworth in England, and it remains a landmark text.

Introduction to the *Travels*

THE ATTENTION OF A TRAVELLER, should be particularly turned, in the first place, to the various works of Nature, to mark the distinctions of the climates he may explore, and to offer such useful observations on the different productions as may occur. Men and manners undoubtedly hold the first rank — whatever may contribute to our existence is also of equal importance, whether it be found in the animal or vegetable kingdoms; neither are the various articles, which tend to promote the happiness and convenience of mankind, to be disregarded. How far the writer of the following sheets has succeeded in furnishing information on these subjects, the reader will be capable of determining. From the advantages the journalist enjoyed under his father John Bartram, botanist to the king of Great-Britain, and fellow of the Royal Society, it is hoped that his labours

From *The Travels of William Bartram* (1791)

will present new as well as useful information to the botanist and zoologist.

This world, as a glorious apartment of the boundless palace of the sovereign Creator, is furnished with an infinite variety of animated scenes, inexpressibly beautiful and pleasing, equally free to the inspection and enjoyment of all his creatures.

Perhaps there is not any part of creation, within the reach of our observations, which exhibits a more glorious display of the Almighty hand, than the vegetable world. Such a variety of pleasing scenes, ever changing, throughout the seasons, arising from various causes and assigned each to the purpose and use determined.

It is difficult to pronounce which division of the earth, within the polar circles, produces the greatest variety. The tropical division certainly affords those which principally contribute to the more luxurious scenes of splendor, as Myrtus communis, Myrt. caryophyllata, Myrt. pimenta, Caryophylus aromaticus, Laurus cinam. Laurus camphor. Laurus Persica, Nux mosch. Illicium, Camellia, Punica, Cactus melocactus; Cactus grandiflora, Gloriosa superba, Theobroma, Adansonia digitata, Nyctanthes, Psidium, Musa paradisica, Musa sapientum, Garcinia mangostana, Cocos nucifera, Citrus, Citrus aurantium, Cucurbita citrullus, Hyacinthus, Amaryllis, Narcissus, Poinciana pulcherima, Crinum, Cactus cochinellifer.

But the temperate zone (including by far the greater portion of the earth, and a climate the most favourable to the increase and support of animal life, as well as for the exercise and activity of the human faculties) exhibits scenes of infinitely greater variety, magnificence and consequence, with respect to human economy, in regard to the various uses of vegetables.

For instance, Triticum Cereale, which affords us bread, and is termed, by way of eminence, the staff of life, the most pleasant and nourishing food — to all terrestrial animals. Vitis vinifera, whose exhilarating juice is said to cheer the hearts of gods and men. Oryza, Zea, Pyrus, Pyrus malus, Prunus, Pr. cerasus, Ficus, Nectarin, Apricot, Cydonia. Next follow the illustrious families of forest-trees, as the Magnolia grandiflora and Quercus sempervirens, which form the venerated groves and solemn shades, on the Mississippi, Alatamaha and Florida, the magnificent Cupressus disticha of Carolina and Florida, the beautiful Water Oak,[1] whose vast hemispheric head, presents the likeness of a distant grove in the fields and savannas of Carolina. The gigantic Black Oak,[2] Platanus occidentalis, Liquid-amber styra-

[1] Quercus Hemispherica.
[2] Quercus tinctoria.

Andromeda Pulverulenta.

ciflua, Liriodendron tulipifera, Fagus castania, Fagus sylvatica, Juglans nigra, Juglans cinerea, Jug. pecan, Ulmus, Acher sacharinum, of Virginia and Pennsylvania; Pinus phoenix, Pinus toeda, Magnolia acuminata, Nyssa aquatica, Populus heterophylla and the floriferous Gordonia lasianthus, of Carolina and Florida; the exalted Pinus strobus, Pin. balsamica, Pin. abies, Pin. Canadensis, Pin. larix, Fraxinus excelsior, Robinia pseudacacia, Guilandina dioica, Æsculus Virginica, Magnolia acuminata, of Virginia, Maryland, Pennsylvania, New-Jersey, New-York, New-England, Ohio and the regions of Erie and the Illinois; and the aromatic and floriferous shrubs, as Azalea coccinia, Azalea rosea, Rosa, Rhododendron, Kalmia, Syringa, Gardinia, Calcycanthus, Daphne, Franklinia, Styrax and others equally celebrated.

In every order of nature, we perceive a variety of qualities distributed amongst individuals, designed for different purposes and uses, yet it appears evident, that the great Author has impartially distributed his favours to his creatures, so that the attributes of each one seem to be of sufficient importance to manifest the divine and inimitable workmanship. The pompous Palms of Florida, and glorious Magnolia, strike us with the sense of dignity and magnificence; the expansive umbrageous Live-Oak[3] with awful veneration, the Carica papaya, supercilious with all the harmony of beauty and gracefulness; the Lillium superbum represents pride and vanity; Kalmia latifolia and Azalea coccinea, exhibit a perfect show of mirth and gaiety; the Illisium Floridanum, Crinum Floridanum, Convalaria majalis of the Cherokees, and Calycanthus floridus, charm with their beauty and fragrance. Yet they are not to be compared for usefulness with the nutritious Triticum, Zea, Oryza, Solanum tuberosa, Musa, Convolvulous, Batata, Rapa, Orchis, Vitis vinifera, Pyrus, Olea; for clothing, Linum, Canabis, Gossypium, Morus; for medical virtues, Hyssopus, Thymus, Anthemis nobilis, Papaver somniferum, Quinqina, Rheum rhabarbarum, Pisum, &c. though none of these most useful tribes are conspicuous for stateliness, figure or splendor, yet their valuable qualities and virtues, excite love, gratitude and adoration to the great Creator, who was pleased to endow them with such eminent qualities, and reveal them to us for our sustenance, amusement and delight.

But there remain of the vegetable world, several tribes that are distinguished by very remarkable properties, which excite our admiration, some for the elegance, singularity and splendor of their vestment, as the Tulipa, Fritillaria, Colchicum, Primula, Lillium su-

[3] Quercus sempervirens.

perbum, Kalmia, &c. Others astonish us by their figure and disposal
of their vestiture, as if designed only to embellish and please the
observer, as in the Nepenthes distillatoria, Ophrys insectoria, Cypri-
pedium calceolus, Hydrangia quercifolia, Bartramia bracteata, Vi-
burnum Canadense, Bartsea, &c.

Observe these green meadows how they are decorated; they seem
enamelled with the beds of flowers. The blushing Chironia and
Rhexia, the spiral Ophrys with immaculate white flowers, the Limo-
dorum, Arethusa pulcherima, Sarracenia purpurea, Sarracenia gal-
eata, Sarracenia lacunosa, Sarracenia flava. Shall we analyze these
beautiful plants, since they seem cheerfully to invite us? How greatly
the flowers of the yellow Sarracenia represent a silken canopy, the
yellow pendant petals are the curtains, and the hollow leaves are not
unlike the cornucopia or Amaltheas horn, what a quantity of water
a leaf is capable of containing, about a pint! taste of it — how cool
and animating — limpid as the morning dew: nature seems to have
furnished them with this cordated appendage or lid, which turns
over, to prevent a too sudden, and copious supply of water from
heavy showers of rain, which would bend down the leaves, never to
rise again; because their streight parallel nerves, which extend and
support them, are so rigid and fragile, the leaf would inevitably break
when bent down to a right angle; therefore I suppose these waters
which contribute to their supplies, are the rebounding drops or horizontal streams wafted by the winds, which adventitiously find their
way into them, when a blast of wind shifts the lid; see these short
stiff hairs, they all point downwards, which direct the condensed
vapours down into the funiculum; these stiff hairs also prevent the
varieties of insects, which are caught, from returning, being invited
down to sip the mellifluous exuvia, from the interior surface of the
tube, where they inevitably perish; what quantities there are of them!
These latent waters undoubtedly contribute to the support and refreshment of the plant; perhaps designed as a reservoir in case of
long continued droughts, or other casualties, since these plants naturally dwell in low savannas liable to overflows, from rain water: for
although I am not of the opinion that vegetables receive their nourishment, only through the ascending part of the plant, as the stem,
branches, leaves, &c. and that their descending part, as the root and
fibres, only serve to hold and retain them in their places, yet I believe
they imbibe rain and dews through their leaves, stems and branches,
by extremely minute pores, which open on both surfaces of the leaves
and on the branches, which may communicate to little auxiliary ducts
or vessels; or, perhaps the cool dews and showers, by constricting

these pores, and thereby preventing a too free perspiration, may recover and again invigorate the languid nerves, of those which seem to suffer for want of water, in great heats and droughts; but whether the insects caught in their leaves, and which dissolve and mix with the fluid, serve for aliment or support to these kind of plants, is doubtful. All the Sarracenia are insect catchers, and so is the Drossea rotundiflolia.

But admirable are the properties of the extraordinary Dionea muscipula! A great extent on each side of that serpentine rivulet, is occupied by those sportive vegetables — let us advance to the spot in which nature has seated them. Astonishing production! see the incarnate lobes expanding, how gay and ludicrous they appear! ready on the spring to intrap incautious deluded insects, what artifice! there behold one of the leaves just closed upon a struggling fly, another has got a worm, its hold is sure, its prey can never escape — carnivorous vegetable! Can we after viewing this object, hesitate a moment to confess, that vegetable beings are endued with some sensible faculties or attributes, similar to those that dignify animal nature; they are organical, living and self-moving bodies, for we see here, in this plant, motion and volition.

What power or faculty is it, that directs the cirri of the Cucurbita, Momordica, Vitis and other climbers, towards the twigs of shrubs, trees and other friendly support? we see them invariably leaning, extending and like the fingers of the human hand, reaching to catch hold of what is nearest, just as if they had eyes to see with, and when their hold is fixed, to coil the tendril in a spiral form, by which artifice it becomes more elastic and effectual, than if it had remained in a direct line, for every revolution of the coil adds a portion of strength, and thus collected, they are enabled to dilate and contract as occasion or necessity require, and thus by yielding to, and humouring the motion of the limbs and twigs, or other support on which they depend, are not so liable to be torn off by sudden blasts of wind or other assaults; is it sense or instinct that influences their actions? it must be some impulse; or does the hand of the Almighty act and perform this work in our sight?

The vital principle or efficient cause of motion and action, in the animal and vegetable system, perhaps, may be more familiar than we generally apprehend. Where is the essential difference between the seed of peas, peaches and other tribes of plants and trees, and that of oviparous animals? as the eggs of birds, snakes or butterflies, spawn of fish, &c. Let us begin at the source of terrestrial existence. Are not the seed of vegetables, and the eggs of oviparous animals fecundated, or influenced with the vivific principle of life, through the approximation and intimacy of the sexes, and immediately after the eggs and seeds are hatched, the young larva and infant plant, by heat and moisture, rise into existence, increase, and in due time arrive to a state of perfect maturity. The physiologists agree in opinion, that the work of generation in viviparous animals, is exactly similar, only more secret and enveloped. The mode of operation that nature pursues in the production of vegetables, and oviparous animals is infinitely more uniform and manifest, than that which is or can be discovered to take place in viviparous animals.

The most apparent difference between animals and vegetables is, that animals have the powers of sound, and are locomotive, whereas vegetables are not able to shift themselves from the places where nature has planted them: yet vegetables have the power of moving and exercising their members, and have the means of transplanting or colonising their tribes almost over the surface of the whole earth, some seeds, for instance, grapes, nuts, smilax, peas, and others, whose pulp or kernel is food for animals, such seed will remain several days without injuring in stomachs of pigeons and other birds of passage; by this means such sorts are distributed from place to place, even across seas; indeed some seeds require this preparation, by the digestive heat of the stomach of animals, to dissolve and detach the oily, viscid pulp, and to soften the hard shells of others. Small seeds are sometimes furnished with rays of hair or down, and others with thin light membranes attached to them, which serve the purpose of wings, on which they mount upward, leaving the earth, float in the air, and are carried away by the swift winds to very remote regions before they settle on the earth; some are furnished with hooks, which catch hold of the wool and hair of animals passing by them, are by that means spread abroad; other seeds ripen in pericarps, which open with elastic force, and shoot their seed to a very great distance round about; some other seeds, as of the Mosses and Fungi, are so very minute as to be invisible, light as atoms, and these mixing with the air, are wafted all over the world.

The animal creation also, excites our admiration, and equally manifests the almighty power, wisdom and beneficence of the Supreme Creator and Sovereign Lord of the universe; some in their vast size and strength, as the mammoth, the elephant, the whale, the lion and alligator; others in agility; others in their beauty and elegance of colour, plumage and rapidity of flight, have the faculty of moving and living in the air; others for their immediate and indispensable use and convenience to man, in furnishing means for our clothing and sustenance, and administering to our help in the toils and labours through life; how wonderful is the mechanism of these finely formed, self-moving beings, how complicated their system, yet what unerring uniformity prevails through every tribe and particular species! the effect we see and contemplate, the cause is invisible, incomprehensible, how can it be otherwise? when we cannot see the end or origin of a nerve or vein, while the divisibility of matter or fluid, is infinite. We admire the mechanism of a watch, and the fabric of a piece of brocade, as being the production of art; these merit our admiration, and must excite our esteem for the ingenious artist or modifier, but nature is the work of God omnipotent: and an elephant, even this world is comparatively but a very minute part of his works. If then the visible, the mechanical part of the animal creation, the mere material part is so admirably beautiful, harmonious and incomprehensible, what must be the intellectual system? that inexpressibly more essential principle, which secretly operates within? that which animates the inimitable machines, which gives them motion, impowers them to act, speak and perform, this must be divine and immortal?

I am sensible that the general opinion of philosophers, has distinguished the moral system of the brute creature from that of mankind, by an epithet which implies a mere mechanical impulse, which leads and impels them to necessary actions, without any premeditated design or contrivance, this we term instinct, which faculty we suppose to be inferior to reason in man.

The parental, and filial affections seem to be as ardent, their sensibility and attachment, as active and faithful, as those observed to be in human nature.

When travelling on the East coast of the isthmus of Florida, ascending the South Musquitoe river, in a canoe, we observed numbers of deer and bears, near the banks, and on the islands of the river, the bear were feeding on the fruit of the dwarf creeping Chamerops, (this fruit is of the form and size of dates, and is delicious and nourishing food:) we saw eleven bears in the course of the day, they seemed no way surprized or affrighted at the sight of us; in the evening my hunter, who was an excellent marksman, said that he would shoot one of them, for the sake of the skin and oil, for we had plenty and variety of provisions in our bark. We accordingly, on sight of two of them, planned our approaches, as artfully as possible, by crossing over to the opposite shore, in order to get under cover of a small island, this we cautiously coasted round, to a point, which we apprehended would take us within shot of the bear, but here finding ourselves at too great a distance from them, and discovering that we must openly show ourselves, we had no other alternative to effect our purpose, but making oblique approaches; we gained gradually on our prey by this artifice, without their noticing us, finding ourselves near enough, the hunter fired, and laid the largest dead on the spot, where she stood, when presently the other, not seeming the least moved, at the report of our piece, approached the dead body, smelled, and pawed it, and appearing in agony, fell to weeping and looking upwards, then towards us, and cried out like a child. Whilst our boat approached very near, the hunter was loading his rifle in order to shoot the survivor, which was a young cub, and the slain supposed to be the dam; the continual cries of this afflicted child, bereft of its parent, affected me very sensibly, I was moved with compassion, and charging myself as if accessory to what now appeared to be a cruel murder, and endeavoured to prevail on the hunter to save its life, but to no effect! for by habit he had become insensible to compassion towards the brute creation, being now within a few yards of the harmless devoted victim, he fired, and laid it dead, upon the body of the dam.

If we bestow but a very little attention to the economy of the animal creation, we shall find manifest examples of premeditation, perseverance, resolution, and consummate artifice, in order to effect their purpose. The next morning, after the slaughter of the bears whilst my companions were striking our tent and preparing to re-embark, I resolved to make a little botanical excursion alone; crossing over a narrow isthmus of sand hills which separated the river from the ocean, I passed over a pretty high hill, its summit crested with a few Palm trees, surrounded with an Orange grove; this hill, whose base was washed on one side, by the floods of the Musquitoe river, and the other side by the billows of the ocean, was about one hundred yards diameter, and seemed to be an entire heap of sea hills. I continued along the beach, a quarter of a mile, and came up to a forest of the Agave vivipara (though composed of herbaceous plants, I term it a forest, because their scapes or flower-stems arose erect near 30 feet high) their tops regularly branching in the form of a pyramidal tree, and these plants growing near to each other, occupied a space of ground of several acres: when their seed is ripe they vegetate, and grow on the branches, until the scape dries when the young plants fall to the ground, take root, and fix themselves in the sand: the plant grows to a prodigious size before the scape shoots up from its centre. Having contemplated this admirable grove, I proceeded towards the shrubberies on the banks of the river, and though it was now late in December, the aromatic groves appeared in full bloom. The broad leaved sweet Myrtus, Erythrina corrallodendrum, Cactus cochenellifer, Cacalia suffruticosa, and particularly, Rhizophora conjugata, which stood close to, and in the salt water of the river, were in full bloom, with beautiful white sweet scented flowers, which attracted to them, two or three species of very beautiful butterflies, one of which was black, the upper pair of its wings very long and narrow, marked with transverse stripes of pale yellow, with some spots of a crimson colour near the body. Another species remarkable for splendor, was of a larger size, the wings were undulated and obtusely crenated round their ends, the nether pair terminating near the body, with a long narrow forked tail; the ground light yellow, striped oblique-transversely, with stripes of pale celestial blue, the ends of them adorned with little eyes encircled with the finest blue and crimson, which represented a very brilliant rosary. But those which were the most numerous were as white as snow, their wings large, their ends lightly crenated and ciliated, forming a fringed border, faintly marked with little black crescents, their points downward, with a cluster of little brilliant orbs of blue and crimson, on the nether wings near the body; the numbers were incredible, and there seemed to be scarcely a flower for each fly, multitudinous as they were, besides clouds of them hovering over the mellifluous groves. Besides these papilios [swallowtails], a variety of other insects come in for share, particularly several species of bees.

As I was gathering specimens of flowers from the shrubs, I was greatly surprised at the sudden appearance of a remarkable large spider on a leaf, of the genus Araneus saliens, at sight of me he boldly faced about, and raised himself up as if ready to spring upon me; his body was about the size of a pigeons egg, of a buff colour, which with his legs were covered with short silky hair, on the top of the abdomen was a round red spot or ocellus encircled with black; after I had recovered from the surprise, and observing the wary hunter had retired under cover, I drew near again, and presently discovered that I had surprised him on predatory attempts against the insect tribes, I was therefore determined to watch his proceedings, I soon noticed that the object of his wishes was a large fat bomble bee (apis bombylicus) that was visiting the flowers, and piercing their nectariferous tubes; this cunning intrepid hunter (conducted his subtil approaches, with the circumspection and perseverance of a Siminole, when hunting a deer) advancing with slow steps obliquely, or under cover of dense foliage, and behind the limbs, and when the bee was engaged in probing a flower he would leap nearer, and then instantly retire out of sight, under a leaf or behind a branch, at the same time keeping a sharp eye upon me; when he had now got within two feet of his prey, and the bee was intent on sipping the delicious nectar from a flower, with his back next the spider, he instantly sprang upon him, and grasped him over the back and shoulder, when for some moments they both disappeared, I expected the bee had carried of his enemy, but to my surprise they both together rebounded back again, suspended at the extremity of a strong elastic thread or web, which the spider had artfully let fall, or fixed on the twig, the instant he leaped from it; the rapidity of the bee's wings, endeavouring to extricate himself, made them both together appear as a moving vapor, until the bee became fatigued by whirling round, first one way and then back again; at length, in about a quarter of an hour, the bee quite exhausted by his struggles, and the repeated wounds of the butcher, became motionless, and quickly expired in the arms of the devouring spider, who, ascending the rope with his game, retired to feast on it under cover of leaves; and perhaps before night became himself, the delicious evening repast of a bird or lizard.

Birds are in general social and benevolent creatures; intelligent, ingenious, volatile, active beings; and this order of animal creation consists of various nations, bands or tribes, as may be observed from their different structure, manners and languages or voice, as each nation, though subdivided into many different tribes, retain their general form or structure, a similarity of customs, and a sort of dialect or language, particular to that nation or genus from which they seem to have descended or separated: what I mean by a language in birds, is the common notes or speech, that they use when employed in feeding themselves and their young, calling on one another, as well as their menaces against their enemy; for their songs seem to be musical compositions, performed only by the males, about the time of incubation, in part to divert and amuse the female, entertaining her with melody, &c. this harmony, with the tender solicitude of the male, alleviates the toils, cares and distresses of the female, consoles her in solitary retirement whilst setting, and animates her with affection and attachment to himself in preference to any other. The volatility of their species, and operation of their passions and affections, are particularly conspicuous in the different tribes of the thrush, famous for song; on a sweet May morning we see the red thrushes (turdus rufus) perched on an elevated sprig of the snowy Hawthorn, sweet flowering Crab, or other hedge shrubs, exerting their accomplishments in song, striving by varying and elevating their voices to excel each other, we observe a very agreeable variation, not only in tone but in modulation; the voice of one is shrill, another lively and elevated, others sonorous and quivering. The mock-bird (turdus polyglottos) who excels, distinguishes himself in variety of action as well as air; from a turret he bounds aloft with the celerity of an arrow, as it were to recover or recall his very soul, expired in the last elevated strain. The high forests are filled with the symphony of the song or wood-thrush (turdus minor).

Both sexes of some tribes of birds sing equally fine, and it is remarkable, that these reciprocally assist in their domestic cares, as building their nests and setting on their eggs, feeding and defending their young brood, &c. The oriolus (icterus, Cat.) is an instance in this case, and the female of the icterus minor is a bird of more splendid and gay dress than the male bird. Some tribes of birds will relieve and rear up the young and helpless, of their own and other tribes, when abandoned. Animal substance seems to be the first food of all birds, even the granivorous tribes.

Having passed through some remarks, which appeared of sufficient consequence to be offered to the public, and which were most suitable to have a place in the introduction, I shall now offer such observations as must necessarily occur, from a careful attention to, and investigation of the manners of the Indian nations; being induced, while traveling among them, to associate with them, that I might judge for myself whether they were deserving of the severe censure, which prevailed against them among the white people, that they were incapable of civilization.

In the consideration of this important subject it will be necessary to enquire, whether they were inclined to adopt the European modes of civil society? whether such a reformation could be obtained, without using coercive or violent means? and lastly, whether such a revolution would be productive of real benefit to them, and consequently beneficial to the public? I was satisfied in discovering that they were desirous of becoming united with us, in civil and religious society. It may, therefore, not be foreign to the subject, to point out the propriety of sending men of ability and virtue, under the authority of government, as friendly visitors, into their towns; let these men be instructed to learn perfectly their languages, and by a liberal and friendly intimacy, become acquainted with their customs and usages, religious and civil; their system of legislation and police, as well as their most ancient and present traditions and history. These men thus enlightened and instructed, would be qualified to judge equitably, and when returned to us, to make true and just reports, which might assist the legislature of the United States to form, and offer to them a judicious plan, for their civilization and union with us.

But I presume not to dictate in these high concerns of government, and I am fully convinced that such important matters are far above my ability; the duty and respect we owe to religion and rectitude, the most acceptable incense we can offer to the Almighty, as an atonement for our negligence, in the care of the present and future well being of our Indian brethren, induces me to mention this matter, though perhaps of greater concernment than we generally are aware of.

ALEXANDER WILSON
(1766–1813)

❧ Alexander Wilson's fiercely wholehearted devotion to his projected "collection of all our finest birds" drove him the length and breadth of the young republic in search of his artistic quarry, and kept him going through disappointments that might have stopped most men. The governor of New York, when asked to subscribe to the book Wilson was assembling, answered, "I would not give a hundred dollars for all the birds you intend to describe even had I them alive." The Scot moved his project forward with amazing efficiency, apparently never doubting its ultimate completion and success, and finally, after a decade of mostly single-handed labor, finished America's first accurate and reasonably complete bird guide. Despite reactions like that of the New York governor, Wilson also managed to solicit enough subscriptions to ensure the book's publication.

So interesting is Wilson's story that we are apt to overlook the quality of the work itself. *American Ornithology* has great beauty, both in its art (even Audubon, whose painting was of an entirely different order, was content to use at least one of Wilson's illustrations as a model) and in its written descriptions. The prose is image-filled and evocative, expressing in a purposefully literary way the author's hard-won field knowledge and his passion for his subject.

Wood Thrush (*Turdus Melodus*)

THIS BIRD is represented on the plate of its natural size, and particular attention has been paid to render the figure a faithful likeness

From *American Ornithology* (1808–1814)

of the original. It measures eight inches in length, and thirteen from tip to tip of the expanded wings; the bill is an inch long; the upper mandible, of a dusky brown, bent at the point, and slightly notched; the lower, a flesh colour towards the base; the legs are long, and, as well as the claws, of a pale flesh colour, or almost transparent. The whole upper parts are of a brown fulvous colour, brightening into reddish on the head, and inclining to an olive on the rump and tail; chin, white; throat and breast, white, tinged with a light buff colour, and beautifully marked with pointed spots of black or dusky, running in chains from the sides of the mouth, and intersecting each other all over the breast to the belly, which, with the vent, is of a pure white; a narrow circle of white surrounds the eye, which is large, full, the pupil black, and the iris of a dark chocolate colour; the inside of the mouth is yellow. The male and female of this species, as, indeed, of almost the whole genus of thrushes, differ so little, as scarcely to be distinguished from each other. It is called by some the wood robin, by others the ground robin, and by some of our American ornithologists *Turdus minor,* though, as will hereafter appear, improperly. The present name has been adopted from Mr William Bartram, who seems to have been the first and almost only naturalist who has taken notice of the merits of this bird.

This sweet and solitary songster inhabits the whole of North America, from Hudson's Bay to the peninsula of Florida. He arrives in Pennsylvania about the 20th of April, or soon after, and returns to the south about the beginning of October. The lateness or earliness of the season seems to make less difference in the times of arrival of our birds of passage than is generally imagined. Early in April the woods are often in considerable forwardness, and scarce a summer bird to be seen. On the other hand, vegetation is sometimes no further advanced on the 20th of April, at which time (e.g., this present year, 1807) numbers of wood thrushes are seen flitting through the moist woody hollows, and a variety of the *Motacilla* genus chattering from almost every bush, with scarce an expanded leaf to conceal them. But at whatever time the wood thrush may arrive, he soon announces his presence in the woods. With the dawn of the succeeding morning, mounting to the top of some tall tree that rises from a low thick shaded part of the woods, he pipes his few, but clear and musical notes, in a kind of ecstasy; the prelude or symphony to which strongly resembles the double-tonguing of a German flute, and sometimes the tinkling of a small bell; the whole song consists of five of six parts, the last note of each of which is in such a tone as to leave the conclusion evidently suspended; the finalé is finely managed, and with such charming effect as to soothe and tranquillise the mind, and to seem sweeter and mellower at each successive repetition. Rival songsters, of the same species, challenge each other from different parts of the wood, seeming to vie for softer tones and more exquisite responses. During the burning heat of the day, they are comparatively mute; but in the evening the same melody is renewed, and continued long after sunset. Those who visit our woods, or ride out into the country at these hours, during the months of May and June, will be at no loss to recognise, from the above description, this pleasing musician. Even in dark, wet, and gloomy weather, when scarce a single chirp is heard from any other bird, the clear notes of the wood thrush thrill through the dropping woods, from morning to night; and it may truly be said, that the sadder the day the sweeter is his song.

The favourite haunts of the wood thrush are low, thick shaded hollows, through which a small brook or rill meanders, overhung with alder bushes, that are mantled with wild vines. Near such a scene he generally builds his nest, in a laurel or alder bush. Outwardly it is composed of withered beech leaves of the preceding year, laid at bottom in considerable quantities, no doubt to prevent damp and moisture from ascending through, being generally built in low, wet situations; above these are layers of knotty stalks of withered grass, mixed with mud, and smoothly plastered, above which is laid a slight lining of fine black fibrous roots of plants. The eggs are four, sometimes five, of a uniform light blue, without any spots.

The wood thrush appears always singly or in pairs, and is of a shy, retired, unobtrusive disposition. With the modesty of true merit, he charms you with his song, but is content, and even solicitous, to be concealed. He delights to trace the irregular windings of the brook, where, by the luxuriance of foliage, the sun is completely shut out, or only plays in a few interrupted beams on the glittering surface of the water. He is also fond of a particular species of lichen which grows in such situations, and which, towards the fall, I have uniformly found in their stomachs: berries, however, of various kinds, are his principal food, as well as beetles and caterpillars. The feathers on the hind head are longer than is usual with birds which have no crest; these he sometimes erects; but this particular cannot be observed but on a close examination.

Those who have paid minute attention to the singing of birds know well that the voice, energy, and expression, in the same tribe, differ as widely as the voices of different individuals of the human species, or as one singer does from another. The powers of song, in some individuals of the wood thrush, have often surprised and delighted me. Of these I remember one, many years ago, whose notes I could instantly recognise on entering the woods, and with whom I had been, as it were, acquainted from his first arrival. The top of a large white oak that overhung part of the glen, was usually the favourite pinnacle from whence he poured the sweetest melody; to which I had frequently listened till night began to gather in the woods, and the fireflies to sparkle among the branches. But, alas! in the pathetic language of the poet —

> One morn I missed him on the accustomed hill,
> Along the vale, and on his favourite tree —
> Another came, nor yet beside the rill,
> Nor up the glen, nor in the wood was he.

A few days afterwards, passing along the edge of the rocks, I found fragments of the wings and broken feathers of a wood thrush killed by the hawk, which I contemplated with unfeigned regret, and not without a determination to retaliate on the first of these murderers I could meet with.

That I may not seem singular in my estimation of this bird, I shall subjoin an extract of a letter from a distinguished American gentleman, to whom I had sent some drawings, and whose name, were I at liberty to give it, would do honour to my humble performance, and render any further observations on the subject from me unnecessary.

"As you are curious in birds, there is one well worthy your attention, to be found, or rather heard, in every part of America, and yet scarcely ever to be seen. It is in all the forests from spring to fall, and never but on the tops of the tallest trees, from which it perpetually serenades us with some of the sweetest notes, and as clear as those of the nightingale. I have followed it for miles, without ever but once getting a good view of it. It is of the size and make of the mocking bird, lightly thrush coloured on the back, and a grayish white on the breast and belly. Mr ———, my son-in-law, was in possession of one, which had been shot by a neighbour; he pronounced it a *Muscicapa,* and I think it much resembles the *Mouche rolle de la Martinique,* 8 Buffon, 374, *Pl. enlum,* 568. As it abounds in all the neighbourhood of Philadelphia, you may, perhaps, by patience and perseverance (of which much will be requisite), get a sight, if not a possession, of it. I have, for twenty years, interested the young sportsmen of my neighbourhood to shoot me one, but, as yet, without success."

It may seem strange that neither Sloane, Catesby, Edwards, nor Buffon,[1] all of whom are said to have described this bird, should say anything of its melody; or rather, assert that it had only a single cry or scream. This I cannot account for in any other way than by supposing, what I think highly probable, that this bird has never been figured or described by any of the above authors.

Catesby has, indeed, represented a bird which he calls *Turdus minimus,*[2] but it is difficult to discover, either from the figure or description, what particular species is meant; or whether it be really intended for the wood thrush we are now describing. It resembles, he says, the English thrush; but is less, never sings, has only a single note, and abides all the year in Carolina. It must be confessed that, except the first circumstance, there are few features of the wood thrush in this description. I have searched the woods of Carolina and Georgia in winter for this bird in vain, nor do I believe it ever winters in these States. If Mr Catesby found his bird mute during spring and summer,

---

[1] Wilson's references are to Sir Hans Sloane, *A Voyage to the Island Madera, Barbados, Nieves, S. Christophers and Jamaica,* 1725; Mark Catesby, *The Natural History of Carolina, Florida, and the Bahama Islands* (1731–1748); George Edwards, *A Natural History of Uncommon Birds* (1743–1751); and the Comte de Buffon, *Histoire Naturelle, Générale et Particulière* (1749–1804). — ED.

[2] Catesby, 1, p. 31.

it was not the wood thrush, otherwise he must have changed his very nature. But Mr Edwards has also described and delineated the little thrush,[3] and has referred to Catesby as having drawn and engraved it before. Now this thrush of Edwards I know to be really a differen species; one not resident in Pennsylvania, but passing to the north ii May, and returning the same way in October, and may be distinguished from the true song thrush (*Turdus melodus*) by the spots being much broader, brown, and not descending so far below the breast. It is also an inch shorter, with the cheeks of a bright tawny colour. Mr William Bartram, who transmitted this bird, more than fifty years ago, to Mr Edwards, by whom it was drawn and engraved, examined the two species in my presence; and on comparing them with the one in Edwards, was satisfied that the bird there figured and described is not the wood thrush (*Turdus melodus*), but the tawny-cheeked species above mentioned. This I have never seen in Pennsylvania but in spring and fall. It is still more solitary than the former, and utters, at rare times, a single cry, similar to that of a chicken which has lost its mother. This very bird I found numerous in the myrtle swamps of Carolina in the depth of winter, and I have not a doubt of its being the same which is described by Edwards and Catesby.

As the Count de Buffon has drawn his description from those above mentioned, the same observations apply equally to what he has said on the subject; and the fanciful theory which this writer had formed to account for its want of song, vanishes into empty air; viz., that the song thrush of Europe (*Turdus musicus*), had, at some time after the creation, rambled round by the northern ocean, and made its way to America; that, advancing to the south, it had there (of consequence) become degenerated by change of food and climate, so that its cry is now harsh and unpleasant, "as are the cries of all birds that live in wild countries inhabited by savages."[4]

---

[3] Edwards, p. 296.
[4] Buffon, vol. 3, p. 289. The figure in Pl. enl. 398, has little or no resemblance to the wood thrush, being of a deep green olive above, and spotted to the tail below with long streaks of brown.

John D. Godman

(1794–1830)

~~ Godman's "Rambles" appeared originally in *The Friend,* a Philadelphia weekly, and were written in rather desperate circumstances — the author was suffering from tuberculosis (which would be responsible for his death in two years), and was trying nevertheless to support his family by writing. He may have been the first American to attempt to make a living by writing about nature.

The "Rambles" show the nature essay in what became its most familiar and popular form: a narrative of a walk, usually near to home, in which the author discerns the true depth of interest of ordinary places. A common theme of Godman's, though the present selection is an exception, was the "beneficence of the great Creator, not less displayed in trivial circumstances."

Rambles of a Naturalist: No. IX

THOSE WHO HAVE ONLY LIVED in forest countries, where vast tracts are shaded by a dense growth of oak, ash, chestnut, hickory, and other trees of deciduous foliage, which present the most pleasing varieties of verdure and freshness, can have but little idea of the effect produced on the feelings by aged forests of pine, composed in great degree of a single species, whose towering summits are crowded with one dark green canopy, which successive seasons find unchanged, and nothing but death causes to vary. Their robust and gigantic trunks rise a hundred or more feet high, in purely proportioned columns, before the limbs begin to diverge; and their tops, densely clothed with long bristling foliage, intermingle so closely as

From *Rambles of a Naturalist* (1828)

to allow of but slight entrance to the sun. Hence the undergrowth of such forests is comparatively slight and thin, since none but shrubs and plants that love the shade can flourish under this perpetual exclusion of the animating and invigorating rays of the great exciter of the vegetable world. Through such forests and by the merest footpaths in great part, it was my lot to pass many miles almost every day; and had I not endeavoured to derive some amusement and instruction from the study of the forest itself, my time would have been as fatiguing to me as it was certainly quiet and solemn. But wherever nature is, and under whatever form she may present herself, enough is always proffered to fix attention and produce pleasure, if we will condescend to observe with carefulness. I soon found that even a pine forest was far from being devoid of interest, and shall endeavour to prove this by stating the result of various observations made during the time I lived in this situation.

The common pitch, or as it is generally called Norway pine, grows from a seed which is matured in vast abundance in the large cones peculiar to the pines. This seed is of a rather triangular shape, thick and heavy at the part by which it grows from the cone, and terminating in a broad membranous fan or sail, which, when the seeds are shaken out by the wind, enables them to sail obliquely through the air to great distances. Should an old corn-field, or other piece of ground, be thrown out of cultivation for more than one season, it is sown with the pine seeds by the winds, and the young pines shoot up as closely and compactly as hemp. They continue to grow in this manner until they become twelve or fifteen feet high, until their roots begin to encroach on each other, or until the stoutest and best rooted begin to overtop, so as entirely to shade the smaller. These gradually begin to fail, and finally dry up and perish, and a similar process is continued until the best trees acquire room enough to grow without impediment. Even when the young pines have attained to thirty or forty feet in height, and are as thick as a man's thigh, they stand so closely together that their lower branches, which are all dry and dead, are intermingled sufficiently to prevent any one from passing between the trees without first breaking these obstructions away. I have seen such a wood as that just mentioned covering an old corn-field, whose ridges were still distinctly to be traced, and which an old resident informed me he had seen growing in corn. In a part of this wood, which was not far from my dwelling, I had a delightful retreat, that served me as a private study, or closet, though enjoying all the advantages of the open air. A road that had once passed through the field, and was of course more compacted than any other part, had denied access to the pine seeds for a certain distance, while on each side of it they grew with their usual density. The ground was covered with the soft layer or carpet of dried pine leaves, which gradually and imperceptibly fall throughout the year, making a most pleasant surface to tread on, and rendering the step perfectly noiseless. By beating off with a stick all the dried branches that projected towards the vacant space, I formed a sort of chamber, fifteen or twenty feet long, which above was canopied by the densely mingled branches of the adjacent trees, which altogether excluded or scattered the rays of the sun, and on all sides was so shut in by the trunks of the young trees as to prevent all observation. Hither, during the hot season, I was accustomed to retire, for the purpose of reading or meditation;

and within this deeper solitude, where all was solitary, very many of the subsequent movements of my life were suggested or devised.

From all I could observe, and all the inquiries I could get answered, it appeared that this rapidly growing tree does not attain its full growth until it is eighty or ninety years old, nor does its time of full health and vigour much exceed a hundred. Before this time it is liable to the attacks of insects, but these are of a kind that bore the tender spring shoots to deposit their eggs therein, and their larvæ appear to live principally on the sap, which is very abundant, so that the tree is but slightly injured. But after the pine has attained its acme, it is attacked by an insect which deposits its egg in the body of the tree, and the larva devours its way through the solid substance of the timber; so that, after a pine has been for one or two seasons subjected to these depredators, it will be fairly riddled, and if cut down is unfit for any other purpose than burning. Indeed, if delayed too long, it is poorly fit for firewood, so thoroughly do these insects destroy its substance. At the same time that one set of insects is engaged in destroying the body, myriads of others are at work under the bark, destroying the sap vessels, and the foliage wears a more and more pale and sickly appearance as the tree declines in vigour. If not cut down, it eventually dies, becomes leafless, stripped of its bark, and, as the decay advances, all the smaller branches are broken off, and it stands with its naked trunk and a few ragged limbs, as if bidding defiance to the tempest which howls around its head. Under favourable circumstances, a large trunk will stand in this condition for nearly a century, so extensive and powerful are its roots, so firm

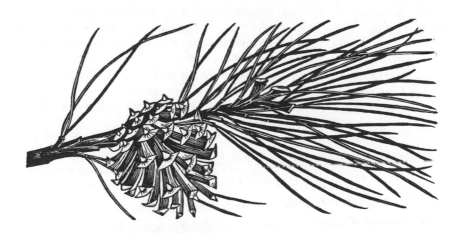

and stubborn the original knitting of its giant frame. At length some storm, more furious than all its predecessors, wrenches those ponderous roots from the soil, and hurls the helpless carcass to the earth, crushing all before it in its fall. Without the aid of fire, or some peculiarity of situation favourable to rapid decomposition, full another hundred years will be requisite to reduce it to its element, and obliterate the traces of its existence. Indeed, long after the lapse of more than that period, we find the heart of the pitch pine still preserving its original form, and from being thoroughly imbued with turpentine, become utterly indestructible except by fire.

If the proprietor attend to the warnings afforded by the woodpecker, he may always cut his pines in time to prevent them from being injured by insects. The woodpeckers run up and around the trunks, tapping from time to time with their powerful bills. The bird knows at once by the sound whether there be insects below or not. If the tree is sound the woodpecker soon forsakes it for another; should he begin to break into the bark, it is to catch the worm, and such trees are at once to be marked for the axe. In felling such pines, I found the woodmen always anxious to avoid letting them strike against neighbouring sound trees, as they said that the insects more readily attacked an injured tree than one whose bark was unbroken. The observation is most probably correct; at least the experience of country folks in such matters is rarely wrong, though they sometimes give very odd reasons for the processes they adopt.

A full grown pine forest is at all times a grand and majestic object to one accustomed to moving through it. Those vast and towering columns, sustaining a waving crown of deepest verdure; those robust and rugged limbs standing forth at a vast height overhead, loaded with the cones of various seasons; and the diminutiveness of all surrounding objects compared with these gigantic children of nature, cannot but inspire ideas of seriousness and even of melancholy. But how awful and even tremendous does such a situation become, when we hear the first wailings of the gathering storm, as it stoops upon the lofty summits of the pine, and soon increases to a deep hoarse roaring, as the boughs begin to wave in the blast, and the whole tree is forced to sway before its power!

In a short time the fury of the wind is at its height, the loftiest trees bend suddenly before it, and scarce regain their upright position ere they are again obliged to cower beneath its violence. Then the tempest literally howls, and amid the tremendous reverberations of thunder, and the blazing glare of the lightning, the unfortunate wanderer hears around him the crash of numerous trees hurled down by the storm, and knows not but the next may be precipitated upon him. More than once have I witnessed all the grandeur, dread, and desolation of such a scene, and have always found safety either by seeking as quickly as possible a spot where there were none but young trees, or if on the main road choosing the most open and exposed situation, out of the reach of the large trees. There, seated on my horse, who seemed to understand the propriety of such patience, I would quietly remain, however thoroughly drenched, until the fury of the wind was completely over. To say nothing of the danger from falling trees, the peril of being struck by the lightning, which so frequently shivers the loftiest of them, is so great as to render any attempt to advance, at such time, highly imprudent.

Like the ox among animals, the pine tree may be looked upon as one of the most universally useful of the sons of the forest. For all sorts of building, for firewood, tar, turpentine, rosin, lampblack, and a vast variety of other useful products, this tree is invaluable to man. Nor is it a pleasing contemplation, to one who knows its usefulness, to observe to how vast an amount it is annually destroyed in this country, beyond the proportion that nature can possibly supply. However, we are not disposed to believe that this evil will ever be productive of very great injury, especially as coal fuel is becoming annually more extensively used. Nevertheless, were I the owner of a pine forest, I should exercise a considerable degree of care in the selection of the wood for the axe.

JOHN JAMES AUDUBON
(1785–1851)

&❧ Audubon was first an artist, second an ornithologist, perhaps, and third a writer. With a dedication matching that of Alexander Wilson, he walked and rode through the young states, alert not only to birds but to the beauty and inexplicable magnetism of wilderness and to the personalities of the human characters he met in the back country. The *Ornithological Biography,* meant as the explanatory text for the magnificent paintings of *The Birds of America,* became also the vehicle for the artist's impressions of this country. Sixty personal essays were interspersed with the ornithological descriptions in the first three volumes of the five-volume set. In "The Great Pine Swamp" (pp. 136–142), Audubon describes his journey to one of the remaining hill-country wetlands in eastern Pennsylvania. The bird biographies, too, are often charged with the artist's instinct for drama, and deeply colored by his personal response to his subject. His description of the wood thrush showcases these qualities.

The Wood Thrush (*Turdus mustelinus*)

KIND READER, you now see before you my greatest favourite of the feathered tribes of our woods. To it I owe much. How often has it revived my drooping spirits, when I have listened to its wild notes in the forest, after passing a restless night in my slender shed, so feebly secured against the violence of the storm, as to shew me the futility of my best efforts to rekindle my little fire, whose uncertain and vacillating light had gradually died away under the destructive weight of the dense torrents of rain that seemed to involve the heavens and

From *Ornithological Biography* (1831)

the earth in one mass of fearful murkiness, save when the red streaks of the flashing thunderbolt burst on the dazzled eye, and, glancing along the huge trunk of the stateliest and noblest tree in my immediate neighbourhood, were instantly followed by an uproar of crackling, crashing, and deafening sounds, rolling their volumes in tumultuous eddies far and near, as if to silence the very breathings of the unformed thought! How often, after such a night, when far from my dear home, and deprived of the presence of those nearest to my heart, wearied, hungry, drenched, and so lonely and desolate as almost to question myself why I was thus situated, when I have seen the fruits of my labours on the eve of being destroyed, as the water, collected into a stream, rushed through my little camp, and forced me to stand erect, shivering in a cold fit like that of a severe ague, when I have been obliged to wait with the patience of a martyr for the return of day, trying in vain to destroy the tormenting moschettoes, silently counting over the years of my youth, doubting perhaps if ever again I should return to my home, and embrace my family! — how often, as the first glimpses of morning gleamed doubtfully amongst the dusky masses of the forest-trees, has there come upon my ear, thrilling along the sensitive cords which connect that organ with the heart, the delightful music of this harbinger of day! — and how fervently, on such occasions, have I blessed the Being who formed the Wood Thrush, and placed it in those solitary forests, as if to console me amidst my privations, to cheer my depressed mind, and to make me feel, as I did, that never ought man to despair, whatever may be his situation, as he can never be certain that aid and deliverance are not at hand.

The Wood Thrush seldom commits a mistake after such a storm as I have attempted to describe; for no sooner are its sweet notes heard than the heavens gradually clear, the bright refracted light rises in gladdening rays from beneath the distant horizon, the effulgent beams increase in their intensity, and the great orb of day at length bursts on the sight. The grey vapour that floats along the ground is quickly dissipated, the world smiles at the happy change, and the woods are soon heard to echo the joyous thanks of their many songsters. At that moment, all fears vanish, giving place to an inspiriting hope. The hunter prepares to leave his camp. He listens to the Wood Thrush, while he thinks of the course which he ought to pursue, and as the bird approaches to peep at him, and learn somewhat of his intentions, he raises his mind towards the Supreme Disposer of events. Seldom, indeed, have I heard the song of this Thrush, without feeling all that tranquillity of mind, to which the

secluded situation in which it delights is so favourable. The thickest and darkest woods always appear to please it best. The borders of murmuring streamlets, overshadowed by the dense foliage of the lofty trees growing on the gentle declivities, amidst which the sun-beams seldom penetrate, are its favourite resorts. There it is, kind reader, that the musical powers of this hermit of the woods must be heard, to be fully appreciated and enjoyed.

The song of the Wood Thrush, although composed of but few notes, is so powerful, distinct, clear, and mellow, that it is impossible for any person to hear it without being struck by the effect which it produces on the mind. I do not know to what instrumental sounds I can compare these notes, for I really know none so melodious and harmonical. They gradually rise in strength, and then fall in gentle cadences, becoming at length so low as to be scarcely audible; like the emotions of the lover, who at one moment exults in the hope of possessing the object of his affections, and the next pauses in suspense, doubtful of the result of all his efforts to please.

Several of these birds seem to challenge each other from different portions of the forest, particularly towards evening, and at that time nearly all the other songsters being about to retire to rest, the notes of the Wood Thrush are doubly pleasing. One would think that each individual is anxious to excel his distant rival, and I have frequently thought that on such occasions their music is more than ordinarily effective, as it then exhibits a degree of skilful modulation quite beyond my power to describe. These concerts are continued for some time after sunset, and take place in the month of June, when the females are sitting.

This species glides swiftly through the woods, whilst on wing, and performs its migrations without appearing in the open country. It is a constant resident in the State of Louisiana, to which the dispersed individuals resort, as to winter quarters, from the different parts of the United States, to which they had gone to breed. They reach Pennsylvania about the beginning or middle of April, and gradually proceed farther north.

Their food consists of different kinds of berries and small fruits, which they procure in the woods, without ever interfering with the farmer. They also occasionally feed on insects and various lichens.

The nest is usually placed in a low horizontal branch of the Dogwood Tree, occasionally on smaller shrubs. It is large, well saddled on the branch, and composed externally of dry leaves of various kinds, with a second bed of grasses and mud, and an internal layer of fine fibrous roots. The eggs are four or five, of a beautiful uniform light blue. The nest is generally found in deep swampy hollows, on the sides of hills.

On alighting on a branch, this Thrush gives its tail a few jets, uttering at each motion a low chuckling note peculiar to itself, and very different from those of the Hermit or Tawny Thrush. It then stands still for a while, with the feathers of the hind part a little raised. It walks and hops along the branches with much ease, and often bends down its head to peep at the objects around. It frequently alights on the ground, and scratches up the dried leaves in search of worms and beetles, but suddenly flies back to the trees, on the least alarm.

The sight of a fox or raccoon causes them much anxiety, and they generally follow these animals at a respectful distance, uttering a mournful *cluck*, well known to hunters. Although, during winter, these birds are numerous in Louisiana, they never form themselves into flocks, but go singly at this period, and only in pairs in the breeding season. They are easily reared from the nest, and sing nearly as well in confinement as while free. Their song is occasionally heard during the whole winter, particularly when the sun reappears after a shower. Their flesh is extremely delicate and juicy, and many of them are killed with the blow-gun.

Having given you a description of the Dogwood before, when I presented that tree in bloom, I have only to say here, that you now see it in its autumnal colouring, adorned with its berries, of which the Wood Thrush is fond.

The Great Pine Swamp

I LEFT PHILADELPHIA, at four in the morning, by the coach, with no other accoutrements than I knew to be absolutely necessary for the jaunt which I intended to make. These consisted of a wooden box, containing a small stock of linen, drawing paper, my journal, colours and pencils, together with 25 pounds of shot, some flints, the due quantum of cash, my gun *Tear-jacket,* and a heart as true to nature as ever.

Our coaches are none of the best, nor do they move with the velocity of those of some other countries. It was eight, and a dark night, when I reached Mauch Chunk, now so celebrated in the Union for its rich coal mines, and eighty-eight miles distant from Philadelphia. I had passed through a very diversified country, part of which was highly cultivated, while the rest was yet in a state of nature, and consequently much more agreeable to me. On alighting, I was shewn to the travellers' room, and on asking for the landlord, saw coming towards me a fine-looking young man, to whom I made known my wishes. He spoke kindly, and offered to lodge and board me at a much lower rate than travellers who go there for the very simple pleasure of being dragged on the railway. In a word, I was fixed in four minutes, and that most comfortably.

No sooner had the approach of day been announced by the cocks of the little village, than I marched out with my gun and note-book, to judge for myself of the wealth of the country. After traversing much ground, and crossing many steep hills, I returned, if not wea-

From *Ornithological Biography* (1831)

ried, at least much disappointed at the extraordinary scarcity of birds. So I bargained to be carried in a cart to the central parts of the Great Pine Swamp, and, although a heavy storm was rising, ordered my conductor to proceed. We winded round many a mountain, and at last crossed the highest. The weather had become tremendous, and we were thoroughly drenched, but my resolution being fixed, the boy was obliged to continue his driving. Having already travelled about fifteen miles or so, we left the turnpike, and struck up a narrow and bad road, that seemed merely cut out to enable the people of the Swamp to receive the necessary supplies from the village which I had left. Some mistakes were made, and it was almost dark, when a post directed us to the habitation of a Mr Jediah Irish, to whom I had been recommended. We now rattled down a steep declivity, edged on one side by almost perpendicular rocks, and on the other by a noisy stream, which seemed grumbling at the approach of strangers. The ground was so overgrown by laurels and tall pines of different kinds, that the whole presented only a mass of darkness.

At length we got to the house, the door of which was already opened, the sight of strangers being nothing uncommon in our woods, even in the most remote parts. On entering, I was presented with a chair, while my conductor was shewn the way to the stable, and on expressing a wish that I should be permitted to remain in the house for some weeks, I was gratified by receiving the sanction of the good woman to my proposal, although her husband was then from home. As I immediately fell a-talking about the nature of the country, and inquired if birds were numerous in the neighbourhood, Mrs Irish, more *au fait* to household affairs than ornithology, sent for a nephew of her husband's, who soon made his appearance, and in whose favour I became at once prepossessed. He conversed like an educated person, saw that I was comfortably disposed of, and finally bade me good-night in such a tone as made me quite happy.

The storm had rolled away before the first beams of the morning sun shone brightly on the wet foliage, displaying all its richness and beauty. My ears were greeted by the notes, always sweet and mellow, of the Wood Thrush and other songsters. Before I had gone many steps, the woods echoed to the report of my gun, and I picked from among the leaves a lovely Sylvia, long sought for, but until then sought for in vain. I needed no more, and standing still for awhile, I was soon convinced that the Great Pine Swamp harboured many other objects as valuable to me.

The young man joined me, bearing his rifle, and offered to accompany me through the woods, all of which he well knew. But I was anxious to transfer to paper the form and beauty of the little bird I had in my hand; and requesting him to break a twig of blooming laurel, we returned to the house, speaking of nothing else than the picturesque beauty of the country around.

A few days passed, during which I became acquainted with my hostess and her sweet children, and made occasional rambles, but spent the greater portion of my time in drawing. One morning, as I stood near the window of my room, I remarked a tall and powerful man alight from his horse, loose the girth of the saddle, raise the latter with one hand, pass the bridle over the head of the animal with the other, and move towards the house, while the horse betook himself to the little brook to drink. I heard some movements in the room below, and again the same tall person walked towards the mills and stores, a few hundred yards from the house. In America, business is the first object in view at all times, and right it is that it should be so. Soon after my hostess entered my room, accompanied by the fine-looking woodsman, to whom, as Mr Jediah Irish, I was introduced. Reader, to describe to you the qualities of that excellent man were vain; you should know him, as I do, to estimate the value of such men in our sequestered forests. He not only made me welcome, but promised all his assistance in forwarding my views.

The long walks and long talks we have had together I never can forget, or the many beautiful birds which we pursued, shot, and admired. The juicy venison, excellent bear flesh, and delightful trout that daily formed my food, methinks I can still enjoy. And then, what pleasure I had in listening to him as he read his favourite Poems of Burns, while my pencil was occupied in smoothing and softening the drawing of the bird before me! Was not this enough to recall to my mind the early impressions that had been made upon it by the description of the golden age, which I here found realized?

The Lehigh about this place forms numerous short turns between the mountains, and affords frequent falls, as well as below the falls deep pools, which render this stream a most valuable one for mills of any kind. Not many years before this date, my host was chosen by the agent of the Lehigh Coal Company, as their mill-wright, and manager for cutting down the fine trees which covered the mountains around. He was young, robust, active, industrious, and persevering. He marched to the spot where his abode now is, with some workmen, and by dint of hard labour first cleared the road mentioned above, and reached the river at the centre of a bend, where he fixed on erecting various mills. The pass here is so narrow that it looks as if formed by the bursting asunder of the mountain, both sides ascending abruptly, so that the place where the settlement was made is in many parts difficult of access, and the road then newly cut was only sufficient to permit men and horses to come to the spot where Jediah and his men were at work. So great, in fact, were the difficulties of access, that, as he told me, pointing to a spot about 150 feet above us, they for many months slipped from it their barrelled provisions, assisted by ropes, to their camp below. But no sooner was the first saw-mill erected, than the axemen began their devastations. Trees one after another were, and are yet, constantly heard falling, during the days; and in calm nights, the greedy mills told the sad tale, that in a century the noble forests around should exist no more. Many mills were erected, many dams raised, in defiance of the impetuous Lehigh. One full third of the trees have already been culled, turned into boards, and floated as far as Philadelphia.

In such an undertaking, the cutting of the trees is not all. They have afterwards to be hauled to the edge of the mountains bordering the river, launched into the stream, and led to the mills over many shallows and difficult places. Whilst I was in the Great Pine Swamp, I frequently visited one of the principal places for the launching of logs. To see them tumbling from such a height, touching here and there the rough angle of a projecting rock, bouncing from it with the elasticity of a foot-ball, and at last falling with awful crash into the river, forms a sight interesting in the highest degree, but impossible for me to describe. Shall I tell you that I have seen masses of these logs heaped above each other to the number of five thousand? I may so tell you, for such I have seen. My friend Irish assured me that at some seasons, these piles consisted of a much greater number, the river becoming in those places completely choked up.

When *freshets* (or floods) take place, then is the time chosen for forwarding the logs to the different mills. This is called a *Frolic*. Jediah Irish, who is generally the leader, proceeds to the upper leap with his men, each provided with a strong wooden handspike, and a short-handled axe. They all take to the water, be it summer or winter, like so many Newfoundland spaniels. The logs are gradually detached, and, after a time, are seen floating down the dancing stream, here striking against a rock and whirling many times round, there suddenly checked in dozens by a shallow, over which they have to be forced with the handspikes. Now they arrive at the edge of a dam, and are again pushed over. Certain numbers are left in each dam, and when the party has arrived at the last, which lies just where my friend Irish's camp was first formed, the drenched leader and his men, about sixty in number, make their way home, find there a healthful repast, and spend the evening and a portion of the night in dancing and frolicking, in their own simple manner, in the most perfect amity, seldom troubling themselves with the idea of the labour prepared for them on the morrow.

That morrow now come, one sounds a horn from the door of the storehouse, at the call of which each returns to his work. The sawyers, the millers, the rafters and raftsmen are all immediately busy. The mills are all going, and the logs, which a few months before were the supporters of broad and leafy tops, are now in the act of being split asunder. The boards are then launched into the stream, and rafts are formed of them for market.

During the summer and autumnal months, the Lehigh, a small river of itself, soon becomes extremely shallow, and to float the rafts would prove impossible, had not art managed to provide a supply of water for this express purpose. At the breast of the lower dam is a curiously constructed lock, which is opened at the approach of the rafts. They pass through this lock with the rapidity of lightning, propelled by the water that had been accumulated in the dam, and which is of itself generally sufficient to float them to Mauch Chunk, after which, entering regular canals, they find no other impediments, but are conveyed to their ultimate destination.

Before population had greatly advanced in this part of Pennsylvania, game of all descriptions found within that range was extremely

abundant. The Elk itself did not disdain to browse on the shoulders of the mountains, near the Lehigh. Bears and the Common Deer must have been plentiful, as, at the moment when I write, many of both kinds are seen and killed by the resident hunters. The Wild Turkey, the Pheasant and the Grouse, are also tolerably abundant; and as to trout in the streams — Ah, reader, if you are an angler, do go there, and try for yourself. For my part, I can only say, that I have been made weary with pulling up from the rivulets the sparkling fish, allured by the struggles of the common grasshopper.

A comical affair happened with the bears, which I shall relate to you, good reader. A party of my friend Irish's raftsmen, returning from Mauch Chunk, one afternoon, through sundry short cuts over the mountains, at the season when the huckle-berries are ripe and plentiful, were suddenly apprised of the proximity of some of these animals, by their snuffing the air. No sooner was this perceived than, to the astonishment of the party, not fewer than eight bears, I was told, made their appearance. Each man, being provided with his short-handled axe, faced about, and willingly came to the scratch; but the assailed soon proved the assailants, and with claw and tooth drove off the men in a twinkling. Down they all rushed from the mountain; the noise spread quickly; rifles were soon procured and shouldered; but when the spot was reached, no bears were to be found; night forced the hunters back to their homes, and a laugh concluded the affair.

I spent six weeks in the Great Pine Forest — Swamp it cannot be called — where I made many a drawing. Wishing to leave Pennsylvania, and to follow the migratory flocks of our birds to the south, I bade adieu to the excellent wife and rosy children of my friend, and to his kind nephew. Jediah Irish, shouldering his heavy rifle, accompanied me, and trudging directly across the mountains, we arrived at Mauch Chunk in good time for dinner. Shall I ever have the pleasure of seeing that good, that generous man again?

At Mauch Chunk, where we both spent the night, Mr White, the civil engineer, visited me, and looked at the drawings which I had made in the Great Pine Forest. The news he gave me of my sons, then in Kentucky, made me still more anxious to move in their direction, and, long before day-break, I shook hands with the goodman of the forest, and found myself moving towards the capital of Pennsylvania, having as my sole companion a sharp frosty breeze. Left to my thoughts, I felt amazed that such a place as the Great Pine Forest should be so little known to the Philadelphians, scarcely any of whom could direct me towards it. How much is it to be regretted, thought I, that the many young gentlemen who are there so much at a loss how to employ their leisure days, should not visit these wild retreats, valuable as they are to the student of nature. How differently would they feel, if, instead of spending weeks in smoothing a useless bow, and walking out in full dress, intent on displaying the make of their legs, to some rendezvous where they may enjoy their wines, they were to occupy themselves in contemplating the rich profusion which nature has poured around them, or even in procuring some desiderated specimen for their *Peale's Museum*, once so valuable and so finely arranged? But alas! no: they are none of them aware of the richness of the Great Pine Swamp, nor are they likely to share the hospitality to be found there.

Night came on, as I was thinking of such things, and I was turned out of the coach in the streets of the fair city, just as the clock struck ten. I cannot say that my bones were much rested, but not a moment was to be lost. So I desired a porter to take up my little luggage, and leading him towards the nearest wharf, I found myself soon after gliding across the Delaware, towards my former lodgings in the Jerseys. The lights were shining from the parallel streets as I crossed them, all was tranquil and serene, until there came the increasing sound of the Baltimore steamer, which, for some reason unknown to me, was that evening later than usual in its arrival. My luggage was landed, and carried home by means of a bribe. The people had all retired to rest, but my voice was instantly recognised, and an entrance was afforded to me.

Thomas Nuttall
(1786–1859)

&❦ Nuttall was one of the great field men in American natural history. Like many of his persuasion and passion, he went absolutely his own way and was regarded by "society" as something of an eccentric. He traveled over a good deal of the United States and what was then the Louisiana Territory and Mexico, botanizing and studying the habits of birds and animals. He also ranged happily from one branch of natural science to the next. When he turned his full attention to birds, so clear and concise were his descriptions that *A Manual of the Ornithology of the United States and Canada,* published in 1832, remained the leading American bird book for most of the rest of the nineteenth century. In its depiction of the interplay of physiology, behavior, and habitat, Nuttall's introduction anticipates later ecological insights.

Introduction

OF ALL THE CLASSES OF ANIMALS by which we are surrounded in the ample field of nature, there are none more remarkable in their appearance and habits than the feathered inhabitants of the air. They play around us like fairy spirits, elude approach in an element which defies our pursuit, soar out of sight in the yielding sky, journey over our heads in marshalled ranks, dart like meteors in the sunshine of summer, or seeking the solitary recesses of the forest and the waters, they glide before us like beings of fancy. They diversify the still landscape with the most lively motion and beautiful association; they come and go with the change of the season, and as their actions are

From *A Manual of the Ornithology of the United States and Canada* (1832)

directed by an uncontrollable instinct of provident nature, they may be considered as concomitant with the beauty of the surrounding scene. With what grateful sensations do we involuntarily hail the arrival of these faithful messengers of spring and summer, after the lapse of the dreary winter, which compelled them to forsake us for more favored climes. Their songs, now heard from the leafy groves and shadowy forests, inspire delight, or recollections of the pleasing past, in every breast. How volatile, how playfully capricious, how musical and happy, are these roving sylphs of nature, to whom the air, the earth, and the waters are almost alike habitable. Their lives are spent in boundless action; and nature, with an omniscient benevolence, has assisted and formed them for this wonderful display of perpetual life and vigor, in an element almost their own.

If we draw a comparison between these inhabitants of the air and the earth, we shall perceive that, instead of the large head, formidable jaws armed with teeth, the capacious chest, wide shoulders, and muscular legs of the quadrupeds; they have bills, or pointed jaws destitute of teeth; a long and pliant neck, gently swelling shoulders, immovable vertebræ; the fore-arm attenuated to a point, and clothed with feathers, forming the expansive wing, and thus fitted for a different species of motion; likewise the wide-extended tail, to assist the general provision for buoyancy throughout the whole anatomical frame. For the same general purpose of lightness, exists the contrast of slender bony legs and feet. So that, in short, we perceive in the whole conformation of this interesting tribe, a structure wisely and curiously adapted for their destined motion through the air. Lightness and buoyancy appear in every part of the structure of birds; to this end nothing contributes more than the soft and delicate plumage with which they are so warmly clothed; and though the wings, or great organs of aërial motion by which they swim, as it were, in the atmosphere, are formed of such light materials, yet the force with which they strike the air is so great as to impel their bodies with a rapidity unknown to the swiftest quadruped. The same grand intention of forming a class of animals to move in the ambient desert they occupy above the earth, is likewise visible in their internal structure. Their bones are light and thin, and all the muscles diminutive, but those appropriated for moving the wings. The lungs are placed near to the back-bone and ribs; and the air is not, as in other animals, merely confined to the pulmonary organs, but passes through, and is then conveyed into a number of membranous cells on either side the external region of the heart, communicating with others situated beneath the chest. In some birds these cells are continued down the wings, extending even to the pinions, bones of the thighs, and other parts of the body, which can be distended with air at the pleasure or necessity of the animal. This diffusion of air is not only intended to assist in lightening and elevating the body, but also appears necessary to prevent the stoppage or interruption of respiration, which would otherwise follow the rapidity of their motion through the resisting atmosphere; and thus the Ostrich, though deprived of the power of flight, runs almost with the swiftness of the wind, and requires, as he possesses, the usual resources of air conferred on other birds. Were it possible for man to move with the rapidity of a Swallow, the resistance of the air, without some such peculiar provision as in birds, would quickly bring on suffocation. The superior vital heat of this class of beings is likewise probably due to this greater aëration of the vital fluid.

Birds, as well as quadrupeds, may be generally distinguished into two great classes from the food on which they are destined to subsist; and may, consequently, be termed carnivorous and granivorous. Some also hold a middle nature, or partake of both. The granivorous and herbivorous birds are provided with larger and longer intestines than those of the carnivorous kinds. Their food, consisting chiefly of grain of various sorts, is conveyed whole into the craw or first stomach, where it is softened and acted upon by a peculiar glandular secretion thrown out upon its surface; it is then again conveyed into a second preparatory digestive organ; and finally transmitted into the true stomach or gizzard, formed of two strong muscles, connected externally with a tendinous substance, and lined internally with a thick membrane of great power and strength; and in this place the unmasticated food is at length completely triturated, and prepared for the operation of the gastric juice. The extraordinary powers of the gizzard in comminuting food, to prepare it for digestion, almost exceeds the bounds of credibility. Turkeys and common fowls have been made to swallow sharp angular fragments of glass, metallic tubes, and balls armed with needles, and even lancets, which were found broken and compressed without any apparent pain to the subjects, or wounds in the stomach. The gravel pebbles swallowed by this class of birds with so much avidity, thus appear useful in bruising and comminuting the grain they feed on, and preparing it for the solvent action of the digestive organs.

Those birds which live chiefly on grain and vegetable substances, partake in a degree of the nature and disposition of herbivorous quadrupeds. In both, the food and the provision for its digestion, are very similar. Alike distinguished for sedentary habits and gentleness of manners, their lives are harmlessly and usefully passed in collecting seeds and fruits, and ridding the earth of noxious and destructive insects; they live wholly on the defensive with all the feathered race, and are content to rear and defend their offspring from the attacks of their enemies. It is from this tractable and gentle race, as well as from the amphibious or aquatic tribes, that man has long succeeded in obtaining useful and domestic species, which, from their prolificacy and hardihood, afford a vast supply of wholesome and nutritious food. Of these, the Hen, originally from India; the Goose, Duck, and Pigeon of Europe; the Turkey of America; and the Pintado or Guinea-Hen of Africa, are the principal: to which may also be added, as less useful, or more recently naturalized, the Peacock of India; the Pheasant of the same country; the Chinese and Canada Goose; the Muscovy Duck; and the European Swan.

Carnivorous birds, by many striking traits, evince the destiny for which they have been created; they are provided with wings of great length, supported by powerful muscles, which enable them to fly with energy, and soar with ease at the loftiest elevations in which they are visible. They are armed with strong and hooked bills; and with the sharp and formidable claws of the tiger; they are also further distinguished by their large heads, short necks, strong muscular thighs in aid of their retractile talons, and a sight so piercing, as to enable them, while soaring at the greatest height, to perceive their prey, upon which they sometimes descend, like an arrow, with undeviating aim. In these birds the stomach is smaller than in the granivorous kinds, and their intestines are shorter. Like beasts of prey, they are of a fierce and unsociable nature; and so far from herding together like the inoffensive tribes, they drive even their offspring from the eyry, and seek habitually the shelter of desert rocks, neglected ruins, or the solitude of the darkest forest, from whence they utter loud, terrific, or piercing cries, in accordance with the gloomy rage and inquietude of their insatiable desires.

Besides these grand divisions of the winged nations, there are others, which, in their habits and manners, might be compared to the amphibious animals, as they live chiefly on the water, and feed on its productions. To enable them to swim and dive in quest of their aquatic food, their toes are connected by broad membranes or webs, with which, like oars, they strike the water, and are impelled with force. In this way even the seas, lakes, and rivers, abounding with fish, insects, and seeds, swarm with birds of various kinds, which all obtain an abundant supply. There are other aquatic birds, frequenting marshes and the margins of lakes, rivers, and the sea, which seem to partake of an intermediate nature between the land and water tribes. Some of these feed on fishes and reptiles; others, with long and sensible bills and extended necks, seek their food in wet and muddy marshes. These birds are not made for swimming; but, familiar with water, they wade, and many follow the edge of the retiring waves of the sea, gleaning their insect prey at the recession of the tides: for this kind of life nature has provided them with long legs, bare of feathers even above the knees; their toes, unconnected by webs, are only partially furnished with membranous appendages, just sufficient to support them on the soft and boggy grounds they frequent. To this tribe belong the Cranes, Snipes, Sandpipers, Woodcocks, and many others.

In comparing the senses of animals in connexion with their instinct, we find that of *sight* to be more extended, more acute, and more distinct in birds, in general, than in quadrupeds. I say, in general, for there are some birds, such as the Owls, whose vision is less clear than that of quadrupeds; but this rather results from the extreme sensibility of the eye; which, though dazzled with the glare of full day, nicely distinguishes even small objects, by the aid of twilight. In all birds the organ of sight is furnished with two membranes, an external and internal, additional to those which occur in the human subject. The former (*membrana nictitans*) or external membrane, is situated in the larger angle of the eye; and is, in fact, a second and more transparent eye-lid, whose motions are directed at pleasure, and its use, besides occasionally cleaning and polishing the cornea, is to temper the excess of light, and adjust the quantity admitted to the extreme delicacy of the organ. The other membrane, situated at the bottom of the eye, appears to be an expansion of the optic nerve, which receiving more immediately the impressions of the light, must be much more sensible than in other animals; and consequently the sight is in birds far more perfect, and embraces a wider range. Facts and observations bear out this conclusion, for a Sparrow-Hawk, while hovering in the air, perceives a lark or other small bird sitting on the ground, at twenty times the distance that such an object would be visible to a man or dog. A Kite, which soars beyond the reach of human vision, yet distinguishes a lizard, field-mouse, or bird, and from this lofty station selects the tiny object of his prey, descending upon it in nearly a perpendicular line. But it may also be added, that this prodigious extent of vision is likewise accompanied with equal accuracy and clearness; for the eye can dilate or contract, be shaded or exposed, depressed or made protuberant, so as readily to assume the precise form suited to the degree of light and the distance of the object; the organ thus answering, as it were, the purpose of a self-adjusting telescope, with a shade for examining the most luminous and dazzling objects; and hence the Eagle is often seen to ascend to the higher regions of the atmosphere, gazing on the unclouded sun, as on an ordinary and familiar object.

The rapid motions executed by birds, have also a reference to the perfection of their vision; for, if nature, while she endowed them with great agility and vast muscular strength, had left them as short-sighted as ourselves, their latent powers would have availed them nothing; and the dangers of a perpetually impeded progress would have repressed or extinguished their ardor. We may then, in general, consider the celerity with which an animal moves, as a just indication of the perfection of its vision. A bird, therefore, shooting swiftly through the air, must undoubtedly see better than one which slowly describes a waving tract. The weak-sighted Bat, flying carefully through bars of willow, even when the eyes were extinguished, may seem to suggest an exception to this rule of relative velocity and vision; but in this case, as in that of some blind individuals of the human species, the exquisite auditory apparatus seems capable of supplying the defect of sight. Nor are the flickerings of the Bat, constantly performed in a narrow circuit, at all to be compared to the distant and lofty soarings of the Eagle, or the wide wanderings of the smaller birds, who often annually pass and repass from the arctic circle to the equator.

The idea of motion, and all the other ideas connected with it, such as those of relative velocities, extent of country, the proportional height of eminences, and of the various inequalities that prevail on the surface, are therefore more precise in birds, and occupy a large share of their conceptions, than in the grovelling quadrupeds. Nature would seem to have pointed out this superiority of vision, by the more conspicuous and elaborate structure of its organ; for in birds the eye is larger in proportion to the bulk of the head than in quadrupeds; it is also more delicate and finely fashioned, and the impressions it receives must consequently excite more vivid ideas.

Another cause of difference in the instincts of birds and quad-rupeds, is the nature of the element in which they live. Birds know better than man, the degrees of resistance in the air, its temperature at different heights, its relative density, and many other particulars, probably, of which we can form no adequate conception. They fore-see more than we, and indicate better than our weather-glasses, the changes which happen in that voluble fluid; for often have they contended with the violence of the wind, and still oftener have they borrowed the advantage of its aid. The Eagle, soaring above the clouds, can at will escape the scene of the storm, and in the lofty region of calm, far within the aërial boundary of eternal frost,[1] enjoy a serene sky and a bright sun, while the terrestrial animals remain involved in darkness, and opposed to all the fury of the tempest. In twenty-four hours it can change its climate, and sailing over different countries, it will form a picture exceeding the powers of the pencil or the imagination. The quadruped knows only the spot where it feeds, its valley, mountain, or plain; it has no conception of the expanse of surface, or of remote distances, and generally no desire to push forward its excursions beyond its immediate wants. Hence remote journeys and extensive migrations are as rare among quadrupeds, as they are frequent among birds. It is this desire, founded on their acquaintance with foreign countries, on the consciousness of their expeditious course, and on their foresight of the changes that will happen in the atmosphere, and the revolutions of seasons, that prompts them to retire together at the powerful suggestions of an unerring instinct. When their food begins to fail, or the cold and heat to incommode them, their innate feelings and latent powers urge them to seek the necessary remedy for the evils that threaten their being. The inquietude of the old is communicated to the young; and collecting in troops, by common consent, influenced by the same general wants, impressed with the approaching changes in the circumstances of their existence, they give way to the strong reveries of instinct, and wing their way over land and sea to some distant and better country.

Comparing animals with each other, we soon perceive that *smell,* in general, is much more acute among the quadrupeds than among the birds. Even the pretended scent of the Vulture is imaginary, as he does not perceive the tainted carrion, on which he feeds, through a wicker basket, though its odor is as potent as in the open air. This choice also of decaying flesh, is probably regulated by his necessities, and the deficiency of his muscular powers to attack a living, or even tear in pieces a recent prey. The structure of the olfactory organ, in birds, is obviously inferior to that of quadrupeds; the external nostrils are wanting, and those odors which might excite sensation have access only to the duct leading from the palate: and even in those, where the organ is disclosed, the nerves, which take their origin from it, are far from being so numerous, so large, or so expanded as in the quadrupeds. We may, therefore, regard *touch* in man, *smell* in the

[1] The mean heights of eternal frost, under the equator, and at the latitude of 30° and 60°, are respectively 15,207; 11,484, and 3,818 feet.

quadruped, and *sight* in birds, as respectively the three most perfect senses, which exercise a general influence on the character.

After sight, the most perfect of the senses in birds appears to be *hearing,* which is even superior to that of the quadrupeds, and scarcely exceeded in the human species. We perceive with what facility they retain and repeat tones, successions of notes, and even discourse; we delight to listen to their unwearied songs, to the incessant warbling of their tuneful affection. Their ear and throat are more ductile and powerful than in other animals, and their voice more capacious and generally agreeable. A Crow, which is scarcely more than the thousandth part the size of an ox, may be heard as far, or farther; the Nightingale can fill a wider space with its music than the human voice. This prodigious extent and power of sound depend entirely on the structure of their organs; but the support and continuance of their song result solely from their internal emotions.

The windpipe is wider and stronger in birds than in any other class of animals, and usually terminates below in a large cavity that augments the sound. The lungs too have greater extent, and communicate with internal cavities, which are capable of being expanded with air, and, besides lightening the body, give additional force to the voice. Indeed the formation of the thorax, the lungs, and all the organs connected with these, seem expressly calculated to give force and duration to their utterance.

Another circumstance, showing the great power of voice in birds, is the distance at which they are audible in the higher regions of the atmosphere. An Eagle may rise at least to the height of 17,000 feet, for it is there just visible. Flocks of Storks and Geese may mount still higher, since, notwithstanding the space they occupy, they soar almost out of sight; their cry will therefore be heard from an altitude of more than three miles, and is at least four times as powerful as the voice of men and quadrupeds.

Sweetness of voice and melody of song are qualities, which in birds are partly natural and partly acquired. The facility with which they catch and repeat sounds, enables them not only to borrow from each other, but often even to copy the more difficult inflections and tones of the human voice, as well as of musical instruments. It is remarkable, that, in the tropical regions, while the birds are arrayed in the most glowing colors, their voices are hoarse, grating, singular, or terrific. Our sylvan Orpheus, the Mocking-bird, the Brown Thrush, the Warbling Flycatcher; as well as the Linnet, the Thrush, the Blackbird, and the Nightingale of Europe, preëminent for song, are all of the plainest colors and weakest tints.

The natural tones of birds, setting aside those derived from education, express the various modifications of their wants and passions; they change even according to the different times and circumstances. The females are much more silent than the males; they have cries of pain or fear, murmurs of inquietude or solicitude, especially for their young; but song is generally withheld from them. The song of the male is inspired by tender emotion, he chants his affectionate lay with a sonorous voice, and the female replies in feeble accents. The Nightingale, when he first arrives in the spring, without his mate, is silent; he begins his lay in low, faltering, and unfrequent airs; and it is not until his consort sits on her eggs, that his enchanting melody is complete; he then tries to relieve and amuse her tedious hours of incubation, and warbles more pathetically and variably his amorous and soothing tale. In a state of nature this propensity for song only continues through the breeding season, for after that period it either entirely ceases, becomes enfeebled, or loses its sweetness.

Conjugal fidelity and parental affection are among the most conspicuous traits of the feathered tribes. The pair unite their labors in preparing for the accommodation of their expected progeny; and during the time of incubation, their participation of the same cares and solicitudes continually augments their mutual attachment. When the young appear, a new source of care and pleasure opens to them, still strengthening the ties of affection; and the tender charge of rearing and defending their infant brood requires the joint attention of both parents. The warmth of first affection is thus succeeded by calm and steady attachment, which by degrees extends, without suffering any diminution, to the rising branches of the family.

This conjugal union, in the rapacious tribe of birds, the Eagles and Hawks, as well as with the Ravens and Crows, continues commonly through life. Among many other kinds it is also of long endurance, as we may perceive in our common Pewee and the Blue-bird, who year after year continue to frequent and build in the same cave, box, or hole in the decayed orchard tree. But, in general, this association of the sexes expires with the season, after it has completed the intentions of reproduction, in the preservation and rearing of the offspring. The appearance even of sexual distinction, often vanishes in the autumn, when both the parents and their young are then seen in the same humble and oblivious dress. When they arrive again amongst us in the spring, the males in flocks, often by themselves, are clad anew in their nuptial livery; and with vigorous songs, after the cheerless silence in which they have passed the winter, they now seek out their mates, and warmly contest the right to their exclusive favor.

With regard to food, birds have a more ample latitude than quadrupeds; flesh, fish, amphibia, reptiles, insects, fruits, grain, seeds, roots, herbs; in a word, whatever lives or vegetates. Nor are they very select in their choice, but often catch indifferently at what they can most easily obtain. Their sense of taste appears indeed much less acute than in quadrupeds; for, if we except such as are carnivorous, their tongue and palate are, in general, hard, and almost cartilaginous. Sight and scent can alone direct them, though they possess the latter in an inferior degree. The greater number swallow without tasting; and mastication, which constitutes the chief pleasure in eating, is entirely wanting to them. As their horny jaws are unprovided with teeth, the food undergoes no preparation in the mouth, but is swallowed in unbruised and untasted morsels. Yet there is reason to believe, that the first action of the stomach, or its preparatory *ventriculus,* affords in some degree the ruminating gratification of taste, as after swallowing food, in some insectivorous and carnivorous birds, the motion of the mandibles, exactly like that of ordinary tasting, can hardly be conceived to exist without conveying some degree of gratifying sensation.

The clothing of birds varies with the habits and climates they inhabit. The aquatic tribes, and those which live in northern regions, are provided with an abundance of plumage and fine down; from which circumstance often we may form a correct judgment of their natal regions. In all climates, aquatic birds are almost equally feathered, and are provided with posterior glands containing an oily substance for anointing their feathers, which, aided by their thickness, prevents the admission of moisture to their bodies. These glands are less conspicuous in land-birds, unless, like the fishing Eagles, their habits be to plunge in the water in pursuit of their prey.

The general structure of feathers seems purposely adapted both for warmth of clothing and security of flight. In the wings of all birds which fly, the webs composing the vanes, or plumy sides of the feather, mutually interlock by means of regular rows of slender hair-like teeth, so that the feather, except at and towards its base, serves as a complete and close screen from the weather on the one hand, and as an impermeable oar on the other, when situated in the wing, and required to catch and retain the impulse of the air. In the birds which do not fly, and inhabit warm climates, the feathers are few and thin, and their lateral webs are usually separate, as in the Ostrich, Cassowary, Emu, and extinct Dodo. In some cases feathers seem to pass into the hairs, which ordinarily clothe the quadrupeds, as in the Cassowary, and others; and the base of the bill in many birds is usually surrounded with these capillary plumes.

The greater number of birds cast their feathers annually, and appear to suffer much more from it than the quadrupeds do from a similar change. The best fed fowl ceases at this time to lay. The season of moulting is generally the end of summer or autumn, and their feathers are not completely restored till the spring. The male sometimes undergoes, as we have already remarked, an additional moult towards the close of summer; and among many of the waders and web-footed tribes, as Sandpipers, Plovers, and Gulls, both sexes experience a moult twice in the year, so that their summer and winter livery appears wholly different.

The strategems and contrivances instinctively employed by birds for their support and protection, are peculiarly remarkable; in this way those which are weak are enabled to elude the pursuit of the strong and rapacious. Some are even screened from the attacks of their enemies by an arrangement of colors assimilated to the places which they most frequent for subsistence and repose: thus the Wryneck is scarcely to be distinguished from the tree on which it seeks its food; or the Snipe from the soft and springy ground which it frequents. The Great Plover finds its chief security in stony places, to which its colors are so nicely adapted, that the most exact observer may be deceived. The same resort is taken advantage of by the Night-Hawk, Partridge, Plover, and the American Quail, the young brood of which squat on the ground, instinctively conscious of being nearly invisible, from their close resemblance to the broken ground on which they lie, and trust to this natural concealment. The same kind of deceptive and protecting artifice is often employed by birds to conceal, or render the external appearance of their nests ambiguous. Thus the European Wren forms its nest externally of hay, if against a hay-rick; covered with lichens, if the tree chosen is so clad; or made of green moss, when the decayed trunk in which it is built, is thus covered; and then, wholly closing it above, leaves only a concealed entry in the side. Our Humming-bird, by external patches of lichen, gives her nest the appearance of a moss-grown knot. A similar artifice is employed by our Yellow Breasted Flycatcher or Vireo, and others. The Golden-Crowned Thrush (*Sylvia aurocapilla*) makes a nest like an oven, erecting an arch over it, so perfectly resembling the tussuck in which it is concealed, that it is only discoverable by the emotion of the female when startled from its covert.

The Butcher-bird is said to draw around him his feathered victims by treacherously imitating their notes. The Kingfisher of Europe is believed to allure his prey by displaying the brilliancy of his colors, as he sits near some sequestered place on the margin of a rivulet; the fish, attracted by the splendor of his fluttering and expanded wings, are detained, while the wily fisher takes an unerring aim.[2] The Erne, and our Bald Eagle, gain a great part of their subsistence by watching the success of the Fish-Hawk, and robbing him of his finny prey as soon as it is caught. In the same way also the rapacious Burgomaster or Glaucus Gull (*Larus glaucus*) of the North, levies his tribute of food from all the smaller species of his race, who knowing his strength and ferocity, are seldom inclined to dispute his piratical claims. Several species of Cuckoo, and the Cow-Troopial of America, habitually deposit their eggs in the nests of other small birds, to whose deceived affection are committed the preservation and rearing of the parasitic and vagrant brood. The instinctive arts of birds are numerous; but treachery, like that which obtains in these parasitic species, is among the rarest expedients of nature in the feathered tribes; though not uncommon among some insect families.

The art displayed by birds in the construction of their temporary habitations, or nests, is also deserving of passing attention. Among the Gallinaceous tribe, including our land domestic species, as well as the aquatic and wading kinds, scarcely any attempt at a nest is made. The birds which swarm along the sea-coast, often deposit their eggs on the bare ground, sand, or slight depressions in shelving rocks; governed alone by grosser wants, their mutual attachment is feeble or nugatory, and neither art nor instinct prompts attention to the construction of a nest, the less necessary, indeed, as the young take to the water as soon as hatched, and early release themselves from parental dependence. The habits of the other aquatic birds are not dissimilar to these; yet it is singular to remark, that while our common geese and ducks, like domestic fowls, have no permanent selective attachment for their mates, the Canadian Wild-goose, the Eider-duck, and some others, are constantly and faithfully paired through the season; so that this neglect of comfortable accommodation for the young in the fabrication of an artificial nest, common to these with the rest of their tribe, has less connexion with the requisition of mutual aid, than with the hardy and precocious habits of these un-musical, coarse, and retiring birds. It is true, that some of them show considerable address, if little of art, in providing security for their brood; in this way some of the Razor-bills (including the Common Puffin) do not trust the exposure of their eggs, like the Gulls, who

---

[2] The bright feathers of this bird enter often successfully, with others, into the composition of the most attractive artificial flies employed by anglers.

rather rely on the solitude of their retreat, than art in its defence; but with considerable labor some of the Alcas form a deep burrow for the security of their eggs and young.

Birds of the same genus differ much in their modes of nidification. Thus the Martin makes a nest within a rough-cast rampart of mud, and enters by a flat opening in the upper edge. The Cliff Swallow of Bonaparte, seen about Portland in Maine and Nova Scotia, as well as in the remote regions of the West, conceals its warm and feathered nest in a receptacle of agglutinated mud, resembling a narrow-necked purse or retort. Another species, in the Indian seas, forms a small receptacle for its young entirely of interlaced gelatinous fibres, provided by the mouth and stomach; these fabrics, stuck in clusters against the rocks, are collected by the Chinese, and boiled and eaten in soups as the rarest delicacy. The Bank-Martin, like the King-Fisher, burrows deep into the friable banks of rivers to secure a depository for its scantily feathered nest. The Chimney-Swallow, originally an inhabitant of hollow trees, builds in empty chimneys a mere nest of agglutinated twigs. The Woodpecker, Nuthatch, Titmouse, and our rural Blue-Bird, secure their young in hollow trees; and the first often gouge and dig through the solid wood with the success and industry of instinctive carpenters, and without the aid of any other chisel than their wedged bills.

But the most consummate ingenuity of ornithal architecture is displayed by the smaller and more social tribes of birds, who, in proportion to their natural enemies, foreseen by nature, are provided with the means of instinctive defence. In this labor both sexes generally unite, and are sometimes occupied a week or more in completing this temporary habitation for their young. We can only glance at a few examples, chiefly domestic; since to give any thing like a general view of this subject of the architecture employed by birds would far exceed the narrow limits we prescribe. And here we may remark, that, after migration, there is no more certain display of the reveries of instinct than what presides over this interesting and necessary labor of the species. And yet so nice are the observable gradations betwixt this innate propensity and the dawnings of reason, that it is not always easy to decide upon the characteristics of one as distinct from the other. Pure and undeviating instincts are perhaps wholly confined to the invertebral class of animals.

In respect to the habits of birds, we well know, that, like the quadrupeds, they possess, though in an inferior degree, the capacity for a certain measure of what may be termed education, or the power of adding to their stock of invariable habits, the additional circumstantial traits of an inferior degree of reason. Thus in those birds who have discovered, like the faithful dog, that humble companion of man, the advantages to be derived from associating round his premises, the regularity of their instinctive habits gives way, in a measure, to improvable conceptions. In this manner our Golden Robin (*Icterus baltimora*) or Fiery Hang-Bird, originally only a native of the wilderness and the forest, is now a constant summer resident in the vicinity of villages and dwellings. From the depending boughs of our towering Elms, like the Oriole of Europe, and the Cassican of tropical America, he weaves his pendulous and purse-like nest of the most tenacious and durable materials he can collect. These naturally consist of the Indian hemp, flax of the silk-weed (*Asclepias* species), and other tough and fibrous substances; but with a ready ingenuity he discovers that real flax and hemp, as well as thread, cotton, yarn, and even hanks of silk, or small strings, and horse and cow hair, are excellent substitutes for his original domestic materials; and in order to be convenient to these accidental resources, a matter of some importance in so tedious a labor, he has left the wild woods of his ancestry, and conscious of the security of his lofty and nearly inaccessible mansion, has taken up his welcome abode in the precincts of our habitations. The same motives of convenience and comfort have had their apparent influence on many more of our almost domestic feathered tribes; the Blue-birds, Wrens, and Swallows, original inhabitants of the woods, are now no less familiar than our Pigeons. The Cat-bird often leaves his native solitary thickets for the convenience and refuge of the garden, and watching, occasionally, the motions of the tenant, answers to his whistle with complaisant mimicry, or in petulant anger scolds at his intrusion. The Common Robin, who never varies his simple and coarse architecture; tormented by the parasitic Cuckoo, or the noisy Jay, who seek at times to rob him of his progeny; for protection, has been known fearlessly to build his nest within a few yards of the blacksmith's anvil, or on the stern timbers of an unfinished vessel, where the carpenters were still employed in their noisy labors. That sagacity obtains its influence over unvarying instinct in these and many other familiar birds, may readily be conceived, when we observe, that this venturous association with man vanishes with the occasion which required it; for no sooner have the Oriole and Robin reared their young, than their natural suspicion and shyness again return.

Deserts and solitudes are avoided by many kinds of birds. In an extensive country of unvarying surface, or possessing but little variety of natural productions, and particularly where streams and waters are scarce, few of the feathered tribes are to be found. The extensive prairies of the west, and the gloomy and almost interminable forests of the north, as well as the umbrageous, wild, and unpeopled banks of the Mississippi, and other of the larger rivers, no less than the vast pine barrens of the southern states, are nearly without birds, as permanent residents. In crossing the desolate piny glades of the south, with the exception of Creepers, Woodpeckers, Pine Warblers, and flocks of flitting Larks (*Sturnella*), scarcely any birds are to be seen till we approach the meanders of some stream, or the precincts of a plantation. The food of birds being extremely various, they consequently congregate only where sustenance is to be obtained; watery situations and a diversified vegetation is necessary for their support, and convenient for their residence; the fruits of the garden and orchard, the swarms of insects which follow the progress of agriculture, the grain which we cultivate, in short, every thing which contributes to our luxuries and wants, in the way of subsistence, no less than the recondite and tiny enemies, which lessen or attack these various resources, all conduce to the support of the feathered race, which consequently seek out and frequent our settlements, as humble and useful dependents.

The most ingenious and labored nest of all the North American birds, is that of the Orchard Oriole or Troopial. It is suspended or pensile, like that of the Baltimore, but, with the exception of hair, constantly constructed of native materials, the principal of which is a kind of tough grass. The blades are formed into a sort of platted purse, but little inferior to a coarse straw bonnet; the artificial labor bestowed is so apparent, that Wilson humorously adds, that on his showing it to a matron of his acquaintance, betwixt joke and earnest, she asked, "if he thought it could not be taught to darn stockings." Every one has heard of the tailor bird of India (*Sylvia sutoria*); this little architect, by way of saving labor, and gaining security for its tiny fabric, actually, as a seamstress, sows together the edges of two leaves of a tree, in which her nest, at the extremity of the branch, is then secured for the period of incubation. Among the *Sylvias* or Warblers, in which are included the Nightingale, and familiar Robin Redbreast, there is a species inhabiting Florida and the West Indies, the *Sylvia pensilis,* which forms its woven, covered nest to rock in the air at the end of two suspending strings, rather than trust it to the wily enemies by which it is surrounded; the entrance, for security, is also from below, and through a winding vestibule.

Our little cheerful, and almost domestic Wren (*Troglodytes fulvus*), which so often disputes with the Martin and the Blue-Bird the possession of the box, set up for their accommodation in the garden or near the house, in his native resort of a hollow tree, or the shed of some neglected out-house, begins his fabric by forming a barricade of crooked interlacing twigs, a kind of *chevaux-de-frise,* for the defence of his internal habitation, leaving merely a very small entrance at the upper edge; and so pertinacious is the instinct of this little petulant and courageous warbler, that, without perceiving the inutility of his industry, in the artificial mansion prepared for him, he still laboriously encumbers the interior of the box with the same mass of rude sticks. The industry of this little bird, and his affection for his mate, are somewhat remarkable, as he frequently completes his habitation without aid, and then searches out a female on whom to bestow it; but not being always successful, or the premises not satisfactory to his mistress, his labor remains without reward, and he continues to warble out his lay in solitude. The same gallant habit prevails also with our recluse Wren of the marshes. Wilson's Marsh Wren (*Troglodytes palustris*), instead of courting the advantages of a proximity to our dwellings, lives wholly among the reed fens, suspending his mud-plastered and circularly covered nest usually to the stalks of the plant he so much affects. Another marsh species inhabits the low and swampy meadows of our vicinity, (*Troglodytes brevirostris*), and, with ready address, constructs its globular nest wholly of the intertwined sedge-grass of the tussuck on which it is built; these two species never leave their subaquatic retreats but for the purpose of distant migration, and avoid and deprecate in angry twitterings every sort of society but their own.

Among the most extraordinary habitations of birds, illustrative of their instinctive invention, may be mentioned that of the *Bengal Grosbeak,* whose pensile nest, suspended from the lofty boughs of the Indian fig-tree, is fabricated of grass, like cloth, in the form of a large bottle, with the entrance downwards; it consists also of two or three chambers, supposed to be occasionally illuminated by the fire-flies, which, however, only constitute a part of the food it probably conveys for the support of its young. But the most extraordinary instinct of this kind known, is exhibited by the Sociable or Republican Grosbeak (*Ploceus socius,* Cuvier) of the Cape of Good Hope. In one tree, according to Mr. Paterson, there could not be fewer than from 800 to 1000 of these nests, covered by one general roof, resembling that of a thatched house, and projecting over the entrance of the nest. Their common industry almost resembles that of bees. Beneath this roof there are many entrances, each of which forms, as it were, a regular street, with nests on either side, about two inches distant from each other. The material which they employ in this building, is a kind of fine grass, whose seed, also, at the same time, serves them for food.

That birds, besides their predilection for the resorts of men, are also capable of appreciating consequences to themselves and young, scarcely admits the shadow of a doubt: they are capable of communicating their fears, and nicely calculating the probability of danger, or the immunities of favor. We talk of the cunning of the Fox, and the watchfulness of the Weasel; but the Eagle, Hawk, Raven, Crow, Pye, and Blackbird, possess those traits of shrewdness and caution, which would seem to arise from reflection and prudence. They well know the powerful weapons and wiles of civilized man. Without being able to *smell powder,* a vulgar idea, the Crow and Blackbird at once suspect the character of the fatal gun; they will alight on the backs of cattle without any show of apprehension, and the Pye even hops upon them with insulting and garrulous playfulness; but he flies instantly from his human enemy, and seems, by his deprecating airs, aware of the proscription that affects his existence. A man on horseback, or in a carriage, is much less an object of suspicion to those wily birds, than when alone; and I have been frequently both amused and surprised, in the Southern states, by the sagacity of the Common

Blackbirds,[3] in starting from the ploughing field with looks of alarm, at the sight of a white man, as distinct from and more dangerous than the black slave, whose furrow they closely and familiarly followed, for the insect-food it afforded them, without betraying any appearance of distrust. Need we any further proof of the capacity for change of disposition, than that which has so long operated upon our domestic poultry, "those victims," as Buffon slightingly remarks, "which are multiplied without trouble, and sacrificed without regret." How different the habits of our Goose and Duck in their wild and tame condition. Instead of that excessive and timid cautiousness, so peculiar to their savage nature, they keep company with the domestic cattle, and hardly shuffle out of our path; nay, the Gander is a very ban-dog; noisy, gabbling, and vociferous, he gives notice of the stranger's approach, is often the terror of the meddling school-boy, in defence of his fostered brood; and it is reported of antiquity, that by their usual garrulity and watchfulness, they once saved the Roman capitol. Not only is the disposition of these birds changed by domestication, but even their strong instinct to migration, or wandering longings, are wholly annihilated. Instead of joining the airy phalanx which wing their way to distant regions, they grovel contented in the perpetual abundance attendant on their willing slavery. If instinct can thus be destroyed or merged in artificial circumstances, need we wonder that this protecting and innate intelligence is capable also of another change by improvement, adapted to new habits and unnatural restraints. Even without undergoing the slavery of domestication, many birds become fully sensible of immunities and protection; and in the same aquatic and rude family of birds, already mentioned, we may quote the tame habits of the Eider Ducks. In Iceland, and other countries, where they breed in such numbers, as to render their valuable down an object of commerce, they are forbidden to be killed under legal penalty, and, as if aware of this legislative security, they sit on their eggs undisturbed at the approach of man, and are entirely as familiar, during this season of breeding, as our tamed Ducks; nor are they apparently aware of the cheat habitually practised upon them of abstracting the down with which they line their nests, though it is usually repeated until they make the third attempt at incubation. If, however, the last nest, with its eggs and down, to the lining of which the male is now obliged to contribute, be taken away, they sagaciously leave the premises without return. The pious Storks, in Holland, protected by law for their usefulness, build their nests on

[3] *Quiscalus versicolor.*

the tops of houses and churches, often in the midst of cities, in boxes prepared for them, like those for our Martins; and, walking about the streets and gardens, without apprehension of danger, perform the useful office of domestic scavengers.

That birds, like our more sedentary and domestic quadrupeds, are capable of exhibiting attachment to those who feed and attend them, is undeniable. Deprived of other society, some of our more intelligent species, particularly the Thrushes, soon learn to seek out the company of their friends or protectors of the human species. The Brown Thrush and Mocking-bird become, in this way, extremely familiar, cheerful, and capriciously playful; the former, in particular, courts the attention of his master, follows his steps, complains when neglected, flies to him when suffered to be at large, and sings and reposes gratefully perched on his hand; in short, by all his actions he appears capable of real and affectionate attachment; and is jealous of every rival, particularly any other bird, which he persecutes from his presence with unceasing hatred. His petulant dislike to particular objects of less moment is also displayed by various tones and gestures, which soon become sufficiently intelligible to those who are near him, as well as his notes of gratulation and satisfaction. His language of fear and surprise could never be mistaken, and an imitation of his guttural low *tsherr tsherr,* on these occasions, answers as a premonitory warning when any danger awaits him, from the sly approach of cat or squirrel. As I have now descended, as I may say, to the actual biography of one of these birds, which I raised and kept uncaged for some time, I may also add, that besides a playful turn for mischief and interruption, in which he would sometimes snatch off the paper on which I was writing, he had a good degree of curiosity, and was much surprised one day by a large springing beetle or *Elater* (*E. ocellatus*), which I had caught and placed in a tumbler. On all such occasions, his looks of capricious surprise were very amusing; he cautiously approached the glass with fanning and closing wings, and in an under tone confessed his surprise at the address and jumping motions of the huge insect. At length he became bolder, and perceiving it had a relation to his ordinary prey of beetles, he, with some hesitation, ventured to snatch at the prisoner between temerity and playfulness. But when really alarmed or offended, he instantly flew to his loftiest perch, forbid all friendly approaches, and for some time kept up his low and angry *tsherr.* My late friend, the venerable William Bartram, was also much amused by the intelligence displayed by this bird, and relates, that, one which he kept, being fond of hard bread crumbs, found, when they grated his throat, a very rational remedy in softening them, by soaking in this vessel of water; he likewise, by experience, discovered that the painful prick of the wasps on which he fed, could be obviated by extracting their stings. But it would be too tedious and minute to follow out these glimmerings of intelligence, which exist as well in birds as in our most sagacious quadrupeds. The remarkable talent of the Parrot for imitating the tones of the human voice has long been familiar. The most extraordinary and well authenticated account of the actions of one of the common Ash-colored species, is that of a bird which Colonel O'Kelly bought for a hundred guineas at Bristol. This individual not only repeated a great number of sentences, but *answered* many questions, and was able to whistle a variety of tunes. While thus engaged, it beat time with all the appearance of science; and possessed a judgment, or ear so accurate, that, if by chance it mistook a note, it would revert to the bar where the mistake was made, correct itself, and still beating regular time, go again through the whole with perfect exactness. So celebrated was this surprising bird, that an obituary notice of its death appeared in the General Evening Post for the 9th of October, 1802. In this account it is added, that, besides her great musical faculties, she could express her wants articulately, and give her orders in a manner approaching to rationality. She was, at the time of her decease, supposed to be more than thirty years of age. The Colonel was repeatedly offered five hundred guineas a year for the bird, by persons who wished to make a public exhibition of her; but out of tenderness to his favorite, he constantly refused the offer.

The story related by Goldsmith of a Parrot belonging to King Henry the Seventh, is very amusing, and possibly true. It was kept in a room in the palace of Westminster, overlooking the Thames, and had naturally enough learnt a store of boatmen's phrases; one day sporting somewhat incautiously, Poll fell into the river, but had rationality enough, it appears, to make a profitable use of the words she had learnt, and accordingly vociferated, "*A boat! twenty pounds for a boat!*" This welcome sound reaching the ears of a waterman, soon brought assistance to the parrot, who delivered it to the king, with a request to be paid the round sum so readily promised by the bird; but his majesty, dissatisfied with the exorbitant demand, agreed, at any rate, to give him what the bird should now award; in answer to which reference, Poll shrewdly cried, "*Give the knave a groat!*"

The story given by Locke, in his "Essay on the Human Understanding," though approaching closely to rationality, and apparently improbable, may not be a greater effort than could have been accomplished by Colonel O'Kelly's bird. This Parrot had attracted the attention of Prince Maurice, then governor of Brazil, who had a curiosity to witness its powers. The bird was introduced into the room, where sat the prince in company with several Dutchmen. On viewing them, the Parrot exclaimed, in Portuguese, "What a company of white men are here!" Pointing to the prince, they asked, "Who is that man?" to which the Parrot replies, "Some general or other." The prince now asked, "From what place do you come?" The answer was, "From Marignan." "To whom do you belong?" it answered, "To a Portuguese." "What do you do there?" to which the Parrot replied, "I look after chickens!" The prince, now laughing, exclaimed, "*You* look after chickens!" To which Poll pertinently answered, "Yes, *I; —* and I know well enough how to do it"; clucking at the same instant in the manner of a calling brood-hen.

The docility of birds in catching and expressing sounds depends, of course, upon the perfection of their voice and hearing; assisted also by no inconsiderable power of memory. The imitative actions and passiveness of some small birds, such as Goldfinches, Linnets, and Canaries, are, however, quite as curious as their expression of sounds. A Sieur Roman exhibited in England some of these birds, one of which simulated death, and was held up by the tail or claw without showing any active signs of life. A second balanced itself on the head, with its claws in the air. A third imitated a milkmaid going to market, with pails on its shoulders. A fourth mimicked a Venetian girl looking out at a window. A fifth acted the soldier, and mounted guard as a sentinel. The sixth was a cannonier, with a cap on its head, a firelock on its shoulder, and with a match in its claw discharged a small cannon. The same bird also acted as if wounded, was wheeled in a little barrow, as it were, to the hospital; after which it flew away before the company. The seventh turned a kind of windmill; and the last bird stood amidst a discharge of small fireworks, without showing any sign of fear.

A similar exhibition, in which twenty-four Canary birds were the actors, was also shown in London in 1820, by a Frenchman named Dujon; one of these suffered itself to be shot at, and, falling down, as if dead, was put into a little wheelbarrow, and conveyed away by one of its comrades.

The docility of the Canary and Goldfinch is thus, by dint of severe education, put in fair competition with that of the Dog; and we cannot deny to the feathered creation a share of that kind of rational intelligence, exhibited by some of our sagacious quadrupeds, an incipient knowledge of cause and effect far removed from the unimprovable and unchangeable destinies of instinct. Nature, probably, delights less in producing such animated machines than we are apt to suppose; and amidst the mutability of circumstances by which almost every animated being is surrounded, there seems to be a frequent demand for that relieving invention, denied to those animals which are solely governed by inflexible instinct.

The velocity with which birds are able to travel in their aërial element, has no parallel among terrestrial animals; and this powerful capacity for progressive motion, is bestowed in aid of their peculiar wants and instinctive habits. The swiftest horse may perhaps proceed a mile in something less than two minutes, but such exertion is unnatural, and quickly fatal. An Eagle, whose stretch of wing exceeds seven feet, with ease and majesty, and without any extraordinary effort, rises out of sight in less than three minutes, and therefore must fly more than 3,500 yards in a minute, or at the rate of sixty miles in an hour. At this speed a bird would easily perform a journey of 600 miles in a day, since ten hours only would be required, which would allow frequent halts, and the whole of the night for repose. Swallows, and other migratory birds, might therefore pass from Northern Europe to the equator in seven or eight days. In fact, Adanson saw, on the coast of Senegal, swallows that had arrived there on the 9th of October, or eight or nine days after their departure from the colder continent. A Canary Falcon, sent to the Duke of Lerma, returned in sixteen hours from Andalusia to the island of Teneriffe, a distance of 750 miles. The Gulls of Barbadoes, according to Sir Hans Sloane, make excursions in flocks to the distance of more than 200 miles after their food, and then return the same day to their rocky roosts.

If we allow that any natural powers come in aid of the instinct to migration, so powerful and uniform in birds, besides their vast capacity for motion, it must be in the perfection and delicacy of their vision, of which we have such striking examples in the rapacious tribes. It is possible, that at times, they may be directed principally by atmospheric phenomena alone; and hence we find that their appearance is frequently a concomitant of the approaching season, and the wild Petrel of the ocean is not the only harbinger of storm and coming change. The currents of the air, in those which make extensive voyages, are sedulously employed; and hence, at certain seasons, when they are usually in motion, we find their arrival or departure accelerated by a favorable direction of the winds. That birds also should be able to derive advantage in their journeys from the acuteness of their vision, is not more wonderful, than the capacity of a dog to discover the path of his master, for many miles in succession, by the mere scent of his steps. It is said, indeed, in corroboration of this conjecture, that the Passenger or Carrying Pigeon, is not certain to return to the place from whence it is brought, unless it be conveyed in an open wicker basket, admitting a view of the passing scenery. Many of our birds, however, follow instinctively the great valleys and river courses, which tend towards their southern or warmer destination; thus the great valleys of the Connecticut, the Hudson, the Delaware, the Susquehannah, the Santee, and more particularly the vast Mississippi, are often, in part, the leading routes of our migrating birds. But, in fact, mysterious as is the voyage and departure of our birds, like those of all other countries where they remove at all, the destination of many is rendered certain, as soon as we visit the southern parts of the Union, or the adjoining countries of Mexico, to which they have retired for the winter; for now, where they were nearly or wholly unknown in summer, they throng by thousands, and flit before our path like the showering leaves of autumn. It is curious to observe the pertinacity of this adventurous instinct in those, more truly and exclusively insectivorous species, which wholly leave us for the mild and genial regions of the tropics. Many penetrate to their destination through Mexico over land; to these the whole journey is merely an amusing and varied feast; but to a much smaller number, who keep too far toward the sea-coast, and enter the ocean-bound peninsula of Florida, a more arduous aërial voyage is presented; the wide ocean must be crossed, by the young and inexperienced, as well as the old and venturous, before they arrive either at the tropical continent, or its scattered islands. When the wind proves propitious, however, our little voyagers wing their unerring way like prosperous fairies; but, baffled by storms and contrary gales, they often suffer from want, and at times, like the Quails, become victims to the devouring waves. On such unfortunate occasions (as Mr. Bullock[4] witnessed in a voyage near to Vera Cruz late in autumn), the famished travellers familiarly crowd the decks of the vessel, in the hope of obtaining rest and a scanty meal, preparatory to the conclusion of their unpropitious flight.

Superficial observers, substituting their own ideas for facts, are ready to conclude, and frequently assert, that the old and young, before leaving, assemble together for mutual departure; this may be true, in many instances, but in as many more a different arrangement obtains. The young, often instinctively vagrant, herd together in separate flocks previous to their departure, and guided alone by the

---

[4] William Bullock, *Six Months' Residence and Travels in Mexico* (London: J. Murray, 1824).

innate monition of nature, seek neither the aid nor the company of the old; consequently in some countries flocks of young of particular species are alone observed, and in others, far distant, we recognise the old. From parental aid, the juvenile company have obtained all that nature intended to bestow, existence and education; and they are now thrown upon the world among their numerous companions, with no other necessary guide than self-preserving instinct. In Europe it appears that these bands of the young always affect even a warmer climate than the old; the aëration of their blood not being yet complete, they are more sensible to the rigors of cold. The season of the year has also its effect on the movements of birds; thus certain species proceed to their northern destination more to the eastward in the spring; and return from it to the southwestward in autumn.

The habitudes and extent of the migrations of birds admit of considerable variety. Some only fly before the inundating storms of winter, and return with the first dawn of spring; these do not leave the continent, and only migrate in quest of food, when it actually begins to fail. Among these may be named our common Song Sparrow, Chipping Sparrow, Blue-bird, Robin, Pewee, Cedar-bird, Blackbird, Meadow Lark, and many more. Others pass into warmer climates in the autumn, after rearing their young. Some are so given to wandering, that their choice of a country is only regulated by the resources which it offers for subsistence; such are the Pigeons, Herons of several kinds, Snipes, Wild Geese and Ducks, the wandering Albatros, and Waxen Chatterer.

The greater number of birds travel in the night; some species, however, proceed only by day, as the diurnal birds of prey, Crows, Pies, Wrens, Creepers, Cross-bills, Larks, Blue-birds, Swallows, and some others. Those which travel wholly in the night are the Owls, Butcher-birds, Kingfishers, Thrushes, Flycatchers, Night-Hawks, Whip-poor-wills, and also a great number of aquatic birds, whose motions are often principally nocturnal, except in the cold and desolate northern regions, where they usually retire to breed. Other birds are so powerfully impelled by this governing motive to migration, that they stop neither day nor night; such are the Herons, Motacillas, Plovers, Swans, Cranes, Wild Geese, Storks, &c. When untoward circumstances render haste necessary, certain kinds of birds, which ordinarily travel only in the night, continue their route during the day, and scarcely allow themselves time to eat: yet the singing birds, properly so called, never migrate by day, whatever may happen to them. And it may here be inquired, with astonishment, how these feeble but enthusiastic animals are able to pass the time, thus engaged, without the aid of recruiting sleep? But so powerful is this necessity for travel, that its incentive breaks out equally in those which are detained in captivity; so much so, that although, during the day, they are no more alert than usual, and only occupied in taking nourishment, at the approach of night, far from seeking repose, as usual, they manifest great agitation, sing without ceasing in the cage, whether the apartment is lighted or not; and when the moon shines, they appear still more restless, as it is their custom, at liberty, to seek the advantage of its light, for facilitating their route. Some birds, while engaged in their journey, still find means to live without halting; the Swallow, while traversing the sea, pursues its insect prey; those who can subsist on fish, without any serious effort, feed as they pass or graze the surface of the deep. If the Wren, the Creeper, and the Titmouse rest for an instant on a tree to snatch a hasty morsel, in the next they are on the wing, to fulfil their destination. However abundant may be the nourishment which presents itself to supply their wants, in general, birds of passage rarely remain more than two days together in a place.

The cries of many birds, while engaged in their aërial voyage, are such as are only heard on this important occasion, and appear necessary for the direction of those which fly in assembled ranks.

During these migrations, it has been observed, that birds fly ordinarily in the higher regions of the air, except when fogs force them to seek a lower elevation. This habit is particularly prevalent with Wild Geese, Storks, Cranes, and Herons, which often pass at such a height as to be scarcely distinguishable.

We shall not here enter into any detailed description of the manner in which each species conducts its migration; but shall content ourselves with citing the single remarkable example of the motions of the Cranes. Of all migrating birds, these appear to be endowed with the greatest share of foresight. They never undertake the journey alone: throughout a circle of several miles, they appear to communicate the intention of commencing their route. Several days previous to their departure, they call upon each other by a peculiar cry, as if giving warning to assemble at a central point; the favorable moment being at length arrived, they betake themselves to flight, and, in military style, fall into two lines, which, uniting at the summit, form an extended angle with two equal sides. At the central point of the phalanx, the chief takes his station, to whom the whole troop, by their subordination, appear to have pledged their obedience. The commander has not only the painful task of breaking the path through the air, but he has also the charge of watching for the common safety; to avoid the attacks of birds of prey; to range the two lines in a circle, at the approach of a tempest, in order to resist with more effect the squalls which menace the dispersion of the linear ranks; and, lastly, it is to their leader that the fatigued company look up to appoint the most convenient places for nourishment and repose. Still, important as is the station and function of the aërial director, its existence is but momentary. As soon as he feels sensible of fatigue, he cedes his place to the next in the file, and retires himself to its extremity. During the night, their flight is attended with considerable noise; the loud cries which we hear, seem to be the marching orders of the chief, answered by the ranks who follow his commands. Wild Geese, and several kinds of Ducks, also make their aërial voyage nearly in the same manner as the Cranes. The loud call of the passing Geese, as they soar securely through the higher regions of the air, is familiar to all; but as an additional proof of their sagacity and caution, we may remark, that when fogs in the atmosphere render their flight necessarily low, they steal along in silence, as if aware of the danger to which their lower path now exposes them.

To assist the efforts of birds, and sustain them through their long journeys, it is often necessary to borrow the aid of the winds; but that this element may assist, it is proper that it meet them; or be in the reverse of its aid to the navigator. This observation is so far verified, that to succeed in the chase of birds upon the water, it is necessary to approach them by cutting the wind upon them; consequently, by the disposition of their wings, they are obliged to come towards the boat, which is also at the same time pushed towards them. Our common Passenger Pigeons and Wild Geese, decided migrators, may be observed, when moving in the largest bodies, flying in a path contrary to the wind. The direction of the winds is then of great importance to the migration of birds, not only as an assistance when favorable, but to be avoided when contrary, as the most disastrous of accidents, when they are traversing the ocean. If the breeze suddenly change, the aërial voyagers tack to meet it, and diverging from their original course, seek the asylum of some land or island, as is the case very frequently with the Quails, who consequently, in their passage across the Mediterranean, at variable times, make a descent in immense numbers on the islands of the Archipelago, where they wait, sometimes for weeks, the arrival of a propitious gale to terminate their journey. And hence we perceive the object of migrating birds, when they alight upon a vessel at sea; it has fallen in their course while seeking refuge from a baffling breeze, or overwhelming storm, and after a few hours of rest, they wing their way to their previous destination. That nature has provided ample means to fulfil the wonderful instinct of these feeble but cautious wanderers, appears in every part of their economy. As the period approaches for their general departure, and the chills of autumn begin to be felt, their bodies begin to be loaded with cellular matter, and at no season of the year are the true birds of passage so fat as at the approach of their migration. The Gulls, Cranes, and Herons, almost proverbially macilent, are at this season loaded with this reservoir of nutriment, which is intended to administer to their support through their arduous and hazardous voyage. With this natural provision, dormant animals also commence their long and dreary sleep through the winter; a nutritious resource, no less necessary in birds while engaged in fulfilling the powerful and waking reveries of instinct.

But if the act of migration surprise us when performed by birds of active power of wing, it is still more remarkable when undertaken by those of short and laborious flight, like the Coots and Rails, who, in fact, perform a part of their route on foot. The Great Penguin (*Alca impennis*), the Guillemot, and the Divers, even make their voyage chiefly by dint of swimming. The young Loons (*Colymbus glacialis*), bred in inland ponds, though proverbially lame (and hence the name of Lom or Loon), without recourse to their wings, which are at this time inefficient, continue their route from pond to pond, floundering over the intervening land by night, until at length they gain some creek of the sea, and finally complete their necessary migration by water.

Birds of passage, both in the old and new continents, are observed generally to migrate south-west in autumn, and to pass to the north-east in spring. Parry [Sir William Edward Parry (1790–1855), Arctic explorer], however, it seems, observed the birds of Greenland proceed to the south-east. This apparent aberration from the usual course, may be accounted for by considering the habits of these aquatic birds. Intent on food and shelter, a part, bending their course over the cold regions of Norway and Russia, seek the shores of Europe; while another division, equally considerable, proceeding south-west, spread themselves over the interior of the United States and the coast and kingdom of Mexico.

This propensity to change their climate, induced by whatever cause, is not confined to the birds of temperate regions; it likewise exists among many of those who inhabit the tropics. Aquatic birds, of several kinds, according to Humboldt [Alexander von Humboldt (1769–1859), German explorer and scientist], cross the line on either side about the time of the periodical rise of the rivers. Waterton

[Charles Waterton (1782–1865), British naturalist], likewise, who spent much time in Demerara [Guyana] and the neighbouring countries, observed, that the visits of many of the tropical birds were periodical. Thus the wonderful Campanero,[5] whose solemn voice is heard, at intervals, tolling like the convent bell, was rare to Waterton, but frequent in Brazil, where they most probably retire to breed. The failure of particular food at any season, in the mildest climate, would be a sufficient incentive to a partial and overland migration with any species of the feathered race.

The longevity of birds is various, and, different from the case of man and quadrupeds, seems to bear but little proportion to the age at which they acquire maturity of character. A few months seems sufficient to bring the bird into full possession of all its native powers; and there are some, as our Marsh Titmouse or Chicadee, which, in fact, as soon as fledged, are no longer to be distinguished from their parents. Land animals generally live six or seven times as long as the period required to attain maturity; but in birds the rate is ten times greater. In proportion to their size, they are also far more vivacious and long-lived, than other animals of the superior class. Our knowledge of the longevity of birds is, however, necessarily limited to the few examples of domesticated species, which we have been able to support through life; the result of these examples is, that our domestic fowls have lived twenty years; Pigeons have exceeded that period; Parrots have attained more than thirty years. Geese live probably more than half a century; a Pelican has lived to eighty years; and Swans, Ravens, and Eagles have exceeded a century: even Linnets, in the unnatural restraints of the cage, have survived for fourteen or fifteen years, and Canaries twenty-five. To account for this remarkable tenacity of life, nothing very satisfactory has been offered; though Buffon is of opinion, that the soft and porous nature of their bones contributes to this end, as the general ossification and rigidity of the system perpetually tends to abridge the boundaries of life.

In a general way it may be considered as essential for the bird to fly, as it is for the fish to swim, or the quadruped to walk; yet in all these tribes there are exceptions to the general habits. Thus among quadrupeds, the Bats fly; the Seals, and other animals of that description, swim; and the Beaver and Otter, with an intermediate locomotive power, swim better than they can walk. So also among birds, the Ostrich, Cassowary, Dodo, and some others, incapable of

---

[5] *Casmarhynchos carunculata.*

flying, are obliged to walk; others, as the Penguins, Dippers, and Razor-bills, fly and swim, but never walk. Some, in fine, like the Birds of Paradise, Swallows, and Humming-birds, can neither walk nor swim, but pass their time chiefly on the wing. A far greater number of birds live on the water than of quadrupeds, for of the latter there are not more than five or six kinds furnished with webbed or oar-like feet; whereas of birds with this structure there are above three hundred. The lightness of their feathers and bones, as well as the boat-like form of their bodies, contributes greatly to facilitate their buoyancy and progress in the water, and their feet serve as oars to propel them.

Thus in whatever way we view the feathered tribes which surround us, we shall find much both to amuse and instruct. We hearken to their songs with renewed delight, as the harbingers and associates of the season they accompany. Their return, after a long absence, is hailed with gratitude to the Author of all existence; and the cheerless solitude of inanimate nature is, by their presence, attuned to life and harmony. Nor do they alone administer to the amusement and luxury of life; faithful aids as well as messengers of the seasons, they associate round our tenements, and defend the various productions of the earth, on which we so much rely for subsistence, from the destructive depredations of myriads of insects, which, but for timely riddance by unnumbered birds, would be followed by a general failure and famine. Public economy and utility, then, no less than humanity, plead for the protection of the feathered race; and the wanton destruction of birds, so useful, beautiful, and amusing, if not treated as such by law, ought to be considered as a crime by every moral, feeling, and reflecting mind.

HENRY DAVID THOREAU
(1817–1862)

❧ In the late winter of 1854, Thoreau finished the final, seventh draft of *Walden*. On March 28, as will be seen in the following selection, he received the first proofs from the printer and began correcting them, becoming conscious, as he noted on March 31, that improvements might still be made. He did finally let them go forth, though, and the book was published on August 9. The journal entries seen here are typical of the later period of Thoreau's life in the preponderance of natural history and weather observations; he appears to have been preparing for a "Book of Concord,"[1] which would give a complete and particular account of the natural year in his home territory.

"Walking," widely regarded as one of the great American essays, was based on a lecture entitled "The Wild," which the author first gave in April, 1851. He repeated the lecture several times, indicating the topic's centrality to him. The *wild* was a concept infinitely rich and unifying to Thoreau's thought, reaching out from the woods and fields and ponds he knew so well to suggest the living quality of the world itself.

Journal: March, 1854
(ÆT. 36)

March 1. Here is our first spring morning according to the almanac. It is remarkable that the spring of the almanac and of nature should correspond so closely. The morning of the 26th was good winter, but

From *The Writings of Henry David Thoreau* (1906).

[1] See William Howarth, *The Book of Concord: Thoreau's Life as a Writer* (New York: Viking, 1982).

there came a plentiful rain in the afternoon, and yesterday and to-day are quite springlike. This morning the air is still, and, though clear enough, a yellowish light is widely diffused throughout the east, now just after sunrise. The sunlight looks and feels warm, and a *fine vapor* fills the lower atmosphere. I hear the phœbe or spring note of the chickadee, and the scream of the jay is perfectly repeated by the echo from a neighboring wood. For some days past the surface of the earth, covered with water, or with ice where the snow is washed off, has shone in the sun as it does only at the approach of spring, methinks. And are not the frosts in the morning more like the early frosts in the fall, — common white frosts?

As for the birds of the past winter: I have seen but three hawks, — one early in the winter and two lately; have heard the hooting owl pretty often late in the afternoon. Crows have not been numerous, but their cawing was heard chiefly in pleasanter mornings. Blue jays have blown the trumpet of winter as usual, but they, as all birds, are most lively in springlike days. The chickadees have been the *prevailing* bird. The partridge common enough. One ditcher tells me that he saw two robins in Moore's Swamp a month ago. I have not seen a quail, though a few have been killed in the thaws. Four or five downy woodpeckers. The white-breasted nuthatch four or five times. Tree sparrows one or more at a time, oftener than any bird that comes to us from the north. Two pigeon woodpeckers, I think, lately. One dead shrike, and perhaps one or two live ones. Have heard of two white owls, — one about Thanksgiving time and one in midwinter. One short-eared owl in December. Several flocks of snow buntings for a week in the severest storm, and in December, last part. One grebe in Walden just before it froze completely. And two brown creepers once in middle of February. Channing says he saw a little olivaceous-green bird lately. I have not seen an *F. linaria,* nor a pine grosbeak, nor an *F. hyemalis* this winter, though the first was the prevailing bird last winter.

In correcting my manuscripts, which I do with sufficient phlegm, I find that I invariably turn out much that is good along with the bad, which it is then impossible for me to distinguish — so much for keeping bad company; but after the lapse of time, having purified the main body and thus created a distinct standard of comparison, I can review the rejected sentences and easily detect those which deserve to be readmitted.

P. M. — To Walden *via* R. W. E.'s.

I am surprised to see how bare Minott's hillside is already. It is already spring there, and Minott is puttering outside in the sun. How wise in his grandfather to select such a site for a house, the summers he has lived have been so much longer! How pleasant the calm season and the warmth — the sun is even like a burning-glass on my back — and the sight and sound of melting snow running down the hill! I look in among the withered grass blades for some starting greenness. I listen to hear the first bluebird in the soft air. I hear the dry clucking of hens which have come abroad.

The ice at Walden is softened, — the skating is gone; with a stick you can loosen it to the depth of an inch, or the first freezing, and turn it up in cakes. Yesterday you could skate here; now only close to the south shore. I notice the redness of the andromeda leaves, but not so much as once. The sand foliage is now in its prime.

March 2. A Corner man tells me that Witherell has seen a bluebird, and Martial Miles thought that he heard one. I doubt it. It may have been given to Witherell to see the first bluebird, so much has been withholden from him.

What produces the peculiar softness of the air yesterday and to-day, as if it were the air of the south suddenly pillowed amid our wintry hills? We have suddenly a different sky, — a different atmos-phere. It is as if the subtlest possible soft vapor were diffused through the atmosphere. Warm air has come to us from the south, but charged with moisture, which will yet distill in rain or congeal into snow and hail.

The sand foliage is vital in its form, reminding me [of] what are called the vitals of the animal body. I am not sure that its arteries are ever hollow. They are rather meandering channels with re-markably distinct sharp edges, formed instantaneously as by magic. How rapidly and perfectly it organizes itself! The material must be sufficiently cohesive. I suspect that a certain portion of clay is nec-essary. Mixed sand and clay being saturated with melted ice and snow, the most liquid portion flows downward through the mass, forming for itself instantly a perfect canal, using the best materials the mass affords for its banks. It digs and builds it in a twinkling. The less fluid portions clog the artery, change its course, and form thick stems and leaves. The lobe principle, — lobe of the ear (*labor, lapsus?*).

On the outside all the life of the earth is expressed in the animal or vegetable, but make a deep cut in it and you find it vital; you find in the very sands an anticipation of the vegetable leaf. No wonder, then, that plants grow and spring in it. The atoms have already learned the law. Let a vegetable sap convey it upwards and you have a vegetable leaf. No wonder that the earth expresses itself outwardly in leaves, which labors with the idea thus inwardly. The overhanging leaf sees here its prototype. The earth is pregnant with law.

The various shades of this sand foliage are very agreeable to the eye, including all the different colors which iron assumes, — brown, gray, yellowish, reddish, and clay-color. Perhaps it produces the greater effect by arranging the sands of the same color side by side, bringing them together.

March 4. A dull, cloudy day.

P. M. — To Walden *via* Hubbard's Wood and foot of Cliff Hill.

The snow has melted very rapidly the past week. There is much bare ground. The checkerberries are revealed, — *somewhat* shrivelled many of them. I look along the ditches and brooks for tortoises and frogs, but the ditches are still full of dirty ice, and they are not yet seen in the brooks. In Hubbard's maple swamp I see the evergreen leaves of the gold-thread as well as the mitchella and large pyrola. I begin to sniff the air and smell the ground. In the meadow beyond I see some still fresh and perfect pitcher-plant leaves, and everywhere the green and reddish radical leaves of the golden senecio, whose fragrance when bruised carries me back or forward to an incredible season. Who would believe that under the snow and ice lie still — or in midwinter — some green leaves which, bruised, yield the same odor that they do when their yellow blossoms spot the meadows in June? Nothing so realizes the summer to me now. This past winter the sphagnum (?) in swamps and meadows has been frost-bitten and blackened, but last winter it was fresh and handsome. I see nowadays, the ground being laid bare, great cracks in the earth revealed, a third of an inch wide, running with a crinkling line for twenty rods or more through the pastures and under the walls, — frost-cracks of the past winter. Sometimes they are revealed through ice four or five inches thick over them. I observed to-day where a crack had divided a piece of bark lying over it with the same irregular and finely meandering line, *sometimes* forking. Yesterday I saw a wasp slowly stretching himself and, I think, a fly, outside of Minott's house in the sun, by his wood-shed. In the dry pasture under the Cliff Hill, the radical leaves of the johnswort are now revealed everywhere in pretty radiating wreaths flat on the ground, with leaves recurved, reddish above, green beneath, and covered with dewy drops. I can no longer get on to the river ice. I do not find any willow catkins started. A red maple which I cut bleeds somewhat, — only the upper side the cut however. Is not this the earliest distinct motion of the spring? This stood in water. Other trees were dry. Found a geiropodium (?), its globe now transparent, with the vermilion-colored remnants of others

(?) lying in jelly about. In dry pastures I see that fungus — is it? — split into ten or twelve rays like a star and curved backward around

a white bag or inner membrane. Were they not the seeds of rose-hips which I saw abundantly in some creature's dung? The various cladonias are now very plump and erect, not only exposed to view, the ground being bare, but flourishing on account of the abundant moisture, — some light, some dark green, and various more dusky shades. In one or two places on the snow under the Cliffs I noticed more than a half-pint of partridge-droppings within a diameter of six inches. Were these all dropped in one night by one bird, or in the course of several nights, or by many birds? I saw that they had eaten the buds of the small blueberry *vacillans*. In their manure was what looked like woody fibres; may have been fibres of leaves. I am surprised to see how fresh and tender is the wintergreen bud, almost pure white. Was it so two months ago? It looks as if it had started under the snow. What is that gray beetle of which I found many under the bark of a large dead white pine, five eighths of an inch long, within an elliptical sort of log fort seven eighths of an inch or more in diameter piled around, of fibres of the sap-wood, perhaps one eighth or one tenth of an inch high, with some red bark chankings? Sometimes a curious chrysalis instead, like a very narrow and long bandbox with flat and parallel top and bottom, but highest at one end like a coffin. Also some white grubs stretch themselves, and some earwig-shaped creatures under the bark. I find that the ice of Walden has melted or softened so much that I sink an inch or more at every step, and hardly anywhere can I cut out a small cake, the water collects so fast in [the] hole. But at last, in a harder and drier place, I succeeded. It was now fifteen and a half inches thick, having lost about an inch and a half. Though the upper side was white and rotten and saturated with water for four or five inches, the under surface was still perfectly smooth and so far unchanged, yet ready to flake off, and did so readily in my hand, in flakes a half-inch to an inch thick, leaving the irregular, undulating surface with which I am familiar. But this side was comparatively unchanged and hard, though for two and three quarters inches, measuring upwards, it was whitish, then for two and a half inches remarkably clear (free from air-bubbles) and hard. Then by successive layers it grew more white and soft till you reached the upper surface. I think that that slight white ice beneath the clear and dark may have been produced by the recent warmth of the water, though this is doubtful. At any rate this year the ice has melted *much* more above than beneath. Least of all between two and three quarters and five inches from the under side.

March 5. Sunday. Channing, talking with Minott the other day about his health, said, "I suppose you'd like to die now." "No," said Minott, "I've toughed it through the winter, and I want to stay and hear the bluebirds once more."

The patches of bare ground grow larger and larger, of snow less and less; even after a night you see a difference. It is a clear morning with some wind beginning to rise, and for the first time I see the water looking blue on the meadows.

Has not the johnswort two lives, in winter sending out radical shoots which creep flat on the ground under the snow, in the summer shooting upward and blossoming?

P. M. — To Upper Nut Meadow.

The river is breaking up. The meadows are already partly bare, for it has only been cold enough to form a thin ice on them since this last freshet, and the old ice still lies concealed on the bottom. Great fields of thick ice from the channel, or between the channel and meadows, are driven by the wind against the thick ice on the channel. Hence the meadow ice *appears* to break up first. The waves dash against the edge of the ice and eat into it fast.

As I go along on the snow under Clamshell Hill I hear it sing around me, being melted next the ground. This is a spring sound. I cannot yet see the marchantia (?) in the ditches, for they are yet filled with ice or flooded. I see no horse-tail (unless one) nor flags, etc., yet started in Nut Meadow, nor any minnows out. This brook has run clear of ice a long time. Near Jenny's its sides are strewn with the wreck of angelica stems and asters. I go along looking at its deep, sometimes yellow, shelving bottom, sprinkled with red pebbles. In the upper meadow the sweet-gale grows rankly along its edges, slanted over the water almost horizontally, so as frequently to meet and conceal it altogether. It is here a dark and sluggish water, comparatively shallow, with a muddy bottom. This sweet-gale is now full of fruit. This and the water andromeda are wild plants, as it were driven to the water's edge by the white man. Saw a wood tortoise at the bottom. A reptile out of the mud before any bird, and probably quadruped. Not yet a frog, I think. The down of some willow catkins by this brook *may have* started forward this spring, though it is doubtful. Those which look most forward now will not be so a fortnight hence. It grew colder before I left. I saw some crystals beginning to shoot on the pools between the tussocks, shaped like feathers or fancoral, — the most delicate I ever saw. Thus even ice begins with crystal leaves, and birds' feathers and wings are leaves, and trees and rivers with intervening earth are vast leaves.

Saw a small blackish caterpillar on the snow. Where do they come from? And crows, as I think, migrating northeasterly. They came in loose, straggling flocks, about twenty to each, commonly silent, a quarter to a half a mile apart, till four flocks had passed, and perhaps there were more. Methinks I see them going southwest in the fall.

March 6. A cool morning. The bare water here and there on the meadow begins to look smooth, and I look to see it rippled by a muskrat. The earth has to some extent frozen dry, for the drying of the earth goes on in the cold night as well as the warm day. The alders and hedgerows are still silent, emit no notes.

P. M. — To Goose Pond.

According to G. Emerson, maple sap sometimes begins to flow in the middle of February, but usually in the second week of March, especially in a clear, bright day with a westerly wind, after a frosty night. The brooks — the swift ones and those in swamps — open before the river; indeed some of the first have been open the better part of the winter. I saw trout glance in the Mill Brook this afternoon, though near its sources, in Hubbard's Close, it is still covered with dark, icy snow, and the river into which it empties has not broken up. Can they have come up from the sea? Like a film or shadow they glance before the eye, and you see where the mud is roiled by them. Saw children checkerberrying in a meadow. I see the skunk-cabbage started about the spring at head of Hubbard's Close, amid the green grass, and what looks like the first probing of the skunk. The snow is now all off on meadow ground, in thick evergreen woods, and on the south sides of hills, but it is still deep in sprout-lands, on the north sides of hills, and generally in deciduous woods. In sprout-lands it is melted beneath, but upheld by the bushes. What bare ground we have now is due then not so much to the increased heat of the sun and warmth of the air as to the little frost there was in the ground in so many localities. This remark applies with less force, however, to the south sides of hills. The ponds are hard enough for skating again. Heard and saw the first blackbird, flying east over the Deep Cut, with a *tchuck, tchuck,* and finally a split whistle.

March 7. P. M. — To Annursnack.

I did not mention the drifts yesterday. Most of the snow left on bare, dry level ground consists of the remains of drifts, particularly along fences, — most on the south side. Also much that looks like snow is softened ice in the lower parts of fields. Looking from Annursnack, there is no perceptible difference as to snow between the north and south prospects, though the north one is not extensive; but the snowiest view is westward. Has this anything to do with there being most snow inland? All the sides of steep hills are likely to be bare, washed bare by rain (?). I do not know why there should be so much snow in sprout-lands and deciduous woods, unless it is because the sun has had less chance to thaw the frosts which yet have been thick there.

It is remarkable how true each plant is to its season. Why should not the fringed gentian put forth early in the spring, instead of holding in till the latter part of September? I do not perceive enough difference in the temperature. How short a time it is with us! I see many little white or dirty white puffballs, yellowish inside, commonly less than an inch in diameter, on bare cultivated fields, and, in pastures, some great chocolate-colored ones (within). Both yield their dust. Heard the first bluebird, — something like *pe-a-wor,* — and then other slight warblings, as if farther off. Was surprised to see the bird within seven or eight rods on the top of an oak on the orchard's edge under the hill. But he appeared silent, while I heard others faintly warbling and twittering far in the orchard. When he flew I heard no more, and then I suspected that he had been ventriloquizing; as if he hardly dared upon his mouth yet, while there was so much winter left. It is an overcast and moist but rather warm afternoon. He revisits the apple trees, and appears to find some worms. Probably not till now was his food to be found abundantly. Saw some fuzzy gnats in the air. Saw where a partridge had been eating many prinos berries, now black and shrivelled. I suspect that they devour a great bulk, which has but little nutriment. The radical leaves of the pinweeds are like the johnswort with leaves reflexed, — most of them closer and finer. They appear unaffected by frost. The radical leaves of the crowfoot everywhere are the commonest green, as soon as the snow goes off. You can hardly tell when it begins to spring. Saw mountain cranberry near Brooks's pigeon-place, very flat on the pasture, raying out from a centre six feet each way, more than three quarters of an inch thick in the middle. Did not know it was so woody. This one of the *winter-reds,* perfectly fresh and glossy. The river *channel* is nearly open everywhere. Saw, on the alders by the riverside front of Hildreth's, a song sparrow, quirking its tail. It flew across the river to the willows, and soon I heard its well-known dry *tchip, tchip.* Saw, methinks, what I called ephemeræ last spring, — one on the water, three quarters of an inch long, narrow, gray-winged, several segments [?] curved on the back.

On winter-rye field, top of Annursnack, what looked like a *very large* hard core of a buttonwood ball — same color. Broke it with a stone and found it full of dark earth. Was it not my pigeon's-egg fungus turned dark and hardened?

March 8. Steady rain on the roof in the night, suggesting April-like warmth. This will help melt the snow and ice and take the frost out of the ground.

What pretty wreaths the mountain cranberry makes, curving upward at the extremity! The leaves are now a dark, glossy red, and wreath and all are of such a shape as might fitly be copied in wood or stone or architectural foliages.

I wrote a letter for an Irishman night before last, sending for his wife in Ireland to come to this country. One sentence which he dictated was, "Don't mind the rocking of the vessel, but take care of the children that they be not lost overboard."

Lightning this evening, after a day of successive rains.

March 9. A. M. — Clearing up.

Water is fast taking place of ice on the river and meadows, and morning and evening we begin to have some smooth water prospects. Saw this morning a muskrat sitting "in a round form on the ice," or, rather, motionless like the top of a stake or a mass of muck on the edge of the ice. He then dove for a clam, whose shells he left on the ice beside him.

Boiled a handful of rock-tripe (*Umbilicaria Muhlenbergii*) — which Tuckerman [Edward Tuckerman (1817–1886), American lichenologist.] says "was the favorite Rock-Tripe in Franklin's Journey" — for more than an hour. It produced a *black* pulp, looking *somewhat* like boiled tea leaves, and was insipid like rice or starch. The dark water in which it was boiled had a bitter taste and was slightly gelatinous.

The pulp was not positively disagreeable to the palate. The account in "The Young Voyageurs"[1] is correct.

P. M. — To Great Meadows.

Peter H. says that he saw gulls (?) and sheldrakes about a month ago, when the meadow was flooded. I detect the trout minnows not an inch long by their quick motions or quirks, soon concealing themselves. The river channel is open, but there is a very *thin* ice of recent formation over the greater part of the meadows. It is a still, moist, louring day, and the water is smooth. Saw several flocks of large grayish and whitish or speckled ducks, — I suppose the same that P. calls sheldrakes. They, like ducks commonly, incline to fly in a line about an equal distance apart. I hear the common sort of quacking from them. It is pleasant to see them at a distance alight on the water with a slanting flight, launch themselves, and sail along so stately. The pieces of ice, large and small, drifting along, help to conceal them, supply so many objects on the water. There is this last night's ice on the surface, but the old ice still at the bottom of the meadows. In the spaces of still open water I see the reflection of the hills and woods, which for so long I have not seen, and it gives expression to the face of nature. The face of nature is lit up by these reflections in still water in the spring. Sometimes you see only the top of a distant hill reflected far within the meadow, where a dull-gray field of ice intervenes between the water and the shore.

March 10. Misty rain, rain, — the third day of more or less rain.

P. M. — C. Miles road *via* Clamshell Hill.

Misty and mizzling. The radical leaves of the shepherd's-purse are common and fresh, also that early thistle by Nut Meadow Brook, with much down webbed, holding the mist in drops. Each alder catkin has a clear drop at the end, though the air is filled with mist merely, which from time to time is blown in my face and I put up my umbrella. The bæomyces is very perfect and handsome to-day. It occurs to me that heavy rains and sudden meltings of the snow, such as we had a fortnight ago (February 26th), before the ground is thawed, so that all the water, instead of being soaked up by the ground, flows rapidly into the streams and ponds, is necessary to swell and break them up. If we waited for the direct influence of the sun on the ice and the influence of such water as would reach the river under other circumstances, the spring would be very much

[1] [By Captain Mayne Reid.]

delayed. In the violent freshet there is a mechanic force added to the chemic. The willow catkins on the Miles [road] I should say had decidedly started since I was here last, and are all peeping from under their scales conspicuously. At present I should say that the vegetable kingdom showed the influence of the spring as much in the air as in the water, — that is, in the flowing of the sap, the skunk-cabbage buds, and the swelling of the willow catkins. I have detected very little, if anything, starting in brooks or ditches, for the first have far overflowed their banks and [are] full of rapid and sandy water, and the latter are still frequently full of ice. But probably that depends on the year, whether open or not. Saw a skunk in the Corner road, which I followed sixty rods or more. Out now about 4 P. M., — partly because it is a dark, foul day. It is a slender black (and white) animal, with its back remarkably arched, standing high behind and carrying its head low; runs, even when undisturbed, with a singular teeter or undulation, like the walking of a Chinese lady. Very slow; I hardly have to run to keep up with it. It has a long tail, which it

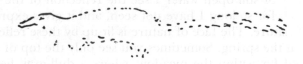

regularly erects when I come too near and prepares to discharge its liquid. It is white at the end of the tail, and the hind head and a line on the front of the face, — the rest black, except the flesh-colored nose (and I think feet). The back is more arched and the fore and hind feet nearer together than in my sketch. It tried repeatedly to get into the wall, and did not show much cunning. Finally it steered, apparently, for an old skunk or woodchuck hole under a wall four rods off, and got into it, — or under the wall, at least — for it was stopped up, — and there I view at leisure close to. It has a remarkably long, narrow, pointed head and snout, which enable it to make those deep narrow holes in the earth by which it probes for insects. Its eyes have an innocent, childlike, bluish-black expression. It made a singular loud patting sound repeatedly, on the frozen ground under the wall, undoubtedly with its fore feet (I saw only the upper part of the animal), which reminded me of what I have heard about your stopping and stamping in order to stop the skunk. Probably it has to do with its getting its food, — patting the earth to get the insects or worms. Though why it did so then I know not.

   Its track was small, round, showing the nails, a little less than an inch in diameter, alternate five or six inches by two or two and a half, sometimes two feet together. There is something pathetic in such a sight, — next to seeing one of the human aborigines of the country. I respect the skunk as a human being in a very humble sphere. I have no doubt they have begun to probe already where the ground permits, — or as far as it does. But what have they eat all winter?

The weather is almost April-like. We always have much of this rainy, drizzling, misty weather in early spring, after which we expect to hear geese.

March 11. Fair weather after three rainy days. Air full of birds, — bluebirds, song sparrows, chickadee (phœbe notes), and blackbirds. Song sparrows toward the water, with at least two kinds of variations of their strain hard to imitate. *Ozit, ozit, ozit, psa te-te te-te-te ter twe ter* is one; the other began *chip chip che we*, etc., etc. Bluebirds' warbling curls in elms.

Shall the earth be regarded as a graveyard, a necropolis, merely, and not also as a granary filled with the seeds of life? Is not its fertility increased by this decay? A fertile compost, not exhausted sand.

On Tuesday, the 7th, I heard the first song sparrow chirp, and saw it flit silently from alder to alder. This pleasant morning after three days' rain and mist, they generally forthburst into sprayey song from the low trees along the river. The developing of their song is gradual but sure, like the expanding of a flower. This is the first *song* I have heard.

P. M. — To Cliffs.

River higher than any time in the winter, I think, yet, there being some ice on the meadows and the tops of reflected trees being seen along its edges, Aunt thought the river had gone down and that this was the ground. Muskrats are driven out of their holes. Heard one's loud plash behind Hubbard's. It comes up, brown striped with wet. I could detect its progress beneath in shallow water by the bubbles which came up. I believe I saw to-day, and have for some time seen, lizards in water, wiggling away more swiftly than tadpoles or frogs. From the hill the river and meadow is about equally water and ice, — rich blue water and islands or continents of white ice — no longer ice in place — blown from this side or that. The distant mountains are all white with snow while our landscape is nearly bare. Another year I must observe the alder and willow sap as early as the middle of February at least. Fair Haven covered with ice. Saw a hawk. Goodwin saw a ground squirrel a fortnight ago and heard robin this morning. He has caught skunks in traps set for minks with a piece of muskrat. Says the fox and skunk eat huckleberries, etc. Nowadays, where snow-banks have partly melted against the banks by the road-side in low ground, I see in the grass numerous galleries where the mice or moles have worked in the winter.

March 12. A. M. — Up railroad to woods.

We have white frosts these mornings. This is the blackbird morning. Their sprayey notes and *conqueree* ring with the song sparrows' jingle all along the river. Thus gradually they acquire confidence to sing. It is a beautiful spring morning. I hear *my* first robin peep distinctly at a distance on some higher trees, — oaks or ?, — on a high key. No singing yet. I hear from an apple tree a faint cricketlike chirp, and a sparrow darts away, flying far, *dashing from side to side.* I think it must be the white-in-tail, or grass finch. Saw either a large mouse or a ground squirrel on the snow near the edge of the wood, — probably the former. I hear a jay loudly screaming *phe-phay phe-phay,* — a loud, shrill chickadee's *phebe.* Now I see and hear the lark sitting with head erect, neck outstretched, in the middle of a pasture, and I hear another far off singing. Sing when they first come. All these birds do their warbling especially in the still, sunny hour after sunrise, as rivers twinkle at their sources. Now is the time to be abroad and hear them, as you detect the slightest ripple in smooth water. As with tinkling sounds the sources of streams burst their icy fetters, so the rills of music begin to flow and swell the general quire of spring. Memorable is the warm light of the spring sun on russet fields in the morning.

A new feature is being added to the landscape, and that is expanses and reaches of blue water.

C. says he saw a gull to-day.

P. M. — To Ball's Hill along river.

My companion tempts me to certain licenses of speech, *i.e.* to reckless and sweeping expressions which I am wont to regret that I have used. That is, I find that I have used more harsh, extravagant, and cynical expressions concerning mankind and individuals than I intended. I find it difficult to make to him a sufficiently moderate statement. I think it is because I have not his sympathy in my sober and constant view. He asks for a paradox, an eccentric statement, and too often I give it to him.

Saw some small ducks, black and white, — perhaps teal or widgeons. This great expanse of deep-blue water, deeper than the sky, why does it not blue my soul as of yore? It is hard to soften me now.

I see no gulls myself. The time was when this great blue scene would have tinged my spirit more. Now is the season to look for Indian relics, the sandy fields being just bared. I stand on the high lichen covered and colored (greenish) hill beyond Abner Buttrick's; I go further east and look across the meadows to Bedford, and see that peculiar scenery of March, in which I have taken so many rambles, the earth just bare and beginning to be dry, the snow lying on the north sides of hills, the gray deciduous trees and the green pines soughing in the March wind — they look now as if deserted by a companion, the snow. When you walk over bare lichen-clad hills, just beginning to be dry, and look afar over the blue water on the meadows, you are beginning to break up your winter quarters and plan adventures for the new year. The scenery is like, yet unlike, November; you have the same barren russet, but now, instead of a dry, hard, cold wind, a peculiarly soft, moist air, or else a raw wind. Now is the reign of water. I see many crows on the meadow by the water's edge these days. It is astonishing how soon the ice has gone out of the river, but it still lies on the bottom of the meadow. Is it peculiar to the song sparrow to dodge behind and hide in walls and the like? Toward night the water becomes smooth and beautiful. Men are eager to launch their boats and paddle over the meadows.

The spring birds have come a little earlier this year than last, methinks, and I suspect the spring may be earlier in the air, yet there is more ice and snow and frozen ground still, because the winter has been so much more severe.

I am surprised to find that water froze pretty thick in my chamber the night of the 14th of March, '53, after a fire in the evening, and that they were at work on the ice at Loring's on the 16th. This is very different weather. The ice is all out of the river proper, and all spoiled even on Walden.

March 13. To Boston.

C. says he saw skater insects to-day. Harris tells me that those gray insects within the little log forts under the bark of the dead white pine, which I found about a week ago, are *Rhagium lineatum.* Bought a telescope to-day for eight dollars. Best military spyglass with six slides, which shuts up to about same size, fifteen dollars, and very powerful. Saw the squares of achromatic glass from Paris which Clark(e?) uses; fifty-odd dollars apiece, the larger. It takes two together, one called the flint. These French glasses all one quality of glass. My glass tried by Clark and approved. Only a part of the object (?) glass available. Bring the edge of the diaphragm against middle of the light, and your nail on object glass in line with these shows what is cut off. Sometimes may enlarge the hole in diaphragm. But, if you do so, you may have to enlarge the hole in diaphragm near small end, which must be exactly as large as the pencil of light there. As the diameter of the pencil is to the diameter of the available portion of the object glass, so is the power, — so many times it magnifies. A good glass because the form of the blurred object is the same on each side of the focus, — *i.e.*, shoved in or drawn out. C. was making a glass for Amherst College.

March 14. A. M. — Threatening rain after clear morning.

Great concert of song sparrows in willows and alders along Swamp Bridge Brook by river. Hardly hear a *distinct* strain. Couples chasing each other, and some tree sparrows with them.

R. W. E. saw a small bird in the woods yesterday which reminded him of the parti-colored warbler.

P. M. — To Great Meadows.

Raw thickening mists, as if preceding rain.

Counted over forty robins with my glass in the meadow north of Sleepy Hollow, in the grass and on the snow. A large company of fox-colored sparrows in Heywood's maple swamp close by. I heard their loud, sweet, canary-like whistle thirty or forty rods off, sounding richer than anything yet; some on the bushes singing, *twee twee twa twa ter tweer tweer twa*, — this is the scheme of it only, there being no dental grit to it. They were shy, flitting before me, and I heard a slight susurrus where many were busily scratching amid the leaves of the swamp, without seeing them, and also saw many indistinctly. Wilson never heard but one sing, their common note there being a *cheep*. Saw fresh tracks in what looked like a woodchuck's hole. No ice visible as I look over the meadows from Peter's, though it lies at the bottom.[2] Scared up four black ducks from the flooded meadow on the right of the roadway as you go to Peter's. The water being rough on the meadows, they had apparently sought this smooth and shallow place shut in by the woods.

Alder scales are visibly loosened, their lower edges (*i.e.* as they hang) showing a line of yellowish or greenish. The pads in open warm ditches are now decidedly the greatest growth of this season, though I am not sure how much is due to last fall.

From within the house at 5.30 P. M. I hear the loud honking of geese, throw up the window, and see a large flock in disordered

[2] [Queried in pencil.]

harrow flying more directly north or even northwest than usual. Raw, thick, misty weather.

March 15. Pleasant morning, unexpectedly. Hear on the alders by the river the *lill lill lill lill* of the first *F. hyemalis,* mingled with song sparrows and tree sparrows. The sound of Barrett's sawmill in the still morning comes over the water very loud. I hear that peculiar, interesting loud hollow tapping of a woodpecker from over the water.

I am sorry to think that you do not get a man's most effective criticism until you provoke him. Severe truth is expressed with some bitterness.

J. Farmer tells me his dog started up a lark last winter completely buried in the snow.

Painted my boat.

March 16. A. M. — Another fine morning.

Willows and alders along watercourses all alive these mornings and ringing with the trills and jingles and warbles of birds, even as the waters have lately broken loose and tinkle below, — song sparrows, blackbirds, not to mention robins, etc., etc. The song sparrows are very abundant, peopling each bush, willow, or alder for a quarter of a mile, and pursuing each other as if now selecting their mates. It is their song which especially fills the air, made an incessant and undistinguishable trill and jingle by their numbers. I see ducks afar, sailing on the meadow, leaving a long furrow in the water behind them. Watch them at leisure without scaring them, with my glass; observe their free and undisturbed motions. Some dark-brown partly on water, alternately dipping with their tails up, partly on land. These I think may be summer ducks.[3] Others with bright white breasts, etc., and black heads about same size or larger, which may be golden-eyes, *i.e.* brass-eyed whistlers.[4] They dive and are gone some time, and come up a rod off. At first I saw but one, then, a minute after, three. The first phœbe near the water is heard.

Saw and heard honey-bees about my boat in the yard, attracted probably by the beeswax in the grafting-wax which was put on it a year ago. It is warm weather. A thunder-storm in the evening.

March 17. *Friday.* A remarkably warm day for the season; too warm while surveying without my greatcoat; almost like May heats.

---

[3] Were they not females of the others?
[4] Probably both sheldrakes. *Vide* April 6 and 7, 1855.

4 P. M. — To Cliffs.

The grass is *slightly* greened on south bank-sides, — on the south side of the house. It begins to be windy. Saw a small gyrinus at the brook bridge behind Hubbard's Grove. The first tinge of green appears to be due to moisture more than to direct heat. It is not on bare dry banks, but in hollows where the snow melts last that it is most conspicuous. Fair Haven is open for half a dozen rods about the shores. If this weather holds, it will be entirely open in a day or two.

March 18. *Saturday.* Very high wind this forenoon; began by filling the air with a cloud of dust. Never felt it shake the house so much; filled the house with dust through the cracks; books, stove, papers covered with it. Blew down Mr. Frost's chimney again. Took up my boat, a very heavy one, which was lying on its bottom in the yard, and carried it two rods. The white caps of the waves on the flooded meadow, seen from the window, are a rare and exciting spectacle, — such an angry face as our Concord meadows rarely exhibit. Walked down the street to post-office. Few inhabitants out more than in a rain. Elms bending and twisting and thrashing the air as if they would come down every moment. I was cautious about passing under them. Yet scarcely a rotten limb in the street. The highest winds occur neither in summer, when the trees are covered with leaves, nor in winter, when they may be covered with ice. Saw a flattened toad on the sidewalk. Could it have been last year's?[5]

P. M. — Walked round by the west side of the river to Conantum.

Wind less violent. C. has already seen a yellow-spotted tortoise in a ditch. (Two sizable elms by river in Merrick's pasture blown down, roots being rotted off on water side.) The willow catkins this side M. Miles's five eighths of an inch long and show some red. Poplar catkins nearly as large, color somewhat like a gray rabbit. Old barn blown down on Conantum. It fell regularly, like a weak box pushed over,

without moving its bottom, the roof falling upon it a little to leeward. The hay is left exposed, but does not blow away. The river was at its height last night. Before this we saw many robins and sparrows under

[5] Guess not.

Clamshell Hill for shelter. Birds seek warm and sheltered places in such weather. It is very cold and freezing, this wind. The water has been blown quite across the Hubbard's Bridge causeway in some places and incrusted the road with ice. Before looking this way we had seen the whitened shore from Lupine Hill. It is blown and dashes

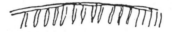

against the willows and incrusts them with ice, sometimes to the height of three feet, with icicles shaped like bulls' horns, especially observable where many osiers stand together, and from the more horizontal osiers, etc., depend icicles, five or six inches long, very regularly, looking exactly like coarse rakes, apparently not the result

of melting but of the spray and water blown or dashed upon them: only more regular. A very wintry sight.

The water is in many places blown a rod on to the shore and frozen. Saw where a woodchuck (probably) had dug out quite a pile of gravel in the side of a hill.

March 19. Sunday. Cold and windy. The meadow ice bears where shallow. William Rice 2d (?) saw a woodchuck last Sunday. Met his father in Walden Woods, who described a flock of crows he had just seen which followed him "eying down, eying down."

Saw in Mill Brook behind Shannon's three or four shiners[6] (the first), poised over the sand with a distinct longitudinal light-colored line midway along their sides and a darker line below it. This is a noteworthy and characteristic lineament, or cipher, or hieroglyphic, or type, of spring. You look into some clear, sandy-bottomed brook, where it spreads into a deeper bay, yet flowing cold from ice and snow not far off, and see, indistinctly poised over the sand on invisible fins, the outlines of a shiner, scarcely to be distinguished from the

[6] Minnows?

sands behind it, as if it were transparent, or as [if] the material of which it was builded had all been picked up from them. Chiefly distinguished by the lines I have mentioned.

Goodwin killed a pigeon yesterday.

Flint's Pond almost entirely open, — much more than Fair Haven.

March 21. *Tuesday.* At sunrise to Clamshell Hill.

River skimmed over at Willow Bay last night. Thought I should find ducks cornered up by the ice; they get behind this hill for shelter. Saw what looked like clods of plowed meadow rising above the ice. Looked with glass and found it to be more than thirty black ducks asleep with their heads in their backs, motionless, and thin ice formed about them. Soon one or two were moving about slowly. There was an open space, eight or ten rods by one or two. At first all within a space of apparently less than a rod [in] diameter. It was 6.30 A. M, and the sun shining on them, but bitter cold. How tough they are! I crawled far on my stomach and got a near view of them, thirty rods off. At length they detected me and quacked. Some got out upon the ice, and when I rose up all took to flight in a great straggling flock which at a distance looked like crows, in no order. Yet, when you see two or three, the parallelism produced by their necks and bodies steering the same way gives the idea of order.

March 22. *Wednesday.* P. M. — Launch boat and paddle to Fair Haven.

Still very cold. The most splendid show of ice chandeliers, casters, hour-glasses (½) that I ever saw or imagined about the piers of the bridges, surpassing any crystal, so large. Rather like the bases of

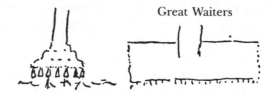

Great Waiters

columns, — terraced pedestals, that is it, — the prototypes of the ornaments of the copings and capitals. Perfect and regular, sharp, cone-shaped drops hang from the first figure a few inches above the water. I should have described it then. It would have filled many pages. Scared up my flock of black ducks and counted forty together.

See crows along the water's edge. What do they eat? Saw a small black duck with glass, — a dipper (?). Fair Haven still covered and frozen anew in part. Shores of meadow strewn with cranberries. The now silvery willow catkins (notwithstanding the severe cold) shine along the shore, over the cold water, and C. thinks some willow osiers decidedly more yellow.

March 23. Thursday. Snows and rains a little. The birds in yard active now, — hyemalis, tree sparrow, and song sparrow. The hyemalis jingle easily distinguished. Hear all together on apple trees these days. Minott confesses to me to-day that he has not been to Boston since the last war, or 1815. Aunt said that he had not been ten miles from home since; that he has not been to Acton since Miss Powers [?] lived there; but he declared that he had been there to cornwallis and musters. When I asked if he would like to go to Boston, he answered he was going to another Boston

March 24. Fair again, the snow melting. Great flocks of hyemalis drifting about with their jingling note. The same ducks under Clamshell Hill. The elm buds were apparently expanded before this cold, which began on the 18th. Goose Pond half open. Flint's has perhaps fifteen or twenty acres of ice yet about shores. Can hardly tell when it is open this year. The black ducks — the most common that I see — are the only ones whose note I know or hear, — a hoarse, croaking quack. How shy they are!

March 25, Saturday. Cold and windy.
   Down river in boat to Great Meadows.
   Freezes on oars. Too cold and windy almost for ducks. They are in the smoother open water (free from ice) under the lee of hills. Got a boat-load of driftwood, — rails, bridge timber, planks, etc. White maple buds bursting, making trees look like some fruit trees with blossom-buds.
   Is not the small duck or two I see one at a time and flying pretty high a teal? Willow osiers near Mill Brook mouth I am almost certain have acquired a fresher color; at least they surprise me at a distance by their green passing through yellowish to red at top.

March 26. River froze over at Lily Bay.[7]

---

[7] ["Lily" is crossed out in pencil and "Willow?" substituted (the interrogation-point being Thoreau's).]

March 27. Saw a hawk — probably marsh hawk — by meadow.

March 28. P. M. — To White Pond.

Coldest day for a month or more, — severe as almost any in the winter. Saw this afternoon either a snipe or a woodcock; it appeared rather small for the last.[8] Pond opening on the northeast. A flock of hyemalis drifting from a wood over a field incessantly for four or five minutes, — thousands of them, notwithstanding the cold. The fox-colored sparrow sings sweetly also. Saw a small slate-colored hawk, with wings transversely mottled beneath, — probably the sharp-shinned hawk.

Got first proof of "Walden."

March 29. *Wednesday.* P. M. — To Fair Haven.

Coldest night. Pump froze so as to require thawing. Saw two marsh hawks (?), white on rump. A gull of pure white, — a wave of foam in the air. How simple and wave-like its outline, the outline of the wings presenting two curves, between which the tail is merely the

point of junction, — all wing like a birch scale; tail remarkably absorbed.

Saw two white-throated, black-beaked divers fly off swiftly low over the water, with black tips of wings curved short downward. Afterward saw one scoot along out from the shore upon the water and dive;

and that was the last I could see of him, though I watched four or five minutes. Fair Haven half open; channel wholly open. See thin cakes of ice at a distance now and then blown up on their edges and glistening in the sun. Had the experience of arctic voyagers amid the floe ice on a small scale. Think I saw a hen-hawk, — two circling over Cliffs.

[8] Probably a snipe.

March 30. 6 A. M. — To Island.

First still hour since the afternoon of the 17th. March truly came in like a lamb and went out like a lion this year. Remarkably and continuously pleasant weather from the very first day till the 18th. Apparently an early spring, — buds and birds well advanced, — then suddenly very severe cold and high winds cold enough to skim the river over in broad places at night, and commencing with the greatest and most destructive gale for many a year, felt far and wide; and it has never ceased to blow since till this morning. Vegetation is accordingly put back. The ground these last cold (thirteen) days has been about bare of snow, but frozen. Some had peas and potatoes in before it. First half of month very pleasant and mild spring weather, last half severe winter cold and high winds. The water at its highest, — not very high, — this month on the 17th. Ducks have been lurking in sheltered places not frozen. Robins feed along the edge of the river. At the Island I see and hear this morning the cackle of a pigeon woodpecker at the hollow poplar; had heard him tapping distinctly from my boat's place ¼ + of a mile. Great flocks of tree sparrows and some *F. hyemalis* on the ground and trees on the Island Neck, making the air and bushes ring with their jingling. The former — some of them — say somewhat like this: *a che che, ter twee twee, tweer tweer twa.* It sounded like a new bird. The black ducks seem always to rise with that loud, hoarse croaking — quacking. The river early is partly filled with thin, floating, hardly cemented ice, occasionally turned on its edge by the wind and sparkling in the sun. If the sun had kept out of the way one day in the past fortnight, I think the river would have frozen to bear.

Read an interesting article on Étienne Geoffroy Saint-Hilaire, the friend and contemporary of Cuvier, though opposed to him in his philosophy. He believed species to be variable. In looking for anatomical resemblances he found that he could not safely be guided by function, form, structure, size, color, etc., but only by the relative position and mutual dependence of organs. Hence his *Le Principe des Connexions* and his maxim, "An organ is sooner destroyed than transposed," — "Un organ est plutôt altéré, atrophié, anéanti, que transposé." A principal formula of his was, "Unity of Plan, Unity of Composition." (In the *Westminster Review,* January, 1854.)

March 31. Weather changes at last to drizzling.

In criticising your writing, trust your fine instinct. There are many things which we come very near questioning, but do not question. When I have sent off my manuscripts to the printer, certain objectionable sentences or expressions are sure to obtrude themselves on my attention with force, though I had not consciously suspected them before. My critical instinct then at once breaks the ice and comes to the surface.

Walking

I wish to speak a word for Nature, for absolute freedom and wildness, as contrasted with a freedom and culture merely civil, — to regard man as an inhabitant, or a part and parcel of Nature, rather than a member of society. I wish to make an extreme statement, if so I may make an emphatic one, for there are enough champions of civilization: the minister, and the school-committee, and every one of you will take care of that.

I have met with but one or two persons in the course of my life who understood the art of Walking, that is, of taking walks, — who had a genius, so to speak, for *sauntering:* which word is beautifully derived "from idle people who roved about the country, in the Middle Ages, and asked charity, under pretence of going *à la Sainte Terre,*" to the Holy Land, till the children exclaimed, "There goes a *Sainte-Terrer,*" a Saunterer, — a Holy-Lander. They who never go to the Holy Land in their walks, as they pretend, are indeed mere idlers and vagabonds; but they who do go there are saunterers in the good sense, such as I mean. Some, however, would derive the word from *sans terre,* without land or a home, which, therefore, in the good sense, will mean, having no particular home, but equally at home everywhere. For this is the secret of successful sauntering. He who sits still in a house all the time may be the greatest vagrant of all; but the saunterer, in the good sense, is no more vagrant than the meandering river, which is all the while sedulously seeking the shortest course to the sea. But I prefer the first, which, indeed, is the most probable derivation. For every walk is a sort of crusade, preached by some Peter the Hermit in us, to go forth and reconquer this Holy Land from the hands of the Infidels.

It is true, we are but faint-hearted crusaders, even the walkers, nowadays, who undertake no persevering, never-ending enterprises. Our expeditions are but tours, and come round again at evening to the old hearth-side from which we set out. Half the walk is but retracing our steps. We should go forth on the shortest walk, perchance, in the spirit of undying adventure, never to return, — prepared to send back our embalmed hearts only as relics to our desolate kingdoms. If you are ready to leave father and mother, and brother and sister, and wife and child and friends, and never see them again, — if you have paid your debts, and made your will and settled all your affairs, and are a free man, then you are ready for a walk.

To come down to my own experience, my companion and I, for I sometimes have a companion, take pleasure in fancying ourselves knights of a new, or rather an old, order, — not Equestrians or Chevaliers, not Ritters or Riders, but Walkers, a still more ancient and honorable class, I trust. The chivalric and heroic spirit which once belonged to the Rider seems now to reside in, or perchance to have subsided into, the Walker, — not the Knight, but Walker Errant. He is a sort of fourth estate, outside of Church and State and People.

We have felt that we almost alone hereabouts practised this noble art; though, to tell the truth, at least, if their own assertions are to be received, most of my townsmen would fain walk sometimes, as I do, but they cannot. No wealth can buy the requisite leisure, freedom, and independence, which are the capital in this profession. It comes only by the grace of God. It requires a direct dispensation from Heaven to become a walker. You must be born into the family of the Walkers. *Ambulator nascitur, non fit.* Some of my townsmen, it is true, can remember and have described to me some walks which they took ten years ago, in which they were so blessed as to lose themselves for half an hour in the woods; but I know very well that they have confined themselves to the highway ever since, whatever pretensions they may make to belong to this select class. No doubt they were elevated for a moment as by the reminiscence of a previous state of existence, when even they were foresters and outlaws.

> "When he came to grene wode,
> In a mery mornynge,
> There he herde the notes small
> Of byrdes mery syngynge.

> "It is ferre gone, sayd Robyn,
> That I was last here;
> Me lyste a lytell for to shote
> At the donne dere."

I think that I cannot preserve my health and spirits, unless I spend four hours a day at least — and it is commonly more than that — sauntering through the woods and over the hills and fields, absolutely free from all worldly engagements. You may safely say, A penny for your thoughts, or a thousand pounds. When sometimes I am reminded that the mechanics and shopkeepers stay in their shops not only all the forenoon, but all the afternoon too, sitting with crossed legs, so many of them, — as if the legs were made to sit upon, and not to stand or walk upon, — I think that they deserve some credit for not having all committed suicide long ago.

I, who cannot stay in my chamber for a single day without acquiring some rust, and when sometimes I have stolen forth for a walk at the eleventh hour of four o'clock in the afternoon, too late to redeem the day, when the shades of night were already beginning to be mingled with the daylight, have felt as if I had committed some sin to be atoned for, — I confess that I am astonished at the power of endurance, to say nothing of the moral insensibility, of my neighbors who confine themselves to shops and offices the whole day for weeks and months, ay, and years almost together. I know not what manner of stuff they are of, — sitting there now at three o'clock in the afternoon, as if it were three o'clock in the morning. Bonaparte may talk of the three-o'clock-in-the-morning courage, but it is nothing to the courage which can sit down cheerfully at this hour in the afternoon over against one's self whom you have known all the morning, to starve out a garrison to whom you are bound by such strong ties of sympathy. I wonder that about this time, or say between four and five o'clock in the afternoon, too late for the morning papers and too early for the evening ones, there is not a general explosion heard up and down the street, scattering a legion of antiquated and house-bred notions and whims to the four winds for an airing, — and so the evil cure itself.

How womankind, who are confined to the house still more than men, stand it I do not know; but I have ground to suspect that most of them do not *stand* it at all. When, early in a summer afternoon, we have been shaking the dust of the village from the skirts of our garments, making haste past those houses with purely Doric or Gothic fronts, which have such an air of repose about them, my companion whispers that probably about these times their occupants are all gone to bed. Then it is that I appreciate the beauty and the glory of architecture, which itself never turns in, but forever stands out and erect, keeping watch over the slumberers.

No doubt temperament, and, above all, age, have a good deal to do with it. As a man grows older, his ability to sit still and follow in-door occupations increases. He grows vespertinal in his habits as the evening of life approaches, till at last he comes forth only just before sundown, and gets all the walk that he requires in half an hour.

But the walking of which I speak has nothing in it akin to taking exercise, as it is called, as the sick take medicine at stated hours, —

as the swinging of dumbbells or chairs; but is itself the enterprise and adventure of the day. If you would get exercise, go in search of the springs of life. Think of a man's swinging dumbbells for his health, when those springs are bubbling up in far-off pastures unsought by him!

Moreover, you must walk like a camel, which is said to be the only beast which ruminates when walking. When a traveller asked Wordsworth's servant to show him her master's study, she answered, "Here is his library, but his study is out of doors."

Living much out of doors, in the sun and wind, will no doubt produce a certain roughness of character, — will cause a thicker cuticle to grow over some of the finer qualities of our nature, as on the face and hands, or as severe manual labor robs the hands of some of their delicacy of touch. So staying in the house, on the other hand, may produce a softness and smoothness, not to say thinness of skin, accompanied by an increased sensibility to certain impressions. Perhaps we should be more susceptible to some influences important to our intellectual and moral growth, if the sun had shone and the wind blown on us a little less; and no doubt it is a nice matter to proportion rightly the thick and thin skin. But methinks that is a scurf that will fall off fast enough, — that the natural remedy is to be found in the proportion which the night bears to the day, the winter to the summer, thought to experience. There will be so much the more air and sunshine in our thoughts. The callous palms of the laborer are conversant with finer tissues of self-respect and heroism, whose touch thrills the heart, than the languid fingers of idleness. That is mere sentimentality that lies abed by day and thinks itself white, far from the tan and callus of experience.

When we walk, we naturally go to the fields and woods: what would become of us, if we walked only in a garden or a mall? Even some sects of philosophers have felt the necessity of importing the woods to themselves, since they did not go to the woods. "They planted groves and walks of Platanes," where they took *subdiales ambulationes* in porticos open to the air. Of course it is of no use to direct our steps to the woods, if they do not carry us thither. I am alarmed when it happens that I have walked a mile into the woods bodily, without getting there in spirit. In my afternoon walk I would fain forget all my morning occupations and my obligations to society. But it sometimes happens that I cannot easily shake off the village. The thought of some work will run in my head, and I am not where my body is, — I am out of my senses. In my walks I would fain return to my senses. What business have I in the woods, if I am thinking of something out of the woods? I suspect myself, and cannot help a shudder, when I find myself so implicated even in what are called good works, — for this may sometimes happen.

My vicinity affords many good walks; and though for so many years I have walked almost every day, and sometimes for several days together, I have not yet exhausted them. An absolutely new prospect is a great happiness, and I can still get this any afternoon. Two or three hours' walking will carry me to as strange a country as I expect ever to see. A single farm-house which I had not seen before is sometimes as good as the dominions of the King of Dahomey. There is in fact a sort of harmony discoverable between the capabilities of the landscape within a circle of ten miles' radius, or the limits of an afternoon walk, and the threescore years and ten of human life. It will never become quite familiar to you.

Nowadays almost all man's improvements, so called, as the building of houses, and the cutting down of the forest and of all large trees, simply deform the landscape, and make it more and more tame and cheap. A people who would begin by burning the fences and let the forest stand! I saw the fences half consumed, their ends lost in the middle of the prairie, and some worldly miser with a surveyor looking after his bounds, while heaven had taken place around him, and he did not see the angels going to and fro, but was looking for an old post-hole in the midst of paradise. I looked again, and saw him standing in the middle of a boggy, stygian fen, surrounded by devils, and he had found his bounds without a doubt, three little stones, where a stake had been driven, and looking nearer, I saw that the Prince of Darkness was his surveyor.

I can easily walk ten, fifteen, twenty, any number of miles, commencing at my own door, without going by any house, without crossing a road except where the fox and the mink do: first along by the river, and then the brook, and then the meadow and the wood-side. There are square miles in my vicinity which have no inhabitant. From many a hill I can see civilization and the abodes of man afar. The farmers and their works are scarcely more obvious than woodchucks and their burrows. Man and his affairs, church and state and school, trade and commerce, and manufactures and agriculture, even politics, the most alarming of them all, — I am pleased to see how little space they occupy in the landscape. Politics is but a narrow field, and that still narrower highway yonder leads to it. I sometimes direct the traveller thither. If you would go to the political world, follow the great road, — follow that market-man, keep his dust in your eyes, and it will lead you straight to it; for it, too, has its place merely, and does not occupy all space. I pass from it as from a beanfield into the forest, and it is forgotten. In one half-hour I can walk off to some portion of the earth's surface where a man does not stand from one year's end to another, and there, consequently, politics are not, for they are but as the cigar-smoke of a man.

The village is the place to which the roads tend, a sort of expansion of the highway, as a lake of a river. It is the body of which roads are the arms and legs, — a trivial or quadrivial place, the thoroughfare and ordinary of travellers. The word is from the Latin *villa*, which, together with *via*, a way, or more anciently *ved* and *vella*, Varro derives from *veho*, to carry, because the villa is the place to and from which things are carried. They who got their living by teaming were said *vellaturam facere*. Hence, too, apparently, the Latin word *vilis* and our vile; also *villain*. This suggests what kind of degeneracy villagers are liable to. They are wayworn by the travel that goes by and over them, without travelling themselves.

Some do not walk at all; others walk in the highways; a few walk across lots. Roads are made for horses and men of business. I do not travel in them much, comparatively, because I am not in a hurry to get to any tavern or grocery or livery-stable or depot to which they lead. I am a good horse to travel, but not from choice a roadster. The landscape-painter uses the figures of men to mark a road. He would not make that use of my figure. I walk out into a Nature such as the old prophets and poets, Menu, Moses, Homer, Chaucer, walked in. You may name it America, but it is not America: neither Americus Vespucius, nor Columbus, nor the rest were the discoverers of it. There is a truer account of it in mythology than in any history of America, so called, that I have seen.

However, there are a few old roads that may be trodden with profit, as if they led somewhere now that they are nearly discontinued. There is the Old Marlborough Road, which does not go to Marlborough now, methinks, unless that is Marlborough where it carries me. I am the bolder to speak of it here, because I presume that there are one or two such roads in every town.

THE OLD MARLBOROUGH ROAD

> Where they once dug for money,
> But never found any;
> Where sometimes Martial Miles
> Singly files,
> And Elijah Wood,
> I fear for no good:

No other man,
Save Elisha Dugan, —
O man of wild habits,
Partridges and rabbits,
Who hast no cares
Only to set snares,
Who liv'st all alone,
Close to the bone,
And where life is sweetest
Constantly eatest.
When the spring stirs my blood
With the instinct to travel,
I can get enough gravel
On the Old Marlborough Road.
Nobody repairs it,
For nobody wears it;
It is a living way,
As the Christians say.
Not many there be
Who enter therein,
Only the guests of the
Irishman Quin,
What is it, what is it,
But a direction out there,
And the bare possibility
Of going somewhere?
Great guide-boards of stone,
But travellers none;
Cenotaphs of the towns
Named on their crowns.
It is worth going to see
Where you *might* be.
What king
Did the thing,
I am still wondering;
Set up how or when,
By what selectmen,
Gourgas or Lee,
Clark or Darby?
They 're a great endeavor
To be something forever;
Blank tablets of stone,
Where a traveller might groan,

And in one sentence
Grave all that is known;
Which another might read,
In his extreme need.
I know one or two
Lines that would do,
Literature that might stand
All over the land,
Which a man could remember
Till next December,
And read again in the spring,
After the thawing.
If with fancy unfurled
You leave your abode,
You may go round the world
By the Old Marlborough Road.

At present, in this vicinity, the best part of the land is not private property; the landscape is not owned, and the walker enjoys comparative freedom. But possibly the day will come when it will be partitioned off into so-called pleasure-grounds, in which a few will take a narrow and exclusive pleasure only, — when fences shall be multiplied, and man-traps and other engines invented to confine men to the *public* road, and walking over the surface of God's earth shall be construed to mean trespassing on some gentleman's grounds. To enjoy a thing exclusively is commonly to exclude yourself from the true enjoyment of it. Let us improve our opportunities, then, before the evil days come.

What is it that makes it so hard sometimes to determine whither we will walk? I believe that there is a subtile magnetism in Nature, which, if we unconsciously yield to it, will direct us aright. It is not indifferent to us which way we walk. There is a right way; but we are very liable from heedlessness and stupidity to take the wrong one. We would fain take that walk, never yet taken by us through this actual world, which is perfectly symbolical of the path which we love to travel in the interior and ideal world; and sometimes, no doubt, we find it difficult to choose our direction, because it does not yet exist distinctly in our idea.

When I go out of the house for a walk, uncertain as yet whither I will bend my steps, and submit myself to my instinct to decide for me, I find, strange and whimsical as it may seem, that I finally and inevitably settle southwest, toward some particular wood or meadow or deserted pasture or hill in that direction. My needle is slow to

settle, — varies a few degrees, and does not always point due southwest, it is true, and it has good authority for this variation, but it
always settles between west and south-southwest. The future lies that
way to me, and the earth seems more unexhausted and richer on
that side. The outline which would bound my walks would be, not a
circle, but a parabola, or rather like one of those cometary orbits
which have been thought to be non-returning curves, in this case
opening westward, in which my house occupies the place of the sun.
I turn round and round irresolute sometimes for a quarter of an
hour, until I decide, for the thousandth time, that I will walk into
the southwest or west. Eastward I go only by force; but westward I
go free. Thither no business leads me. It is hard for me to believe
that I shall find fair landscapes or sufficient wildness and freedom
behind the eastern horizon. I am not excited by the prospect of a
walk thither; but I believe that the forest which I see in the western
horizon stretches uninterruptedly towards the setting sun, and that
there are no towns nor cities in it of enough consequence to disturb
me. Let me live where I will, on this side is the city, on that the
wilderness, and ever I am leaving the city more and more, and
withdrawing into the wilderness. I should not lay so much stress on
this fact, if I did not believe that something like this is the prevailing
tendency of my countrymen. I must walk toward Oregon, and not
toward Europe. And that way the nation is moving, and I may say
that mankind progress from east to west. Within a few years we have
witnessed the phenomenon of a southeastward migration, in the
settlement of Australia; but this affects us as a retrograde movement,
and, judging from the moral and physical character of the first generation of Australians, has not yet proved a successful experiment.
The eastern Tartars think that there is nothing west beyond Thibet.
"The world ends there," say they; "beyond there is nothing but a
shoreless sea." It is unmitigated East where they live.

We go eastward to realize history and study the works of art and
literature, retracing the steps of the race; we go westward as into the
future, with a spirit of enterprise and adventure. The Atlantic is a
Lethean stream, in our passage over which we have had an opportunity to forget the Old World and its institutions. If we do not
succeed this time, there is perhaps one more chance for the race left
before it arrives on the banks of the Styx; and that is in the Lethe of
the Pacific, which is three times as wide.

I know not how significant it is, or how far it is an evidence of
singularity, that an individual should thus consent in his pettiest walk
with the general movement of the race; but I know that something

akin to the migratory instinct in birds and quadrupeds, — which, in some instances, is known to have affected the squirrel tribe, impelling them to a general and mysterious movement, in which they were seen, say some, crossing the broadest rivers, each on its particular chip, with its tail raised for a sail, and bridging narrower streams with their dead, — that something like the *furor* which affects the domestic cattle in the spring, and which is referred to a worm in their tails, — affects both nations and individuals, either perennially or from time to time. Not a flock of wild geese cackles over our town, but it to some extent unsettles the value of real estate here, and, if I were a broker, I should probably take that disturbance into account.

> "Then longen folk to gon on pilgrimages,
> And palmeres for to seken strange strondes."

Every sunset which I witness inspires me with the desire to go to a West as distant and as fair as that into which the sun goes down. He appears to migrate westward daily, and tempt us to follow him. He is the Great Western Pioneer whom the nations follow. We dream all night of those mountain-ridges in the horizon, though they may be of vapor only, which were last gilded by his rays. The island of Atlantis, and the islands and gardens of the Hesperides, a sort of terrestrial paradise, appear to have been the Great West of the ancients, enveloped in mystery and poetry. Who has not seen in imagination, when looking into the sunset sky, the gardens of the Hesperides, and the foundation of all those fables?

Columbus felt the westward tendency more strongly than any before. He obeyed it, and found a New World for Castile and Leon. The herd of men in those days scented fresh pastures from afar.

> "And now the sun had stretched out all the hills,
> And now was dropped into the western bay;
> At last *he* rose, and twitched his mantle blue;
> To-morrow to fresh woods and pastures new."

Where on the globe can there be found an area of equal extent with that occupied by the bulk of our States, so fertile and so rich and varied in its productions, and at the same time so habitable by the European, as this is? Michaux, who knew but part of them, says that "the species of large trees are much more numerous in North America than in Europe; in the United States there are more than one hundred and forty species that exceed thirty feet in height; in France there are but thirty that attain this size." Later botanists more than confirm his observations. Humboldt came to America to realize his youthful dreams of a tropical vegetation, and he beheld it in its greatest perfection in the primitive forests of the Amazon, the most gigantic wilderness on the earth, which he has so eloquently described. The geographer Guyot, himself a European, goes farther, — farther than I am ready to follow him; yet not when he says, — "As the plant is made for the animal, as the vegetable world is made for the animal world, America is made for the man of the Old World. . . . The man of the Old World sets out upon his way. Leaving the highlands of Asia, he descends from station to station towards Europe. Each of his steps is marked by a new civilization superior to the preceding, by a greater power of development. Arrived at the Atlantic, he pauses on the shore of this unknown ocean, the bounds of which he knows not, and turns upon his footprints for an instant." When he has exhausted the rich soil of Europe, and reinvigorated himself, "then recommences his adventurous career westward as in the earliest ages." So far Guyot.

From this western impulse coming in contact with the barrier of the Atlantic sprang the commerce and enterprise of modern times. The younger Michaux, in his "Travels West of the Alleghanies in 1802," says that the common inquiry in the newly settled West was, " 'From what part of the world have you come?' As if these vast and fertile regions would naturally be the place of meeting and common country of all the inhabitants of the globe."

To use an obsolete Latin word, I might say, *Ex Oriente lux; ex Occidente* FRUX. From the East light; from the West fruit.

Sir Francis Head, an English traveller and a Governor-General of Canada, tells us that "in both the northern and southern hemispheres of the New World, Nature has not only outlined her works on a larger scale, but has painted the whole picture with brighter and more costly colors than she used in delineating and in beautifying the Old World. . . . The heavens of America appear infinitely higher, the sky is bluer, the air is fresher, the cold is intenser, the moon looks larger, the stars are brighter, the thunder is louder, the lightning is vivider, the wind is stronger, the rain is heavier, the mountains are higher, the rivers longer, the forests bigger, the plains broader." This statement will do at least to set against Buffon's account of this part of the world and its productions.

Linnæus said long ago, "Nescio quæ facies *læta, glabra* plantis Americanis: I know not what there is of joyous and smooth in the aspect of American plants"; and I think that in this country there are no, or at most very few, *Africanæ bestiæ*, African beasts, as the Romans called them, and that in this respect also it is peculiarly fitted for the habitation of man. We are told that within three miles of the centre of the East-Indian city of Singapore, some of the inhabitants are annually carried off by tigers; but the traveller can lie down in the woods at night almost anywhere in North America without fear of wild beasts.

These are encouraging testimonies. If the moon looks larger here than in Europe, probably the sun looks larger also. If the heavens of America appear infinitely higher, and the stars brighter, I trust that these facts are symbolical of the height to which the philosophy and poetry and religion of her inhabitants may one day soar. At length, perchance, the immaterial heaven will appear as much higher to the American mind, and the intimations that star it as much brighter. For I believe that climate does thus react on man, — as there is something in the mountain-air that feeds the spirit and inspires. Will not man grow to greater perfection intellectually as well as physically under these influences? Or is it unimportant how many foggy days there are in his life? I trust that we shall be more imaginative, that our thoughts will be clearer, fresher, and more ethereal, as our sky, — our understanding more comprehensive and broader, like our plains, — our intellect generally on a grander scale, like our thunder and lightning, our rivers and mountains and forests, — and our hearts shall even correspond in breadth and depth and grandeur to our inland seas. Perchance there will appear to the traveller something, he knows not what, of *læta* and *glabra*, of joyous and serene, in our very faces. Else to what end does the world go on, and why was America discovered?

To Americans I hardly need to say, —

"Westward the star of empire takes its way."

As a true patriot, I should be ashamed to think that Adam in paradise was more favorably situated on the whole than the backwoodsman in this country.

Our sympathies in Massachusetts are not confined to New England; though we may be estranged from the South, we sympathize with the West. There is the home of the younger sons, as among the Scandinavians they took to the sea for their inheritance. It is too late to be studying Hebrew; it is more important to understand even the slang of to-day.

Some months ago I went to see a panorama of the Rhine. It was like a dream of the Middle Ages. I floated down its historic stream in something more than imagination, under bridges built by the Romans, and repaired by later heroes, past cities and castles whose

very names were music to my ears, and each of which was the subject
of a legend. There were Ehrenbreitstein and Rolandseck and Co-
blentz, which I knew only in history. They were ruins that interested
me chiefly. There seemed to come up from its waters and its vine-
clad hills and valleys a hushed music as of Crusaders departing for
the Holy Land. I floated along under the spell of enchantment, as if
I had been transported to an heroic age, and breathed an atmosphere
of chivalry.

Soon after, I went to see a panorama of the Mississippi, and as I
worked my way up the river in the light of to-day, and saw the
steamboats wooding up, counted the rising cities, gazed on the fresh
ruins of Nauvoo, beheld the Indians moving west across the stream,
and, as before I had looked up the Moselle, now looked up the Ohio
and the Missouri, and heard the legends of Dubuque and of We-
nona's Cliff, — still thinking more of the future than of the past or
present, — I saw that this was a Rhine stream of a different kind;
that the foundations of castles were yet to be laid, and the famous
bridges were yet to be thrown over the river; and I felt that *this was
the heroic age itself*, though we know it not, for the hero is commonly
the simplest and obscurest of men.

The West of which I speak is but another name for the Wild; and
what I have been preparing to say is, that in Wildness is the preservation of the world. Every tree sends its fibres forth in search of the
Wild. The cities import it at any price. Men plough and sail for it.
From the forest and wilderness come the tonics and barks which
brace mankind. Our ancestors were savages. The story of Romulus
and Remus being suckled by a wolf is not a meaningless fable. The
founders of every State which has risen to eminence have drawn their
nourishment and vigor from a similar wild source. It was because the
children of the Empire were not suckled by the wolf that they were
conquered and displaced by the children of the Northern forests who
were.

I believe in the forest, and in the meadow, and in the night in
which the corn grows. We require an infusion of hemlock-spruce or
arbor-vitæ in our tea. There is a difference between eating and
drinking for strength and from mere gluttony. The Hottentots ea-
gerly devour the marrow of the koodoo and other antelopes raw, as
a matter of course. Some of our Northern Indians eat raw the marrow
of the Arctic reindeer, as well as various other parts, including the
summits of the antlers, as long as they are soft. And herein, perchance, they have stolen a march on the cooks of Paris. They get

what usually goes to feed the fire. This is probably better than stall-fed beef and slaughter-house pork to make a man of. Give me a wildness whose glance no civilization can endure, — as if we lived on the marrow of koodoos devoured raw.

There are some intervals which border the strain of the wood-thrush, to which I would migrate, — wild lands where no settler has squatted; to which, methinks, I am already acclimated.

The African hunter Cummings tells us that the skin of the eland, as well as that of most other antelopes just killed, emits the most delicious perfume of trees and grass. I would have every man so much like a wild antelope, so much a part and parcel of Nature, that his very person should thus sweetly advertise our senses of his presence, and remind us of those parts of Nature which he most haunts. I feel no disposition to be satirical, when the trapper's coat emits the odor of musquash even; it is a sweeter scent to me than that which commonly exhales from the merchant's or the scholar's garments. When I go into their wardrobes and handle their vestments, I am reminded of no grassy plains and flowery meads which they have frequented, but of dusty merchants' exchanges and libraries rather.

A tanned skin is something more than respectable, and perhaps olive is a fitter color than white for a man, — a denizen of the woods. "The pale white man!" I do not wonder that the African pitied him. Darwin the naturalist says, "A white man bathing by the side of a Tahitian was like a plant bleached by the gardener's art, compared with a fine, dark green one, growing vigorously in the open fields."

Ben Jonson exclaims, —

"How near to good is what is fair!"

So I would say, —

How near to good is what is *wild!*

Life consists with wildness. The most alive is the wildest. Not yet subdued to man, its presence refreshes him. One who pressed forward incessantly and never rested from his labors, who grew fast and made infinite demands on life, would always find himself in a new country or wilderness, and surrounded by the raw material of life. He would be climbing over the prostrate stems of primitive forest-trees.

Hope and the future for me are not in lawns and cultivated fields, not in towns and cities, but in the impervious and quaking swamps. When, formerly, I have analyzed my partiality for some farm which

I had contemplated purchasing, I have frequently found that I was attracted solely by a few square rods of impermeable and unfathomable bog, — a natural sink in one corner of it. That was the jewel which dazzled me. I derive more of my subsistence from the swamps which surround my native town than from the cultivated gardens in the village. There are no richer parterres to my eyes than the dense beds of dwarf andromeda (*Cassandra calyculata*) which cover these tender places on the earth's surface. Botany cannot go farther than tell me the names of the shrubs which grow there, — the high blueberry, panicled andromeda, lamb-kill, azalea, and rhodora, — all standing in the quaking sphagnum. I often think that I should like to have my house front on this mass of dull red bushes, omitting other flower plots and borders, transplanted spruce and trim box, even gravelled walks, — to have this fertile spot under my windows, not a few imported barrow-fulls of soil only to cover the sand which was thrown out in digging the cellar. Why not put my house, my parlor, behind this plot, instead of behind that meagre assemblage of curiosities, that poor apology for a Nature and Art, which I call my front-yard? It is an effort to clear up and make a decent appearance when the carpenter and mason have departed, though done as much for the passer-by as the dweller within. The most tasteful front-yard fence was never an agreeable object of study to me; the most elaborate ornaments, acorn-tops, or what not, soon wearied and disgusted me. Bring your sills up to the very edge of the swamp, then, (though it may not be the best place for a dry cellar,) so that there be no access on that side to citizens. Front-yards are not made to walk in, but, at most, through, and you could go in the back way.

Yes, though you may think me perverse, if it were proposed to me to dwell in the neighborhood of the most beautiful garden that ever human art contrived, or else of a dismal swamp, I should certainly decide for the swamp. How vain, then, have been all your labors, citizens, for me!

My spirits infallibly rise in proportion to the outward dreariness.

Give me the ocean, the desert, or the wilderness! In the desert, pure air and solitude compensate for want of moisture and fertility. The traveller Burton says of it, — "Your *morale* improves; you become frank and cordial, hospitable and single-minded. . . . In the desert, spirituous liquors excite only disgust. There is a keen enjoyment in a mere animal existence." They who have been travelling long on the steppes of Tartary say, — "On reëntering cultivated lands, the agitation, perplexity, and turmoil of civilization oppressed and suffocated us; the air seemed to fail us, and we felt every moment as if about to die of asphyxia." When I would recreate myself, I seek the darkest wood, the thickest and most interminable, and, to the citizen, most dismal swamp. I enter a swamp as a sacred place, — a *sanctum sanctorum*. There is the strength, the marrow of Nature. The wildwood covers the virgin mould, — and the same soil is good for men and for trees. A man's health requires as many acres of meadow to his prospect as his farm does loads of muck. There are the strong meats on which he feeds. A town is saved, not more by the righteous men in it than by the woods and swamps that surround it. A township where one primitive forest waves above, while another primitive forest rots below, — such a town is fitted to raise not only corn and potatoes, but poets and philosophers for the coming ages. In such a soil grew Homer and Confucius and the rest, and out of such a wilderness comes the Reformer eating locusts and wild honey.

To preserve wild animals implies generally the creation of a forest for them to dwell in or resort to. So is it with man. A hundred years ago they sold bark in our streets peeled from our own woods. In the very aspect of those primitive and rugged trees, there was, methinks, a tanning principle which hardened and consolidated the fibres of men's thoughts. Ah! already I shudder for these comparatively degenerate days of my native village, when you cannot collect a load of bark of good thickness, — and we no longer produce tar and turpentine.

The civilized nations — Greece, Rome, England — have been sustained by the primitive forests which anciently rotted where they stand. They survive as long as the soil is not exhausted. Alas for human culture! little is to be expected of a nation, when the vegetable mould is exhausted, and it is compelled to make manure of the bones of its fathers. There the poet sustains himself merely by his own superfluous fat, and the philosopher comes down on his marrow-bones.

It is said to be the task of the American "to work the virgin soil," and that "agriculture here already assumes proportions unknown everywhere else." I think that the farmer displaces the Indian even because he redeems the meadow, and so makes himself stronger and in some respects more natural. I was surveying for a man the other day a single straight line one hundred and thirty-two rods long, through a swamp, at whose entrance might have been written the words which Dante read over the entrance to the infernal regions, — "Leave all hope, ye that enter," — that is, of ever getting out again; where at one time I saw my employer actually up to his neck and swimming for his life in his property, though it was still winter. He had another similar swamp which I could not survey at all, because it was completely under water, and nevertheless, with regard to a third swamp, which I did *survey* from a distance, he remarked to me, true to his instincts, that he would not part with it for any consideration, on account of the mud which it contained. And that man intends to put a girdling ditch round the whole in the course of forty months, and so redeem it by the magic of his spade. I refer to him only as the type of a class.

The weapons with which we have gained our most important victories, which should be handed down as heirlooms from father to son, are not the sword and the lance, but the bush-whack, the turf-cutter, the spade, and the bog-hoe, rusted with the blood of many a meadow, and begrimed with the dust of many a hard-fought field. The very winds blew the Indian's cornfield into the meadow, and pointed out the way which he had not the skill to follow. He had no better implement with which to intrench himself in the land than a clamshell. But the farmer is armed with plough and space.

In Literature it is only the wild that attracts us. Dullness is but another name for tameness. It is the uncivilized free and wild thinking in "Hamlet" and the "Iliad," in all the Scriptures and Mythologies, not learned in the schools, that delights us. As the wild duck is more swift and beautiful than the tame, so is the wild — the mallard — thought, which 'mid falling dews wings its way above the fens. A truly good book is something as natural, and as unexpectedly and unaccountably fair and perfect, as a wild flower discovered on the prairies of the West or in the jungles of the East. Genius is a light which makes the darkness visible, like the lightning's flash, which perchance shatters the temple of knowledge itself, — and not a taper lighted at the hearth-stone of the race, which pales before the light of common day.

English literature, from the days of the minstrels to the Lake Poets, — Chaucer and Spenser and Milton, and even Shakespeare, included, — breathes no quite fresh and in this sense wild strain. It is an essentially tame and civilized literature, reflecting Greece and Rome. Her wilderness is a green-wood, — her wild man a Robin Hood. There is plenty of genial love of Nature, but not so much of Nature herself. Her chronicles inform us when her wild animals, but not when the wild man in her, became extinct.

The science of Humboldt is one thing, poetry is another thing. The poet to-day, notwithstanding all the discoveries of science, and the accumulated learning of mankind, enjoys no advantage over Homer.

Where is the literature which gives expression to Nature? He would be a poet who could impress the winds and streams into his service, to speak for him; who nailed words to their primitive senses, as farmers drive down stakes in the spring, which the frost has heaved; who derived his words as often as he used them, — transplanted them to his page with earth adhering to their roots; whose words were so true and fresh and natural that they would appear to expand like the buds at the approach of spring, though they lay half-smothered between two musty leaves in a library, — ay, to bloom and bear fruit there, after their kind, annually, for the faithful reader, in sympathy with surrounding Nature.

I do not know of any poetry to quote which adequately expresses this yearning for the Wild. Approached from this side, the best poetry is tame. I do not know where to find in any literature, ancient or modern, any account which contents me of that Nature with which even I am acquainted. You will perceive that I demand something which no Augustan nor Elizabethan age, which no *culture*, in short, can give. Mythology comes nearer to it than anything. How much more fertile a Nature, at least, has Grecian mythology its root in than English literature! Mythology is the crop which the Old World bore before its soil was exhausted, before the fancy and imagination were affected with blight; and which it still bears, wherever its pristine vigor is unabated. All other literatures endure only as the elms which overshadow our houses; but this is like the great dragon-tree of the Western Isles, as old as mankind, and, whether that does or not, will endure as long; for the decay of other literatures makes the soil in which it thrives.

The West is preparing to add its fables to those of the East. The valleys of the Ganges, the Nile, and the Rhine, having yielded their crop, it remains to be seen what the valleys of the Amazon, the Plate, the Orinoco, the St. Lawrence, and the Mississippi will produce. Perchance, when, in the course of ages, American liberty has become a fiction of the past, — as it is to some extent a fiction of the present, — the poets of the world will be inspired by American mythology.

The wildest dreams of wild men, even, are not the less true, though they may not recommend themselves to the sense which is most common among Englishmen and Americans to-day. It is not every truth that recommends itself to the common sense. Nature has a place for the wild clematis as well as for the cabbage. Some expressions of truth are reminiscent, — others merely *sensible,* as the phrase is, — others prophetic. Some forms of disease, even, may prophesy forms of health. The geologist has discovered that the figures of serpents, griffins, flying dragons, and other fanciful embellishments of heraldry, have their prototypes in the forms of fossil species which were extinct before man was created, and hence "indicate a faint and shadowy knowledge of a previous state of organic existence." The Hindoos dreamed that the earth rested on an elephant, and the elephant on a tortoise, and the tortoise on a serpent; and though it may be an unimportant coincidence, it will not be out of place here to state, that a fossil tortoise has lately been discovered in Asia large enough to support an elephant. I confess that I am partial to these wild fancies, which transcend the order of time and development. They are the sublimest recreation of the intellect. The partridge loves peas, but not those that go with her into the pot.

In short, all good things are wild and free. There is something in a strain of music, whether produced by an instrument or by the human voice, — take the sound of a bugle in a summer night, for instance, — which by its wildness, to speak without satire, reminds me of the cries emitted by wild beasts in their native forests. It is so much of their wildness as I can understand. Give me for my friends and neighbors wild men, not tame ones. The wildness of the savage is but a faint symbol of the awful ferity with which good men and lovers meet.

I love even to see the domestic animals reassert their native rights, — any evidence that they have not wholly lost their original wild habits and vigor; as when my neighbor's cow breaks out of her pasture early in the spring and boldly swims the river, a cold, gray tide, twenty-five or thirty rods wide, swollen by the melted snow. It is the buffalo crossing the Mississippi. This exploit confers some dignity on the herd in my eyes, — already dignified. The seeds of instinct are preserved under the thick hides of cattle and horses, like seeds in the bowels of the earth, an indefinite period.

Any sportiveness in cattle is unexpected. I saw one day a herd of a dozen bullocks and cows running about and frisking in unwieldy sport, like huge rats, even like kittens. They shook their heads, raised their tails, and rushed up and down a hill, and I perceived by their horns, as well as by their activity, their relation to the deer tribe. But, alas! a sudden loud *Whoa!* would have damped their ardor at once, reduced them from venison to beef, and stiffened their sides and sinews like the locomotive. Who but the Evil One has cried, "Whoa!" to mankind? Indeed, the life of cattle, like that of many men, is but a sort of locomotiveness; they move a side at a time, and man, by his machinery, is meeting the horse and ox half-way. Whatever part the whip has touched is thenceforth palsied. Who would ever think of a *side* of any of the supple cat tribe, as we speak of a *side* of beef?

I rejoice that horses and steers have to be broken before they can be made the slaves of men, and that men themselves have some wild oats still left to sow before they become submissive members of society. Undoubtedly, all men are not equally fit subjects for civilization; and because the majority, like dogs and sheep, are tame by inherited disposition, this is no reason why the others should have their natures broken that they may be reduced to the same level. Men are in the main alike, but they were made several in order that they might be various. If a low use is to be served, one man will do nearly or quite as well as another; if a high one, individual excellence is to be regarded. Any man can stop a hole to keep the wind away, but no other man could serve so rare a use as the author of this illustration did. Confucius says, — "The skins of the tiger and the leopard, when they are tanned, are as the skins of the dog and the sheep tanned." But it is not the part of a true culture to tame tigers, any more than it is to make sheep ferocious; and tanning their skins for shoes is not the best use to which they can be put.

When looking over a list of men's names in a foreign language, as of military officers, or of authors who have written on a particular subject, I am reminded once more that there is nothing in a name. The name Menschikoff, for instance, has nothing in it to my ears more human than a whisker, and it may belong to a rat. As the names of the Poles and Russians are to us, so are ours to them. It is as if they had been named by the child's rigmarole, — *Iery wiery ichery van, tittle-tol-tan.* I see in my mind a herd of wild creatures swarming over the earth, and to each the herdsman has affixed some barbarous sound in his own dialect. The names of men are of course as cheap and meaningless as *Rose* and *Tray*, the names of dogs.

Methinks it would be some advantage to philosophy, if men were named merely in the gross, as they are known. It would be necessary only to know the genus, and perhaps the race or variety, to know the individual. We are not prepared to believe that every private soldier in a Roman army had a name of his own, — because we have not supposed that he had a character of his own. At present our only true names are nicknames. I knew a boy who, from his peculiar energy, was called "Buster" by his playmates, and this rightly supplanted his Christian name. Some travellers tell us that an Indian had no name given him at first, but earned it, and his name was his fame; and among some tribes he acquired a new name with every new exploit. It is pitiful when a man bears a name for convenience merely, who has earned neither name nor fame.

I will not allow mere names to make distinctions for me, but still see men in herds for all them. A familiar name cannot make a man less strange to me. It may be given to a savage who retains in secret his own wild title earned in the woods. We have a wild savage in us, and a savage name is perchance somewhere recorded as ours. I see that my neighbor, who bears the familiar epithet William, or Edwin, takes it off with his jacket. It does not adhere to him when asleep or in anger, or aroused by any passion or inspiration. I seem to hear pronounced by some of his kin at such a time his original wild name in some jaw-breaking or else melodious tongue.

Here is this vast, savage, howling mother of ours, Nature, lying all around, with such beauty, and such affection for her children, as the leopard; and yet we are so early weaned from her breast to society, to that culture which is exclusively an interaction of man on man, — a sort of breeding in and in, which produces at most a merely English nobility, a civilization destined to have a speedy limit.

In society, in the best institutions of men, it is easy to detect a certain precocity. When we should still be growing children, we are already little men. Give me a culture which imports much muck from the meadows, and deepens the soil, — not that which trusts to heating manures, and improved implements and modes of culture only!

Many a poor sore-eyed student that I have heard of would grow faster, both intellectually and physically, if, instead of sitting up so very late, he honestly slumbered a fool's allowance.

There may be an excess even of informing light. Niépce, a Frenchman, discovered "actinism," that power in the sun's rays which produces a chemical effect, — that granite rocks, and stone structures, and statues of metal, "are all alike destructively acted upon during the hours of sunshine, and, but for provisions of Nature no less wonderful, would soon perish under the delicate touch of the most subtile of the agencies of the universe." But he observed that "those bodies which underwent this change during the daylight possessed the power of restoring themselves to their original conditions during the hours of night, when this excitement was no longer influencing them." Hence it has been inferred that "the hours of darkness are as necessary to the inorganic creation as we know night and sleep are to the organic kingdom." Not even does the moon shine every night, but gives place to darkness.

I would not have every man nor every part of a man cultivated, any more than I would have every acre of earth cultivated: part will be tillage, but the greater part will be meadow and forest, not only serving an immediate use, but preparing a mould against a distant future, by the annual decay of the vegetation which it supports.

There are other letters for the child to learn than those which Cadmus invented. The Spaniards have a good term to express this wild and dusky knowledge, — *Gramática parda,* tawny grammar, — a kind of mother-wit derived from that same leopard to which I have referred.

We have heard of a Society for the Diffusion of Useful Knowledge. It is said that knowledge is power; and the like. Methinks there is equal need of a Society for the Diffusion of Useful Ignorance, what we will call Beautiful Knowledge, a knowledge useful in a higher sense: for what is most of our boasted so-called knowledge but a conceit that we know something, which robs us of the advantage of our actual ignorance? What we call knowledge is often our positive ignorance; ignorance our negative knowledge. By long years of patient industry and reading of the newspapers — for what are the libraries of science but files of newspapers? — a man accumulates a myriad facts, lays them up in his memory, and then when in some spring of his life he saunters abroad into the Great Fields of thought, he, as it were, goes to grass like a horse, and leaves all his harness behind in the stable. I would say to the Society for the Diffusion of Useful Knowledge, sometimes, — Go to grass. You have eaten hay long enough. The spring has come with its green crop. The very cows are driven to their country pastures before the end of May; though I have heard of one unnatural farmer who kept his cow in the barn and fed her on hay all the year round. So, frequently, the Society for the Diffusion of Useful Knowledge treats its cattle.

A man's ignorance sometimes is not only useful, but beautiful, — while his knowledge, so called, is oftentimes worse than useless, besides being ugly. Which is the best man to deal with, — he who knows nothing about a subject, and, what is extremely rare, knows that he knows nothing, or he who really knows something about it, but thinks that he knows all?

My desire for knowledge is intermittent; but my desire to bathe my head in atmospheres unknown to my feet is perennial and constant. The highest that we can attain to is not Knowledge, but Sympathy with Intelligence. I do not know that this higher knowledge amounts to anything more definite than a novel and grand surprise on a sudden revelation of the insufficiency of all that we called Knowledge before, — a discovery that there are more things in heaven and earth than are dreamed of in our philosophy. It is the lighting up of the mist by the sun. Man cannot *know* in any higher sense than this, any more than he can look serenely and with impunity in the face of the sun:Ωζ τὶ νοῶν, οὐ κεῖνον νοήσειζ, — "You will not perceive that, as perceiving a particular thing," say the Chaldean Oracles.

There is something servile in the habit of seeking after a law which we may obey. We may study the laws of matter at and for our convenience, but a successful life knows no law. It is an unfortunate discovery certainly, that of a law which binds us where we did not know before we were bound. Live free, child of the mist, — and with respect to knowledge we are all children of the mist. The man who takes the liberty to live is superior to all the laws, by virtue of his relation to the law-maker. "That is active duty," says the Vishnu Purana, "which is not for our bondage; that is knowledge which is for our liberation: all other duty is good only unto weariness; all other knowledge is only the cleverness of an artist."

It is remarkable how few events or crises there are in our histories; how little exercised we have been in our minds; how few experiences we have had. I would fain be assured that I am growing apace and rankly, though my very growth disturb this dull equanimity, — though it be with struggle through long, dark, muggy nights or seasons of gloom. It would be well, if all our lives were a divine tragedy even, instead of this trivial comedy or farce. Dante, Bunyan, and others, appear to have been exercised in their minds more than we: they were subjected to a kind of culture such as our district schools and colleges do not contemplate. Even Mahomet, though many may scream at his name, had a good deal more to live for, ay, and to die for, than they have commonly.

When, at rare intervals, some thought visits one, as perchance he is walking on a railroad, then indeed the cars go by without his hearing them. But soon, by some inexorable law, our life goes by and the cars return.

"Gentle breeze, that wanderest unseen,
And bendest the thistles round Loira of storms,
Traveller of the windy glens,
Why hast thou left my ear so soon?"

While almost all men feel an attraction drawing them to society, few are attracted strongly to Nature. In their relation to Nature men appear to me for the most part, notwithstanding their arts, lower than the animals. It is not often a beautiful relation, as in the case of the animals. How little appreciation of the beauty of the landscape there is among us! We have to be told that the Greeks called the world Κόσμος, Beauty, or Order, but we do not see clearly why they did so, and we esteem it at best only a curious philological fact.

For my part, I feel that with regard to Nature I live a sort of border life, on the confines of a world into which I make occasional and transient forays only, and my patriotism and allegiance to the State into whose territories I seem to retreat are those of a moss-trooper. Unto a life which I call natural I would gladly follow even a will-o'-the-wisp through bogs and sloughs unimaginable, but no moon nor fire-fly has shown me the causeway to it. Nature is a personality so vast and universal that we have never seen one of her features. The walker in the familiar fields which stretch around my native town sometimes finds himself in another land than is described in their owners' deeds, as it were in some faraway field on the confines of the actual Concord, where her jurisdiction ceases, and the idea which the word Concord suggests ceases to be suggested. These farms which I have myself surveyed, these bounds which I have set up appear dimly still as through a mist; but they have no chemistry to fix them; they fade from the surface of the glass; and the picture which the painter painted stands out dimly from beneath. The world with which we are commonly acquainted leaves no trace, and it will have no anniversary.

I took a walk on Spaulding's Farm the other afternoon. I saw the setting sun lighting up the opposite side of a stately pine wood. Its golden rays straggled into the aisles of the wood as into some noble hall. I was impressed as if some ancient and altogether admirable and shining family had settled there in that part of the land called Concord, unknown to me, — to whom the sun was servant, — who had not gone into society in the village, — who had not been called on. I saw their park, their pleasure-ground, beyond through the wood, in Spaulding's cranberry-meadow. The pines furnished them with gables as they grew. Their house was not obvious to vision; the trees grew through it. I do not know whether I heard the sounds of a suppressed hilarity or not. They seemed to recline on the sunbeams. They have sons and daughters. They are quite well. The farmer's cart-path, which leads directly through their hall, does not in the least put them out, — as the muddy bottom of a pool is sometimes seen through the reflected skies. They never heard of Spaulding, and do not know that he is their neighbor, — notwithstanding I heard him whistle as he drove his team through the house. Nothing can equal the serenity of their lives. Their coat of arms is simply a lichen. I saw it painted on the pines and oaks. Their attics were in the tops of the trees. They are of no politics. There was no noise of labor. I did not perceive that they were weaving or spinning. Yet I did detect, when the wind lulled and hearing was done away, the finest imaginable sweet musical hum, — as of a distant hive in May, which perchance was the sound of their thinking. They had no idle thoughts, and no one without could see their work, for their industry was not as in knots and excrescences embayed.

But I find it difficult to remember them. They fade irrevocably out of my mind even now while I speak and endeavor to recall them, and recollect myself. It is only after a long and serious effort to recollect my best thoughts that I become again aware of their cohabitancy. If it were not for such families as this, I think I should move out of Concord.

We are accustomed to say in New England that few and fewer pigeons visit us every year. Our forests furnish no mast for them. So, it would seem, few and fewer thoughts visit each growing man from year to year, for the grove in our minds is laid waste, — sold to feed unnecessary fires of ambition, or sent to mill, and there is scarcely a twig left for them to perch on. They no longer build nor breed with us. In some more genial season, perchance, a faint shadow flits across the landscape of the mind, cast by the *wings* of some thought in its vernal or autumnal migration, but, looking up, we are unable to detect the substance of the thought itself. Our winged thoughts are turned to poultry. They no longer soar, and they attain only to a Shanghai and Cochin-China grandeur. Those *gra-a-ate thoughts,* those *gra-a-ate men* you hear of!

We hug the earth, — how rarely we mount! Methinks we might elevate ourselves a little more. We might climb a tree, at least. I found my account in climbing a tree once. It was a tall white pine, on the top of a hill; and though I got well pitched, I was well paid for it, for I discovered new mountains in the horizon which I had never seen before, — so much more of the earth and the heavens. I might have walked about the foot of the tree for threescore years and ten, and yet I certainly should never have seen them. But, above all, I discovered around me, — it was near the end of June, — on the ends of the topmost branches only, a few minute and delicate red cone-like blossoms, the fertile flower of the white pine looking heavenward. I carried straightway to the village the topmost spire, and showed it to stranger jurymen who walked the streets, — for it was court-week, — and to farmers and lumber-dealers and wood-choppers and hunters, and not one had ever seen the like before, but they wondered as at a star dropped down. Tell of ancient architects finishing their works on the tops of columns as perfectly as on the lower and more visible parts! Nature has from the first expanded the minute blossoms of the forest only toward the heavens, above men's heads and unobserved by them. We see only the flowers that are under our feet in the meadows. The pines have developed their delicate blossoms on the highest twigs of the wood every summer for ages, as well over the heads of Nature's red children as of her white ones; yet scarcely a farmer or hunter in the land has ever seen them.

Above all, we cannot afford not to live in the present. He is blessed over all mortals who loses no moment of the passing life in remembering the past. Unless our philosophy hears the cock crow in every barn-yard within our horizon, it is belated. That sound commonly reminds us that we are growing rusty and antique in our employments and habits of thought. His philosophy comes down to a more recent time than ours. There is something suggested by it that is a newer testament, — the gospel according to this moment. He has not fallen astern; he has got up early, and kept up early, and to be where he is is to be in season, in the foremost rank of time. It is an expression of the health and soundness of Nature, a brag for all the world, — healthiness as of a spring burst forth, a new fountain of the Muses, to celebrate this last instant of time. Where he lives no fugitive slave laws are passed. Who has not betrayed his master many times since last he heard that note?

The merit of this bird's strain is in its freedom from all plaintiveness. The singer can easily move us to tears or to laughter, but where is he who can excite in us a pure morning joy? When, in doleful dumps, breaking the awful stillness of our wooden sidewalk on a Sunday, or, perchance, a watcher in the house of mourning, I hear a cockerel crow far or near, I think to myself, "There is one of us well, at any rate," — and with a sudden gush return to my senses.

*

We had a remarkable sunset one day last November. I was walking in a meadow, the source of a small brook, when the sun at last, just before setting, after a cold gray day, reached a clear stratum in the horizon, and the softest, brightest morning sunlight fell on the dry grass and on the stems of the trees in the opposite horizon, and on the leaves of the shrub-oaks on the hill-side, while our shadows stretched long over the meadow eastward, as if we were the only motes in its beams. It was such a light as we could not have imagined a moment before, and the air also was so warm and serene that nothing was wanting to make a paradise of that meadow. When we reflected that this was not a solitary phenomenon, never to happen again, but that it would happen forever and ever an infinite number of evenings, and cheer and reassure the latest child that walked there, it was more glorious still.

The sun sets on some retired meadow, where no house is visible, with all the glory and splendor that it lavishes on cities, and, perchance, as it has never set before, — where there is but a solitary marsh-hawk to have his wings gilded by it, or only a musquash looks out from his cabin, and there is some little black-veined brook in the midst of the marsh, just beginning to meander, winding slowly round a decaying stump. We walked in so pure and bright a light, gilding the withered grass and leaves, so softly and serenely bright, I thought I had never bathed in such a golden flood, without a ripple or a murmur to it. The west side of every wood and rising ground gleamed like the boundary of Elysium, and the sun on our backs seemed like a gentle herdsman driving us home at evening.

So we saunter toward the Holy Land, till one day the sun shall shine more brightly than ever he has done, shall perchance shine into our minds and hearts, and light up our whole lives with a great awakening light, as warm and serene and golden as on a bank-side in autumn.

JOHN MUIR
(1838–1914)

&. The water ouzel, a bird Muir initially met in his grand "first summer in the Sierra" in 1869, pleased him to the heart with its absolute embodiment of wildness. His description of the bird is notable for its synthesis of expository writing, scientific accuracy, and pure, unsentimental love, and for its author's unmistakable identification with his subject. His sense of a deeper import in his experience of this bird first surfaced in a letter to his early adviser, Mrs. Jeanne Carr, in 1874: "I have ouzel tales to tell. . . . I am hopelessly and forever a mountaineer. . . . Civilization and fever and all the morbidness that has been hooted at me have not dimmed my glacial eye, and I care to live only to entice people to look at Nature's loveliness. My own special self is nothing."

The Water-Ouzel

THE WATERFALLS of the Sierra are frequented by only one bird, — the Ouzel or Water Thrush (*Cinclus Mexicanus*, Sw.). He is a singularly joyous and lovable little fellow, about the size of a robin, clad in a plain waterproof suit of bluish gray, with a tinge of chocolate on the head and shoulders. In form he is about as smoothly plump and compact as a pebble that has been whirled in a pot-hole, the flowing contour of his body being interrupted only by his strong feet and bill, the crisp wing-tips, and the up-slanted wren-like tail.

Among all the countless waterfalls I have met in the course of ten years' exploration in the Sierra, whether among the icy peaks, or warm foot-hills, or in the profound yosemitic cañons of the middle

From *The Mountains of California* (1894)

region, not one was found without its Ouzel. No cañon is too cold for this little bird, none too lonely, provided it be rich in falling water. Find a fall, or cascade, or rushing rapid, anywhere upon a clear stream, and there you will surely find its complementary Ouzel, flitting about in the spray, diving in foaming eddies, whirling like a leaf among beaten foam-bells; ever vigorous and enthusiastic, yet self-contained, and neither seeking nor shunning your company.

If disturbed while dipping about in the margin shallows, he either sets off with a rapid whir to some other feeding-ground up or down the stream, or alights on some half-submerged rock or snag out in the current, and immediately begins to nod and courtesy like a wren, turning his head from side to side with many other odd dainty movements that never fail to fix the attention of the observer.

He is the mountain streams' own darling, the humming-bird of blooming waters, loving rocky ripple-slopes and sheets of foam as a bee loves flowers, as a lark loves sunshine and meadows. Among all the mountain birds, none has cheered me so much in my lonely wanderings, — none so unfailingly. For both in winter and summer he sings, sweetly, cheerily, independent alike of sunshine and of love, requiring no other inspiration than the stream on which he dwells. While water sings, so must he, in heat or cold, calm or storm, ever attuning his voice in sure accord; low in the drought of summer and the drought of winter, but never silent.

During the golden days of Indian summer, after most of the snow has been melted, and the mountain streams have become feeble, — a succession of silent pools, linked together by shallow, transparent currents and strips of silvery lacework, — then the song of the Ouzel is at its lowest ebb. But as soon as the winter clouds have bloomed, and the mountain treasuries are once more replenished with snow, the voices of the streams and ouzels increase in strength and richness until the flood season of early summer. Then the torrents chant their noblest anthems, and then is the flood-time of our songster's melody. As for weather, dark days and sun days are the same to him. The voices of most song-birds, however joyous, suffer a long winter eclipse; but the Ouzel sings on through all the seasons and every kind of storm. Indeed no storm can be more violent than those of the waterfalls in the midst of which he delights to dwell. However dark and boisterous the weather, snowing, blowing, or cloudy, all the same he sings, and with never a note of sadness. No need of spring sunshine to thaw *his* song, for it never freezes. Never shall you hear anything wintry from *his* warm breast; no pinched cheeping, no wavering notes between sorrow and joy; his mellow, fluty voice is ever tuned to downright gladness, as free from dejection as cock-crowing.

It is pitiful to see wee frost-pinched sparrows on cold mornings in the mountain groves shaking the snow from their feathers, and hopping about as if anxious to be cheery, then hastening back to their hidings out of the wind, puffing out their breast-feathers over their toes, and subsiding among the leaves, cold and breakfastless, while the snow continues to fall, and there is no sign of clearing. But the Ouzel never calls forth a single touch of pity; not because he is strong to endure, but rather because he seems to live a charmed life beyond the reach of every influence that makes endurance necessary.

One wild winter morning, when Yosemite Valley was swept its length from west to east by a cordial snow-storm, I sallied forth to see what I might learn and enjoy. A sort of gray, gloaming-like darkness filled the valley, the huge walls were out of sight, all ordinary sounds were smothered, and even the loudest booming of the falls was at times buried beneath the roar of the heavy-laden blast. The loose snow was already over five feet deep on the meadows, making extended walks impossible without the aid of snow-shoes. I found no great difficulty, however, in making my way to a certain ripple on the river where one of my ouzels lived. He was at home, busily gleaning his breakfast among the pebbles of a shallow portion of the margin, apparently unaware of anything extraordinary in the weather. Presently he flew out to a stone against which the icy current was beating, and turning his back to the wind, sang as delightfully as a lark in springtime.

After spending an hour or two with my favorite, I made my way across the valley, boring and wallowing through the drifts, to learn as definitely as possible how the other birds were spending their time. The Yosemite birds are easily found during the winter because all of them excepting the Ouzel are restricted to the sunny north side of the valley, the south side being constantly eclipsed by the great frosty shadow of the wall. And because the Indian Cañon groves, from their peculiar exposure, are the warmest, the birds congregate there, more especially in severe weather.

I found most of the robins cowering on the lee side of the larger branches where the snow could not fall upon them, while two or three of the more enterprising were making desperate efforts to reach the mistletoe berries by clinging nervously to the under side of the snow-crowned masses, back downward, like woodpeckers. Every now and then they would dislodge some of the loose fringes of the snow-crown, which would come sifting down on them and send them screaming back to camp, where they would subside among their companions with a shiver, muttering in low, querulous chatter like hungry children.

Some of the sparrows were busy at the feet of the larger trees gleaning seeds and benumbed insects, joined now and then by a robin weary of his unsuccessful attempts upon the snow-covered berries. The brave woodpeckers were clinging to the snowless sides of the larger boles and overarching branches of the camp trees, making short flights from side to side of the grove, pecking now and then at the acorns they had stored in the bark, and chattering aimlessly as if unable to keep still, yet evidently putting in the time in a very dull way, like storm-bound travelers at a country tavern. The hardy nut-hatches were threading the open furrows of the trunks in their usual industrious manner, and uttering their quaint notes, evidently less distressed than their neighbors. The Steller jays were of course making more noisy stir than all the other birds combined; ever coming and going with loud bluster, screaming as if each had a lump of melting sludge in his throat, and taking good care to improve the favorable opportunity afforded by the storm to steal from the acorn stores of the woodpeckers. I also noticed one solitary gray eagle braving the storm on the top of a tall pine-stump just outside the main grove. He was standing bolt upright with his back to the wind, a tuft of snow piled on his square shoulders, a monument of passive endurance. Thus every snow-bound bird seemed more or less uncomfortable if not in positive distress. The storm was reflected in every gesture, and not one cheerful note, not to say song, came from a single bill; their cowering, joyless endurance offering a striking contrast to the spontaneous, irrepressible gladness of the Ouzel, who could no more help exhaling sweet song than a rose sweet fragrance. He *must* sing though the heavens fall. I remember noticing the distress of a pair of robins during the violent earthquake of the year 1872, when the pines of the Valley, with strange movements, flapped and waved their branches, and beetling rock-brows came thundering down to the meadows in tremendous avalanches. It did not occur to me in the midst of the excitement of other observations to look for the ouzels, but I doubt not they were singing straight on through it all, regarding the terrible rock-thunder as fearlessly as they do the booming of the waterfalls.

What may be regarded as the separate songs of the Ouzel are exceedingly difficult of description, because they are so variable and at the same time so confluent. Though I have been acquainted with my favorite ten years, and during most of this time have heard him sing nearly every day, I still detect notes and strains that seem new to me. Nearly all of his music is sweet and tender, lapsing from his round breast like water over the smooth lip of a pool, then breaking farther on into a sparkling foam of melodious notes, which glow with subdued enthusiasm, yet without expressing much of the strong, gushing ecstasy of the bobolink or skylark.

The more striking strains are perfect arabesques of melody, composed of a few full, round, mellow notes, embroidered with delicate trills which fade and melt in long slender cadences. In a general way his music is that of the streams refined and spiritualized. The deep booming notes of the falls are in it, the trills of rapids, the gurgling of margin eddies, the low whispering of level reaches, and the sweet tinkle of separate drops oozing from the ends of mosses and falling into tranquil pools.

The Ouzel never sings in chorus with other birds, nor with his kind, but only with the streams. And like flowers that bloom beneath the surface of the ground, some of our favorite's best song-blossoms never rise above the surface of the heavier music of the water. I have often observed him singing in the midst of beaten spray, his music completely buried beneath the water's roar; yet I knew he was surely singing by his gestures and the movements of his bill.

His food, as far as I have noticed, consists of all kinds of water insects, which in summer are chiefly procured along shallow margins. Here he wades about ducking his head under water and deftly turning over pebbles and fallen leaves with his bill, seldom choosing to go into deep water where he has to use his wings in diving.

He seems to be especially fond of the larvæ of mosquitos, found in abundance attached to the bottom of smooth rock channels where the current is shallow. When feeding in such places he wades upstream, and often while his head is under water the swift current is deflected upward along the glossy curves of his neck and shoulders, in the form of a clear, crystalline shell, which fairly encloses him like a bell-glass, the shell being broken and re-formed as he lifts and dips his head; while ever and anon he sidles out to where the too powerful current carries him off his feet; then he dexterously rises on the wing and goes gleaning again in shallower places.

But during the winter, when the stream-banks are embossed in snow, and the streams themselves are chilled nearly to the freezing-point, so that the snow falling into them in stormy weather is not wholly dissolved, but forms a thin, blue sludge, thus rendering the current opaque — then he seeks the deeper portions of the main rivers, where he may dive to clear water beneath the sludge. Or he repairs to some open lake or mill-pond, at the bottom of which he feeds in safety.

When thus compelled to betake himself to a lake, he does not plunge into it at once like a duck, but always alights in the first place upon some rock or fallen pine along the shore. Then flying out thirty or forty yards, more or less, according to the character of the bottom, he alights with a dainty glint on the surface, swims about, looks down, finally makes up his mind, and disappears with a sharp stroke of his wings. After feeding for two or three minutes he suddenly reappears, showers the water from his wings with one vigorous shake, and rises abruptly into the air as if pushed up from beneath, comes back to his perch, sings a few minutes, and goes out to dive again; thus coming and going, singing and diving at the same place for hours.

The Ouzel is usually found singly; rarely in pairs, excepting during the breeding season, and *very* rarely in threes or fours. I once observed three thus spending a winter morning in company, upon a small glacier lake, on the Upper Merced, about 7500 feet above the level of the sea. A storm had occurred during the night, but the morning sun shone unclouded, and the shadowy lake, gleaming darkly in its setting of fresh snow, lay smooth and motionless as a mirror. My camp chanced to be within a few feet of the water's edge, opposite a fallen pine, some of the branches of which leaned out over the lake. Here my three dearly welcome visitors took up their station, and at once began to embroider the frosty air with their delicious melody, doubly delightful to me that particular morning, as I had been somewhat apprehensive of danger in breaking my way down through the snow-choked cañons to the lowlands.

The portion of the lake bottom selected for a feeding-ground lies at a depth of fifteen or twenty feet below the surface, and is covered

with a short growth of algæ and other aquatic plants, — facts I had previously determined while sailing over it on a raft. After alighting on the glassy surface, they occasionally indulged in a little play, chasing one another round about in small circles; then all three would suddenly dive together, and then come ashore and sing.

The Ouzel seldom swims more than a few yards on the surface, for, not being web-footed, he makes rather slow progress, but by means of his strong, crisp wings he swims, or rather flies, with celerity under the surface, often to considerable distances. But it is in withstanding the force of heavy rapids that his strength of wing in this respect is most strikingly manifested. The following may be regarded as a fair illustration of his power of sub-aquatic flight. One stormy morning in winter when the Merced River was blue and green with unmelted snow, I observed one of my ouzels perched on a snag out in the midst of a swift-rushing rapid, singing cheerily, as if everything was just to his mind; and while I stood on the bank admiring him, he suddenly plunged into the sludgy current, leaving his song abruptly broken off. After feeding a minute or two at the bottom, and when one would suppose that he must inevitably be swept far down-stream, he emerged just where he went down, alighted on the same snag, showered the water-beads from his feathers, and continued his unfinished song, seemingly in tranquil ease as if it had suffered no interruption.

The Ouzel alone of all birds dares to enter a white torrent. And though strictly terrestrial in structure, no other is so inseparably related to water, not even the duck, or the bold ocean albatross, or the stormy-petrel. For ducks go ashore as soon as they finish feeding in undisturbed places, and very often make long flights overland from lake to lake or field to field. The same is true of most other aquatic birds. But the Ouzel, born on the brink of a stream, or on a snag or boulder in the midst of it, seldom leaves it for a single moment. For, notwithstanding he is often on the wing, he never flies overland, but whirs with rapid, quail-like beat above the stream, tracing all its windings. Even when the stream is quite small, say from five to ten feet wide, he seldom shortens his flight by crossing a bend, however abrupt it may be; and even when disturbed by meeting some one on the bank, he prefers to fly over one's head, to dodging out over the ground. When, therefore, his flight along a crooked stream is viewed endwise, it appears most strikingly wavered — a description on the air of every curve with lightning-like rapidity.

The vertical curves and angles of the most precipitous torrents he traces with the same rigid fidelity, swooping down the inclines of cascades, dropping sheer over dizzy falls amid the spray, and ascend-

ing with the same fearlessness and ease, seldom seeking to lessen the
steepness of the acclivity by beginning to ascend before reaching the
base of the fall. No matter though it may be several hundred feet in
height he holds straight on, as if about to dash headlong into the
throng of booming rockets, then darts abruptly upward, and, after
alighting at the top of the precipice to rest a moment, proceeds to
feed and sing. His flight is solid and impetuous, without any inter-
mission of wing-beats, — one homogeneous buzz like that of a laden
bee on its way home. And while thus buzzing freely from fall to fall,
he is frequently heard giving utterance to a long outdrawn train of
unmodulated notes, in no way connected with his song, but corre-
sponding closely with his flight in sustained vigor.

Were the flights of all the ouzels in the Sierra traced on a chart,
they would indicate the direction of the flow of the entire system of
ancient glaciers, from about the period of the breaking up of the ice-
sheet until near the close of the glacial winter; because the streams
which the ouzels so rigidly follow are, with the unimportant exceptions of a few side tributaries, all flowing in channels eroded for them
out of the solid flank of the range by the vanished glaciers, — the
streams tracing the ancient glaciers, the ouzels tracing the streams.
Nor do we find so complete compliance to glacial conditions in the
life of any other mountain bird, or animal of any kind. Bears frequently accept the pathways laid down by glaciers as the easiest to
travel; but they often leave them and cross over from cañon to cañon.
So also, most of the birds trace the moraines to some extent, because
the forests are growing on them. But they wander far, crossing the
cañons from grove to grove, and draw exceedingly angular and
complicated courses.

The Ouzel's nest is one of the most extraordinary pieces of bird
architecture I ever saw, odd and novel in design, perfectly fresh and
beautiful, and in every way worthy of the genius of the little builder.
It is about a foot in diameter, round and bossy in outline, with
a neatly arched opening near the bottom, somewhat like an old-
fashioned brick oven, or Hottentot's hut. It is built almost exclusively
of green and yellow mosses, chiefly the beautiful fronded hypnum
that covers the rocks and old drift-logs in the vicinity of waterfalls.
These are deftly interwoven, and felted together into a charming
little hut; and so situated that many of the outer mosses continue to
flourish as if they had not been plucked. A few fine, silky-stemmed
grasses are occasionally found interwoven with the mosses, but, with
the exception of a thin layer lining the floor, their presence seems
accidental, as they are of a species found growing with the mosses
and are probably plucked with them. The site chosen for this curious

mansion is usually some little rock-shelf within reach of the lighter particles of the spray of a waterfall, so that its walls are kept green and growing, at least during the time of high water.

No harsh lines are presented by any portion of the nest as seen in place, but when removed from its shelf, the back and bottom, and sometimes a portion of the top, is found quite sharply angular, because it is made to conform to the surface of the rock upon which and against which it is built, the little architect always taking advantage of slight crevices and protuberances that may chance to offer, to render his structure stable by means of a kind of gripping and dovetailing.

In choosing a building-spot, concealment does not seem to be taken into consideration; yet notwithstanding the nest is large and guilelessly exposed to view, it is far from being easily detected, chiefly because it swells forward like any other bulging moss-cushion growing naturally in such situations. This is more especially the case where the nest is kept fresh by being well sprinkled. Sometimes these romantic little huts have their beauty enhanced by rock-ferns and grasses that spring up around the mossy walls, or in front of the door-sill, dripping with crystal beads.

Furthermore, at certain hours of the day, when the sunshine is poured down at the required angle, the whole mass of the spray enveloping the fairy establishment is brilliantly irised; and it is through so glorious a rainbow atmosphere as this that some of our blessed ouzels obtain their first peep at the world.

Ouzels seem so completely part and parcel of the streams they inhabit, they scarce suggest any other origin than the streams themselves; and one might almost be pardoned in fancying they come direct from the living waters, like flowers from the ground. At least, from whatever cause, it never occurred to me to look for their nests until more than a year after I had made the acquaintance of the birds themselves, although I found one the very day on which I began the search. In making my way from Yosemite to the glaciers at the heads of the Merced and Tuolumne rivers, I camped in a particularly wild and romantic portion of the Nevada cañon where in previous excursions I had never failed to enjoy the company of my favorites, who were attracted here, no doubt, by the safe nesting-places in the shelving rocks, and by the abundance of food and falling water. The river, for miles above and below, consists of a succession of small falls from ten to sixty feet in height, connected by flat, plume-like cascades that go flashing from fall to fall, free and almost channelless, over waving folds of glacier-polished granite.

On the south side of one of the falls, that portion of the precipice which is bathed by the spray presents a series of little shelves and tab-lets caused by the development of planes of cleavage in the granite, and by the consequent fall of masses through the action of the water. "Now here," said I, "of all places, is the most charming spot for an Ouzel's nest." Then carefully scanning the fretted face of the precipice through the spray, I at length noticed a yellowish moss-cushion, grow-ing on the edge of a level tablet within five or six feet of the outer folds of the fall. But apart from the fact of its being situated where one acquainted with the lives of ouzels would fancy an Ouzel's nest ought to be, there was nothing in its appearance visible at first sight, to distin-guish it from other bosses of rock-moss similarly situated with refer-ence to perennial spray; and it was not until I had scrutinized it again and again, and had removed my shoes and stockings and crept along the face of the rock within eight or ten feet of it, that I could decide certainly whether it was a nest or a natural growth.

In these moss huts three or four eggs are laid, white like foam-bubbles; and well may the little birds hatched from them sing water songs, for they hear them all their lives, and even before they are born.

I have often observed the young just out of the nest making their odd gestures, and seeming in every way as much at home as their experienced parents, like young bees on their first excursions to the flower fields. No amount of familiarity with people and their ways seems to change them in the least. To all appearance their behavior is just the same on seeing a man for the first time, as when they have seen him frequently.

On the lower reaches of the rivers where mills are built, they sing on through the din of the machinery, and all the noisy confusion of dogs, cattle, and workmen. On one occasion, while a wood-chopper was at work on the river-bank, I observed one cheerily singing within reach of the flying chips. Nor does any kind of unwonted disturbance put him in bad humor, or frighten him out of calm self-possession. In passing through a narrow gorge, I once drove one ahead of me from rapid to rapid, disturbing him four times in quick succession where he could not very well fly past me on account of the narrowness of the channel. Most birds under similar circumstances fancy them-selves pursued, and become suspiciously uneasy; but, instead of grow-ing nervous about it, he made his usual dippings, and sang one of his most tranquil strains. When observed within a few yards their eyes are seen to express remarkable gentleness and intelligence; but they seldom allow so near a view unless one wears clothing of about the same color as the rocks and trees, and knows how to sit still. On one occasion, while rambling along the shore of a mountain lake, where the birds, at least those born that season, had never seen a man, I sat down to rest on a large stone close to the water's edge, upon which it seemed the ouzels and sandpipers were in the habit of alighting when they came to feed on that part of the shore, and some of the other birds also, when they came down to wash or drink. In a few minutes, along came a whirring Ouzel and alighted on the stone beside me, within reach of my hand. Then suddenly observing me, he stooped nervously as if about to fly on the instant, but as I remained as motionless as the stone, he gained confidence, and looked me steadily in the face for about a minute, then flew quietly to the outlet and began to sing. Next came a sandpiper and gazed at me with much the same guileless expression of eye as the Ouzel. Lastly, down with a swoop came a Steller's jay out of a fir-tree, probably with the intention of moistening his noisy throat. But instead of sitting confidingly as my other visitors had done, he rushed off at once, nearly tumbling heels over head into the lake in his suspicious confusion, and with loud screams roused the neighborhood.

Love for song-birds, with their sweet human voices, appears to be more common and unfailing than love for flowers. Every one loves flowers to some extent, at least in life's fresh morning, attracted by them as instinctively as humming-birds and bees. Even the young Digger Indians have sufficient love for the brightest of those found growing on the mountains to gather them and braid them as decorations for the hair. And I was glad to discover, through the few Indians that could be induced to talk on the subject, that they have names for the wild rose and the lily, and other conspicuous flowers, whether available as food or otherwise. Most men, however, whether savage or civilized, become apathetic toward all plants that have no other apparent use than the use of beauty. But fortunately one's first instinctive love of songbirds is never wholly obliterated, no matter what the influences upon our lives may be. I have often been delighted to see a pure, spiritual glow come into the countenances of hard business-men and old miners, when a song-bird chanced to alight near them. Nevertheless, the little mouthful of meat that swells out the breasts of some song-birds is too often the cause of their death. Larks and robins in particular are brought to market in hundreds. But fortunately the Ouzel has no enemy so eager to eat his little body as to follow him into the mountain solitudes. I never knew him to be chased even by hawks.

An acquaintance of mine, a sort of foot-hill mountaineer, had a pet cat, a great, dozy, overgrown creature, about as broad-shouldered as a lynx. During the winter, while the snow lay deep, the mountaineer sat in his lonely cabin among the pines smoking his pipe and wearing the dull time away. Tom was his sole companion, sharing his bed, and sitting beside him on a stool with much the same drowsy expression of eye as his master. The good-natured bachelor was content with his hard fare of soda-bread and bacon, but Tom, the only creature in the world acknowledging dependence on him, must needs be provided with fresh meat. Accordingly he bestirred himself to contrive squirrel-traps, and waded the snowy woods with his gun, making sad havoc among the few winter birds, sparing neither robin, sparrow, nor tiny nut-hatch, and the pleasure of seeing Tom eat and grow fat was his great reward.

One cold afternoon, while hunting along the river-bank, he noticed a plain-feathered little bird skipping about in the shallows, and immediately raised his gun. But just then the confiding songster began to sing, and after listening to his summery melody the charmed hunter turned away, saying, "Bless your little heart, I can't shoot you, not even for Tom."

Even so far north as icy Alaska, I have found my glad singer. When I was exploring the glaciers between Mount Fairweather and the Stikeen River, one cold day in November, after trying in vain to force a way through the innumerable icebergs of Sum Dum Bay to the great glaciers at the head of it, I was weary and baffled and sat resting in my canoe convinced at last that I would have to leave this part of my work for another year. Then I began to plan my escape to open water before the young ice which was beginning to form should shut me in. While I thus lingered drifting with the bergs, in the midst of these gloomy forebodings and all the terrible glacial desolation and grandeur, I suddenly heard the well-known whir of an Ouzel's wings, and, looking up, saw my little comforter coming straight across the ice from the shore. In a second or two he was with me, flying three times round my head with a happy salute, as if saying, "Cheer up, old friend; you see I'm here, and all's well." Then he flew back to the shore, alighted on the topmost jag of a stranded iceberg, and began to nod and bow as though he were on one of his favorite boulders in the midst of a sunny Sierra cascade.

The species is distributed all along the mountain-ranges of the Pacific Coast from Alaska to Mexico, and east to the Rocky Mountains. Nevertheless, it is as yet comparatively little known. Aububon and Wilson did not meet it. Swainson was, I believe, the first naturalist to describe a specimen from Mexico. Specimens were shortly afterward procured by Drummond near the sources of the Athabasca

River, between the fifty-fourth and fifty-sixth parallels; and it has been collected by nearly all of the numerous exploring expeditions undertaken of late through our Western States and Territories; for it never fails to engage the attention of naturalists in a very particular manner.

Such, then, is our little cinclus, beloved of every one who is so fortunate as to know him. Tracing on strong wing every curve of the most precipitous torrents from one extremity of the Sierra to the other; not fearing to follow them through their darkest gorges and coldest snow-tunnels; acquainted with every waterfall, echoing their divine music; and throughout the whole of their beautiful lives interpreting all that we in our unbelief call terrible in the utterances of torrents and storms, as only varied expressions of God's eternal love.

JOHN BURROUGHS

(1837–1921)

&ampersand; In his pioneering study, *The Development of the Natural History Essay in American Literature* (1924), Philip Marshall Hicks declared John Burroughs' work to be the culmination of the genre. Loren C. Owings, in his important recent (1976) bibliography, *Environmental Values, 1860–1972*, writes that Burroughs "occupies the central place in the history of American nature writing." These judgments may be correct, at least historically. Certainly, Burroughs was immensely popular: his books sold prodigiously well, and he himself became a nationally revered symbol of nature wisdom. Streams of visitors came to his Hudson River Valley retreat, as to a shrine. More accessible than Thoreau, and not nearly so wild as Muir, he wrote with disarming simplicity about his country walks and wildlife sightings. He brought the "ramble" to its quintessential expression.

Burroughs was also a philosophical essayist. He defended his own "desultory habits" of nature study, as he described them, as more likely to absorb truth than a hard-science approach, but he perceived that science had in fact opened up a whole new view of the world. His later works build to a comprehensive naturalistic philosophy that included the scientific point of view. Burroughs' rather serene accommodation of the new openness of view indicates that the farm boy from the Catskills, indifferently educated, had persevered and earned his own understanding of science's implications, and that the popular, woodsy ramble-taker whose books had sold over a million and a half copies was also a thinker in all seriousness.

The Natural Providence

I

WHAT UNTHINKING PEOPLE call design in nature is simply the reflection of our inevitable anthropomorphism. Whatever they can use, they think was designed for that purpose — the air to breathe, the water to drink, the soil to plant. It is as if they thought the notch in the mountains was made for the road to pass over, or the bays and harbor for the use of cities and shipping. But in inorganic nature the foot is made to fit the shoe and not the reverse. We are cast in the mould of the environment. If the black cap of the nuthatch which comes to the maple-tree in front of my window and feeds on the suet I place there were a human thinking-cap, the bird would see design in the regular renewal of that bit of suet; he would say, "Some one or something puts that there for me"; but he helps himself and asks no questions. The mystery does not trouble him. Why should not I, poor mortal, feel the same about these blessings and conveniences around me of which I hourly partake, and which seem so providential? Why do not I, with my thinking-cap, infer that some one or something is thinking about me and my well-being? The mass of mankind does draw this inference, and it is well for them to do so. But the case of the bird is different. The bit of suet that I feed on is not so conspicuously something extra, something added to the tree; it is a part of the tree; it is inseparable from it. I am compelled, as it were, to distil it out of the tree, so that instead of being the act of a special providence, it is the inevitable benefaction of the general providence of nature. What the old maple holds for me is maple-sugar, but it was not put there for me; it is there just the same, whether I want it or not; it is a part of the economy of the tree; it is a factor in its own growth; the tree is not thinking of me (pardon the term), but of itself. Of course this does not make my debt to it, and my grounds for thankfulness, any the less real, but it takes it out of the category of events such as that which brings the suet to the nuthatch. The Natural Providence is not intermittent, it is perennial; but it takes no thought of me or you. It is life that is flexible and adaptive, and not matter and force. "We do not," says Renan, "remark in the universe any sign of deliberate and thoughtful action. We may affirm that no action of this sort has existed for millions of centuries."

From *Accepting the Universe: Essays in Naturalism* (1920)

I think we may affirm more than that — we may affirm that it never existed. Some vestige of the old theology still clung to Renan's mind — there was a day of creation in which God set the universe going, and then left it to run itself; the same vestige clung to Darwin's mind and led him to say that in the beginning God must have created a few species of animals and vegetables and then left them to develop and populate the world.

Says Renan, "When a chemist arranges an experiment that is to last for years, everything which takes place in his retort is regulated by the laws of absolute unconsciousness; which does not mean that a will has not intervened at the beginning of the experiment, and that it will not intervene at the end." There was no beginning nor will there be any ending to the experiment of creation; the will is as truly there in the behavior of the molecules at one time as at another. The effect of Renan's priestly training and associations clings to him like a birthmark.

In discussing these questions our plumb-line does not touch bottom, because there is no bottom. "In the infinite," says Renan with deeper insight, "negations vanish, contradictions are merged"; in other words, opposites are true. Where I stand on the surface of the sphere is the center of that surface, but that does not prevent the point where you stand being the center also. Every point is a center, and the sky is overhead at one place as at another; opposites are true.

The moral and intellectual worlds present the same contradictions or limitations — the same relatively of what we call truth.

Nature's ways — which with me is the same as saying God's ways — are so different from ours; "no deliberate and thoughtful action," as Renan puts it, no economy of time or material, no short cuts, no cutting-out of non-essentials, no definite plan, no specific ends, few straight lines or right angles; her streams loiter and curve, her forces are unbridled; no loss or gain; her accounts always balance; the loss at one point, or with one form, is a gain with some other — all of which is the same as saying that there is nothing artificial in Nature. All is Natural, all is subject to the hit-and-miss method. The way Nature trims her trees, plants her forests, sows her gardens, is typical of the whole process of the cosmos. God is no better than man because man is a part of God. From our human point of view he is guilty of our excesses and shortcomings. Time does not count, pain does not count, waste does not count. The wonder is that the forests all get planted by this method, the pines in their places, the spruces in theirs, the oaks and maples in theirs; and the trees get trimmed in due time, now and then, it is true, by a very wasteful method. A tree doctor could save and prolong the lives of many of them. The small fountains and streams all find their way to larger streams, and these to still larger, and these to lakes or to the sea, and the drainage system of the continents works itself out with engineering exactitude. The decay of the rocks and the formation of the soil come about in due time, but not in man's time. In all the grand processes and transformations of nature the element of time enters on such a scale as to dwarf all human efforts.

II

When we say of a thing or an event that it was a chance happening, we do not mean that it was not determined by the laws of matter and force, but we mean it was not the result of the human will, or of anything like it, it was not planned or designed by conscious intelligence. Chance in this sense plays a very large part in nature and in life. Though the result of irrefragable laws, the whole non-living world about us shows no purpose or forethought in our human sense. For instance, we are compelled to regard the main features of the earth as matters of chance, the distribution of land and water, of islands and continents, of rivers, lakes, seas, mountains and plains, valleys and hills, the shapes of the continents; that there is more land in the northern hemisphere than in the southern, more land at the South Pole than at the North, is a matter of chance. The serpentine course of a stream through an alluvial plain, a stream two yards wide, winding and ox-bowing precisely as does the Mississippi, is a matter of chance. The whole geography of a country, in fact, is purely a matter of chance, and not the result of anything like human forethought. The planets themselves — that Jupiter is large and Mercury small; that Saturn has rings; that Jupiter has seven moons; that the Earth has one; that other planets have none; that some of the planets are in a condition to sustain life as we know it, for example, Venus, Earth, and probably Mars; that some revolve in more elliptical orbits than others; that Mercury and Venus apparently always keep the same side toward the sun — all these things are matters of chance. It is easy to say, as did our fathers, that God designed it thus and so, but how are we to think of an omnipotent and omniscient Being as planning such wholesale destruction of his own works as occurs in the cosmic catastrophes which the astronomers now and then witness in the sidereal universe, or even as occur on the earth, when earthquakes and volcanoes devastate fair lands or engulf the islands of the sea? Why should such a Being design a desert, or invent a tornado, or ordain that some portion of the earth's surface should have almost perpetual rain and another portion almost perpetual drought? In Hawaii I saw islands that were green and fertile on one end from daily showers, while the other end, ten miles away, was a rough barren rock, from the entire absence of showers. Were the trade winds designed to bring the vapors of the sea to the tropic lands?

In following this line of thought we, of course, soon get where no step can be taken. Is the universe itself a chance happening? Such a proposition is unthinkable, because something out of nothing is unthinkable. Our experience in this world develops our conceptions of time and space, and to set bounds to either is an impossible task. We say the cosmos must always have existed, and there we stop. We have no faculties to deal with the great ultimate problems.

We are no better off when we turn to the world of living things. Here we see design, particular means adapted to specific ends. Shall we say that a bird or a bee or a flower is a chance happening, as is the rainbow or the sunset cloud or a pearl or a precious stone? Is man himself a chance happening? Here we are stuck and cannot lift our feet. The mystery and the miracle of vitality, as Tyndall called it, is before us. Here is the long, hard road of evolution, the push and the unfolding of life through countless ages, something more than the mechanical and the accidental, though these have played a part; something less than specific plan and purpose, though we seem to catch dim outlines of these.

Spontaneous variations, original adaptations, a never-failing primal push toward higher and more complex forms — how can we, how shall we, read the riddle of it all? How shall we account for man on purely naturalistic grounds?

The consistent exponent of variation cannot go into partnership with supernaturalism. Grant that the organic split off from the inorganic by insensible degrees, yet we are bound to ask what made it split off at all? — and how it was that the first unicellular life contained the promise and the potency of all the life of to-day? Such questions take us into deep waters where our plummet-line finds no bottom. It suits my reason better to say there is no solution than to accept a solution which itself needs solution, and still leaves us where we began.

The adjustment of non-living bodies to each other seems a simple matter, but in considering the adaptations of living bodies to one another, and to their environment, we are confronted with a much harder problem. Life is an active principle, not in the sense that gravity and chemical reactions are active principles, but in a quite different sense. Gravity and chemical reactions are always the same, inflexible and uncompromising; but life is ever variable and adaptive; it will take half a loaf if it cannot get a whole one. Gravity answers yea and nay. Life says, "Probably; we will see about it; we will try again to-morrow." The oak-leaf will become an oak-ball to accommodate an insect that wants a cradle and a nursery for its young; it will develop one kind of a nursery for one insect and another kind for a different insect.

III

As far as I have got, or ever hope to get, toward solving the problem of the universe is to see clearly that it is insoluble. One can arrive only at negative conclusions; he comes to see that the problem cannot be dealt with in terms of our human experience and knowledge. But what other terms have we? Our knowledge does not qualify us in any degree to deal with the Infinite. The sphere has no handle to take hold of, and the Infinite baffles the mind in the same way. Measured by our human standards, it is a series of contradictions. The method of Nature is a haphazard method, yet behold the final order and completeness! How many of her seeds she trusts to the winds and the waters, and her fertilizing pollens and germs also! And the winds and the waters do her errands, with many failures, of course, but they hit the mark often enough to serve her purpose. She provides lavishly enough to afford her failures.

When we venture upon the winds and the waters with our crafts, we aim to control them, and we reach our havens only when we do control them.

What is there in the method of Nature that answers to the human will in such matters? Nothing that I can see; yet her boats and her balloons reach their havens — not all of them, but enough of them for her purpose. Yet when we apply the word "purpose" or "design" to Nature, to the Infinite, we are describing her in terms of the finite, and thus fall into contradictions. Still, the wings and balloons and hooks and springs in the vegetable world are for a specific purpose — to scatter the seed far from the parent plant. Every part and organ and movement of a living body serves a purpose to that organism. The mountain lily looks straight up to the sky; the meadow lily looks down to the earth; undoubtedly each flower finds its advantage in its own attitude, but what that advantage is, I know not. If Nature planned and invented as man does, she would attain to mere unity and simplicity. It is her blind, prodigal, haphazard methods that result

in her endless diversity. When she got a good wing for the seed of a
tree, such as that of the maple, she would, if merely efficient, give
this to the seeds of other similar trees; but she gives a different wing
to the ash, to the linden, to the elm, the pine, and the hemlock, while
to some she gives no wings at all. The nut-bearing trees, such as the
oaks, the beeches, the walnuts, and the hickories, have no wings,
except such as are afforded them by the birds and beasts that feed
upon them and carry them away. And here again Nature has a
purpose in the edible nut which tempts some creatures to carry it
away. If all the nuts were devoured, the whole tribe of nut-bearing
trees would in time be exterminated, and Nature's end defeated. But
in a world of conflicting forces like ours, chance plays an important
part; many of the nuts get scattered, and not all devoured. The
hoarding-up propensities of certain birds and squirrels result in the
planting of many oaks and chestnuts and beeches.

The inherent tendency to variation in organic life, together with
Nature's hit-and-miss method, account for her endless variety on the
same plane, as it were, as that of her many devices for disseminating
her seeds. One plan of hook or barb serves as well as another, —
that of bidens as well as that of hound's-tongue, — yet each has a
pattern of its own. The same may be said of the leaves of the trees:
their function is to expose the juices of the tree to the chemical action
of light and air; yet behold what an endless variety in their shape,
size, and structure! This is the way of the Infinite — to multiply
endlessly, to give a free rein to the physical forces and let them
struggle with one another for the stable equilibrium to which they
never, as a whole, attain; to give the same free rein to the organic
forces and let their various forms struggle with one another for the
unstable equilibrium which is the secret of their life.

The many contingencies that wait upon the circuit of the physical
forces and determine the various forms of organic matter — rocks,
sand, soil, gravel, mountain, plain — all shifting and changing endlessly — wait upon the circuit of the organic forces and turn the life
impulse into myriad channels, and people the earth with myriads of
living forms, each accidental from our limited point of view, while
all are determined by irrefragable laws. The contradictions in such
statements are obvious and are inevitable when the finite tries to
measure or describe the ways of the Infinite.

The waters of the globe are forever seeking the repose of a dead
level, but when they attain it, if they ever do, the world will be dead.
Behold what a career they have in their circuit from the sea to the
clouds and back to the earth in the ministering rains, and then to the

sea again through the streams and rivers! The mantling snow with its exquisite crystals, the grinding and transporting glaciers, the placid or plowing and turbulent rivers, the sparkling and refreshing streams, the cooling and renewing dews, the softening and protecting vapors, wait upon this circuit of the waters through the agency of the sun, from the sea, through the sky and land, back to the sea again. Yes, and all the myriad forms of life also. This circuit of the waters drives and sustains all the vital machinery of the globe.

Why and how the sun and the rain bring the rose and the violet, the peach and the plum, the wheat and the rye, and the boys and the girls, out of the same elements and conditions that they bring the thistles and the tares, the thorn and the scrub, the fang and the sting, the monkey and the reptile, is the insoluble mystery.

If Nature aspires toward what we call the good in man, does she not equally aspire toward what we call the bad in thorns and weeds and reptiles? May we not say that good is our good, and bad is our bad, and that there is, and can be, no absolute good and no absolute bad, any more than there can be an absolute up or an absolute down?

How haphazard, how fortuitous and uncalculated is all this business of the multiplication of the human race! What freaks, what failures, what monstrosities, what empty vessels, what deformed limbs, what defective brains, what perverted instincts! It is as if in the counsels of the Eternal it had been decided to set going an evolutionary impulse that should inevitably result in man, and then leave him to fail or flourish just as the ten thousand contingencies of the maelstrom of conflicting earth forces should decide, so that whether a

man become a cripple or an athlete, a fool or a philosopher, a satyr
or a god, is largely a matter of chance. Yet the human brain has
steadily grown in size, human mastery over nature has steadily increased, and chance has, upon the whole, brought more good to man
than evil. Optimism is a final trait of the Eternal.

And the taking-off of man, how haphazard, how fortuitous it all
is! His years shall be threescore and ten; but how few, comparatively,
reach that age, how few live out half their days! Disease, accident,
stupidity, superstition, cut him off at all ages — in infancy, in childhood, in youth, in manhood; his whole life is a part of the flux and
uncertainty of things. No god watches over him aside from himself
and his kind, no atom or molecule is partial to him, gravity crushes
him, fire burns him, the floods drown him as readily as they do vipers
and vermin. He takes his chances, he gains, and he loses, but Nature
treats him with the same impartiality that she treats the rest of her
creatures. He runs the same gantlet of the hostile physical forces, he
pays the same price for his development; but his greater capacity for
development — to whom or what does he owe that? If we follow
Darwin we shall say natural selection, and natural selection is just as
good a god as any other. No matter what we call it, if it brought man
to the head of creation and put all things (nearly all) under his feet,
it is god enough for anybody. At the heart of it there is still a mystery
we cannot grasp. The ways of Nature about us are no less divine
because they are near and familiar. The illusion of the rare and the
remote, science dispels. Of course we are still trying to describe the
Infinite in terms of the finite.

IV

We are so attached to our kind, and so dependent upon them, that
most persons feel homeless and orphaned in a universe where no
suggestion of sympathy and interest akin to our own comes to us
from the great void. A providence of impersonal forces, the broad-
cast, indiscriminate benefits of nature, kind deeds where no thought
of kindness is, well-being as the result of immutable law — all such
ideas chill and disquiet us, until we have inured ourselves to them.
We love to fancy that we see friendly hands and hear friendly voices
in nature. It is easy to make ourselves believe that the rains, the
warmth, the fruitful seasons, are sent by some Being for our especial
benefit. The thought that we are adapted to nature and not nature
made or modified to suit us, is distasteful to us. It rubs us the wrong

way. We have long been taught to believe that there is air because we have lungs, and water because we need it to drink, and light because we need it to see. Science takes this conceit out of us. The light begat the eye, and the air begat the lungs.

In the universe, as science reveals it to us, sensitive souls experience the cosmic chill; in the universe as our inevitable anthropomorphism shapes it for us, we experience the human glow. The same anthropomorphism has in the past peopled the woods and fields and streams and winds with good and evil spirits, and filled the world with cruel and debasing superstitions; but in our day we have got rid of all of this; we have abolished all gods but one. This one we still fear, and bow down before, and seek to propitiate — not with offerings and sacrifices, but with good Sunday clothes and creeds and pew-rents and praise and incense and surplices and ceremonies. What Brocken shadows our intense personalism casts upon nature! We see the gigantic outlines of our own forms, and mistake them for a veritable god. But as we ourselves are a part of nature, so this humanizing tendency of ours is also a part of nature, a part of human nature — not valid and independent, like the chemical and physical forces, but as valid and real as our dreams, our ideas, our aspirations. All the gods and divinities and spirits with which man has peopled the heavens and the earth are a part of Nature as she manifests herself in our subjective selves. So there we are, on a trail that ends where it began. We condemn one phase of nature through another phase of nature that is active in our own minds. How shall we escape this self-contradiction? As we check or control the gravity without us by the power of the gravity in our own bodies, so our intelligence must sit in judgment on phases of the same Universal Intelligence manifested in outward nature.

It is this recognition of an intelligence in nature akin to our own that gives rise to our anthropomorphism. We recognize in the living world about us the use of specific means to specific ends, and this we call intelligence. It differs from our own in that it is not selective and intensive in the same way. It does not take short cuts; it does not aim at human efficiency; it does not cut out waste and delay and pain. It is the method of trial and error. It hits its mark because it hits all marks. Species succeed because the tide that bears them on is a universal tide. It is not a river, but an ocean current. Nature progresses, but not as man does by discarding one form and adapting a higher. She discards nothing; she keeps all her old forms and ways and out of them evolves the higher; she keeps the fish's fin, while she perfects the bird's wing; she preserves the invertebrate, while she fashions the vertebrate; she achieves man, while she preserves the monkey. She gropes her way like a blind man, but she arrives because all goals are hers. Perceptive intelligence she has given in varying degrees to all creatures, but reasoning intelligence she has given to man alone. I say "given," after our human manner of speaking, when I mean "achieve." There is no giving in Nature — there is effort and development. There is interchange and interaction, but no free gifts. Things are bought with a price. The price of the mind of man — who can estimate what it has been through the biological and geological ages? — a price which his long line of antecedent forms has paid in struggle and suffering and death. The little that has been added to the size of his brain since the Piltdown man and the Neanderthal man — what effort and pain has not that cost? We pay for what we get, or our forbears paid for it. They paid for the size of our brains, and we pay for our progress in knowledge.

V

The term "religion" is an equivocal and much-abused word, but I am convinced that no man's life is complete without some kind of an emotional experience that may be called religious. Not necessarily so much a definite creed or belief as an attraction and aspiration toward the Infinite, or a feeling of awe and reverence inspired by the contemplation of this wonderful and mysterious universe, something to lift a man above purely selfish and material ends, and open his soul to influences from the highest heavens of thought.

Religion in some form is as natural to man as are eating and sleeping. The mysteries of life and the wonder and terror of the world in which he finds himself, arouse emotions of awe and fear and worship in him as soon as his powers of reflection are born. In man's early history religion, philosophy, and literature are one. He worships before he investigates; he builds temples before he builds schoolhouses or civic halls. He is, of course, superstitious long before he is scientific; he trembles before the supernatural long before he has mastered the natural. The mind of early man was synthetic as our emotions always are; it lumped things, it did not differentiate and classify. The material progress of the race has kept pace with man's power of analysis — the power to separate one thing from another, to resolve things into their component parts and recombine them to serve his own purposes. He gets water power, steam power, electric power, by separating a part from the whole and placing his machinery where they tend to unite again.

Science tends more and more to reveal to us the unity that underlies the diversity of nature. We must have diversity in our practical
lives; we must seize Nature by many handles. But our intellectual
lives demand unity, demand simplicity amid all this complexity. Our
religious lives demand the same. Amid all the diversity of creeds and
sects we are coming more and more to see that religion is one, that
verbal differences and ceremonies are unimportant, and that the
fundamental agreements are alone significant. Religion as a key or
passport to some other world has had its day; as a mere set of
statements or dogmas about the Infinite mystery it has had its day.
Science makes us more and more at home in this world, and is coming
more and more, to the intuitional mind, to have a religious value.
Science kills credulity and superstition, but to the well-balanced mind
it enhances the feeling of wonder, of veneration, and of kinship which
we feel in the presence of the marvelous universe. It quiets our fears
and apprehensions, it pours oil upon the troubled waters of our lives,
and reconciles us to the world as it is. The old fickle and jealous
gods begotten by our fears and morbid consciences fall away, and the
new gods of law and order, who deal justly if mercilessly, take their
places.

"The mind of the universe which we share," is a phrase of Thoreau's — a large and sane idea which shines like a star amid his many
firefly conceits and paradoxes. The physical life of each of us is a
part or rill of the universal life about us, as surely as every ounce of
our strength is a part of gravity. With equal certainty, and under the
same law, our mental lives flow from the fountain of universal mind,
the cosmic intelligence which guides the rootlets of the smallest plant
as it searches the soil for the elements it needs, and the most minute
insect in availing itself of the things it needs. It is this primal current
of life, the two different phases of which we see in our bodies and
in our minds, that continues after our own special embodiments of
it have ceased; in it is the real immortality. The universal mind does
not die, the universal life does not go out. The jewel that trembles
in the dewdrop, the rain that lends itself to the painting of the
prismatic colors of the bow in the clouds, pass away, but their fountainhead in the sea does not pass away. The waters may make the
wonderful circuit through the clouds, the air, the earth, and the cells
and veins of living things, any number of times — now a globule
of vapor in the sky, now a starlike crystal in the snow, now the painted
mist of a waterfall, then the limpid current of a mountain brook —
and still the sea remains unchanged. And though the life and mentality of the globe passes daily and is daily renewed, the primal source
of those things is as abounding as ever. It is not you and I that are

immortal; it is Creative Energy, of which we are a part. Our immortality is swallowed up in this.

The poets, the prophets, the martyrs, the heroes, the saints — where are they? Each was but a jewel in the dew, the rain, the snowflake — throbbing, burning, flashing with color for a brief time and then vanishing, adorning the world for a moment and then caught away in the great abyss. "O spendthrift Nature!" our hearts cry out; but Nature's spending is only the ceaseless merging of one form into another without diminution of her material or blurring of her types. Flowers bloom and flowers fade, the seasons come and the seasons go, men are born and men die, the world mourns for its saints and heroes, its poets and saviors, but Nature remains and is as young and spontaneous and inexhaustible as ever. Where is the comfort in all this to you and to me? There is none, save the comfort or satisfaction of knowing things as they are. We shall feel more at ease in Zion when we learn to distinguish substance from shadow, and to grasp the true significance of the world of which we form a part. In the end each of us will have had his day, and can say as Whitman does,

"I have positively appeared. That is enough."

In us or through us the Primal Mind will have contemplated and enjoyed its own works and will continue to do so as long as human life endures on this planet. It will have achieved the miracle of the Incarnation, and have tasted the sweet and the bitter, the victories and the defeats of evolution. The legend of the birth and life of Jesus is but this everpresent naturalism written large with parable and miracle on the pages of our religious history. In the lives of each of us the supreme reality comes down to earth and takes on the human form and suffers all the struggles and pains and humiliations of mortal, finite life. Even the Christian theory of the vicarious atonement is not without its basis of naturalism. Men, through disease and ignorance and half knowledge, store up an experience that saves future generations from suffering and failure. We win victories for our descendants, and bring the kingdom nearer for them by the devils and evil spirits we overcome.

LIBERTY HYDE BAILEY
(1858–1954)

✌ Nature writing built on the rural, middle ground runs a risk of complacency. The environment is seductively pleasant. But if the writer looks at the trends — for the last century and a half, centralization and mechanization of farms, and accelerating depopulation of the rural zone itself — and if he looks at the plight of the working farmer, he will likely go deeper.

Liberty Bailey, a farm horticulturist, editor, dean of agriculture, and philosopher, did just that. He lived through the tipping of the American balance from an agrarian to an industrial society and on into the downward environmental slide of the twentieth century, and he thought long about the human implications of these large historical movements. In several influential books, he examined the relations between city and country, the values that were being lost in the urban ascendance, and the possibility of a relationship with nature that was both spiritually right and practically sustainable. He was one of the early "deep ecologists" of the modern era.

The Habit of Destruction

THE FIRST OBSERVATION that must be apparent to all men is that our dominion has been mostly destructive.

We have been greatly engaged in digging up the stored resources, and in destroying vast products of the earth for some small kernel that we can apply to our necessities or add to our enjoyments. We excavate the best of the coal and cast away the remainder; blast the

From *The Holy Earth* (1915)

minerals and metals from underneath the crust, and leave the earth raw and sore; we box the pines for turpentine and abandon the growths of limitless years to fire and devastation; sweep the forests with the besom of destruction; pull the fish from the rivers and ponds without making any adequate provision for renewal; exterminate whole races of animals; choke the streams with refuse and dross; rob the land of its available stores, denuding the surface, exposing great areas to erosion.

Nor do we exercise the care and thrift of good housekeepers. We do not clean up our work or leave the earth in order. The remnants and accumulation of mining-camps are left to ruin and decay; the deserted phosphate excavations are ragged, barren, and unfilled; vast areas of forested lands are left in brush and waste, unthoughtful of the future, unmindful of the years that must be consumed to reduce the refuse to mould and to cover the surface respectably, uncharitable to those who must clear away the wastes and put the place in order; and so thoughtless are we with these natural resources that even the establishments that manufacture them — the mills, the factories of many kinds — are likely to be offensive objects in the landscape, unclean, unkempt, displaying the unconcern of the owners to the obligation that the use of the materials imposes and to the sensibilities of the community for the way in which they handle them. The burden of proof seems always to have been rested on those who partake little in the benefits, although we know that these non-partakers have been real owners of the resources; and yet so undeveloped has been the public conscience in these matters that the blame — if blame there be — cannot be laid on one group more than on the other. Strange it is, however, that we should not have insisted at least that those who appropriate the accumulations of the earth should complete their work, cleaning up the remainders, leaving the areas wholesome, inoffensive, and safe. How many and many are the years required to grow a forest and to fill the pockets of the rocks, and how satisfying are the landscapes, and yet how desperately soon may men reduce it all to ruin and to emptiness, and how slatternly may they violate the scenery!

All this habit of destructiveness is uneconomic in the best sense, unsocial, unmoral.

Society now begins to demand a constructive process. With care and with regard for other men, we must produce the food and the other supplies in regularity and sufficiency; and we must clean up after our work, that the earth may not be depleted, scarred, or repulsive.

Yet there is even a more defenseless devastation than all this. It is the organized destructiveness of those who would make military domination the major premise in the constitution of society, accompanying desolation with viciousness and violence, ravaging the holy earth, disrespecting the works of the creator, looking toward extirpation, confessing thereby that they do not know how to live in cooperation with their fellows; in such situations, every new implement of destruction adds to the guilt.

In times past we were moved by religious fanaticism, even to the point of waging wars. Today we are moved by impulses of trade, and we find ourselves plunged into a war of commercial frenzy; and as it has behind it vaster resources and more command of natural forces, so is it the most ferocious and wasteful that the race has experienced, exceeding in its havoc the cataclysms of earthquake and volcano. Certainly we have not yet learned how to withstand the prosperity and the privileges that we have gained by the discoveries of science; and certainly the morals of commerce have not given us freedom or mastery. Rivalry that leads to arms is a natural fruit of unrestrained rivalry in trade.

Man has dominion, but he has no commission to devastate: And the Lord God took the man, and put him into the garden of Eden to dress it and to keep it.

Verily, so bountiful hath been the earth and so securely have we drawn from it our substance, that we have taken it all for granted as if it were only a gift, and with little care or conscious thought of the consequences of our use of it.

The New Hold

WE MAY DISTINGUISH three stages in our relation to the planet, — the collecting stage, the mining stage, and the producing stage. These overlap and perhaps are nowhere distinct, and yet it serves a purpose to contrast them.

At first man sweeps the earth to see what he may gather, — game, wood, fruits, fish, fur, feathers, shells on the shore. A certain social and moral life arises out of this relation, seen well in the woodsmen and the fishers — in whom it best persists to the present day — strong, dogmatic, superstitious folk. Then man begins to go beneath

From *The Holy Earth* (1915)

the surface to see what he can find, — iron and precious stones, the gold of Ophir, coal, and many curious treasures. This develops the exploiting faculties, and leads men into the uttermost parts. In both these stages the elements of waste and disregard have been heavy.

Finally, we begin to enter the productive stage, whereby we secure supplies by controlling the conditions under which they grow, wasting little, harming not. Farming has been very much a mining process, the utilizing of fertility easily at hand and the moving-on to lands unspoiled of quick potash and nitrogen. Now it begins to be really productive and constructive, with a range of responsible and permanent morals. We rear the domestic animals with precision. We raise crops, when we will, almost to a nicety. We plant fish in lakes and streams to some extent but chiefly to provide more game rather than more human food, for in this range we are yet mostly in the collecting or hunter stage. If the older stages were strongly expressed in the character of the people, so will this new stage be expressed; and so is it that we are escaping the primitive and should be coming into a new character. We shall find our rootage in the soil.

This new character, this clearer sense of relationship with the earth, should express itself in all the people and not exclusively in farming people and their like. It should be a popular character — or a national character if we would limit the discussion to one people — and not a class character. Now, here lies a difficulty and here is a reason for writing this book: the population of the earth is increasing, the relative population of farmers is decreasing, people are herding in cities, we have a city mind, and relatively fewer people are brought into touch with the earth in any real way. So is it incumbent on us to take special pains — now that we see the new time — that all the people, or as many of them as possible, shall have contact with the earth and that the earth righteousness shall be abundantly taught.

I hasten to say that I am not thinking of any back-to-the-farm movement to bring about the results we seek. Necessarily, the proportion of farmers will decrease. Not so many are needed, relatively, to produce the requisite supplies from the earth. Agriculture makes a great contribution to human progress by releasing men for the manufactures and the trades. In proportion as the ratio of farmers decreases is it important that we provide them the best of opportunities and encouragement: they must be better and better men. And if we are to secure our moral connection with the planet to a large extent through them, we can see that they bear a relation to society in general that we have overlooked.

Even the farming itself is changing radically in character. It ceases to be an occupation to gain sustenance and becomes a business. We apply to it the general attitudes of commerce. We must be alert to see that it does not lose its capacity for spiritual contact.

How we may achieve a more widespread contact with the earth on the part of all the people without making them farmers, I shall endeavor to suggest as I proceed; in fact, this is my theme. Dominion means mastery; we may make the surface of the earth much what we will; we can govern the way in which we shall contemplate it. We are probably near something like a stable occupancy. It is not to be expected that there will be vast shifting of cities as the contest for the mastery of the earth proceeds, — probably nothing like the loss of Tyre and Carthage, and of the commercial glory of Venice. In fact, we shall have a progressive occupancy. The greater the population, the greater will be the demands on the planet; and, moreover, every new man will make more demands than his father made, for he will want more to satisfy him. We are to take from the earth much more than we have ever taken before, but it will be taken in a new way and with better intentions. It will be seen, therefore, that we are not here dealing narrowly with an occupation but with something very fundamental to our life on the planet.

We are not to look for our permanent civilization to rest on any species of robber-economy. No flurry of coal-mining, or gold-fever, or rubber-collecting in the tropics, or excitement of prospecting for new finds or even locating new lands, no ravishing of the earth or monopolistic control of its bounties, will build a stable society. So is much of our economic and social fabric transitory. It is not by accident that a very distinct form of society is developing in the great farming regions of the Mississippi Valley and in other comparable places; the exploiting and promoting occupancy of those lands is passing and a stable progressive development appears. We have been obsessed of the passion to cover everything at once, to skin the earth, to pass on, even when there was no necessity for so doing. It is a vast pity that this should ever have been the policy of government in giving away great tracts of land by lottery, as if our fingers would burn if we held the lands inviolate until needed by the natural process of settlement. The people should be kept on their lands long enough to learn how to use them. But very well: we have run with the wind, we have staked the lands; now we shall be real farmers and real conquerors. Not all lands are equally good for farming, and some lands will never be good for farming; but whether in Iowa, or New England, or old Asia, farming land may develop character in the people.

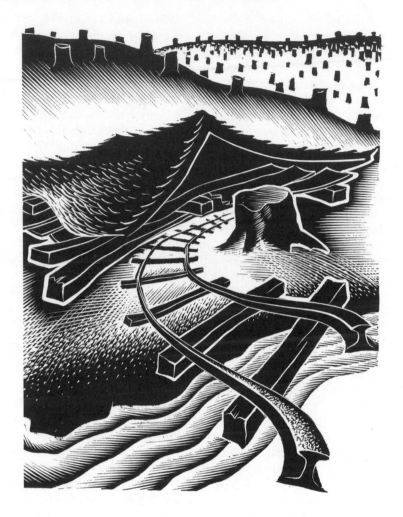

My reader must not infer that we have arrived at a permanent agriculture, although we begin now to see the importance of a permanent land occupancy. Probably we have not yet evolved a satisfying husbandry that will maintain itself century by century, without loss and without the ransacking of the ends of the earth for fertilizer materials to make good our deficiencies. All the more is it important that the problem be elevated into the realm of statesmanship and of morals. Neither must he infer that the resources of the earth are to be locked up beyond contact and use (for the contact and use will be morally regulated). But no system of brilliant exploitation, and no accidental scratching of the surface of the earth, and no easy appropriation of stored materials can suffice us in the good days to come. City, country, this class and that class, all fall and merge before the common necessity.

It is often said that the farmer is our financial mainstay; so in the good process of time will he be a moral mainstay, for ultimately finance and social morals must coincide.

The gifts are to be used for service and for satisfaction, and not for wealth. Very great wealth introduces too many intermediaries, too great indirectness, too much that is extrinsic, too frequent hindrances and superficialities. It builds a wall about the man, and too often does he receive his impressions of the needs of the world from satellites and sycophants. It is significant that great wealth, if it contributes much to social service, usually accomplishes the result by endowing others to work. The gift of the products of the earth was "for meat": nothing was said about riches.

Yet the very appropriation or use of natural resources may be the means of directing the mind of the people back to the native situations. We have the opportunity to make the forthcoming development of water-power, for example, such an agency for wholesome training. Whenever we can appropriate without despoliation or loss, or without a damaging monopoly, we tie the people to the backgrounds.

In the background is the countryman; and how is the countryman to make use of the rain and the abounding soil, and the varied wonder of plant and animal amidst which he lives, that he may arrive at kinship? We are teaching him how to bring some of these things under the dominion of his hands, how to measure and to weigh and to judge. This will give him the essential physical mastery. But beyond this, how shall he take them into himself, how shall he make them to be of his spirit, how shall he complete his dominion? How shall he become the man that his natural position requires of him? This will come slowly, ah, yes! — slowly. The people — the great striving self-absorbed throng of the people — they do not know what we mean when we talk like this, they hear only so many fine words. The naturist knows that the time will come slowly, — not yet are we ready for fulfillment; he knows that we cannot regulate the cosmos, or even the natural history of the people, by enactments. Slowly: by removing handicaps here and there; by selection of the folk in a natural process, to eliminate the unresponsiveness; by teaching, by suggestion; by a public recognition of the problem, even though not one of us sees the end of it.

I hope my reader now sees where I am leading him. He sees that I am not thinking merely of instructing the young in the names and habits of birds and flowers and other pleasant knowledge, although this works strongly toward the desired end; nor of any movement merely to have gardens, or to own farms, although this is desirable provided one is qualified to own a farm; nor of rhapsodies on the beauties of nature. Nor am I thinking of any new plan or any novel kind of institution or any new agency; rather shall we do better to escape some of the excessive institutionalism and organization. We are so accustomed to think in terms of organized politics and education and religion and philanthropies that when we detach ourselves we are said to lack definiteness. It is the personal satisfaction in the earth to which we are born, and the quickened responsibility, the whole relation, broadly developed, of the man and of all men, — it is this attitude that we are to discuss.

The years pass and they grow into centuries. We see more clearly. We are to take a new hold.

The Brotherhood Relation

A CONSTRUCTIVE and careful handling of the resources of the earth is impossible except on a basis of large co-operation and of association for mutual welfare. The great inventions and discoveries of recent time have extensive social significance.

Yet we have other relations than with the physical and static materials. We are parts in a living sensitive creation. The theme of evolution has overturned our attitude toward this creation. The living creation is not exclusively man-centred: it is bio-centric. We perceive the essential continuity in nature, arising from within rather than from without, the forms of life proceeding upwardly and onwardly in something very like a mighty plan of sequence, man being one part in the process. We have genetic relation with all living things, and our aristocracy is the aristocracy of nature. We can claim no gross superiority and no isolated self-importance. The creation, and not man, is the norm. Even now do we begin to guide our practises and our speech by our studies of what we still call the lower creation. We gain a good perspective on ourselves.

If we are parts in the evolution, and if the universe, or even the earth, is not made merely as a footstool, or as a theatre for man, so do we lose our cosmic selfishness and we find our place in the plan

From *The Holy Earth* (1915)

of things. We are emancipated from ignorance and superstition and small philosophies. The present widespread growth of the feeling of brotherhood would have been impossible in a self-centred creation: the way has been prepared by the discussion of evolution, which is the major biological contribution to human welfare and progress. This is the philosophy of the oneness in nature and the unity in living things.

The Spiritual Contact with Nature

A USEFUL CONTACT with the earth places man not as superior to nature but as a superior intelligence working in nature as a conscious and therefore as a responsible part in a plan of evolution, which is a continuing creation. It distinguishes the elemental virtues as against the acquired, factitious, and pampered virtues. These strong and simple traits may be brought out easily and naturally if we incorporate into our schemes of education the solid experiences of tramping, camping, scouting, farming, handcraft, and other activities that are not mere refinements of subjective processes.

Lack of training in the realities drives us to find satisfaction in all sorts of make-believes and in play-lives. The "movies" and many other developments of our time make an appeal wholly beyond their merits, and they challenge the methods and intentions of education.

There are more fundamental satisfactions than "thrills." There is more heart-ease in frugality than in surfeit. There is no real relish except when the appetite is keen. We are now provided with all sorts of things that nobody ever should want.

The good spiritual reaction to nature is not a form of dogmatism or impressionism. It results normally from objective experience, when the person is ready for it and has good digestion. It should be the natural emotion of the man who knows his objects and does not merely dream about them. There is no hallucination in it. The remedy for some of the erratic "futurism" and other forms of illusion is to put the man hard against the facts: he might be set to studying bugs or soils or placed between the handles of a plow until such time as objects begin to take their natural shape and meaning in his mind.

It is not within my purview here to consider the abstract righteous relation of man to the creation, nor to examine the major emotions

From *The Holy Earth* (1915)

that result from a contemplation of nature. It is only a very few of the simpler and more practical considerations that I may suggest.

The training in solid experience naturally emphasizes the righteousness of plain and simple eating and drinking, and of frugality and control in pleasures. Many of the adventitious pleasures are in the highest degree pernicious and are indications of weakness.

Considering the almost universal opinion that nature exhibits the merciless and relentless struggle of an eye for an eye and a tooth for a tooth, it is significant that one of the most productive ways of training a youth in sensitiveness and in regard for other creatures is by means of the nature contact. Even if the person is taught that the strong and ferocious survive and conquer, he nevertheless soon comes to have the tenderest regard for every living thing if he has the naturist in him. He discards the idea that we lose virility when we cease to kill, and relegates the notion to the limbo of deceits. This only means that unconsciously he has experienced the truth in nature, and in practice has discarded the erroneous philosophy contained in books even though he may still give these philosophies his mental assent.

It is exactly among the naturists that the old instinct to kill begins to lose its force and that an instinct of helpfulness and real brotherhood soon takes its place. From another source, the instinct to kill dies out among the moralists and other people. And yet it is passing strange how this old survival — or is it a reversion? — holds its place amongst us, even in the higher levels. The punishment of a life for a life is itself a survival. Entertainment even yet plays upon this old memory of killing, as in books of adventure, in fiction, in playgames of children, and worst of all on the stage where this strange anachronism, even in plays that are not historic, is still portrayed in pernicious features and in a way that would rouse any community and violate law if it were enacted in real life.

It is difficult to explain these survivals when we pretend to be so much shocked by the struggle for existence. We must accept the struggle, but we ought to try to understand it. The actual suffering among the creatures as the result of this struggle is probably small, and the bloody and ferocious contest that we like to picture to ourselves is relatively insignificant. There is a righteous element in the struggle; or, more truthfully, the struggle itself is right. Every living and sentient thing persists by its merit and by its right. It persists within its sphere, and usually not in the sphere of some other creature. The weeding-out process is probably related in some way with adaptability, but only remotely with physical strength. It is a process of applying the test. The test is applied continuously, and not in some violent upheaval.

If one looks for a moral significance in the struggle for existence, one finds it in the fact that it is a process of adjustment rather than a contest in ambition.

The elimination of the unessentials and of the survivals of a lower order of creation that have no proper place in human society, is the daily necessity of the race. The human struggle should not be on the plane of the struggle in the lower creation, by the simple fact that the human plane is unlike; and those who contend that we should draw our methods of contest from wild nature would therefore put us back on the plane of the creatures we are supposed to have passed. If there is one struggle of the creeping things, if there is one struggle of the fish of the sea and another of the beasts of the field, and still another of the fowls of the air, then surely there must be still another order for those who have dominion.

HENRY BESTON

(*1888–1968*)

❧ Few books seem as distilled as *The Outermost House*. The shapes of its sentences are carefully wrought, pared to the essence, and its poetic stopping-short in the face of ultimate matters shows the author's regard for the power of his subject. In literary form, Beston enacted the respect for nature he recommended to his readers, and in his evocative imagery, the sensuous participation he also advised.

Beston had bought the dune land for his Cape Cod cottage in 1925, and when the house was ready, he moved in to spend a year alone. His wife Elizabeth Coatsworth, herself a poet, later wrote, "It was on the dunes that he found himself as a writer." Though nearsighted and somewhat hard of hearing, Beston had placed himself supremely well; he learned to perceive what was before him with an aesthete's heightened sensitivity, and to feel its implications as a poet-philosopher. The "Fo'castle," his cottage, was designated a National Literary Landmark in 1964. In 1978, it was broken up and washed out to sea in a great winter storm.

Night on the Great Beach

I

OUR FANTASTIC CIVILIZATION has fallen out of touch with many aspects of nature, and with none more completely than with night. Primitive folk, gathered at a cave mouth round a fire, do not fear night; they fear, rather, the energies and creatures to whom night gives power; we of the age of the machines, having delivered ourselves of nocturnal enemies, now have a dislike of night itself. With

From *The Outermost House* (1928)

lights and ever more lights, we drive the holiness and beauty of night back to the forests and the sea; the little villages, the crossroads even, will have none of it. Are modern folk, perhaps, afraid of night? Do they fear that vast serenity, the mystery of infinite space, the austerity of stars? Having made themselves at home in a civilization obsessed with power, which explains its whole world in terms of energy, do they fear at night for their dull acquiescence and the pattern of their beliefs? Be the answer what it will, to-day's civilization is full of people who have not the slightest notion of the character or the poetry of night, who have never even seen night. Yet to live thus, to know only artificial night, is as absurd and evil as to know only artificial day.

Night is very beautiful on this great beach. It is the true other half of the day's tremendous wheel; no lights without meaning stab or trouble it; it is beauty, it is fulfilment, it is rest. Thin clouds float in these heavens, islands of obscurity in a splendour of space and stars: the Milky Way bridges earth and ocean; the beach resolves itself into a unity of form, its summer lagoons, its slopes and uplands merging; against the western sky and falling bow of sun rise the silent and superb undulations of the dunes.

My nights are at their darkest when a dense fog streams in from the sea under a black, unbroken floor of cloud. Such nights are rare, but are most to be expected when fog gathers off the coast in early summer; this last Wednesday night was the darkest I have known. Between ten o'clock and two in the morning three vessels stranded on the outer beach — a fisherman, a four-masted schooner, and a beam trawler. The fisherman and the schooner have been towed off, but the trawler, they say, is still ashore.

I went down to the beach that night just after ten o'clock. So utterly black, pitch dark it was, and so thick with moisture and trailing showers, that there was no sign whatever of the beam of Nauset; the sea was only a sound, and when I reached the edge of the surf the dunes themselves had disappeared behind. I stood as isolate in that immensity of rain and night as I might have stood in interplanetary space. The sea was troubled and noisy, and when I opened the darkness with an outlined cone of light from my electric torch I saw that the waves were washing up green coils of sea grass, all coldly wet and bright in the motionless and unnatural radiance. Far off a single ship was groaning its way along the shoals. The fog was compact of the finest moisture; passing by, it spun itself into my lens of light like a kind of strange, aërial, and liquid silk. Effin Chalke, the new coast guard, passed me going north, and told me that he had had news at the halfway house of the schooner at Cahoon's.

It was dark, pitch dark to my eye, yet complete darkness, I imagine, is exceedingly rare, perhaps unknown in outer nature. The nearest natural approximation to it is probably the gloom of forest country buried in night and cloud. Dark as the night was here, there was still light on the surface of the planet. Standing on the shelving beach, with the surf breaking at my feet, I could see the endless wild uprush, slide, and withdrawal of the sea's white rim of foam. The men at Nauset tell me that on such nights they follow along this vague crawl of whiteness, trusting to habit and a sixth sense to warn them of their approach to the halfway house.

Animals descend by starlight to the beach. North, beyond the dunes, muskrats forsake the cliff and nose about in the driftwood and weed, leaving intricate trails and figure eights to be obliterated by the day; the lesser folk — the mice, the occasional small sand-coloured toads, the burrowing moles — keep to the upper beach and leave their tiny footprints under the overhanging wall. In autumn skunks, beset by a shrinking larder, go beach combing early in the night. The animal is by preference a clean feeder and turns up his nose at rankness. I almost stepped on a big fellow one night as I was walking north to meet the first man south from Nauset. There was a scamper, and the creature ran up the beach from under my feet; alarmed he certainly was, yet was he contained and continent. Deer are frequently seen, especially north of the light. I find their tracks upon the summer dunes.

Years ago, while camping on this beach north of Nauset, I went for a stroll along the top of the cliff at break of dawn. Though the path followed close enough along the edge, the beach below was often hidden, and I looked directly from the height to the flush of sunrise at sea. Presently the path, turning, approached the brink of the earth precipice, and on the beach below, in the cool, wet rosiness of dawn, I saw three deer playing. They frolicked, rose on their hind legs, scampered off, and returned again, and were merry. Just before sunrise they trotted off north together down the beach toward a hollow in the cliff and the path that climbs it.

Occasionally a sea creature visits the shore at night. Lone coast guardsmen, trudging the sand at some deserted hour, have been startled by seals. One man fell flat on a creature's back, and it drew away from under him, flippering toward the sea, with a sound "half-way between a squeal and a bark." I myself once had rather a start. It was long after sundown, the light dying and uncertain, and I was walking home on the top level of the beach and close along the slope descending to the ebbing tide. A little more than halfway to the Fo'castle a huge unexpected something suddenly writhed horribly in

the darkness under my bare foot. I had stepped on a skate left
stranded by some recent crest of surf, and my weight had momentarily annoyed it back to life.

Facing north, the beam of Nauset becomes part of the dune night.
As I walk toward it, I see the lantern, now as a star of light which
waxes and wanes three mathematic times, now as a lovely pale flare
of light behind the rounded summits of the dunes. The changes in
the atmosphere change the colour of the beam; it is now whitish,
now flame golden, now golden red; it changes its form as well, from
a star to a blare of light, from a blare of light to a cone of radiance
sweeping a circumference of fog. To the west of Nauset I often see
the apocalyptic flash of the great light at the Highland reflected on
the clouds or even on the moisture in the starlit air, and, seeing it, I
often think of the pleasant hours I have spent there when George
and Mary Smith were at the light and I had the good fortune to visit
as their guest. Instead of going to sleep in the room under the eaves,
I would lie awake, looking out of a window to the great spokes of
light revolving as solemnly as a part of the universe.

All night long the lights of coastwise vessels pass at sea, green lights
going south, red lights moving north. Fishing schooners and flounder
draggers anchor two or three miles out, and keep a bright riding
light burning on the mast. I see them come to anchor at sundown,
but I rarely see them go, for they are off at dawn. When busy at
night, these fishermen illumine their decks with a scatter of oil flares.
From shore, the ships might be thought afire. I have watched the
scene through a night glass. I could see no smoke, only the waving
flares, the reddish radiance on sail and rigging, an edge of reflection
overside, and the enormous night and sea beyond.

One July night, as I returned at three o'clock from an expedition
north, the whole night, in one strange, burning instant, turned into
a phantom day. I stopped and, questioning, stared about. An enormous meteor, the largest I have ever seen, was consuming itself in
an effulgence of light west of the zenith. Beach and dune and ocean
appeared out of nothing, shadowless and motionless, a landscape
whose every tremor and vibration were stilled, a landscape in a
dream.

The beach at night has a voice all its own, a sound in fullest
harmony with its spirit and mood — with its little, dry noise of sand
forever moving, with its solemn, overspilling, rhythmic seas, with its
eternity of stars that sometimes seem to hang down like lamps from
the high heavens — and that sound the piping of a bird. As I walk
the beach in early summer my solitary coming disturbs it on its nest,

and it flies away, troubled, invisible, piping its sweet, plaintive cry. The bird I write of is the piping plover, *Charadrius melodus,* sometimes called the beach plover or the mourning bird. Its note is a whistled syllable, the loveliest musical note, I think, sounded by any North Atlantic bird.

Now that summer is here I often cook myself a camp supper on the beach. Beyond the crackling, salt-yellow driftwood flame, over the pyramid of barrel staves, broken boards, and old sticks all atwist with climbing fire, the unseen ocean thunders and booms, the breaker sounding hollow as it falls. The wall of the sand cliff behind, with its rim of grass and withering roots, its sandy crumblings and erosions, stands gilded with flame; wind cries over it; a covey of sandpipers pass between the ocean and the fire. There are stars, and to the south Scorpio hangs curving down the sky with ringed Saturn shining in his claw.

Learn to reverence night and to put away the vulgar fear of it, for, with the banishment of night from the experience of man, there vanishes as well a religious emotion, a poetic mood, which gives depth to the adventure of humanity. By day, space is one with the earth and with man — it is his sun that is shining, his clouds that are floating past; at night, space is his no more. When the great earth, abandoning day, rolls up the deeps of the heavens and the universe, a new door opens for the human spirit, and there are few so clownish that some awareness of the mystery of being does not touch them as they gaze. For a moment of night we have a glimpse of ourselves and of our world islanded in its stream of stars — pilgrims of mortality, voyaging between horizons across eternal seas of space and time. Fugitive though the instant be, the spirit of man is, during it, ennobled by a genuine moment of emotional dignity, and poetry makes its own both the human spirit and experience.

II

At intervals during the summer, often enough when the tides are high and the moon is near the full, the surf along the beach turns from a churn of empty moonlit water to a mass of panic life. Driven in by schools of larger fish, swarms of little fish enter the tumble of the surf, the eaters follow them, the surf catches them both up and throws them, mauled and confused, ashore.

Under a sailing moon, the whole churn of sea close off the beach vibrates with a primeval ferocity and intensity of life; yet is this war of rushing mouth and living food without a sound save for the breaking of the seas. But let me tell of such a night.

I had spent an afternoon ashore with friends, and they had driven me to Nauset Station just after nine o'clock. The moon, two days from the full, was very lovely on the moors and on the channels and flat, moon-green isles of the lagoon; the wind was southerly and light. Moved by its own enormous rhythms, the surf that night was a stately incoming of high, serried waves, the last wave alone breaking. This inmost wave broke heavily in a smother and rebound of sandy foam, and thin sheets of seethe, racing before it up the beach, vanished endlessly into the endless thirst of the sands. As I neared the surf rim to begin my walk to the southward, I saw that the beach close along the breakers, as far as the eye would reach, was curiously atwinkle in the moonlight with the convulsive dance of myriads of tiny fish. The breakers were spilling them on the sands; the surf was aswarm with the creatures; it was indeed, for the time being, a surf of life. And this surf of life was breaking for miles along the Cape.

Little herring or mackerel? Sand eels? I picked a dancer out of the slide and held him up to the moon. It was the familiar sand eel or sand launce, *Ammodytes americanus,* of the waters between Hatteras and Labrador. This is no kin of the true eels, though he rather resembles one in general appearance, for his body is slender, eel-like, and round. Instead of ending bluntly, however, this "eel" has a large, well-forked tail. The fish in the surf were two and three inches long.

Homeward that night I walked barefooted in the surf, watching the convulsive, twinkling dance, now and then feeling the squirm of

a fish across my toes. Presently something occurred which made me
keep to the thinnest edge of the foam. Some ten feet ahead, an
enormous dogfish was suddenly borne up the beach on the rim of a
slide of foam; he moved with it unresisting while it carried him; the
slide withdrawing and drying up, it rolled him twice over seaward;
he then twisted heavily, and another minor slide carried him back
again to shore. The fish was about three feet long, a real junior shark,
purplish black in the increasing light — for the moon was moving
west across the long axis of the breakers — and his dark, important
bulk seemed strange in the bright dance of the smaller fish about
him.

It was then that I began to look carefully at the width of gathering
seas. Here were the greater fish, the mouths, the eaters who had
driven the "eels" ashore to the edge of their world and into ours.
The surf was alive with dogfish, aswarm with them, with the rush,
the cold bellies, the twist and tear of their wolfish violence of life. Yet
there was but little sign of it in the waters — a rare fin slicing past,
and once the odd and instant glimpse of a fish embedded like a fly
in amber in the bright, overturning volute of a wave.

Too far in, the dogfish were now in the grip of the surf, and
presently began to come ashore. As I walked the next half mile every
other breaker seemed to leave behind its ebb a mauled and stranded
sharklet feebly sculling with his tail. I kicked many back into the seas,
risking a toe, perhaps; some I caught by the tails and flung, for I did
not want them corrupting on the beach. The next morning, in the
mile and three quarters between the Fo'castle and the station, I
counted seventy-one dogfish lying dead on the upper beach. There
were also a dozen or two skates — the skate is really a kind of shark
— which had stranded the same night. Skates follow in many things,
and are forever being flung upon these sands.

I sat up late that night at the Fo'castle, often putting down the
book I read to return to the beach.

A little after eleven came Bill Eldredge to the door, with a grin on
his face and one hand held behind his back. "Have you ordered tomorrow's dinner yet?" said he. "No." "Well, here it is," and Bill produced a fine cod from behind his back. "Just found him right in
front of your door, alive and flopping. Yes, yes, haddock and cod
often chase those sand eels in with the bigger fish; often find them
on the beach about this time of the year. Got any place to keep him?
Let me have a piece of string and I'll hang him on your clothesline.
He'll keep all right." With a deft unforking of two fingers, Bill drew
the line through the gills, and as he did so the heavy fish flopped

noisily. No fear about him being dead. Make a nice chowder. Bill stepped outside; I heard him at the clothesline. Afterward we talked till it was time for him to shoulder his clock and Coston case again, pick up his watch cap, whistle in his little black dog, and go down over the dune to the beach and Nauset Station.

There were nights in June when there was phosphorescence in the surf and on the beach, and one such night I think I shall remember as the most strange and beautiful of all the year.

Early this summer the middle beach moulded itself into a bar, and between it and the dunes are long, shallow runnels into which the ocean spills over at high tide. On the night I write of, the first quarter of the moon hung in the west, and its light on the sheets of incoming tide coursing thin across the bar was very beautiful to see. Just after sundown I walked to Nauset with friends who had been with me during the afternoon; the tide was still rising, and a current running in the pools. I lingered at the station with my friends till the last of sunset had died, and the light upon the planet, which had been moonlight mingled with sunset pink, had cleared to pure cold moon.

Southward, then, I turned, and because the flooded runnels were deep close by the station, I could not cross them and had to walk their inner shores. The tide had fallen half a foot, perhaps, but the breakers were still leaping up against the bar as against a wall, the greater ones still spilling over sheets of vanishing foam.

It grew darker with the westing of the moon. There was light on the western tops of the dunes, a fainter light on the lower beach and the breakers; the face of the dunes was a unity of dusk.

The tide had ebbed in the pools, and their edges were wet and dark. There was a strange contrast between the still levels of the pool and the seethe of the sea. I kept close to the land edge of the lagoons, and as I advanced my boots kicked wet spatters of sand ahead as they might have kicked particles of snow. Every spatter was a crumb of phosphorescence; I walked in a dust of stars. Behind me, in my footprints, luminous patches burned. With the double-ebb moonlight and tide, the deepening brims of the pools took shape in smouldering, wet fire. So strangely did the luminous speckles smoulder and die and glow that it seemed as if some wind were passing, by whose breath they were kindled and extinguished. Occasional whole breakers of phosphorescence rolled in out of the vague sea — the whole wave one ghostly motion, one creamy light — and, breaking against the bar, flung up pale sprays of fire.

A strange thing happens here during these luminous tides. The phosphorescence is itself a mass of life, sometimes protozoan its origin, sometimes bacterial, the phosphorescence I write of being probably the latter. Once this living light has seeped into the beach, colonies of it speedily invade the tissues of the ten thousand thousand sand fleas which are forever hopping on this edge of ocean. Within an hour the grey bodies of these swarming amphipods, these useful, ever hungry sea scavengers (*Orchestia agilis; Talorchestia megaloph-thalma*), show phosphorescent pin points, and these points grow and unite till the whole creature is luminous. The attack is really a disease, an infection of light. The process had already begun when I arrived on the beach on the night of which I am writing, and the luminous fleas hopping off before my boots were an extraordinary sight. It was curious to see them hop from the pool rims to the upper beach, paling as they reached the width of peaceful moonlight lying land-ward of the strange, crawling beauty of the pools. This infection kills them, I think; at least, I have often found the larger creature lying dead on the fringe of the beach, his huge porcelain eyes and water-grey body one core of living fire. Round and about him, disregarding, ten thousand kinsmen, carrying on life and the plan of life, ate of the bounty of the tide.

III

All winter long I slept on a couch in my larger room, but with the coming of warm weather I have put my bedroom in order — I used it as a kind of storage space during the cold season — and returned to my old and rather rusty iron cot. Every once in a while, however, moved by some obscure mood, I lift off the bedclothing and make up the couch again for a few nights. I like the seven windows of the larger room, and the sense one may have there of being almost out-of-doors. My couch stands alongside the two front windows, and from my pillow I can look out to sea and watch the passing lights, the stars rising over ocean, the swaying lanterns of the anchored fishermen, and the white spill of the surf whose long sound fills the quiet of the dunes.

Ever since my coming I have wanted to see a thunderstorm bear down upon this elemental coast. A thunderstorm is a "tempest" on the Cape. The quoted word, as Shakespeare used it, means lightning and thunder, and it is in this old and beautiful Elizabethan sense that the word is used in Eastham. When a schoolboy in the Orleans or the Wellfleet High reads the Shakespearean play, its title means to him exactly what it meant to the man from Stratford; elsewhere in

America, the term seems to mean anything from a tornado to a blizzard. I imagine that this old significance of the word is now to be found only in certain parts of England and Cape Cod.

On the night of the June tempest, I was sleeping in my larger room, the windows were open, and the first low roll of thunder opened my eyes. It had been very still when I went to bed, but now a wind from the west-nor'west was blowing through the windows in a strong and steady current, and as I closed them there was lightning to the west and far away. I looked at my watch; it was just after one o'clock. Then came a time of waiting in the darkness, long minutes broken by more thunder, and intervals of quiet in which I heard a faintest sound of light surf upon the beach. Suddenly the heavens cracked open in an immense instant of pinkish-violet lightning. My seven windows filled with the violent, inhuman light, and I had a glimpse of the great, solitary dunes staringly empty of familiar shadows; a tremendous crash then mingled with the withdrawal of the light, and echoes of thunder rumbled away and grew faint in a returning rush of darkness. A moment after, rain began to fall gently as if someone had just released its flow, a blessed sound on a roof of wooden shingles, and one I have loved ever since I was a child. From a gentle patter the sound of the rain grew swiftly to a drumming roar, and with the rain came the chuckling of water from the eaves. The tempest was crossing the Cape, striking at the ancient land on its way to the heavens above the sea.

Now came flash after stabbing flash amid a roaring of rain, and heavy thunder that rolled on till its last echoes were swallowed up in vast detonations which jarred the walls. Houses were struck that night in Eastham village. My lonely world, full of lightning and rain, was strange to look upon. I do not share the usual fear of lightning, but that night there came over me, for the first and last time of all my solitary year, a sense of isolation and remoteness from my kind. I remember that I stood up, watching, in the middle of the room. On the great marshes the lightning surfaced the winding channels with a metallic splendour and arrest of motion, all very strange through windows blurred by rain. Under the violences of light the great dunes took on a kind of elemental passivity, the quiet of earth enchanted into stone, and as I watched them appear and plunge back into a darkness that had an intensity of its own I felt, as never before, a sense of the vast time, of the thousands of cyclic and uncounted years which had passed since these giants had risen from the dark ocean at their feet and given themselves to the wind and the bright day.

Fantastic things were visible at sea. Beaten down by the rain, and sheltered by the Cape itself from the river of west wind, the offshore brim of ocean remained unusually calm. The tide was about halfway up the beach, and rising, and long parallels of low waves, forming close inshore, were curling over and breaking placidly along the lonely, rain-drenched miles. The intense crackling flares and quiverings of the storm, moving out to sea, illumined every inch of the beach and the plain of the Atlantic, all save the hollow bellies of the little breakers, which were shielded from the light by their overcurling crests. The effect was dramatic and strangely beautiful, for what one saw was a bright ocean rimmed with parallel bands of blackest advancing darkness, each one melting back to light as the wave toppled down upon the beach in foam.

Stars came out after the storm, and when I woke again before sunrise I found the heavens and the earth rainwashed, cool, and clear. Saturn and the Scorpion were setting, but Jupiter was riding the zenith and paling on his throne. The tide was low in the marsh channels; the gulls had scarcely stirred upon their gravel banks and bars. Suddenly, thus wandering about, I disturbed a song sparrow on her nest. She flew to the roof of my house, grasped the ridgepole, and turned about, apprehensive, inquiring . . . 'tsiped her monosyllable of alarm. Then back toward her nest she flew, alighted in a plum bush, and, reassured at last, trilled out a morning song.

DONALD CULROSS PEATTIE
(*1898–1964*)

\ After spending five relatively unsuccessful years in France as an aspiring writer, Peattie returned to Depression-era America with his young family. "Refugees" was the term he later used for them. They went to live at "The Grove," his wife's family's property in Illinois. The Grove was distinguished by some noble trees, surrounded by prairie grass, and steeped in a century-long tradition of caring stewardship. Despite these surroundings, Peattie suffered through a long season of spiritual and creative drought, several months in duration, which finally broke only at the sound of a vesper sparrow's song one June night.

Peattie heard in that song's "piercing sweetness" a heartbeat, as he later wrote, the heartbeat of "the America that was here before we Americans came to it." He began to work freshly now, awakened to a deeper dimension in nature writing than in the work he had once prepared for his newspaper columns. By the next winter, he had finished *An Almanac for Moderns*. In its recognition of the modern, existential human position, the book reflected the dry months its author had endured. It also registered the affirmation that is inherent in the songs of birds, the insistent calling of frogs, the push of life that brings mayflies and human beings into existence. The *Almanac* was a victory, gaining for Peattie a significant literary prize and launching his successful career as an interpreter of the natural world.

March

March Eighth. It is fifteen years ago now that I set off with another boy in the first rapture of an Appalachian spring, to look for the

From *An Almanac for Moderns* (1935)

flower called Shortia, the flower that Michaux discovered in some high glen of the Blue Ridge, and that was lost again for a century. One winter dusk it was, in 1788, when Michaux with his silent Indian guides was hastening back to a camp upon a nameless roaring mountain river, that he stopped a moment to pluck a single plant, a little leaf like galax, bearing still a fruit pod. He took it up, and left it in his herbarium in Paris, unidentified. But he never returned to study it, for he was destined to die far from his beloved Blue Ridge, under the killing suns of Madagascar.

And there in France, decades later, it was found by Asa Gray — a plant that no one could name, an American flower that no American had ever seen. The specimen tormented Gray; the hope of finding the plant green and growing went always with him thereafter, on expeditions through the Blue Ridge, to Mt. Mitchell, Grandfather, Roan, the Great Smokies — everywhere his friends and students sought it too. In an old book of Japanese flower prints Gray discovered its counterpart, and understood then that it belonged to one of those strange genera exclusive to the mountains of Japan and to our southern Appalachians. Still it remained elusive, until one evening just ninety-nine years after Michaux had stopped in the dusk to cull it, Charles Sargent (the grand old man of trees) chanced upon it in a dark ravine below Highlands, North Carolina.

There too I found it, in the wild, sad glen dominated by the roar of an angry river, its white foamy bells tumbling down the bank under the perpetual gloom of the laurel's shade.

March Ninth.   There is no explaining, to those who cannot feel it, the call, the fascination, the feeling in the bones like a tropism, to go plant hunting in the renewing year. I can never forget the bubbling excitement of my first botanical trip, when I too set out to look for Shortia — rediscovered now innumerable times, but what of that? Is it any less exciting when you first see land after a stormy ocean voyage, because a thousand others too have seen Finisterre rising out of the blue, a trembling mirage, a hope, a deception, a fact, a continent! Linnæus on his way to Lapland was not happier than the youngster starting off across the mountains, lost to railroads, inns, beds, houses, and even, at times, to food, to look not only for Shortia but for all the Blue Ridge held that spring of trillium, deliciously fragrant, of long-spurred violet, mountain saxifrage and gentian-colored bluets.

I feel the calling still in bones grown older, and not less poignantly because I have no longer the time nor liberty nor quite the light-heartedness to yield to it, and on this blue and green day step off

the edge of the known and vanish into some wilderness without telling where I go. But alas, there is no wilderness left for me. It is not that fifteen years ago the Blue Ridge was truly any wilder, but only that the world was younger, and I expected more of its rewards.

March Tenth. On this day did the cardinal open the morning with a great cry down in the valley below my house, "Three Cheers! Three Cheers!" The wrens are chuckling about private business of their own. Even the starlings have put on a black sheen of the courting plumage, and in the broken voices of street boys call out on the flesh and the devil, with their spring song of "Sweet Beelzebub!"

The elms are backward, and the crocuses look bullied by the wind; the oaks are still asleep. It is the hour, though, when creatures have the same aching restlessness that we call spring fever. Grackles spatter through the woods. I caught a sway-backed old white horse in the act of taking two gamboling steps in the pasture. There is a fine tumult from distant poultry that means that the hens' Grand Turk has lifted the curtain of their apartment. The salamanders have crept out to mate, in that detached, cool-blooded way of theirs, and by tomorrow their eggs may be in the pools.

March Eleventh. I have said that much of life and perhaps the best of it is not quite "nice." The business of early spring is not; it transpires in nakedness and candor, under high empty skies. Almost all the first buds to break their bonds send forth not leaves but frank catkins, or in the maple sheer pistil and stamen, devoid of the frilled trimmings of petals. The cedar sows the wind with its pollen now, because it is a relict of an age before bees, and it blooms in a month essentially barren of winged pollinators. The wood frogs, warmed like the spring flowers by the swift-heating earth, return to the primordial element of water for their spawning, and up from the oozy bottoms rise the pond frogs, to make of the half-world of the marges one breeding ground.

It is a fact that the philosopher afoot must not forget, that the astonishing embrace of the frog-kind, all in the eery green chill of earliest March, may be the attitude into which the tender passion throws these batrachians, but it is a world away from warm-blooded mating. It is a phlegmatic and persisting clasping, nothing more. It appears to be merely a reminder to the female that death brings up the rear of life's procession. When after patient hours he quits her, the female goes to the water to pour out her still unfertilized eggs. Only then are they baptized with the fecundating complement of the mate.

It is a startling bit of intelligence for the moralists, but the fact seems to be that sex is a force not necessarily concerned with reproduction; back in the primitive one-celled animals there are individuals that fuse without reproducing in consequence; the reproduction in those lowly states is but a simple fission of the cell, a self-division. It seems then that reproduction has, as it were, fastened itself on quite another force in the world; it has stolen a ride upon sex, which is a principle in its own right.

March Twelfth.   Today winter has returned in a tantrum. The ponds, turned bitter gray, look as if ice would gather on them again, and in the high leafless hardwood groves the wind flings about and stamps on the trembling shoots of wildflowers; it takes the wood in a fury, setting up a great roaring upon a single tone, high overhead, as if it had found the keynote of the trees and were vibrating them to the root. So, house-bound and angry for it, I add a few words less pleasing, perhaps, to the moralists than what has gone before.

A long survey of the ascent of sex has shown all who ever made it that the purpose of this awe-inspiring impulsion is nothing more, nor less, than the enrichment of life. Reproduction purely considered gets on a great deal better without anything so chancy as mating. What sex contributes to it is the precious gift of variation, as a result of commingling. And as variety is the spice of life, it has come to be — thanks to the invitation of sex which creatures accept with such eagerness — one of life's chief characteristics. Thus sex is what the lover has always wished to believe, a worthy end in itself. It is to be revered for its own sake, and the very batrachians know it.

March Thirteenth.   It is a complaint of the poets that men of science concern themselves not at all with beauty. But the scientists mind their own business, and they know that all men mean something different by beauty. Rodin preferred men with broken noses, old hags of the street; Romney liked handsome high-born children. To speak broadly, the variety of life is its beauty; you may choose out of that as you will.

In the age of piety, it was supposed that the purpose of living beauty was to be useful. No less a man than Darwin proposed the idea of sexual selection. The breast of a grosbeak was colored to win a mate, the catbird sang in competition with his fellows to win the little female away from them, and thus the whole duty of birds — to be fruitful and multiply — was advanced. You may pretend so if you like, but it is not demonstrable. It is even to be doubted that the color of the flowers serves any such righteous purpose as attracting the bee; many flower-haunting insects seem blind to color. The beauty of a butterfly's wing, the beauty of all things, is not a slave to purpose, a drudge sold to futurity. It is excrescence, superabundance, random ebullience, and sheer delightful waste to be enjoyed in its own high right.

March Fourteenth.   I set forth on this high-promising day for the hills, but the slope of the land drew me downward; the brook, running toward the river, led me on, and I walked as a man who knows that the day has something in store for him, something it would disclose. Before very long I was at the lowest level in this neighborhood, on the springy turf, full of green spears of coarse grass, of the river meadows. The sunlight hung in the misty willows. *Pee-yeep . . . pee-yeep* came the sweet metallic clink of the spring peepers, but when I tried to stalk them, ever so quietly, I was forestalled, surrounded by silence, a man alone on the wild useless bottom land, under the remote candor of the skies that arched the marsh and me. *Pee-yeep* — like the horizon, the sweet melancholy sound receded or closed up behind me.

Among a penciling of last year's reeds, upon the very marge, I stood and saw the frog's eggs in the water. Laid only today, perhaps, the dark velvety globules in their sphere of silver jelly shine softly up at me, reminding me that a year ago I was seeing them in this same pond, and proposing to have their secret. Well, the Ides of March

are here, they say. Can I recite the ritual of their ancient free-
masonry?

March Fifteenth.   I lift from the chill and cloudy waters of the woodland marsh a bit of frog's egg jelly, and the very feel of it on my
fingers is dubious and suggestive. I accept without even cortical re-
pulsion the sensation of their mucous envelope, for I have grown
used by now to the gelatinous feel that conveys the very nature of
protoplasm. This plasmic feel, traveling up from my nerve ends, asks
questions now of my brain.

Suppose that these eggs are so fresh-laid that they are still unfe-
cundated; are they yet come to life? At what instant does individual
life begin? Usually, we deem, from the moment that sperm meets
egg. Before that happens are the ova half alive? Or do they not
simply represent pure potentiality, such as Aristotle meant when he
called the rock in the quarry, awaiting the sculptor's chisel, potentiality?

It is just here that the mechanistic biologists have sought to drive
in their wedge. They removed the frog's eggs before they were
fecundated, and essayed to stimulate them "into life" without benefit
of fatherhood. And they discovered that chemicals, or even a mere
pinprick in the nucleus, would start the unfertilized egg cell to dividing and developing. In a few brief weeks the half-orphan tadpoles
were grown to clamorous, croaking frogs!

March Sixteenth.   Almost it seems as if the great mechanist, Jacques
Loeb, and the clever laboratory man, Bataillon, had found the break
in the charmed circle of life.

But the vitalists are ready, with the well taken reply that because a
chemical or a mechanical irritation will stimulate the unfertilized frog
eggs to develop parthenogenetically — that is, by immaculate conception — it does not follow that conception is but a physico-chemical
process as Loeb has boldly stated. For in their preoccupations with
acids and needle pricks, the mechanists have forgotten to examine
the most remarkable feature of all — the nature of the egg itself. All
that the needle and the reagent did was to release the forces of
cleavage, development and metabolism that were already stored
within the egg. The closed, charmed circle of life remains intact, was
never broken.

Behold Driesch grinding the eggs of Loeb's favorite sea urchin up
between plates of glass, pounding and breaking and deforming them
in every way. And when he ceased from thus abusing them, they
proceeded with their orderly and normal development. Is any ma-

chine conceivable, Driesch asks, which could thus be torn down into parts and have each part continue to act like a whole machine? Could any machine have its parts all disarranged and transposed, and still have them act normally? One cannot imagine it. But of the living egg, fertilized or not, we can say that there lie latent within it all the potentialities presumed by Aristotle, and all of the sculptor's dream of form, yes, and the very power in the sculptor's arm.

March Seventeenth. So at the end of it all we come to a truce between the old wrestlings of a mechanistic with a vitalistic view of life. We grant, and gladly, with a sense of kinship to the great elements and forces, that life is built of the same star-stuff as the rest of the universe. It obeys physical and chemical laws. But I am of those who believe that it is a law in itself.

A thing is either alive or it isn't; there is nothing that is almost alive. There is but the remotest possibility of the origin of life by spontaneous generation, and every likelihood that Arrhenius is right when he dares to claim that life is a cosmic phenomenon, something that drifts between the spheres, like light, and like light transiently descends upon those fit to receive it. Life is a phenomenon, *sui generis,* a primal fact in its own right, like energy. Cut flesh or wood how you like, hack at them in a baffled fury — you cannot find life itself, you can only see what it built out of the lifeless dust. Can you see energy in a cresting wave, a shaft of spring sunlight? No, energy is but a name for something absolutely primal which we cannot analyze or comprehend but only measure in science and depict in art. Life, too, is an ineffable, like thought. It is the glory on the earth.

March Eighteenth. Now all life renews, in its hopes and in its threats, in its strict needs and in all that superabundance that we call by the name of beauty. In the same place where last I found them, the pale watery shoots of Equisetum rise; buds of flowers open, all crumpled like babies' hands; the phœbes have returned to the nests at the mouth of the cave, where before they bred and where poignant accidents befell them. With a touching hopefulness all things renew themselves, not undismayed, perhaps, by the terror and chanciness of fate, but because, God help them, they can do no other.

For life is a green cataract; it is an inundation, a march against the slings of death that counts no costs. Still it advances, waving its inquisitive antennæ, flaunting green banners. Life is adventure in experience, and when you are no longer greedy for the last drop of it, it means no more than that you have set your face, whether you know it or not, to the day when you shall depart without a backward look. Those who look backward longingly to the end die young, at whatever age.

March Nineteenth. I go to the cellar for the last logs in my woodpile, and disclose a family of mice who have trustingly taken up residence there. Their tiny young, all ears and belly, mere little sacks of milk in a furless skin, lie there blind and helpless, five little tangible, irrepressible evidences of some moment, not so many nights ago, when in between the walls of my house there took place an act to which I am not so egotistic as to deny the name of love.

But it is not this which moves me, but the look in the mother's eyes as she stares up at me, her tail to the wall, all power of decision fled from her. There I read, in her agonized glance, how precious is life even to her. She entreats me not to take it from her. She does not know of pity in the world, so has no hope of it. But life — no matter how one suffers in it, hungers, flees, and fights — life is her religion.

How can we ever hope, then, to commensurate this thing which we too share, when it is its own cause, its own reason for being, when, as soon as we are challenged to stand and deliver it, we tremble and beg, like the trapped mouse?

March Twentieth. To the terror that faces mice and men, a man at least can find an answer. This will be his religion.

Now how may a man base all his faith on Nature when in Nature there is no certain end awaiting the ambition of his race? When all is flux and fleet, the great flood tides of spring that are like to drown him, and the final neap tide of decease? How take comfort from the brave new greening of the grass, when grass must wither, or in the first eery whistle of the meadow larks, saying that life is "sweet-to-you, so sweet to you"? For life is not sweet to all men. It brings some blind into this world and of others requires blood and tears. The sun toward which man turns his face is a brief candle in the universe. His woman and his children are mortal as the flowers.

But it is not life's generosity, so capricious, that makes one man happy. It is rather the extent of his gratitude to life.

I say that it touches a man that his tears are only salt, and that the tides of youth rise, and, having fallen, rise again. Now he has lived to see another spring and to walk again beneath the faintly greening trees. So, having an ear for the uprising of sap, for the running of blood, having an eye for all things done most hiddenly, and a hand in the making of those small dear lives that are not built with hands, he lives at peace with great events.

RACHEL CARSON
(1907–1964)

ૐ Rachel Carson has affected our time perhaps more profoundly than any other modern nature writer. Her best-known work, *Silent Spring* (1962), is a revolutionary text, educating its readers to "see" at the hidden but crucial cellular and genetic levels, and to realize that our consumer and lifestyle choices are of real and even urgent importance to the health of the natural world which sustains us. These are two significant ingredients of modern ecological awareness.

So important has *Silent Spring* been that we may tend to overlook Carson's other books and the lyric science that made them best sellers. They too have affected perception; it might even be argued that with their dramatic emphasis on relationships of all kinds (wind and water, for example, to take an illustration close at hand), Carson's popular books on the sea promoted just the kind of understanding that would be required for *Silent Spring*. These widely read books continue to give both pleasure and instruction, reminding inhabitants of an increasingly sheltered civilization about the great natural forces that continue to shape life on earth.

Wind and Water

The wind's feet shine along the sea.
SWINBURNE

AS THE WAVES roll in toward Lands End on the westernmost tip of England they bring the feel of the distant places of the Atlantic.

From *The Sea Around Us* (rev. ed., 1961)

Moving shoreward above the steeply rising floor of the deep sea, from dark blue water into troubled green, they pass the edge of 'soundings' and roll up over the continental shelf in confused ripplings and turbulence. Over the shoaling bottom they sweep landward, breaking on the Seven Stones of the channel between the Scilly Isles and Lands End, coming in over the sunken ledges and the rocks that roll out their glistening backs at low water. As they approach the rocky tip of Lands End, they pass over a strange instrument lying on the sea bottom. By the fluctuating pressure of their rise and fall they tell this instrument many things of the distant Atlantic waters from which they have come, and their messages are translated by its mechanisms into symbols understandable to the human mind.

If you visited this place and talked to the meteorologist in charge, he could tell you the life histories of the waves that are rolling in, minute by minute and hour after hour, bringing their messages of far-off places. He could tell you where the waves were created by the action of wind on water, the strength of the winds that produced them, how fast the storm is moving, and how soon, if at all, it will become necessary to raise storm warnings along the coast of England. Most of the waves that roll over the recorder at Lands End, he would tell you, are born in the stormy North Atlantic eastward from Newfoundland and south of Greenland. Some can be traced to tropical storms on the opposite side of the Atlantic, moving through the West Indies and along the coast of Florida. A few have rolled up from the southernmost part of the world, taking a great-circle course all the way from Cape Horn to Lands End, a journey of 6000 miles.

On the coast of California wave recorders have detected swell from as great a distance, for some of the surf that breaks on that coast in summer is born in the west-wind belt of the Southern Hemisphere. The Cornwall recorders and those in California, as well as a few on the east coast of America, have been in use since the end of the Second World War. These experiments have several objects, among them the development of a new kind of weather forecasting. In the countries bordering the North Atlantic there is no practical need to turn to the waves for weather information because meteorological stations are numerous and strategically placed. The areas in which the wave recorders are presently used have served rather as a testing laboratory to develop the method. It will soon be ready for use in other parts of the world, for which there are no meteorological data except those the waves bring. Especially in the Southern Hemisphere, many coasts are washed by waves that have come from lonely, unvisited parts of the ocean, seldom crossed by vessels, off the normal routes of the air lines. Storms may develop in these remote places, unobserved, and sweep down suddenly on mid-ocean islands or exposed coasts. Over the millions of years the waves, running ahead of the storms, have been crying a warning, but only now are we learning to read their language. Or only now, at least, are we learning to do so scientifically. There is a basis in folklore for these modern achievements in wave research. To generations of Pacific Island natives, a certain kind of swell has signaled the approach of a typhoon. And centuries ago, when peasants on the lonely shores of Ireland saw the long swells that herald a storm rolling in upon their coasts, they shuddered and talked of death waves.

Now our study of waves has come of age, and on all sides we can find evidence that modern man is turning to the waves of the sea for practical purposes. Off the Fishing Pier at Long Branch, New Jersey, at the end of a quarter-mile pipeline on the bed of the ocean, a wave-recording instrument silently and continuously takes note of the arrival of waves from the open Atlantic. By electric impulses transmitted through the pipeline, the height of each wave and the interval between succeeding crests are transmitted to a shore station and automatically recorded as a graph. These records are carefully studied by the Beach Erosion Board of the Army Corps of Engineers, which is concerned about the rate of erosion along the New Jersey coast.

Off the coast of Africa, high-flying planes recently took a series of overlapping photographs of the surf and the areas immediately offshore. From these photographs, trained men determined the speed of the waves moving in toward the shore. Then they applied a mathematical formula that relates the behavior of waves advancing into shallow water to the depths beneath them. All this information provided the British government with usable surveys of the depths off the coast of an almost inaccessible part of its empire, which could have been sounded in the ordinary way only at great expense and with endless difficulty. Like much of our new knowledge of waves, this practical method was born of wartime necessity.

Forecasts of the state of the sea and particularly the height of the surf became regular preliminaries to invasion in the Second World War, especially on the exposed beaches of Europe and Africa. But application of theory to practical conditions was at first difficult; so was the interpretation of the actual effect of any predicted height of surf or roughness of sea surface on the transfer of men and supplies between boats or from boats to beaches. This first attempt at practical military oceanography was, as one naval officer put it, a 'most fright-

ening lesson' concerning the 'almost desperate lack of basic information on the fundamentals of the nature of the sea.'

As long as there has been an earth, the moving masses of air that
we call winds have swept back and forth across its surface. And as
long as there has been an ocean, its waters have stirred to the passage
of the winds. Most waves are the result of the action of wind on
water. There are exceptions, such as the tidal waves sometimes produced by earthquakes under the sea. But the waves most of us know
best are wind waves.

It is a confused pattern that the waves make in the open sea — a
mixture of countless different wave trains, intermingling, overtaking,
passing, or sometimes engulfing one another; each group differing
from the others in the place and manner of its origin, in its speed,
its direction of movement; some doomed never to reach any shore,
others destined to roll across half an ocean before they dissolve in
thunder on a distant beach.

Out of such seemingly hopeless confusion the patient study of
many men over many years has brought a surprising amount of
order. While there is still much to be learned about waves, and much
to be done to apply what is known to man's advantage, there is a
solid basis of fact on which to reconstruct the life history of a wave,
predict its behavior under all the changing circumstances of its life,
and foretell its effect on human affairs.

Before constructing an imaginary life history of a typical wave, we
need to become familiar with some of its physical characteristics. A
wave has height, from trough to crest. It has length, the distance
from its crest to that of the following wave. The period of the wave
refers to the time required for succeeding crests to pass a fixed point.
None of these dimensions is static; all change, but bear definite
relations to the wind, the depth of the water, and many other matters.
Furthermore, the water that composes a wave does not advance with
it across the sea; each water particle describes a circular or elliptical
orbit with the passage of the wave form, but returns very nearly to
its original position. And it is fortunate that this is so, for if the huge
masses of water that comprise a wave actually moved across the sea,
navigation would be impossible. Those who deal professionally in the
lore of waves make frequent use of a picturesque expression — the
'length of fetch.' The 'fetch' is the distance that the waves have run,
under the drive of a wind blowing in a constant direction, without
obstruction. The greater the fetch, the higher the waves. Really large
waves cannot be generated within the confined space of a bay or a
small area. A fetch of perhaps 600 to 800 miles, with winds of gale
velocity, is required to get up the largest ocean waves.

Now let us suppose that, after a period of calm, a storm develops far out in the Atlantic, perhaps a thousand miles from the New Jersey coast where we are spending a summer holiday. Its winds blow irregularly, with sudden gusts, shifting direction but in general blowing shoreward. The sheet of water under the wind responds to the changing pressures. It is no longer a level surface; it becomes furrowed with alternating troughs and ridges. The waves move toward the coast, and the wind that created them controls their destiny. As the storm continues and the waves move shoreward, they receive energy from the wind and increase in height. Up to a point they will continue to take to themselves the fierce energy of the wind, growing in height as the strength of the gale is absorbed, but when a wave becomes about a seventh as high from trough to crest as the distance to the next crest it will begin to topple in foaming whitecaps. Winds of hurricane force often blow the tops off the waves by their sheer violence; in such a storm the highest waves may develop after the wind has begun to subside.

But to return to our typical wave, born of wind and water far out in the Atlantic, grown to its full height on the energy of the winds, with its fellow waves forming a confused, irregular pattern known as a 'sea.' As the waves gradually pass out of the storm area their height diminishes, the distance between successive crests increases, and the 'sea' becomes a 'swell,' moving at an average speed of about 15 miles an hour. Near the coast a pattern of long, regular swells is substituted for the turbulence of open ocean. But as the swell enters shallow water a startling transformation takes place. For the first time in its existence, the wave feels the drag of shoaling bottom. Its speed slackens, crests of following waves crowd in toward it, abruptly its height increases and the wave form steepens. Then with a spilling, tumbling rush of water falling down into its trough, it dissolves in a seething confusion of foam.

An observer sitting on a beach can make at least an intelligent guess whether the surf spilling out onto the sand before him has been produced by a gale close offshore or by a distant storm. Young waves, only recently shaped by the wind, have a steep, peaked shape even well out at sea. From far out on the horizon you can see them forming whitecaps as they come in; bits of foam are spilling down their fronts and boiling and bubbling over the advancing face, and the final breaking of the wave is a prolonged and deliberate process. But if a wave, on coming into the surf zone, rears high as though gathering all its strength for the final act of its life, if the crest forms all along its advancing front and then begins to curl forward, if the whole mass of water plunges suddenly with a booming roar into its trough — then you may take it that these waves are visitors from some very distant part of the ocean, that they have traveled long and far before their final dissolution at your feet.

What is true of the Atlantic wave we have followed is true, in general, of wind waves the world over. The incidents in the life of a wave are many. How long it will live, how far it will travel, to what manner of end it will come are all determined, in large measure, by the conditions it meets in its progression across the face of the sea. For the one essential quality of a wave is that it moves; anything that retards or stops its motion dooms it to dissolution and death.

Forces within the sea itself may affect a wave most profoundly. Some of the most terrible furies of the ocean are unleashed when tidal currents cross the path of the waves or move in direct opposition to them. This is the cause of the famous 'roosts' of Scotland, like the one off Sumburgh Head, at the southernmost tip of the Shetland Islands. During northeasterly winds the roost is quiescent, but when the wind-born waves roll in from any other quarter they encounter the tidal currents, either streaming shoreward in flood or seaward on the ebb. It is like the meeting of two wild beasts. The battle of the waves and tides is fought over an area of sea that may be three miles wide when the tides are running at full strength, first off Sumburgh Head, then gradually shifting seaward, subsiding only with the temporary slackening of the tide. 'In this confused, tumbling, and bursting sea, vessels often become entirely unmanageable and sometimes founder,' says the *British Islands Pilot,* 'while others have been tossed about for days together.' Such dangerous waters have been personified in many parts of the world by names that are handed down through generations of seafaring men. As in the time of our grandfathers and of their grandfathers, the Bore of Duncansby and the Merry Men of Mey rage at opposite ends of the Pentland Firth, which separates the Orkney Islands from the northern tip of Scotland. The sailing directions for the Firth in the *North Sea Pilot* for 1875 contained a warning to mariners, which is repeated verbatim in the modern *Pilot:*

> Before entering the Pentland Firth all vessels should be prepared to batten down, and the hatches of small vessels ought to be secured even in the finest weather, as it is difficult to see what may be going on in the distance, and the transition from smooth water to a broken sea is so sudden that no time is given for making arrangements.

Both roosts are caused by the meeting of swells from the open ocean and opposing tidal currents, so that at the east end of the Firth the Bore of Duncansby is to be feared with easterly swells and a flood tide, and at the west end the Merry Men of Mey stage their revelries with the ebb tides and a westerly swell. Then, according to the *Pilot*, 'a sea is raised which cannot be imagined by those who have never experienced it.'

Such a rip may offer protection to the near-by coast by the very fury and uncompromisingness of the struggle between waves and tide. Thomas Stevenson long ago observed that as long as the Sumburgh roost was breaking and cresting heavily off the Head there was little surf on shore; once the strength of the tide was spent and it could no longer run down the seas a heavy surf rolled in against the coast and rose to great heights on the cliffs. And in the western Atlantic, the confused and swiftly running tidal currents at the mouth of the Bay of Fundy offer such strong opposition to waves approaching from any quarter from southwest to southeast that such surf as develops within the Bay is almost entirely local in its origin.

Out in the open sea, a train of waves encountering a hostile wind may be rapidly destroyed, for the power that created a wave may also destroy it. So a fresh trade wind in the Atlantic has often flattened out the swells as they rolled down from Iceland toward Africa. Or a friendly wind, suddenly springing up to blow in the direction the waves are moving, may cause their height to increase at the rate of a foot or two per minute. Once a group of moving ridges has been created, the wind has only to fall into the troughs between them to push up their crests rapidly.

Rocky ledges, shoals of sand or clay or rock, and coastal islands in the mouths of bays all play their part in the fate of the waves that advance toward shore. The long swells that roll from the open ocean toward the shores of northern New England seldom reach it in full strength. Their energy is spent in passing over that great submerged highland known as Georges Bank, the crests of whose highest hills approach the surface over the Cultivator Shoals. The hindrance of these submarine hills, and of the tidal currents that swirl around and across them, robs the long ocean swells of their power. Or islands scattered within a bay or about its mouth may so absorb the strength of the waves that the head of the bay is free from surf. Even scattered reefs off a coast may offer it great protection, by causing the highest waves to break there, so that they never reach the shore.

Ice, snow, rain — all are enemies of the waves and under proper conditions may knock down a sea or cushion the force of surf on a beach. Within loose pack ice a vessel may count on smooth seas even if a gale is raging and surf is breaking heavily about the edges of the

pack. Ice crystals forming in the sea will smooth the waves by increasing the friction between water particles; even the delicate, crystalline
form of a snowflake has such an effect on a smaller scale. A hail
storm will knock down a rough sea, and even a sudden downpour
of rain may often turn the surface of the ocean to oiled-silk smoothness, rippling to the passage of the swells.

The divers of ancient times who carried oil in their mouths to
release beneath the surface when rough water made their work difficult were applying what every seaman today knows — that oil appears to have a calming effect on the free waves of the open ocean.
Instructions for the use of oil in emergencies at sea are carried by
most official sailing directions of maritime nations. Oil has little effect
on surf, however, once the dissolution of the wave form has begun.

In the Southern Ocean where the waves are not destroyed by
breaking on any beach, the great swells produced by the westerly
winds roll around and around the world. Here the longest waves,
and those with the greatest sidewise expanse of crest, are formed.
Here, it might be supposed, the highest waves would also be found.
Yet there is no evidence that the waves of the Southern Ocean
surpass the giants of any other ocean. A long series of reports culled
from the publications of engineers and ships' officers show that waves
higher than 25 feet from trough to crest are rare in all oceans.
Storm waves may grow twice as high, and if a full gale blows long
enough in one direction to have a fetch of 600 to 800 miles, the
resulting waves may be even higher. The greatest possible height of
storm waves at sea is a much debated question, with most textbooks
citing a conservative 60 feet, and mariners stubbornly describing
much higher waves. Throughout the century that has followed the
report of Dumont d'Urville that he encountered a wave 100 feet
high off the Cape of Good Hope, science generally has viewed such
figures with skepticism. Yet there is one record of a giant wave
which, because of the method of measurement, seems to be accepted
as reliable.

In February 1933 the U.S.S. *Ramapo,* while proceeding from Ma-
nila to San Diego, encountered seven days of stormy weather. The
storm was part of a weather disturbance that extended all the way
from Kamchatka to New York and permitted the winds an unbroken
fetch of thousands of miles. During the height of the storm the
Ramapo maintained a course running down the wind and with the
sea. On 6 February the gale reached its fiercest intensity. Winds of
68 knots came in gusts and squalls, and the seas reached mountainous
height. While standing watch on the bridge during the early hours
of that day, one of the officers of the *Ramapo* saw, in the moonlight,

a great sea rising astern to a level above an iron strap on the crow's nest of the mainmast. The *Ramapo* was on even keel and her stern was in the trough of the sea. These circumstances made possible an exact line of sight from the bridge to the crest of the wave, and simple mathematical calculations based on the dimensions of the ship gave the height of the wave. It was 112 feet.

Waves have taken their toll of shipping and of human life on the open sea, but it is around the shorelines of the world that they are most destructive. Whatever the height of storm waves at sea, there is abundant evidence, as some of the case histories that follow will show, that breaking surf and the upward-leaping water masses from thundering breakers may engulf lighthouses, shatter buildings, and hurl stones through lighthouse windows anywhere from 100 to 300 feet above the sea. Before the power of such surf, piers and breakwaters and other shore installations are fragile as a child's toys.

Almost every coast of the world is visited periodically by violent storm surf, but there are some that have never known the sea in its milder moods. 'There is not in the world a coast more terrible than this!' exclaimed Lord Bryce of Tierra del Fuego, where the breakers roar in upon the coast with a voice that, according to report, can be heard 20 miles inland on a still night. 'The sight of such a coast,' Darwin had written in his diary, 'is enough to make a landsman dream for a week about death, peril, and shipwreck.'

Others claim that the Pacific coast of the United States from northern California to the Straits of Juan de Fuca has a surf as heavy as any in the world. But it seems unlikely that any coast is visited more wrathfully by the sea's waves than the Shetlands and the Orkneys, in the path of the cyclonic storms that pass eastward between Iceland and the British Isles. All the feeling and the fury of such a storm, couched almost in Conradian prose, are contained in the usually prosaic *British Islands Pilot*:

> In the terrific gales which usually occur four or five times in every year all distinction between air and water is lost, the nearest objects are obscured by spray, and everything seems enveloped in a thick smoke; upon the open coast the sea rises at once, and striking upon the rocky shores rises in foam for several hundred feet and spreads over the whole country.
>
> The sea, however, is not so heavy in the violent gales of short continuance as when an ordinary gale has been blowing for many days; the whole force of the Atlantic is then beating against the shores of the Orkneys, rocks of many tons in weight are lifted from their beds, and the roar of the surge may be heard for twenty miles; the breakers rise to the height of 60 feet, and the broken sea on the North Shoal,

which lies 12 miles northwestward of Costa Head, is visible at Skail and Birsay.

The first man who ever measured the force of an ocean wave was Thomas Stevenson, father of Robert Louis. Stevenson developed the instrument known as a wave dynamometer and with it studied the waves that battered the coast of his native Scotland. He found that in winter gales the force of a wave might be as great as 6000 pounds to the square foot. Perhaps it was waves of this strength that destroyed the breakwater at Wick on the coast of Scotland in a December storm in 1872. The seaward end of the Wick breakwater consisted of a block of concrete weighing more than 800 tons, bound solidly with iron rods to underlying blocks of stone. During the height of this winter gale the resident engineer watched the onslaught of the waves from a point on the cliff above the breakwater. Before his incredulous eyes, the block of concrete was lifted up and swept shoreward. After the storm had subsided divers investigated the wreckage. They found that not only the concrete monolith but the stones it was attached to had been carried away. The waves had torn loose, lifted, and bodily moved a mass weighing not less than 1350 tons, or 2,700,000 pounds. Five years later it became clear that this feat had been a mere dress rehearsal, for the new pier, weighing about 2600 tons, was then carried away in another storm.

A list of the perverse and freakish doings of the sea can easily be compiled from the records of the keepers of lights on lonely ledges at sea, or on rocky headlands exposed to the full strength of storm surf. At Unst, the most northern of the Shetland Islands, a door in the lighthouse was broken open 195 feet above the sea. At the Bishop Rock Light, on the English Channel, a bell was torn away from its attachment 100 feet above high water during a winter gale. About the Bell Rock Light on the coast of Scotland one November day a heavy ground swell was running, although there was no wind. Suddenly one of the swells rose about the tower, mounted to the gilded ball atop the lantern, 117 feet above the rock, and tore away a ladder that was attached to the tower 86 feet above the water. There have been happenings that, to some minds, are tinged with the supernatural, like that at the Eddystone Light in 1840. The entrance door of the tower had been made fast by strong bolts, as usual. During a night of heavy seas the door was broken open *from within,* and all its iron bolts and hinges were torn loose. Engineers say that such a thing happens as a result of pneumatic action — the sudden back draught created by the recession of a heavy wave combined with an abrupt release of pressure on the outside of the door.

On the Atlantic coast of the United States, the 97-foot tower on Minot's Ledge in Massachusetts is often completely enveloped by masses of water from breaking surf, and an earlier light on this ledge was swept away in 1851. Then there is the often quoted story of the December storm at Trinidad Head Light on the coast of northern California. As the keeper watched the storm from his lantern 196 feet above high water, he could see the near-by Pilot Rock engulfed again and again by waves that swept over its hundred-foot crest. Then a wave, larger than the rest, struck the cliffs at the base of the light. It seemed to rise in a solid wall of water to the level of the lantern, and it hurled its spray completely over the tower. The shock of the blow stopped the revolving of the light.

Along a rocky coast, the waves of a severe storm are likely to be armed with stones and rock fragments, which greatly increase their destructive power. Once a rock weighing 135 pounds was hurled high above the lightkeeper's house on Tillamook Rock on the coast of Oregon, 100 feet above sea level. In falling, it tore a 20-foot hole through the roof. The same day showers of smaller rocks broke many panes of glass in the lantern, 132 feet above the sea. The most amazing of such stories concerns the lighthouse at Dunnet Head, which stands on the summit of a 300-foot cliff at the southwestern entrance to Pentland Firth. The windows of this light have been broken repeatedly by stones swept from the cliff and tossed aloft by waves.

For millennia beyond computation, the sea's waves have battered the coastlines of the world with erosive effect, here cutting back a cliff, there stripping away tons of sand from a beach, and yet again, in a reversal of their destructiveness, building up a bar or a small island. Unlike the slow geologic changes that bring about the flooding of half a continent, the work of the waves is attuned to the brief span of human life, and so the sculpturing of the continent's edge is something each of us can see for ourselves.

The high clay cliff of Cape Cod, rising at Eastham and running north until it is lost in the sand dunes near Peaked Hill, is wearing back so fast that half of the ten acres which the Government acquired as a site for the Highland Light has disappeared, and the cliffs are said to be receding about three feet a year. Cape Cod is not old, in geologic terms, being the product of the glaciers of the most recent Ice Age, but apparently the waves have cut away, since its formation, a strip of land some two miles wide. At the present rate of erosion, the disappearance of the outer cape is foredoomed; it will presumably occur in another 4000 or 5000 years.

The sea's method on a rocky coast is to wear it down by grinding, to chisel out and wrench away fragments of rock, each of which becomes a tool to wear away the cliff. And as masses of rock are undercut, a whole huge mass will fall into the sea, there to be ground in the mill of the surf and to contribute more weapons for the attack. On a rocky shore this grinding and polishing of rocks and fragments of rocks goes on incessantly and audibly, for the breakers on such a coast have a different sound from those that have only sand to work with — a deep-toned mutter and rumble not easily forgotten, even by one who strolls casually along such a beach. Few people have heard the sounds of the surf mill practically from within the sea, as described by Henwood after his visit to a British mine extending out under the ocean:

When standing beneath the base of the cliff, and in that part of the mine where but nine feet of rock stood between us and the ocean, the heavy roll of the larger boulders, the ceaseless grinding of the pebbles, the fierce thundering of the billows, with the crackling and boiling as they rebounded, placed a tempest in its most appalling form too vividly before me ever to be forgotten. More than once doubting the protection of our rocky shield we retreated in affright; and it was only after repeated trials that we had confidence to pursue our investigations.[1]

Great Britain, an island, has always been conscious of that 'powerful marine gnawing' by which her coasts are eaten away. An old map dated 1786 and prepared by the county surveyor, John Tuke, gives a long list of lost towns and villages on the Holderness Coast. Among them are notations of Hornsea Burton, Hornsea Beck, and Hartburn — 'washed away by the sea'; of Ancient Withernsea, Hyde, or Hythe — 'lost by the sea.' Many other old records allow comparison of present shorelines with former ones and show astonishing annual rates of cliff erosion on many parts of the coast — up to 15 feet at Holderness, 19 feet between Cromer and Mundesley, and 15 to 45 feet at Southwold. 'The configuration of the coastline of Great Britain,' one of her present engineers writes, 'is not the same for two consecutive days.'

And yet we owe some of the most beautiful and interesting shoreline scenery to the sculpturing effect of moving water. Sea caves are almost literally blasted out of the cliffs by waves, which pour into crevices in the rocks and force them apart by hydraulic pressure. Over the years the widening of fissures and the steady removal of fine rock particles in infinite number result in the excavation of a cave. Within such a cavern the weight of incoming water and the strange suctions and pressures caused by the movements of water in an enclosed space may continue the excavation upward. The roofs of such caves (and of overhanging cliffs) are subjected to blows like those from a battering ram as the water from a breaking wave is hurled upward, most of the energy of the wave passing into this smaller mass of water. Eventually a hole is torn through the roof of the cave, to form a spouting horn. Or, on a narrow promontory, what began as a cave may be cut through from side to side, so that a natural bridge is formed. Later, after years of erosion, the arch may fall, leaving the seaward mass of rock to stand alone — one of the strange, chimneylike formations known as a stack.

The sea waves that have fixed themselves most firmly in the human imagination are the so-called 'tidal waves.' The term is popularly applied to two very different kinds of waves, neither of which has any relation to the tide. One is a seismic sea wave produced by

[1] From *Transactions*, Geol. Soc. Cornwall, vol. 5, 1843.

undersea earthquakes; the other is an exceptionally vast wind or storm wave — an immense mass of water driven by winds of hurricane force far above the normal high-water line.

Most of the seismic sea waves, now called 'tsunamis,' are born in the deepest trenches of the ocean floor. The Japanese, Aleutian, and Atacama trenches have each produced waves that claimed many human lives. Such a trench is, by its very nature, a breeder of earthquakes, being a place of disturbed and uneasy equilibrium, of buckling and warping downward of the sea floor to form the deepest pits of all the earth's surface. From the historic records of the ancients down to the modern newspaper, the writings of man contain frequent mention of the devastation of coastal settlements by these great waves that suddenly rise out of the sea. One of the earliest of record rose along the eastern shores of the Mediterranean in A.D. 358, passing completely over islands and low-lying shores, leaving boats on the housetops of Alexandria, and drowning thousands of people. After the Lisbon earthquake of 1755, the coast at Cadiz was visited by a wave said to have been 50 feet higher than the highest tide. This came about an hour after the earthquake. The waves from this same disturbance traveled across the Atlantic and reached the West Indies in 9½ hours. In 1868, a stretch of nearly 3000 miles of the western coast of South America was shaken by earthquakes. Shortly after the most violent shocks, the sea receded from the shore, leaving ships that had been anchored in 40 feet of water stranded in mud; then the water returned in a great wave, and boats were carried a quarter of a mile inland.

This ominous withdrawal of the sea from its normal stand is often the first warning of the approach of seismic sea waves. Natives on the beaches of Hawaii on the first of April 1946 were alarmed when the accustomed voice of the breakers was suddenly stilled, leaving a strange quiet. They could not know that this recession of the waves from the reefs and the shallow coastal waters was the sea's response to an earthquake on the steep slopes of a deep trench off the island of Unimak in the Aleutian chain, more than 2000 miles away; or that in a matter of moments the water would rise rapidly, as though the tide were coming in much too fast, but without surf. The rise carried the ocean waters 25 feet or more above the normal levels of the tide. According to an eyewitness account:

> The waves of the tsunami swept toward shore with steep fronts and great turbulence . . . Between crests the water withdrew from shore, exposing reefs, coastal mud-flats, and harbor bottoms for distances up

to 500 feet or more from the normal strand-line. The outflow of the water was rapid and turbulent, making a loud hissing, roaring, and rattling noise. At several places houses were carried out to sea, and in some areas even large rocks and blocks of concrete were carried out onto the reefs . . . People and their belongings were swept to sea, some being rescued hours later by boats and life rafts dropped from planes.[2]

In the open ocean the waves produced by the Aleutian quake were only about a foot or two high and would not be noticed from vessels. Their length, however, was enormous, with a distance of about 90 miles between succeeding crests. It took the waves less than five hours to reach the Hawaiian chain, 2300 miles distant, so they must have moved at an average speed of about 470 miles per hour. Along eastern Pacific shores, they were recorded as far into the Southern Hemisphere as Valparaiso, Chile, the distance of 8066 miles from the epicenter being covered by the waves in about 18 hours.

This particular occurrence of seismic sea waves had one result that distinguished it from all its predecessors. It set people to thinking that perhaps we now know enough about such waves and how they behave that a warning system could be devised which would rob them of the terror of the unexpected. Seismologists and specialists on waves and tides co-operated, and now such a system has been established to protect the Hawaiian Islands. A network of stations equipped with special instruments is scattered over the Pacific from Kodiak to Pago Pago and from Balboa to Palau. There are two phases of the warning system. One is based on a new audible alarm at seismograph stations operated by the United States Coast and Geodetic Survey, which calls instant attention to the fact that an earthquake has occurred. If it is found that the epicenter of the quake is under the ocean and so might produce seismic sea waves, a warning is sent to observers at selected tide stations to watch their gauges for evidence of the passage of the racing tsunamis. (Even a very small seismic wave can be identified by its peculiar period, and though it may be small at one place, it may reach dangerous heights at another.) When seismologists in Honolulu are notified that an undersea earthquake has occurred and that its waves have actually been recorded at certain stations, they can calculate when the waves will arrive at any point between the epicenter of the quake and the Hawaiian Islands. They can then issue warnings for the evacuation of beaches and waterfront areas. And so, for the first time in history, there is an organized effort to prevent these ominous waves from

[2]From *Annual Rept.*, Smithsonian Inst., 1947.

racing undetected over the empty spaces of the Pacific, to roar up suddenly on some inhabited shore.[3]

The storm waves that sometimes rise over low-lying coast lands in hurricane zones belong in the class of wind waves, but unlike the waves of ordinary winds and storms, they are accompanied by a rise of the general water level, called a storm tide. The rise of water is often so sudden that it leaves no possibility of escape. Such storm waves claim about three-fourths of the lives lost by tropical hurricanes. The most notable disasters from storm waves in the United States have been those at Galveston, Texas, on 8 September, 1900, on the lower Florida Keys on 2 and 3 September, 1935, and the catastrophic rise of water accompanying the New England hurricane of 21 September, 1938. The most fearful destruction by hurricane waves within historic time occurred in the Bay of Bengal on 7 October, 1737, when 20,000 boats were destroyed and 300,000 people drowned.[4]

There are other great waves, usually called 'rollers,' that periodically rise on certain coasts and batter them for days with damaging

[3]From the time of its establishment up to 1960, the warning system has issued eight alerts warning residents of the Hawaiian Islands of the approach of seismic waves. On three of these occasions, waves of major proportions have in fact struck the islands. None have been so large or so destructive, however, as those of May 23, 1960, which spread out across the Pacific from their place of origin in violent earthquakes on the coast of Chile. Without such warning the loss of life would almost certainly have been enormous. As soon as the seismograph at the Honolulu Observatory recorded the first of the Chilean quakes the system went into operation. Reports from the scattered tide stations gave ample notice that a seismic wave had formed and was spreading out across the Pacific. By early news bulletins and later by an official "sea wave warning" the Observatory alerted residents of the area and predicted the time the wave would arrive and the areas to be affected. These predictions proved to be accurate within reasonable limits, and although property damage was heavy, loss of life was limited to the few who disregarded the warnings. Sea wave activity was reported as far west as New Zealand and as far north as Alaska. The Japanese coasts were struck by heavy waves. Although the United States warning system does not now include other nations, officials at Honolulu sent to Japan warnings of the wave which, unfortunately, were disregarded.

The warning system now (in 1960) consists of eight seismograph stations at points on both eastern and western shores of the Pacific and on certain islands, and of twenty widely scattered wave stations, four of which are equipped with automatic wave detectors. The Coast and Geodetic Survey feels that additional wave-reporting tide stations would improve the effectiveness of the system. Its principal defect now, however, is the fact that it is not possible to predict the height of a wave as it reaches any particular shore, and therefore the same alert must be issued for all approaching seismic waves. Research on methods of forecasting wave height is therefore needed. Even with its present limitations, however, the system has filled so great a need that there is strong international interest in extending it to other parts of the world.

[4]The flood of ocean waters that overwhelmed the coast of the Netherlands on February 1, 1953, deserves a place in the history of great storm waves. A winter gale that formed

surf. These, too, are wind waves, but they are related to changes in barometric pressure over the ocean, perhaps several thousand miles distant from the beaches on which the waves eventually arrive. Low-pressure areas — like the one south of Iceland — are notorious storm breeders, their winds lashing the sea into great waves. After the waves leave the storm area they tend to become lower and longer and after perhaps thousands of miles of travel across the sea they become transformed into the undulations known as a ground swell. These swells are so regular and so low that often they are unnoticed as they pass through the short, choppy, new-formed waves of other areas. But when a swell approaches a coast and feels beneath it the gradually shoaling bottom, it begins to 'peak up' into a high, steep wave; within the surf zone the steepening becomes abruptly accentuated, a crest forms, breaks, and a great mass of water plunges downward.

Winter swell on the west coast of North America is the product of storms that travel south of the Aleutians into the Gulf of Alaska. Swell reaching this same coast during the summer has been traced back to its origin in the Southern Hemisphere belt of the 'roaring forties,' several thousand miles south of the equator. Because of the direction of the prevailing winds, the American east coast and the Gulf of Mexico do not receive the swell from far distant storms.

The coast of Morocco has always been particularly at the mercy of swell, for there is no protected harbor from the Strait of Gibraltar southward for some 500 miles. The rollers that visit the Atlantic islands of Ascension, St. Helena, South Trinidad, and Fernando de Noronha are historic. Apparently the same sort of waves occur on the South American coast near Rio de Janeiro, where they are known as *resacas;* others of kindred nature, having run their course from storms in the west-wind belt of the South Pacific, attack the shores of the Paumotos Islands; still others have been responsible for the well-known 'surf days' that plague the Pacific coast of South America. According to Robert Cushman Murphy, it was formerly the custom

---

west of Iceland swept across the Atlantic and into the North Sea. All its force was ultimately brought to bear on the first land mass to obstruct the course of its center — the southwestern corner of Holland. The storm-driven waves and tides battered against the dikes in such bitter violence that these ancient defenses were breached in a hundred places, through which the flood rushed in to inundate farms and villages. The storm struck on Saturday, January 31, and by midday of Sunday one-eighth of Holland was under water. The toll included about half a million acres of Holland's best agricultural land — ravaged by water and permeated with salt — thousands of buildings, hundreds of thousands of live stock, and an estimated 1400 people. In all the long history of Holland's struggle against the sea, there has been no comparable assault by ocean waters.

of shipmasters in the guano trade to demand a special allowance for
a certain number of days during which the loading of their vessels
would be interrupted by the swell. On such surf days 'mighty rollers
come pouring over the sea wall, and have been known to carry away
forty-ton freight cars, to uproot concrete piers, and to twist iron rails
like wire.'

The slow progression of swell from its place of origin made it
possible for the Moroccan Protectorate to establish a service for the
prediction of the state of the sea. This was done in 1921, after long
and troublesome experience with wrecked vessels and wharves. Daily
telegraphic reports of the condition of the sea give advance notice of
troublesome surf days. Warned of the approach of swells, ships in
port may seek safety in the open sea. Before this service was established, the port of Casablanca had once been paralyzed for seven
months, and St. Helena had seen the wreckage of practically all the
ships in her harbor on one or more occasions. Modern wave-recording instruments like those now being tested in England and the
United States will soon provide even greater security for all such
shores.

It is always the unseen that most deeply stirs our imagination, and
so it is with waves. The largest and most awe-inspiring waves of the
ocean are invisible; they move on their mysterious courses far down
in the hidden depths of the sea, rolling ponderously and unceasingly.
For many years it was known that the vessels of Arctic expeditions
often became almost trapped and made headway only with difficulty
in what was called 'dead water' — now recognized as internal waves
at the boundary between a thin surface layer of fresh water and the
underlying salt water. In the early 1900's several Scandinavian hy-
drographers called attention to the existence of submarine waves,
but another generation was to elapse before science had the instruments to study them thoroughly.

Now, even though mystery still surrounds the causes of these great
waves that rise and fall, far below the surface, their oceanwide occurrence is well established. Down in deep water they toss submarines
about, just as their surface counterparts set ships to rolling. They
seem to break against the Gulf Stream and other strong currents in
a deep-sea version of the dramatic meeting of surface waves and
opposing tidal currents. Probably internal waves occur wherever
there is a boundary between layers of dissimilar water, just as the
waves we see occur at the boundary between air and sea. But these
are waves such as never moved at the surface of the ocean. The water
masses involved are unthinkably great, some of the waves being as
high as 300 feet.

Of their effect on fishes and other life of the deep sea we have only the faintest conception. Swedish scientists say that the herring are carried or drawn into some of the fiords of Sweden when the deep internal waves roll over the submerged sills and into the fiords. In the open ocean, we know that the boundary between water masses of different temperatures or salinities is often a barrier that may not be passed by living creatures, delicately adjusted to certain conditions. Do these creatures themselves then move up and down with the roll of the deep waves? And what happens to the bottom fauna of the continental slope, adjusted, it may be, to water of unchanging warmth? What is their fate when the waves move in from a region of arctic cold, rolling like a storm surf against those deep, dark slopes? At present we do not know. We can only sense that in the deep and turbulent recesses of the sea are hidden mysteries far greater than any we have solved.

JOSEPH WOOD KRUTCH
(1893–1970)

&2 When he turned his full attention to natural history in the 1950s, Joseph Wood Krutch approached the tricky, complex subject of animal consciousness with particular care. He rejected interpretations that smacked of any sort of mysticism, yet he could not accept a purely mechanistic view of life and mind. Surely there must be more to a bird's song than an automatonlike announcement of territory. For himself, he wanted above all simply to see clearly: "What I am after is less to meet God face to face than really to take in a beetle, a frog, or a mountain lion when I meet one." Because of this caution and essential sincerity, Krutch's comparisons of man and animals, his analysis of evolution, and his thoughts on man's place in the spectrum of life tend to carry weight. His nature essays, particularly those built on the remarkable adaptations of life to desert conditions, have been some of the most influential of recent decades.

The Meaning of Awareness

THE YOU AND THE ME

FOR NINE LONG YEARS a large salamander lived her sluggish life in a damp terrarium on my window sill. Before I assumed responsibility for her health and welfare she had lived through a different life — not as different as the life of a butterfly is from that of a caterpillar, but different enough. Once she had lived in water and breathed it. Like her parents before her she still had to keep her skin damp, but now she seldom actually went into the water.

From *The Great Chain of Life* (1956)

Before she was even an egg her father and her mother, prompted by some no doubt unconscious memory, had left the damp moss or leaves they had normally preferred since achieving maturity and had climbed down into some pond or pool to mate. The prompt result was a cluster of eggs embedded in a mass of jelly much like that which surrounds the eggs of common American frogs. These eggs had hatched into tadpoles easily distinguishable from those destined to become frogs or toads by the two plumes waving from their shoulders — gills for breathing the water which frogs manage to get along without even though they too are temporarily water-breathers.

Most of my specimen's subsequent history was much like that of the young frogs themselves. Legs had budded, and though the tail had not disappeared the plumes had withered away while lungs fit for air-breathing had developed. Sally, as I called her, had then left the water and become a land animal. All this took place quite gradually without any radical dissolution of the organism as a whole, as in the case of the caterpillar, and without the intervention of that dead sleep from which the caterpillar woke to find himself somebody else. Far back in time, Sally's direct ancestors had been the first vertebrates to risk coming to land, and she recapitulated their history.

The rest of my salamander's life was very uneventful but not much more so than it would have been had I left her to her own devices. In fact, returning to the water is almost the only interesting thing the amphibia ever *do*. By comparison with even the butterflies — who lead very uneventful lives as insects go — the amphibia are dull creatures indeed, seemingly without enterprise, aspiration, or any conspicuous resourcefulness.

If you or I had been permitted a brief moment of consciousness sometime about the middle of the Mesozoic era, when the amphibia and the insects were both flourishing, we well might have concluded that the latter were the more promising experiment. I doubt that we would have been very likely to pick out a salamander as our ancestor. Yet the evidence seems pretty definite that nature knew better and that it is from him we come. In Old Testament terms, Amphibia begat Reptile, Reptile begat Mammal, Mammal begat Man.

Even before the Mesozoic was over the beetles were far ahead of the salamanders so far as the techniques of living are concerned. "What," we might well have asked, "do the amphibia have that the insects do not?" What potentiality in them was responsible for the fact that, given the whole Cenozoic still to develop in, the one got no farther than the bee and the ant, while the other has ended — if this is indeed the end — in man?

*

Perhaps if that anticipatory visit had lasted long enough we could finally have guessed the answer as easily as it can be guessed today by anyone who has kept both insects and salamanders in captivity and has observed one great difference between them. The insect goes very expertly about his business. But not even those insects who go very expertly about their very complicated business give any sign of awareness of anything not directly connected with that immediate business.

It is not merely that they are absolutely, or almost absolutely, incapable of learning anything. A salamander cannot learn very much either. But the salamander has some awareness of the world outside himself and he has, therefore, the true beginnings of a self — as we understand the term. A butterfly or a beetle does not. Hence you can make a pet out of a salamander — at least to the extent necessary to fulfill the minimum definition of that word. He will come to depend upon you, to profit from your ministrations, and to expect them at appropriate times. An insect is never more than a captive. If you help him he does not know it and he will never come to depend upon your ministrations. He does not even know that you exist. And because of what that implies, a whole great world of experience was opened up to the hierarchy of vertebrates from the salamander on up and has remained closed to the insect.

Seen from the outside, the ants who keep cows, practice agriculture, make war, and capture slaves suggest human beings more strongly than any vertebrate lower than the apes. But if we could see from the inside, the psyche of even the sluggish salamander in my window terrarium would be different. In some dim way she has connected me with herself and I am part of her life.

My old housekeeper used to assure me pridefully from time to time: "She knows me." That, I am afraid, was a bit of overinterpretation. I doubt very seriously that Sally could tell me and my housekeeper apart. But if either one of us approached the terrarium she would rise heavily on her short legs and amble slowly in the direction of the familiar object. We were associated in what little mind she had with the prospect of food.

Was this, many will ask, more than a mere reflex action? Did any such consciousness as I have been assuming really exist? I will not answer that question in the affirmative as positively as many would answer it in the negative. But the consciousness which is so acute in us must have begun dimly somewhere and to me it seems probable that it had already begun at least as far back as the salamanders who lie, though remotely, on our own direct line of descent.

Yet if Sally just barely achieved the status of a pet she fell considerably short of being what we call a domesticated animal. Considerably more awareness of the world around her and considerably more capacity to make an individual adaptation to it would be necessary for that. But because dogs and cats and horses — all of whom have, like us, a salamander in their ancestry — have that considerably greater awareness, they can live a considerable part of our lives and come to seem actual members of our family. Even they are not nearly as ingenious as bees or ants. But we recognize their nearer kinship to us.

Those ants have a culture not only analogous to ours in certain respects but one also far older than ours, since the social insects have been civilized for a much longer time — perhaps thirty times longer — than we have. This was possible because they had settled down biologically — i.e., had ceased to evolve organically — long before we did. And since they were not changing rapidly, they had time to mature and to settle irrevocably into habits and customs, while we are even now still experimenting wildly — discarding habits and techniques every decade or two.

By ant standards we have never had any traditions loyally adhered to. Their so-called virtues — industry, selfless devotion to the good of the community, etc. — are so strikingly superior to ours that certain fanatical critics of human nature and its ways have implied that these creatures whom the biologist calls "lower" are morally "better" than we, and have hoped that in a few million years we might become more like them. Even without going that far and leaving ourselves resolutely out of it as obviously *hors concours,* we may still find ourselves raising again the outrageous question already alluded to. By what right do we call the ants "lower" than, say, a member of a wolf pack? On what basis is the hierarchy established?

Ask that question of a biologist and he will give you ready reasons satisfactory to himself. Anatomically, the insects are simpler. They show very little adaptability. They cannot learn as readily as a wolf can. They can't change their habits very much. They have come to a dead end. They have been precisely what they are for a very long time and will remain that for a very long time to come. "Progress" is something they no longer know anything about. And they are not "intelligent."

All these statements are true enough, but like so many biological distinctions and standards they seem just a little remote. To say that an animal is a compulsory protein feeder is, as we remarked once before, perfectly accurate but has little to do with the rich complex of meanings the word "animal" suggests to the human being who hears it. In certain contexts it is fine. In other contexts — the context of a poem, for instance — it isn't.

Indisputable accuracy does not make it much more satisfactory than Plato's definition of man — a two-legged animal without feathers. Man is certainly that and no other animal is. His definition establishes a criterion that is infallible, but also entirely irrelevant. Apply the test and you will never mistake a wolf or a bird for a man or even mistake a primate — always more or less four-footed — for one of your fellow citizens. This really is a sure way of telling your friends from the apes. But then, you would not be very likely to make a mistake anyway. The definition is perfect but also meaningless.

The explanation a biologist would give why a wolf is "higher" than an ant is almost equally unsatisfactory, because it does not seem to involve the thing on the basis of which we make our judgment. Should they reverse themselves tomorrow and give new reasons in similar terms for deciding that the ant is "higher" we would go right on feeling that he is not. On what, then, is this feeling based if not upon any good scientific criteria? What kind of distinctions appeal to us as genuinely meaningful?

Suppose you play the childish game. Suppose you ask yourself which you would rather be — a farmer ant or a robin. Only the perverse would hesitate. "A robin, of course." But why? What it would come to would certainly be something like this: "Because being a robin would be more fun. Because the robin exhibits the joy of life. Because he seems to be glad to be a robin and because it is hard to believe that an ant is glad to be what he is." Of course we can't say positively that he isn't. We cannot understand his language and he may be proclaiming to the world of other ants with what ecstasy he contemplates the fact that he is one of them. But he cannot communicate with us, and, justifiably or not, we find it hard to believe that he is glad.

Privately, biologists often share our prejudice. But few, I am afraid, would agree to classify animals as "higher" or "lower" on any such basis. They would reply, and rightly so far as biology is concerned, that to say a robin is higher than an ant because he has more joy in living is to cease to be scientific. Also, some might think that it smacks of immoral hedonism. Nevertheless a hierarchy ordered on that basis is meaningful in human terms as the scientific one is not.

If the joy of living is the most enviable good any of the lower animals can attain to and at least the second-best available to man

himself, that implies in both a more general capacity which can only be called "awareness" — something that is different from intelligence as usually defined and not perfectly equatable with logic, or insight, or adaptability; also something the salamander has more of than the ant has. There is no way of measuring it, and even the psychologist would be for that reason rather loath to take it much into consideration or even to admit that it exists as distinguished from reason, insight, and the rest. That it does exist in human beings, any contemplative man knows from his own experience.

The best solver of puzzles is not necessarily the man most aware of living. The animal who most skillfully adapts himself to the conditions for survival is not necessarily the one who has the greatest joy in living. And from the standpoint of one kind of interest in living creatures it is perfectly legitimate to think of them as "high" or "low" in proportion to the degree of awareness they exhibit.

We can freely admit that the ant's technique of making a living is far more advanced than that of the bird or, indeed, of any vertebrate animal except man. We can see that some species of ants have reached what in terms of human history corresponds to an agricultural society, whereas there is no vertebrate who is not still a mere nomad hunter. But living — as some men have got around to telling themselves — can be more important than making a living. And making a living seems to be all the ant does, while the robin and many another vertebrate live abundantly.

Yes, I say to myself, the "higher" animals really are higher. Even the sluggish, dim-witted salamander, cold-blooded but vertebrate and with the beginnings of a vertebrate brain, is "higher" than the industrious ant. But it is not for any of the objective reasons either the biologist or the social anthropologist will consent to give that I call him so.

It is because even the salamander has some sort of awareness the insects have not; because, unlike them, he is on his way to intelligence, on his way to pain and pleasure, on his way to courage, and even to a sense of honor as the bighorn is beginning to feel it; on his way to Love, which the birds, bungling parents though they are, can feel and the wise wasp cannot. On the way to the joy of life, which only one or more of these things can make possible.

Once you admit this fact there is something obviously wrong with the orthodox view of the aims and methods of that evolutionary process through which both the blindly efficient ant and the blunderingly emotional bird arrived at their present state. According to that orthodox view "survival value" is the key to everything. But though intelligence does have an obvious survival value, it is by no means obvious that it works any better than the instinct of the insect. As for the emotions, their survival value is not always obvious at all. And if you want to include man in the scheme of evolution, it is so far from obvious that the complexities of civilized emotional and intellectual life have any survival value at all that many recent philosophers have suspected them of being fatal handicaps instead.

This is a fact that raises a question for the evolutionist. If the survival value of intelligence is real enough though no greater than that of instinct, if many of our emotions and the kind of awareness upon which they depend have no obvious survival value at all, then why have certain animals developed both to such a high degree? Why, for that matter, have either they or we developed them at all? Doubtless an intelligent *individual* has a better chance of individual survival than a merely instinctive one. But if nature is careful of the type, careless of the individual, then why should that weigh anything in the scales?

Darwin himself formulated a "law." No organism, he said, ever develops a characteristic beyond the point where it is useful for survival. But, as we have been asking, how useful in that sense is intelligence or even consciousness? Doesn't instinct have an even higher survival value?

It is pretty generally recognized that the insects are the most successful organisms on earth. It is also generally recognized that they get along either with the dimmest consciousness and intelligence, or perhaps without any at all. It is even believed by many that they lost a good deal of what they once had because instinct proved to have a higher survival value. If all this is true does it not suggest that orthodox evolutionism may be in one respect wrong? Does it not suggest that nature (or whatever you want to call it) puts a value on things which do not have any simple survival value? Is it not possible that mammals look after their young with bumbling consciousness rather than with the expertness of instinct because nature has, in some way, been interested not merely in the survival of the fittest, but in "the fittest" for something more than mere survival.

This last question, in a somewhat different form, was actually asked and then left unanswered in the earliest days of Darwinism. Alfred Russel Wallace, generously acknowledged by Darwin as the co-propounder of the theory of natural selection, steadily and from the beginning maintained one difference with his more famous co-worker. It was not and could not be demonstrated, he said, that natural selection could account for "the higher qualities of man." Most notable among these "higher qualities" was, he maintained, the moral sense.

No doubt some manifestations of it had a survival value in society. But not all of them. Man's willingness, sometimes at least, not only to sacrifice himself but to sacrifice himself and others for an ideal, his human conviction that "survival value" is not the only value, did not in themselves have any "survival value." How then could they have arisen if it was, as Darwin said, the inviolable rule of nature that no organism can develop what is not biologically useful to it? An all-inclusive explanation of the phenomenon of life in terms of natural selection would have to account somehow for the very conception of "values which have no survival value." And no such inclusive explanation is forthcoming.

For the most part this question has been simply brushed aside by orthodox evolutionists. Along with other related questions it has been kept alive chiefly by "mere men of letters" — by Samuel Butler, Bergson, Bernard Shaw, and the rest. But it will not down. And there are even signs that some scientists, perhaps especially the neurologists, are less sure than they once were that the mechanistic explanation of all the phenomena of living matter is complete. But if nature has been working toward something besides survival, what is it?

Julian Huxley, one of the most enlightened of present-day evolutionists, has tangled with the question. Evolution, he says, implies progress. But in what does "progress" consist? Certainly, as he admits, it includes something more than a mere progressive increase in the amount of living matter on the earth. That could be achieved by the simplest forms. Nature "wants" not merely more organisms but more complex organisms. But how can it want them if they do not survive more abundantly? Greater complexity implies, he says, "improvement." But what constitutes an "improved" organism? Not, he says, mere complexity itself but a complexity which opens the way to further "improvement." That, it seems, simply closes the circle. The question of what constitutes "improvement" and what sort of values other than mere survival value nature does recognize is still unanswered.

Perhaps the only way to escape from the dilemma that a Huxley recognizes is to make an assumption bolder than he would probably be willing to accept. But the difficulties do vanish if we are willing to accept the possibility that what nature has been working toward is not merely survival; that, ultimately, it is not survival itself but Consciousness and Intelligence *themselves* — partly at least for their own sake.

If Nature has advanced from the inanimate to the animate; if she "prefers" the living to the lifeless and the forms of life which survive rather to those that perish; then there is nothing which forbids the assumption that she also "prefers" conscious intelligence to blind instinct; that just as complex organization was developed even though it had no obvious survival value for the species, so also the awareness of itself which complex organization made possible is also one of her goals.

Whenever man's thinking starts with himself rather than with his possible origins in lower forms of life he usually comes to the conclusion that consciousness is the primary fact. "I think therefore I am" seems to be the most inescapably self-evident of propositions. Only when he starts as far away from himself as possible can he get into the contrary habit of assuming what the nineteenth century did assume: namely, that his own mind is so far from being the most significant thing in the universe that it has no substantial significance at all, being a mere illusion, some sort of insubstantial by-product of those ultimate realities which are unconscious, automatic, and mechanical.

Ever since the seventeenth century, science actually has tended to begin as far away from man himself as possible, while metaphysics has continued to start with man's own mind. Hence the undoubted fact that for a long time, at least, science and metaphysics either grew farther and farther apart, or, as with the positivists, metaphysics simply surrendered to science and tended to become no more than an abstractly stated theory of the validity of science. Yet, as we have just seen, science and positivism leave certain stubborn questions unanswered. Perhaps these questions will ultimately have to be attacked again and from the older point of view.

Aristotle is the acknowledged father of natural history. But because Aristotle lived in an age when it still seemed natural to start with the human mind itself, he reached the conclusion that at least so far as man himself is concerned Contemplation is what he is "for." And if Aristotle had had any clear idea of evolution he would certainly have supposed that a more and more complete awareness, not mere survival, was what nature was aiming at.

Most present-day biologists, following the lead of the nineteenth century, have no patience with any such metaphysical notions. When you come right down to it man is, they say, an animal; and there is only one thing that any animal is "for" — namely, survival and reproduction. Some animals accomplish this purpose in one way and some in another. Man's way happens to involve some consciousness of what he is doing and of why he does it. But that is a mere accident. If what we call intelligence had not had a high survival value it would never have developed. And one of the consequences of this fact is that man is most successful when he uses his intelligence to facilitate his survival. Thinking, or even awareness, for its own sake is a biological mistake. What he is "for" is *doing,* certainly not mooning over what he has done — unless of course that mooning has survival value, as under certain circumstances it may.

What we have been asking is, then, simply this: How good is the evidence — even their own kind of evidence — which those who take this position can offer in its support? If they are right, then man ought biologically to be the most successful of all animals. No other ought to flourish so exuberantly or have a future which, biologically, looks so bright. But what grounds do we really have for believing anything like that to be the real state of affairs? Does conscious intelligence really work any better than instinct?

No doubt you and I are the most successful of the mammals. When we take possession of any part of this earth the others go into a decline. No bear or wolf, no whale or buffalo, can successfully compete with us. But that doesn't really mean much, because all the mammals are creatures who have already started down the road we have followed so much farther than they. To some considerable extent they too are conscious, intelligent, capable of learning much from experience. Like us they are born with mental slates which, if not entirely blank, have much less written on them than is indelibly inscribed before birth on the nervous systems of many a "lower" animal.

Obviously if you are going to have to depend upon conscious intelligence, then it is an advantage to have that conscious intelligence highly developed. The other mammals over whom we triumph so easily have to fight us chiefly with inferior versions of our own weapons and it is no wonder that they lose. But what of the creatures who learn little or nothing, who can hardly be said to be capable of thought, who are conscious only dimly if at all? Are they really, from the biological standpoint, any less "successful" than we or the other mammals? Can they be said to "succeed" any less well? Are they deprived of anything except consciousness itself?

It is certainly not evident that they are. As a matter of fact the insects are the only conspicuous creatures indubitably holding their own against man. When he matches wits with any of the lower mammals they always lose. But when he matches his wit against the instinct and vitality of the insects he merely holds his own, at best. An individual insect is no match for an individual man. But most species of insects have done very well at holding their own as a species against him. And if you believe the biologists it is only with the prosperity of the species that Nature, or evolution, has ever, or could ever, concern herself.

Who is the more likely to be here on what evolution calls tomorrow — i.e., ten million years hence? Certainly the chance that man will have destroyed himself before then seems greater than the chance that the insects will have done so. Their instincts seem not to have created for them the difficulties and the dangers man's intelligence and emotion have created for him. They have been here much longer than he and it certainly seems not improbable that they will remain here much longer also. As a matter of fact the bacteria are even more "successful" than the insects. There are far more of them alive at this moment than there are of even insects, and it is even more difficult to imagine them ever extinct. If survival is the only thing that counts in nature then why or how did any life higher than that of a bacterium ever come into being?

No answer to that question seems possible unless we are willing to assume that for Nature herself, as well as for us, the instinct of the insect is "better" than the vegetative life of the bacterium, and the conscious concern of the bird for its offspring better than the unconscious efficiency of the wasp. Yet vegetation is not better than instinct and consciousness is not better than instinct if the only criterion is survival value. And if man's mind does not help him to survive more successfully than creatures having no mind at all, then what on earth can it be for? Can it be for anything except itself? Can its value be other than absolute rather than instrumental?

The bird and the man are more successful than the wasp only if you count their consciousness as, itself, some kind of success. The "purpose" of parental concern cannot be merely the successful rearing of offspring, because that can be accomplished quite as successfully without any consciousness at all.

Is it not possible, then, that Aristotle was right, that contemplation is not only the true end of man but the end that has been pursued ever since vertebrates took the road leading to a keener and keener consciousness? Have we been trying to understand the meaning of evolution by beginning at the wrong end? Is it possible that, for instance, the real, the only true "purpose" served by conscious concern over the young is the fact that out of it comes parental love itself? Has what evolution worked toward been not "survival" but "awareness"? Is the ultimate answer to the question "Why is a bungling mammal higher than an efficient wasp" simply that it is higher because it can experience parental love? Was it this, rather than mere survival, that nature was after all along?

PETER MATTHIESSEN
(*1927–*   )

8❧ Besides natural history and other kinds of essays, Peter Matthiessen writes novels, and along with nature study he practices formal meditation. Not surprisingly, his descriptive prose is characterized by movement and drama; his wild animals reveal character; and his images often have both the clarity of absolute suchness and the relational power of focusing instantly a complex scene. They are, in a word, ecological. He is also a careful compiler of facts, as shown first in *Wildlife in America* (1959), recently updated and revised and still an indispensable text.

Many of the observations in *The Wind Birds,* from which the following essay is taken, are drawn from experiences on the author's home ground of eastern Long Island — the tide flats and ponds, the beach, and the plowed and planted land as well. The far-traveling "wind birds" bring to this area, as to every one of their stopping places, a sense of the great migrations and the distant, wild reaches of the planet.

The Wind Birds: Chapter 11

Voices of plover.
I stare
Into the darkness of the star-lit promontory.

BASHŌ (17th century)

Through throats where many rivers meet, the curlews cry,
Under the conceiving moon, on the high chalk hill. . . .

DYLAN THOMAS, "In the White Giant's Thigh"

MOST SHOREBIRDS leave the breeding grounds before the adverse days round to the fore, and those that do not are rarely driven southward by cold weather. Surfbirds, rock sandpipers, and black turnstones, waiting for low tides at Wrangell Inlet, keep company all winter on the docks and warehouse roofs of Petersburg, Alaska;[1] other surfbirds winter on hot tropic coasts. So long as there is food, in other words, a remarkable range of temperature can be sustained, and food may still be plentiful when the wind birds rise from the moon rim of the northern waters and fly toward the southern stars. While not as strong as the spring impulse, the migratory urge of fall causes several species to leave behind the rich crowberry crops and intertidal zones of the maritime North Atlantic summer for the high winds and hungry sea of a long transoceanic crossing.

Favorable winds are less crucial than was once assumed. A gale may discourage the flocks from setting out, but once the migrants are aloft and underway, streaming across the stars of wild night skies, they will fly into the teeth of adverse winds. There is much evidence that strong winds are preferred to windlessness, providing the lift that carries the birds for hours over land and sea.

The frequency with which the wind birds rest at sea is still debated. While many species have been seen to alight and swim on sheltered water, good sight records of shorebirds alighted on the ocean — always excepting the red and northern phalaropes — are virtually nonexistent. Nevertheless, in May of 1907, an experienced naturalist[2] saw a migration of "near a thousand" willets resting on the open sea of the Grand Banks; since the birds were so close that they had to flutter up from the path of the ship, it is hard to believe that this

From *The Wind Birds* (1973)
[1]Ira N. Gabrielson and Frederick C. Lincoln, *Birds of Alaska* (Harrisburg, Pa.: Stackpole, 1959).
[2]George B. Grinnell, "Willets in Migration," *The Auk* 33 (1916): 198–99.

well-marked species could have been mistaken for anything else. (The size of the willet flock and its location southeast of Newfoundland is almost as astonishing as the mass settlement upon the sea; that the flock had gone astray in fog and passed east of a destination in Nova Scotia is my own unsatisfactory explanation.)

Present opinion is that while many species can and will rest on the surface if necessary, they do not often do so out of choice, nor can they survive long if the sea is rough. (Whales and sea turtles, before their great numbers were reduced by commercial slaughter, may have provided resting points throughout the tropic seas; the red phalarope, at least, has been seen to use both animals in this manner.[3]) Thus the gale winds that sometimes carry shorebirds far off course and scatter the immature and inexperienced to strange coasts must also drown them in considerable numbers. Winds have carried ocean birds so far inland and southbound birds so far into the north that, tired and disoriented, the impulse toward migration spent, they linger where they find themselves: in a great storm of November 1888 this fate befell large flocks of killdeer, few of which managed to survive the long Massachusetts winter.

But true invasions — in which meaningful numbers of a certain species, strayed or stormborne, establish a breeding population far beyond their usual range — are very rare: the only bird species which have invaded the North American land mass within the memory of man are the fieldfare, a European thrush blown to Greenland in a 1937 storm and now resident at the island's southwestern tip, and the cattle egret, an Afro-Asian species which, after millennia in its natural range, now seems intent on populating the whole world.

Among shorebirds, the closest thing to a North American invasion occurred in 1927. Large flocks of lapwings known to have left England for Ireland on the night of December 18–19 were overtaken by fog and violent winds, and by December 20 appeared in thousands throughout the Maritime Provinces of Canada, from Baffin Island to New Brunswick.[4] Had they arrived at a benign time of year, a few might have established themselves, but in a very few days the last of them died of cold and hunger. A few greater golden plover turn up in late May every year near Stephenville Crossing, Newfoundland,[5] but where they nest — their nearest known breeding ground is Iceland — remains a mystery.

[3]Ralph S. Palmer. Conversation with the author.
[4]Richard H. Pough, *Audubon Water Bird Guide* (New York: Doubleday, 1951).
[5]Ralph S. Palmer, species accounts in *The Shorebirds of North America*, ed. G. D. Stout (New York: Viking, 1967).

Ruffs and curlew sandpipers appear regularly on our North Atlantic coast (the first ruff was recorded before the Civil War, on Long Island; since then it has turned up at least once in every state from Maine to North Carolina), although the prevailing winds are set against them; redshanks and other European birds come also. But the obstacles against westward wandering across the Atlantic are great, and it may be that some of the accidental visitors do not come direct from Europe but from southward points on their migration route, riding the east winds of the Canary Current or the tropical storms that build off the coast of Africa. This possibility might help explain why that great wanderer, the curlew sandpiper, which breeds in central and eastern Siberia (a first North American nesting was reported in 1962, from the vicinity of Point Barrow[6]) but winters as far west as Africa, turns up not on the Pacific coast, as one might expect, but on the Atlantic seaboard. It is also possible "that a few individuals may migrate in fall from their Siberian nesting grounds east by way of Alaska and Canada to the Atlantic seaboard — a route used by certain shorebirds breeding in tundra country. . . ."[7]

North American birds, conversely, have no trouble getting lost, riding rapidly to Europe on the strong westerlies of the North Atlantic; the jet streams of high altitudes would blow them there in a matter of hours. New World visitors, especially in Great Britain, are comparatively abundant (bird-watchers are also abundant in Britain, but this does not entirely account for the high incidence of accidentals), and the most frequent visitors by far are the Charadrii. Yellowlegs of both species go regularly to Europe, as do the long-billed dowitcher and solitary sandpiper. But the commonest wanderer, with sixty-two recorded sightings, is the pectoral sandpiper, which goes too far in so many other directions as well.

A more surprising chronic stray is the buff-breasted sandpiper. Like the stilt sandpiper, the buff-breast has very narrow migration lanes, clinging close to the 100th meridian, and it ventures even more rarely than its kinsman as far east as the Atlantic coast: in the spring, it is so faithful to its route that the majority of buff-breast migrants cross the Gulf of Mexico[8] and alight in certain fields near Rockport, Texas, then make a second long-distance flight to certain fields near Edmonton, Alberta, being very uncommon at other likely places in

[6]John Bull, *Birds of the New York Area* (New York: Harper & Row, 1964).
[7]Ibid.
[8]George G. Williams, "Do Birds Cross the Gulf of Mexico in Spring?" *The Auk* 62 (1945), 98–111; and George M. Lowery, Jr., "Evidence of Trans-Gulf Migration," *The Auk* 63 (1946), 175–211.

between. But while the prudent stilt sandpiper has remained a home-body, daring but one recorded visit across the Atlantic,[9] the far-flung buff-breast of the fall has delighted and surprised new friends not only in England but in France, Switzerland, Heligoland, and Egypt; it has been said[10] that the autumn buff-breast is more likely to turn up in England than in "any area of similar size in eastern North America."

Other anomalies have been noted[11] among transatlantic vagrants. Species common on the coast (cf. semipalmated sandpiper) and also those which make long transoceanic migrations (cf. golden plover) cross the Atlantic far *less* often than several species of more inland distribution (buff-breasted and upland sandpipers), whereas species which breed in the western Nearctic (cf. long-billed dowitcher) wander *more* commonly to Europe than those breeding farther east (cf. short-billed dowitcher): the pectoral sandpiper of Siberia and Alaska is eight times as common in England as the Baird's sandpiper, even though the Baird's nests as close as Greenland. The theory is that the western nesters, which mainly strike eastward before heading south, are more apt to carry on to England than species which set out on a more southerly course at the beginning of migration: the same tendency, in reverse, may in part account for the 1927 invasion of lapwings, populations of which migrate west to Ireland in the autumn. (Spring records in Britain of the buff-breasted and Baird's sandpipers and the northern phalarope, which in this season are extremely rare on the Atlantic coast of North America, may represent individuals which strayed from South America to Africa, then proceeded north. The killdeer, unlike all other species, visits Britain most commonly in *winter*, perhaps in consequence of its luckless habit of being blown back north by winter storms.)

Shorebird wanderers have not been limited to European travel. The Hudsonian godwit has flown at least twelve times to New Zealand, a place so removed from its natural haunts that one must suppose that it followed the bar-tailed godwits which belong there. (The Hudsonian godwit and several other North American shore-birds recorded in New Zealand have never been recorded in Australia, but a few hundred miles away;[12] whether this is a tribute to the bird-watchers of New Zealand or a phenomenon of zoogeography is not yet known.) In 1953 the sharp-tailed sandpiper of Siberia,

[9]Henry M. Hall, *A Gathering of Shorebirds* (New York: Devin-Adair, 1960).
[10]T.C.T. Nisbet, "Wader Migration in North America and Its Relation to Transatlantic Crossings," *British Birds* 52 (1949), 205–15.
[11]Ibid.
[12]Jean Dorst, *The Migration of Birds* (Boston: Houghton Mifflin, 1962).

which occurs in migration in northwest Alaska and winters in the southwest Pacific, turned up at Tristan da Cunha,[13] a small volcanic peak of a submerged mountain range in the Atlantic wastes between Africa and South America. The red phalarope has found itself as far inland as Kansas and Colorado, while a jaçana has alighted on a ship forty miles at sea, off the coast of Surinam.[14] Young long-billed dowitchers, Wilson's phalaropes, and western willets straggle east-ward in late summer as far as the Atlantic seaboard (fall willets at Sagaponack are more likely to be westerns than not), a form of juvenile wandering analogous to the northward explorations of young summer egrets. Post-juvenile dispersion, as it is called, cannot be accounted for on the basis of food alone; in many creatures besides man, the young are more adventurous and less set in their ways, and thus prone to disorganized behavior.

The westerly winds of the northern land mass that account for a general west-east drift of autumn migrants may also explain this curious characteristic of shorebird distribution — that almost none of them winter west or even southwest of their breeding grounds.[15] Even those long-billed dowitchers and pectoral sandpipers that breed in Siberia return east to North America before migrating southward, and the European ringed plover that breeds in Baffin Island goes east again to Europe before moving on to its winter latitudes.

The exceptions to the rule are three, and two of these, the marbled godwit and the avocet, migrate to both ocean coasts, then southward, wintering east as well as west of their summer range. The third exception is the mountain plover. In one of the most rigid and least

[13]Ibid.
[14]A. W. Schorger, "Jaçana Taken at Sea," *The Auk* 63 (1946): 255.
[15]Dorst, *The Migration of Birds.*

explicable of all migrations, this plover travels southwest six hundred miles from its breeding grounds on the Great Plains, across the Rockies and the Coast Ranges of California; many of the arrivals in California then proceed south into northern Mexico, a region reached easily from the Great Plains without the trouble of negotiating two north-south ranges of high mountains. (Despite its name, which was given it only because the first specimen was taken in the Rocky Mountain foothills, this bird is not partial to mountains; it is a bird of short-grass country and would be better named the plains plover.) So fixed is it in its habits that though it breeds in Montana and Wyoming, it has never been recorded in the adjoining state of Idaho, nor in Nevada, nor in Oregon.[16]

Except for those species like the surfbird, wandering tattler, and black turnstone which rarely or never leave the Pacific perimeter, the great majority of the Alaskan nesters travel a kind of transcontinental migration, flying southeast to Hudson Bay or the Atlantic Ocean before proceeding southward. This is markedly true of the western sandpiper, which breeds in northern and western Alaska and the Chukchi Peninsula of Siberia and winters chiefly in the Carolinas, and of the Eskimo curlew, Hudsonian godwit, and white-rumped sandpiper, which commonly perform the ocean flight from the Canadian Maritimes to South America.

Similarly, a number of buff-breasted sandpipers move east to Hudson Bay and onward, much less commonly, to the coast. From the coast the buff-breast apparently heads southwest again, across the Appalachians (it is not known to migrate through the South Atlantic states) to Central America, then southeast again to the Argentine. This odd zigzag route may be shared by the scattering of Baird's sandpipers that come east in the fall migrations, for their movements are also obscure once they leave the North Atlantic. There are few records of the Baird's sandpiper in the southeastern states and the West Indies.

Not all migrants, in other words, select the shortest route, much less the easiest. The Baird's sandpiper, quite apart from its zigzag course, migrates commonly along mountain chains in both the Andes and Rockies which would serve as barriers to ordinary birds; it has been seen flying busily along in the rarefied air at thirteen thousand feet. Similarly, the pectoral sandpiper has been recorded at thirteen thousand feet in Colorado and twelve thousand feet in Argentina.

[16]American Ornithologists' Union, *The A.O.U. Check-list of North American Birds* (New York: American Ornithologists' Union, 1957).

The Mongolian plover, which, like the rufous-necked sandpiper, crosses occasionally from Asia to breed on Alaska's Seward Peninsula, may nest at three miles above sea level in the Himalayas. (Godwits and curlews have been sighted at close to twenty thousand feet in the same range, but these birds were presumably crossing the north-south barrier.)

While it may be that only the Baird's and pectoral sandpipers use the great cordilleras as a migration route, many wind birds migrate at high altitudes when conditions favor them. This would seem particularly logical for those that migrate after dark. The moon illumines coasts and rivers that serve as guidelines even in the night, and when the clouds close over, the night fliers may rise to high clear altitudes, their course oriented to the stars.

The sun is also used as a point of orientation — and certain shore-birds travel in the day as well as at night — but the majority of the smaller migrants prefer darkness. In daylight, when the sun consumes the precious energies needed for flight, it is more economical to feed and rest; at night, the air is apt to be more stable, and fewer predators are abroad. (Migrating birds, in the intensity of their journey, are notably unwary and may view with detachment small reductions of their number by hawk or prowling coon. But shorebirds can usually outmaneuver hawks in the rare instances when they cannot outfly them. On several occasions I have watched a peregrine falcon in pursuit of shorebirds, but the only victim was a lone yellowlegs caught low over the Sagaponack flats; it was knocked spinning to the ground like an old feathered pinwheel. The falcon, out of apathy or inexperience, did not turn fast enough to pin it down, nor did it pursue the wind bird very far when the latter pulled itself together and took off again with an impressive turn of speed.)

The night fliers rest well into the twilight, and most are aloft a short time after dark. Just before midnight, the migration reaches its peak; then a telescope trained on the moon can watch the steady stream across the sky. Before dawn, the tired birds have dropped onto other margins, hundreds of miles south. There they may rest a day, a fortnight, or a month, depending on food, weather, and the skies remaining between this point and their destination.

How birds orient themselves during migration remains the greatest of the unsolved questions in avian studies. The young of the distance fliers, starting southward without guidance on journeys of thousands of miles, must have at least an innate sense of primary direction. (A distinction should be made between directional sense, in which the bird, transplanted five hundred miles west of its intended route, will theoretically arrive five hundred miles west of its destination, and true homing ability, possessed by a few species, which would permit them to compensate for this displacement by the time they had arrived at their home latitudes. Most migrants do not seem to allow for wind displacement after their course is set; but they can apparently adjust the course, once arrived at a resting point, and have been observed[17] to return east or west again before proceeding southward.) Sense of direction, in adult birds, is probably supplemented by high-altitude search and by acute visual memory, which permits them to return to a given point once they arrive within a wide radius of the area. It is also supplemented by an internal timing mechanism, not yet understood, which gives the migrant some kind of azimuth bearing, using the sun or stars.

For reasons of food and prevailing winds, the golden plover which came up from the Argentine in spring by way of Peru and Yucatán, perhaps, or flew from Peru to the Gulf Coast and proceeded up the Mississippi Valley, does not return by the same route. Most though not all will complete an elliptical migration, the southbound arc of which takes them from their nesting grounds southeast across the continent to western New England and Delaware — a few go as far east as Nova Scotia and even Labrador — and on out across the open sea to South America; those that are seen at Sagaponack and elsewhere on the North Atlantic coast are probably deflected there by fog or storm.

The Eskimo curlew also made an elliptical or "loop" migration, and the Hudsonian godwit and white-rumped sandpiper make one still. But these three species may rest at Bermuda and in the Antilles, where the golden plover is quite rare: the first place that the plover turns up commonly is the Guianas. (The Eskimo curlew, on the other hand, was uncommon in Guiana, and it has been suggested[18] that this species flew a kind of "great circle" course, making its first landfall south of Cape San Roque in easternmost Brazil and possibly flying on southwest to the interior savannas without alighting.)

Yet even assuming an advanced navigational ability, how does one explain why many young golden plover, as if in defiance of the directional sense inherited from their parents, fail to follow the southeastward path that the adult birds have taken a few weeks earlier, choosing instead to take, in reverse, the path that brought the adults

---

[17]David Lack, "Migration Across the Sea," *Ibis* 101 (1959), 374–99.
[18]James C. Greenway, Jr., *Extinct and Vanishing Birds of the World* (New York: American Committee for International Wildlife Protection, 1958).

north? The choice of the interior route spares the young birds the
awesome transoceanic flight of the adults, so that they may live to
make that flight another year, but no known theory of migration can
explain this choice except one so startling that to recognize it would
be acknowledgment of an historic and continuing failure to comprehend the life dimensions: a few authorities, dissatisfied with all other
explanations, have wondered if the young migratory bird *inherits* a
topographic knowledge of the globe (an inherited knowledge of the
constellations has already been established[19]), or at least of that seg-
ment of it that the bird must span each spring and autumn.[20]

The great overseas flights add the question of ocean navigation to
the problem of orientation. Assuming that migrants use topographic
features to refine a course based primarily on an inherited sense of
direction, what landmarks prevent the wind bird which spans the
gray trackless reaches of the sea from being carried far off course,
or otherwise losing itself so irremediably that it must inevitably burn
its strength and drop into the water, to flutter and blink and float a
little before drifting down like a dead leaf into the void?

The ocean itself gives its mute signs — the cloud lines, for example,
registering a change in air temperature and humidity in the region,
say, of the Equatorial Current; or the long lines of sargassum weed
and spindrift that betray the wind patterns; or the high cumulus
which, looming over island outposts beyond the horizon, are visible
to high-flying birds a hundred miles away. But all these signs presume
fair weather and prevailing winds; if the voyager depends on them,
then should it be caught at sea by heavy fog or overcast or even
windlessness, it may be doomed. Considering the mixed conditions
that the wind birds meet successfully in annual journeys of fifteen
thousand miles or more, one should not underestimate their chances;
yet good as a bird's orientation is, it cannot spare a large percentage
of each species that one fatal mistake of navigation. Mere sense of
direction seems inadequate. Without visual aids to correct its compass,
a gale might cause the unlucky bird to miss or overshoot its target,
as in the case of the ill-fated lapwings that flew to Canada.

And so there remains a mystery, and one pores anew over refuted
theories based on bird sensitivity to the atmosphere's electric waves
or to the guidelines of the earth's magnetic fields. Birds have been
carried to far places in revolving cages or sent aloft with magnets

[19]Roger Tory Peterson and James Fisher, *The World of Birds* (New York: Doubleday, 1963).
[20]Joel C. Welty, *The Life of Birds* (New York: Knopf, 1963).

fastened to their heads, without noticeable impairment of their homing ability. No experiment has ever proved that a bird can orient
itself magnetically (although pigeons and many other birds have
pectens or magnetic sensors in each eye),[21] but neither can the possibility be discarded, for the talent has been demonstrated in the
otherwise ungifted common mud snail of our own Atlantic Coast.[22]

The combination of abilities and experience doubtless differs from
species to species. Certain sedentary birds have no homing ability
whatsoever, while certain seabirds perform feats of navigation which
confound the theorists, especially those who have left no place for
metaphysics. None of the theories or combinations of theories presently considered reasonable provides an explanation of how a shear-
water released in Venice, on a sea that none of its species ever visit,
could and did return on an unfamiliar east-west bearing, across the
European land mass in all likelihood, to its nesting ledge on a skerry
in the Irish Sea, not in the season following but in twelve and a half
days. There is no reason to suppose that a shorebird put to an
equivalent test could not perform as well; and in regard to such a
mystery the exact scientists must do much better than they have done
in the way of rigorous explanation if the rest of us, the awestruck
individuals who still glimpse fine strange happenings through the
screen of words and facts, are not to continue calling mystery by its
proper name.

   The departure of curlew from a given place often occurs just prior
to a storm, and in ancient days, in England, the curlew's cry, the
plover's whistle boded no man any good. Of the golden plover it was
said in Lancashire that its sad whistle was the plaint of errant souls
— not any old souls but the souls of those Jews who had lent a hand
at the Crucifixion. In North England, curlews and whimbrels were
called "Gabriel's hounds"; the name whimbrel comes from "whim-
pernel," which, in the Durham Household Book of 1530, refers to a
habit attributed to it of houndlike whimperings.[23] Both birds were
known as harbingers of death, and in the sense that they are birds
of passage, that in the wild melodies of their calls, in the breath of
vast distance and bare regions that attends them, we sense intimations
of our own mortality, there is justice in the legend. Yet it is not the
death sign that the curlews bring, but only the memory of life, of a
high beauty passing swiftly, as the curlew passes, leaving us in solitude
on an empty beach, with summer gone, and a wind blowing.

[21]William G. Conway, correspondence and conversations with the author.
[22]Dorst, *The Migration of Birds.*
[23]E. A. Armstrong, *Folklore of Birds* (Boston: Houghton Mifflin, 1959).

EDWARD HOAGLAND
(1932–   )

❧ Few writers about nature, perhaps, are less sentimental than
Edward Hoagland. He seems to write in constant awareness of the
pitfalls of genteel emotion — the Thompson Seton of *Lives of the
Hunted,* say, might be cautionary — and yet he is drawn to the wild,
he exults in it. The hills of Vermont, the jumbled mountains of British
Columbia, or simply the lean, efficient bodies of predators seem to
bring Hoagland's senses alive and to give dimension and even hope
to his thought. In working on *Notes from the Century Before* (1969), he
spent as much time as he could with veterans of the wilderness,
people who had lived their lives breathing pure air and looking at
mountains. The scope of their stories, the scope of the field they
lived in, and a certain emotional clarity to their lives were profoundly
attractive. Among the animals, Hoagland has a particular fondness
for the big cats, a feeling registered in the brilliant imagery of his
first novel, *Cat Man* (1955).

Hailing the Elusory Mountain Lion

THE SWAN SONG sounded by the wilderness grows fainter, ever
more constricted, until only sharp ears can catch it at all. It fades to
a nearly inaudible level, and yet there never is going to be any one
time when we can say right *now* it is gone. Wolves meet their maker
in wholesale lots, but coyotes infiltrate eastward, northward, southeastward. Woodland caribou and bighorn sheep are vanishing fast,
but moose have expanded their range in some areas.

Mountain lions used to have practically the run of the Western

From *Walking the Dead Diamond River* (1973)

Hemisphere, and they still do occur from Cape Horn to the Big Muddy River at the boundary of the Yukon and on the coasts of both oceans, so that they are the most versatile land mammal in the New World, probably taking in more latitudes than any other four-footed wild creature anywhere. There are perhaps only four to six thousand left in the United States, though there is no place that they didn't once go, eating deer, elk, pikas, porcupines, grasshoppers, and dead fish on the beach. They were called mountain lions in the Rockies, pumas (originally an Incan word) in the Southwestern states, cougars (a naturalist's corruption of an Amazonian Indian word) in the Northwest, panthers in the traditionalist East — "painters" in dialect-proud New England — or catamounts. The Dutchmen of New Netherland called them tigers, red tigers, deer tigers, and the Spaniards *leones* or *leopardos*. They liked to eat horses — wolves preferred beef and black bears favored pork — but as adversaries of mankind they were overshadowed at first because bears appeared more formidable and wolves in their howling packs were more flamboyant and more damaging financially. Yet this panoply of names is itself quite a tribute, and somehow the legends about "panthers" have lingered longer than bear or wolf tales, helped by the animal's own limber, far-traveling stealth and as a carry-over from the immense mythic force of the great cats of the Old World. Though only Florida among the Eastern states is known for certain to have any left, no wild knot of mountains or swamp is without rumors of panthers; nowadays people delight in these, keeping their eyes peeled. It's wishful, and the wandering, secretive nature of the beast ensures that even Eastern panthers will not soon be certifiably extinct. An informal census among experts in 1963 indicated that an island of twenty-five or more may have survived in the New Brunswick–Maine–Quebec region, and Louisiana may still have a handful, and perhaps eight live isolated in the Black Hills of South Dakota, and the Oklahoma panhandle may have a small colony — all outside the established range in Florida, Texas, and the Far West. As with the blue whale, who will be able to say when they have been eliminated?

"Mexican lion" is another name for mountain lions in the border states — a name that might imply a meager second-best rating there yet ties to the majestic African beasts. Lions are at least twice as big as mountain lions, measuring by weight, though they are nearly the same in length because of the mountain lion's superb long tail. Both animals sometimes pair up affectionately with mates and hunt in tandem, but mountain lions go winding through life in ones or twos, whereas the lion is a harem-keeper, harem-dweller, the males eventually becoming stay-at-homes, heavy figureheads. Lions enjoy the grassy flatlands, forested along the streams, and they stay put, engrossed in communal events — roaring, grunting, growling with a racket like the noise of gears being stripped — unless the game moves on. They sun themselves, preside over the numerous kibbutz young, sneeze from the dust, and bask in dreams, occasionally waking up to issue reverberating, guttural pronouncements which serve notice that they are now awake.

Mountain lions spirit themselves away in saw-toothed canyons and on escarpments instead, and when conversing with their mates they coo like pigeons, sob like women, emit a flat slight shriek, a popping bubbling growl, or mew, or yowl. They growl and suddenly caterwaul into falsetto — the famous scarifying, metallic scream functioning as a kind of hunting cry close up, to terrorize and start the game. They ramble as much as twenty-five miles in a night, maintaining a large loop of territory which they cover every week or two. It's a solitary, busy life, involving a survey of several valleys, many deer herds. Like tigers and leopards, mountain lions are not sociably inclined and don't converse at length with the whole waiting world, but they are even less noisy; they seem to speak most eloquently with their feet. Where a tiger would roar, a mountain lion screams like a castrato. Where a mountain lion hisses, a leopard would snarl like a truck stuck in snow.

Leopards are the best counterpart to mountain lions in physique and in the tenor of their lives. Supple, fierce creatures, skilled at concealment but with great self-assurance and drive, leopards are bolder when facing human beings than the American cats. Basically they are hot-land beasts and not such remarkable travelers individually, though as a race they once inhabited the broad Eurasian land mass all the way from Great Britain to Malaysia, as well as Africa. As late as the 1960s, a few were said to be still holding out on the shore of the Mediterranean at Mount Mycale, Turkey. (During a forest fire twenty years ago a yearling swam the narrow straits to the Greek island Samos and holed up in a cave, where he was duly killed — perhaps the last leopard ever to set foot in Europe on his own.) Leopards are thicker and shorter than adult mountain lions and seem to lead an athlete's indolent, incurious life much of the time, testing their perfected bodies by clawing tree trunks, chewing on old skulls, executing acrobatic leaps, and then rousing themselves to the semi-weekly antelope kill. Built with supreme hardness and economy, they make little allowance for man — they don't see him as different. They relish the flesh of his dogs, and they run up a tree when hunted and then sometimes spring down, as heavy as a chunk of iron wrapped in a flag. With stunning, gorgeous coats, their tight, dervish faces carved in a snarl, they head for the hereafter as if it were just one more extra-emphatic leap — as impersonal in death as the crack of the rifle was.

The American leopard, the jaguar, is a powerfully built, serious fellow, who, before white men arrived, wandered as far north as the Carolinas, but his best home is the humid basin of the Amazon. Mountain lions penetrate these ultimate jungles too, but rather thinly, thriving better in the cooler, drier climate of the untenanted pampas and on the mountain slopes. They are blessed with a pleasant but undazzling coat, tan except for a white belly, mouth and throat, and some black behind the ears, on the tip of the tail and at the sides of the nose, and so they are hunted as symbols, not for their fur. The cubs are spotted, leopardlike, much as lion cubs are. If all of the big cats developed from a common ancestry, the mountain lions' specialization has been unpresumptuous — away from bulk and savagery to traveling light. Toward deer, their prey, they may be as ferocious as leopards, but not toward chance acquaintances such as man. They sometimes break their necks, their jaws, their teeth, springing against the necks of quarry they have crept close to — a fate in part resulting from the circumstance that they can't ferret out the weaker individuals in a herd by the device of a long chase, the way wolves do; they have to take the luck of the draw. None of the cats possess enough lung capacity for grueling runs. They depend upon shock tactics, bursts of speed, sledge-hammer leaps, strong collarbones for hitting power, and shearing dentition, whereas wolves employ all the advantages of time in killing their quarry, as well as the numbers and gaiety of the pack, biting the beast's nose and rump — the technique of a thousand cuts — lapping the bloody snow. Wolves sometimes even have a cheering section of flapping ravens accompanying them, eager to scavenge after the brawl.

It's a risky business for the mountain lion, staking the strength and impact of his neck against the strength of the prey animal's neck. Necessarily, he is concentrated and fierce; yet legends exist that mountain lions have irritably defended men and women lost in the wilderness against marauding jaguars, who are no friends of theirs, and (with a good deal more supporting evidence) that they are susceptible to an odd kind of fascination with human beings. Sometimes they will tentatively seek an association, hanging about a campground or following a hiker out of curiosity, perhaps, circling around and bounding up on a ledge above to watch him pass. This mild modesty has helped preserve them from extinction. If they have been unable to make any adjustments to the advent of man, they haven't suicidally opposed him either, as the buffalo wolves and grizzlies did. In fact, at close quarters they seem bewildered. When treed, they don't breathe a hundred-proof ferocity but puzzle over what to do. They're too light-bodied to bear down on the hunter and kill him easily, even if they should attack — a course they seem to have no inclination for. In this century in the United States only one person, a child of thirteen, has been killed by a mountain lion; that was in 1924. And they're informal animals. Lolling in an informal sprawl on a high limb, they can't seem to summon any Enobarbus-like front of resistance for long. Daring men occasionally climb up and toss lassos about a cat and haul him down, strangling him by pulling from two directions, while the lion, mortified, appalled, never does muster his fighting aplomb. Although he could fight off a pack of wolves, he hasn't worked out a posture to assume toward man and his dogs. Impotently, he stiffens, as the dinosaurs must have when the atmosphere grew cold.

Someday hunting big game may come to be regarded as a form of vandalism, and the remaining big creatures of the wilderness will skulk through restricted reserves wearing radio transmitters and numbered collars, or bearing stripes of dye, as many elephants already do, to aid the busy biologists who track them from the air. Like a vanishing race of trolls, more report and memory than a reality, they will inhabit children's books and nostalgic articles, a special glamour attaching to those, like mountain lions, that are geographically incalculable and may still be sighted away from the preserves. Already we've become enthusiasts. We want game about us — at least at a summer house; it's part of privileged living. There is a precious privacy about seeing wildlife, too. Like meeting a fantastically dressed mute on the road, the fact that no words are exchanged and that *he's* not going to give an account makes the experience light-hearted; it's wholly ours. Besides, if anything out of the ordinary happened, we know we can't expect to be believed, and since it's rather fun to be disbelieved — fishermen know this — the privacy is even more complete. Deer, otter, foxes are messengers from another condition of life, another mentality, and bring us tidings of places where we don't go.

Ten years ago at Vavenby, a sawmill town on the North Thompson River in British Columbia, a frolicsome mountain lion used to appear at dusk every ten days or so in a bluegrass field alongside the river. Deer congregated there, the river was silky and swift, cooling the

summer air, and it was a festive spot for a lion to be. She was thought
to be a female, and reputedly left tracks around an enormous territory to the north and west — Raft Mountain, Battle Mountain, the
Trophy Range, the Murtle River, and Mahood Lake — territory on
an upended, pelagic scale, much of it scarcely accessible to a man by
trail, where the tiger lilies grew four feet tall. She would materialize
in this field among the deer five minutes before dark, as if checking
in again, a habit that may have resulted in her death eventually,
though for the present the farmer who observed her visits was keeping his mouth shut about it. This was pioneer country; there were
people alive who could remember the time when poisoning the carcass of a cow would net a man a pile of dead predators — a family
of mountain lions to bounty, maybe half a dozen wolves, and both
black bears and grizzlies. The Indians considered lion meat a delicacy,
but they had clans which drew their origins at the Creation from
ancestral mountain lions, or wolves or bears, so these massacres
amazed them. They thought the outright bounty hunters were crazy
men.

Even before Columbus, mountain lions were probably not distributed in saturation numbers anywhere, as wolves may have been.
Except for the family unit — a female with her half-grown cubs —
each lion seems to occupy its own spread of territory, not as a result
of fights with intruders but because the young transients share the
same instinct for solitude and soon sheer off to find vacant mountains
and valleys. A mature lion kills only one deer every week or two,
according to a study by Maurice Hornocker in Idaho, and therefore
is not really a notable factor in controlling the local deer population.
Rather, it keeps watch contentedly as that population grows, sometimes benefitting the herds by scaring them onto new wintering
grounds that are not overbrowsed, and by its very presence warding
off other lions.

This thin distribution, coupled with the mountain lion's taciturn
habits, make sighting one a matter of luck, even for game officials
located in likely country. One warden in Colorado I talked to had
indeed seen a pair of them fraternizing during the breeding season.
He was driving a jeep over an abandoned mining road, and he passed
two brown animals sitting peaceably in the grass, their heads close
together. For a moment he thought they were coyotes and kept
driving, when all of a sudden the picture registered that they were
cougars! He braked and backed up, but of course they were gone. He
was an old-timer, a man who had crawled inside bear dens to pull
out the cubs, and knew where to find clusters of buffalo skulls in the

recesses of the Rockies where the last bands had hidden; yet this cryptic instant when he was turning his jeep round a curve was the only glimpse — unprovable — that he ever got of a mountain lion.

Such glimpses usually are cryptic. During a summer I spent in Wyoming in my boyhood, I managed to see two coyotes, but both occasions were so fleeting that it required an act of faith on my part afterward to feel sure I had seen them. One of the animals vanished between rolls of ground; the other, in rougher, stonier, wooded country, cast his startled gray face in my direction and simply was gone. Hunching, he swerved for cover, and the brush closed over him. I used to climb to a vantage point above a high basin at twilight and watch the mule deer steal into the meadows to feed. The grass grew higher than their stomachs, the steep forest was close at hand, and they were as small and fragile-looking as filaments at that distance, quite human in coloring, gait and form. It was possible to visualize them as a naked Indian hunting party a hundred years before — or not to believe in their existence at all, either as Indians or deer. Minute, aphid-sized, they stepped so carefully in emerging, hundreds of feet below, that, straining my eyes, I needed to tell myself constantly that they were deer; my imagination, left to its own devices with the dusk settling down, would have made of them a dozen other creatures.

Recently, walking at night on the woods road that passes my house in Vermont, I heard footsteps in the leaves and windfalls. I waited, listening — they sounded too heavy to be anything less than a man, a large deer or a bear. A man wouldn't have been in the woods so late, my dog stood respectfully silent and still, and they did seem to shuffle portentously. Sure enough, after pausing at the edge of the road, a fully grown bear appeared, visible only in dimmest outline, staring in my direction for four or five seconds. The darkness lent a faintly red tinge to his coat; he was well built. Then, turning, he ambled off, almost immediately lost to view, though I heard the noise of his passage, interrupted by several pauses. It was all as concise as a vision, and since I had wanted to see a bear close to my own house, being a person who likes to live in a melting pot, whether in the city or country, and since it was too dark to pick out his tracks, I was grateful when the dog inquisitively urinated along the bear's path, thereby confirming that at least I had witnessed *something*. The dog seemed unsurprised, however, as if the scent were not all that remarkable, and, sure enough, the next week in the car I encountered a yearling bear in daylight two miles downhill, and a cub a month later. My farmer neighbors were politely skeptical of my accounts, having themselves caught sight of only perhaps a couple of bears in all their lives.

So it's with sympathy as well as an awareness of the tricks that enthusiasm and nightfall may play that I have been going to nearby towns seeking out people who have claimed at one time or another to have seen a mountain lion. The experts of the state — game wardens, taxidermists, the most accomplished hunters — emphatically discount the claims, but the believers are unshaken. They include some summer people who were enjoying a drink on the back terrace when the apparition of a great-tailed cat moved out along the fringe of the woods on a deer path; a boy who was hunting with his .22 years ago near the village dump and saw the animal across a gully and fired blindly, then ran away and brought back a search party, which found a tuft of toast-colored fur; and a state forestry employee, a sober woodsman, who caught the cat in his headlights while driving through Victory Bog in the wildest corner of the Northeast Kingdom. Gordon Hickok, who works for a furniture factory and has shot one or two mountain lions on hunting trips in the West, saw one cross U.S. 5 at a place called Auger Hole near Mount Hor. He tracked it with dogs a short distance, finding a fawn with its head gnawed off. A high-school English teacher reported seeing a mountain lion cross another road, near Runaway Pond, but the hunters who quickly went out decided that the prints were those of a big bobcat, splayed impressively in the mud and snow. Fifteen years ago a watchman in the fire tower on top of Bald Mountain had left grain scattered in the grooves of a flat rock under the tower to feed several deer. One night, looking down just as the dusk turned murky, he saw two slim long-tailed lions creep out of the scrubby border of spruce and inspect the rock, sniffing deer droppings and dried deer saliva. The next night, when he was in his cabin, the dog barked and, looking out the window, again he saw the vague shape of a lion just vanishing.

A dozen loggers and woodsmen told me such stories. In the Adirondacks I've also heard some persuasive avowals — one by an old dog-sled driver and trapper, a French Canadian; another by the owner of a tourist zoo, who was exhibiting a Western cougar. In Vermont perhaps the most eager rumor buffs are some of the farmers. After all, now that packaged semen has replaced the awesome farm bull and so many procedures have been mechanized, who wants to lose *all* the adventure of farming? Until recently the last mountain lion known to have been killed in the Northeast was recorded in 1881 in Barnard, Vermont. However, it has been learned that probably another one was shot from a tree in 1931 in Mundleville, New Bruns-

wick, and still another trapped seven years later in Somerset County in Maine. Bruce S. Wright, director of the Northeastern Wildlife Station (which is operated at the University of New Brunswick with international funding), is convinced that though they are exceedingly rare, mountain lions are still part of the fauna of the region; in fact, he has plaster casts of tracks to prove it, as well as a compilation of hundreds of reported sightings. Some people may have mistaken a golden retriever for a lion, or may have intended to foment a hoax, but all in all the evidence does seem promising. Indeed, after almost twenty years of search and study, Wright himself finally saw one.

The way these sightings crop up in groups has often been pooh-poohed as greenhorn fare or as a sympathetic hysteria among neighbors, but it is just as easily explained by the habit mountain lions have of establishing a territory that they scout through at intervals, visiting an auspicious deer-ridden swamp or remote ledgy mountain. Even at such a site a successful hunt could not be mounted without trained dogs, and if the population of the big cats was extremely sparse, requiring of them long journeys during the mating season, and yet with plenty of deer all over, they might not stay for long. One or two hundred miles is no obstacle to a Western cougar. The cat might inhabit a mountain ridge one year, and then never again.

Fifteen years ago, Francis Perry, who is an ebullient muffin of a man, a farmer all his life in Brownington, Vermont, saw a mountain lion "larger and taller than a collie, and grayish yellow" (he had seen them in circuses). Having set a trap for a woodchuck, he was on his way to visit the spot when he came over a rise and, at a distance of fifty yards, saw the beast engaged in eating the dead woodchuck. It bounded off, but Perry set four light fox traps for it around the woodchuck. Apparently, a night or two later the cat returned and got caught in three of these, but they couldn't hold it; it pulled free, leaving the marks of a struggle. Noel Perry, his brother, remembers how scared Francis looked when he came home from the first episode. Noel himself saw the cat (which may have meant that Brownington Swamp was one of its haunts that summer), once when it crossed a cow pasture on another farm the brothers owned, and once when it fled past his rabbit dogs through underbrush while he was training them — he thought for a second that its big streaking form was one of the dogs. A neighbor, Robert Chase, also saw the animal that year. Then again last summer, for the first time in fifteen years, Noel Perry saw a track as big as a bear's but round like a mountain lion's, and Robert's brother, Larry Chase, saw the actual cat several times one summer evening, playing a chummy hide-and-seek with him in the fields.

Elmer and Elizabeth Ambler are in their forties, populists politically, and have bought a farm in Glover to live the good life, though he is a truck driver in Massachusetts on weekdays and must drive hard in order to be home when he can. He's bald, with large eyebrows, handsome teeth and a low forehead, but altogether a strong-looking, clear, humane face. He is an informational kind of man who will give you the history of various breeds of cattle or a talk about taxation in a slow and musical voice, and both he and his wife, a purposeful, self-sufficient redhead, are fascinated by the possibility that they live in the wilderness. Beavers inhabit the river that flows past their house. The Amblers say that on Black Mountain nearby hunters "disappear" from time to time, and bears frequent the berry patches in their back field — they see them, their visitors see them, people on the road see them, their German shepherds meet them and run back drooling with fright. They've stocked their farm with horned Herefords instead of the polled variety so that the creatures can "defend themselves." Ambler is intrigued by the thought that apart from the danger of bears, someday "a cat" might prey on one of his cows. Last year, looking out the back window, his wife saw through binoculars an animal with a flowing tail and "a cat's gallop" following a line of trees where the deer go, several hundred yards uphill behind the house. Later, Ambler went up on snowshoes and found tracks as big as their shepherds'; the dogs obligingly ran alongside. He saw walking tracks, leaping tracks and deer tracks marked with blood going toward higher ground. He wonders whether the cat will ever attack him. There are plenty of bobcats around, but they both say they know the difference. The splendid, nervous *tail* is what people must have identified in order to claim they have seen a mountain lion.

I, too, cherish the notion that I may have seen a lion. Mine was crouched on an overlook above a grass-grown, steeply pitched wash in the Alberta Rockies — a much more likely setting than anywhere in New England. It was late afternoon on my last day at Maligne Lake, where I had been staying with my father at a national-park chalet. I was twenty; I could walk forever or could climb endlessly in a sanguine scramble, going out every day as far as my legs carried me, swinging around for home before the sun went down. Earlier, in the valley of the Athabasca, I had found several winter-starved or wolf-killed deer, well picked and scattered, and an area with many elk antlers strewn on the ground where the herds had wintered safely, dropping their antlers but not their bones. Here, much higher up, in the bright plenitude of the summer, I had watched two wolves and a stately bull moose in one mountain basin, and had been up on the caribou barrens on the ridge west of the lake and brought back the talons of a hawk I'd found dead on the ground. Whenever I was watching game, a sort of stopwatch in me started running. These were moments of intense importance and intimacy, of new intimations and aptitudes. Time had a jam-packed character, as it does during a mile run.

I was good at moving quietly through the woods and at spotting game, and was appropriately exuberant. The finest, longest day of my stay was the last. Going east, climbing through a luxuriant terrain of up-and-down boulders, brief brilliant glades, sudden potholes fifty feet deep — a forest of moss-hung lodgepole pines and firs and spare, gaunt spruce with the black lower branches broken off — I came upon the remains of a young bear, which had been torn up and shredded. Perhaps wolves had cornered it during some imprudent excursion in the early spring. (Bears often wake up while the snow is still deep, dig themselves out and rummage around in the neighborhood sleepily for a day or two before bedding down again under a fallen tree.) I took the skull along so that I could extract the teeth when I got hold of some tools. Discoveries like this represent a superfluity of wildlife and show how many beasts there are scouting about.

I went higher. The marmots whistled familially; the tall trees wilted to stubs of themselves. A pretty stream led down a defile from a series of openings in front of the ultimate barrier of a vast mountain wall which I had been looking at from a distance each day on my outings. It wasn't too steep to be climbed, but it was a barrier because my energies were not sufficient to scale it and bring me back the same night. Besides, it stretched so majestically, surflike above the lesser ridges, that I liked to think of it as the Continental Divide.

On my left as I went up this wash was an abrupt, grassy slope that enjoyed a southern exposure and was sunny and windblown all winter, which kept it fairly free of snow. The ranger at the lake had told me it served as a wintering ground for a few bighorn sheep and for a band of mountain goats, three of which were in sight. As I approached laboriously, these white, pointy-horned fellows drifted up over a rise, managing to combine their retreat with some nippy good grazing as they went, not to give any pursuer the impression that they had been pushed into flight. I took my time too, climbing to locate the spring in a precipitous cleft of rock where the band did most of its drinking, and finding the shallow, high-ceilinged cave where the goats had sheltered from storms, presumably for generations. The floor was layered with rubbery droppings, tramped down and sprinkled with tufts of shed fur, and the back wall was checkered with footholds where the goats liked to clamber and perch. Here and there was a horn lying loose — a memento for me to add to my collection from an old individual that had died a natural death, secure in the band's winter stronghold. A bold, thriving family of pack rats emerged to observe me. They lived mainly on the nutritives in the droppings, and were used to the goats' tolerance; they seemed astonished when I tossed a stone.

I kept scrabbling along the side of the slope to a section of outcroppings where the going was harder. After perhaps half an hour, crawling around a corner, I found myself faced with a bighorn ram who was taking his ease on several square yards of bare earth between large rocks, a little above the level of my head. Just as surprised as I, he stood up. He must have construed the sounds of my advance to be those of another sheep or goat. His horns had made a complete curl and then some; they were thick, massive and bunched together like a high Roman helmet, and he himself was muscly and military, with a grave-looking nose. A squared-off, middle-aged, trophy-type ram, full of imposing professionalism, he was at the stage of life when rams sometimes stop herding and live as rogues.

He turned and tried a couple of possible exits from the pocket where I had found him, but the ground was badly pitched and would require a reeling gait and loss of dignity. Since we were within a national park and obviously I was unarmed, he simply was not inclined to put himself to so much trouble. He stood fifteen or twenty feet above me, pushing his tongue out through his teeth, shaking his head slightly and dipping it into charging position as I moved closer by a step or two, raising my hand slowly toward him in what I proposed as a friendly greeting. The day had been a banner one since the beginning, so while I recognized immediately that this meeting would be a valued memory, I felt as natural in his company as if he were a friend of mine reincarnated in a shag suit. I saw also that he was going to knock me for a loop, head over heels down the steep slope, if I sidled nearer, because he did not by any means feel as expansive and exuberant at our encounter as I did. That was the chief difference between us. I was talking to him with easy gladness, and beaming; he was not. He was unsettled and on his mettle, waiting for me to move along, the way a bighorn sheep waits for a predator to move on in a wildlife movie when each would be evenly matched in a contest of strength and position. Although his warlike nose and high bone helmet, blocky and beautiful as weaponry, kept me from giving in to my sense that we were brothers, I knew I could stand there for a long while. His coat was a down-to-earth brown, edgy with muscle, his head was that of an unsmiling veteran standing to arms, and despite my reluctance to treat him as some sort of boxed-in prize, I might have stayed on for half the afternoon if I hadn't realized that I had other sights to see. It was not a day to dawdle.

I trudged up the wash and continued until, past tree line, the terrain widened and flattened in front of a preliminary ridge that formed an obstacle before the great roaring, silent, surflike mountain wall that I liked to think of as the Continental Divide, although it wasn't. A cirque separated the preliminary ridge from the ultimate divide, which I still hoped to climb to and look over. The opening into this was roomy enough, except for being littered with enormous boulders, and I began trying to make my way across them. Each was boat-sized and rested upon underboulders; it was like running in place. After tussling with this landscape for an hour or two, I was limp and sweating, pinching my cramped legs. The sun had gone so low that I knew I would be finding my way home by moonlight in any case, and I could see into the cirque, which was big and symmetrical and presented a view of sheer barbarism; everywhere were these cruel boat-sized boulders.

Giving up and descending to the goats' draw again, I had a drink from the stream and bathed before climbing farther downward. The grass was green, sweet-smelling, and I felt safely close to life after that sea of dead boulders. I knew I would never be physically younger or in finer country; even then the wilderness was singing its swan song. I had no other challenges in mind, and though very tired, I liked looking up at the routes where I'd climbed. The trio of goats had not returned, but I could see their wintering cave and the cleft in the rocks where the spring was. Curiously, the bighorn ram had not left; he had only withdrawn upward, shifting away from the outcroppings to an open sweep of space where every avenue of escape was available. He was lying on a carpet of grass and, lonely pirate that he was, had his head turned in my direction.

It was from this same wash that looking up, I spotted the animal I took to be a mountain lion. He was skulking among some outcroppings at a point lower on the mountainside than the ledges where the ram originally had been. A pair of hawks or eagles were swooping at him by turns, as if he were close to a nest. The slant between us was steep, but the light of evening was still more than adequate. I did not really see the wonderful tail — that special medallion — nor was he particularly big for a lion. He was gloriously catlike and slinky, however, and so indifferent to the swooping birds as to seem oblivious of them. There are plenty of creatures he wasn't: he wasn't a marmot, a goat or other grass-eater, a badger, a wolf or coyote or fisher. He *may* have been a big bobcat or a wolverine, although he looked ideally lion-colored. He had a cat's strong collarbone structure for hitting, powerful haunches for vaulting, and the almost mystically small head mountain lions possess, with the gooseberry eyes. Anyway, I believed him to be a mountain lion, and standing quietly I watched him as he inspected in leisurely fashion the ledge that he was on and the one under him savory with every trace of goat — frosty-colored with the white hairs they'd shed. The sight was so dramatic that it seemed to be happening close to me, though in fact he and the hawks or eagles, whatever they were, were miniaturized by distance.

If I'd kept motionless, eventually I could have seen whether he had the proper tail, but such scientific questions had no weight next to my need to essay some kind of communication with him. It had been exactly the same when I'd watched the two wolves playing together a couple of days before. They were above me, absorbed in their game of noses-and-paws. I had recognized that I might never witness such a scene again, yet I couldn't hold myself in. Instead of talking and raising my arm to them, as I had with the ram, I'd shuffled forward impetuously as if to say *Here I am!* Now, with the lion, I tried hard to dampen my impulse and restrained myself as long as I could. Then I stepped toward him, just barely squelching a cry in my throat but lifting my hand — as clumsy as anyone who is trying to attract attention.

At that, of course, he swerved aside instantly and was gone. Even the two birds vanished. Foolish, triumphant and disappointed, I hiked on down into the lower forests, gargantuanly tangled, another life zone — not one which would exclude a lion but one where he would not be seen. I'd got my second wind and walked lightly and softly, letting the silvery darkness settle around me. The blowdowns were as black as whales; my feet sank in the moss. Clearly this was as crowded a day as I would ever have, and I knew my real problem would not be to make myself believed but rather to make myself understood at all, simply in reporting the story, and that I must at least keep the memory straight for myself. I was so happy that I was unerring in distinguishing the deer trails going my way. The forest's night beauty was supreme in its promise, and I didn't hurry.

ANNIE DILLARD
(1945–   )

🐦 The American nature essay has often been religious, in the small-"r" sense — looking for meaning, looking for the power in things or behind them, looking to see if nature can tell us how to live. Annie Dillard continues this tradition, showing that for all our particular knowledge, we still, if we are honest, experience life as a series of questions. Dillard's exquisite images and similes mark her close attention to nature; her simultaneously conveyed sense of the fragility of existence heightens the value of the moment.

Nightwatch

I STOOD IN THE LUCAS MEADOW in the middle of a barrage of grasshoppers. There must have been something about the rising heat, the falling night, the ripeness of grasses — something that mustered this army in the meadow where they have never been in such legions before. I must have seen a thousand grasshoppers, alarums and excursions clicking over the clover, knee-high to me.

I had stepped into the meadow to feel the heat and catch a glimpse of the sky, but these grasshoppers demanded my attention, and became an event in themselves. Every step I took detonated the grass. A blast of bodies like shrapnel exploded around me; the air burst and whirred. There were grasshoppers of all sizes, grasshoppers yellow, green and black, short-horned, long-horned, slant-faced, band-winged, spur-throated, cone-headed, pygmy, spotted, striped and barred. They sprang in salvos, dropped in the air, and clung unevenly to stems and blades with their legs spread for balance, as

From *Pilgrim at Tinker Creek* (1974)

redwings ride cattail reeds. They clattered around my ears; they ricocheted off my calves with an instant clutch and release of tiny legs.

I was in shelter, but open to the sky. The meadow was clean, the world new, and I washed by my walk over the waters of the dam. A new, wild feeling descended upon me and caught me up. What if these grasshoppers were locusts, I thought; what if I were the first man in the world, and stood in a swarm?

I had been reading about locusts. Hordes of migrating locusts have always appeared in arid countries, and then disappeared as suddenly as they had come. You could actually watch them lay eggs all over a plain, and the next year there would be no locusts on the plain. Entomologists would label their specimens, study their structure, and never find a single one that was alive — until years later they would be overrun again. No one knew in what caves of clouds the locusts hid between plagues.

In 1921 a Russian naturalist named Uvarov solved the mystery. Locusts are grasshoppers: they are the same animal. Swarms of locusts are ordinary grasshoppers gone berserk.

If you take ordinary grasshoppers of any of several species from any of a number of the world's dry regions — including the Rocky Mountains — and rear them in glass jars under crowded conditions, they go into the migratory phase. That is, they turn into locusts. They literally and physically change from Jekyll to Hyde before your eyes. They will even change, all alone in their jars, if you stimulate them by a rapid succession of artificial touches. Imperceptibly at first, their wings and wing-covers elongate. Their drab color heightens, then saturates more and more, until it locks at the hysterical locust yellows and pinks. Stripes and dots appear on the wing-covers; these deepen to a glittering black. They lay more egg-pods than grasshoppers. They are restless, excitable, voracious. You now have jars full of plague.

Under ordinary conditions, inside the laboratory and out in the deserts, the eggs laid by these locusts produce ordinary solitary grasshoppers. Only under special conditions — such as droughts that herd them together in crowds near available food — do the grasshoppers change. They shun food and shelter and seek only the jostle and clack of their kind. Their ranks swell; the valleys teem. One fine day they take to the air.

In full flight their millions can blacken the sky for nine hours, and when they land, it's every man to your tents, O Israel. "A fire devoureth before them; and behind them a flame burneth: the land is as the garden of Eden before them, and behind them a desolate wilderness; yea, and nothing shall escape them." One writer says that if you feed one a blade of grass, "the eighteen components of its jaws go immediately into action, lubricated by a brown saliva which looks like motor oil." Multiply this action by millions, and you hear a new sound: "The noise their myriad jaws make when engaged in their work of destruction can be realized by any one who has fought a prairie fire or heard the flames passing along before a brisk wind, the low crackling and rasping." Every contour of the land, every twig, is inches deep in bodies, so the valleys seethe and the hills tremble. Locusts: it is an old story.

A man lay down to sleep in a horde of locusts, Will Barker says. Instantly the suffocating swarm fell on him and knit him in a clicking coat of mail. The metallic mouth parts meshed and pinched. His friends rushed in and woke him at once. But when he stood up, he was bleeding from the throat and wrists.

The world has locusts, and the world has grasshoppers. I was up to my knees in the world.

Not one of these insects in this meadow could change into a locust under any circumstance. I am King of the Meadow, I thought, and raised my arms. Instantly grasshoppers burst all around me, describing in the air a blur of angular trajectories which ended in front of my path in a wag of grasses. As *if* I were king, dilly-dilly.

A large gray-green grasshopper hit with a clack on my shirt, and stood on my shoulder, panting. "Boo," I said, and it clattered off. It landed on a grass head several yards away. The grass bucked and sprang from the impact like a bronc, and the grasshopper rode it down. When the movement ceased, I couldn't see the grasshopper.

I walked on, one step at a time, both instigating and receiving this spray of small-arms fire. I had to laugh. I'd been had. I wanted to see the creatures, and they were gone. The only way I could see them in their cunning was to frighten them in their innocence. No charm or cleverness of mine could conjure or draw them; I could only flush them, triggering the grossest of their instincts, with the physical bluntness of my passage. To them I was just so much trouble, a horde of commotion, like any rolling stone. Wait! Where did you go? Does not any one of you, with your eighteen mouthparts, wish to have a word with me here in the Lucas meadow? Again I raised my arms: there you are. And then gone. The grasses slammed. I was exhilarated, flush. I was the serf of the meadow, exalted; I was the bride who waits with her lamp filled. A new wind was stirring; I had received the grasshoppers the way I received this wind. All around the meadow's rim the highest trees heaved soundlessly.

I walked back toward the cottage, maneuvering the whole squadron from one end of the meadow to the other. I'd been had all along by grasshoppers, muskrats, mountains — and like any sucker, I come back for more. They always get you in the end, and when you know it from the beginning, you have to laugh. You come for the assault, you come for the flight — but really you know you come for the laugh.

This is the fullness of late summer now; the green of what is growing and grown conceals. I can watch a muskrat feed on a bank for ten minutes, harvesting shocks of grass that bristle and droop from his jaws, and when he is gone I cannot see any difference in the grass. If I spread the patch with my hands and peer closely, I am hard put to locate any damage from even the most intense grazing. Nothing even looks trampled. Does everything else but me pass so lightly? When the praying mantis egg cases hatched in June, over a period of several days, I watched the tiny translucent mantises leap about leggily on the egg case, scraggle down the hedge's twigs, and disappear in the grass. In some places I could see them descend in a line like a moving bridge from stem to ground. The instant they crossed the horizon and entered the grass, they vanished as if they had jumped off the edge of the world.

Now it is early September, and the paths are clogged. I look to water to see sky. It is the time of year when a honeybee beats feebly at the inside back window of every parked car. A frog flies up for every foot of bank, bubbles tangle in a snare of blue-green algae, and Japanese beetles hunch doubled on the willow leaves. The sun thickens the air to jelly; it bleaches, flattens, dissolves. The skies are a milky haze — nowhere, do-nothing summer skies. Every kid I see has a circular grid on his forehead, a regular cross-hatching of straight lines, from spending his days leaning into screen doors.

I had come to the Lucas place to spend a night there, to let come what may. The Lucas place is paradise enow. It has everything: old woods, young woods, cliffs, meadows, slow water, fast water, caves. All it needs is a glacier extending a creaking foot behind the cottage. This magic garden is just on the other side of the oxbow in Tinker Creek; it is secluded because it is hard to approach. I could have followed the rock cliff path through the old woods, but in summer that path is wrapped past finding in saplings, bushes, kudzu, and poison oak. I could have tacked down the shorn grass terraces next to the cliff, but to get there I would have had to pass a vicious dog, who is waiting for the day I forget to carry a stick. So I planned on going the third way, over the dam.

I made a sandwich, filled a canteen, and slipped a palm-sized flashlight into my pocket. Then all I had to do was grab a thin foam pad and my sleeping bag, walk down the road, over the eroded clay hill where the mantis laid her eggs, along the creek downstream to the motorbike woods, and through the woods' bike trail to the dam.

I like crossing the dam. If I fell, I might not get up again. The dam is three or four feet high; a thick green algae, combed by the drag and sudden plunge of the creek's current, clings to its submersed, concrete brim. Below is a jumble of fast water and rocks. But I face this threat every time I cross the dam, and it is always exhilarating. The tightest part is at the very beginning. That day as always I faced the current, planted my feet firmly, stepped sideways instead of striding, and I soon emerged dripping in a new world.

Now, returning from my foray into the grasshopper meadow, I was back where I started, on the bank that separates the cottage from the top of the dam, where my sleeping bag, foam pad, and sandwich lay. The sun was setting invisibly behind the cliffs' rim. I unwrapped the sandwich and looked back over the way I had come, as if I could have seen the grasshoppers spread themselves again over the wide meadow and hide enfolded in its thickets and plush.

This is what I had come for, just this, and nothing more. A fling of leafy motion on the cliffs, the assault of real things, living and still, with shapes and powers under the sky — this is my city, my culture, and all the world I need. I looked around.

What I call the Lucas place is only a part of the vast Lucas property. It is one of the earliest clearings around here, a garden in the wilderness; every time I cross the dam and dry my feet on the bank, I feel like I've just been born. Now to my right the creek's dammed waters were silent and deep, overhung by the reflecting bankside tulip and pawpaw and ash. The creek angled away out of sight upstream; this was the oxbow, and the dam spanned its sharpest arc. Downstream the creek slid over the dam and slapped along sandstone ledges and bankside boulders, exhaling a cooling breath of mist before disappearing around the bend under the steep wooded cliff.

I stood ringed and rimmed in heights, locked and limned, in a valley within a valley. Next to the cliff fell a grassy series of high terraces, suitable for planting the hanging gardens of Babylon. Beyond the terraces, forest erupted again wherever it could eke a roothold on the sheer vertical rock. In one place, three caves cut into the stone vaults, their entrances hidden by honeysuckle. One of the caves was so small only a child could enter it crawling; one was big enough to explore long after you have taken the initiatory turns that shut out the light; the third was huge and shallow, filled with cut wood and chicken wire, and into its nether wall extended another tiny cave in which a groundhog reared her litter this spring.

Ahead of me in the distance I could see where the forested cliffs mined with caves gave way to overgrown terraces that once must have been cleared. Now they were tangled in saplings swatched in honeysuckle and wild rose brambles. I always remember trying to fight my way up that steepness one winter when I first understood that even January is not muscle enough to subdue the deciduous South. There were clear trails through the undergrowth — I saw once I was in the thick of it — but they were rabbit paths, unfit for anyone over seven inches tall. I had emerged scratched, pricked, and panting in the Lucas peach orchard, which is considerably more conveniently approached by the steep gravel drive that parallels the creek.

In the flat at the center of all this rimrock was the sunlit grasshopper meadow, and facing the meadow, tucked up between the grass terrace and the creek's dam, was the heart of the city, the Lucas cottage.

I stepped to the porch. My footfall resounded; the cliffs rang back the sound, and the clover and grasses absorbed it. The Lucas cottage was in fact mostly porch, airy and winged. Gray-painted two-by-fours wobbled around three sides of the cottage, split, smashed, and warped long past plumb. Beams at the porch's four corners supported a low, peaked roof that vaulted over both the porch and the cottage impartially, lending so much importance to the already huge porch that it made the cottage proper seem an afterthought, as Adam seems sometimes an afterthought in Eden. For years an old inlaid chess table with a broken carved pedestal leaned against the cottage on one wing of the porch; the contrasting brown patches of weathered inlay curled up in curves like leaves.

The cottage was scarcely longer than the porch was deep. It was a one-room cottage; you could manage (I've thought this through again and again — building more spartan mansions, o my soul) a cot, a plank window-desk, a chair (two for company, as the man says), and some narrow shelves. The cottage is mostly windows — there are

five — and the windows are entirely broken, so that my life inside
the cottage is mostly Tinker Creek and mud dauber wasps.

It's a great life — luxurious, really. The cottage is wired for elec-
tricity; a bare-bulb socket hangs from the unfinished wood ceiling.
There is a stovepipe connection in the roof. Beyond the porch on
the side away from the creek is a big brick fireplace suitable for
grilling whole steers. The steers themselves are fattening just five
minutes away, up the hill and down into the pasture. The trees that
shade the cottage are walnuts and pecans. In the spring the edge of
the upstream creek just outside the cottage porch comes up in yellow
daffodils, all the way up to the peach orchard.

That day it was dark inside the cottage, as usual; the five windows framed five films of the light and living world. I crunched to the creekside window, walking on the layer of glass shards on the floor, and stood to watch the creek lurch over the dam and round the shaded bend under the cliff, while bumblebees the size of ponies fumbled in the fragrant flowers that flecked the bank. A young cottontail rabbit bounded into view and froze. It crouched under my window with its ears flattened to its skull and its body motionless, the picture of adaptive invisibility. With one ridiculous exception. It was so very young, and its shoulder itched so maddeningly, that it whapped away at the spot noisily with a violent burst of a hind leg — and then resumed its frozen alert. Over the dam's drop of waters, two dog-faced sulphur butterflies were fighting. They touched and parted, ascending in a vertical climb, as though they were racing up an invisible spiraling vine.

All at once something wonderful happened, although at first it seemed perfectly ordinary. A female goldfinch suddenly hove into view. She lighted weightlessly on the head of a bankside purple thistle and began emptying the seedcase, sowing the air with down.

The lighted frame of my window filled. The down rose and spread in all directions, wafting over the dam's waterfall and wavering between the tulip trunks and into the meadow. It vaulted towards the orchard in a puff; it hovered over the ripening pawpaw fruit and staggered up the steep-faced terrace. It jerked, floated, rolled, veered, swayed. The thistledown faltered toward the cottage and gusted clear to the motorbike woods; it rose and entered the shaggy arms of pecans. At last it strayed like snow, blind and sweet, into the pool of the creek upstream, and into the race of the creek over rocks down. It shuddered onto the tips of growing grasses, where it poised, light, still wracked by errant quivers. I was holding my breath. Is this where we live, I thought, in this place at this moment, with the air so light and wild?

The same fixity that collapses stars and drives the mantis to devour her mate eased these creatures together before my eyes: the thick adept bill of the goldfinch, and the feathery, coded down. How could anything be amiss? If I myself were lighter and frayed, I could ride these small winds, too, taking my chances, for the pleasure of being so purely played.

The thistle is part of Adam's curse. "Cursed is the ground for thy sake; in sorrow shalt thou eat of it all the days of thy life; Thorns also and thistles shall it bring forth to thee." A terrible curse: But does the goldfinch eat thorny sorrow with the thistle, or do I? If this furling air is fallen, then the fall was happy indeed. If this creekside

garden is sorrow, then I seek martyrdom. This crown of thorns sits
light on my skull, like wings. The Venetian Baroque painter Tiepolo
painted Christ as a red-lipped infant clutching a goldfinch; the goldfinch seems to be looking around in search of thorns. Creation itself
was the fall, a burst into the thorny beauty of the real.

The goldfinch here on the fringed thistletop was burying her head
with each light thrust deeper into the seedcase. Her fragile legs
braced to her task on the vertical, thorny stem; the last of the thistledown sprayed and poured. Is there anything I could eat so lightly,
or could I die so fair? With a ruffle of feathered wings the goldfinch
fluttered away, out of range of the broken window's frame and toward
the deep blue shade of the cliffs where late fireflies already were
rising alight under trees. I was weightless; my bones were taut skins
blown with buoyant gas; it seemed that if I inhaled too deeply, my
shoulders and head would waft off. Alleluia.

Later I lay half out of my sleeping bag on a narrow shelf of flat
ground between the cottage porch and the bank to the dam. I lay
where a flash flood would reach me, but we have had a flood; the
time is late. The night was clear; when the fretwork of overhead
foliage rustled and parted, I could see the pagan stars.

Sounds fell all about me; I vibrated like still water ruffed by wind.
Cicadas — which Donald E. Carr calls "the guns of August" — were
out in full force. Their stridulations mounted over the meadow and
echoed from the rim of cliffs, filling the air with a plaintive, mysterious urgency. I had heard them begin at twilight, and was struck
with the way they actually do "start up," like an out-of-practice or-
chestra, creaking and grinding and all out of synch. It had sounded
like someone playing a cello with a wide-toothed comb. The frogs
added their unlocatable notes, which always seem to me to be so
arbitrary and anarchistic, and crickets piped in, calling their own
tune which they have been calling since the time of Pliny, who noted
bluntly of the cricket, it "never ceaseth all night long to creak very
shrill."

Earlier a bobwhite had cried from the orchardside cliff, now here,
now there, and his round notes swelled sorrowfully over the meadow.
A bobwhite who is still calling in summer is lorn; he has never found
a mate. When I first read this piece of information, every bobwhite
call I heard sounded tinged with desperation, suicidally miserable.
But now I am somehow cheered on my way by that solitary signal.
The bobwhite's very helplessness, his obstinate Johnny-two-noted-
ness, takes on an aura of dogged pluck. God knows what he is

thinking in those pendant silences between calls. God knows what I am. But: bob*white*. (Somebody showed me once how to answer a bobwhite in the warbling, descending notes of the female. It works like a charm. But what can I do with a charmed circle of male bobwhites but weep? Still, I am brutalized enough that I give the answering call occasionally, just to get a rise out of the cliffs, and a bitter laugh.) Yes, it's tough, it's tough, that goes without saying. But isn't waiting itself and longing a wonder, being played on by wind, sun, and shade?

In his famous *Camping and Woodcraft*, Horace Kephart sounds a single ominous note. He writes in parentheses: "Some cannot sleep well in a white tent under a full moon." Every time I think of it, I laugh. I like the way that handy woodsy tip threatens us with the thrashings of the spirit.

I was in no tent under leaves, sleepless and glad. There was no moon at all; along the world's coasts the sea tides would be springing strong. The air itself also has lunar tides: I lay still. Could I feel in the air an invisible sweep and surge, and an answering knock in my lungs? Or could I feel the starlight? Every minute on a square mile of this land — on the steers and the orchard, on the quarry, the meadow, and creek — one ten thousandth of an ounce of starlight spatters to earth. What percentage of an ounce did that make on my eyes and cheeks and arms, tapping and nudging as particles, pulsing and stroking as waves? Straining after these tiny sensations, I nearly rolled off the world when I heard, and at the same time felt through my hips' and legs' bones on the ground, the bang and shudder of distant freight trains coupling.

Night risings and fallings filled my mind, free excursions carried out invisibly while the air swung up and back and the starlight rained. By day I had watched water striders dimple and jerk over the deep bankside water slowed by the dam. But I knew that sometimes a breath or call stirs the colony, and new forms emerge with wings. They cluster at night on the surface of their home waters and then take to the air in a rush. Migrating, they sail over meadows, under trees, cruising, veering towards a steady gleam in a flurry of glistening wings: "phantom ships in the air."

Now also in the valley night a skunk emerged from his underground burrow to hunt pale beetle grubs in the dark. A great horned owl folded his wings and dropped from the sky, and the two met on the bloodied surface of earth. Spreading over a distance, the air from that spot thinned to a frail sweetness, a tinctured wind that bespoke real creatures and real encounters at the edge . . . events, events. Over my head black hunting beetles crawled up into the high limbs of trees, killing more caterpillars and pupae than they would eat.

I had read once about a mysterious event of the night that is never far from my mind. Edwin Way Teale described an occurrence so absurd that it vaults out of the world of strange facts and into that startling realm where power and beauty hold sovereign sway.

The sentence in Teale is simple: "On cool autumn nights, eels hurrying to the sea sometimes crawl for a mile or more across dewy meadows to reach streams that will carry them to salt water." These are adult eels, silver eels, and this descent that slid down my mind is the fall from a long spring ascent the eels made years ago. As one-inch elvers they wriggled and heaved their way from the salt sea up the coastal rivers of America and Europe, upstream always into "the quiet upper reaches of rivers and brooks, in lakes and ponds — sometimes as high as 8,000 feet above sea level." There they had lived without breeding "for at least eight years." In the late summer of the year they reached maturity, they stopped eating, and their dark color vanished. They turned silver; now they are heading to the sea. Down streams to rivers, down rivers to the sea, south in the North Atlantic where they meet and pass billions of northbound elvers, they are returning to the Sargasso Sea, where, in floating sargassum weed in the deepest waters of the Atlantic, they will mate, release their eggs, and die. This, the whole story of eels at which I have only just hinted, is extravagant in the extreme, and food for another kind of thought, a thought about the meaning of such wild, incomprehensible gestures. But it was feeling with which I was concerned under the walnut tree by the side of the Lucas cottage and dam. My mind was on that meadow.

Imagine a chilly night and a meadow; balls of dew droop from the curved blades of grass. All right: the grass at the edge of the meadow begins to tremble and sway. Here come the eels. The largest are five feet long. All are silver. They stream into the meadow, sift between grasses and clover, veer from your path. There are too many to count. All you see is a silver slither, like twisted ropes of water falling roughly, a one-way milling and mingling over the meadow and slide to the creek. Silver eels in the night: a barely-made-out seething as far as you can squint, a squirming, jostling torrent of silver eels in the grass. If I saw that sight, would I live? If I stumbled across it, would I ever set foot from my door again? Or would I be seized to join that compelling rush, would I cease eating, and pale, and abandon all to start walking?

Had this place always been so, and had I not known it? There were blowings and flights, tossings and heaves up the air and down to grass. Why didn't God let the animals in Eden name the man; why didn't I wrestle the grasshopper on my shoulder and pin him down till he called my name? I was thistledown, and now I seemed to be grass, the receiver of grasshoppers and eels and mantises, grass the windblown and final receiver.

For the grasshoppers and thistledown and eels went up and came down. If you watch carefully the hands of a juggler, you see they are almost motionless, held at precise angles, so that the balls seem to be of their own volition describing a perfect circle in the air. The ascending arc is the hard part, but our eyes are on the smooth and curving fall. Each falling ball seems to trail beauty as its afterimage, receding faintly down the air, almost disappearing, when lo, another real ball falls, shedding its transparent beauty, and another. . . .

And it all happens so dizzyingly fast. The goldfinch I had seen was asleep in a thicket; when she settled to sleep, the weight of her breast locked her toes around her perch. Wasps were asleep with their legs hanging loose, their jaws jammed into the soft stems of plants. Everybody grab a handle: we're spinning headlong down.

I am puffed clay, blown up and set down. That I fall like Adam is not surprising: I plunge, waft, arc, pour, and dive. The surprise is how good the wind feels on my face as I fall. And the other surprise is that I ever rise at all. I rise when I receive, like grass.

I didn't know, I never have known, what spirit it is that descends into my lungs and flaps near my heart like an eagle rising. I named it full-of-wonder, highest good, voices. I shut my eyes and saw a tree stump hurled by wind, an enormous tree stump sailing sideways across my vision, with a wide circular brim of roots and soil like a tossed top hat.

And what if those grasshoppers had been locusts descending, I thought, and what if I stood awake in a swarm? I cannot ask for more than to be so wholly acted upon, flown at, and lighted on in throngs, probed, knocked, even bitten. A little blood from the wrists and throat is the price I would willingly pay for that pressure of clacking weights on my shoulders, for the scent of deserts, groundfire in my ears — for being so in the clustering thick of things, rapt and enwrapped in the rising and falling real world.

EDWARD ABBEY

(*1927–*   )

&. Edward Abbey is deeply concerned, especially in his early work, with attaining a clarified and true perception of wilderness, and just as profoundly interested in actually acting to preserve it. He has made an influential statement of the some of the central themes in modern nature literature. Abbey's statement is by turns darkly humorous, rippingly satiric, straight-on blunt, and poetically lyrical. Few American essayists, perhaps, have surpassed this writer's range of tones, which somehow he has brought together as the voice of one maverick persona.

The Great American Desert

IN MY CASE it was love at first sight. This desert, all deserts, any desert. No matter where my head and feet may go, my heart and my entrails stay behind, here on the clean, true, comfortable rock, under the black sun of God's forsaken country. When I take on my next incarnation, my bones will remain bleaching nicely in a stone gulch under the rim of some faraway plateau, way out there in the back of beyond. An unrequited and excessive love, inhuman no doubt but painful anyhow, especially when I see my desert under attack. "The one death I cannot bear," said the Sonoran-Arizonan poet Richard Shelton. The kind of love that makes a man selfish, possessive, irritable. If you're thinking of a visit, my natural reaction is like a rattlesnake's — to warn you off. What I want to say goes something like this.

Survival Hint #1: Stay out of there. Don't go. Stay home and read

From *The Journey Home: Some Words in Defense of the American West* (1977)

a good book, this one for example. The Great American Desert is an awful place. People get hurt, get sick, get lost out there. Even if you survive, which is not certain, you will have a miserable time. The desert is for movies and God-intoxicated mystics, not for family recreation.

Let me enumerate the hazards. First the Walapai tiger, also known as conenose kissing bug. *Triatoma protracta* is a true bug, black as sin, and it flies through the night quiet as an assassin. It does not attack directly like a mosquito or deerfly, but alights at a discreet distance, undetected, and creeps upon you, its hairy little feet making not the slightest noise. The kissing bug is fond of warmth and like Dracula requires mammalian blood for sustenance. When it reaches you the bug crawls onto your skin so gently, so softly that unless your senses are hyperacute you feel nothing. Selecting a tender point, the bug slips its conical proboscis into your flesh, injecting a poisonous anesthetic. If you are asleep you will feel nothing. If you happen to be awake you may notice the faintest of pinpricks, hardly more than a brief ticklish sensation, which you will probably disregard. But the bug is already at work. Having numbed the nerves near the point of entry the bug proceeds (with a sigh of satisfaction, no doubt) to withdraw blood. When its belly is filled, it pulls out, backs off, and waddles away, so drunk and gorged it cannot fly.

At about this time the victim awakes, scratching at a furious itch. If you recognize the symptoms at once, you can sometimes find the bug in your vicinity and destroy it. But revenge will be your only satisfaction. Your night is ruined. If you are of average sensitivity to a kissing bug's poison, your entire body breaks out in hives, skin aflame from head to toe. Some people become seriously ill, in many cases requiring hospitalization. Others recover fully after five or six hours except for a hard and itchy swelling, which may endure for a week.

After the kissing bug, you should beware of rattlesnakes; we have half a dozen species, all offensive and dangerous, plus centipedes, millipedes, tarantulas, black widows, brown recluses, Gila monsters, the deadly poisonous coral snakes, and giant hairy desert scorpions. Plus an immense variety and near-infinite number of ants, midges, gnats, bloodsucking flies, and blood-guzzling mosquitoes. (You might think the desert would be spared at least mosquitoes? Not so. Peer in any water hole by day: swarming with mosquito larvae. Venture out on a summer's eve: The air vibrates with their mournful keening.) Finally, where the desert meets the sea, as on the coasts of Sonora and Baja California, we have the usual assortment of obnoxious marine life: sandflies, ghost crabs, stingrays, electric jellyfish, spiny sea urchins, man-eating sharks, and other creatures so distasteful one prefers not even to name them.

It has been said, and truly, that everything in the desert either stings, stabs, stinks, or sticks. You will find the flora here as venomous, hooked, barbed, thorny, prickly, needled, saw-toothed, hairy, stickered, mean, bitter, sharp, wiry, and fierce as the animals. Something about the desert inclines all living things to harshness and acerbity. The soft evolve out. Except for sleek and oily growths like the poison ivy — oh yes, indeed — that flourish in sinister profusion on the dank walls above the quicksand down in those corridors of gloom and labyrinthine monotony that men call canyons.

We come now to the third major hazard, which is sunshine. Too much of a good thing can be fatal. Sunstroke, heatstroke, and dehydration are common misfortunes in the bright American Southwest. If you can avoid the insects, reptiles, and arachnids, the cactus and the ivy, the smog of the southwestern cities, and the lung fungus of the desert valleys (carried by dust in the air), you cannot escape the desert sun. Too much exposure to it eventually causes, quite literally, not merely sunburn but skin cancer.

Much sun, little rain also means an arid climate. Compared with the high humidity of more hospitable regions, the dry heat of the desert seems at first not terribly uncomfortable — sometimes even pleasant. But that sensation of comfort is false, a deception, and therefore all the more dangerous, for it induces overexertion and an insufficient consumption of water, even when water is available. This leads to various internal complications, some immediate — sunstroke, for example — and some not apparent until much later. Mild but prolonged dehydration, continued over a span of months or years, leads to the crystallization of mineral solutions in the urinary tract, that is, to what urologists call urinary calculi or kidney stones. A disability common in all the world's arid regions. Kidney stones, in case you haven't met one, come in many shapes and sizes, from pellets smooth as BB shot to highly irregular calcifications resembling asteroids, Vietcong shrapnel, and crown-of-thorns starfish. Some of these objects may be "passed" naturally; others can be removed only by means of the Davis stone basket or by surgery. Me — I was lucky; I passed mine with only a groan, my forehead pressed against the wall of a pissoir in the rear of a Tucson bar that I cannot recommend.

You may be getting the impression by now that the desert is not the most suitable of environments for human habitation. Correct. Of all the Earth's climatic zones, excepting only the Antarctic, the deserts are the least inhabited, the least "developed," for reasons that should now be clear.

You may wish to ask, Yes, okay, but among North American deserts which is the *worst?* A good question — and I am happy to attempt to answer.

Geographers generally divide the North American desert — what was once termed "the Great American Desert" — into four distinct regions or subdeserts. These are the Sonoran Desert, which comprises southern Arizona, Baja California, and the state of Sonora in Mexico; the Chihuahuan Desert, which includes west Texas, southern New Mexico, and the states of Chihuahua and Coahuila in Mexico; the Mojave Desert, which includes southeastern California and small portions of Nevada, Utah, and Arizona; and the Great Basin Desert, which includes most of Utah and Nevada, northern Arizona, northwestern New Mexico, and much of Idaho and eastern Oregon.

Privately, I prefer my own categories. Up north in Utah somewhere is the canyon country — places like Zeke's Hole, Death Hollow, Pucker Pass, Buckskin Gulch, Nausea Crick, Wolf Hole, Mollie's Nipple, Dirty Devil River, Horse Canyon, Horseshoe Canyon, Lost Horse Canyon, Horsethief Canyon, and Horseshit Canyon, to name only the more classic places. Down in Arizona and Sonora there's the cactus country; if you have nothing better to do, you might take a look at High Tanks, Salome Creek, Tortilla Flat, Esperero ("Hoper") Canyon, Holy Joe Peak, Depression Canyon, Painted Cave, Hell Hole Canyon, Hell's Half Acre, Iceberg Canyon, Tiburon (Shark) Island, Pinacate Peak, Infernal Valley, Sykes Crater, Montezuma's Head, Gu Oidak, Kuakatch, Pisinimo, and Baboquivari Mountain, for example.

Then there's The Canyon. *The* Canyon. The Grand. That's one world. And North Rim — that's another. And Death Valley, still another, where I lived one winter near Furnace Creek and climbed the Funeral Mountains, tasted Badwater, looked into the Devil's Hole, hollered up Echo Canyon, searched for and never did find Seldom Seen Slim. Looked for *satori* near Vana, Nevada, and found a ghost town named Bonnie Claire. Never made it to Winnemucca. Drove through the Smoke Creek Desert and down through Big Pine and Lone Pine and home across the Panamints to Death Valley again — home sweet home that winter.

And which of these deserts is the worst? I find it hard to judge. They're all bad — not half bad but all bad. In the Sonoran Desert, Phoenix will get you if the sun, snakes, bugs, and arthropods don't. In the Mojave Desert, it's Las Vegas, more sickening by far than the Glauber's salt in the Death Valley sinkholes. Go to Chihuahua and you're liable to get busted in El Paso and sandbagged in Ciudad Juárez — where all old whores go to die. Up north in the Great Basin Desert, on the Plateau Province, in the canyon country, your heart will break, seeing the strip mines open up and the power plants rise where only cowboys and Indians and J. Wesley Powell ever roamed before.

Nevertheless, all is not lost; much remains, and I welcome the prospect of an army of lug-soled hiker's boots on the desert trails. To save what wilderness is left in the American Southwest — and in the American Southwest only the wilderness is worth saving — we are going to need all the recruits we can get. All the hands, heads, bodies, time, money, effort we can find. Presumably — and the Sierra Club, the Wilderness Society, the Friends of the Earth, the Audubon Society, the Defenders of Wildlife operate on this theory — those who learn to love what is spare, rough, wild, undeveloped, and unbroken will be willing to fight for it, will help resist the strip miners, highway builders, land developers, weapons testers, power producers, tree chainers, clear cutters, oil drillers, dam beavers, subdividers — the list goes on and on — before that zinc-hearted, termite-brained, squint-eyed, nearsighted, greedy crew succeeds in completely californicating what still survives of the Great American Desert.

So much for the Good Cause. Now what about desert hiking itself, you may ask. I'm glad you asked that question. I firmly believe that one should never — I repeated *never* — go out into that formidable wasteland of cactus, heat, serpents, rock, scrub, and thorn without careful planning, thorough and cautious preparation, and complete — never mind the expense! — *complete* equipment. My motto is: Be Prepared.

That is my belief and that is my motto. My practice, however, is a little different. I tend to go off in a more or less random direction myself, half-baked, half-assed, half-cocked, and half-ripped. Why? Well, because I have an indolent and melancholy nature and don't care to be bothered getting all those *things* together — all that bloody *gear* — maps, compass, binoculars, poncho, pup tent, shoes, first-aid kit, rope, flashlight, inspirational poetry, water, food — and because anyhow I approach nature with a certain surly ill-will, daring Her to make trouble. Later when I'm deep into Natural Bridges Natural Moneymint or Zion National Parkinglot or say General Shithead National Forest Land of Many Abuses why then, of course, when it's a bit late, then I may wish I had packed that something extra: matches perhaps, to mention one useful item, or maybe a spoon to eat my gruel with.

If I hike with another person it's usually the same; most of my friends have indolent and melancholy natures too. A cursed lot, all of them. I think of my comrade John De Puy, for example, sloping along for mile after mile like a goddamned camel — indefatigable — with those J. C. Penney hightops on his feet and that plastic pack on his back he got with five books of Green Stamps and nothing inside it but a sketchbook, some homemade jerky and a few cans of green chiles. Or Douglas Peacock, ex-Green Beret, just the opposite. Built like a buffalo, he loads a ninety-pound canvas pannier on his back at trailhead, loaded with guns, ammunition, bayonet, pitons and carabiners, cameras, field books, a 150-foot rope, geologist's sledge, rock samples, assay kit, field glasses, two gallons of water in steel canteens, jungle boots, a case of C-rations, rope hammock, pharmaceuticals in a pig-iron box, raincoat, overcoat, two-man mountain tent, Dutch oven, hibachi, shovel, ax, inflatable boat, and near the top of the load and distributed through side and back pockets, easily accessible, a case of beer. Not because he enjoys or needs all that weight — he may never get to the bottom of that cargo on a ten-day outing — but simply because Douglas uses his packbag for general storage both at home and on the trail and prefers not to have to rearrange everything from time to time merely for the purposes of a hike. Thus my friends De Puy and Peacock; you may wish to avoid such extremes.

A few tips on desert etiquette:

1. Carry a cooking stove, if you must cook. Do not burn desert wood, which is rare and beautiful and required ages for its creation (an ironwood tree lives for over 1,000 years and juniper almost as long).

2. If you must, out of need, build a fire, then for God's sake allow it to burn itself out before you leave — do not bury it, as Boy Scouts and Campfire Girls do, under a heap of mud or sand. Scatter the ashes; replace any rocks you may have used in constructing a fireplace; do all you can to obliterate the evidence that you camped here. (The Search & Rescue Team may be looking for you.)

3. Do not bury garbage — the wildlife will only dig it up again. Burn what will burn and pack out the rest. The same goes for toilet paper: Don't bury it, *burn it*.

4. Do not bathe in desert pools, natural tanks, *tinajas,* potholes. Drink what water you need, take what you need, and leave the rest for the next hiker and more important for the bees, birds, and animals — bighorn sheep, coyotes, lions, foxes, badgers, deer, wild pigs, wild horses — whose *lives* depend on that water.

5. Always remove and destroy survey stakes, flagging, advertising signboards, mining claim markers, animal traps, poisoned bait, seismic

exploration geophones, and other such artifacts of industrialism. The men who put those things there are up to no good and it is our duty to confound them. Keep America Beautiful. Grow a Beard. Take a Bath. Burn a Billboard.

Anyway — why go into the desert? Really, why do it? That sun, roaring at you all day long. The fetid, tepid, vapid little water holes slowly evaporating under a scum of grease, full of cannibal beetles, spotted toads, horsehair worms, liver flukes, and down at the bottom, inevitably, the pale cadaver of a ten-inch centipede. Those pink rattlesnakes down in The Canyon, those diamondback monsters thick as a truck driver's wrist that lurk in shady places along the trail, those unpleasant solpugids and unnecessary Jerusalem crickets that scurry on dirty claws across your face at night. Why? The rain that comes down like lead shot and wrecks the trail, those sudden rockfalls of obscure origin that crash like thunder ten feet behind you in the heart of a dead-still afternoon. The ubiquitous buzzard, so patient — but only so patient. The sullen and hostile Indians, all on welfare. The ragweed, the tumbleweed, the Jimson weed, the snakeweed. The scorpion in your shoe at dawn. The dreary wind that blows all spring, the psychedelic Joshua trees waving their arms at you on moonlight nights. Sand in the soup du jour. Halazone tablets in your canteen. The barren hills that always go up, which is bad, or down, which is worse. Those canyons like catacombs with quicksand lapping at your crotch. Hollow, mummified horses with forelegs casually crossed, dead for ten years, leaning against the corner of a barbed-wire fence. Packhorses at night, iron-shod, clattering over the slickrock through your camp. The last tin of tuna, two flat tires, not enough water and a forty-mile trek to Tule Well. An osprey on a cardón cactus, snatching the head off a living fish — always the best part first. The hawk sailing by at 200 feet, a squirming snake in its talons. Salt in the drinking water. Salt, selenium, arsenic, radon and radium in the water, in the gravel, in your bones. Water so hard it bends light, drills holes in rock and chokes up your radiator. Why go there? Those places with the hardcase names: Starvation Creek, Poverty Knoll, Hungry Valley, Bitter Springs, Last Chance Canyon, Dungeon Canyon, Whipsaw Flat, Dead Horse Point, Scorpion Flat, Dead Man Draw, Stinking Spring, Camino del Diablo, Jornado del Muerto . . . Death Valley.

Well then, why indeed go walking into the desert, that grim ground, that bleak and lonesome land where, as Genghis Khan said of India, "the heat is bad and the water makes men sick"?

Why the desert, when you could be strolling along the golden beaches of California? Camping by a stream of pure Rocky Mountain spring water in colorful Colorado? Loafing through a laurel slick in the misty hills of North Carolina? Or getting your head mashed in the greasy alley behind the Elysium Bar and Grill in Hoboken, New Jersey? Why the desert, given a world of such splendor and variety?

A friend and I took a walk around the base of a mountain up beyond Coconino County, Arizona. This was a mountain we'd been planning to circumambulate for years. Finally we put on our walking shoes and did it. About halfway around this mountain, on the third or fourth day, we paused for a while — two days — by the side of a stream, which the Navajos call Nasja because of the amber color of the water. (Caused perhaps by juniper roots — the water seems safe enough to drink.) On our second day there I walked down the stream, alone, to look at the canyon beyond. I entered the canyon and followed it for half the afternoon, for three or four miles, maybe, until it became a gorge so deep, narrow and dark, full of water and the inevitable quagmires of quicksand, that I turned around and looked for a way out. A route other than the way I'd come, which was crooked and uncomfortable and buried — I wanted to see what was up on top of this world. I found a sort of chimney flue on the east wall, which looked plausible, and sweated and cursed my way up through that until I reached a point where I could walk upright, like a human being. Another 300 feet of scrambling brought me to the rim of the canyon. No one, I felt certain, had ever before departed Nasja Canyon by that route.

But someone had. Near the summit I found an arrow sign, three feet long, formed of stones and pointing off into the north toward those same old purple vistas, so grand, immense, and mysterious, of more canyons, more mesas and plateaus, more mountains, more cloud-dappled sun-spangled leagues of desert sand and desert rock, under the same old wide and aching sky.

The arrow pointed into the north. But what was it pointing *at*? I looked at the sign closely and saw that those dark, desert-varnished stones had been in place for a long, long, time; they rested in compacted dust. They must have been there for a century at least. I followed the direction indicated and came promptly to the rim of another canyon and a drop-off straight down of a good 500 feet. Not that way, surely. Across this canyon was nothing of any unusual interest that I could see — only the familiar sun-blasted sandstone, a few scrubby clumps of blackbrush and prickly pear, a few acres of nothing where only a lizard could graze, surrounded by a few square miles of more nothingness interesting chiefly to horned toads. I returned to the arrow and checked again, this time with field glasses, looking away for as far as my aided eyes could see toward the north, for ten, twenty, forty miles into the distance. I studied the scene with care, looking for an ancient Indian ruin, a significant cairn, perhaps an abandoned mine, a hidden treasure of some inconceivable wealth, the mother of all mother lodes. . . .

But there was nothing out there. Nothing at all. Nothing but the desert. Nothing but the silent world.

That's why.

WENDELL BERRY

(*1934–*   )

&. More than most of us, perhaps, Wendell Berry is a man with a strong sense of place, writing out of working contact with his home ground — to be specific, a farm in Kentucky. In his writing, insights into interconnectedness flow from both epiphanic experience (see "A Native Hill" in *The Long-Legged House,* for example) and sober, assessing judgment, as in the following essay. His farming is not a country gentleman's pastime but a continuing study in which networks of connections reveal themselves, until farming, finally, stands as instructive about our entire relationship with the natural world. A conservator and renewer of soil, Berry is also, not surprisingly, conservative in temperament. What might not be so readily noticed is that his intense localism frees him from the wider provincialism of mass culture and allows him to be, against the mobile and dis-placed contemporary scene, radical on diverse matters. It is worth noting that Berry has written at some length, in praise and thoughtful analysis, of both Gary Snyder and Edward Abbey.

The Making of a Marginal Farm

ONE DAY in the summer of 1956, leaving home for school, I stopped on the side of the road directly above the house where I now live. From there you could see a mile or so across the Kentucky River Valley, and perhaps six miles along the length of it. The valley was a green trough full of sunlight, blue in its distances. I often stopped here in my comings and goings, just to look, for it was all familiar to me from before the time my memory began: woodlands and pastures

From *Recollected Essays* (*1965–1980*)

on the hillsides; fields and croplands, wooded slew-edges and hollows in the bottoms; and through the midst of it the tree-lined river passing down from its headwaters near the Virginia line toward its mouth at Carrollton on the Ohio.

Standing there, I was looking at land where one of my great-great-great-grandfathers settled in 1803, and at the scene of some of the happiest times of my own life, where in my growing-up years I camped, hunted, fished, boated, swam, and wandered — where, in short, I did whatever escaping I felt called upon to do. It was a place where I had happily been, and where I always wanted to be. And I remember gesturing toward the valley that day and saying to the friend who was with me: "That's all I need."

I meant it. It was an honest enough response to my recognition of its beauty, the abundance of its lives and possibilities, and of my own love for it and interest in it. And in the sense that I continue to recognize all that, and feel that what I most need is here, I can still say the same thing.

And yet I am aware that I must necessarily mean differently — or at least a great deal more — when I say it now. Then I was speaking mostly from affection, and did not know, by half, what I was talking about. I was speaking of a place that in some ways I knew and in some ways cared for, but did not live in. The differences between knowing a place and living in it, between cherishing a place and living responsibly in it, had not begun to occur to me. But they are critical differences, and understanding them has been perhaps the chief necessity of my experience since then.

I married in the following summer, and in the next seven years lived in a number of distant places. But, largely because I continued to feel that what I needed was here, I could never bring myself to want to live in any other place. And so we returned to live in Kentucky in the summer of 1964, and that autumn bought the house whose roof my friend and I had looked down on eight years before, and with it "twelve acres more or less." Thus I began a profound change in my life. Before, I had lived according to expectation rooted in ambition. Now I began to live according to a kind of destiny rooted in my origins and in my life. One should not speak too confidently of one's "destiny"; I use the word to refer to causes that lie deeper in history and character than mere intention or desire. In buying the little place known as Lanes Landing, it seems to me, I began to obey the deeper causes.

We had returned so that I could take a job at the University of

Kentucky in Lexington. And we expected to live pretty much the usual academic life: I would teach and write; my "subject matter" would be, as it had been, the few square miles in Henry County where I grew up. We bought the tiny farm at Lanes Landing, thinking that we would use it as a "summer place," and on that understanding I began, with the help of two carpenter friends, to make some necessary repairs on the house. I no longer remember exactly how it was decided, but that work had hardly begun when it became a full-scale overhaul.

By so little our minds had been changed: this was not going to be a house to visit, but a house to live in. It was as though, having put our hand to the plow, we not only did not look back, but could not. We renewed the old house, equipped it with plumbing, bathroom, and oil furnace, and moved in on July 4, 1965.

Once the house was whole again, we came under the influence of the "twelve acres more or less." This acreage included a steep hillside pasture, two small pastures by the river, and a "garden spot" of less than half an acre. We had, besides the house, a small barn in bad shape, a good large building that once had been a general store, and a small garage also in usable condition. This was hardly a farm by modern standards, but it was land that could be used, and it was unthinkable that we would not use it. The land was not good enough to afford the possibility of a cash income, but it would allow us to grow our food — or most of it. And that is what we set out to do.

In the early spring of 1965 I had planted a small orchard; the next spring we planted our first garden. Within the following six or seven years we reclaimed the pastures, converted the garage into a hen-house, rebuilt the barn, greatly improved the garden soil, planted berry bushes, acquired a milk cow — and were producing, except for hay and grain for our animals, nearly everything that we ate: fruit, vegetables, eggs, meat, milk, cream, and butter. We built an outbuilding with a meat room and a food-storage cellar. Because we did not want to pollute our land and water with sewage, and in the process waste nutrients that should be returned to the soil, we built a composting privy. And so we began to attempt a life that, in addition to whatever else it was, would be responsibly agricultural. We used no chemical fertilizers. Except for a little rotenone, we used no insecticides. As our land and our food became healthier, so did we. And our food was of better quality than any that we could have bought.

We were not, of course, living an idyll. What we had done could not have been accomplished without difficulty and a great deal of work. And we had made some mistakes and false starts. But there was great satisfaction, too, in restoring the neglected land, and in feeding ourselves from it.

Meanwhile, the forty-acre place adjoining ours on the downriver side had been sold to a "developer" who planned to divide it into lots for "second homes." This project was probably doomed by the steepness of the ground and the difficulty of access, but a lot of bulldozing — and a lot of damage — was done before it was given up. In the fall of 1972, the place was offered for sale and we were able to buy it.

We now began to deal with larger agricultural problems. Some of this new land was usable; some would have to be left in trees. There were perhaps fifteen acres of hillside that could be reclaimed for pasture, and about two and a half acres of excellent bottomland on which we would grow alfalfa for hay. But it was a mess, all of it badly neglected, and a considerable portion of it badly abused by the developer's bulldozers. The hillsides were covered with thicket growth; the bottom was shoulder high in weeds; the diversion ditches had to be restored; a bulldozed gash meant for "building sites" had to be mended; the barn needed a new foundation, and the cistern a new top; there were no fences. What we had bought was less a farm than a reclamation project — which was now, with a later purchase, grown to seventy-five acres.

While we had only the small place, I had got along very well with a Gravely "walking tractor" that I owned, and an old Farmall A that I occasionally borrowed from my Uncle Jimmy. But now that we had increased our acreage, it was clear that I could not continue to depend on a borrowed tractor. For a while I assumed that I would buy a tractor of my own. But because our land was steep, and there was already talk of a fuel shortage — and because I liked the idea — I finally decided to buy a team of horses instead. By the spring of 1973, after a lot of inquiring and looking, I had found and bought a team of five-year-old sorrel mares. And — again by the generosity of my Uncle Jimmy, who has never thrown any good thing away — I had enough equipment to make a start.

Though I had worked horses and mules during the time I was growing up, I had never worked over ground so steep and problematical as this, and it had been twenty years since I had worked a team over ground of any kind. Getting started again, I anticipated every new task with uneasiness, and sometimes with dread. But to my relief and delight, the team and I did all that needed to be done that year, getting better as we went along. And over the years since then, with that team and others, my son and I have carried on our farming the way it was carried on in my boyhood, doing everything with our horses except baling the hay. And we have done work in places and in weather in which a tractor would have been useless. Experience has shown us — or re-shown us — that horses are not only a satisfactory and economical means of power, especially on such small places as ours, but are probably *necessary* to the most conservative use of steep land. Our farm, in fact, is surrounded by potentially excellent hillsides that were maintained in pasture until tractors replaced the teams.

Another change in our economy (and our lives) was accomplished in the fall of 1973 with the purchase of our first wood-burning stove. Again the petroleum shortage was on our minds, but we also knew that from the pasture-clearing we had ahead of us we would have an abundance of wood that otherwise would go to waste — and when that was gone we would still have our permanent wood lots. We thus expanded our subsistence income to include heating fuel, and since then have used our furnace only as a "backup system" in the coldest weather and in our absences from home. The horses also contribute significantly to the work of fuel-gathering; they will go easily into difficult places and over soft ground or snow where a truck or a tractor could not move.

As we have continued to live on and from our place, we have slowly begun its restoration and healing. Most of the scars have now been

mended and grassed over, most of the washes stopped, most of the buildings made sound; many loads of rocks have been hauled out of the fields and used to pave entrances or fill hollows; we have done perhaps half of the necessary fencing. A great deal of work is still left to do, and some of it — the rebuilding of fertility in the depleted hillsides — will take longer than we will live. But in doing these things we have begun a restoration and a healing in ourselves.

I should say plainly that this has not been a "paying proposition." As a reclamation project, it has been costly both in money and in effort. It seems at least possible that, in any other place, I might have had little interest in doing any such thing. The reason I have been interested in doing it here, I think, is that I have felt implicated in the history, the uses, and the attitudes that have depleted such places as ours and made them "marginal."

I had not worked long on our "twelve acres more or less" before I saw that such places were explained almost as much by their human history as by their nature. I saw that they were not "marginal" because they ever were unfit for human use, but because in both culture and character *we* had been unfit to use them. Originally, even such steep slopes as these along the lower Kentucky River Valley were deep-soiled and abundantly fertile; "jumper" plows and generations of carelessness impoverished them. Where yellow clay is at the surface now, five feet of good soil may be gone. I once wrote that on some of the nearby uplands one walks as if "knee-deep" in the absence of the original soil. On these steeper slopes, I now know, that absence is shoulder-deep.

That is a loss that is horrifying as soon as it is imagined. It happened easily, by ignorance, indifference, "a little folding of the hands to sleep." It cannot be remedied in human time; to build five feet of soil takes perhaps fifty or sixty thousand years. This loss, once imagined, is potent with despair. If a people in adding a hundred and fifty years to itself subtracts fifty thousand from its land, what is there to hope?

And so our reclamation project has been, for me, less a matter of idealism or morality than a kind of self-preservation. A destructive history, once it is understood as such, is a nearly insupportable burden. Understanding it is a disease of understanding, depleting the sense of efficacy and paralyzing effort, unless it finds healing work. For me that work has been partly of the mind, in what I have written, but that seems to have depended inescapably on work of the body and of the ground. In order to affirm the values most native and necessary to me — indeed, to affirm my own life as a thing decent in possibility — I needed to know in my own experience that this place did not have to be abused in the past, and that it can be kindly and conservingly used now.

With certain reservations that must be strictly borne in mind, our work here has begun to offer some of the needed proofs.

Bountiful as the vanished original soil of the hillsides may have been, what remains is good. It responds well — sometimes astonishingly well — to good treatment. It never should have been plowed (some of it never should have been cleared), and it never should be plowed again. But it can be put in pasture without plowing, and it will support an excellent grass sod that will in turn protect it from erosion, if properly managed and not overgrazed.

Land so steep as this cannot be preserved in row crop cultivation. To subject it to such an expectation is simply to ruin it, as its history shows. Our rule, generally, has been to plow no steep ground, to maintain in pasture only such slopes as can be safely mowed with a horse-drawn mower, and to leave the rest in trees. We have increased the numbers of livestock on our pastures gradually, and have carefully rotated the animals from field to field, in order to avoid overgrazing. Under this use and care, our hillsides have mended and they produce more and better pasturage every year.

As a child I always intended to be a farmer. As a young man, I gave up that intention, assuming that I could not farm and do the other things I wanted to do. And then I became a farmer almost unintentionally and by a kind of necessity. That wayward and necessary becoming — along with my marriage, which has been intimately a part of it — is the major event in my life. It has changed me profoundly from the man and the writer I would otherwise have been.

There was a time, after I had left home and before I came back, when this place was my "subject matter." I meant that too, I think, on the day in 1956 when I told my friend, "That's all I need." I was regarding it, in a way too easy for a writer, as a mirror in which I saw myself. There was obviously a sort-of narcissism in that — and an inevitable superficiality, for only the surface can reflect.

In coming home and settling on this place, I began to *live* in my subject, and to learn that living in one's subject is not at all the same as "having" a subject. To live in the place that is one's subject is to pass through the surface. The simplifications of distance and mere observation are thus destroyed. The obsessively regarded reflection is broken and dissolved. One sees that the mirror was a blinder; one can now begin to see where one is. One's relation to one's subject ceases to be merely emotional or esthetical, or even merely critical, and becomes problematical, practical, and responsible as well. Because it must. It is like marrying your sweetheart.

Though our farm has not been an economic success, as such success is usually reckoned, it is nevertheless beginning to make a kind of economic sense that is consoling and hopeful. Now that the largest expenses of purchase and repair are behind us, our income from the place is beginning to run ahead of expenses. As income I am counting the value of shelter, subsistence, heating fuel, and money earned by the sale of livestock. As expenses I am counting maintenance, newly purchased equipment, extra livestock feed, newly purchased animals, reclamation work, fencing materials, taxes, and insurance.

If our land had been in better shape when we bought it, our expenses would obviously be much smaller. As it is, once we have completed its restoration, our farm will provide us a home, produce our subsistence, keep us warm in winter, and earn a modest cash income. The significance of this becomes apparent when one considers that most of this land is "unfarmable" by the standards of conventional agriculture, and that most of it was producing nothing at the time we bought it.

And so, contrary to some people's opinion, it *is* possible for a family to live on such "marginal" land, to take a bountiful subsistence and some cash income from it, and, in doing so, to improve both the land and themselves. (I believe, however, that, at least in the present economy, this should not be attempted without a source of income other than the farm. It is now extremely difficult to pay for the best of farmland by farming it, and even "marginal" land has become unreasonably expensive. To attempt to make a living from such land is to impose a severe strain on land and people alike.)

I said earlier that the success of our work here is subject to reservations. There are only two of these, but both are serious.

The first is that land like ours — and there are many acres of such land in this country — can be conserved in use only by competent knowledge, by a great deal more work than is required by leveler land, by a devotion more particular and disciplined than patriotism, and by ceaseless watchfulness and care. All these are cultural values and resources, never sufficiently abundant in this country, and now almost obliterated by the contrary values of the so-called "affluent society."

One of my own mistakes will suggest the difficulty. In 1974 I dug a small pond on a wooded hillside that I wanted to pasture occasionally. The excavation for that pond — as I should have anticipated, for I had better reason than I used — caused the hillside to slump both above and below. After six years the slope has not stabilized, and more expense and trouble will be required to stabilize it. A small hillside farm will not survive many mistakes of that order. Nor will a modest income.

The true remedy for mistakes is to keep from making them. It is not in the piecemeal technological solutions that our society now offers, but in a change of cultural (and economic) values that will encourage in the whole population the necessary respect, restraint, and care. Even more important, it is in the possibility of settled families and local communities, in which the knowledge of proper means and methods, proper moderations and restraints, can be handed down, and so accumulate in place and stay alive; the experience of one generation is not adequate to inform and control its actions. Such possibilities are not now in sight in this country.

The second reservation is that we live at the lower end of the Kentucky River watershed, which has long been intensively used, and is increasingly abused. Strip mining, logging, extractive farming, and the digging, draining, roofing, and paving that go with industrial and urban "development," all have seriously depleted the capacity of the watershed to retain water. This means not only that floods are higher and more frequent than they would be if the watershed were healthy, but that the floods subside too quickly, the watershed being far less a sponge, now, than it is a roof. The floodwater drops suddenly out of the river, leaving the steep banks soggy, heavy, and soft. As a result, great strips and blocks of land crack loose and slump, or they give way entirely and disappear into the river in what people here call "slips."

The flood of December 1978, which was unusually high, also went down extremely fast, falling from banktop almost to pool stage within a couple of days. In the aftermath of this rapid "drawdown," we lost a block of bottomland an acre square. This slip, which is still crumbling, severely damaged our place, and may eventually undermine two buildings. The same flood started a slip in another place, which threatens a third building. We have yet another building situated on a huge (but, so far, very gradual) slide that starts at the river, and, aggravated by two state highway cuts, goes almost to the hilltop. And we have serious river bank erosion the whole length of our place.

What this means is that, no matter how successfully we may control erosion on our hillsides, our land remains susceptible to a more serious cause of erosion that we cannot control. Our river bank stands literally at the cutting edge of our nation's consumptive economy. This, I think, is true of many "marginal" places — it is true, in fact, of many places that are not marginal. In its consciousness, ours is an upland society; the ruin of watersheds, and what that involves and means, is little considered. And so the land is heavily taxed to subsidize an "affluence" that consists, in reality, of health and goods stolen from the unborn.

Living at the lower end of the Kentucky River watershed is what is now known as "an educational experience" — and not an easy one. A lot of information comes with it that is severely damaging to the reputation of our people and our time. From where I live and work, I never have to look far to see that the earth does indeed pass away. But however that is taught, and however bitterly learned, it is something that should be known, and there is a certain good strength in knowing it. To spend one's life farming a piece of earth so passing is, as many would say, a hard lot. But it is, in an ancient sense, the human lot. What saves it is to love the farming.

JOHN HAINES
(1924–   )

꩜ Nature literature is a literature of place, and in our time that is one of its quietly revolutionary characteristics. To talk of nature writing is to talk of the sense of place — the way the weather and the light and the animals and birds and the lay of the land are somehow present in the words, making the life of the book. But what is this sense, exactly? What is it that happens in the mind that allies us to a piece of country?

John Haines, who is best known as a poet, has pondered the matter of place from a perspective of isolation and solitude unusual among contemporary writers. This essay, which first appeared in *Inland Boat* (1979), was later included in *Living Off the Country*, one of the books in the highly regarded "Poets on Poetry" series published by the University of Michigan Press.

The Writer as Alaskan:
Beginnings and Reflections

I

AS A POET I was born in a particular place, a hillside overlooking the Tanana River in central Alaska, where I built a house and lived for the better part of twenty-two years. It was there, in the winter of 1947–48, that I began writing poems seriously, and there many years later that I wrote my first mature poems. Many things went into the making of those poems and the others I've written since: the air of

From *Living Off the Country: Essays on Poetry and Place* (1981)

the place, its rocks, soil, and water; snow and ice; human history, birds, animals, and insects. Other things, surely, not directly related to the place: the words of other poets learned once, forgotten, and remembered again. Old stories from childhood, voices out of dreams. Images, a way of seeing learned partly from several years' study as a painter and sculptor. And human relationship, life shared with another person whose existence mingled with my own, so that we saw the world as one person. But it was finally the place itself that provided the means of unifying all of these into a single experience.

I must have carried in myself from an early age some vague design of such a place and such a life. I grew up more or less homeless, moved from place to place, and came, I think, to regard all residence and all relationships as only temporary. It would naturally follow that I nourished in myself a great wish for something more permanent. What I got from that early life was a good sense of geography, but also great insecurity and uncertainty about who I was. I think I knew then that I would have to find a specific place and be born over again as my own person.

Why I chose that particular place rather than another probably can't be answered completely. I might have gone elsewhere and become a very different poet and person. But there was, most likely, no other region where I might have had that original experience of the North American wilderness. Unlike other "wilderness" areas, Alaska in those days seemed open-ended. I could walk north from my homestead at Richardson all the way to the Arctic Ocean and never cross a road nor encounter a village. This kind of freedom may no longer be available, but at that time it gave to the country a limitlessness and mystery hard to find now on this planet.

From the first day I set foot in interior Alaska, and more specifically on Richardson Hill, I knew I was home. Something in me identified with that landscape. I had come, let's say, to the dream place. Not exactly, of course, for there never was an exact place, but here was something so close to it that I could accept it at once. I think such a recognition must be rare, and I was extremely fortunate to have it happen in the way that it did. Such a purity of feeling, of joy and of being in the right place, I have not often felt since.

What that experience meant to me, in terms of self-discovery and the sort of work I was to do, could be told at great length, but I will try only to suggest in this essay some of the most important features of its personal significance.

There was, first of all, the experience of the wilderness itself, of finding life on more basic terms than those given me without thought as a child. This may seem like a strange thing to say, but perhaps it will make better sense if I link it to a more general theme. At times it becomes necessary for people to turn away from their cultural origins and return for a while to an older and simpler existence. One of the consequences of having a language and a culture is that these begin to exist for themselves in place of the original things we once lived by. Words become abstract, institutions and customs become unrelated to anything necessary or authentic. And they begin subtly to sap vitality from us; we begin to live falsely, and after a while we find it necessary to turn away from them and find ourselves once more in the hard, irreducible world of natural things — of rock and water, fire and wood, flesh and blood.

So here, on a steep hillside, seventy miles from Fairbanks, was a place to begin. It was for me the beginning of what I have come to understand as the myth-journey of humankind. This life of food gathering, of making for ourselves out of what we can find around us, this is what we have come from and will return to. The Scottish poet, Edwin Muir, speaks in terms of the biblical Fall from Paradise, and he may be right. Think of what we have done to the earth and to ourselves — this fallen kingdom, the landscapes we make everywhere, devoid of beauty and grandeur. I can still remember the intensity of my feeling, of actual pain and outrage, seeing the landscape of southern California once more after twelve years in the wilderness. I saw it slowly, as I drove south from Alaska, through Canada — the accumulating ruin of the North American landscape.

I had when younger a habit of mind, of dreaminess, a vague drifting through the world. I was naturally observant, but unfocused. Living as I did there at Richardson, limited by circumstances to a small area, I found it necessary to learn more and more about it in order to get a living from it. I was forced to pay attention, to learn in detail many things of a kind I could not have learned if I had stayed only briefly in the country or had lived there in easier circumstances. I learned quickly, because it was an adventure for me, a young person from the city unused to knowing any place intimately, to distinguish actual things, particular and exact, from the vague and general character of the world. Words began to fasten themselves to what I saw. I learned the names of the things to be found there, characteristic of the subarctic the world over: the forest trees and shrubs, their kinds and uses, what made good building material or fuel, and what did not; what could be eaten, preserved, and put up for later use. I began for the first time to make things for myself, to build shelters, to weave nets, to make sleds and harness, and to train animals for work. I learned to hunt, to watch, and to listen, to think like a moose, if need be, or a marten, or a lynx. I watched the river, and saw in its gray and swirling water, heavy with silt, the probable trace of salmon, and knew where to set my nets. I read the snow and what was written there. I became familiar with the forms of frost, the seeding of the grasses, the early swelling of the birch leaves. I watched a tree, no bigger than my wrist when I first built there, grow tenfold over the years, until I had to cut away its branches from the rain gutters of the house.

Digging in the soil, picking away the rock, uprooting stumps, I became in time a grower of things sufficient to feed myself and another. Slowly finding my way into the skills of hunter and trapper, I understood what blood and bone, hide and muscle, marrow and sinew really are; not as things read about, but as things touched and handled until they became as familiar to me as my own skin. Land itself came alive for me as it never had before, more alive sometimes than the people who moved about on it. I learned that it is land, *place,* that makes people, provides for them the possibilities they will have of becoming something more than mere lumps of sucking matter. We today who live so much from the inheritance of land and culture do not understand this as well as we need to. Few of us these days are really residents anywhere, in the deep sense of that term. We live off the surface of things and places, the culture as well as the land; ours is a derivative life: we take what we find without thought, without regard for origin or consequences, unaware for the most part that the resources, both natural and cultural, are fast diminishing.

These were big lessons, basic things, and I was a long time assimilating them and understanding their significance. Never really privileged in youth, I was never in actual want, either. Like most people in our society, I did not know what it was to be hungry, to look for food and find myself short when I needed it most. That old life, unchanged for centuries, in time with the seasons, the rising and setting of the sun, the coming and going of birds and animals, the sources of food and light, became for me not a passage in a book of histories, but a matter of daily occurrence, a way still vital and full of meaning. I grew to feel that if civilization failed, I could still make my way, and in general, thrive. I still feel that way, though I am old enough to know that it would not be as easy for me now as it was twenty or thirty years ago.

The place in which I settled, Richardson, which included Banner Creek and the nearby Tenderfoot area, had been a thriving gold rush camp from around 1905 until the late years of the First World War. As with many such settlements, conditions rapidly changed; the easy gold was mined, and people left for another camp, another strike. By the time I came there in 1947, only six or eight of the older residents still lived along the creeks, or in the hills above the Tanana. Most of the old buildings were gone, and it was only by listening to what the residents told me that I learned something of the history of Richardson. And what I learned seemed to confirm what Thomas Hardy said once in respect to local life, long residence in a certain place, and the changes he had witnessed in his own lifetime.

> The change at the root of this has been the recent supplanting of the class of stationary cottagers, who carried on the local traditions and humours, by a population of more or less migratory labourers, which has led to a break of continuity in local history, more fatal than any other thing to the preservation of legend, folk-lore, close inter-social relations, and eccentric individualities. For these the indispensible conditions of existence are attachment to the soil of one particular spot by generation after generation.[1]

What I found at Richardson was a late beginning of just that local condition of which Hardy is speaking. The few gold rush survivors, men and women, could not have been living in the area for more than fifty years, but in their memories and the stories they told, full of humor and spite, already the place had begun to acquire the dimensions of myth. Each of the persons I came to know before the last of them died in the late 1960s had a clarity of outline, a distinctiveness of temperament that only simplicity and a certain isolation allow human character. For the first time in my life I became aware of individuals, in all their quirkiness and singularity. I was fortunate indeed, for what I found has by now nearly vanished from American life, and in its place all life takes on the same bland mediocrity one finds so plentiful in the suburbs. It may be true, as I sometimes find reason to believe, that this change has been more than just a sign of deterioration in social life. In order for a new form of life to occupy a place, another must die. When our imaginations have grown enough, perhaps we will understand that for us the local must one day include the continent, and finally the planet itself. It seems likely that nothing else will allow us to thrive as a species. But it is also true that meanwhile we are painfully aware that an honored and durable way of life has disappeared, leaving an empty place in our lives.

[1] Preface to *Far from the Madding Crowd* (Greenwich, Conn.: Fawcett, 1960).

It would be easy to say that something of the cold and clarity of the land, and much of the rest I have been talking about, just somehow got into the poems I wrote while I lived there. In a way this is true, but there is more to it. It was an awakening, profound and disturbing. Everything was so new to me that it was like finding myself for the first time with my feet on the earth. To the extent that it was possible for me, I entered the original mystery of things, the great past out of which we came. I saw the midwinter sun sink in a cleft of the mountains to the south, and I felt I had learned a great secret. The winter solstice was an actual event, and it came on with a menace and a grandeur much older than a date on the Christian calendar.

But most important, as I have already suggested, was the meeting of place and dream. Without my being entirely conscious of it, this place and this life were what I had wanted more than any other thing. All doors seemed to open there; things hidden away, brooded upon for years, came to life: the owls I sketched as a child, the grass flowing on the hillside, the lynx track in the snow. When I was a small boy, five or six years old, my father read to me on winter evenings from Kipling's *Jungle Books*. Something took shape then and there in my mind: the wolf in the mouth of the cave, ready for the night's hunting, the forest coming awake, and far away the village of men. Thirty years went by, and that shape surfaced in a poem, "Book of the Jungle," from *Winter News.*

> The animal, rising at dusk
> from its bed in the trampled
> grass —
>   this is how it all began.
>
> Far off the shaggy tribesmen
> listened and fed their fires
> with thorns.
>
> Secret paths of the forest,
> when did your children walk
> unarmed, clothed only
> with the shadows of leaves?
>
> We are still kneeling
> and listening,
> as from the edge of a field
> there rises sometimes at evening
> the snort of a rutting bull.

Poetry seems to have been a natural response to my living there. My first winter in the cabin at Richardson, unable for some reason to paint, I began attempting poems in which I could express some of my feeling for this place I was coming to know, amazed at all I was seeing and learning. The poems were not, of course, very good. They were hardly poems at all. I had a lot to learn, about writing and about myself. To really know the place, I had to live there, build there, become intimate with it and know it for a long time, before I could say anything about it that would be personal and distinctive. It was nearly ten years before I wrote anything that satisfied me.

On that hillside, remote from many distractions, it was possible for me to see things, all things, more clearly, and to think in a quiet that is hard to come by these days. The events of my life seemed to reach into both past and future. Sometimes on a fall evening, looking out on that great valley, the route of migrations, I saw, or in some way felt, a future invasion of the continent — some force out of Asia, as in the not-so-remote past. In a poem called "Foreboding" I tried to convey something of the essence of this feeling, call it a vision if you like: a suggestion of an event still to come.

> Something immense and lonely
> divides the earth at evening.
>
> For nine long years I have watched
> from an inner doorway:
> as in a confused vision,
> manlike figures approach, cover
> their faces, and pass on,
> heavy with iron and distance.
>
> There is no sound but the wind
> crossing the road, filling
> the ruts with a dust as fine as chalk.
>
> Like the closing of an inner door,
> the day begins its dark
> journey, across nine bridges
> wrecked one by one.

I hope it will be clearer from this brief description how much and in what ways those years at Richardson formed me as a person and as a poet. There is one part of it I have hardly mentioned, and that concerns the two women who lived there with me much of the time, and one in particular. It seems only honest in an account of this sort

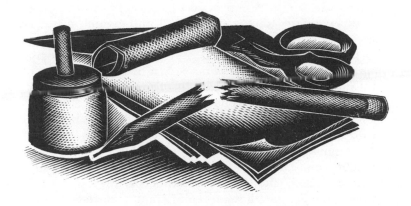

not to have it appear that I was alone all the time, or that whatever was done I did all by myself. Without that companionship and support, physical and emotional, it seems unlikely that I would have gotten through those years, deprived as in some ways they were; and it seems to me not the least of things that I did finally learn to live with another human being.

It is still a place I go back to, in mind and in spirit, though it seems I cannot return to it fully in fact. The material it gave me is still part of my life, and I go back to it in poems and in prose, trying to understand as well as I can the significance of what happened to me there. The experience was so powerful that it has influenced everything else I have done. Probably I measure everything else against it. Of all things I have and am, it is something I do not lose. While writing parts of this essay I could see on a table before me a broken sandstone seed mortar that I dug up from a field in California a few years ago. When I found it I was out early in the morning, looking at some Indian rock paintings not far from where I was camped with my wife and a group of schoolchildren. Such things, and the landscapes of which they are part, would not have for me the significance they do if I had not explored for myself during those years in Alaska something of the original life of the continent.

But I no longer live at Richardson. In more ways than one, perhaps, that life is gone. Place for me has shifted from the north country wilderness to a house in suburban California; from there to some rocks in the arid California foothills, to the rainy outlines of a city in the Northwest, and to a windy street in Missoula, Montana. These

places have added to the sum of what I have been; and then, returning to some enduring stillness in my life, I find myself once more in
a familiar setting of broad river and sunlit hill. Behind all I write
there is a landscape, partly idealized, perhaps, upon which the human
figure, my own or another's, acts out a part of its life. That original
place still sustains me. It gave me a way of perceiving the world that
I might not have acquired otherwise, and not least, a solitude in
which I could learn to listen to my own voice. But as I have tried to
show, I do not think that place, outer place, alone can account for
this. There must be another place, and that is within the person
himself. When that interior place, formed out of dream and fantasy,
and by intense imagination, finds its counterpart in a physical landscape, then some genuine human reality can be created.

The homestead at Richardson provided a place of departure from
which I might go out into the world forearmed. On the evidence of
my own experience, I believe that one of the most important metaphors of our time is the journey out of wilderness into culture, into
the forms of our complicated and divided age, with its intense con-
fusions and deceptions. The eventual disintegration of these cultural
forms returns us once more to the wilderness. This journey can be
seen both as fall and as reconciliation. And place, once again, means
actual place, but also a state of mind, of consciousness. Once that
place is established, we carry it with us, as we do a sense of ourselves.

II

As D. H. Lawrence has told us, there is a "spirit of place." In any
landscape or region on the map, there is a potential life to be lived.
The place itself offers certain possibilities, and these, combined with
the capacities of those who come there, produce after a while certain
kinds of life. In human terms, these may be, among other things,
religions, art forms, architecture, stories, and myths, and sometimes
the absence of them. This is much clearer when we look at tribal
societies that have survived with little change for centuries. But it
may still be true for us, mobile, and in some ways innovative contemporary people that we are. Place makes people; in the end it makes
everything. Strong efforts may be made to deny the place, to silence
the authentic, but the spirit of things will break through that silence
to speak, if necessary, in strained and deformed accents. William
Carlos Williams, in his book, *In the American Grain,* attempted to
define what he felt had gone wrong with America from the start —

the inability or refusal to recognize what was actually under our feet, or in the air, and to live by that. Instead we fell back on the old names for things, familiar responses to whatever lay beyond our power to see. The meaning of what he found is still with us, as potent as ever.

What do we find here in Alaska? Something absolutely new in American experience. Though it resembles all previous encounters of a people with a new country, for Americans (the great majority of people in the United States and in Canada) it is profoundly new. If we wish to read about the North, not as sensation or bald news report, we must go to Scandinavian literature, to the Russians, or to some extent, to the Canadians. I have found it clearest and strongest in the writings of Norwegian and Swedish authors, in the books of Hamsun, Vesaas, Lagerlof, and others. Strange and exotic to the experience of a southerner: the brief, intense summers, the long, sunless winters. In Edwin Muir's account of his early years in the Orkney Islands, I recognized the North: the long shadows over the treeless islands, the barely setting sun of midsummer. My second summer in Alaska I sat on the porch of my cabin at Richardson in the evenings and read through *Kristin Lavransdätter*, Sigrid Undset's trilogy on life in medieval Norway. And there on the page was the North I was coming to know. The book and the sound of the river below the house mingled, and my being there had that much more meaning for me. This is what real literature does, it seems to me; it enhances the place, the conditions under which we live, and we are more alive thereby. But there is little in English that carries the authentic mark of having been made in the North.

It is not only the land itself that faces us in the North today, as real as that is, but the entire drama of European life on this continent reenacted at a pace that leaves us stunned and gasping. The experience is hard to come to grips with; there are few names for it, and too many old responses. We see Alaska through clichés to save us from thinking: "The Last Frontier," "The Great Land." What do these really mean, aside from a great opportunity to grab? "North to the Future," that preposterous slogan once flaunted on the state auto license plates: the whole thing is a travel agent's invention. There *is* no place called Alaska, just as there is hardly anything today that can be identified as California. But of course there was, and is, such a place, though it can scarcely be found any longer for what we have done to it, and are beginning to do here. What I read about Alaska in magazines is for the most part the superficial message of the tourist — he who comes to gape, but not to understand.

How long might it take a people living here to be at home in their landscape, and to produce from that experience things that could be recognized anywhere as literature of the first rank? Several hundred years? A few generations? We know from history how long a people have lived in a land and then found ways to express that living in song and the other forms of art. Closeness is needed, long residence, intimacy of a sort that demands a certain daring and risk: a surrender, an abandonment, or just a sense of somehow being stuck with it. Whatever it is that is needed, it can't be merely willed. And much of what we say about it will be conditional; in the end it will depend on the right circumstances and on the genius of a few individuals who know what they want to do, and whose material and direction cannot be predicted. All we can do is to project a few apparent needs and conditions.

The Alaskan writer faces a double task: to see, to feel, and to interpret the place itself, and then to relate that experience to what he knows of the world at large. Not simply to describe the place and what is in it (though valuable, this has been done many times already); but to give this material a life in imagination, a vitality beyond mere appearances. This alone allows the place to be seen and felt by an audience whose members are everywhere. It is not, in the end, Alaska, a place where a few people can live in perpetual self-congratulation, but humankind we are talking about. What we do and say here touches everywhere the common lot of people.

The Alaskan writer faces in addition a difficulty which is everywhere around us, and whose effect can be seen in much of the writing of today. The way we live nowadays seems intended to prevent closeness to anything outside this incubator world we have built around us. Within it, individuals face an increasingly impoverished inner world. It seems all too characteristic of us as a people that we tend to limit and confine ourselves, to specialize and restrict. We prefer anything to openness. The sort of intimacy, of being available to the land in Alaska, to the things it can reveal to one willing to stay, to observe and listen, this is prevented, or at least it is blunted, by the life most people come here to live, a life no different than one they would live anywhere. It requires of them no change, but especially no inner change. The weather is colder, the days a little longer, or shorter, but life comes boxed in the same meager pattern. To one seeing it after some absence, it seems a strange and lonely place; it is as if here, finally, the dream of frontier America must face itself. There is nowhere else to go, and it may be that deep down we are afraid that it is already a failure so enormous that we have no words for it. This furious industry over the face of the land is a distraction, and in the end it will hide nothing. If Alaska is the last frontier it may be because it represents the last full-scale attempt in North America to build a society worthy of human life, worthy of the claims made for America at the beginning. The weight of the past is heavy, and old habits hold on. The natives in Alaska have already formed themselves into "corporations"; the name is significant in that it is really *business* that runs our lives, and we are all conscripts to a system that divides and demeans us.

To see what is here, right in front of us: nothing would seem easier or more obvious, yet few things are more difficult. There are unmistakable signs that something may be dying among us: that capacity to see the world, to recognize the "other" and admit it into our lives. Invisible walls shut us out, or shut us in, and we make them stronger and thicker by the day. This may sound entirely negative, but it is frankly what I read in much that is written today. The poet Robert Bly made the observation not long ago that what most poets write about these days is not what is out there in the world, but what is passing through their own heads, filled with shapes and designs already known. Moving from the city to the country, writing about fields and ponds and hayricks doesn't change anything, though it may be a gesture of sorts. Likewise, moving from a city "outside" to another city in Alaska isn't likely to change anything either. Something else is needed, a change of an entirely different kind, and this can take place only within the individual — but by implication it would also take place between the individual and his environment.

The world of the poet has shrunk many times since the days when Wallace Stevens and William Carlos Williams took for their concern the whole of life, or at least the whole life of a place. The world with which the contemporary poet characteristically concerns himself or herself resembles the self-limited world of the adolescent. It is a deliberate limitation that comes, I believe, from despair, as if the meaning of our situation, the weight of the disasters that threaten us, is so huge that we cannot find words for it, nor perhaps even emotions. Therefore we shrink, become deliberately small and trivial, and chatter about nothing at all, huddled like apes before a storm.

An original literature is possible in Alaska, but much is against it, everything perhaps except the place itself. There is the inevitable provinciality of a newly settled place, the self-protectiveness of unsure people who tend to feel threatened by anything "outside" and possibly superior to themselves. The Alaskan writer must learn to live with the knowledge that what he or she writes may be recognized by only a few people, and the better we write the fewer those few will be. In Alaska, as in our society generally, the average person just isn't listening, and probably doesn't care. This may be unpleasant, but it is true. Everyman has no longer a culture, but sports and entertainment. Money and power are the chief motives in American life, not decency and justice, nor humanistic values generally.

I realize that there is another side to this, and that is the obvious and willing care on the part of groups and individuals to learn what the land can teach, and to live by that learning. Strong efforts are being made to rescue large areas of Alaska from the destruction inevitably following on the rapid settling of a land. Some of us, at least, are trying to change our way of living, to be more in accord with the realities that face us. These efforts matter, though they reflect the concern of relatively few people.

In January, 1976, I went on a 900 mile trip through interior and south central Alaska. In spite of the many gloomy reports being written at the time, I saw that the oil pipeline after all had not changed the land very much. The old impression of its vastness, and, in winter, at least, of the uninhabitability of much of it, is still there, and will be, I suspect, for a long time to come. That big land out there abides, as always. Projects like Alyeska are not yet the ruin of Alaska. Away from the cities, what impressed me most was how little the land has changed since I first saw it over thirty years ago. Works and days seem lost in that immensity, so much so that one feels a mixture of awe, gratitude, and a little fear: fear of what *could* happen if all restraint on settlement and development were removed.

We can hardly look to the arts for the specific answers to the difficulties that beset us, for they generally provide none. They can, however, reveal to us a range of possible human responses to life, show us what it is like to be alive now, feeling and thinking. And genuine literature shows, as only great writings and art do show, the significant shapes that lie behind appearances. We can learn from past and living examples, poets and writers whose work owes some authentic quality to the North. What does it mean to be in this place at this time? How does it relate to what is happening in the world elsewhere? It is no longer possible to live in Alaska, or anywhere else, and keep out the world. We are in it, for better or worse. One might make a categorical statement: no significant literature can be written now that does not include in its subject the human predicament everywhere.

Literature must embody some truth, in what is said and the way it is said, if it is to have any meaning for us now and in the future. And this is why, for Alaska, clichés about the "last frontier" will not do. The truth of our times, bitter and disheartening as it may turn out to be, must be faced. Honesty and imagination are needed. What counts finally in a work are not novel and interesting things, though these can be important, but the absolutely authentic. I think that there *is* a spirit of place, a presence asking to be expressed; and sometimes when we are lucky as writers, and quiet in a way few of us want to be anymore, a voice enters our own, becomes mingled with it, and we speak with a force and clarity not otherwise heard.

We live in a world, that great "other" made up of nature, the wilderness, the universe. At the same time we are compelled, because we are human and vulnerable, to make for ourselves, in imagination and in fact, another world in which we can feel at home, yet not too far removed from that other. One of the functions of the writer, the poet, is to reconcile us to our lot; in the words of William Carlos Williams, "by metaphor to reconcile the people and the stones": to tell us a story in such a way that we become the characters in a tale we can believe in. Isn't this what writing, storytelling, and the arts generally are all about? The money making, the market, "success," and all the rest of it are beside the point, though they may seem important enough from time to time. Alaska needs a literature as a matter of practical necessity, of self-identification. "A culture without dreams is finished. It has nothing to motivate it."[2]

A literature is made of many things, not just a few outstanding names and works, and there is room for all kinds of writing. But what has most concerned me in this essay is that literature so distinctive that it belongs unmistakably to a certain place and yet speaks for all places. It ought to be the task of the Alaskan writer to understand this, and to seek to embody it in his or her work. Otherwise, what Alaska produces as literature may go on being notable for its hymns to Mount McKinley, dead odes to dead salmon, superficial accounts of "life on the last frontier," or finally, at best, very thin copies of the many poems and stories written anywhere in this country today. My concern is with the writer who wishes above all to come to terms in some way with the truth of our times. Everything tries to prevent this, to offer instead easy rewards for saying the obvious and already known. I suppose that what this means is that the writing, the best of it, should have some commitment beyond the private self. This seems not to be a time in which anyone has a right to expect a seriousness of the kind I am asking for, but anything less will not be enough.

[2] Joseph Campbell, "Man and Myth," in *Voices and Visions*, ed. Sam Keen (New York: Harper and Row, 1974), p. 79.

We need to be as clear as possible about the world we live in, and to have some ideas about our place in it; to understand and to accept, if necessary, the limitations that living on a finite and exhaustible planet imposes on us. Perhaps here in Alaska is an opportunity to deepen that understanding. It is another *place,* where we can stand and see the world and ourselves. The literature that is to come will bear the mark of an urgency, a seriousness that recognizes the dangers and choices held out to us by our involvement with the earth. And it may now and then be possible to recover, in a new land, something of that first morning of existence, when we looked at the world and saw, without motives, how beautiful it is.

BARRY LOPEZ

(1945–   )

&. "Animal rights," currently a controversial subject for both discussion and action, may seem superficially like just another special-interest focus. But to read Barry Lopez is to surmise that the topic is much bigger than our political arena. Lopez expressed the essential seriousness of the man-animal issue in *Of Wolves and Men* (1978), first investigating wolves as they live their lives and then analyzing both the symbolism they inspire in our minds and our mostly sorry, neurotic treatment of them in recent times. He examined the curiously intense, specist outlook that is apparently characteristic of many of us. *Arctic Dreams* (1986) also dwelt on our consciousness of wild animals; the way we see them reveals choices of the highest moral significance.

Renegotiating the Contracts

IN AN ESSAY in *Harper's* magazine several years ago, Lewis Lapham wrote that democracy was an experiment, a flawed enterprise that required continued human attention if it was going to serve us well. The philosophy behind our relationship with animals in the Western world is also flawed, and in need of continued attention.

To put this in the most basic terms, our relationships with wild animals were once contractual — principled agreements, established and maintained in a spirit of reciprocity and mythic in their pervasiveness. Among hunting peoples in general in the northern hemisphere, these agreements derived from a sense of mutual obligation and courtesy.

From *Parabola* (Spring, 1983)

Over the past two decades, in particular, our contemporary relationships with wild animals have been energetically scrutinized by
anthropologists, moral philosophers, and field biologists. A renewed
interest in the mythologies and values of hunting peoples has caused
us to question the moral basis for a continuation of hunting by
industrialized cultures. Tests to determine the lethal dosages of consumer products and the corrosiveness of cosmetics in animal labo-
ratories, the commercial harvest of infant harp seals, and research
on cetacean brains have all provoked heated debate over animal
rights. A proliferation of animal images in advertising, and their
dominant presence in children's stories, have brought thinkers such
as Paul Shepard to wonder how animals affect the very way we
conceptualize.

We once thought of animals as not only sentient but as congruent
with ourselves in a world beyond the world we can see, one structured
by myth and moral obligation, and activated by spiritual power. The
departure from the original conception was formalized in Cartesian
dualism — the animal was a soulless entity with which people could
not have a moral relationship — and in Ruskin's belief that to find
anything but the profane and mechanistic in the natural world was
to engage in a pathetic fallacy. Both these ideas seem short-sighted
and to have not served us well.

Today, commerce raises perhaps the most strenuous objection to
the interference of animals — their mere presence, their purported
rights — in human activity. Wilderness areas the world over, the only
places where animals are free of the social and economic schemes of
men, are consistently violated for their wealth of timber, minerals,
and hydrocarbons; and to fill zoos. Fundamentalist religions and
reductionist science deny — or persist in regarding as "outdated" —
the aboriginal aspects of our relationships with animals; and deny
that animals themselves have any spiritual dimension.

If we have embarked on a shared path in reevaluating this situation
as humanists and scientists, it has been to inquire how we are going
to repair the original contracts. These agreements were abrogated
during the agricultural, scientific, and industrial revolutions with a
determined degradation of the value of animal life. Acts once inde-
fensible became, over the centuries, only what was acceptable or
expeditious. Such a reconsideration bears sharply on the fate of zoos
and the future of animal experimentation, but it is also fundamentally
important to us as creatures. Whatever wisdom we have shown in
deriving a science of ecology, whatever insight we have gained from
quantum mechanics into the importance of *relationships* (rather than

the mere existence of *things*), urge us to consider these issues without calculation and passionately. We must examine a deep and long-lived insult.

I believe there are two failures to face. I speak with the view of someone who regards human beings as a Pleistocene species rather than a twentieth-century phenomenon; and who also believes that to set aside our relationships with wild animals as inconsequential is to undermine our regard for the other sex, other cultures, other universes. Animals exist apart from us, and the balance here between self-esteem and a prejudice directed toward what is different is one of the most rarefied and baffling issues in anthropology. Our own direction as a culture has been to enhance self-esteem *and* to dismantle prejudice by eradicating ignorance. No culture, however, including our own, with its great admiration for compassion and the high value it places on a broad education, has erased prejudice. (No one for that matter has proved it a worthless aspect of cultural evolution and survival.) What is required — or our Western venture is for naught — is to rise above prejudice to a position of respectful regard toward everything that is different from ourselves and not innately evil.

The two ways we have broken with animals are clear and could easily be the focus of our repair. One is that we have simply lost contact with them. Our notions of animal life are highly intellectualized, and no longer checked by daily contact with their environs. Our conceptions of them are not only bookish but stagnant, for, once discovered, we do not permit them to evolve as cultures. We allow them very little grace, enterprise, or individual variation. On the basis of even my own meager field experience — with wolves in Alaska, with mountain lion in Arizona, and with muskoxen, polar bear, and narwhal in the Canadian Arctic — this is a major blind spot in our efforts to erase ignorance. By predetermining categories of relevant information, by dismissing what cannot be easily quantified, by designing research to flatter the predilection of sponsors or defeat the political aims of a special interest group — field biologists have complained to me of both — we have produced distorted and incomplete images of animals.

We have created, further, mathematical models of ecosystems we only superficially grasp and then set divisions of government to managing the lives of the affected animals on the basis of these abstractions. We come perilously close in this to the worst moments of our history, to events we regret most deeply: the subjugation of races, the violent persecution of minority beliefs, the waging of war. With animals, all that saves us here is Descartes' convenience. Of course, some believe him right and regard this as firm ethical ground. But we skirt such imperious condescension here, such hubris, that we cannot help but undermine our principles of behavior toward ourselves, toward each other.

Some doubt the validity or the pertinence of these themes. But I have often heard, at grave and hopeful meetings, eloquent talk of the intellectual and social crises of our times — suppression of personality in a patriarchal society; the inhumane thrust of industry; the colonial designs of Russian or American foreign policy. With the change of only a word or two people could have been speaking of animals. The prejudices inform each other.

If the first failure is one of principle, where our attitudes toward animals have become those of owners and our knowledge skewed because we no longer meet with them and rarely enter their landscapes, the second is a failure of imagination. We have largely lost our understanding of where in an adult life to fit the awe and mystery that animals excite. This sensibility is still maintained in some fashion, however, by many aboriginal peoples and I would suggest, again on the basis of my own short time with Eskimos, that to step beyond a superficial acquaintance with such people is to enter a realm of understanding where what has meant human survival for the past 40,000 years remains clear. Here the comprehension of fundamental human needs and their application — how to live a successful life — is revealed continuously in story, often in stories of human encounters with animals. These stories employ the prosaic to announce the profound, the profound to reveal the ineffable. They balance reassuringly the unfathomable and the concrete. In our age we prefer analysis, not awe; but historically, human beings have subsisted as much on the mystery and awe inspired by animals as they have on the actual flesh of the caribou or the salmon. They have actively sought them in the hunting experience and have preserved them in their oral literatures.

The cultivation of mystery and awe keeps the human capacity for metaphor alive. And a capacity for metaphor allows us to perceive several layers of meaning in a story about, say, a polar bear; to perceive animals not only as complex physiological organisms but as part of a coherent and shared landscape.

Our second failure with animals, then, has been to banish them from our minds, as though they were not capable of helping us with our predicaments, the myriad paradoxes of our existence. It is as though we had told the polar bear that his solitary life and the

implacable hunger that makes him a persistent and resourceful hunter have no meaning for us. I believe this is a false sophistication of mind, and ultimately destructive.

A convenience of rational thought allows me to say there are but two places where our relationships with animals have been severed; audacity perhaps moves me to state that we must repair these breaks. I say so out of years of coming and going in a world inhabited largely by animals and aboriginal peoples, and out of repeated contact with human despair and loneliness in my own culture. What we do to animals troubles us — the horror of laboratory experiment, trophy shooting, factory farming; and our loss of contact with them leaves us mysteriously bereaved. If we could establish an atmosphere of respect in our relationships, simple awe for the complexities of animals' lives, I think we would feel revived as a species. And we would know more, deeply more, about what we are fighting for when we raise our voices against tyranny of any sort.

I am aware of having written here without reference to the incidents of day-to-day life by which most of us corroborate our beliefs. I think of several images. There is a group of sea ducks called scoters. They are dark, thick-bodied birds. With the exception of the males, who have bright, oddly shaped bills, they are of undistinguished coloration. The casual spring visitor to Cape Cod or to Cape Flattery would very likely see a few, but we know little about them. Like the ribbon seal and the narwhal, we cannot easily find them again once they leave these accustomed meeting places. So they are not really known to us.

Taxonomists took years to finally differentiate the spotted seal (*Phoca largha*) from the harbor seal (*Phoca vitulina*). They distrusted the statements of Eskimos in the same Bering Sea region who had always separated the two seals on the basis of their ice-related behavior. Now the scientists speak like Yup'ik men about the matter.

A marine biologist, armed with a prestigious grant, went to Hawaii to study a certain crab. The animal's behavior was so utterly different from what he had imagined it would be (from reading the literature) that his research proposal made no sense. To maintain his credibility he abandoned the experiment rather than restructure his conception of the animal.

One morning, walking through fresh snow, looking for mountain lion tracks on the north rim of the Grand Canyon, a biologist with years of this behind him said to me suddenly, "It's not in the data." I looked at him. "It's not in the data," he reiterated. With his hands he made a motion to indicate his head, his chest. "It's here. What I know is here." We went on in silence. "But as a field biologist," I said, "you must offer data or — ." "We are not biologists," he answered. "We are historians."

A final moment. In the Sea of Labrador one summer a sperm whale approached our ship head-on. I was standing in the bow with a retired Danish master mariner. The calm green sea broke over the whale's brow as he closed on us at ten or twelve knots. His approach was unwavering. I wondered out loud to my companion if they were aware on the bridge of our collision course. The whale surged past suddenly to port, crashing across our bow wave. I turned around — the mate shrugged from the superstructure several hundred feet away: who knows? The retired captain had not moved. He had not loosened the tenacious grip he had on the ship's rail. He slowly began to tell me a story about a convoy in the North Atlantic in 1942, the night they were torpedoed.

If we are to locate animals again at the complicated ethical and conceptual level of our ancestors, where they seem to have such a bearing on our state of mental health, we must decide what obligations and courtesies we will be bound by. The hunting contracts of our ancestors are no longer appropriate, just as their insight into natural history is no longer superior to our own at every point. These are to be new contracts. They must represent a new decorum, born of our aboriginal attachment to ancestral landscapes, our extraordinary learning, and the evolution of our culture from Altamira and Lascaux to the chambers of Washington, D.C. and the corridors of the Metropolitan Museum of Art.

Enormous as these steps are to contemplate, we seem in diverse ways to have firm hold of a beginning. The best of our books and films reflect a wider-than-Western, wider-than-purely-scientific, more-than-utilitarian view of animals. Moral philosophers are at work in a scholarly remodeling of Western philosophy in this area. And some people choose now to vacation among snow geese in northern California or among egrets and roseate spoonbills in Florida, as well as among the pyramids, or creations of the Medici.

However new agreements are drawn up, they must reflect as the old ones did an atmosphere of mutual regard, some latitude for mystery, and a sense of hope. As a European people we have taken great intellectual risks and made at various times penetrating insights — Leibnitz's calculus, Darwin's theory of natural selection, Heisenberg's uncertainty principle, Levi-Strauss's anthropology. We have in common with all other people in the world an understanding of how animals inform our intellectual, physical, aesthetic, and spiritual lives. From this reservoir of knowledge and sensitivity we could hope to forge a new covenant, fiercely honest, with other creatures.

In the time I have spent with native peoples in North America I have observed a deceptively simple event — how superstition, a slight, seemingly irrational prohibition, will be used to undercut arrogance in a young, headstrong hunter. To see it once is to be reminded forever that all life is a great gamble; wisdom is not simply erudition; and to behave in an irrational manner can, in fact, be life-enhancing. We tore up the animal contracts when the animals got in the way of our agriculture, our husbandry, and our science. We are now tearing up and rewriting our contracts with native peoples, because they block our political and industrial development. We cannot keep doing this. We will find ourselves with a false and miserable existence, a hollow probity, isolated far from our roots.

We will never find a way home until we find a way to look the caribou, the salmon, the lynx, and the white-throated sparrow in the face, without guile, with no plan of betrayal. We have to decide, again, after a long hiatus, how we are going to behave. We have to decide again to be impeccable in our dealings with the elements of our natural history.

JOHN HAY

(1915–   )

&❧ John Hay's latest book, *The Immortal Wilderness* (1987), presents a culminating insight. In several highly regarded natural histories, such as *Spirit of Survival* (1974) and *The Run* (1979), he has depicted the complex workings of nature; now the understanding which has underlain these earlier studies is the explicit theme: wilderness is not simply an officially designated "area," it is the very texture of our true, natural lives. It is the whole, interpenetrating system of things — "the earth's immortal genius." To many readers this may appear as a revolutionary concept. Hay's method as a writer, all along, has been to reveal this larger, perhaps unfamiliar wilderness in images of ordinary things and experiences. He has also been forthright and accessible in describing his own education in nature. Most of his books have come out of his years on Cape Cod, where he stands in a long and honorable tradition of nature writers drawn by the sweep of sky and sea toward elemental themes. In the selection that follows, Hay moves inland and into the equally mind-expanding lives of trees.

Custodians of Space

THE EXPLOITATION OF TREES has led us from rags to riches, and here we are suspended on our precarious height, regarding the developed ground where the great trees used to flourish and wondering how far we may have to back down. To be able to lay low the greatest deciduous forest on earth, once occupying a large part of this continent, was no mean feat. What subsequent inventions could ever exceed that ax-wielding test of progress!

From *The Immortal Wilderness* (1987)

New Hampshire, where I spent much of my boyhood, is tree country, and the white pine, which favors regions of moderate to heavy snowfall, is one of its dominant species. I remember one stand, bordering a wooded road, that had been left to grow and had reached a considerable height. The pines formed vaulted aisles like a Gothic cathedral. I looked up and they sang in my spirit as the wind swished through their long, fine needles swinging in the light.

The great hurricane of 1938 cut a swath through inland New England and hit our lakeside area head on. All those cathedral pines and others pluming by the lake shore for a hundred years or more went down like so many matchsticks. My father, who loved trees, came up from New York where he worked to view the damage, sat down by the road, and cried. But since this is a land of trees — in the character and quality of the light they are adapted to, and in the cold and stony soil which the old time farmers cleared and plowed — it is also irrepressible.

In some areas where white pines had grown in on abandoned fields and then been knocked down by the hurricane, they were succeeded by an understory of beech trees, with smooth, silvery gray trunks reminiscent of marine fish, or shining white birch, or sugar maples and ash. Following their pattern, the pines seeded into open clearings and unused pasture land, taking the opportunity to reclaim thousands of acres for themselves.

Either as farmland or original forest, these northern farmlands exacted their tribute from human beings, certainly their respect. They forced a hard life and cantankerous natures on the natives. The long, dark, snowy winters and the short growing season, which to trees are perfectly natural, are not easy on human dispositions. But at least the people were molded by the place they lived in. As Wendell Berry put it, in *The Unsettling of America:* "If we do not live where we work, and when we work, we are wasting our lives and our work, too."

One fall afternoon I was walking down the lower slopes of a minor mountain. It was toward sundown and, since it was now December, getting much colder. Behind me, a screech owl wailed in the shadow of a belt of brilliantly white birch that lay between mixed evergreens and hardwoods. Otherwise the air was still. I walked out into a clearing, where there had once been a small farm, with nothing left but a cellar hole and open fields before it, that was crowded with white pine seedlings. Below that, a long stone wall descended to a cold, clear, rocky brook perpetually sounding. I could feel the edges of an overload of freezing air that was about to fall and turn the grasses white. The ground, too, seemed withheld, waiting in silent strength.

The original house, I knew, had a sometimes grim understanding with the north. A combat had been waged here between life and its limits. People had been close-mouthed in the process. "Nothing to recommend," I heard them say. But they were centered in time and place, and there was a tall sky and long hills to look out on and remember. Give them credit for the way all seasons indentured them.

They had left their doorstep behind them, a great slab of granite, and a big sugar maple. Its broad-beamed trunk, covered with shaggy, deeply ridged, gray bark, stood over the cellar hole like a reliable ancestor and descendant. The field where they had grown corn and vegetables was returning to its original symmetry. The wilderness air had its way. A chorus of crows responded as cold, rushing waters fell toward the base of the hills. Soon, blue stars would shine out in the well of night. I listened to a silence that followed me away.

There are occasions when you can hear the mysterious language of the earth, in water, or coming through the trees, emanating from the mosses, seeping through the undercurrents of the soil, but you have to be willing to wait and receive. And there is a planetary silence behind it that defines the unseen quality of existence, as on a day when the white pines — one of the founders of America — are loaded with snow and nothing stirs. They seem to say: "What more do you want to know?" What more, indeed, can we know?

There was a white pine of fair height standing on a knoll over a little ravine that cut the hillside slopes above the lake, an area where my father had introduced many species of rock plants between the granite boulders. It was in that tree that I built a platform from which to view the world along with the red squirrels. I inhaled its resinous scent. The wind blew through the branches, sounding like the sea, and what distant worlds I imagined there I can no longer remember, although they probably included the walls of Jericho and the plains of Araby. White pine wood, soft and clean and easy to cut, also sent me on other voyages. I built a houseboat of it, a flat-bottomed boat with uptilted bow and stern and a cabin. It was powered by a Johnson outboard, or a long oar when the motor failed, with which I drove it slowly forward, and from it I fished for black bass and explored all the inlets and corners of the eleven-mile-long lake.

Having the mind of a mole, I built tunnels in the hillside below my treehouse. I built trenches there, too, being war-minded, and awaited attack. The fringe of woods along the water's edge sounded with the liquid note of thrushes in the twilight. The lake itself made music

with its wavelets for much of the year, except when it was iced over. They slapped at the timbers of our boat dock, or at the rocks along the shore, and they lapped at the edge of the ice in early winter. At times a stiff wind sprang up to chop the lake's surface to pieces, while at others the waters were wide, limpid, and glassy. I watched thunderstorms come in from the direction of Blue Mountain to the north, and the gathering noble blue-blackness would suddenly roll in overhead and the rain splashed across the lake, which ran with corrugated ripples, while the gods let loose their thunder and their bolts of lightning. If I was caught out in the open and there was no time to reach the house, I would go in under the pine for shelter. It is an unfortunate man or woman who has never loved a tree.

The power of forests is in that wild darkness the white settlers tried to get rid of; it never meant annihilation but stability. Trees, it has to be said, are "savages." They grow sick, they suffer from abuse and man's polluting tides, they inevitably die, as we do, when their span of life is finished; they are also uncompromising primitives, as anyone trying to make his way through a dense spruce forest will understand. In us, too, is the savage richness we override. Without those deep foundations, we would not understand the earth and would die out from lack of nutrition. Although it may temporarily satisfy millions of people, manufacturing goods and services beyond their need, a civilization that treats the trees as if they were inert ciphers, part of the numbers game, abandons the depth that builds community and invites vast areas of local sadness and vacancy.

In southern Mexico there is a remnant tribe of Mayans called the Lacadones. Their lives were always intimately dependent on the great mahogany forests that had lasted since the Mayan civilization died;

but in recent years most of the great trees, now exploitable commodities, have been cut down. In *The Last Lords of the Palenque,* the tribal leader Chan Kin, then in his eighties, speaks in this way:

"What the people of the city do not realize," he says in a heavy voice, "is that the roots of all living things are tied together. When a mighty tree is felled, a star falls from the sky. Before one chops down a mahogany, one should ask permission of the guardian of the forest, and one should ask permission of the guardian of the stars. Hachäkyum made the trees, and he also made the stars, and he made them from the same sand and clay, ashes and lime. When the great trees are cut down, the rain ends, and the forest turns to weeds and grass. In El Real, six hours from here, which used to be forest before the trees were felled, the top soil erodes and disappears, the streams have dried up, and the corn that grows there is stunted and dry. All becomes dry, not only here but in the highland as well — not only in this heaven, but the higher heavens above. Such is the punishment of Hachäkyum. I know that soon we must all die — all of us, not only the *hach winik.* There is too much cold in the world now, and it has worked its way into the hearts of all living creatures and down into the roots of the grass and the trees. But I am not afraid. What saddens me is that I must live to see the felling of the trees and the drying up of the forest, so that all the animals die, one after the other, and only the snakes live and thrive in the thickets."[1]

The more the forests are destroyed, the more we turn into separatists, strangers in our own home. We lose our companions. We lose our way, because an age where all things are expendable makes it increasingly hard to identify what we need, and for that, reason is not enough. You cannot follow trees if they are not in you, but only in your way.

I once set out on a camping trip along the Deerfield River in Vermont. We had made our way to the campsite through woods made darker by a coming storm. We forded stony streams, slipped over wet logs, and tramped over shallow duff at the river's edge, while the wind kept increasing in intensity. Along the route were a number of big maples, covered with the yellow leaves of autumn, that made me very conscious of their presence. They had been growing there for a long time, stubborn roots probing piles of schist and a stretching skin of soil, until they had attained an eminence, affecting the character of everything around them.

---

[1] Victor Perera and Robert D. Bruce, *The Last Lords of the Palenque* (Little, Brown, 1982), p. 86.

The wind grew wilder and the skies blacker. The waters of the lake we were to camp by were whipped and torn, and finally intermittent showers changed to full and unrelenting rain. We packed up the tents and trekked back in the evening over trails that had been turned into running streams. We skirted the river, deep, wide, and danger-ous, running down between woodland banks with a drawing power of its own, full of torrents and torment; it seemed to be gathering the growing darkness into itself. The wind hit the maples with a wild fury, so that their leaf masses whirled like a fire in the sky. The great storm, like the trees themselves, heightened the expressive unity of the region, its endurance, its stress, its ceaseless cohabitation. I was conscious of the power of interaction there, of bright leaves sensing change in the measure of seasons, of dark leaves and decay, and of all the transmutations unknown to me but carried by the creatures in the soil, and manifested in strange forms like the slime molds that moved on the trees.

We define our confused and disorderly world in terms of extremes we are unable to reconcile: war and peace, order and disorder, health and disease, life and death. Forests, on the other hand, have always contained these opposites in the unity of their being. Their wounds and malignancies are gradually healed. Wildness takes such care of wildness that it must always be the earth's criterion of health.

Trees stand deep within a kind of knowing that surpasses human knowledge. We are running too fast to absorb it. To go so far beyond them is to lose the sense of a community that thrives on the unities of the world. One day I was climbing up Sunset Hill, which overlooks Lake Sunapee, where we lived. (Sunapee, with various other spelling, such as *soo-ni-pee,* was an Indian name for wild geese.) A light rain was falling, coming in with a southeast wind. Most of the leaves on the trees had changed to copper, bronze, and brownish yellow, or they had eddied off into the wind. A pearly gray mist stole between the trees and hung over outcroppings of granite. The wind would occasionally push little shreds of cloud across the trail. I passed through a gaunt, dark belt of spruce with splintered arms that had haunted me as a child. I had imagined wolves running through them. Now the trees were filled with a slow-moving, sea-gray atmosphere.

As the light rain fell through the clearings and was filtered through the trees, the whole region had been changed by the watery atmo-sphere. There were countless new adjustments, recognitions, and responses set in motion everywhere. The hills and its woodlands received all outer weather with inner calm, and much art of its own. I watched while a junco, slate-gray and white like rocks and clouds, whisked and darted around in the underbrush and then alighted on the low branch of a spruce. I saw a raindrop suspended from a waxy needle in front of me, as it was swelling and about to fall. Water drop and junco, instead of being two separate and separable phenomena, became simply and easily allied. I was quite ready to say that a bird was like a raindrop.

The less we are able to admit common feelings into our relationship with trees, the more impoverished we become: it must indicate a deforestation of the spirit. Strangely enough, their least understood qualities lie in the sensate natures they share with the rest of life. When I walk through cut over areas where pasture birch, young sugar maples or white pines are growing back, I sense that they have a will of their own, an ability to come back that is more than automatic. After all, they are providers. They nurture multiplicity, from root to crown. Just as every life that associates with trees must communicate in one form or another, so trees themselves seem to respond to each other. We have hardly started to explore our mutual chemistry. On a high and open night in the winter, all blazing with the laddered, climbing stars, it is not accidental that the branches of the trees should reach and gesture as they do, or that one's spine should tingle at the lineup of the constellations. We were both constructed to that end.

It is December again, and the snow filters down through the air, while the wind picks up. Grainy-trunked ash, white and pinkish birch, dark green hemlock, ironwood trees with crinkly bark, all stand together in the snow laden wind. The higher branches creak and crack as they scrape or butt each other. They make a sound now and then like the tapping of a woodpecker. One tree suddenly sings like a bird, a singing note that is kindred to the wind, a sound that moves with air and snow, as we ourselves have voices that move in harmony at times with some deep, far off foundation for sound.

These trees might tell us where to whet our minds and appetites and examine our credentials for sight and hearing. They are keepers, not just of a wilderness apart, a reserve for the benefit of study and ecological research, but of a testing ground. A real acquaintance with them is more than good enough for the grace that living asks of us.

So in that uncompromising beauty of the arctic cold, you can walk where they stand on the hill tops and watch the wonderful sweeping by of snow like smoke, with its visible particles bouncing, racing, intercirculating, on and on, with immortal energy.

Bibliography

Notes

Index

Bibliography

The following booklists, as students of the field will recognize, are far from exhaustive. The field is indeed vast — there exists, for example, a bibliography on just one mountain range, the Adirondacks, which comes to 354 pages, and covers only materials published through 1955! (It takes a 198-page supplement to continue the Adirondack coverage just ten years further, to 1965.) So, clearly, I have made a selection here, attempting to gauge literary worth, cultural and historical significance, and intellectual challenge, along with other qualities.

Primary Materials

This section includes natural history essays; "rambles"; essays of travel, adventure, and solitude in nature; and accounts of farm and country living. The intent here, simply, is to list the best American nature writing.

Abbey, Edward (1927–   ). *Abbey's Road.* New York: Dutton, 1979.
  The "road not taken" by most of us. The pieces collected here are defiantly anarchistic, in the best, positive, encouraging sense of the term, and also humorous, in a way that few if any nature essays have ever been. Allegiance to wild nature is the one value never satirized.
————. *Appalachian Wilderness.* New York: Dutton, 1970.
  Intimate, almost tactile photographs by Eliot Porter and a dark, no-punches-pulled "Epilogue" on strip mining and other abuses by Harry M. Caudill complement Abbey's descriptions of the Great Smoky Mountains.
————. *Cactus Country.* New York: Time-Life, 1973.
  The Sonoran Desert, seen through the eyes of a confirmed desert rat (one who honors above all the birthright of freedom, and likes humanity "in moderation"). There is a good deal of natural history information here, although the author states, "I am not a naturalist; what I hope to evoke through words here is the way things *feel* on stormy desert afternoons, the exact shade of color in shadows on the warm rock, the brightness of October, the rust and silence and echoes of human history along dusty desert roads, the fragrance of burning mesquite, and a few other simple, ordinary, inexplicable things like that."

———. *Desert Solitaire.* New York: McGraw-Hill, 1968; Simon & Schuster, 1970 (Touchstone Books); Layton, Utah: Peregrine Smith, 1980 (Literature of the American Wilderness); New York: Ballantine, 1985.

After the fashion of Thoreau, Abbey sharpens his narrative of solitude in nature by boiling several seasons down to one, and several years of philosophical reflection down to a few potent questions. His perception of the desert is determinedly frameless and unconventional, as is his commentary on civilization. A work steadily gaining "classic" status.

———. *Down the River.* New York: Dutton, 1982.

A gathering of articles, including a searching personal reflection on Henry David Thoreau and, in "Thus I Reply to René Dubos," one of the important wilderness essays of the present day.

———. *The Journey Home: Some Words in Defense of the American West.* New York: Dutton, 1977.

The energy of outrage, directed at real, on-the-ground evils; tender lyricism toward all that is innocent, wild, and threatened; the charm of a self-deprecating literary persona; and some of the most vigorous revolutionary humanism in contemporary nature writing. (See selection, pp. 346–355.) "The Second Rape of the West" is in effect all italics, and it needs to be.

———. *Slickrock.* With photographs by Philip Hyde. San Francisco: Sierra Club, 1971.

Southern Utah's canyon country in its vulnerable beauty, described and defended with passion. Abbey notes with wonder the obsession for paved roads, and counters that poverty of outlook by demonstrating a more leisurely pace. Philip Hyde's photographs and comments do the same. A "coffee-table" book with heart and spirit.

Allen, Durward (1910–   ). *Wolves of Minong: Their Vital Role in a Wild Community.* Boston: Houghton Mifflin, 1979.

An illustration of how a "limited" ecological study — in this case of the small wolf population of Isle Royale National Park and its relationship with the moose of the island — can blossom into an ecological vision including the human perspective. Includes provocative commentary: "In degree each of us has become the hyperkinetic victim of an overpopulated range, overused living space, competition for increasingly scarce resources, and the harassment of sounds that invade every attempt to be alone."

Anderson, Edgar (1897–1969). *Landscape Papers.* Edited by Bob Callahan. Berkeley: Turtle Island Foundation, 1976.

A collection of short essays on the subject of paying attention to one's surroundings, whether they are a wildflower preserve or a crowded city. The author was not an absolutist in his views of nature or wilderness. He felt we should be learning how to preserve leaf mold in urban parks, for example, as a practical means of adapting to the world and honoring it. "If one accepts Man as a part of Nature there is always something to be found."

Audubon, John James (1785–1851). *Ornithological Biography, or An Account of the Habits of the Birds of the United States of America.* 5 vols. Philadelphia:

J. Dobson, 1831 (vol. 1); Boston: Hilliard, Gray & Co., 1835 (vol. 2); Edinburgh: A. & C. Black, 1835–39 (vols. 3–5).

Chatty, personal, and discursive notes on birds and the American scene, meant to accompany the great plates of *The Birds of America*. The gold under the surface here is Audubon's field knowledge. He uses the phrase "closet naturalists" for those who believe, for example, that the hen turkey doesn't have a beard. Aubudon's enthusiasm and love for nature radiate from many of these pages. (See selecting, pp. 132–142.)

Audubon, Maria R. (1843–1925). *Aubudon and His Journals.* 2 vols. New York: Scribner's, 1897; Dover, 1960, 1986.

Maria, the artist's granddaughter, included in Volume 1 seventy-odd pages of biographical and autobiographical material, which (subsequent studies have shown) should be interpreted with caution. The journals are lively, and marked by Audubon's quick and observant outlook, for instance his immediate perception of a difference in song between eastern and western meadowlarks, and his speculation therefrom that he might be dealing with separate species. The "Episodes" in Volume 2 reprint, with one important addition ("My Style of Drawing Birds"), the sketches of American character and landscape published in the first three volumes of the *Ornithological Biography.*

Austin, Mary (1868–1934). *The Flock.* Boston: Houghton Mifflin, 1906.

Folk life, which for Austin meant life connected to, and sensitive to, a "home place" out in the bright, clear air of the semi-arid West. Following sheep across the wilderness is seen here as a healthy and fundamental activity with a mystical dimension. "There is a look about men who come from sojourning in that country, as if the sheer nakedness of the land had somehow driven the soul back upon its elemental impulses."

———. *The Land of Journeys' Ending.* New York: Century, 1924; Tucson: University of Arizona Press, 1983.

After two decades in what people call "the world," or "the real world," Austin turned back toward the dry, wild spaces. She toured Arizona and New Mexico, and here portrays the deep, attracting power of the desert. Her stance is oracular and generalizing, but there are strong passages of pure, and some may say awakened, perception.

———. *The Land of Little Rain.* Boston: Houghton Mifflin, 1903; Albuquerque: University of New Mexico Press, 1974.

This was Austin's first book, radiant with just-learned facts and truths. The title idea becomes a central ecological insight, organizing and clarifying the author's observations.

———. *The Lands of the Sun.* Boston: Houghton Mifflin, 1927; originally published as *California, the Land of the Sun* (New York: Macmillan, 1914).

A survey, almost a travelogue, but done with the Austin intensity and aura of portent. "The way to learn the mesa life is to sit still, and to sit still, and to keep on sitting still."

Bailey, Liberty Hyde (1858–1954). *The Country-Life Movement.* New York: Macmillan, 1911.

Since the farmer is "the ultimate conservator of the resources of the earth. . . . in contact with the original and raw materials," civilization has deep and permanent need of him. Bailey shows us there is more to agriculture, much more, than production of food.

———. *The Harvest of the Year to the Tiller of the Soil.* New York: Macmillan, 1927.

Part 1, "The Situation," summarizes the transformation of America from agrarian to industrial times, and warns against what Bailey calls "corporationism"—what we would call agribusiness today. Part 2, "The Incomes," consists of pithy, reflective essays on the satisfactions of farm life lived with a broader awareness of nature.

———. *The Holy Earth.* New York: Macmillan, 1915; The Christian Rural Fellowship, 1943.

This work conveys Bailey's reverence for the earth and for knowledge, independence, good tools, and honest work. All of these virtues, though "the days of homespun are gone," may still be combined in farm life of the higher sort. (See selection, pp. 247–257.)

———. *The Outlook to Nature.* New York: Macmillan, 1905.

Essays on the corrective, enlarging effect of the outward look. Bailey evokes the sky and the weather and the lay of the land poetically, as basic elements of consciousness and spirituality. "Evolution: The Quest of Truth" goes beneath controversy to the issues of open-mindedness and our basic ability to correct our views and actions.

Baker, Ray Stannard (1870–1946). *The Countryman's Year.* Garden City, N.Y.: Doubleday, Doran, 1936.

Journal entries and quietly offered aphorisms, based on life in rural Massachusetts. This may be one of the most modest of the books on country life; the author keeps his eye on small matters and common things, and the cumulative effect is of a profound, alert calmness.

Bakker, Elna (1921–   ). *An Island Called California.* Berkeley: University of California Press, 1971.

A well-written ecological "pilot" to the major biomes of the state, and a guide to what the author calls "intelligent appreciation" as the foundation of conservation. Includes a useful bibliography.

Bandelier, Fanny, trans. *The Journey of Alvar Nuñez Cabeza de Vaca.* New York: A. S. Barnes, 1905.

A brief, very brief, list of the birds and animals Cabeza de Vaca saw during his eight-year travail, and the first report of bison to reach Europe. Cabeza de Vaca's account also gives evidence for a rather impressive population density of Indians, even in the dry Southwest.

Bartram, John. *See* Cruickshank, Helen Gere, ed., and Darlington, William.

Bartram, William (1739–1823). *Travels Through North and South Carolina, Georgia, East and West Florida, the Cherokee Country, the Extensive Territories of the Muscogulges, or Creek Confederacy, and the Country of the Choctaws.* Philadelphia: James & Johnson, 1791; New Haven: Yale University Press, 1958 (Naturalist's Edition, edited by Francis Harper); Layton, Utah: Peregrine Smith, 1980.

Early reviews of Bartram's *Travels* were none too favorable, and there was no American edition, after the first, for 136 years. But this book is still alive. Bartram displayed an innocent, overflowing joy in what he saw, and he noticed parallels, analogies, and relations in the natural world, and saw the implications of these for philosophy. A primary document of American natural history and nature writing. (See selection, pp. 107–119.) *See also* Ewan, Joseph, ed.

Bates, Marston (1906–1974). *The Forest and the Sea.* New York: Random House, 1960.

An introductory (but challenging) course in the biosphere and the methods and theories of biology, conducted with wit and grace. The author recognized similarities between biological patterns in the tropical forest and the sea.

———. *A Jungle in the House: Essays in Natural and Unnatural History.* New York: Walker, 1970.

Two years' worth of Bates's columns from *Natural History* magazine, showing wonderfully broad scientific curiosity and his desire to communicate clearly and wittily. The "jungle" in the title is a conservatory and greenhouse he developed into a kind of outsized terrarium housing tropical plants and animals, including seven species of hummingbirds.

Bedichek, Roy (1878–1959). *Adventures with a Texas Naturalist.* Garden City, N.Y.: Doubleday, 1947.

J. Frank Dobie (see p. 415) referred to Bedichek as "an earth man," his term of highest praise. This book regards simple items such as fences with an open, category-bridging attention; the "adventures" are thought-journeys into progressively deeper levels of relationship and complexity.

———. *Karankaway Country.* Garden City, N.Y.: Doubleday, 1950; Austin, Texas: University of Texas Press, 1974.

The Gulf Coast of Texas, and much, much else. Bedichek found that to discuss the decline in shellfish intelligently, he had to present facts on stream- and nutrient-flow; this opened up the subject of dams, and land use, and eventually man's role on earth. Everything is connected.

———. *The Sense of Smell.* Garden City, N.Y.: Doubleday, 1960.

The "most enduring of all the senses" is important to consciousness but lacks popular recognition of its importance and scientific standing. To correct this state of affairs, Bedichek presents a natural history of olfaction in immense detail from myriad sources, including remarkable accounts of "sensitives" like Helen Keller. His survey is not limited to humans. The concluding chapters examine some effects of industrialism and pollution.

Beebe, William. *Edge of the Jungle.* New York: Holt, 1921; Duell, Sloan and Pearce, 1950.

A sequel to *Jungle Peace* (1918–see below); Beebe shares the "thrill of discovery and the artistic delight" of learning the labyrinthine diversity of Guiana. The area described here had been colonized and worked over at intervals, beginning around 1613, but the jungle was reestablishing itself as a wilderness, and the opportunities for study were endless. Beebe's attitude was, "Who can be bored for a moment . . . ?"

———. *High Jungle*. New York: Duell, Sloan and Pearce, 1949.
Beebe goes uphill here, to the Venezuelan cloud forest, and recounts interesting phenomena seen in three years' study during the 1940s. The account is evenly balanced between natural history and the sociology and humor of field-station naturalists' lives.

———. *Jungle Days*. New York: Putnam's, 1925.
A "chain of jungle life" (predation, scavengers' consumption of carrion, and so on) takes on deeper implications when the author extends it to include his own comprehension and the making and reading of his book. The chapter on "Old-time People" is an interesting speculation on evolution and the earliest divergence of apes and hominids.

———. *Jungle Peace*. New York: Holt, 1918.
The "great green wonderland" of the moist tropical forest in British Guiana, where Beebe established the Tropical Research Station of the New York Zoological Society. The peace of the jungle, which Beebe describes as "beyond all telling," contrasts greatly with popular images.

———. *The Log of the Sun: A Chronicle of Nature's Year*. Garden City, N.Y.: Garden City Publishing Co., 1905; Norwood, Pa.: Telegraph Books, 1982.
Short essays, most of them on the model of the "ramble," appreciating on a fairly elementary level wildlife's adaptations to the seasons of the temperate zone. Many of the pieces are about birds, and some adopt the bird's point of view, taking care to preserve logic and factuality.

———. *Unseen Life of New York: As a Naturalist Sees It*. New York: Duell, Sloan and Pearce; Boston: Little, Brown, 1953.
Beebe examines the "creatures which pass in the night or swim in the depths, or which fly too high or too fast for our eyesight, or whose small size requires a microscope to become visible to us." In this unusual guide Beebe also covers prehistoric animals and more recently extirpated species such as the timber wolf and wood bison. This book helps to establish New York City as a bioregion.

Bent, Arthur Cleveland (1866–1954). *Life Histories of North American Birds*. 20 vols. Washington, D.C.: U.S. Government (Smithsonian Institution Bulletins), 1919–1968.
Immense compendia of facts, travelers' and biologists' notes, aesthetic appreciations, curious incidents and anecdotes, and many passages of fine writing, *passim*. This is truly a life work. The volumes encompass so much, and are referred to so often and so much as a matter of course, that they have attained among students of bird life the status of something very like scripture. Although a few of the observers' reports need to be taken with a grain of salt, they are an indispensable resource for the study of American ecological history.
The volumes are:

———. *Life Histories of North American Birds of Prey*. Washington, D.C.: U.S.

Government, 1937–38 (Smithsonian Institution Bulletins 167, 170); New York: Dover, 1961.

———. *Life Histories of North American Blackbirds, Orioles, Tanagers, and Allies.* Washington, D.C.: U.S. Government, 1958 (Smithsonian Institution Bulletin 211); New York: Dover, 1965.

———. *Life Histories of North American Cardinals, Grosbeaks, Buntings, Towhees, Finches, Sparrows, and Allies.* Washington, D.C.: U.S. Government, 1968 (Smithsonian Institution Bulletin 237); New York: Dover, 1968.

———. *Life Histories of North American Cuckoos, Goatsuckers, Hummingbirds, and Their Allies.* Washington, D.C.: U.S. Government, 1940 (Smithsonian Institution Bulletin 176); New York: Dover, 1964.

———. *Life Histories of North American Diving Birds.* Washington, D.C.: U.S. Government, 1919 (Smithsonian Institution Bulletin 107); New York: Dover, 1963.

———. *Life Histories of North American Flycatchers, Larks, Swallows, and Their Allies.* Washington, D.C.: U.S. Government, 1942 (Smithsonian Institution Bulletin 179); New York: Dover, 1963.

———. *Life Histories of North American Gallinaceous Birds.* Washington, D.C.: U.S. Government, 1932 (Smithsonian Institution Bulletin 162); New York: Dover, 1963.

———. *Life Histories of North American Gulls and Terns.* Washington, D.C.: U.S. Government, 1921 (Smithsonian Institution Bulletin 113); New York: Dover, 1963.

———. *Life Histories of North American Jays, Crows, and Titmice.* Washington, D.C.: U.S. Government, 1946 (Smithsonian Institution Bulletin 191); New York: Dover, 1964.

———. *Life Histories of North American Marsh Birds.* Washington, D.C.: U.S. Government, 1926 (Smithsonian Institution Bulletin 135); New York: Dover, 1963.

———. *Life Histories of North American Nuthatches, Wrens, Thrashers, and Their Allies.* Washington, D.C.: U.S. Government, 1948 (Smithsonian Institution Bulletin 195); New York: Dover, 1964.

———. *Life Histories of North American Petrels and Pelicans and Their Allies.* Washington, D.C.: U.S. Government, 1922 (Smithsonian Institution Bulletin 121); New York: Dover, 1964.

———. *Life Histories of North American Shore Birds.* 2 vols. Washington, D.C.: U.S. Government, 1927, 1929 (Smithsonian Institution Bulletins 142, 146); New York: Dover, 1962.

———. *Life Histories of North American Thrushes, Kinglets, and Their Allies.* Washington, D.C.: U.S. Government, 1949 (Smithsonian Institution Bulletin 196); New York: Dover, 1964.

———. *Life Histories of North American Wagtails, Shrikes, Vireos, and Their Allies.* Washington, D.C.: U.S. Government, 1950 (Smithsonian Institution Bulletin 197); New York: Dover, 1965.

———. *Life Histories of North American Wildfowl.* 2 vols. Washington, D.C.:

U.S. Government, 1923, 1925 (Smithsonian Institution Bulletins 126, 130); New York: Dover, 1962.

———. *Life Histories of North American Woodpeckers.* Washington, D.C.: U.S. Government, 1939 (Smithsonian Institution Bulletin 174); New York: Dover, 1964.

———. *Life Histories of North American Wood Warblers.* Washington, D.C.: U.S. Government, 1953 (Smithsonian Institution Bulletin 203); New York: Dover, 1963.

Berry, Wendell (1934–   ). *A Continuous Harmony: Essays Cultural and Agricultural.* New York: Harcourt Brace Jovanovich, 1972.

Berry affirms the possibility of moral and practical redemption, and believes that this recovery, both personally and culturally, may be begun in humble, working contact with nature. "What I have been preparing at such length to say is that there is only one value: the life and health of the world."

———. *The Gift of Good Land.* Berkeley: North Point Press, 1981.

In this sequel to *The Unsettling of America,* the author goes traveling, to conferences where there isn't much of practical value being said, and to cared-for places where ecologically responsible farming has survived. In the title essay he proposes an interpretation of the Bible and Christianity in which land stewardship is central. This essay unifies all the travels and examples at a moral center. Berry asks, "Is there . . . any such thing as a Christian strip mine?"

———. *The Long-Legged House.* New York: Harcourt, Brace & World, 1969; Audubon Society/Ballantine, 1971.

Berry had settled himself by 1969; this book shows both a definite geographic and moral focus. From his position on the land, he rakes the false and destructive ways of place-less culture — "nature-consuming," the war in Vietnam, and the horror of strip mining. He also describes, positively, where he lives and what he lives for.

Beston, Henry (1888–1968). *Especially Maine: The Natural World of Henry Beston from Cape Cod to the Saint Lawrence.* Edited by Elizabeth Coatsworth. Brattleboro, Vt.: Stephen Greene, 1970.

An informative Foreword and selections from many letters add biographical depth to this Beston "reader." Coatsworth, the author's wife, offers useful insights. "He sometimes spent an entire morning on a single sentence, unable to go on until he was completely satisfied with both words and cadence, which he considered equally important."

———. *Herbs and the Earth.* Garden City, N.Y.: Doubleday, Doran, 1935; Doubleday, 1961, 1973.

This is Beston at his most domestic, perhaps, tending and describing with delectation his herb garden and his twelve favorite herbs — but the fresh winds and the great swing of the seasons move through even this small, cultivated space. The outlook, that is the looking outward, is pure Beston, and his wife reported in *Especially Maine* that he "considered the last passages in this book the best he had ever written."

————. *Northern Farm: A Chronicle of Maine.* New York: Rinehart, 1948.
Rhythmically poetic prose, conveying the distinctive Beston sensitivity to weather and the seasons and the feel of the landscape. The author relishes what is earned and traditional, enjoys his neighbors, and anathematizes the machine era and its projected "chromium millennium" — "What a really appalling future!"

————. *The Outermost House.* Garden City, N.Y.: Doubleday, 1928; New York: Rinehart, 1949, 1962; Ballantine, 1971.
A year on the Great Beach of Cape Cod: one of our literature's classic evocations of just what a year might naturally mean. (See selection, pp. 258–268.

————. *The St. Lawrence.* New York: Farrar & Rinehart, 1942 (Rivers of America Series).
The natural and human history of the great northern river, "flowing in vague and enormous motion to the east." This book also celebrates wildness: in some of the more remote stretches of the St. Lawrence, in 1942, "all sign and show of industrial perversion has melted from sight. It is the America of Audubon. . . ."

Bird, Isabella (1831–1904). *A Lady's Life in the Rocky Mountains.* New York: Putnam's, 1879–80; Norman: University of Oklahoma Press, 1960.
A no-nonsense, non-Romantic account of the autumn and early winter of 1873, which Bird, an Englishwoman, spent in and around Estes Park, Colorado. She cowboyed some, and climbed Longs Peak, and appreciated the beauty of the mountains.

Bohn, David (1938–   ). *Rambles Through an Alaskan Wild: Katmai and the Valley of the Smokes.* Santa Barbara: Capra, 1979.
Bohn, a photographer, records his strong feeling for wilderness and his desire that it be left alone. He is intensely conscious that even his photography and writing violate to some degree his leave-it-alone principle. The photographs reproduced here, though, will seem, to most viewers, acts of reverence.

Bolles, Frank (1856–1894). *From Blomidon to Smoky, and Other Papers.* Boston: Houghton Mifflin, 1894.
Tours in Nova Scotia and Cape Breton Island, prompting more reflection than the author's rambles in Massachusetts and New Hampshire. "The spell of the wilderness grew stronger upon me, and when, suddenly, I thought how many wearied souls there were in great cities who would love to see this beautiful, hidden spot, something akin to shame for my own race came also into my mind. If man came here, would he not destroy?"

————. *Land of the Lingering Snow.* Boston: Houghton Mifflin, 1891.
Brief essays in journal style, describing walks, carriage rides, and boating excursions, most of them in the vicinity of Boston. The author delights in atmospheric and psychological effects of seasonal changes, and presents very fine evocations of bird songs.

Borland, Hal (1900–1978). *Beyond Your Doorstep: A Handbook to the Country.* New York: Knopf, 1962.

A friendly guide to nature study, based on the Connecticut countryside near Borland's home and including interpretive commentary on land use. This is a primer on identification and on the observation of relationships.

――――. *Countryman: A Summary of Belief*. Philadelphia: Lippincott, 1965.

A year's worth of observations and reflections, in which the author's land in Connecticut inspired him to consider human nature and our particular moment in time. This yearbook also sums up Borland's lifetime philosophical affirmations.

――――. *The Enduring Pattern*. New York: Simon & Schuster, 1959.

Posing the questions, "*What is man? Where did he come from? What is his relationship to all the other forms of life around him?*", Borland sketches the earth's natural history and finds in it a great, inclusive system, constantly developing. Many of the illustrations are drawn from the area surrounding the author's country home in Connecticut.

――――. *Hill Country Harvest*. Philadelphia: Lippincott, 1967.

Notes on natural history and country living in what the author describes as a "somewhat remote corner of New England." Borland writes that "most of man's troubles are man-made," and recommends a slower pace — walking or even sitting still.

――――. *Homeland: A Report from the Country*. Philadelphia: Lippincott, 1969.

These essays are columns from *The Progressive*, 1963–68, and may be seen as fever for the political mind. In these "dispatches," as Borland calls them, as if he were a kind of foreign correspondent, he affirms his belief that "the country — the uncultivated land and the remaining remnants of wilderness as well as the farmland — is essential to the whole nation's sense of proportion and its perspective."

――――. *Sundial of the Seasons: A Selection of Outdoor Editorials from The New York Times*. Philadelphia: Lippincott, 1964.

A year's worth of brief essays — most are just three paragraphs long — arranged in the traditional order, spring to spring.

Bowden, Charles (1945–   ). *Blue Desert*. Tucson: University of Arizona Press, 1986.

The dark side of Sun Belt hedonism. Violence and sleaze are held up against the ideal of desert clarity and sparseness. "Everything a desert tortoise is — calm, a homebody, long-lived, patient, quiet — the people of the Southwest are not."

Bradbury, John (1768–1823). *Travels in the Interior of America in the Years 1809, 1810, and 1811*. London: Sherwood, Neely, and Jones, 1819; Lincoln: University of Nebraska Press, 1986.

Accompanying the Astorians (see p. 45) partway, the English botanist Bradbury described some of the "wild productions of the Missouri Territory," such as grapes, persimmons, pawpaws and strawberries, and recorded that a denizen of St. Louis could purchase a turkey or a quarter of venison for a quarter of a dollar. He was also one of the first to note that in the Midwest wolves were "already becoming scarce, and will soon disappear," and that "large tracts" of land were in the hands of speculators.

Brewer, William H. (1828–1910). *See* Farquhar, Francis P., ed.

Brewster, William (1851–1919). *Concord River*. Cambridge: Harvard University Press, 1937.

Although he was a founder of the American Ornithologists' Union and served as president of the Massachusetts Audubon Society for several years, Brewster's prose suggests that these titles were of little importance to anyone whose goal was to simply watch a bird and see it truly. On his game-preserve farm, he saw and heard keenly. "Repeatedly of late I have heard a male Bluebird warbling to its mate in tones exquisitely soft and tender, and so low as to be audible only a few yards away."

———. *October Farm*. Cambridge: Harvard University Press, 1936.

Brewster owned about 300 acres of varied, interesting land at Concord, Massachusetts, over which he walked with what must have been the greatest patience and watchfulness. His journal, which is the source of both *October Farm* and *Concord River,* has headings like "Sharp-shinned hawk catches a Robin" and "Remarkable Bird Concert." The episodes recorded are unadorned and unexpectedly moving.

Bromfield, Louis (1896–1956). *From My Experience: The Pleasures and Miseries of Life on a Farm*. New York: Harper, 1955.

This is "chapter three" of the Malabar story (see *Malabar Farm,* below). A vision of a restored society, founded ultimately on humus- and mulch-enriched soil, is Bromfield's guiding thought, but he is no fanatic. Bromfield cautions against both chemicalism and organicism, as religions. The final chapter, "The White Room," is a fine autobiographical essay in which the author looks beyond material success.

———. *Malabar Farm*. New York: Harper, 1948; Ballantine, 1970; Mattituck, N.Y.: Aeonian Press, 1978.

This is "chapter two" of the Malabar story. The farm has grown to 1,000 acres; the soil has been rejuvenated, largely by the "great healer" — grass; and Bromfield has developed some ideas on how a family-sized farm might survive in the modern era. The keys, he predicts, will be planning and specialization. In the larger dimension, Bromfield shows how the health of the land connects directly to world peace.

———. *Pleasant Valley*. New York: Harper, 1945.

A successful writer living in France, Bromfield in the late 1930s was looking for "real continuity, real love of one's country, real permanence." He returned to the Ohio countryside where he had grown up, bought three adjacent farms, set up a community modeled in part on the collective farm of Russia (but with himself, "as capitalist, . . . substituted for the state"), and began the agrarian ideal by restoring the soil's fertility.

Brooks, Paul (1909–   ). *Roadless Area*. New York: Knopf, 1964.

One of the early texts that contributed to the awakening to wilderness and environmental values in general in the 1960s. The framework here is narratives of trips into wilderness areas taken by the author and his wife; the gist of the book is a positive, ecological concept of wilderness, quietly radical.

Brown, Bruce. *Mountain in the Clouds: A Search for the Wild Salmon.* New York: Simon & Schuster, 1982.

The author walks and wades, mostly on the Olympic Peninsula, looking for wild salmon (as opposed to hatchery-produced ones), and fills out his narratives with historical information. He brings our sorry history of mistreatment of the salmon and their habitat into immediate, unforgettable focus through strong images. Dams, logging, road-building, nuclear power plants, and heavy commercial fishing have cut deeply into what was once a staggeringly beautiful abundance, but wherever conditions are at all favorable, the salmon still attempt to fulfill their ancient urges.

Burdick, Arthur J. (1858– ?). *The Mystic Mid-Region.* New York: Putnam's, 1904.

The Mohave Desert and its peculiar, compelling attraction — beyond mineral riches, the author says — to the old-style prospectors.

Burroughs, John (1837–1921). *Locusts and Wild Honey.* Boston: Houghton, Osgood, 1879; reprinted in *The Complete Writings of John Burroughs*, vol. 3. New York: Wm. H. Wise, 1924.

The focus on natural history is sharper and more particular than in *Wake-Robin* or *Winter Sunshine* (see below). This collection includes a comparison of European and American bird songs: ours are softer but wilder, according to the author. A week's camping in the Catskills had a bracing effect: "I was leg-weary and foot-sore, but a fresh, hardy feeling had taken possession of me that lasted for weeks."

———. *Signs and Seasons.* Boston: Houghton Mifflin, 1886; reprinted in *The Complete Writings of John Burroughs*, vol. 8. New York: Wm. H. Wise, 1924. Sketches of how birds and other animals fare in a hard winter, of birds' nests and the dangers they are exposed to, and of camping in the Maine wilderness are notable here, but perhaps the most substantial chapter deals with the proper habits of observation.

———. *Time and Change.* Boston: Houghton Mifflin, 1912; reprinted in *The Complete Writings of John Burroughs*, vol. 15. New York: Wm. H. Wise, 1924. Evolution is the theme. "I am sure I was an evolutionist in the abstract, or by the quality and complexion of my mind, before I read Darwin, but to become an evolutionist in the concrete, and accept the doctrine of the animal origin of man, has not for me been an easy matter." In a chapter on Yosemite, Burroughs stretches himself to take in the wild scene, and writes a more excited prose than usual.

———. *Wake-Robin.* New York: Hurd and Houghton, 1871; reprinted in *The Complete Writings of John Burroughs*, vol. 1. New York: Wm. H. Wise, 1924. Burroughs' first book of nature essays. *Wake-Robin* established him as the reader's congenial companion and observer of the near woods and fields. At this time, in 1871, he had not yet read Darwin, and his concept of nature lacked the acceptance of predation and death and the breadth and serenely comprehensive tone of his mature writings. Also at this time, he carried a gun and used it frequently.

———. *Ways of Nature.* Boston: Houghton Mifflin, 1905; reprinted in *The*

Complete Writings of John Burroughs, vol. 11. New York: Wm. H. Wise, 1924. Written soon after the "nature-faker" controversy (see p. 66), this volume sets forth Burroughs' thoughts on the instincts and probable consciousness of some of the other animals. His ideas represent an amalgam of native compassion and fellow-feeling, leanings toward a vitalist and transcendental view, and a recognition of the great powers of the scientific method and attitude.

————. *Winter Sunshine.* New York: Hurd and Houghton, 1875; reprinted in *The Complete Writings of John Burroughs,* vol. 2. New York: Wm. H. Wise, 1924.
Early, charming sketches, including appreciations of the winter skies and atmosphere of Washington, D.C., and the activities of foxes and skunks. The last chapters are on England and Ireland, where Burroughs had gone on government business, and it is evident that the author much preferred his native land.

Caras, Roger (1928–   ). *The Endless Migrations.* New York: Dutton, 1985.
This book might profitably be read alongside Donald Griffin's *Bird Migration.* Caras's dramatic, narrative approach conveys the wonder and majesty of mass movements. Birds, butterflies, whales, turtles, eels, bats, salmon, and others are the actors; the book presents a strong image of the planet netted with complex routes, and living bodies and consciousnesses following them.

————. *The Forest.* New York: Holt, Rinehart and Winston, 1979.
Ecology lessons, given vividly through narratives centering on a 200-foot western hemlock and a golden eagle.

Carrighar, Sally (1898–1985). *Icebound Summer.* New York: Knopf, 1953.
The blossoming of summer life in the Arctic, as experienced by several birds and mammals. This book has a wider compass, both geographically and temporally, than *Beetle Rock* or *Teton Marsh* (see below), and thus suggests the earth's great patterns of wind and water more strongly. The human presence is also more evident. Carrighar took pains to make her writing ethologically and ecologically respectable; she also had a fine dramatic sense. The account here of the golden plover's migration is as compelling as many a novel.

————. *One Day at Teton Marsh.* New York: Knopf, 1947; Lincoln: University of Nebraska Press, 1969.
A September day's happenings at a beaver pond in Jackson Hole, Wyoming, given from various animals' points of view and recorded with a certain overall narrative push. Each actor's responses to the environment — the taste of a mayfly to a trout, or aspen bark to a beaver, or the feel of the water to an otter — seem realistically grounded in natural history facts, and in the aggregate, give a remarkably vivid and complete picture of a biotic community.

————. *One Day on Beetle Rock.* New York: Knopf, 1944.
A June day on and around a two-acre outcrop of granite in the Sierra Nevada. The characters — Weasel, Coyote, Deer, Grouse, Lizard, and

others — demonstrate the author's intense awareness of wild creatures, and the way their lives impinge on one another's. The personalities described, and the inside views, appear as plausible extrapolations from observed behavior.

————. *The Twilight Seas.* New York: Weybright and Talley, 1975.
An inside narrative of a blue whale's life, told with imaginative feeling for the tactile delight of the ocean and with careful buttressing of scientific fact. "Whaleness was utter freedom, no gravity and no walls." A strong critique of whaling gives the book's title a disturbing dimension.

————. *Wild Heritage.* Boston: Houghton Mifflin, 1965.
An informed view of several aspects of animal behavior — courtship, aggression, play, dominance, and the effects of crowding, among other topics — that are both interesting in themselves and of possible application to the human circumstance.

————. *Wild Voice of the North.* Garden City, N.Y.: Doubleday, 1959.
Carrighar was engaged in a study of lemmings and was living in Nome, Alaska, when she acquired Bobo, a Siberian Husky. Over the years of their friendship she learned much from Bobo about animal behavior and the range of animal emotion and intelligence.

Carson, Rachel (1907–1964). *The Edge of the Sea.* Boston: Houghton Mifflin, 1955.
The shoreline, one of the most interesting and productive ecotones on earth, is interpreted "in terms of that essential unity that binds life to the earth." Carson covers rock shores, sand beaches, and coral reefs, taking her examples from the Atlantic Coast of America. Her own response to beauty and her sense of the interconnecting patterns in nature are prominent here.

————. *The Sea Around Us.* New York: Oxford University Press, 1950; Simon & Schuster, 1958; rev. ed., Oxford University Press, 1961.
A huge, indeed encircling subject, given point and intelligibility by exposition of particulars and by carefully shaped and cadenced prose. There have been gains in knowledge since this book's most recent, revised edition, but there has been no clearer presentation of the big picture. The moral point of view is quiet but firm. Of oceanic islands like Laysan and Midway, where exotic and destructive species were casually introduced, Carson writes, "In a reasonable world men would have treated these islands as precious possessions, as natural museums filled with beautiful and curious works of creation, valuable beyond price because nowhere in the world are they duplicated." (See also selection, pp. 277–295.)

————. *Under the Sea-Wind: A Naturalist's Picture of Ocean Life.* New York: Oxford University Press, 1941, 1952.
Framed as a series of narratives and vignettes of shore and ocean life, this book dramatizes food chains and other ecological relationships. Focal animals — a pair of sanderlings, a young mackerel, and an eel — grant the coherence of a story line, but entirely without "nature faking." There is a moving account of purse-seining at night, which might be read alongside Robinson Jeffers' great poem, "The Purse-Seine." The glossary consists of

remarkably concise descriptions of birds, fish, invertebrates, and geologic features — a kind of mini-encyclopedia of prominent elements in the littoral and pelagic realms.

Catesby, Mark (1682–1749). *Hortus Britanno-Americanus; or, a Curious Collection of Trees and Shrubs, The Produce of the British Colonies in North America; Adapted to the Soil and Climate of England.* London: W. Richardson and S. Clark, 1763.
A catalog of 85 American trees and shrubs, with instructions on transporting them to England for transplanting.

————. *The Natural History of Carolina, Florida and the Bahama Islands.* 2 vols. London: Printed at the expense of the author, 1731–1743. Appendix, 1748.
One of the major primary texts of the pre-systematic era. Beautifully done plates and a text impressive for its thoroughness (given the state of science at the time) mark these volumes.

Catlin, George (1796–1872). *Letters and Notes on the Manners, Customs, and Conditions of the North American Indians, Written During Eight Years' Travel Amongst the Wildest Tribes of Indians in North America.* New York: Wiley and Putnam, 1841.
Includes a prescient observation on the coming demise of the buffalo, and a "splendid contemplation" of a "*nation's Park,*" in which Indians would be forever free to live as they had, "amid the fleeting herds of elks and buffaloes."

Chadwick, Douglas. *A Beast the Color of Winter: The Mountain Goat Observed.* San Francisco: Sierra Club, 1983.
Oreamnos americanus and its perfect fit with the mountains it inhabits. The author's research in Montana began in 1971 and continued for seven years. The book gives a full natural history portrait of the mountain goat and makes a strong argument for wilderness in its presentation of the impacts of logging and road development.

Colby, William E., ed. *John Muir's Studies in the Sierra.* San Francisco: Sierra Club, 1960.
These are Muir's glacier articles, originally published in the 1870s in *The Overland Monthly.* Even at his most scientific, working out the proofs for Sierran glaciation, Muir managed to convey the wild, thrilling beauty of the ice-sculptured mountains.

Colvin, Verplanck (1847–1920). *Report on the Topographical Survey of the Adirondack Wilderness of New York, for the Year 1873.* Albany: Weed, Parsons, 1874.
Vicissitudes of survey work in a good cause (Colvin was a strong advocate of preservation for the Adirondacks), and in the midst of difficulties, appreciation for wilderness beauty. "The Adirondack wilderness may be considered the wonder and glory of New York. It is a vast *natural* park, one immense and silent forest, curiously and beautifully broken by the gleaming waters of a myriad of lakes, between which rugged mountain ranges rise as a sea of granite billows."

Cooper, David J. *Brooks Range Passage.* Seattle: The Mountaineers, 1982.

A long solo adventure, including building and using a log raft. The author subsisted in part on roots and berries, and (after intentionally bringing only minimal rain gear) came to terms with the Alaskan weather. The book has the flavor of solitude and wilderness, and little if any self-dramatization.

Cooper, Susan Fenimore (1813–1894). *Rural Hours.* New York: G. P. Putnam, 1850; rev. ed., Boston: Houghton Mifflin, 1887; Syracuse, N.Y.: Syracuse University Press, 1968.

A distinct sense of place — the environs of Otsego Lake in New York — emerges from journal-like entries arranged on the classic seasonal basis. Miss Cooper walked a great deal, and was not shy about taking moonlight rambles or venturing out in below-zero weather. She knew her birds, was acutely conscious of the feel of the day's atmosphere and light, and was a careful student of natural history. A memorable image is created here when the author measures a large downed pine with her parasol. *Rural Hours* includes a detailed description of a New York State farm household of the late 1840s, and perceptive notes on local plant geography.

Craighead, Frank (1916–   ). *Track of the Grizzly.* San Francisco: Sierra Club, 1979.

An immense amount of time in the field, and carefully planned research procedures, give this Yellowstone-based study its authority. It is also marked by broad knowledge of the ecosystem in general and its threatened integrity. "What is at stake is not just the grizzly, but the steady, often unnoticed attrition of the countless life forms, both plant and animal, that compose our complex biosphere and keep it functioning."

Crèvecoeur, Hector St. John de (1735–1813). *Letters from an American Farmer.* London: T. Davies, 1782; Philadelphia: Mathew Carey, 1793; New York: Dutton, 1912, 1951; New American Library, 1963.

The author's happy years (1769–1778) on his farm in Orange County, New York, set the dominant tone for these emotionally positive essays. There is both evocative detail ("Often when I plough my low ground, I place my little boy on a chair which screws to the beam of the plough — its motion and that of the horses please him, he is perfectly happy and begins to chat") and broad generalization about farm life, the frontier, and America.

————. *Sketches of Eighteenth Century America.* Edited by Henri L. Bourdin, Ralph H. Gabriel, and Stanley T. Williams. New Haven: Yale University Press, 1925.

Here Crèvecoeur, the "emotional prototype" of the American, as D. H. Lawrence described him, puts the farm up against the reality of finance, and graphically describes land abuse. He also notices the "most beautiful curves" made in the air by a bald eagle trying to escape a kingbird's attack, and sympathizes to a degree with blackbirds swarming onto the farmers' cornfields: ". . . are they not the children of the great Creator as well as we? They are entitled to live and get their food wherever they can get it."

Crisler, Lois (?–1971). *Arctic Wild.* New York: Harper, 1958.

The experiences of a husband and wife in the Brooks Range, as they gradually became more intimate with the wild and demanding place and with its wildlife — especially a group of wolves they came to know. A contribution to the debunking of the Little-Red-Riding-Hood concept of wolves.

Cruickshank, Helen Gere, ed. (1907–   ). *John and William Bartram's America: Selections from the Writings of the Philadelphia Naturalists.* New York: Devin-Adair, 1957.

A most useful introduction and collection—certainly the most accessible gathering of John Bartram's matter-of-fact journal accounts.

Darlington, William (1782–1863). *Memorials of John Bartram and Humphry Marshall.* Philadelphia: Lindsay & Blakiston, 1849.

Includes a history of American botany to the mid-nineteenth century, and a large, interesting selection of John Bartram's correspondence.

Dillard, Annie (1945–   ). *Pilgrim at Tinker Creek.* New York: Harper & Row, 1974.

Observation of nature here opens up profound questions about life and death, meaning, and identity. To the author, Tinker Creek in Virginia represents the universe in all its spiritual complexity. A pilgrim watching for keys and signs, she examines very closely the experience of ostensibly small and ordinary things. One of the most influential of contemporary books on natural history. (See selection, pp. 334–345.)

———. *Teaching a Stone to Talk: Expeditions and Encounters.* New York: Harper & Row, 1982.

Sensitive travel essays, carrying on in a wider geographic scope many of the themes of *Pilgrim at Tinker Creek.*

Dobie, J. Frank (1888–1964). *The Mustangs.* Boston: Little, Brown, 1952.

A paean to freedom above all, but also a work of historical and natural-historical acumen and research. Should be read with Hope Ryden's *America's Last Wild Horses* (1970, 1978) as necessary background.

———. *Rattlesnakes.* Boston: Little, Brown, 1965.

As animals going about their business, rattlesnakes deserve the interested, even-handed, folkloristically sophisticated treatment they get here. Of necessity, given the record of our relations with the rattlesnakes, this collection of experiences and tales offers almost as much material for an investigation of human nature as for a summary look at the pit vipers in genus *Crotalus.*

———. *The Voice of the Coyote.* Boston: Little, Brown, 1949; Lincoln: University of Nebraska Press, 1961.

A thoroughly "maverick," thoroughly engaging work of scholarship and homage, in which Don Coyote is honored for being his clever, surviving self. Dobie blasts "jukebox culture" with glee and righteousness. The book is illustrated by Olaus Murie.

Douglas, William O. (1898–1980). *Farewell to Texas: A Vanishing Wilderness.* New York: McGraw-Hill, 1967.

A pained but still hopeful survey of the state, from the Big Thicket to the western plains and mountains. As Douglas saw it, the frontier ethos was still firmly in the ascendant — in the saddle, so to speak: "Conservationists of Texas [are] a lonely lot." But there are *some,* and hope springs eternal.

————. *My Wilderness: East to Katahdin.* Garden City, N.Y.: Doubleday, 1961. Rambles of a sensitive man in wild areas ranging from Utah to Maine, and plain talk about overgrazing, the political power of livestock interests, and governmental insufficiency and mistakes. Douglas believed in the restorative power of wilderness, individually and culturally. A forthright, simply written book, with sharp flashes of both poetic appreciation and rightful anger.

————. *My Wilderness: The Pacific West.* Garden City, N.Y.: Doubleday, 1960. From the Brooks Range to Oregon's Wallowas, with stops in the Sierra Nevada, central Idaho, and lingering stays in the justice's home country of Washington state. As the author hikes and boats, he pays close attention to his surroundings and to threats against wilderness. Beautifully illustrated by Francis Lee Jaques.

Dubkin, Leonard (1904–   ). *Enchanted Streets: The Unlikely Adventures of an Urban Nature Lover.* Boston: Little, Brown, 1947. Finding himself suddenly unemployed, the author returned to a youthful fascination, natural history. Even in Chicago, there was plenty to enchant him. Lying in the grass of a park, climbing a tree for a closer look at sparrows, then having a new job for four weeks and quitting it, Dubkin came to a certain perspective on himself as a potential interpreter of the importance of nature to the modern, working world.

————. *My Secret Places: One Man's Love Affair with Nature in the City.* New York: McKay, 1972. Reminiscences of Chicago when there were still "secret" (undeveloped) places. The book becomes the record of an awful decline, as the author attempts to revisit scenes of powerful experiences (the yard described so lovingly in *The Natural History of a Yard* is now a parking lot, for example). The result is a considerably darker book than *Enchanted Streets* or the *Yard* study (see below).

————. *The Natural History of a Yard.* Chicago: Henry Regnery, 1955. The subject is the small grass plot of an apartment hotel on Chicago's north side, "surrounded by a [two-foot-high] privet hedge, with an elm tree in the back." Not a very promising subject, but Dubkin goes into it slowly and carefully over a three-year study, relying almost solely on his own observation, and finds a surprising richness. This book is a testimony to the endurance of several species, our own included.

Dutton, Clarence E. (1841–1912). *Report on the Geology of the High Plateaus of Utah.* Washington, D.C.: U.S. Government, 1880. A government surveyor with a job to do, the author nonetheless responded deeply to the dramatic wilderness of southern Utah. He described the 12,000-foot Tushar range with both geological accuracy and poetic enthusiasm, as "a composite structure, its northern half being a wild bristling cordillera of grand dimensions and altitudes, crowned with snowy peaks, while the southern half is conspicuously tabular."

————. *Tertiary History of the Grand Cañon District.* Washington, D.C.: U.S. Government, 1882; Layton, Utah: Peregrine Smith, 1977.

Geology and wilderness appreciation, along with an argument for a non-traditional mode of perception when viewing something as difficult to categorize as the Grand Canyon. "Forms so new to the culture of civilized races and so strongly contrasted with those which have been the ideals of thirty generations of white men cannot indeed be appreciated after the study of a single hour or day" Dutton recommended realism in description, over "fancy" or metaphor.

Dwight, Timothy (1752–1817). *Travels in New England and New York*. New Haven: T. Dwight, 1821–1822; reprinted in 4 vols., edited by Barbara Miller Solomon, Cambridge: Harvard University Press, 1969.

Journals of a man with very wide interests and a keen eye. In his ecological history, *Changes in the Land*, William Cronon writes, "anyone interested in New England ecology could do no better than to read Dwight from cover to cover."

Eckert, Allan W. (1931–   ). *Wild Season*. Boston: Little, Brown, 1967.

Astonishing activity in the month of May, unveiled at a modest, ordinary lake in the Midwest. Eckert describes growth, predation, human cruelty and pity, and the intricacy of ecological relationships with unsentimental objectivity.

Eckstein, Gustav (1890–1981). *Lives*. New York: Harper, 1932.

A unusual book, describing lives of laboratory rats, cockroaches, canaries, turtles, a green parrot, and a university groundskeeper with strong empathy and an uncompromising sense of democracy: these lives are just as vital and interesting and just as much to be respected as the observer's own. Eckstein writes elliptically, which has the effect of removing the usual anthropomorphic and egoistic embroidery and putting the reader directly in touch with the subject at hand.

Ehrlich, Gretel (1946–   ). *The Solace of Open Spaces*. New York: Viking, 1985.

An appreciation of the vastness and rigor of Wyoming's high plains country, and of the people whose lives have been shaped by its elemental forces.

Eiseley, Loren (1907–1977). *The Firmament of Time*. New York: Atheneum, 1960.

Six lectures on evolution, on man's perception of the process, and on mind and ideas, one of the most interesting of the last being the concept of "natural." Within these reflections, which are presented with Eiseley's great respect for the elusiveness of truth and his sense of the primacy of the inner life, there is a clear, biography-centered history of evolutionary interpretation over the past three centuries.

———. *The Immense Journey*. New York: Random House, 1957.

A personal record of explorations into paleontological and anthropological time, back toward the *Urschleim* that was once thought to be a transitional form between nonliving and living matter. The investigations serve as map coordinates, so to speak, for placing man in the scheme of things. One of the author's central beliefs is that "the most enormous extension of vision of which life is capable" is "the projection of itself into other lives." This ability is necessary, Eiseley feels, for the imaginative and intellectual "immense journey" into evolutionary time.

———. *The Night Country.* New York: Scribner's, 1971.

There are dimensions to life, certain uneasinesses in particular, that daylight thinking seemingly cannot encompass. This "night country," which the author began entering at an early age, is perhaps the source of his slanted but thoroughly sane outlook.

———. *The Star Thrower.* New York: Times Books, 1978; Harcourt Brace Jovanovich, 1979.

An anthology of Eiseley's work, most of it chosen by Eiseley during the year before his death. The volume, edited by Kenneth Heuer, includes a fine appreciation by W. H. Auden, two interesting essays on Thoreau by Eiseley, and a selection of the author's early poems.

———. *The Unexpected Universe.* New York: Harcourt, Brace & World, 1969.

The creativity of nature, its endless possibility and open-endedness, described with awe and with a poet's distrust of pat answers. "The world contains, for all its seeming regularity, a series of surprises resembling those that in childhood terrorized us by erupting on springs from closed boxes." These surprises may even be found in the study of the past; in one chapter Eiseley looks anew at Pleistocene and Permian glaciation, to find immense implications for human evolution.

Emerson, Ralph Waldo (1803–1882). *Nature.* Boston: J. Munroe, 1836; Houghton Mifflin, 1902; Indianapolis: Bobbs-Merrill, 1948; Boston: Beacon Press, 1986 (facsimile of first edition).

One of the seminal texts in American nature writing and nature philosophy. Emerson argued persuasively that individual experience is universal in essence and that experience "in the woods" is full of potential for clarity and enlightenment. It was once fashionable to disdain Emerson for a certain alleged unreality, but the list of writers influenced by *Nature* would be very long indeed.

Engberg, Robert, and Donald Wesling, eds. *John Muir: To Yosemite and Beyond.* Madison: University of Wisconsin Press, 1980.

A valuable collation of letters, journal entries, and lesser-known writings, extending Muir's own *Story of My Boyhood and Youth* (1913; see p. 57) through 1875. The editors' framing of the selections and their interpretations of Muir's thought are informative.

Errington, Paul (1902–1962). *Of Men and Marshes.* New York: Macmillan, 1957.

An introduction to the study of wetlands, written with a strong sense of their beauty and importance. The text centers on the glaciated country of the north-central states and is founded on the idea that "greater familiarity with marshes on the part of more people could give man a truer and more wholesome view of himself in relation to Nature." Errington praises wildness, and laments the fact that by 1957 more than three-fourths of the aboriginal wetlands of America had been damaged or drained.

———. *Of Predation and Life.* Ames: Iowa State University Press, 1967.

Many years of close observation, here focused chiefly on muskrats, mink, and bobwhite quail in north-central locations, provided the author with remarkable opportunities for insight into the fluidity and complexity of predator-prey relationships. After what amounted to a lifetime in the field, all of his conclusions were tentative.

Evans, Howard Ensign (1919–   ). *Life on a Little Known Planet*. New York: Dutton, 1968; Chicago: University of Chicago Press, 1984.

We don't know much, and yet we presume so greatly. Evans, a museum curator and research entomologist, says "Few groups are better suited to demonstrate how little we know about our planet than the insects — how little the experts know, and how very little of this knowledge has reached 'the man on the street.'" The author attempts to improve this by recounting in informal style some fascinating entomological items: flash patterns in male fireflies, mimicry in several species, the flight muscles of flies, the unusual mating habits of bedbugs, and much else, all written with clarity and wit. Evans concludes with a survey of pressing environmental matters, a plea for diversity, and a response to *Silent Spring* that seems oddly inadequate.

———. *Wasp Farm*. Garden City, N.Y.: Natural History Press, 1963; Doubleday, 1973.

An engrossing natural history of wasps, based in part on the author's observations on an eight-acre farm in upstate New York. Evans says that "the twentieth century belongs to the laboratory scientists," but this course in wasp biology and evolution takes the reader into the field where the living wasps are.

Ewan, Joseph, ed. *William Bartram: Botanical and Zoological Drawings, 1756–1788*. Philadelphia: American Philosophical Society, 1968.

Beautiful, sensitive, caring work, reproduced from the Fothergill album in the British Museum. (John Fothergill was Bartram's English patron.) William Bartram was, as editor Ewan points out, "the first native-born American artist-naturalist"; his art, like his writing, deserves greater appreciation.

Farb, Peter (1929–1980). *Living Earth*. New York: Harper, 1959.

A lively introduction to the "hidden world" of soil, organized on the basis of forest, grassland, and desert, showing the complexity of "soil societies" and the importance of soil to manifold ecological relationships. "The soil is the seat of abundance on earth, a massive machinery for keeping the chemical stuff of the planet in constant circulation."

Farquhar, Francis P., ed. *Up and Down California in 1860–1864*. Berkeley: University of California Press, 1966. Selections from the unpublished writings of William H. Brewer (1828–1910).

Brewer, a member of the California Survey (whose charge was a complete geological accounting of the state's lands), was a graduate of the Sheffield Scientific School of Yale University. His descriptions of pristine, near-pristine, and already-besmirched California landscapes are always scientifically precise and often touched with enthusiasm.

Finch, Robert (1943–   ). *Common Ground: A Naturalist's Cape Cod*. Boston: Godine, 1981.

Every place, however extensively studied, is new to one who comes newly to it. Finch's impetus: "I felt that living with nature in the late twentieth century must mean more than turning down the thermostat and meeting state sanitary codes." So he explored Cape Cod at a walking pace, hearing the woodcock's spring vocalizations, trying to save an injured junco, and exploring the aftermath of the great winter storm of 1978, among other adventures in learning.

————. *Outlands: Journeys to the Outer Edges of Cape Cod*. Boston: Godine, 1986.

These essays in personal experience are marked by a sharp, imagistic sense of place and a philosophically low-keyed, even anti-portentous tone. "North Beach Journal" is one of the finer contemporary essays on solitude.

————. *The Primal Place*. New York: Norton, 1983.

Concentrating upon the author's neighborhood, on Cape Cod but not especially near the ocean (the surf is rarely heard in this book — unusual for a Cape Cod natural history), these essays show a developing sense of home ground — a "primal place." From that center, one may venture outward with a certain authenticity and reference.

Flagg, Wilson (1805–1884). *Studies in the Field and Forest*. Boston: Little, Brown, 1857.

"Rambles" concentrating on the aesthetics of different scenes and landscapes. "What do we care for a scene, however beautiful, which is so tame as to afford no exercise for the imagination? Rocks, by increasing the inequalities of the surface, proportionally multiply the ideas and images which are associated with landscape."

————. *The Woods and By-Ways of New England*. Boston: James R. Osgood, 1872.

"It is delightful to enter by chance upon one of these old roads, when it will carry you half a day's journey on foot, without the intrusion upon your sight of a steam-factory or a railroad station." The book consists of short, three- to seven-page essays on such subjects as "Foliage" and "A Summer Night in the Woods," and is marked by the author's fondness for the pastoral. But there is also some bite here, and a critical view of what was happening to the American landscape: "The preservation of the forests in a certain ratio over the whole territory ought to be the subject of immediate legislation in all the States."

Fletcher, Colin (1922–   ). *The Complete Walker*. New York: Knopf, 1970; rev. ed., as *The New Complete Walker*, 1974; rev. ed., as *The Complete Walker III*, 1984.

This is a guide to equipment and techniques, but Fletcher makes it abundantly clear, through sharply drawn vignettes and extended philosophical commentary, that the real core of backpacking in the wilderness is not having tools or covering miles, but truly being there.

————. *The Man Who Walked Through Time*. New York: Knopf, 1968.

Walking the length of the Grand Canyon on a route at varying elevations from rim to river gave the author an ideal opportunity to ponder time and earth history, and his own place in and response to nature.

————. *The Thousand-Mile Summer.* Berkeley: Howell-North, 1964; New York: Random House (Vintage Books), 1987.

Fletcher backpacked from the Mexican border to the California-Oregon line, traversing deserts and the length of the Sierra Nevada, relishing open country and open time, and especially enjoying evenings in camp after a long, capacity-stretching day.

Fosburgh, Hugh (1916–1976). *A Clearing in the Wilderness.* Garden City, N.Y.: Doubleday, 1969.

"Baker's Clearing" in the Adirondacks, created in 1854, is a seventy-acre opening. Living there gave the author opportunity to comment on the Adirondacks' "incredible capacity to rejuvenate themselves." He argued that intelligent logging may make for a various and productive mix of environments.

Frémont, John Charles (1813–1890). *Report on the Exploring Expedition to the Rocky Mountains in the Year 1842 and North California in the Years 1843–44.* Washington: U.S. Senate, 1845.

Although Frémont was always going somewhere (in both a geographic and political sense), he did take the time to write some energetic descriptions of mountain scenery. The depictions of the Wind River Range of Wyoming are perhaps the high point, literarily, of this report.

Gilbert, Bil (1927–   ). *Our Nature.* Lincoln: University of Nebraska Press, 1986.

Written in a style that is both humorous and knowing when it deals with man and self, and objective and respectful when nature is the subject, the magazine essays collected here are sophisticated but not slick. Gilbert takes pains to make personal contact with his subjects — retracing some of John Franklin's peregrinations in the Far North, for example — and he keeps our environmental moment firmly in the reader's mind.

————. *The Weasels: A Sensible Look at a Family of Predators.* New York: Pantheon, 1970.

The subtitle is accurate. With a comprehensive natural history of the weasel family, Gilbert interweaves a logical, anti-anthropomorphic analysis of predation. He lays waste to several superstitions about the weasel family and holds up some human foibles to humorous witness.

Godman, John D. (1794–1830). *American Natural History.* 2 vols. Philadelphia: Carey & Lea, 1826; Stoddert & Atherton, 1828–1831; R. W. Pomeroy, 1842.

Godman, a medical doctor, centered his descriptions of the quadrupeds of America on anatomy, building outward from the bodies of animals to their behavior and what would later be called their ecological "niche." This careful and responsible work, which has been unfairly overlooked, also promotes the scientific approach — as opposed to folklore and prejudice — and displays an objective attitude toward predation. This enlightened view places Godman about a century ahead of his time.

————. *Rambles of a Naturalist.* Philadelphia: T. T. Ash, 1833. Also found in

vol. 2 of the 1828–31 and 1842 editions of *American Natural History.*
Careful instruction in the small and near-at-hand. This is one of the earliest
examples of the ramble — a durable subgenre in American nature writing.
As in later rambles, the lecture is based on paying close attention to
"common" scenes that are usually passed over. (See selection, pp. 127–
131.)

Gould, Stephen Jay (1941–   ). *Ever Since Darwin: Reflections in Natural
History.* New York: Norton, 1977.
Pointing out that Darwinism is by no means fully accepted — or understood — the author examines what is so difficult about the theory. Darwin
saw no purpose or direction to evolution; this helps make evolutionary
theory an "antidote to our cosmic arrogance," as Gould says, and also helps
make it a trying interpretation. The essays here (first published as columns
in *Natural History* magazine) add up to a thorough treatment of evolution
and its effects on human thought and self-concept.

————. *The Flamingo's Smile.* New York: Norton, 1985.
"Evolution is one of the half-dozen shattering ideas that science has developed to overturn past hopes and assumptions, and to enlighten our
current thoughts." It is a more personal idea than quantum theory or
relativity, Gould argues. In this collection of *Natural History* columns, a
major theme is the possibility that a collision with an asteroid, or a shower
of comets, brought about major changes in earth's patterns of life; there
follows an interesting discussion about "what it means to say that life is the
product of a contingent past. . . ."

————. *The Panda's Thumb: More Reflections in Natural History.* New York:
Norton, 1980.
Evolutionary theory, because it embodies the "duality in natural history —
richness in particularities and potential union in underlying explanation,"
excites the author's mind profoundly. These essays, drawn from Gould's
columns in *Natural History,* suggest natural history's rightful standing in
intellectual life as a discipline demanding imagination and the highest
powers of synthesis.

Graustein, Jeannette E., ed. *Nuttall's Travels into the Old Northwest: An Unpublished 1810 Diary.* In *Chronica Botanica,* vol. 14. Waltham, Mass.: Chronica
Botanica Company, 1950–51.
The record of a long, difficult, and lonely journey — from Philadelphia to
Detroit, to the Mandan villages, and downstream to St. Louis and New
Orleans. It is the travel diary of a young man, as yet rather inexperienced
in the American fauna and flora, and its natural history consists mainly of
lists. But the author's dedication and bravery shine through. Suffering
from "ague" (malaria), he tried bleeding, cathartics, and emetics, somehow
managing to keep traveling and continue learning.

Graves, John (1920–   ). *From a Limestone Ledge.* New York: Knopf, 1980.
Essays originally published in *Texas Monthly,* describing life on a country
place with a light, ironic touch.

————. *Goodbye to a River.* New York: Knopf, 1960.

The author canoes down a stretch of the Brazos River in Texas, a section of the stream under sentence of dam construction, and reflects about time and loss and progress. He describes the rich and varied wildlife and calls up the lives of former inhabitants and settlers, weaving the elements of his story subtly, so that in the end the reader realizes that what is being lost is indeed nothing less than a world.

———. *Hard Scrabble: Observations on a Patch of Land.* New York: Knopf, 1974.
Graves bought the first part of his country place in 1960, and over the years came to a sense of the requirements, and certainly the pleasures and pains, of living beyond the easy-service zone. He writes of his acquisition of knowledge entirely without self-praise.

Griffin, Donald (1915–   ). *Bird Migration.* Garden City, N.Y.: Doubleday, 1964; Dover, 1974.
The facts on velocity, range, altitude, timing, navigation, and the theories on why and how birds migrate are set forth patiently here, and thoroughly. But the author is also aware of the deeper dimensions of life's fit with the earth and its seasons. One of the book's most stirring passages describes Griffin's flight in a light plane alongside some migrants, trying to learn, trying to sense their world.

———. *Animal Thinking.* Cambridge: Harvard University Press, 1984.
"The aim of this book," Griffin explains, "is to rekindle scientific interest in the conscious mental experiences of animals." To do this, Griffin must subvert the reigning behaviorist-mechanist theories by presenting voluminous data showing that the thoughts and feelings of other species are real, verifiable items. There are, of course, some profound philosophical questions inherent in this investigation. A remarkably provocative study.

Grosart, Alexander B., ed. *The Poems and Literary Prose of Alexander Wilson.* 2 vols. Paisley, Scotland: Alex. Gardner, 1876.
A compendious collection of Wilson's work, prefaced by an admiring introduction by the editor. Grosart says of Wilson's bird descriptions, several of which are included here, "You have painstaking technical accuracy; but besides, a tender, delicate, lingering over their habits which is most taking." Wilson's letters give interesting detail on American country life during the first decade of the 19th century.

Haines, John (1924–   ). *Living Off the Country: Essays on Poetry and Place.* Ann Arbor: University of Michigan Press, 1981.
Twenty years on a homestead in Alaska gave Haines a standpoint. He came into his own as a poet there ("there" means Alaska, and also what he describes as "the hard irreducible world of natural things — of rock and water, fire and wood, flesh and blood") and from that place and state of mind come his estimates of what is not centered or tied to any sense of place, in particular modern culture and a good deal of modern poetry. The essays here seem illusionless about both wilderness and civilization; they also vivify the "old ways" of mankind in sudden, poetic images. (See selection, pp. 366–380.)

————. *Other Days: Selection from a Work in Progress.* Port Townsend, Wash.: Graywolf, 1981.

Succinct, lyrical vignettes and reflections drawn from the author's life in Alaska. He describes the coming of spring, the singing of wolves, and the suddenness with which getting lost can occur. The images carry a weight of thought and a certain dreamlike quality, as if what is perceptible to the eye or ear stopped just short of explaining itself and yet unmistakably indicated meaning, leading the mind on.

Hakluyt, Richard (1552–1616). *The Principal Navigations, Voyages, Traffiques and Discoveries of the English Nation.* New York: Dutton, 1927.

Volume 6 includes Thomas Heriot's "A briefe and true report of the new found land of Virginia," a sixteenth-century man of science's attempt to describe paradise soberly. "Walnut trees, as I have said before very many, some have bene seene excellent faire timber of foure and five fadome [fathoms], and above fourescore foote streight without bough."

Hall, Donald (1928–   ). *String Too Short to Be Saved.* New York: Viking, 1961.

The old ways and character of small-farm America. The author spent his growing-up summers on his grandparents' farm in New Hampshire, watching and listening. In maturity, he returned and found that it all still rang true.

Halle, Louis J. (1910–   ). *Birds Against Men.* New York: Viking, 1938.

Halle is sensitive to the impact of modern man on the natural world, and entirely sympathetic to his bird subjects here, whose natural innocence and simple following of the dictates of their natures he finds instructive. As for man, Halle observes, "By his own militant energy, by the sweat of his brow and the labor of his hands, he has found riches. But he has not found peace." In these essays there is a strong feeling for the individual selves of the birds described.

————. *Spring in Washington.* New York: William Sloane, 1947; Harper, 1957.

"To snatch the passing moment and examine it for signs of eternity is the noblest of occupations. It is Olympian. Therefore I undertook to be monitor of the Washington seasons, when the government was not looking." This beautiful book is a tribute to the nature threading through even the most chest-thumpingly monumental of cities. "The discovery of spring each year, after the winter's hibernation, is like a rediscovery of the universe."

Hamilton, Gail [Mary Abigail Dodge] (1833–1896). *Country Living and Country Thinking.* Boston: Ticknor and Fields, 1862.

Confiding, spirited essays, more or less well connected to country life. The author's proclivities were for philosophy and social comment rather than nature study. The essay on "Men and Women," whose connection to country living is not evident, is a strong assertion of the author's feminist point of view.

Hay, John (1915–   ). *The Great Beach.* Garden City, N.Y.: Doubleday, 1964.

The Outer Beach of Cape Cod, where light and space and the sounds of the surf and the birds conspire to awaken an elemental consciousness. In one memorable chapter, the author takes a three-day walk down the beach, between the dunes and the sea, responding to the wild and evocative scene.

————. *Nature's Year.* Garden City, N.Y.: Doubleday, 1961.

"I drove to Cape Cod with travelers from everywhere" is this book's first sentence; what follows is a record of learning a place, coming to be at home there. One of the early texts, possibly, in the modern literature of bio-regionalism and re-inhabitation.

————. *The Immortal Wilderness.* New York: Norton, 1987.

The myriad signals and adjustments of species and habitats, complexly and perfectly tuned to each other; the inspiring odysseys of alewives, terns, and monarch butterflies; the fit and health of the whole, and the dismaying estrangement from this of the modern human way. Hay affirms, "We do not own intelligence; it is an attribute of the planet, together with all of the fine degrees of perception and awareness in living things. . . ." (See selection, pp. 389–395.)

————. *In Defense of Nature.* Boston: Little, Brown, 1969.

The author, recognizing certain symptoms in himself, makes a critique of progress-engrossed, uprooted, "free agent" modern man and affirms what could be a saving allegiance to nature and wildness. "As we diminish our environment, both physically and in terms of our attitude toward it, so we diminish our range of attention. Half the beauties of the world are no longer seen." Hay wonders, "What will we be when left to nothing but our own devices!"

————. *The Run.* New York: Norton, 1979.

Hay describes the alewives' great journeys, emblematic of nature's long cycles and patterns, abundance, and survival despite remorseless attrition. As he looks down into a New England brook in springtime, he stands in awe of what might be learned from these patterns.

————. *Spirit of Survival: A Natural and Personal History of Terns.* New York: Dutton, 1974.

A gathering of information on migration, courtship, nesting, communication, care and feeding of young, and other matters, illuminated by a profound personal response to this attractive family of birds. "I kept moving toward them, listening to them, not as if they were entirely alien factors, but as if we had a collateral relationship whose depths were beyond conscious knowledge."

————. *The Undiscovered Country.* New York: Norton, 1982.

This is a book about learning "the proprieties of the earth," the living system of connections of each to all. Hay describes his own movement toward recognition of these proprieties. "How wild and wonderful it is," he exclaims, "to be out in open territory with everything to learn!" This, precisely, is the undiscovered country.

Higginson, Thomas Wentworth (1823–1911). *Outdoor Studies: Poems*; vol. 6, *The Writings of Thomas Wentworth Higginson.* Cambridge: Riverside, 1900.

Half a dozen essays are added here to a reprinting of *The Procession of the*

Flowers. In one, "Saints and Their Bodies," the author praises physical fitness and activity and accuses Americans of becoming a soft, indoor breed. The essay was originally published in 1858. "Footpaths," another notable essay, is built on this idea: "Civilization is tiresome and enfeebling, unless we occasionally give it the relish of a little outlawry, and approach, in imagination at least, the zest of a gypsy life."

————. *The Procession of the Flowers*. New York: Longmans, Green, 1897.
Higginson is wary of affectation and sentimentality, and holds that "Nature is not didactic, but simply healthy." The author's impressionistic style seems appropriate to his refusal to pin nature down too tightly. "My Out-Door Study" touches on some of the same ground, genteelly, as Thoreau covered in "Walking" (see pp. 194–220).

Hoagland, Edward (1932–   ). *The Courage of Turtles*. New York: Random House, 1970; San Francisco: North Point, 1985.
The author is energized by a two-part existence, one in New York City and the other in Vermont, and derives sophisticated insights from playing the parts off one another. Four of the essays here touch on this gray-green dialectic. Attracted to country characters and old-time ways, the author nevertheless has no sentimental desire to turn the clock back.

————. *Notes from the Century Before: A Journal of British Columbia*. New York: Random House, 1969; San Francisco: North Point, 1982.
The author spent a glorious summer — the summer of 1966 — in back-country British Columbia, interviewing old-timers. Surrounded by lush greenness and seemingly limitless wilderness, their lives had been slow-paced and self-sufficient and in some ways "rangier" than they might have been "outside." Hoagland realizes such richness is being cut back swiftly, and hurries to get the record down. The situation has obvious tragic dimensions, but in the face of our dark progress the account glows with affirmation.

————. *Red Wolves and Black Bears*. New York: Random House, 1976.
Hoagland gives a sharp sense of where we are, in our rush into what certainly looks to be a tamer future. In Hoagland's hands, a subject like the difference between field study and "black-box" biology blossoms into a subtly done commentary on our entire relationship with nature. The author's subjects here could be temptations to preach, but he resists.

————. *Walking the Dead Diamond River*. New York: Random House, 1973; San Francisco: North Point, 1985.
Five essays in this collection, including the outstanding "Hailing the Elusory Mountain Lion" (see pp. 319–333), convey the keen, pleasurable sense of a long hike in good country. Hoagland straightforwardly warns, "All factions have reason to worry if the broad majority of citizens lose that mysterious sense of felicity and exuberance they once had in the presence of natural grandeur — the feeling of having known it before, of being linked to it via thousands of centuries before they were born — and simply stop caring."

Hoover, Helen (1910–   ). *The Gift of the Deer*. New York: Knopf, 1966.

The author describes herself as an "alien" in the Minnesota forest, separated from it by many generations of civilized humanity, but her knowledgeable sympathy for wild creatures does not speak of alienation. This is an account of the relationship Hoover and her husband Ade (who illustrated the book) developed with a family of white-tailed deer. Though attached to the deer, the author understands and values the role of the predators in the area, especially, and crucially, the wolves.

————. *A Place in the Woods.* New York: Knopf, 1969.

The day-to-day changes involved in moving from Chicago to a cabin in the North Woods are not small things, but they did not prevent the Hoovers from coming into an appreciative relationship with the wilderness around them.

————. *The Years of the Forest.* New York: Knopf, 1973.

A chronicle of the Hoovers' finding and improving their place in the north woods of Minnesota. There are life-enhancing adventures with wild animals, very considerable practicalities to master, and a reorientation toward work and money. This book contains, in between the lines, an interesting essay on freedom.

Hubbell, Sue (1935–   ). *A Country Year: Living the Questions.* New York: Random House, 1986; Harper & Row, 1987.

A record of living in the Ozarks, tending some 300 hives of bees, and looking well at the natural world. At fifty, the author was divorced and set about "building a new kind of order . . . at peace with herself and the world around her." She does her own truck maintenance, knows how to use a come-along, and writes in a plain, untranscendental style. There is good natural history information here on bats, bees, copperheads, brown recluse spiders, and much else; autobiographical revelations come along slowly, in patches, as the account develops.

James, George Wharton (1858–1923). *California, Romantic and Beautiful.* Boston: Page, 1914.

James was perhaps more of a booster than a serious or reflective writer, but he did respond to wilderness. The theme of what might be called renewal of the self through scenery is prominent in his work, and has autobiographical roots.

————. *Utah, Land of Blossoming Valleys.* Boston: Page, 1922.

In this book, something like an extended travel brochure, James praises the "good work" of irrigation.

————. *The Wonders of the Colorado Desert.* Boston: Little, Brown, 1906.

In the desert, James had found recovery and health after a personal crisis. He recommended the desert for its absolute honesty. "There is no knowing of self in the whirl of the cities." This is his most substantial book.

Janovy, John (1937–   ). *Back in Keith County.* Lincoln: University of Nebraska Press, 1983.

Occasional glimpses of the Nebraska sandhills and their natural history, but the concentration here is on the author and his friends and students, on their way to or from the field.

————. *Keith County Journal*. New York: St. Martins, 1980.

Nuggets of Nebraska prairieland natural history set within, and partially integrated with, personal notes and stories.

Jefferson, Thomas (1743–1826). *Notes on the State of Virginia*. Paris: 1784–85; Chapel Hill: University of North Carolina Press, 1955; New York: Penguin, 1981.

A careful, diplomatic demolition of the Comte de Buffon's suppositions (see p. 36) on the degeneracy of American life forms, a compilation of natural history facts from the author's own study and reading, and a bit of personal narrative relating an experience at the Virginia Natural Bridge probably qualify parts of this wide-ranging book as early natural history essays.

Johnson, Josephine (1910–   ). *The Inland Island*. New York: Simon & Schuster, 1969.

The journal of a year on an old Ohio farm, in which the beauty and encouragement and essential sanity of nature are somewhat darkened by the author's sense of human and national decline. She states, "We are dying of preconceptions, outworn rules, decaying flags, venomous religions, and sentimentalities. We need a new world." The Vietnam War casts a shadow over this account, but on December 31, the last entry reads, "It went down to zero in the night. And the new year began with awesome clarity."

Jones, Charles (1932–   ). *The Gifting Birds: Toward an Art of Having Place and Being Animal*. Salt Lake City: Dream Garden, 1985.

Notes on various places, including southern Arizona ("finest solitude I had ever known"), San Gregorio Beach in California, the Arctic coast near Point Barrow, and Hawaii. The theme is the impact that place has on consciousness and the mind.

Josselyn, John (?–1675). *An Account of Two Voyages to New-England, Made During the Years 1638, 1663*. London: G. Widdows, 1674; Boston: William Veazie, 1865.

A haphazard diary of odd little occurrences and adventures, mixed in with natural history notes. An example of the author's curious approach: "I never heard of any mischief that snakes did [Josselyn differentiates "snakes" from "Rattle-snakes"], they kill them sometimes for their skins and bones to make hatbands of, their skins likewise worn as a Garter is an excellent remedie against the cramp." But there are also passages of what should probably be called ecological insight.

————. *New-England's Rarities Discovered*. London: G. Widdows, 1672; also in Edward Tuckerman, ed., *Transactions and Collections of the American Antiquarian Society*, vol. 4. Boston: John Wilson & Son, 1860; Boston: Massachusetts Historical Society, 1972 (facsimile of first edition).

In this book, his first, Josselyn presents rather brief lists of birds and animals, and quaint ideas ("The skin of a gripe [bald eagle], drest with the doun on, is good to wear upon the stomach, for the pain and coldness of it"), and also good detail on plants and their virtues, and a useful account of changes in the land already underway.

Kalm, Peter (1716–1779). *Peter Kalm's Travels in North America.* 2 vols. Edited by Adolph B. Benson. New York: Wilson-Erickson, 1937; Dover, 1966.

A most useful historical reference. The Delaware River was still of drinking-water quality in 1748, but the forests of New Jersey were being hard hit to supply the market for "black walnut and oak planks for ships." The countryside around Philadelphia, as seen by Kalm, confirms the most positive agrarian traditions, but already there were losses in wildlife, perceptible to oldtimers whom he met and interviewed. Kalm was a traveler with a utilitarian eye (looking out for plants that could be transported to Sweden), and his account has a sober, factual solidity.

Kappel-Smith, Diana. *Wintering.* Boston: Little, Brown, 1984; New York: McGraw-Hill, 1986.

From a farm in northern Vermont, emotionally forthright reflections on the experience of the seasons. Moments of contact with the earth provide sustenance through the winter. After an earthquake, and after drilling for a water well and finding limestone 120 feet down, "Suddenly everything that I am exploring — live, surface, things — seems fragmentary, insecurely perched, hardly worth the ticket. I am seated on miles of living rock."

Kent, Rockwell (1882–1971). *N. by E.* New York: Random House, 1930; Harcourt Brace, 1930.

A stormy and difficult passage by sail to Greenland, climaxing in shipwreck on a rocky shore; the dénouement, however, is Kent's post-disaster awakening to the beauty of the wild, spare surroundings. Camping out on the tundra, walking in occasionally to a tiny settlement, the author found perception renewed. "How rich in everything was Greenland! . . . [T]hen human kind seemed what it ought to be."

———. *Wilderness: A Journal of Quiet Adventure in Alaska.* New York: Putnam's, 1920.

The artist and his son Rockwell III (nine years old at the time) spent six months on Fox Island, just off the Kenai Peninsula, in the winter of 1918–1919. Kent's informal, forthright style conveys the sense of place and weather with clarity, and characterizes the relationship between father and son simply and profoundly. "The still, deep cup of the wilderness is potent with wisdom. Only to have tasted it is to have have moved a lifetime forward to a finer youth." A beautiful book.

Kieran, John (1892–1981). *Footnotes on Nature.* Garden City, N.Y.: Doubleday, 1947.

Rambles with a "strolling group" of friends, mostly in the vicinity of New York City, suggesting the delight in nature and the flavor of camaraderie of Izaak Walton's *The Compleat Angler.* The quarry here is usually birds. Written with charmingly self-effacing wit.

———. *A Natural History of New York City.* Boston: Houghton Mifflin, 1959.

Modestly, the author writes that he has "touched on some of the easily observed divisions of plant and animal life that occur within the city limits." One might wonder how a place with 25,000 people per square mile, notoriously overtopped with asphalt and concrete, could be of much natural history interest. This book shows how it could, in detail.

Kinkead, Eugene (1906–   ). *A Concrete Look at Nature: Central Park (and Other) Glimpses.* New York: Quadrangle/New York Times, 1974.
Most of the pieces here describe rambles in New York City, including bird walks and tree walks that may surprise the reader with their richness of things to see.

King, Clarence (1842–1901). *Mountaineering in the Sierra Nevada.* Boston: James R. Osgood, 1872; New York: Scribner's, 1902; Norton, 1935; Philadelphia: Lippincott, 1963; Lincoln: University of Nebraska Press, 1970.
Entertaining adventures in the Sierra, clear lectures on geology, and perceptive and humorous accounts of mountain characters. The most consciously literary production of the California Survey team.

————. *Systematic Geology.* Washington: U.S. Government, 1878.
A remarkably lucid overview of the landscape between Cheyenne, Wyoming, and Carson City, Nevada, covering a 100-mile swath of country as representative. King's vigorous prose conveys the drama of geologic history as revealed by present landforms.

King, Thomas Starr (1824–1864). *The White Hills.* Boston: Crosby, Nichols, 1860.
Concentrating upon views and viewpoints, this book guides the traveler toward New Hampshire's White Mountains from every point of the compass. The emphasis is entirely visual. "One can hardly conceive what heightened charm a very little cultivation on the sides of a mountain will add to the landscape."

Knowler, Donald (1946–   ). *The Falconer of Central Park.* Princeton: Karz-Cohl, 1984.
A British birder comes to New York City and is mugged early on, but continues birding in Central Park, making sharp observations on the human scene and entering in this journal-like account lyrical descriptions of birds, weather, and the seasons.

Krutch, Joseph Wood (1893–1970). *The Best Nature Writing of Joseph Wood Krutch.* New York: Morrow, 1970; Pocket Books, 1971.
A good selection, made by the author and introduced by an essay that describes nature writing as science with a human, caring face and that also recounts Krutch's own beginnings in the genre.

————. *The Desert Year.* New York: William Sloane, 1952; Viking, 1963.
Essays in desert natural history, derived from the author's life-changing sabbatical year in Arizona. A major pleasure here is Krutch's growing sense of wonder and delight, and his depth of response to other creatures' consciousness and emotions. The chapter "A Bird in the Bush," in which Krutch writes, "A bird in the bush is worth two in the hand," is a penetrating examination of the unfeeling kind of biological science.

————. *The Forgotten Peninsula.* New York: William Sloane, 1961.
Baja California, when it *was* forgotten. Krutch described himself as a traveler "so struck by its wildness and its beauty that he returned again and again." This travel book contains astute observations on progress, inspired by Krutch's glimpses into a slower, materially poorer, yet richer world.

————. *The Grand Canyon*. New York: William Sloane, 1958.

Instruction in ecology — for example, the differentiation between squirrels that live on the north and south rims of the canyon — and the canyon's clear demonstration of Merriam's "life-zone" theory. Krutch declares himself among those "who find themselves seeing it more vividly when nature is not merely a spectacle but a phenomenon interpretable in terms of the infinitely complex and subtle processes of which the spectacle is an outward and visible sign. And I have never found either the beauty or the wonder diminished."

————. *The Great Chain of Life*. Boston: Houghton Mifflin, 1956, 1978.

The author's immense command of historical and literary reference is brought to bear on some of the most instructive aspects of the biosphere. Working from an evolutionary standpoint, Krutch attempts to place consciousness and feeling within the overall biological context. His reflections on happiness and joy are provocative. (See selection, pp. 296–307.)

————. *The Voice of the Desert*. New York: William Sloane, 1954.

The adaptations of desert wildlife to heat and aridity lead the author to considerations on man's place, and to a critique of mechanical behaviorism as a theory of nature. The book also includes a plea for an attitude more profound than mere conservation. Krutch argues, "The wisest, the most enlightened, the most remotely long-seeing exploitation of resources is not enough, for the simple reason that the whole concept of exploitation is so false and so limited that in the end it will defeat itself and the earth will have been plundered no matter how scientifically and farseeingly the plundering has been done."

LaBastille, Anne (1938–   ). *Beyond Black Bear Lake*. New York: Norton, 1987.

In this sequel to *Woodswoman* (see below), a stronger environmental concern is evident. Much had happened in ten years, but the central themes remain in place. The author built a second cabin for $130.75. It is called "Thoreau II."

————. *Woodswoman*. New York: Dutton, 1976.

Getting to know the Adirondacks close up, in all seasons, learning how to live alone, and learning how to live in "an ecologically sound manner" in the wilderness. The author honestly relates her fears and occasional loneliness, and her impatience for spring.

Lambourne, Alfred (1850–1926). *Our Inland Sea: The Story of a Homestead*. Salt Lake City: The Deseret News, 1909.

Lambourne, a poet of some power and a landscape artist in the tradition of Albert Bierstadt, lived alone for fourteen months on Gunnison Island in the Great Salt Lake. "I shall see the great phenomena of nature," he wrote early in his stay, and though he did spend some time looking at the mainland through his telescope, he also responded to the spareness of the island and to the dramatic movement of storms across the lake.

Lanner, Ronald (1930–   ). *The Piñon Pine: A Natural and Cultural History*. Reno: University of Nevada Press, 1981.

A good example of how to write popular natural history without writing down. This forestry professor's account of a most interesting tree examines its ecological settings and describes its uses and its beauty and appeal. The book includes pine-nut recipes supplied by the author's wife Harriette.

———. *Trees of the Great Basin.* Reno: University of Nevada Press, 1984.

A thorough survey, illustrated with drawings by Christine Rasmuss as well as several fine photographs, and studded with little-known facts revealing the ecological complexity of an area often regarded as a wasteland or military testing ground. This is a basic reference text and, for its clarity and depth of appreciation for its subject, a pleasure to read.

Lawson, John (?–1721). *A New Voyage to Carolina.* Edited by Hugh T. Lefler. Chapel Hill: University of North Carolina Press, 1967. (Originally published in 1709.)

In the first decade of the 18th century Lawson went inland into Carolina on a journey of over 500 miles, going from one Indian tribe to the next. His journal gives plentiful information on animals' lives (though he did not look as closely as Catesby would, later, at the hog-nosed snake, and though he believed female opossums bore their young at the nipples). He studied Indians minutely, describing their physiques and their ways of life in vivid detail.

LeConte, Joseph (1823–1901). *A Journal of Ramblings Through the High Sierra of California.* San Francisco: Francis & Valentine, 1875; Sierra Club, 1930, 1960.

A summer pack trip in the year 1870, with a geology professor from the University of California. The author describes the lay of the land and its likely geological history, and pays an early tribute to the charisma and intelligence of John Muir, whom LeConte met in Yosemite Valley.

Lehmberg, Paul (1946–   ). *In the Strong Woods: A Season Alone in the North Country.* New York: St. Martins, 1980.

From the kitchen table of a cabin at Nym Lake, Minnesota, the author reflects on solitude, work and its relation to contemplation, and his own life, and finds himself able to come to a major decision.

Leopold, Aldo (1887–1948). *Round River.* Edited by Luna Leopold. New York: Oxford University Press, 1953.

Early journals, with many of the entries about hunting. This would be a good text for the argument that a hunter's awareness is related to ecological consciousness.

———. *A Sand County Almanac.* New York: Oxford University Press, 1949.

One of the modern classics, setting forth in elegantly economical prose the author's own journey toward ecological understanding, the necessity of wilderness to civilization, and (perhaps most revolutionary of his ideas) the need for a "land ethic."

Leydet, François (1927–   ). *The Coyote, Defiant Songdog of the West.* Norman: University of Oklahoma Press, 1977.

Focusing on the relationship of coyote and man, and more pointedly on what is called "predator control," Leydet describes the wonderful adaptability of the coyote. On the human side are those who respect and appreciate the animal, and also those who dedicate much of their lives and a good deal of the public's money to a campaign of eradication. The extent of the war on coyotes, and the perverse energy with which it is prosecuted, may surprise some readers.

Longgood, William (1917–   ). *The Queen Must Die and Other Affairs of Bees and Men.* New York: Norton, 1985.
A beekeeper's thoughts on the life of the hive, with interesting, non-clichéd comparisons and contrasts to human life. The descriptions of bee physiology and behavior are splendidly clear, yet suggest the "mystery and poetry" which the author believes are at the heart of the subject.

Lopez, Barry (1945–   ). *Arctic Dreams.* New York: Scribner's, 1986.
This is a book with much to say about perception. Perception, Lopez explains, may be shaped and limited by preconceptions, psychic needs, and material wants — these are some of our "dreams." It may also, on occasion, and revealing an admirable human potential, be clear. As Lopez sees them, the objects of perception (whether they are a horned lark, an Eskimo, an oil-rig worker, or a musk ox) retain their inherent dignity and standing in the world. A spiritually democratic state is disclosed in the process. The author travels over great stretches of the Arctic, seeing well and meditating upon the great choice that is behind our eyes.

———. *Crossing Open Ground.* New York: Scribner's, 1988.
A collection of essays unified by Lopez's stance of passionate respect for the natural world and by the exquisite attention he pays to things like the sound of music in the Grand Canyon, a wolverine story in Alaska, and an actual wolverine entering his camp. "Bob and I stood up, as though someone important had walked in. . . ." Similes seem to leap up before his wide-awake perception. The spectacle of nature does not appear here so much as a resource for writing, however, but as intense moral instruction. "The Passing Wisdom of Birds" has the weight of a major essay in the quest for an ecologically responsible human position.

———. *Of Wolves and Men.* New York: Scribner's, 1978.
A wide-ranging book that brings in biology, ethology, mythology, folklore, and history; the author's insights into the relationship between wolves and men from each angle of vision are penetrating. A strong indictment of human shortsightedness and fear emerges, but the fellow-feeling that permeates the book offers evidence of a different, better attitude. The section on American anti-wolf hysteria, both individual and government-sponsored, makes its point by understatement.

Lueders, Edward (1923–   ). *The Clam Lake Papers: A Winter in the North Woods.* New York: Harper & Row, 1977.
In a small cabin near Clam Lake, Wisconsin, the author becomes intensely self- and word-conscious as winter deepens. "I am less and less stimulated by the observation of my surroundings, and I find myself turning my observations more and more inward." A major quest here is for an understanding of metaphor and the basic processes of consciousness.

McMullen, James P. (1943–   ). *Cry of the Panther: Quest of a Species.* Engle-

wood, Fla.: Pineapple Press, 1984; New York: McGraw-Hill, 1985.
A Vietnam veteran throws his guns into a river, then spends years searching for the Florida cougar, hoping to see and know the health that a living
big cat in a living ecosystem would epitomize.

McNamee, Thomas (1947–   ). *The Grizzly Bear.* New York: Knopf, 1984;
McGraw-Hill, 1986.
The author's style is nearly conversational, and the organization somewhat
episodic, but this book offers a solid natural history of grizzlies and a
stimulating interpretation of bear-man interaction. The book focuses on
the Greater Yellowstone ecosystem and includes criticism of the Park Service and of lax local prosecution of poachers.

McNulty, Faith (1918–   ). *The Wildlife Stories of Faith McNulty.* Garden City,
N.Y.: Doubleday, 1980.
Close-up accounts of animals the author has encountered, studied, and in
some cases lived with, written in high consciousness of the great, endan-
gering power of the modern human way of life. This is an informative
and reflective book of essays, in which "The Whooping Crane," a gem of
concerned reportage, is perhaps the centerpiece. The book ought to have
a more accurate title.

McPhee, John (1931–   ). *Basin and Range.* New York: Farrar, Straus &
Giroux, 1981.
A wide-ranging introductory course in earth history, strung along I-80 in
part and using its roadcuts to make lecture points. The focus is on Nevada
and the Great Basin, where the parallel, north-south mountain ranges
appear to McPhee like stretch marks on the earth's crust. Highly informative prose, with sentences taking unforeseen but eminently logical turns.

———. *Coming into the Country.* New York: Farrar, Straus & Giroux, 1977;
Bantam, 1979.
A portrait of Alaska, including a wilderness idyll (a float trip on the Salmon
River), telling snapshots of movers and shakers, and more extended ac-
counts of back-country settlers — many of whom, here, appear to desire
both wilderness and a fossil-fuel-powered lifestyle.

———. *The Pine Barrens.* New York: Farrar, Straus & Giroux, 1968; special
ed. 1981, with photographs by Bill Curtsinger.
A surprisingly intact quasi-wilderness in the center of the northeast industrial corridor, with a cast of interesting characters. The focus here, and
typically so for McPhee, is sociological and personal, but there is also
information on such matters as berries, the giant aquifer underneath the
Barrens, fire and its effects upon forest succession, and the birds of the
area.

———. *Rising from the Plains.* New York: Farrar, Straus & Giroux, 1986.
A fascinating geological tour of Wyoming, with biographies of David Love
(the "Grand Old Man of Rocky Mountain Geology") and his mother, a
Wellesley graduate turned rancher.

Madson, John (1923–   ). *Up on the River.* New York: Schocken, 1985.
The Mississippi between St. Louis and St. Paul, as the heart of the country
and the home of wildlife and an abundance of human "characters."

————. *Where the Sky Began: Land of the Tallgrass Prairie.* Boston: Houghton Mifflin, 1982; San Francisco: Sierra Club, 1985.
A natural and recent human history of the easternmost grasslands of North America, covering soils, weather, ecological complexity, and the impact of settlement and conversion. A most useful appendix lists natural and restored tallgrass reserves in twelve states.

Marsh, Philip M., ed. *The Prose of Philip Freneau.* New Brunswick, N.J.: Scarecrow, 1955.
A thoroughly political writer, and, in Marsh's words, a "thoroughgoing Rousseauistic romanticist," Freneau wrote a number of newspaper essays in the late 18th and early 19th centuries, criticizing civilization from the standpoint of the "Philosopher of the Forest" and that of "Tomo-Cheeki," a fictional Indian. Freneau's theme was that a simple life in the forest gave rise to democratic and tolerant feelings.

Marshall, Robert (1901–1939). *Arctic Wilderness.* Berkeley: University of California Press, 1956; reprinted in 1970 as *Alaska Wilderness.*
In his youth, Marshall lamented being born too late for Lewis-and-Clark-style adventure and exploration. But four expeditions to the Brooks Range gave him plenty of opportunity to ford rivers, hike enormous distances, be tested by weather, and climb nameless mountains to gaze off over thousands of square miles of wilderness. This is a fast-moving, exhilarating account.

Maslow, Jonathan Evan. *Bird of Life, Bird of Death: A Naturalist's Journey Through a Land of Political Turmoil.* New York: Simon & Schuster, 1986.
A search for the resplendent quetzal, ancient symbol of freedom and the national symbol of Guatemala, a country where vultures now prosper famously. The author reports that the highland cloud-forest habitat of the quetzal has shrunk to some 2,500 square kilometers.

Matthiessen, Peter (1927–   ). *Sand Rivers.* New York: Viking, 1981.
An expedition in 1979 into the Selous Game Reserve in Tanzania, the largest wildlife reservation in Africa and a wilderness of almost primeval intactness.

————. *The Snow Leopard.* New York: Viking, 1978.
The story of a long, physically and spiritually demanding trek in a remote section of Nepal, undertaken not long after the death of the author's wife. The narrative is bell-clear and strongly evocative of a world of bright mountain light, snow, and rock.

————. *The Shorebirds of North America.* New York: Viking, 1967; reprinted in part as *The Wind Birds,* 1973.
A most interesting group of birds, given thorough and appreciative treatment. Matthiessen's eleven chapters covering the history, physiology, and habits of the "wind birds" (see selection, pp. 308–318) are written in a prose as elegant and precise as a flight of phalaropes. Robert Clem's paintings and Ralph S. Palmer's "Species Accounts," found in the 1967 edition, are also scientifically trustworthy and touched with the poetry that shorebirds seem to inspire. A beautiful book in all respects. The revised edition, *The Wind Birds,* is illustrated by Robert Gillmor.

————. *The Tree Where Man Was Born.* New York: Crescent, 1972.

In preserved portions of East Africa, we can still see a "glimpse of the earth's morning." The author conveys this auroral freshness not only in descriptions of wildlife, but also in portraits of humans. A book revealing high awareness of both the moment and the ancient, interlocked story of Africa and man. Eliot Porter's photographs are also superb.

Maximilian, Alexander Philip (1782–1867). *Travels in the Interior of North America, 1832–1834*. Vols. 22, 23, and 24 in Reuben Gold Thwaites, ed., *Early Western Travels*. Cleveland: Arthur H. Clark, 1906.
The Prince of Wied-Neuwied on the Rhine, Maximilian had the means and the leisure to take a slow journey up the Missouri and to winter over at the Mandan villages on his way home. He studied the abundant wildlife and the Indians with deep interest, and recorded one of the most compelling accounts of early travel in the West. His descriptions of cranes, buffalo, and wolves are memorable, in part because his writing speaks to the ear as well as the eye.

Merriam, Florence A. (1863–1948). *A-Birding on a Bronco*. Boston: Houghton Mifflin, 1896.
Two springtimes in southern California just north of San Diego were the source of these pleasant, well-written birdwatching narratives. Merriam, the author of authoritative bird guides and later the winner of a major scientific prize in ornithology, knew her birds. Her writing expresses strong fellow-feeling as well.

Michaux, F. André (1770–1855), and Thomas Nuttall (1786–1859). *The North American Sylva*. 5 vols. Philadelphia: Rice, Rutter, 1865. Vols. 1–3 by Michaux, 4, 5 by Nuttall.
Two great field men survey the trees of North America with scientific thoroughness and with delight. Nuttall's "Preface" expresses his love for the wild, American places he had known, as do his narratives of events during his botanical explorations in the West.

Mills, Enos (1870–1922). *The Spell of the Rockies*. Boston: Houghton Mifflin, 1911.
High adventures in the mountains, including a race with an avalanche that may test readers' credulity, mingled with excellent descriptions of wildlife and logical arguments for forest preservation. Mills was self-educated, an amateur in the high sense, and endlessly curious. "To spend a day in the rain at the source of a stream was an experience I had long desired, for the behavior of the waters in collecting and hurrying down slopes would doubtless show some of Nature's interesting ways."

————. *Wild Animal Homesteads*. Garden City, N.Y.: Doubleday, Page, 1923.
Narratives of animal interaction by a most patient and understanding observer. Mills emphasizes the importance of territory and familiarity with a home range in the lives of his subjects. Two of the essays here demonstrate a talent for satire, when the author compares animal and human ways.

————. *Wild Life on the Rockies*. Boston: Houghton Mifflin, 1909.
This energetic book of observations and adventures was dedicated to John

Muir, and contains many expressions that hark back to Muir, such as, "I lived intensely through ten strong days and nights, and gave to my life new and rare experiences." There are also detailed accounts of the distribution and ecology of various tree species.

———. *Your National Parks*. Boston: Houghton Mifflin, 1917.

A rather general travel guide, supplemented by occasional quotations from John Muir or John Charles Van Dyke. Mills's stand is clear: "Without parks and outdoor life all that is best in civilization will be smothered."

Milne, Lorus (1910–), and Margery Milne (1914–). *The Balance of Nature*. New York: Knopf, 1960.

Modern ecological studies, several of which are reported in detail here, provide concepts, and standards for environmental health, that might help man adjust his numbers and activities to the earth. A valuable handbook, illustrated by Olaus Murie.

———. *A Multitude of Living Things*. New York: Dodd, Mead, 1947.

Clear explications of small, usually unnoticed phenomena: the work of burying (carrion) beetles, the importance of water film (surface tension) on small bodies of water, the lives of animals who spend the daytime under rocks, and more. The opening chapter, not surprisingly, is a guide to slowed-down, patient observation.

———. *The Valley: Meadow, Grove, and Stream*. New York: Harper & Row, 1963.

The "commonplaces" of one's local surroundings — in this case a river valley in New England — reinforce the web of all life. The subtitle is from Wordsworth's "Ode on Intimations of Immortality," and this book provides a scientific gloss on that poem's theme. The immortality is the ecological wholeness in which every mollusk, bird, fish, or human observer participates.

———. *The World of Night*. New York: Harper, 1956.

What happens at night on the desert, in the ocean, in polar regions, in the forest, on the beach, in the jungle, and elsewhere, described in expository prose that is a model of clarity. The often-neglected half of natural history.

Milton, John P. *Nameless Valleys, Shining Mountains: The Record of an Expedition into the Vanishing Wilderness of Alaska's Brooks Range*. New York: Walker, 1970.

A 300-mile, 38-day trek in 1967, across the mountains and down the North Slope to the Arctic Ocean, with the awareness that the oil companies were close behind.

Mitchell, Donald Grant (1822–1908). *My Farm of Edgewood*. New York: Scribner's, 1863.

Careful planning (including the matter of just how far from a city a farm ought to be) enabled the author to make "Edgewood," his farm near New Haven, Connecticut, something of a model. This is mainly a "how-to" book, but Mitchell's many references to literature and philosophy help put the matter of going back to the country into a larger perspective.

———. *Wet Days at Edgewood*. New York: Scribner's, 1865.

Rain and snow keep the author indoors here, and he takes the opportunity to renew his acquaintance with Virgil and other writers of the classical era, medieval and Renaissance authors, and near-contemporaries: writers who all dealt with agricultural and pastoral matters in one way or another.

Mitchell, John Hanson. *Ceremonial Time: Fifteen Thousand Years on One Square Mile.* Garden City, N.Y.: Anchor Press/Doubleday, 1984.

The story of "Scratch Flat," an area near Boston, from the era of the last glaciation. Mitchell covers the known historical events, and renders the area's ecological history clearly, but what interests him most is "that undiscovered country of the nearby, the secret world that lurks beyond the night windows and at the fringes of cultivated backyards." In search of this undocumented dimension of Scratch Flat, he attempts to imagine the sense of place of the area's longest-term inhabitants, the Indians. The quest takes on overtones of a psychic adventure, because the Indian perception implies a wholly different sense of time and self.

Morison, Samuel Eliot, ed. and trans. *Journals and Other Documents on the Life and Voyages of Christopher Columbus.* New York: Heritage Press, 1963.

The reactions of Columbus to his discovery of the New World:

"Saturday, 13 October. This island is very big and very level; and the trees very green, and many bodies of water, and a very big lake in the middle, but no mountain, and the whole of it so green that it is a pleasure to gaze upon. . . ." Columbus was sorry, Morison tells us, that he didn't know the new plants and trees he was seeing — and wrote that this was "what [caused him]the greatest grief in the world. . . ."

Morton, Thomas (1575–1646). *New English Canaan.* London: Charles Green, 1632; reprinted in *Tracts and Other Papers, Relating Principally to the Origin, Settlement, and Progress of the Colonies in North America from the Discovery of the Country to the Year 1776.* Washington: Peter Force, 1838.

Morton says he arrived in the month of June, 1622, with thirty servants "and provision of all sorts fit for a plantation. . . ." While the houses were being built, he "did endeavour to take a survey of the Country: The more I looked, the more I liked it." His book lists prominent wildlife species and makes observations on forest cover, useful to later ecological historians.

Muir, John (1838–1914). *John of the Mountains: The Unpublished Journals of John Muir.* Edited by Linnie Marsh Wolfe. Boston: Houghton Mifflin, 1938; Madison: University of Wisconsin Press, 1979.

Muir's shortest entries here (probably reflecting the level of his interest) describe dinner parties and meetings with well-known people. They come late in the journal; the record of the earlier years, particularly in the early 1870s, is steadily focused on the wilderness, as fruitfully as in any American book.

———. *Letters to a Friend.* Boston: Houghton Mifflin, 1915; Dunwoody, Ga.: Norman S. Berg, 1973.

Jeanne Carr, the wife of Muir's science professor at the University of Wisconsin and something very like a mentor herself to the young Muir, encouraged him to write, both to her and more generally for publication.

These letters stand with the early journal as primary sources on Muir's inner life and developing knowledge of wilderness.

————. *The Mountains of California.* New York: Century, 1894; Garden City, N.Y.: Doubleday, 1961.

Muir's first book, well controlled and put together. It moves from the overview to the particulars with logic, and yet remains mysteriously radiant and ebullient — wild. "A Near View of the High Sierra," "A Wind-Storm in the Forests," and "The Water-Ouzel" (see pp. 221–233) are classic essays, epitomizing Muir's highly individual yet transparent, wilderness-engrossed outlook.

————. *My First Summer in the Sierra.* Boston: Houghton Mifflin, 1911, 1979.

The journal of the baptismal summer of 1869, edited by a Muir who is older but very much alive. In these months he saw his first water ouzels and glacial "erratics," crossed the Sierra Nevada for the first time, stared with awe at summer thunderheads, crept to the edge of Yosemite Falls, and stood face to face with a bear. Muir directed his ecstasy into his notebook, there being no one else to discuss it with:

"June 13. Another glorious Sierra day in which one seems to be dissolved and absorbed and sent pulsing onward we know not where. Life seems neither long nor short, and we take no more heed to save time or make haste than do the trees and stars. This is true freedom, a good practical sort of immortality."

————. *Travels in Alaska.* Boston: Houghton Mifflin, 1917, 1979.

The wild southeastern coast of Alaska, with its gigantic fjords and ice rivers, provided scope for Muir's expansive love of wildness and up-to-date texts for his understanding of glaciation and his sense of the ongoing creation of the world. He reveled in the great land, canoeing 800 miles in one trip, climbing mountains, and taking greater interest than theretofore in native peoples.

————. *Steep Trails.* Boston: Houghton Mifflin, 1918.

A posthumous collection of essays that includes the important essay "Wild Wool," an early effort to describe wilderness not as chaotic or in need of human correction but as reflecting the pure order of the universe. Muir roams to Nevada and Utah, among other places.

————. *The Story of My Boyhood and Youth.* Boston: Houghton Mifflin, 1913, 1938; Madison: University of Wisconsin Press, 1965.

Muir's early years, as seen from the vantage point of a seventy-year-old, appear as a drama of emergence: innate love of wild things and wild places, and freedom of spirit, survive punishingly narrow circumstances.

————. *Studies in the Sierra. See* Colby, William E., ed.

————. *A Thousand-Mile Walk to the Gulf.* Boston: Houghton Mifflin, 1916, 1981.

This is a journal record of Muir's first great solo adventure, a hike from southern Indiana to the Gulf Coast of Florida in the fall of 1867. Less polished literarily than Muir's other works, it records his delight in new botanical scenes and, most interestingly, his growing philosophical independence.

———. *The Yosemite.* New York: Century, 1912; Garden City, N.Y.: Doubleday, 1962.

A guidebook that names the most spectacular features and directs interested walkers to them, but also urges readers to realize the spiritual dimensions of a sacred place. The book concludes with a passionate, biblically thundering defense of Hetch Hetchy as wilderness that ought to be left alone, undammed. *See also* Engberg, Robert, and Donald Wesling, eds.

Murie, Adolph (1899–1973). *The Ecology of the Coyote in the Yellowstone.* U.S. National Park Service, Fauna Series, no. 4. Washington: U.S. Government, 1940.

An important contribution to the adoption of a more ecological point of view in the National Park Service's attitude toward predation. The author walked the back country, observing the behavior of coyotes and documenting their diet by examining several hundred scats. A "base-line" type of study that should be read in conjunction with Dobie's *The Voice of the Coyote* (see p. 415) and Leydet's *The Coyote, Defiant Songdog of the West* (p. 432).

———. *The Grizzlies of Mount McKinley.* Scientific Monograph Series, no. 14. Washington: U.S. Government, 1981; Seattle: University of Washington Press, 1981.

A natural history and historical treatment based upon many seasons in Denali, and written with a depth of feeling and understanding not always seen in professional reports:

"On our initial day in the field in McKinley National Park in 1922, my brother and I were crossing from Jenny Creek over a rise to Savage River on our way to the head of the river. In those days there was no road, the park was all a blessed wilderness, and I have often thought since what a wonderful people we would have been if we had wanted to keep it that way."

———. *A Naturalist in Alaska.* New York: Devin-Adair, 1961.

Encounters with wildlife, showing what kind of adventures a person might have, and what sense of nature and wilderness he or she might develop, if willing to spend a lifetime in the field.

———. *The Wolves of Mount McKinley.* U.S. National Park Service, Fauna Series, no. 5. Washington: U.S. Government, 1944; Seattle: University of Washington Press, 1985.

The first extended scientific study of wolves in the wild, conducted (in the days before radio collars and aerial tracking) by going out and watching and listening.

Murie, Margaret (1902–   ). *Two in the Far North.* New York: Knopf, 1962.

The author gives a vivid reminiscence of her early life in Alaska, her marriage to Olaus Murie, and several of their wilderness trips together, including one to the Sheenjek River in 1956. The feel of untrammeled country and of caring, uncrowded human relationships is strong in these pages.

Murie, Olaus (1889–1963). *The Elk of North America.* Harrisburg, Pa.: Stackpole, 1951, 1957; Jackson, Wyo.: Teton Bookshop, 1979.
An authoritative natural history, with a clear presentation of the historical-
political record and a consideration of the impacts of modern settlement
upon a formerly wide-ranging species. The author's sense of what might
constitute intelligent management of a wilderness animal in a nonwil-
derness world is the result of long pondering of a difficult, many-sided
subject.

————. *Journeys to the Far North.* Palo Alto: The Wilderness Society and
American West Publishing, 1973.
Over a span of forty-seven years of field work, the author made trips to
Labrador, the Hudson Bay country, and several parts of Alaska, studying
wildlife where it lived and experiencing the challenges of the old-time
naturalist's way of life. The essays and journal entries here record explicitly
what many of Murie's technical and professional papers could not dwell
upon: his powerful feelings for wilderness and his artistic response to line,
color, and sound.

Murie, Olaus, and Margaret E. Murie. *Wapiti Wilderness.* New York: Knopf,
1966.
A sequel to *Two in the Far North,* covering the authors' life together in
Jackson Hole, Wyoming, with a strong sense of place. This book contains
some of Olaus Murie's best plain-style writing, and conveys throughout
the Muries' deep response to wild country.

Murphy, Robert Cushman (1887–1973). *Fish-Shape Paumanok.* Philadelphia:
American Philosophical Society, 1964.
A brilliantly ordered lecture on some of the major factors that shaped the
natural history of Long Island, from glaciation to the 1960s, with particular
stress on the effects of Euro-American settlement and population growth
over the past three centuries.

Murphy, Robert W. (1902–1971). *The Peregrine Falcon.* Boston: Houghton
Mifflin, 1963.
The first year in the life of a female peregrine, hatched on the Barren
Grounds of Canada. After the arctic summer, she flies southward into a
strange, dangerous world crowded with humans. The story is told credibly
from the falcon's point of view.

Nabhan, Gary (1952–   ). *The Desert Smells Like Rain: A Naturalist in Papago
Indian Country.* San Francisco: North Point, 1982.
A description of the old ways of the Papago Indians, stressing their adaptations to seasonal abundance and scarcity and their knowledge of the
desert's fine points. The Papagos live in "raw intimacy" with the dry land,
and take nothing for granted.

————. *Gathering the Desert.* Tucson: University of Arizona Press, 1985.
Although the author describes edible plants of the Sonoran Desert, his
focus expands from natural history to a general consideration of the ways
we get our food and what this tells of our whole inhabitation of the earth.
"Gathering" here means taking in, trying to understand, and being ready
in the mind.

BIBLIOGRAPHY

Nelson, Richard K. (1941–   ). *Make Prayers to the Raven: A Koyukon View of the Northern Forest*. Chicago: University of Chicago Press, 1983.

An account of research in Alaska in the 1970s, expressed in terms of what might be called "deep anthropology": "Through the Koyukon, I became aware of a rich and eloquent natural history that extends into realms unknown or ignored in my own culture." "Subsistence" and the natural history knowledge it depends upon are seen here as a fundamentally spiritual way of life.

Nuttall, Thomas (1786–1859). *A Journal of Travels into the Arkansa Territory, During the Year 1819*. Philadelphia: Thos. H. Palmer, 1821; reprinted as vol. 13 in Reuben Gold Thwaites, ed., *Early Western Travels*. Cleveland: Arthur H. Clark, 1905.

Extensive notes on frontier settlements, Indians, and the flora of both riverine forest and prairie. Nuttall forgot his gun at least once, and was known to use the barrel as a digging stick. Parts of this journal have a Garden-of-Eden flavor. Nuttall exulted in the flowering prairie.

———. *A Manual of the Ornithology of the United States and Canada*. Cambridge: Hilliard and Brown, 1832; Boston: Hilliard, Gray, 1840.

The standard "bird book" for most of the 19th century. The introduction (see pp. 143–171) is an important ecological essay, and several of the descriptions are enlivened by Nuttall's extensive field experience and his good ear for songs and calls. *See also* Michaux, F. André, and Thomas Nuttall, p. 436.

Ogburn, Charlton (1911–   ). *The Adventure of Birds*. New York: Morrow, 1976.

What is it about birds, Ogburn asks, that "gave them meaning to man, in the needs of his soul"? Ogburn attempts no abstract formulation, but answers the question from the inside by revealing his own grand passion, a life passion, for birds. This feeling makes the chapters on avian physiology and behavior come alive; here, and in a most fascinating essay on bird song, Ogburn enlarges and poeticizes these subjects with a sense of earth and woods and weather. Much of the book derives from the author's own experience, a good deal of that in the vicinity of Washington, D.C.

———. *The Winter Beach*. New York: Morrow, 1966; Simon & Schuster, 1971; Morrow (Quill), 1979.

Winter tours of Mt. Desert Island, Cape Ann, Cape Cod, Long Island, Assateague, and the Outer Banks, with informed commentary on the areas' geological history and present ecological condition. The quiet (all of these East Coast areas are crowded in summer), the sense of impending storm, and the hardiness of wintering birds are prominent themes, as is the meretriciousness of "development." The author also speculates on the ultimate philosophical origins of the calamitous changes he recounts.

Olson, Sigurd F. (1899–1982). *Listening Point*. New York: Knopf, 1958.

Home in the North Woods, on a point of shelving granite at the edge of a lake bordered with pines and birches. The sounds come clearly — far-off rapids in the quiet of the night, the call of a loon, and the distance-sweetened hooting of a steam locomotive. The peacefulness of wild country is conveyed well by Olson's unadorned sentences.

———. *Runes of the North.* New York: Knopf, 1963.

Runes, to Olson, are narratives with the touch of the wilderness, awakening the "inner world," the "earth wisdom which since the beginning of man's rise from the primitive has nourished his visions and dreams." The personal accounts here come from northern lands — northern waters, more precisely — from Minnesota to Alaska, and speak of the elemental attractiveness of clean lakeside rock, clear water, wind in the pines, and the voice of the loon.

———. *The Singing Wilderness.* New York: Knopf, 1956.

The Quetico-Superior country of northern Minnesota and Ontario, still a wilderness, sings to the spirit: " . . . the music can even be heard in the soft guttering of an open fire or in the beat of rain on a tent, and sometimes not until long afterward when, like an echo out of the past, you know it was there in some quiet place or when you were doing some simple thing in the out-of-doors." Here Olson records moments like that in his notably straightforward prose, arranging them on the calendar of the northern seasons.

Packard, Winthrop (1862–1943). *Wild Pastures.* Boston: Small, Maynard, 1909.

The soul of gentility. "The most beautiful place which can be found on earth of a June morning is a New England pasture. . . ." The author noted, however, that the "trolley tripper" had come to even the most secluded ponds near the hallowed pastures, and now "builds his bungalows on its shore, sinks his tin cans in its waters, and scares the bullfrogs with his phonograph."

———. *Wildwood Ways.* Boston: Small, Maynard, 1909.

Pleasant rambles with a *Boston Transcript* columnist, out into the winter countryside. Packard made forthright, copious use of the pathetic fallacy, and looked always for what could quicken the sense of magic or what he called "fairyland." But he also paid close attention to the building of a hornets' nest, and protested against the pollution of streams.

———. *Wood Wanderings.* Boston: Small, Maynard, 1910.

Relaxed, agreeable, genteel essays, mostly about rural and semirural parts of eastern Massachusetts. "Among Autumn Leaves" has some fine descriptions of trees and colors.

Page, Jake (1936–   ). *Pastorale: A Natural History of Sorts.* New York: Norton, 1985.

Observations on keeping pets, gardening, and modern technology, and on various curiosities of nature and hair-splitting predilections of human nature, such as the American Ornithologists' Union's imperial re-naming of several bird species. Much of the commentary is written with wry wit, and most of it is drawn from the author's country life on an acre in Virginia.

Peattie, Donald Culross (1898–1964). *An Almanac for Moderns.* New York: Putnam's, 1935; Boston: David R. Godine, 1980.

In 1950, Joseph Wood Krutch thought that Peattie was "perhaps the most widely read of all contemporary American nature writers." The *Almanac* consists of 365 one-page essays, most suggested by the date or season (see p. 269). Many reveal the author's concern with evolution and other theories of life's origin and development. He interweaves thoughts on philosophical matters with descriptions of bird song and the progression of the seasons, and with excellent thumbnail sketches of figures like Linnaeus, Thoreau, and Muir, occasioned by their birthdays. The book is for "moderns" by virtue of its up-to-date understanding of the natural universe and its realization that science has changed the very ground of thought.

————. *A Book of Hours*. New York: Putnam's, 1937.
One contemplative spring day: the special, natural quality of each of the hours, as marked by the activity of birds and animals, and recorded in the mythic, anciently derived thoughts of men. At each hour something is noted that might, to a receptive mind, reveal the meaningfulness abiding in the world.

————. *Flowering Earth*. New York: Putnam's, 1939.
A vision of earth as knit together by the "green society" of plants that makes animal life possible. In this essay on ecology, a strongly participative point of view (which makes this book something different from mere autobiography) enlivens the text. Peattie makes topics such as photosynthesis indubitably real, and also miraculous.

————. *A Natural History of Trees of Eastern and Central America*. Boston: Houghton Mifflin, 1950; New York: Bonanza Books, n.d.
An immensely detailed handbook, giving clear descriptions (including a key to genera and species) and full historical information. For certain species of large utilitarian importance, such as white pine and sugar maple, the descriptions amount to essays in human ecology.

————. *A Natural History of Western Trees*. Boston: Houghton Mifflin, 1953.
The first words of this 750-page manual are "The sylva of western North America is the most impressive and humanly significant in the world." The text, both poetically evocative and deep with scholarly information, lives up to the charge implicit in those words.

————. *The Road of a Naturalist*. Boston: Houghton Mifflin, 1941; G. K. Hall, 1986.
The "road" here is the author's life, described in terms of formative moments, and also, concurrently, an account of a trip by car through several western habitat types. "Since Walden," the penultimate chapter, offers reflections on nature writing in which Peattie defends science and realism. In the shadow of impending war (World War II), science and realism seemed to the author the most substantial grounds for hope.

Perrin, Noel (1927–   ). *First Person Rural: Essays of a Sometime Farmer*. New York: Penguin, 1980.
Emphasis on practical matters, described with a droll, self-deprecating attitude, as Perrin learns how to choose a pickup truck, sell firewood in New York City (a funny tale), and buy a chainsaw.

————. *Second Person Rural: More Essays of a Sometime Farmer.* Boston: Godine, 1980; New York: Penguin, 1981.

There is relaxed wit here, much of it playing off the contrast between native New Englander and recent arrival, and an occasional sharp comment serving to keep the back-to-the-country scene firmly real.

————. *Third Person Rural: Further Essays of a Sometime Farmer.* Boston: Godine, 1983.

Regional mystique is very evident in these pieces, but not slavishly revered. The "Country Calendar" is a record of the New England seasons, as the author has known them, acutely and practically. The subsequent essays, gathered from various journals, continue Perrin's humorous, astute autobiography and his examination of farm and country mores.

Peterson, Roger Tory (1908–   ). *Birds Over America.* New York: Dodd, Mead, 1948.

Birding rambles from many parts of the country, showing that the sense of discovery inherent in birding is there even for an authority. Peterson observes, "The appeal of birds seems to be greater the more life is restrained." Illustrated with over a hundred photos by the author.

Platt, Rutherford (1894–1975). *The Great American Forest.* Englewood Cliffs, N.J.: Prentice-Hall, 1965.

Annie Dillard has called this "one of the most interesting books ever written." Done in an energetic, informal style, it covers forest ecology, the mechanics of water and trace-element transport, photosynthesis, and the importance of soil and humus; interspersed with this information are several dramatic renderings of historical incidents (such as Alexander Mackenzie's great overland trip to the Pacific in 1793) that took place in forested country. The final chapter, "Our Vanishing Wilderness," is a passionate cry for preservation.

————. *This Green World.* New York: Dodd, Mead, 1942.

A course in botany, taught with enthusiasm. Platt creates a large, ecological understanding of what a plant is and does. A simple and useful key to tree identification is included.

Powell, John Wesley (1834–1902). *The Exploration of the Colorado River.* Washington: U.S. Government, 1875; Chicago: University of Chicago Press, 1957; New York: Dover, 1961.

A present-tense account of the great downriver adventure of Powell and his men in 1869, full of drama and suspense. Powell appreciated the splendor and sublimity of the great canyons he drifted through.

Proenneke, Richard. *One Man's Wilderness.* Edited by Sam Keith. Anchorage: Alaska Northwest, 1973.

Proenneke did what many have dreamed of: he built a cabin by himself in the wilderness of the Alaska Peninsula and lived sensibly and well for many years, abiding by the constraints of the land and weather. His journal reflects calmness and practicality and a deep, compassionate interest in wildlife.

Pruitt, William O., Jr. (1922–   ). *Animals of the North.* New York: Harper & Row, 1967.

Pruitt shows the "rugged" North in its true fragility, via narratives describing what a sharply seasonal life is like for voles, hares, wolves, caribou, and others. The "Moose People" of former times are contrasted pointedly with modern-day invaders having little or no knowledge of taiga and tundra ecology.

Pyle, Robert Michael. *Wintergreen: Listening to the Land's Heart.* New York: Scribner's, 1986; Boston: Houghton Mifflin, 1988.

The author lives among the Willapa Hills, a small, cut-over range near the mouth of the Columbia River, a place not much studied by naturalists nor hiked in by recreationists. In the tradition of Gilbert White of Selborne, Pyle finds much to study and enjoy on his chosen home ground. He also finds much to lament, in particular the brutal destructiveness of clearcut logging carried on by corporate giants. Though the area has been ravaged, and its human culture, now that the logging boom is over, appears "senescent," its grass does revive in beautiful greenness each winter, a metaphor for hope.

Quammen, David (1948–   ). *Natural Acts: A Sidelong View of Science & Nature.* New York: Schocken, 1985.

Most of the pieces here are from the author's columns in *Outside* magazine. Quammen has an eye for odd facts, and takes delight in revealing how even the oddest may become instructive of nature's ways. The essays are written in an informal, "sidelong" manner; Quammen, whose main vocation is writing novels, states that he is a follower of science rather than a scientist.

Ribaut, Jean (c. 1520–1565). *The Whole & True Discouerye of Terra Florida.* A facsimile reprint of the London edition of 1563. Deland, Fla.: The Florida State Historical Society, 1927.

Cruising northward along the Florida coast in May, 1562, Ribaut (in good European explorer fashion) named the rivers he came upon: the "Seine," the "Somme," the "Loire," etc. But at another level he responded deeply to the teeming wildlife of "this incomperable lande," and to its utter, and as he saw it, God-"endued" wildness.

Rich, Louise Dickinson (1903–   ). *The Natural World of Louise Dickinson Rich.* New York: Dodd, Mead, 1962.

Essays covering the author's life in three environments — southeastern Massachusetts; northwestern Maine, where she spent fifteen years in wild country; and finally the coast of Maine, where she moved after her husband's death. Rich displays humor and a slightly ironic view of herself as a countrywoman, and quietly reflects on our place in the natural scheme of things: "Perhaps all [of man's] other achievements are less than this, that he watches, and makes the record, and tries to find the meaning."

———. *We Took to the Woods.* Philadelphia: Lippincott, 1942.

A full life, lived with relish, in northwestern Maine: pines, water, storms, and the delicious quiet after a forty-inch snowfall; hot summer days, "characters," and making-do.

Richardson, Wyman (1896–1953). *The House on Nauset Marsh.* New York: Norton, 1955.

Brief essays on life at a vacation place in Cape Cod, by a Boston physician and Harvard Medical School professor. Encounters with birds, including several with the rare gyrfalcon, tally the seasons.

Roberts, David (1943–). *Moments of Doubt, and Other Mountaineering Writings*. Seattle: The Mountaineers, 1986.
A collection of twenty essays spanning the author's career as a climber and stressing motivations and feelings — the "human element." The title essay recounts, soberly, the climbing accidents that Roberts has witnessed or been a part of.

———. *The Mountain of My Fear*. New York: Vanguard, 1968.
An ascent of Mt. Huntington in the Alaska Range, rendered in intense prose: the author describes "an unwitnessable challenge in an inhuman place," where a snow cave illuminated by candles "seemed the only island of safety in a limitless sea of night."

Robinson, Rowland Evans (1833–1900). *In New England Fields and Woods*. Boston: Houghton Mifflin, 1896; Rutland, Vt.: Charles E. Tuttle, 1937.
Sinclair Lewis, in a Foreword to the 1937 edition, praised Robinson's work for keeping alive the "simplicities of the old democratic life" found in the country in Vermont. The sketches here cover the seasonal changes and some of the familiar birds and animals of Vermont, and describe an excursion to view once again the vivid and whole woods of youth, only to find them logged off.

Roosevelt, Theodore (1858–1919). *Hunting Trips of a Ranchman: Hunting Trips on the Prairie and in the Mountains*. New York: The Review of Reviews Company, 1904 (Statesman Edition). Originally published by Co-operative Publication Society, New York, 1882, and by Putnam's, New York, 1885.
There are hints of the condition of the northern plains in the 1880s — bison and wolves almost gone, coyotes rare, elk diminishing rapidly — and some natural history information, such as the habits of sharp-tailed grouse, but the weight of detail here is on the techniques of the hunt.

———. *The Wilderness Hunter*. New York: Putnam's, 1893.
Although Roosevelt boasts that "it has been [his] good-luck to kill every kind of game properly belonging to the United States," he tempers his enthusiasm with a certain amount of restraint: "It is always lawful to kill dangerous or noxious animals, like the bear, cougar, and wolf; but other game should only be shot when there is need of the meat, or for the sake of an unusually fine trophy."

Roueche, Berton (1911–). *The River World and Other Explorations*. New York: Harper & Row, 1978.
Essays that first appeared in *The New Yorker*, including interesting accounts of the fossil beds in Florissant, Colorado, bananas, apples, and an exciting ocean voyage with a group of Eskimos.

———. *What's Left: Reports on a Diminishing America*. Boston: Little, Brown, 1969.
These essays, which originally appeared in *The New Yorker*, have a point: some beautiful places (such as the C. & O. towpath along the Potomac

River, the Islandia Keys in Florida, and the Current River in the Ozarks) are indeed "left," but urgently in need of protection.

Rowell, Galen (1940–   ), ed. *The Vertical World of Yosemite.* Berkeley: The Wilderness Press, 1974.

An anthology of writing about climbing that offers more than vertigo and derring-do.

Rudloe, Jack. *The Living Dock at Panacea.* New York: Knopf, 1977.

Engaging narratives based on Rudloe's marine-specimen business in the fishing village of Panacea, Florida. Adventures featuring sharks and heavy weather, coping with bureaucracy and barnacles, and other elements in the working day of the author provide natural history information and show the writer's sense of wonder at the Gulf's abundant life. Upon inspection, the company dock itself is revealed as an interesting ecosystem.

———. *Time of the Turtle.* New York: Knopf, 1979.

Personal encounters with sea turtles are the framework here for the author's presentation of the natural history of these animals, their powerful presence in folklore, and their too-often shabby treatment at the hands of *Homo sapiens.* A brief but telling description of Haiti, where Rudloe had gone to look for the beautiful hawksbill turtle, presages a world overcrowded with desperately needy humans.

Rusho, W. L., ed. *Everett Ruess: Vagabond for Beauty.* Layton, Utah: Gibbs M. Smith, 1983.

The solitary wanderings (1914–1935?) of Everett Ruess in the desert remain emblematic of the quest for wilderness and the ultimate. In this "life and letters," Ruess's artistic talent and moral sincerity come through as clearly as the country he walked and rode through.

Russell, Franklin (1922–   ). *The Hunting Animal.* New York: Harper & Row, 1983.

Narratives on hunting, stalking, predation, and aloneness. Gradually the picture widens to suggest the deep importance of predation in maintaining healthy ecosystems, and beyond that to speculate on the kinds of bonds that may exist between hunted and hunter.

———. *Searchers at the Gulf.* New York: Norton, 1970.

Fictionalized and poeticized natural history of the Gulf of St. Lawrence, built on the central metaphor of the Gulf itself as a super-organism. Russell brings out the time-tested synchronicity of all aspects of the ecosystem. "Interdependence was the touchstone. . . ."

———. *Watchers at the Pond.* New York: Knopf, 1961; Boston: Godine, 1981.

Alternately sliding into the viewpoints of red-tailed hawk, snowshoe hare, muskrat, or raven, then giving information in straight, expository style, the author makes the complex life of the pond intensely interesting. This novelistic treatment has been criticized on certain factual points.

———. *Wings on the Southwind: Birds & Creatures of the Southern Wetlands.* Birmingham, Ala.: Oxmoor House, 1984.

A celebration of the teeming marshes, bayous, bays, lagoons, swamps, and lakes of the South, particularly the Gulf Coast — "places where the lushness of American nature is still on display." With photographs by Thase Daniel.

Russell, Osborne (1814–1892). *Journal of a Trapper*. Lincoln: University of Nebraska Press, n.d.

There are some poetic appreciations of wilderness here, apparently written in the field (that is, the Rocky Mountain wilderness, 1834–1843). The appendix consists of quaint thumbnail sketches of various animals this trapper encountered. A sensitive journal; evidence that at least one mountain man was not hampered in his responses by the necessities of a dangerous way of life.

Ryden, Hope. *America's Last Wild Horses*. New York: Dutton, 1970. Rev. and updated ed., 1978.

A history of the wild horse in America and a survey of the modern controversy, written with enthusiasm and forthrightly stated personal involvement: "When I first saw wild horses sweeping across a mountain slope, tails and manes streaming, screaming with an exuberance never heard in any pasture, my whole view of modern America brightened."

———. *God's Dog: A Celebration of the North American Coyote*. New York: Viking, 1979.

A highly sympathetic natural history and tribute, much of it based on old-fashioned field observation.

Schaller, George B. (1933–   ). *The Stones of Silence: Journeys in the Himalaya*. New York: Viking, 1980.

High adventures (1969–1975), described in a sober, modest, intense style. The author's quest to observe a snow leopard is a quest to know the complete wilderness. After a fruitless night camped near the object of his search, he writes, "I had learned nothing new that night, but the hours of silence, the celestial beauty of the mountains in the moonlight, and, above all, the knowledge of having been a part of the snow leopard's world filled me with quiet ecstasy."

———. *The Year of the Gorilla*. Chicago: University of Chicago Press, 1964; New York: Ballantine, 1965, 1971.

The result of a pioneering investigation, this book is a demonstration of what may be accomplished in a humane, non-intrusive way in the study of animals, and is a testimony to scientific openness on the part of the author. It stands with Adolph Murie's *The Wolves of Mount McKinley* as revisionist natural history. Schaller's own response to the gorillas and their wilderness home is integral to the account.

Scherman, Katharine. *Spring on an Arctic Island*. Boston: Little, Brown, 1956.

Scherman and her husband, with half a dozen other birders and scientists, spent six eventful weeks on Bylot Island, north of Baffin, watching and listening to the incredible burgeoning of life that marks the Arctic spring. Although the tundra looked "depressingly barren" at first sight, she later wrote, "I can feel it under my feet, bouncy and full of life."

Schorger, A. W. (1884–1972). *The Passenger Pigeon: Its Natural History and Extinction*. Madison: University of Wisconsin Press, 1955; Norman: University of Oklahoma Press, 1973.

A necessary text, and necessarily a sad one:

"Viewed from all angles, the passenger pigeon was the most impressive

species of bird that man has known. Elegant in form and color, graceful
and swift of flight, it moved about and nested in such enormous numbers as to confound the senses. Equally dramatic was its disappearance
from the earth due to the thoughtlessness and insatiable greed of man."

Seton, Ernest Thompson (1860–1946). *The Arctic Prairies*. New York: Scribner's, 1911.
A strongly flavored account of travel and adventure in the vast, wild
neighborhood of Great Slave Lake. The subtitle is "A Canoe-Journey of
2,000 Miles in Search of the Caribou" — plenty of opportunity for Seton
to demonstrate his sincere love of beauty and wildness, especially in beautiful portraits of his favorite rivers, the Nyarling and the Little Buffalo.
He also displays sarcastic wit (usually at the Indians' expense), rails at
mosquitoes, and usually shows himself in good light.

————. *Lives of Game Animals*. 4 vols. Garden City, N.Y.: Doubleday, Doran,
1929.
A complete natural history, constructed of data on size, habits, distribution,
"Record Heads" (of hoofed animals), food, enemies, diseases, and more,
with illustrative narratives of the author's own experiences, these last given
with his customary verve.

Sharp, Dallas Lore (1870–1929). *The Face of the Fields*. Boston: Houghton
Mifflin, 1911.
This is perhaps Sharp's most substantial and penetrating book, containing
essays on death and fear, on his own growth in self-knowledge when forced
to deal with skunks' depredations upon his chickens, on literary nature
writing, on John Burroughs (whom he compares more than favorably with
Thoreau), and on what has later come to be known as the "tragedy of the
commons."

————. *The Lay of the Land*. Boston: Houghton Mifflin, 1908.
Rambles on the author's fourteen-acre Massachusetts farm, and thoughts
on the joy and simplicity of country living: "A farm, of all human habitations, is most of a home. . . ." Sharp takes particular delight in coziness, as
exemplified in animals' preparations for winter and his own provisions for
the season as a farmer.

————. *A Watcher in the Woods*. New York: Century, 1903.
Sharp appreciated the near and accessible scenes that included orchards
and woods roads. Thirty-six species of birds nested within a quarter-mile
of his New England home, and he thought a similar density and variety
could not be achieved in the wilderness. Thus, he felt, there was hope for
a harmonious fitting-in of man.

————. *The Whole Year Round*. Boston: Houghton Mifflin, 1915.
A gathering of essays arranged by the seasons and directed at younger
readers, advising them of special delights to watch for.

Sheldon, Charles (1867–1928). *The Wilderness of Denali: Explorations of a
Hunter-naturalist in Northern Alaska*. New York: Scribner's, 1930.
Although Sheldon killed an appalling number of animals, he was the
earliest promoter of national park status for the Mt. McKinley (Denali)
area. He also had a strong yen for the sublime:

"Alone in an unknown wilderness hundreds of miles from civilization and high on one of the world's most imposing mountains, I was deeply moved by the stupendous mass of the great upheaval, the vast extent of the wild areas below, the chaos of the unfinished surfaces still in process of moulding, and by the crash and roar of the mighty avalanches."

————. *The Wilderness of the North Pacific Coast Islands.* New York: Scribner's, 1912.

Independently wealthy, the author was able to devote several months of each year to hunting. In this book, he describes quests for wapiti, grizzly bears, and caribou. Although he shot a number of grizzlies, he thought that if the bears were exterminated, it would be a deep loss to the wilderness — "perhaps the loss of its very essence."

————. *The Wilderness of the Upper Yukon: A Hunter's Explorations for Wild Sheep in Sub-Arctic Mountains.* New York: Scribner's, 1911.

Self-consciously aware of contradiction in his values, Sheldon declared his love for the animals he killed. A frighteningly assiduous trophy hunter and museum collector, he could foresee a time when lovers of the wilderness would go there strictly for contemplation. This book records his response to the untracked mountains of the Yukon, where he hunted in 1904.

Skutch, Alexander F. (1904–   ). *A Bird Watcher's Adventures in Tropical America.* Austin: University of Texas Press, 1977.

Travels in the neotropics, before the advent of good roads and field guides. Skutch did not use a gun, nor was he out to make a big list; he moved at a leisurely, studying pace and came into close acquaintance with the lush habitats described here.

————. *The Imperative Call: A Naturalist's Quest in Temperate and Tropical America.* Gainesville: University of Florida Press, 1979.

Travels and studies in an autobiographical framework. Skutch describes his good fortune in being able to respond to the call of nature study, and to know tropical environments before their modern decimation. "A Wanderer's Harvest" describes his non-intrusive methods of field study — tedious, but fulfilling.

————. *Life of the Woodpecker.* Santa Monica: Ibis, 1985.

A natural history of one of the most interesting and attractive bird families, delineating habits, habitats, and ecological information on several prominent species.

————. *Nature Through Tropical Windows.* Berkeley: University of California Press, 1983.

The windows of the author's home at Los Cusingos in Costa Rica are screenless and glassless, enabling unobstructed views of the forest outside and the birds who nest close by. Close observation, and consideration of such matters as the ecology of size, the "gentler side of nature," and altruism distinguish this interesting book. "Windows of the Mind," the concluding chapter, is a meditation on isolation and its possible cures.

Slocum, Joshua (1844–1909). *Sailing Alone Around the World.* New York: Century, 1900; Dover, 1956.

The critic Van Wyck Brooks called this book a "nautical equivalent" to *Walden,* and Slocum asserted after his epic circumnavigation of 1895–1898 that he had been "in touch with nature as few have ever been," but the great bulk of his writing is wrapped up in practical details of seamanship — getting from one place to another. He does describe how whales catch small fish, and records that the farther he went, the less able he was to kill, even for the table. Slocum wrote with understated wit. For many readers, *Sailing Alone* is a compelling statement of self-reliance.

Smith, John (1580–1631). *The Generall Historie of Virginia, New England & the Summer Isles, Together with the True Travels, Adventures and Observations, and a Sea Grammar.* 2 vols. London: Michael Sparkes, 1624; New York: Macmillan, 1907.

In major part a promotional tract, this narrative nevertheless presents information rarely encountered elsewhere, such as the size of the Indians' cultivated fields: "some 20 acres, some 40. some 100. some 200." Also: "Neare their habitations is little small wood or old trees on the ground by reason of their burning of them for fire. So that a man may gallop a horse amongst these woods any way, but where the creekes or Rivers shall hinder."

Snyder, Gary (1930–   ). *Earth House Hold.* New York: New Directions, 1969.

Early journals from a fire lookout, along with several penetrating essays, including "Poetry and the Primitive" and the influential "Buddhism and the Coming Revolution," place this book within the philosophically radical wing of American nature writing. An important, influential text.

———. *Turtle Island.* New York: New Directions, 1974.

A book of poetry in the main, this volume also contains "Four Changes" and "The Wilderness," two significant essays on mind, nature, and human ecology.

Stadtfeld, Curtis K. (1935–   ). *From the Land and Back.* New York: Scribner's, 1972.

A heartfelt remembrance of the ways and values of the family farm: "We remember forever that we were once a part of something whole. . . ."

Stansbury, Howard (1806–1863). *Exploration and Survey of the Valley of the Great Salt Lake of Utah.* Philadelphia: Lippincott, Grambo, 1852.

A difficult survey, during which, at times, the author had to dole out water to the party's mules by the cupful. In spite of heat, cold, wind, and thirst, Stansbury appreciated the severe beauty of the Great Basin desert.

Stegner, Wallace (1909–   ). *The Sound of Mountain Water.* Garden City, N.Y.: Doubleday, 1969; Lincoln: University of Nebraska Press, 1985.

A collection of searching, humanistic essays on the broad theme of man and nature, including the quiet and unforgettable "Glen Canyon Submersus." A statement about the permanent flooding of Utah's Glen Canyon (behind Glen Canyon Dam) and the creation of Lake Powell, this essay might make even the most wilderness-indifferent pause.

Steinbeck, John (1902–1968). *The Log from the Sea of Cortez.* New York: Viking, 1951, 1962.

Originally published in 1941 as part of *Sea of Cortez*. A biological expedition to the Gulf of California, on which the author and his mentor Edward Ricketts discussed ecology, evolution, teleology, and much else. Of particular interest are the Darwinian, "nonteleological" conclusions the men reach.

Sugg, Redding S., Jr., ed. *The Horn Island Logs of Walter Inglis Anderson.* Memphis: Memphis State University Press, 1973.

The artist Walter Inglis Anderson (1903–1965) went to Horn Island, a barrier island between the Mississippi Sound and the Gulf of Mexico, quite frequently in the years between 1944 and 1965, using it as a hermitage. Its rich life, described here in his journals, supplied his appetite for images. Editor Sugg's phrase for Anderson is "a Robinson Crusoe with the inclinations of a St. Francis."

Swain, Roger B. (1949–   ). *Earthly Pleasures: Tales from a Biologist's Garden.* New York: Scribner's, 1981; Penguin, 1985.

In these essays from *Horticulture* magazine, the author begins with his small farm and garden in southern New Hampshire and weaves interconnections with all manner of topics, including dung beetles, lightning, road-salting, and energy use.

Teal, John (1929–   ), and Mildred Teal (1928–   ). *Life and Death of the Salt Marsh.* Boston: Little, Brown, 1969; New York: Ballantine, 1969.

A complex and thorough book, paying the tribute of close attention to the "green ribbon" of salt marshes along the East Coast of America. These marshes, "some of the most productive natural areas known," have been under-appreciated and often abused. This book's discussions on filling, pollution, and insect control are amazingly temperate, under the circumstances, but nonetheless alarming.

Teale, Edwin Way (1899–1980). *Autumn Across America.* New York: Dodd, Mead, 1956.

A Tealean journey — that is, relaxed, digressive, and eminently informative — from Cape Cod to the California coast, mostly in the northern tier of states. Thomas Nuttall's impressive contributions, the butterfly concentration at Point Pelee on Lake Erie, Kirtland's warbler in Michigan, and the life history of the pika are some of the many topics held up for the pleasure of leisurely inspection. A strong environmental consciousness surfaces in the author's remarks on the once-proposed Echo Park Dam in Utah.

———. *Journey Into Summer.* New York: Dodd, Mead, 1960.

From New England to the Colorado Rockies, via the Great Lakes, showing the immense variety of summers in America. Teale shows us the best way to travel by car: prepare well, with maps and extensive notes; go easy, looping around; and learn new things each day.

———. *The Lost Woods: Adventures of a Naturalist.* New York: Dodd, Mead, 1945.

Teale notes, "It is curious how some moments have abnormal vitality, how they live on in memory long after later events have faded from the mind." For Teale, the touchstone experience came on a winter day at his grandfather's farm in Indiana, when he and the old man went to the woods by sleigh to gather firewood. Years later, the author was unable to find the exact place — thus the title of this book — but his career, in effect, continually sought to re-create it. (During the journey recorded in *Autumn Across America,* Teale finally learned that the woods had been cut down in 1911).

————. *North with the Spring.* New York: Dodd, Mead, 1951.
Spring advances, gloriously, about fifteen miles per day northward through eastern America. Teale and his wife Nellie kept pace, covering some 17,000 miles and 23 states. The narrative is laced with a vast number of natural history facts and historical notes, recording well the drama of what for most observers is the most exciting season.

————. *Wandering Through Winter.* New York: Dodd, Mead, 1965.
The last in the "American Seasons" series, and the most given to reflection. The natural history information is just as rich as in the previous books — how sand dunes move, how shrikes and sparrow hawks (kestrels) space themselves out on their winter territories, how sleet is formed, and a great deal more — but there is a heightened sense of the historical moment, and more comment on man and nature. Teale warns, "Those who become aroused only when *man* is endangered become aroused too late."

Terres, John K. (1905–   ), ed. *Discovery: Great Moments in the Lives of Outstanding Naturalists.* Philadelphia: Lippincott, 1961.
"I believe that all naturalists at some time in their lives have had one great adventure, and that the shock, ecstasy, beauty, wonder, tragedy, or intellectual illumination of that moment, hour, or day, they carry with them the rest of their lives." Operating on that premise, Terres persuaded thirty-six naturalists to describe their own outstanding experiences. The sense of discovery is strong here; these adult experiences might be studied alongside those discussed in Edith Cobb's *The Ecology of Imagination in Childhood* (New York: Columbia University Press, 1977).

————. *From Laurel Hill to Siler's Bog: The Walking Adventures of a Naturalist.* New York: Hawthorn Books, 1969; Knopf, 1969.
An 800-acre nature preserve in North Carolina, taken in at a walking pace or better still from within a blind, becomes a wilderness of large proportions. Terres argues, and demonstrates here, that it is the receptive mind that makes the "Last Frontier." Informative natural history essays on foxes, flying squirrels, the golden mouse, turkeys, and others.

Thomas, Lewis (1913–   ). *The Lives of a Cell: Notes of a Biology Watcher.* New York: Viking, 1974; Bantam, 1975.
A justly famed book of essays. Thomas begins by noting that man's effort to imagine himself "above the rest of life" has been "his most consistent intellectual exertion down the millennia," and proceeds to describe hundreds of connections that demolish the fantasy of separateness while suggesting a beautiful vision of possibility in expanding consciousness.

————. *The Medusa and the Snail: More Notes of a Biology Watcher.* New York: Viking, 1979.

Brief but penetrating reflections, most of them originally published in *The New England Journal of Medicine,* showing how the study of nature can raise disturbing and humbling questions. The author is keenly aware of the limits of human consciousness and the changeableness of nature, and suggests by this awareness a properly humble position toward the world. Thomas states: "The only solid piece of scientific truth about which I feel totally confident is that we are profoundly ignorant about nature. Indeed, I regard this as the major discovery of the past hundred years of biology."

Thomson, Betty Flanders (1913–   ). *The Changing Face of New England.* New York: Macmillan, 1958; Boston: Houghton Mifflin, 1977.
An ecological history of a much-worked-over yet still appealing landscape. Thomson suggests something of the broad subject of the agency of man on earth in her description of tree succession on abandoned fields. She also responds personally to her subject, creating the "home" feeling of place. "Other plants turn red, but none quite equals the inner light of a sugar maple in full gold and scarlet glory." An absorbing and valuable study.

Thoreau, Henry David (1817–1862). *Cape Cod.* Boston: Ticknor and Fields, 1865; New York: Crowell, 1966.
Three long walks on Cape Cod, in 1849, 1850, and 1855, described with zest, humor, and sociable fellow-feeling for oldtimers. Thoreau's images, as in the opening scenes describing the remains of a shipwreck, are sharp with the sense of discovery. On the Great Beach, "ever and anon a higher wave caused us hastily to deviate from our path, and we looked back on our tracks filled with water and foam. The breakers looked like droves of a thousand wild horses of Neptune, rushing to the shore, with their white manes streaming far behind; and when at length the sun shone for a moment, their manes were rainbow-tinted."

——. *Journals.* Vols. 7–20 of *The Writings of Henry David Thoreau.* Boston: Houghton Mifflin, 1906; Layton, Utah: Gibbs M. Smith, 1984; new ed. (in progress). Princeton: Princeton University Press, 1981—.
The examined life, in the form of a kind of continuing letter to the higher self, and a continuing and intensifying study of nature. The entries of the later years have been criticized as too scientific or as reflecting a drying up of transcendental motivation, but William Howarth's *The Book of Concord: Thoreau's Life as a Writer* (New York: Viking, 1982) and Robert Richardson's *Henry Thoreau: A Life of the Mind* (Berkeley: University of California Press, 1986) point out that Thoreau was engaged in a high, sincere attempt to know himself and his place, a life project which simply needed science to be complete. (See selection, pp. 172–193.)

——. *The Maine Woods.* Boston: Ticknor and Fields, 1864; New York: Crowell, 1961, 1966; Princeton: Princeton University Press, 1972.
A record of three trips, in 1846, 1853, and 1857, on foot and in a "birch" into the wildest portion of New England. Thoreau was sharply conscious of the contrast between the shaggy wilderness of Maine and the smoothed landscapes back home in Concord. He watched his Indian guides closely,

and noted trees, flowers, moose, birds, and the techniques of route-finding. "You carried so much topography in your mind always. . . ." The "Ktaadn" section, describing an expedition to Mt. Katahdin that Thoreau undertook during his second summer at Walden, contains some of his most direct and spontaneous responses to wilderness.

―――. *Walden.* Boston: Ticknor and Fields, 1854; New York: Twayne, 1962 (Variorum Edition, edited by Walter Harding); Princeton: Princeton University Press, 1971.

A world-famous text on simple living as the means and the expression of enlightenment, and one of the purest appreciations of place and the natural that we have. This is a much-worked-on, clarified book which the author put through several drafts, but which retained through the course of refinement its original inspiration and force.

Thwaites, Reuben Gold (1853–1913), ed. *Original Journals of the Lewis and Clark Expedition, 1804–1806.* New York: Dodd, Mead, 1904–1905; Antiquarian Press, 1959.

A document rich in itself, and potent in its ability to suggest the measure of what has happened since. Meriwether Lewis's entries are often reflective and aesthetically sensitive, shaped in a way that approaches at times the intentional quality of more formal essays.

Torrey, Bradford (1843–1912). *Birds in the Bush.* Boston: Houghton Mifflin, 1885.

Pleasant bird rambles, mostly in the Boston area. The author had an excellent ear for bird calls and songs, and in a fine essay describes the opening of his eyes and ears by birds.

―――. *The Foot-Path Way.* Boston: Houghton Mifflin, 1892.

Genial, chatty essays for the most part, commenting on rural scenes the author walks through. But there is acid, too, in Torrey's outrage at hunting, particularly the shooting of shorebirds. "But a man of twenty, a man of seventy, shooting sanderlings, ring plovers, golden plovers, and whatever else comes in his way, not for money, nor primarily for food, but because he enjoys the work! 'A little lower than the angels!' "

Townsend, John Kirk (1809–1851). *Narrative of a Journey Across the Rocky Mountains, to the Columbia River, and a Visit to the Sandwich Islands, Chili, &c.* Philadelphia: Henry Perkins, 1839; also in Reuben Gold Thwaites, ed., *Early Western Travels,* vol. 21, Cleveland: Arthur H. Clark, 1905; Lincoln: University of Nebraska Press, 1978.

The author made the western crossing in the company of Thomas Nuttall in 1834. His account is smooth and urbane, and is focused on pictorial scenes, amounting to something like a tourist's-eye view of the West during the mountain-man era.

Traver, Robert [John Voelker] (1903–   ). *Anatomy of a Fisherman.* New York: McGraw-Hill, 1964; Santa Barbara and Salt Lake City: Peregrine Smith, 1978.

"I fish because I love to; because I love the environs where trout are found, which are invariably beautiful, and hate the environs where crowds of people are found, which are invariably ugly. . . ."

Trefil, James (1938–   ). *Meditations at 10,000 Feet: A Scientist in the Mountains*. New York: Scribner's, 1986.
Interesting lessons in geohistory, loosely based, in part, on walks in the Beartooth Mountains of Montana.
———. *A Scientist at the Seashore*. New York: Scribner's, 1984.
The edge of the sea as seen by a physicist pursuing "law," or the physical principles behind phenomena. "Something as ephemeral and inconsequential as a bubble in the foam leads us to consider the forces that hold the nucleus of the atom together."
Trimble, Stephen (1950–   ). *Longs Peak: A Rocky Mountain Chronicle*. Estes Park, Colo.: Rocky Mountain Nature Association, 1984.
Among local natural histories and nature guides, books most often sold in visitor centers and nearby bookstores, one may encounter not only useful facts and good photographs, but sometimes a deeper sense of the history and meanings of a place, and even a poetic apprehension of its sacredness. *Longs Peak* tells the ecological story of the famous mountain, and the human history (with particular detail on climbing), and goes on to suggest the significance of the peak as a numinous presence in our civilized, flatland lives.
Van Dyke, John Charles (1856–1932). *The Desert*. New York: Scribner's, 1901; Tucson: Arizona Historical Society, 1976; Layton, Utah: Peregrine Smith, 1980.
This is a primary text in the aesthetic and spiritual appreciation of wilderness, written out of solitude, illness, hardship, and exaltation: "What is it that draws us to the boundless and the fathomless? Why should the lovely things of earth — the grasses, the trees, the lakes, the little hills — appear trivial and insignificant when we come face to face with the sea or the desert or the vastness of the midnight sky?"
———. *The Grand Canyon of the Colorado*. New York: Scribner's, 1920.
The author is modest about how closely words or art may approach this particular subject, and his reticence creates an artistic distance from the subject that draws our attention. One of the more successful treatments of a canyon whose scale and wildness make it the archetype of the sublime.
———. *The Mountain*. New York: Scribner's, 1916.
"The great spaces of the wilderness have a quality of beauty about them that no panorama of civilized lands can equal or even suggest." One of the high points of this book is Van Dyke's impressionistic account of a long horseback journey across the plains of Montana toward the Rockies. The text also includes a good deal of the natural history of mountains: mountain-building forces, glaciers, avalanches, and the flora and fauna of high places.
———. *Nature For Its Own Sake*. New York: Scribner's, 1898.
Well-finished lectures on the aesthetics of the wild, with particular, loving attention to the quality of light on the high plains. Van Dyke saw wholeness as the *sine qua non* of beauty, and wholeness nowhere better represented than in wilderness. His writing recalls the Upper Mississippi thirty years earlier, when "all was quite as wild and primeval as one could wish, and

every traveller standing on the deck of the river steamer, as he ascended that stream felt the freshness of the air, the brightness of the light, the unmarred, the unbroken beauty of forest, bluff, and shining water."

———. *The Open Spaces.* New York: Scribner's, 1922.

In part an autobiography, this book emphasizes the mysterious but undeniable sense of connectedness and meaning that the author felt in wild, open situations. It also laments the coming of the automobile (Van Dyke was one of the first to foresee what it would do to Yosemite, for example) and presents, by the way almost, a good deal of natural history. "What a strange feeling, sleeping under the wide sky, that you belong only to the universe. You are back to your habitat, to your original environment, to your native heritage."

Wallace, David Rains (1945–   ). *The Dark Range: A Naturalist's Night Notebook.* San Francisco: Sierra Club, 1978.

Night makes wilderness more challenging, and the little-visited Yolla Bolly Mountains of northern California tend to compound the effect. Narratives of animal night-life in three habitat types are presented. The "Index to Animals and Plants" consists of wonderfully concise and informative definitions.

———. *Idle Weeds: The Life of a Sandstone Ridge.* San Francisco: Sierra Club, 1980.

Wallace narrates the natural history of a year on an "ordinary" wooded ridge in Ohio that has just recently been preserved. The opening and closing essays, characterizing the past and the possible futures of the ridge, are thoughtful.

———. *The Klamath Knot: Explorations of Myth and Evolution.* San Francisco: Sierra Club, 1983.

An essay on evolution, which Wallace calls "the great myth of modern times," illuminated and given specificity by the author's experience and study in the mountain wilderness of northwestern California. The reflections on evolutionary theory arise naturally from notes on the tangle of forested mountains described, making this one of the most definitely place-centered of books on biological theory.

———. *The Untamed Garden and Other Personal Essays.* Columbus: Ohio State University Press, 1986.

These "rambles" show a consistent, even-tempered sensibility. There is a good, nonrighteous investigation of an urban lake (Oakland's Lake Merritt), an interesting essay on the Absaroka–Beartooth Wilderness in Montana, and, in "The Nature of Nature Writing," a survey of the history of the genre and some reflection on its "quiet" revolutionary content.

Warner, William W. (1920–   ). *Beautiful Swimmers: Watermen, Crabs, and the Chesapeake Bay.* Boston: Little, Brown, 1976; New York: Penguin, 1977.

Local history within the ecological context, built on detailed narratives of the blue crab fishery, the kinds of human life founded on the Bay and its now-threatened abundance, and the natural history of the place itself.

Wheeler, William Morton (1865–1937). *Foibles of Insects and Men.* New York: Knopf, 1928.

The introduction to this collection of essays by the great entomologist discusses changing attitudes toward the study of insects, with observations on "Fundamentalists, spiritualists, anti-evolutionists and other confusionists with whom our modern world is so richly provided." "The Physiognomy of Insects" describes body and facial variation among insects, suggesting certain commonalities with human types. Of a variety of East Indian ant equipped with "huge eyes and clipping mandibles," Wheeler writes, "If there are Anthony Comstocks, movie censors and prohibition agents among the ants we might, perhaps, expect them to have just such faces." "Insect Parisitism and Its Peculiarities" and "A Study of the Guest Ant" similarly demonstrate the author's close observation and enlargement of his subjects with suggestive wit.

White, William Chapman (1903–1955). *Adirondack Country.* New York: Duell, Sloane, & Pearce, 1954.

Part of the "American Folkways" series, this survey emphasizes the history and local character of the region. It is also a record of human impacts, of course, and of at least partly successful preservation. Part 8, "Adirondack Year," is a calendar based on natural history.

Whitman, Walt (1819–1892). *Specimen Days.* Philadelphia: D. McKay, 1882; Boston: Godine, 1971.

This autobiography-by-vignette includes some lovely, sun-filled descriptions of summer days at Timber Creek in southern New Jersey, where the poet was recuperating from serious illness.

Williams, Samuel (1743–1817). *The Natural and Civil History of Vermont.* Walpole, N.H.: Thomas and Carlisle, 1794.

A scientifically minded minister, Williams made measurements of soil and air temperature on a regular basis, watched the behavior of animals closely (though he fell into some traditional errors), organized his book to give first and fundamental importance to environmental factors, and espoused a broad, non-anthropocentric outlook. A literate and sophisticated early American text, too often overlooked.

Williams, Terry Tempest. *Pieces of White Shell: A Journey to Navajoland.* New York: Scribner's, 1984.

The journey of a museum curator whose "knowledge of earth is literal," into a land where things are not that simple. "I quietly kept on walking," the author writes, and the eventual enlargement of view that she gains makes even a museum collection take on life.

Wilson, Alexander (1766–1813). *American Ornithology; or, the Natural History of the Birds of the United States.* 9 vols. Philadelphia: Bradford & Inskeep, 1808–1814; reprinted in 3 vols., New York: Collins & Co., and Philadelphia: Harrison Hall, 1828–1829.

The first large-scale, nearly complete treatment of American birds. Wilson's enthusiasm shines through these pages, showing the springs of motivation of nature study. Donald Culross Peattie wrote of Wilson: "As an observer his patience was infinite, his attention faultless; he had the gift of accuracy that lifts him right out of the rank of the dilettante into the highest realms of science." (See selection, pp. 120–125.)

Wilson, Edward O. (1929–   ). *Biophilia.* Cambridge: Harvard University Press, 1984.

Wilson's presentation of biology in a way that is simultaneously heartfelt and mechanistic will likely challenge some readers. His "rough map of innovation in science" begins thus: "You start by loving a subject." The starting point here is the author's tropical research, in particular his fascination with insect life.

Wood, William (flourished 1629–1635). *New England's Prospect.* London: I. Bellamie, 1634; Amherst: University of Massachusetts Press, 1977.

A keen and judicious observer of wildlife, soil fertility, and Indians, Wood looked steadily outward beyond the literal pale of the infant Puritan settlement. His account is refreshing for its point of view, which was quite unusual for the time, and is presented in sturdy, interesting prose. His description of a flight of passenger pigeons is a moving glimpse of the original America. (See selection, pp. 95–106.)

Wright, Billie. *Four Seasons North: A Journal of Life in the Alaskan Wilderness.* New York: Harper & Row, 1973.

The author describes the experiences she and her husband shared in the Brooks Range about a hundred miles above the Arctic Circle: living in a miner's cabin, laying in two or three caribou and a moose for their winter meat, trapping and shooting wolves that threatened to compete with them for food, picking berries, trying out new recipes. Mrs. Wright attains what she calls *koviashuktok,* the quality of being here and now in her environment. She warns against others trying the same life on for size — she believes the Arctic's "delicately balanced ecological life" could not take the impact.

Wright, Mabel Osgood (1859–1934). *The Friendship of Nature: A New England Chronicle of Birds and Flowers.* New York: Macmillan, 1894.

The months of nature's year, lovingly recounted with homey details: "eight acres of rolling ground, and in the centre a plainly cheerful house. . . ." The author subscribes to the agrarian theme — "Farms near at hand, farms on the slopes, farms standing boldly against the horizon, and over all the white wings of the dove of peace are folded" — but the main thing here is her ready response to light and wind and color, and the songs of birds, all contributing to a great and enveloping friendship with nature.

Wright, William H. (1856–1934). *The Grizzly Bear: The Narrative of a Hunter-Naturalist, Historical, Scientific and Adventurous.* New York: Scribner's, 1909.

Part 1 is history and taxonomy, and includes an account of the remarkable James Capen ("Grizzly") Adams; Part 2 covers the author's own often amazing experiences with bears, including several hunting expeditions; and Part 3, on the "character and habits of the grizzly," concludes with Wright's advice to the reader to go to the wilderness without a gun. "He will learn more about [the grizzly] in one season than he will in a lifetime of hunting to kill." This admonition was founded in the author's own experience.

Young, Louise B. (1919–   ). *The Blue Planet: A Celebration of Earth.* Boston: Little, Brown, 1983; New York: New American Library, 1984.

Young describes the earth as a whole, geophysically: "If we could watch a time-lapse movie of the planet's history, we could see an amazing drama of change and development: mountains being created and destroyed, sea-floor ejected along ocean ridges and consumed again at the trenches, canyons being carved by turbulent rivers, new continents split from old ones and set adrift to wander around the planet." The author provides just such a "time-lapse" account.

Zwinger, Ann (1925   ). *Beyond the Aspen Grove*. New York: Harper & Row, 1970, 1981.
West of Colorado Springs, on forty acres at an elevation of 8,300 feet, the author and her husband built a summer place, and she began to learn the natural history of the area. This book is a pleasant mixture of family reminiscences and botany and zoology notes, illustrated by Mrs. Zwinger's fine drawings.
———. *A Desert Country Near the Sea: A Natural History of the Cape Region of Baja California*. New York: Harper & Row, 1983.
The author wanders at a leisurely pace but with intense attention from mountaintop down to the undersea world, giving detailed accounts of several different habitats along the way. A land once regarded as barren is found to be astonishingly diverse and rich.
———. *Run, River, Run*. New York: Harper & Row, 1975.
The author walks and paddles the length of the Green River, from its origins high in the Wind River range of Wyoming to its confluence with the Colorado River in Utah. Along the way, she describes interesting elements in the river's natural history, names and analyzes threats to its integrity, and responds to solitude and wildness.
———. *Wind in the Rock*. New York: Harper & Row, 1978.
Rambles into five dramatic canyons in southern Utah, with particular attention to solitude, quiet, the very interesting natural history of the area, and the impact of modern man. Illustrated by the author's delicate, precise drawings.
Zwinger, Ann (1925–), and Edwin Way Teale (1899–1980). *A Conscious Stillness: Two Naturalists on Thoreau's Rivers*. New York: Harper & Row, 1982.
Zwinger and Teale alternate, she concentrating on Thoreau's "river of ripples," the Assabet, and he on the "river of reflections," the Sudbury. They canoe together down one stream or the other, noting the geological, hydrological, botanical, and historical changes that have occurred over time. They see disheartening signs of pollution much of the way, now, but also remnants of wildness. Autobiographical passages by Teale are forthright and interesting.
Zwinger, Ann, and Beatrice Willard (1925–). *Land Above the Trees*. New York: Harper & Row, 1972.
American alpine ecology, focusing on the plants of the tundra but also highlighting Zwinger's responses to the openness, the weather, and the light, and offering strong commentary on the alpine zone's vulnerability. A most useful text.

Secondary Studies

This section includes philosophical essays on man and nature, critical interpretations of nature literature, and histories and anthologies. Some of the
most far-reaching philosophical speculation on man and nature, as well as
what seem to me the most useful scholarly sources, can be found here.

Adams, Alexander (1917–1984). *Eternal Quest: The Story of the Great Naturalists.* New York: Putnam, 1969.
A history of the natural sciences, presented in narrative fashion through
biographies of significant figures: Aristotle, Pliny, Copernicus, Linnaeus,
Darwin, and others. Audubon and Wilson are also included. The interpretive theme is that creativity, curiosity, and intuition vie, often dramatically,
with the inertia of authority.

Allen, Durward (1910–   ). *Our Wildlife Legacy.* New York: Funk & Wagnalls, 1954.
An excellent history of wildlife and wildlife management in the United
States, folded into a presentation of the major principles of population
study, ecology, and wildlife conservation. The study is marked by its emphasis on habitat health and its clear acknowledgment of the rightful place
of predators in the natural scheme. Like Aldo Leopold's *A Sand County
Almanac,* but with more supporting detail, it extends the lessons of American wildlife history to the realm of ethics: "I suspect that . . . curious,
impartial sympathy toward *all* creatures, regardless of their diet, is an
attitude of the cultivated mind. It is a measure of man's civilization."

Anderson, Edgar (1897–1969). *Plants, Man, and Life.* Boston: Little, Brown,
1952.
An exploration of interrelationships, focusing on such aspects of "economic
botany" as crops, weeds, monoculture, and diverse planting. Anderson
presents a provocative discussion of efficiency in agriculture, based on his
study of a low-maintenance, "primitive" garden in Guatemala.

Bailey, Liberty Hyde (1858–1954). *The State and the Farmer.* New York: Macmillan, 1908.
Bailey saw that power had concentrated in the city and the national government, but hoped that through skillful diversification and simple awareness (paying more attention to the value of woodlots, for example, and
being wary of centralist moves like school consolidation) farmers could
survive the great shift.

Bakeless, John (1894–1978). *The Eyes of Discovery.* Philadelphia: Lippincott,
1950; New York: Dover, 1961.
Explorers' responses to the aboriginal American environment. Such records have remained alive, affecting our literature profoundly. Bakeless
found the appreciators among the first Europeans here — Cartier, Rad-
isson, and others — and he noted too the preoccupations that blinded so
many.

Baron, Robert C., and Elizabeth Darby Junkin, eds. *Of Discovery and Destiny:*

An Anthology of American Writers and the American Land. Golden, Colo.: Fulcrum, 1986.

"In this anthology we have included what we think are whispers of the creation of this peculiar American character, this character that has always looked outside of itself for peace and in hope of ever more possibility."

Bates, Marston (1906–1974). *The Nature of Natural History.* New York: Scribner's, 1950; rev. ed., 1962

Natural history, which Bates describes as a "growing point of science," "an area of science of immediate concern to all of us," and also a reasonably accessible kind of knowledge, might be the means for developing an attitude attuned to ecological relationships and conservation. In this basic ecological essay, Bates discusses taxonomy, community, and evolution, and enters a plea for the respectability of the term "naturalist."

Beebe, William (1877–1962). *The Book of Naturalists: An Anthology of the Best Natural History.* New York: Knopf, 1944.

The introduction presents events in chronological order, with no strongly developed theme, but the selections, ranging from Aristotle to Rachel Carson, give a sense of the growth and inherent adventure of natural science.

Bergon, Frank, ed. *The Wilderness Reader.* New York: New American Library, 1980.

An anthology of well-known and not-so-well-known selections, introduced by an overview of the literary history of American wilderness. Bergon presents a number of useful insights in this history and in the headnotes to the selections.

Berry, Wendell (1934–   ). *The Unsettling of America.* San Francisco: Sierra Club, 1977; New York: Avon, 1978.

Dealing with farming techniques as they manifest world-views, Berry mounts as thorough and unsparing a critique of industrial agriculture as can be found. The central theme is the unity of land care, morality, health, education, public policy, and the indefinable essence called "character." Berry's conclusion seems to be that fragmentation anywhere tends to spread like disease.

Borland, Hal (1900–1978). *The History of Wildlife in America.* Washington, D.C.: National Wildlife Federation, 1975.

A large-format book with many illustrations, surveying major happenings clearly. Its conclusion is that we have come to our senses to a degree, and through intelligent management may provide a livable world for wildlife.

——, ed. *Our Natural World: The Land and Wildlife of America as Seen and Described by Writers Since the Country's Discovery.* Garden City, N.Y.: Doubleday, 1965.

A generous selection, organized by "The Scene" (The Woodlands, The Watery Places, The Plains and Deserts, and The Mountains) and "The Life" (Animals, Birds, Insects, and Plants and Trees).

Bowden, Charles (1945–   ). *Killing the Hidden Waters.* Austin: University of Texas Press, 1977.

The modern-day mining of groundwater in Arizona and Texas, supported by fossil-fuel energy and accompanied by a singular faith, here contrasted with the old, unsubsidized ways of the Papago and Comanche.

Brooks, Paul (1909–   ). *The House of Life: Rachel Carson at Work.* Boston: Houghton Mifflin, 1972.

A moving study. Passages from many letters, together with personal reminiscences, give insight into Carson's philosophy and her never-easy life as a writer. This biography rises to high drama in describing the genesis, writing, and reception of *Silent Spring.*

———. *The Pursuit of Wilderness.* Boston: Houghton Mifflin, 1971.

Crucial moments in the dawning environmental consciousness of the 1960s. Brooks records "certain key battles for wilderness" in the North Cascades, Alaska, the Everglades, and Africa, showing how they illustrate the profound choices we must make. There are some hard but unfortunately true words here for the U.S. Forest Service and the Army Corps of Engineers.

———. *Speaking for Nature.* Boston: Houghton Mifflin, 1980; San Francisco: Sierra Club, 1983.

Brooks surveys the careers and influence of some fifty-eight American writers about nature since Thoreau's time, arguing for their large effect upon culture and public policy. Lesser-known figures such as Wilson Flagg and Florence Merriam are included, and there are fresh views of the greats. A valuable source book, suggesting an interpretation of American history.

———. *The View from Lincoln Hill.* Boston: Houghton Mifflin, 1976.

The human-ecological history of Lincoln, Masssachusetts. In 1976, there were only four farmers left in Lincoln; the town had become a suburb of Boston. Through careful planning, however, a process whose roots went back all the way to the colonial era, open space and a degree of rural atmosphere had been preserved. "Standards of value traditionally associated with rural New England no longer look as quaint as they did a generation ago."

Burroughs, John (1837–1921). *Accepting the Universe.* Boston: Houghton Mifflin, 1920; reprinted in vol. 21, *The Complete Writings of John Burroughs.* New York: Wm. H. Wise, 1924.

An eighty-year-old's lucid exposition of his semi-Darwinian, naturalistic, reverent philosophy. In the final chapter, Burroughs closed his writing career as he had opened it, with a marveling, yet perceptive tribute to Walt Whitman. (See selection, pp. 234–246.)

Carson, Rachel (1907–1964). *Silent Spring.* Boston: Houghton Mifflin, 1962, 1988; New York: Fawcett Crest, 1964; Ballantine, 1982.

A major text, still valuable, still urgent. Carson assembled the evidence painstakingly, showing by careful reasoning and ecological insight just what a chemicalized environment would mean. History and further investigation have borne out her analysis. "How many a man has dated a new era in his life from the reading of a book," Thoreau wrote; this may one day be said of America and *Silent Spring.*

Clough, Wilson O. (1894–   ). *The Necessary Earth: Nature and Solitude in American Literature.* Austin: University of Texas Press, 1964.
The American land, and life on the frontier, as sources of the newness, vitality, and distinctiveness of American literature. Clough stresses the American habit of "direct reference to experience."

Coues, Elliott (1842–1899). *Biogen: A Speculation on the Origin and Nature of Life.* Boston. Estes and Lauriat, 1884.
"Biogen" means "soul-stuff." It is the mysterious vital principle which, Coues writes, is "inscrutable." In this lecture we see a scientist, one of the important American ornithologists, placing limits on the scientific method. Pure reason, to the author, is "a lamp which finally serves not to light the way, but only to make the darkness visible."

Cronon, William (1954–   ). *Changes in the Land: Indians, Colonists, and the Ecology of New England.* New York: Hill & Wang, 1983.
Cronon offers documentation, and a carefully stated overview, on the transition from the diversity of pre-colonial New England to the more regularized systems under European management. He does not absolve the Indians of a certain complicity (perhaps circumstantially forced) in the new market system. This study might serve as a model for ecological histories of other areas affected by European conquest, or indeed any region undergoing profound transformations.

Cutright, Paul Russell (1897–   ). *Lewis and Clark: Pioneering Naturalists.* Urbana: University of Illinois Press, 1969.
A narrative of the expedition, emphasizing the natural history aspects. Lewis's observations often contained minute detail (the number of feathers in a grouse's tail, for example), and also provided benchmark descriptions of unspoiledness. Cutright believes Lewis "had a distinct flair for literary composition."

Dasmann, Raymond F. (1919–   ). *The Last Horizon.* New York: Macmillan, 1963.
Biome by biome, Dasmann examines the process of homogenization, by which the wild diversity and the cultural diversity of the earth are reduced to the industrial model, and contemplates the possibility of a thoroughly tamed world.

Devall, Bill (1938–   ), and George Sessions (1938–   ). *Deep Ecology.* Layton, Utah: Gibbs M. Smith, 1985.
"Shallow" ecology, devoted to intelligent management of natural resources, is anthropocentric at heart. It tends to cover over the fundamental problem — alienation from nature — with a confident gloss of purposeful activity; people are surprised when things keep getting worse. To practice deep ecology, the authors say, is to take a new-old orientation to nature, one of belonging: "We need to accept the invitation to the dance." The authors mount a vigorous critique of the presently dominant world-view, leaving hardly a pillar unshaken, and they present a many-sided, carefully attributed introduction to the deeper position. One of the most useful features of this book is its command of bibliographic sources.

Durrenberger, Robert W. (1918–   ). *Environment and Man: A Bibliography.* Palo Alto: National Press Books, 1970.

Emphasizes, but is not limited to, books and articles from the 1960s. Arranged alphabetically, then by means of numbers, into 46 subject categories. Though "literature" is not one of these, the list's accent on environmental concern makes it a useful source for anyone tracing the recent literary history of man and the environment.

Egerton, Frank N. (1936–   ), ed. *History of American Ecology.* New York: Arno Press, 1977.

Pays tribute to Peter Kalm, Samuel Williams, Alexander Wilson, and Ralph Waldo Emerson as forerunners in the development of the ecological perspective.

Ehrenfeld, David (1938–   ). *The Arrogance of Humanism.* New York: Oxford University Press, 1978, 1981.

The preposterous claims of the anthropocentrist-mechanist mentality, and the faith this religion inspires in the masses, are surveyed here with wit, logic, passion, and finally compassion. Against the specist cult of certainty the author proposes two humbling laws: "1. Most scientific discoveries and technological inventions can be developed in such a way that they are capable of doing great damage to human beings, their cultures, and their environments. 2. If a discovery or a technology can be used for evil purposes, it will be so used."

Eiseley, Loren (1907–1977). *Darwin's Century: Evolution and the Men Who Discovered It.* Garden City, N.Y.: Doubleday, 1958, 1961.

A course of lectures on the scientific and philosophical challenge that may have marked a watershed in human thought. An essential background text.

Ekirch, Arthur A., Jr. (1915–   ). *Man and Nature in America.* New York: Columbia University Press, 1963.

A history of American ideas about nature, and an account of the changing human ecology of this country that in some part results from those ideas. This is a cautionary book, calling for an examination of anthropocentrism. The vicious circle of "greater production and greater consumption" is discussed, and the author makes a reasoned plea for reviving the concepts of harmony and balance.

Elman, Robert (1930–   ). *First in the Field: America's Pioneering Naturalists.* New York: Mason/Charter, 1977.

A well-informed survey of the careers and contributions of Catesby, the Bartrams, Wilson, Audubon, Agassiz, Powell, and Burroughs — the latter not for additions to scientific knowledge but for popularizing natural history at a crucial time in American history.

Ewan, Joseph, and Nesta Ewan. *John Banister and His Natural History of Virginia, 1678–1692.* Urbana: University of Illinois Press, 1970.

Banister, who had an M.A. from Oxford, spent fourteen years in Virginia and was, according to the Ewans, "America's first resident naturalist." His drawings, covering thirty-two pages here, are delicate and detailed, and his projected "Natural History of Virginia" might have been a landmark. The authors' chronology of American natural history, 1650–1753, complementing the one by Joseph Ewan, ed., in *William Bartram: Botanical and Zoological Drawings* (see p. 419), is most useful.

Feduccia, Alan (1943–   ). *Catesby's Birds of Colonial America.* Chapel Hill: University of North Carolina Press, 1985.
A superb modern edition of Catesby's bird plates, with useful ancillary information on just how many species the early naturalists saw, and how well they knew their birds.

Foerster, Norman (1887–1972). *Nature in American Literature: Studies in the Modern View.* New York: Macmillan, 1923.
Foerster treats Bryant, Whittier, Emerson, Thoreau, Lowell, Whitman, Lanier, Muir, and Burroughs as exemplary and influential nature writers. He presents interesting insights into Thoreau's sensuousness, and describes Burroughs' "temperamental laxity" and his "rudderless" books, while praising his sincerity. A dated but still significant study.

Frick, George Frederick (1925–   ), and Raymond Phineas Stearns (1904–1970). *Mark Catesby, the Colonial Audubon.* Urbana: University of Illinois Press, 1961.
Offering as much as we are likely to learn about Catesby's life, this study is particularly good on the place of his work in American natural history.

Glacken, Clarence J. (1909–   ). *Traces on the Rhodian Shore: Nature and Culture in Western Thought from Ancient Times to the End of the Eighteenth Century.* Berkeley: University of California Press, 1967.
An immense, scholarly examination of three ideas: the thought that the earth was designed for man; the concept that the moral and social dimensions of human life are influenced by nature; and the realization that man is a significant agent of ecological change.

Graber, Linda. *Wilderness as Sacred Space.* Washington, D.C.: Association of American Geographers, 1976.
Graber's thesis is that wilderness appreciation and the drive to preserve wildlands are basically religious phenomena. She asks why wilderness should generate religiously potent imagery, and answers that it is because wilderness is "Wholly Other" to modern man. The analysis tends to be reductive, perhaps even hobby-horsical, but is nonetheless of interest.

Graham, Frank, Jr. (1925–   ). *Since Silent Spring.* Boston: Houghton Mifflin, 1970; New York: Fawcett Crest, 1970.
Graham pays tribute to the astuteness and courage of Rachel Carson, and brings the story of pesticides and herbicides eight years further along, giving evidence that the venality of pesticide promoters had not much abated, and that the fence-sitting, and worse, of academics and bureaucrats continued. By 1970, though, there were indications of organized resistance to mindless spraying of chemicals.

Griffin, Susan (1943–   ). *Woman and Nature: The Roaring Inside Her.* New York: Harper & Row, 1978.
Griffin describes what she calls the unnatural history of patriarchy's alien-

ated, abstract, egoistic, reductionist, world-fragmenting arrogance of power. The good side is the emergence of a feminine, natural outlook, answering to a "green and still living" possibility. "This earth is my sister. . . ."

Hanley, Wayne (1915–   ). *Natural History in America: From Mark Catesby to Rachel Carson*. New York: Quadrangle/New York Times, 1977.
Modestly describing himself as a "compiler," Hanley intersperses longish passages from the works of great American naturalists with a running historical commentary. His remarks on the influence of Linnaeus and the major contributions of Wilson, Audubon, and Nuttall are helpful in building the historical overview.

Hazard, Lucy Lockwood (1890–   ). *The Frontier in American Literature*. New York: Crowell, 1927.
A consideration of American writing in light of the "frontier thesis" of Frederick Jackson Turner, with interesting insights on Transcendentalist thought, which Hazard believed to be heavily influenced by the "frontier" condition of American life. Her linkage of John Winthrop, Ralph Waldo Emerson, and George F. Babbitt is a stimulating concept.

Hicks, Philip Marshall (1885–   ). *The Development of the Natural History Essay in American Literature*. Philadelphia: University of Pennsylvania, 1924.
Hicks argues that the natural history essay is properly limited to "scientifically accurate observations of the life history of the lower orders of nature," and does not include "the essay inspired merely by an aesthetic or sentimental delight in nature in general; the narrative of travel, where the observation is only incidental; and the sketch which is concerned solely with description of scenery." He covers nearly everyone of importance from Captain John Smith to John Burroughs, giving extremely high significance to Burroughs ("the chief contributor to the literature of this field") and — oddly — not mentioning John Muir at all.

Huth, Hans (1892–   ). *Nature and the American: Three Centuries of Changing Attitudes*. Berkeley: University of California Press, 1957.
Steps along the way, and influential thinkers, recounted in scholarly fashion: Jefferson, the Bartrams, Crèvecoeur, Wilson, Bryant, Cooper, the Hudson River School, the Transcendentalists, Catlin, G. P. Marsh (with the publication of *Man and Nature* in 1864 seen here as a turning point), and so on. The author appears to accept dams and the Tennessee Valley Authority uncritically, as conservation measures, but the parts of this study covering the 18th and 19th centuries are eminently useful.

Jackson, John B. (1909–   ). *Landscapes: Selected Writings of J. B. Jackson*. Edited by Ervin H. Zube. Amherst: University of Massachusetts Press, 1970.
Humanistic landscape-criticism, founded in impressive historical knowledge of our culture's relationship with nature. Includes an interesting comparison of the "anti-urbanism" of Thomas Jefferson and Henry David Thoreau.

Jones, Howard Mumford (1892–1980). *O Strange New World*. New York: Viking, 1964.

This study of the formative years of American culture includes three chapters on the European encounter with American nature: "The Image of the New World" and "The Anti-Image," which open the investigation, and "American Landscape," which concludes it with an analysis of the West and the influence of space upon American values.

Kastner, Joseph (1907–   ). *A Species of Eternity*. New York: Knopf, 1977
Impressively thorough research makes this account of the "virtuoso" period of American natural history a standard reference. Informing Kastner's biographies is a clear sense of American intellectual life and its development. An indispensable work.

———. *A World of Watchers*. New York: Knopf, 1986.
A chatty, anecdotal, informative history of birdwatching in America, written with good humor (on such subjects as bird clubs' exclusiveness, for example) and with a strong sense of what birding has meant, in all seriousness, to this nation historically.

Kohl, Judith, and Herbert Kohl (1937–   ). *The View from the Oak: The Private Worlds of Other Creatures*. San Francisco: Sierra Club, 1977.
Classified as "juvenile literature," but containing sentences like "It is difficult to understand the umwelt of creatures that have different senses and sizes than ours," this book asks the reader to go beyond the usual perceptual borders. A useful educational guide for all ages.

Kolodny, Annette (1941–   ). *The Land Before Her: Fantasy and Experience of the American Frontiers, 1630–1860*. Chapel Hill: University of North Carolina Press, 1984.
An analysis of symbolic landscapes and fantasies, showing women's responses to the American frontiers. For many women, the image of the garden was central: ". . . the garden implied home and community, not [as for many of the male fantasies depicted in the author's *The Lay of the Land*] privatized erotic mastery." This book offers a fresh look at American history with regard to the land.

———. *The Lay of the Land: Metaphor as Experience and History in American Life and Letters*. Chapel Hill: University of North Carolina Press, 1975.
This careful study examines the personification of the New World landscape as feminine, and ponders the effects of this continuing metaphor.

Krutch, Joseph Wood (1893–1970), ed. *Great American Nature Writing*. New York: William Sloane, 1950.
The eighty-page "Prologue" to this anthology, an invaluable essay, describes the philosophical preconditions of modern nature writing. Krutch traces the history of the idea of oneness with nature and the accompanying attitude of fellow-feeling; he finds the move toward an ecological view nothing less than an "intellectual revolution." There is analysis of the concept of the sublime, of mechanism, of Linnaean science versus Cartesian, and of the influence of certain divines like John Ray.

LaBastille, Anne (1938–   ). *Women and Wilderness*. San Francisco: Sierra Club, 1980.
An interesting study of how women in North America responded to wilderness in the era of settlement and westward movement, how they began

in modern times to go to the wilderness for study and recreation, and what they now do there. It is the story of a kind of revolution. A major portion of the book is profiles of fifteen contemporary women who have had extensive wilderness experience.

LaChapelle, Dolores. *Earth Wisdom*. Los Angeles: Guild of the Tutors, 1978; rev. ed., Silverton, Colo.: Finn Hill Arts, 1984.
A synthesis of anthropological and biological information, philosophy, and personal experience, focused by a provocative intuition. The author's theme is the healing re-connection that is, she believes, yet possible.

Lillard, Richard D. (1909–   ). *The Great Forest*. New York: Knopf, 1947.
A narrative history of America from the standpoint of forests and forest products, including chapters on conservation and labor issues.

Limerick, Patricia Nelson (1951–   ). *Desert Passages: Encounters with the American Deserts*. Albuquerque: University of New Mexico Press, 1985.
Early travelers, up to about the time of John Charles Van Dyke, disliked the unimproved desert; later, Limerick argues, "appreciation supplants dislike." She believes that improvements in transportation gave a "margin of safety," so that twentieth-century Americans "felt safe to appreciate the desert."

Linden, Eugene (1947–   ). *Silent Partners: The Legacy of the Ape Language Experiments*. New York: Times Books, 1986.
Within this account of the decline of the ape language research, and the subsequent "diaspora" of the apes themselves, there is a complex question. What is it that separates humans from other animals? (Language? And if so, what is *that*?) Seen from a chimpanzee's point of view, perhaps, we appear as a "bizarre, moody species." This book is marked by strong, unsentimental compassion for the chimpanzees and gorillas who are the "silent partners" in a human quest for knowledge.

Marsh, George Perkins (1801–1882). *Man and Nature*. New York: Scribner's, 1864; Cambridge: Harvard University Press, 1965.
Marsh analyzed the decline of Mediterranean and Near Eastern civilization in terms of watershed abuse, and warned against a similar mistake in America. He showed that man had become a major force with the ability to change the earth radically. And he proposed the protection of wilderness. This is an early, one might say prescient, text in ecological awareness; Lewis Mumford, writing in *The Brown Decades* (1931), described it as the "fountainhead of the conservation movement."

Marx, Leo (1919–   ). *The Machine in the Garden: Technology and the Pastoral Ideal in America*. New York: Oxford University Press, 1964.
Marx states his purpose as "to describe and evaluate the uses of the pastoral ideal in the interpretation of American experience. I shall be tracing its adaptation to the conditions of life in the New World, its emergence as a distinctly American theory of society, and its subsequent transformation under the impact of industrialism." A major study of gray and green in American art and thought.

Matthiessen, Peter (1927–   ). *Wildlife in America*. New York: Viking, 1959. Rev. and updated ed., New York: Viking, 1987.

Still the most complete record of the impact of three-plus centuries of Euro-American settlement upon the wildlife of North America. Matthiessen allows the often-appalling facts to speak for themselves. Not a heartening book, but a necessary one.

Meeker, Joseph (1932–   ). *The Comedy of Survival.* New York: Scribner's, 1974; rev. ed., Los Angeles: Guild of the Tutors, 1980.

Literary analysis from an ecological standpoint, offering fresh insights into well-known works and, more significantly, setting up a new way of reading. The author associates the tragic hero with nature indifference and general ecological irresponsibility, and the comic stance with humility and survival. A provocative departure.

Merchant, Carolyn (1936–   ). *The Death of Nature: Women, Ecology, and the Scientific Revolution.* San Francisco: Harper & Row, 1980.

From an egalitarian standpoint, Merchant argues, women's liberation and ecological consciousness have much in common. The intellectual revolution that established the modern, mechanistic world-view in the sixteenth and seventeenth centuries denied the traditional, organic world — the female world of nature. Now, "by critically reexamining history from these [egalitarian] perspectives, we may begin to discover values associated with the premodern world that may be worthy of transformation and reintegration into today's and tomorrow's society." This revisionist study will be taken into account in any serious examination of our culture's relationship with the natural world.

Nash, Roderick (1939–   ). *Wilderness and the American Mind.* New Haven: Yale University Press, 1967; rev. ed., 1973; 3rd ed., 1982.

An indispensable historical survey. The later editions make observations on recent developments such as the environmental movement in the 1960s and 1970s and the contemporary crowding of wilderness areas. Nash appears to equate Western man with man in general, in point of attitudes toward the wild, and holds to what might be termed the "full-stomach" theory of wilderness appreciation (veneration of the wild arises *after* certain basic needs have been met). Both these views may be debatable, but the book remains authoritative in its historical analysis.

Osborn, Fairfield (1887–1969). *Our Plundered Planet.* Boston: Little, Brown, 1948.

A sobering work, written at the dawn of the post-war frenzy of development. A world population of some two billion worried Osborn, as did topsoil loss, the increase of degenerative diseases, and the curious faith that science will make everything turn out right.

Osborn, Henry Fairfield (1852–1935). *Impressions of Great Naturalists: Reminiscences of Darwin, Huxley, Balfour, Cope and Others.* New York: Scribner's, 1924.

"I like a naturalist better than a scientist," Professor Osborn wrote, "because there is less of the ego in him, and in a naturalist like Darwin the ego entirely disappears and through his vision we see Nature with the least human aberration." The sketches of John Muir and John Burroughs are influenced by Osborn's ideas on heredity and race — Muir he saw as a representative "Scotch type of soul," and Burroughs, as very English.

Owings, Loren C. (1928–). *Environmental Values, 1860–1972: A Guide to Information Sources.* Detroit: Gale Research Co., 1976.
This well-annotated reference work covers man and nature in America, travelers' accounts by region, American landscape painting, conservation, nature writing and nature study, camping literature, and country living, and does so with a clear focus on philosophy and values. An excellent sourcebook.

Peattie, Donald Culross (1898–1964). *Green Laurels: The Lives and Achievements of the Great Naturalists.* New York: Simon & Schuster, 1936.
Informative background on medieval and Renaissance concepts of nature, and on the life and work of Linnaeus, serve as a kind of prologue to this study of the Bartrams, the two botanists Michaux (father and son), Wilson, Audubon, Thomas Say the entomologist, and others important in American natural history.

———. *Singing in the Wilderness: A Salute to John James Aubudon.* New York: Putnam's, 1935.
Peattie was highly sympathetic to his subject ("Audubon gave everything he had for the most beautiful thing he could see"), freely novelizing scenes and speaking forthrightly of Audubon's importance in his own life. But he was also clear-headed about his methods, astute in his art criticism, and knowledgeable about the middle America of 1805–1825. An honest, accessible biography, very modern in conception.

Porter, Charlotte M. (1948–). *The Eagle's Nest: Natural History and American Ideas, 1812–1842.* Tuscaloosa: University of Alabama Press, 1986.
A survey of the naturalists of the early republic, centering on William Maclure (who completed the first geological survey of the United States, in 1808) and the Philadelphia-based Academy of Natural Sciences. These naturalists were "sons of the Enlightenment," Porter says, and beneficent views of nature came easily to them.

Robertson, David (1937–). *West of Eden: A History of the Art and Literature of Yosemite.* Berkeley: Yosemite Natural History Association and Wilderness Press, 1984.
A model scholarly study of the expression of place. Robertson's criticism suggests the high level at which nature writing may be enjoyed. His treatment of Ansel Adams's work, in the section on photography, likewise elevates the level of discourse.

Ronald, Ann (1939–), ed. *Words for the Wild: The Sierra Club Trailside Reader.* San Francisco: Sierra Club, 1987.
The editor has chosen particularly resonant excerpts from twenty-three American writers, from R. W. Emerson to Barry Lopez; these are accompanied by instructive statements on what these writers have meant to her.

Sauer, Carl Ortwin (1889–1975). *Sixteenth Century North America: The Land and the People as Seen by the Europeans.* Berkeley: University of California Press, 1971.

A recounting of explorations and attempts at settlement, in large part those of the Spanish, with ecological commentary. Sauer describes the Indians' sophisticated agriculture, noting that even on the high plains of present-day west Texas, Native Americans were not purely nomadic.

Savage, Henry (1903–). *Lost Heritage.* New York: Morrow, 1970.
Brief, fact-filled biographies of seven important naturalists: John Lawson, Mark Catesby, the Bartrams, André and François André Michaux, and Alexander Wilson. The text is enriched by a sense of the beauty and intactness (the "lost heritage") of the America these men saw, and given a sharp point by the author's outspoken commentary on the present state of the American environment.

Schmitt, Peter J. (1947–). *Back to Nature: The Arcadian Myth in Urban America.* New York: Oxford University Press, 1969.
Various responses to the urbanization of America, ranging from the retreat to the suburb and hobby farm to nature study in the schools to the popular novel of the wilderness, analyzed as expressions of what the author terms the "Arcadian myth." The approach is slightly patronizing, limiting the depth of the analysis, but the scope and sheer numbers of examples and illustrations are impressive.

Schwartz, William, ed. *Voices for the Wilderness.* New York: Ballantine, 1969.
A collection of papers from Sierra Club biennial wilderness conferences of the 1960s, including some strong essays by David Brower, Joseph Wood Krutch, and Wallace Stegner.

Shepard, Paul (1925–). *Man in the Landscape.* New York: Knopf, 1967.
An historical consideration of views of nature, centered on Western civilization. Contains a spirited inquiry into the roots of our cultural estrangement from nature and an interesting account of the impact of wild, western landscapes upon the Euro-American sensibility.

———. *Nature and Madness.* San Francisco: Sierra Club, 1982.
Describing the role played by encounters with wild nature in the development of personality, Shepard provides a challenging analysis of our culture's historically atypical situation. He traces the development of our estrangement from nature, or "madness," back into the Industrial Revolution, then further into the time of the "desert fathers," and further still into the time of the domestication of plants and animals. Each of these eras provided ideas and practices reinforcing the dualistic, "mad" view of the world, which Shepard describes as a kind of freezing of certain immature, normally superseded attitudes.

———. *The Tender Carnivore and the Sacred Game.* New York: Scribner's, 1973.
The author looks into the life of man before the Neolithic revolution, to see if the hunting and gathering life might provide any useful references for the present crisis. He has harsh words for agriculture and domestication: "The myth that the practice of agriculture engenders respect for the soil does not stand careful examination." This book requires a re-thinking of the term "primitive."

———. *Thinking Animals.* New York: Viking, 1978.

Far from being independent of the other animals, we are profoundly affected by them "in the shaping of personality, identity, and social consciousness." This book makes a many-sided argument for the symbiosis of our awareness and the natural world.

Shepard, Paul, and Barry Sanders. *The Sacred Paw: The Bear in Nature, Myth, and Literature.* New York: Viking, 1985.
Bears have entered deeply into human thought, ritual, symbology, language, and literature. The authors show how and why the bear "strikes a chord in us of fear and caution, curiosity and fascination."

Smallwood, William (1873–1949), and Mabel Smallwood. *Natural History and the American Mind.* New York: Columbia University Press, 1941.
A useful record of the advance of science, particularly informative on the influence, culture-wide, of university curricula in natural history.

Snyder, Gary (1930–   ). *Good, Wild, Sacred.* Hereford, U.K.: Five Seasons Press, 1984.
A clear laying-out and analysis of the terms by which, linguistically and philosophically, we know and judge land. What emerges here is an outline-critique of culture itself, vis-à-vis nature.

Thomas, Lewis (1913–   ). *Late Night Thoughts on Listening to Mahler's Ninth Symphony.* New York: Viking, 1983; Bantam, 1984; Oxford University Press, 1985.
Most of these essays are from *Discover* magazine, and many are meditations on modern developments related to biology and medicine — heart pacemakers, atomic weapons and their possible use and consequences, the Gaia hypothesis, chemical treatments for mental illness, and fraudulent research publications, among others. In the aggregate, they convey a humane view of our time and the human prospect. The shadow of the Bomb is over these essays, but they embody the inherent affirmation of an inquiring mind.

Tobias, Michael (1951–   ), ed. *Deep Ecology.* San Diego: Avant Books, 1985.
A wide-ranging collection of sixteen essays and several poems, most of them pointed toward a new and radically deeper understanding of our ecological situation. There is an excellent survey of the philosophical literature on the subject, by George Sessions, along with a sobering study of our numbers and our pressure on the world, by William R. Catton, Jr., and a provocative investigation of nature and sex, by Dolores LaChapelle, among other pieces of note. Perhaps the root distinction between "shallow ecology" and "deep ecology," at the level of self-concept and identity, will be most clearly seen by comparing the essay "Discriminating Altruisms," by Garrett Hardin, with "Identification as a Source of Deep Ecological Attitudes," by the Norwegian philosopher Arne Naess. Both essays are astute, and in their different ways persuasive.

Tracy, Henry Chester (1876–   ). *American Naturists.* New York: Dutton, 1930.
A history of American nature writing, with commentary on the genre's

cultural significance and on individual writers' distinctive contributions. There are interesting insights here. Of John Muir: "It takes something more than, or other than literary criticism to find and assay the chief values in John Muir's prose." Of Mary Austin: "Deeper and deeper, as one proceeds, he is led into an inner seeing; by word-clues, by wands snatched from the Indian, by subduings of the clamant Western ego, by eye and hand contacts, by yieldings to the silent desert sense. One is ever on the edge of new-seeing."

Trimble, Stephen (1950–   ). *Words from the Land: Encounters with Natural History Writing.* Salt Lake City: Gibbs M. Smith, 1988.

An anthology of contemporary essays, prefaced by a most interesting gathering of comments from some of the authors on their research and writing methods. This wide-ranging introduction will be richly educative for anyone venturing upon criticism of the nature essay.

Turner, Frederick (1937–   ). *Beyond Geography: The Western Spirit Against the Wilderness.* New York: Viking, 1980.

An "essay in spiritual history," arguing that the loss of a mythic sense of life, and its replacement by an historical sense, were factors in Western civilization's alienation from nature. This study suggests origins for the seeming ethical indifference with which the New World was conquered and transfigured.

Vermes, Jean (1907–   ), ed. *The Wilderness Sampler.* Harrisburg, Pa.: Stackpole, 1968.

An anthology including Herman Melville on the "Enchanted Isles" (the Galápagos), Muir on the 1872 earthquake, and other familiar selections from Powell, Audubon, Thoreau, and Burroughs, among thirty authors represented.

West, Herbert Faulkner (1898–1974). *The Nature Writers: A Guide to Richer Reading.* Brattleboro, Vt.: Stephen Daye, 1939.

An annotated booklist, brief but international in scope, preceded by the editor's introduction, which presents a historical overview of nature writing, and a foreword by Henry Beston, which describes the nature writer's function as being like that of the poet: "to give depth and color to the adventure of human life, to touch the imagination of his readers, exalt their sense of beauty and mystery, and fortify in their souls that power of intelligent awareness with which they look out upon their world."

Wheeler, William Morton (1865–1937). *Essays in Philosophical Biology.* Cambridge: Harvard University Press, 1939.

Twelve essays collected from various sources, giving a good idea of Wheeler's range of interests and his philosopher's humane understanding. An anti-pedant and a thinker whose insights into ecological relationships were carefully derived and precisely formulated, Wheeler saw life in a manner both wittily satiric and penetrating. His sense of the term "social" extended "down through the non-living to the very atom with its organization of component electrons." Thus his comparisons of ant and human societies go beyond the obvious deflation of human pride to suggest the understanding that we live in and manifest great natural patterns, greater by far than our narrow conceptions of politics or economics.

Wild, Peter (1940–). *Pioneer Conservationists of Eastern America*. Missoula, Mont.: Mountain Press, 1987.
Critical sketches of fifteen Americans whose pro-environment works have helped shape history, opening up the possibility of a qualitative definition of progress. Under this rubric, Wild treats Ralph Nader and Amory Lovins as modern successors of the Marsh-Olmsted-Roosevelt line. It is by no means sure that conservationists' minority views will ever prevail — ". . . fueled by economics and out of control, the destruction goes on at a far faster pace than the intense but limited efforts at restoration" — but these brief biographies do demonstrate the revolutionary power of ecological conscience. A 43-page bibliography helps make this a most serviceable reference.

———. *Pioneer Conservationists of Western America*. Missoula, Mont.: Mountain Press, 1979.
Profiles of fifteen people, among them John Muir, Mary Austin, Olaus Murie, and David Brower, whose work urges a post-frontier understanding. Introduced by an interestingly straight, philosophical essay by Edward Abbey.

Wilson, David Scofield (1931–). *In the Presence of Nature*. Amherst: University of Massachusetts Press, 1978.
An "American Studies" approach to the significance of natural history in colonial America, concentrating on Jonathan Carver, John Bartram, and Mark Catesby. Wilson makes an interesting and useful distinction between natural history writing and "nature reportage," and studies here an example of the latter, giving John Bartram's prose some of the "serious and sustained scrutiny" he believes it deserves.

Wilson, Edward O. (1929–). *Sociobiology*. Cambridge: Harvard University Press, 1975.
A comprehensive attempt to describe the links between biological evolution and social evolution, written with objectivity and wit. To many students of evolution, this book has Darwinian scope and weight.

Worster, Donald (1941–). *Nature's Economy: The Roots of Ecology*. San Francisco: Sierra Club, 1977; Garden City, N.Y.: Anchor/Doubleday, 1979.
Fascinating intellectual history. Worster shows how ecological thought over the past three centuries has been shaped by large cultural currents, including both Arcadian visions of nature and the stronger "imperial" traditions. His tracing of the interaction of these two streams of thought is masterly. A comprehensive and useful study, whose more philosophical focus makes it an essential text to be read alongside Roderick Nash's *Wilderness and the American Mind* (see p. 471).

Notes

Preface

1. Wayne Hanley, *Natural History in America: From Mark Catesby to Rachel Carson* (New York: Quadrangle/New York Times, 1977), p. xi.
2. Philip Marshall Hicks, *The Development of the Natural History Essay in American Literature* (Philadelphia: University of Pennsylvania, 1924), p. 155.
3. David Robertson, *West of Eden: A History of the Art and Literature of Yosemite* (Berkeley: Yosemite Natural History Association and the Wilderness Press, 1984), p. vi.
4. Edward Abbey, *The Journey Home: Some Words in Defense of the American West* (New York: Dutton, 1977), pp. xii–xiii.
5. Edgar Allan Poe, "J. Fenimore Cooper," in *The Works of Edgar Allan Poe* (New York: A. C. Armstrong, 1900), vol. 6, p. 417.
6. Joyce Carol Oates, "Against Nature," *Antaeus*, no. 57 (Autumn, 1986), p. 236.

1. A Taxonomy of Nature Writing

1. Roger Tory Peterson, *A Field Guide to Western Birds* (Boston: Houghton Mifflin, 1961), p. 223.
2. See Joseph Campbell, *The Hero with a Thousand Faces* (Princeton: Princeton University Press, 1949). I am grateful to Professor Joe Gordon of the Colorado College for pointing out this pattern's ubiquity in nature writing.

3. The American Setting

1. Jean Ribaut, *The Whole & True Discouerye of Terra Florida* (Deland, Fla.: Florida State Historical Society, 1927), pp. 72–73. This is a facsimile reprint of the London edition of 1563.
2. Walter Prescott Webb, *The Great Frontier* (Austin: University of Texas Press, 1979), p. 13. Originally published by Houghton Mifflin, 1952.
3. Henry David Thoreau, "A Natural History of Massachusetts," in Carl Bode, ed., *The Portable Thoreau* (New York: Viking, 1964), p. 56.

4. Francis Harper, ed., *The Travels of William Bartram,* Naturalist's Edition (New Haven: Yale University Press, 1958), pp. li, lvi.
5. Paul Brooks, *Speaking for Nature* (San Francisco: Sierra Club, 1983), p. 285. Originally published by Houghton Mifflin, 1980.
6. Edwin Way Teale, always careful with numbers, estimated that by 1951, 100,000,000 acres of America's marshes had been drained or filled in the course of the country's history. See *North with the Spring* (New York: Dodd, Mead, 1951), p. 134.

4. Beginnings

1. Carl O. Sauer, *Sixteenth Century North America: The Land and the People as Seen by the Europeans* (Berkeley: University of California Press, 1971), p. 57, and also William Cronon, *Changes in the Land* (New York: Hill & Wang, 1983), pp. 25–26.
2. Cecil Jane, ed. and trans., *The Voyages of Christopher Columbus: Being the Journals of His First and Third, and the Letters Concerning His First and Last Voyages* (London: The Argonaut Press, 1930), pp. 153, 160.
3. Thomas Heriot, "A briefe and true report of the new found land of Virginia," in Richard Hakluyt, *The Principal Navigations, Voyages, Traffiques and Discoveries of the English Nation* (New York: Dutton, 1927), vol. 6, pp. 181–182.
4. Thomas Morton, *New English Canaan* (London: Charles Green, 1632), reprinted in *Tracts and Other Papers, Relating Principally to the Origin, Settlement, and Progress of the Colonies in North America from the Discovery of the Country to the Year 1776* (Washington: Peter Force, 1838), p. 47.
5. Ibid., p. 48.
6. Ibid., p. 50.
7. Henry David Thoreau, *Journals* (Boston: Houghton Mifflin, 1906), vol. 7, p. 109.
8. William Wood, *New England's Prospect*, ed. Alden T. Vaughan (Amherst: University of Massachusetts Press, 1977), p. 46. Originally published by I. Bellamie, London, 1634.
9. William Cronon, *Changes in the Land*, p. 127.
10. Peter Matthiessen, *Wildlife in America* (New York: Penguin, 1977), p. 281. Originally published by Viking, 1959.
11. Philip Marshall Hicks, *The Development of the Natural History Essay in American Literature*, p. 15.
12. John Josselyn, *New England's Rarities Discovered*, in Edward Tuckerman, ed., *Transactions and Collections of the American Antiquarian Society* (Boston: John Wilson & Son, 1860), vol. 4, p. 216.
13. See Tuckerman's opinion in *Transactions and Collections*, p. 112.
14. Josselyn, *New England's Rarities*, in *Transactions and Collections*, p. 144.
15. For more on this matter, see Chapter 5, "Commodities of the Hunt," in William Cronon, *Changes in the Land*.

16. John Josselyn, *An Account of Two Voyages to New-England, Made During the Years 1638, 1663* (Boston: William Veazie, 1865), p. 107. Originally published by G. Widdows, London, 1674.

17. Ibid., p. 71.

18. Ibid., p. 72.

19. Ibid., p. 99.

20. John Ray, *The Wisdom of God Manifested in the Works of the Creation* (London: Innys and Manby, 1735), p. 175. Originally published by Samuel Smith, London, 1691.

21. Keith Thomas's *Man and the Natural World: A History of the Modern Sensibility* (New York: Pantheon, 1983) traces the widening of man's views of nature during the crucial time period of 1500–1800, in one of the major source-countries for that widening, England.

22. Joseph Ewan and Nesta Ewan, *John Banister and His Natural History of Virginia, 1678–1692* (Urbana: University of Illinois Press, 1970) p. 63.

23. Joseph Kastner, *A Species of Eternity* (New York: Knopf, 1977), p. 12.

24. George Frederick Frick and Raymond Phineas Stearns, *Mark Catesby, the Colonial Audubon* (Urbana: University of Illinois Press, 1961), p. 7. See also Robert Elman, *First in the Field: America's Pioneering Naturalists* (New York: Mason/Charter, 1977), pp. 9–25.

25. Alan Feduccia, *Catesby's Birds of Colonial America* (Chapel Hill: University of North Carolina Press, 1985), p. 10.

26. Ibid., p. 138.

27. Mark Catesby, *The Natural History of Carolina, Florida, and the Bahama Islands* (London: "Printed at the Expence of the Author," 1743), vol. 2, p. xxxvi.

28. Ibid., p. 56.

29. Ibid., Appendix, p. 13. For an analysis of Catesby's contribution, see David Scofield Wilson, *In the Presence of Nature* (Amherst: University of Massachusetts Press, 1978), pp. 123–159.

30. Adolph B. Benson, ed., *Peter Kalm's Travels in North America* (New York: Wilson-Erickson, 1937), p. 152.

31. Ibid., p. 300.

32. Ibid., p. 153.

33. Ibid., p. 48.

34. Ibid., p. 698.

35. Ibid., p. 707.

36. Crèvecoeur, *Sketches of Eighteenth Century America*, ed. Henri L. Bourdin, Ralph H. Gabriel, and Stanley T. Williams (New Haven: Yale University Press, 1925), p. 39.

37. Ibid., pp. 41–42.

38. Ibid., p. 46.

39. D. H. Lawrence, *Studies in Classic American Literature* (New York: Thomas Seltzer, 1923), p. 33.

40. Crèvecoeur, *Sketches*, p. 77.

41. Ibid., pp. 106–107.

42. Crèvecoeur, *Letters from an American Farmer* (New York: Fox, Duffield, 1904), pp. 253–254.

43. Thomas Jefferson, *Notes on the State of Virginia,* ed. William Peden (Chapel Hill: University of North Carolina Press, 1955), pp. 58–59.

44. Joseph Kastner, *A Species of Eternity,* p. 4.

45. Helen Gere Cruickshank, ed., *John and William Bartram's America: Selections from the Writings of the Philadelphia Naturalists* (New York: Devin-Adair, 1957), p. 13.

46. Francis Harper, ed., *The Travels of William Bartram,* Naturalist's Edition (New Haven: Yale University Press, 1958), p. 133.

47. Ibid., pp. lvii, 38.

48. Ibid., p. 71.

49. Ibid.

50. Samuel Williams, *The Natural and Civil History of Vermont* (Walpole, N.H.: Thomas and Carlisle, 1794), p. viii.

51. Ibid., pp. 121, 86–87, 73.

52. Ibid., p. 131.

53. Reuben Gold Thwaites, ed., *Original Journals of the Lewis and Clark Expedition, 1804–1806* (New York: Dodd, Mead, 1904), vol. 1, part 2, p. 335.

54. Paul Russell Cutright, *Lewis and Clark: Pioneering Naturalists* (Urbana: University of Illinois Press, 1969), p. vii.

55. Alexander B. Grosart, ed., *The Poems and Literary Prose of Alexander Wilson* (Paisley, Scotland: Alex. Gardner, 1876), p. xl. Robert Cantwell's *Alexander Wilson, Naturalist and Pioneer* (Philadelphia: Lippincott, 1961) is the most detailed biography.

56. Grosart, p. 1.

57. Alexander Wilson, *American Ornithology* (Philadelphia: Bradford & Inskeep, 1811), vol. 4, p. 20.

58. Alan Feduccia, *Catesby's Birds of Colonial America,* p. 101.

59. Biographical information is found in Jeannette E. Graustein's study, *Thomas Nuttall, Naturalist: Explorations in America, 1808–1841* (Cambridge: Harvard University Press, 1967). References to Nuttall may be found in Washington Irving, *Astoria,* ed. Edgeley W. Todd (Norman: University of Oklahoma Press, 1964), pp. 143, 144, 170, 201, 215; and in Richard Henry Dana, Jr., *Two Years Before the Mast* (Boston: Houghton Mifflin, 1911), pp. 359–61, 412. *Astoria* was first published in 1836, and *Two Years Before the Mast* in 1840.

60. Jeannette E. Graustein, ed. *Nuttall's Travels into the Old Northwest: An Unpublished 1810 Diary. Chronica Botanica,* vol. 14. (Waltham, Mass.: The Chronica Botanica Company, 1950–1951).

61. Thomas Nuttall, *A Journal of Travels into the Arkansa Territory, During the Year 1819.* In Reuben Gold Thwaites, ed., *Early Western Travels* (Cleveland: Arthur H. Clark, 1905), vol. 13, p. 109. Originally published by Thos. H. Palmer, Philadelphia, 1821.

62. John D. Godman, *American Natural History* (Philadelphia: R. W. Pomeroy, 1842), vol. 1, p. 44. Originally published by Carey & Lea, Philadelphia, 1826.

63. Ibid., p. 205.
64. Ibid., vol. 2, p. 291. *Rambles of a Naturalist* is included in this edition of *American Natural History.*
65. John James Audubon, *Ornithological Biography* (Edinburgh: Adam Black, 1831–1834), vol. 1, p. vii.
66. Ibid., vol. 2, p. 242.
67. Ibid., vol. 1, p. 29.

5. The Age of Thoreau, Muir, and Burroughs

1. Samuel Austin, ed., *The Works of President Edwards* (Worcester, Mass.: Isaiah Thomas, Jr., 1808), vol. 1, pp. 34–35.
2. Ralph Waldo Emerson, "Nature," in Brooks Atkinson, ed., *The Selected Writings of Ralph Waldo Emerson* (New York: Random House, 1940), p. 6. Originally published by J. Munroe, Boston, 1836.
3. Thoreau's original subtitle for *Walden* was "or, Life in the Woods."
4. Bradford Torrey, ed., *Journal*, in *The Writings of Henry David Thoreau* (Boston: Houghton Mifflin, 1906), vol. 1, p. xli.
5. William Howarth, *The Book of Concord* (New York: Viking, 1982), p. 9.
6. See Robert D. Richardson, Jr., *Henry Thoreau: A Life of the Mind* (Berkeley: University of California Press, 1986), pp. 116, 123, 224.
7. Henry David Thoreau, "A Natural History of Massachusetts," p. 34.
8. Ibid.
9. Thoreau, *Journals*, vol. 1, p. 265.
10. Walter Harding, *The Days of Henry Thoreau* (New York: Knopf, 1965), p. 457. This remark has a Buddhistic flavor, and it may be pertinent in this connection that Rick Fields, in *How the Swans Came to the Lake: A Narrative History of Buddhism in America* (Boulder: Shambhala, 1981), writes that Thoreau was "perhaps the first American to explore the nontheistic mode of contemplation which is the distinguishing mark of Buddhism" (pp. 62–63). Reginald H. Blyth, the British student of Zen in literature, considered Thoreau a great man in world history, ranking him only behind J. S. Bach and the Japanese Haiku poet Bashō. "The order is the order of Zen," Blyth explained. R. H. Blyth, *Mumonkan*, in *Zen and Zen Classics* (Tokyo: Hokuseido, 1966), vol. 4, p. 7.
11. Thoreau, *Walden*, ed. J. Lyndon Shanley (Princeton: Princeton University Press, 1971), p. 312.
12. Nuttall, *A Manual of the Ornithology of the United States and Canada* (Boston: Hilliard, Gray, 1840), p. 392. Originally published by Hilliard and Brown, Cambridge, 1832.
13. Thoreau, *Journals*, vol. 4, pp. 190–191.
14. Thoreau, "Walking," *The Atlantic Monthly* 9 (June, 1862), pp. 659, 662, 667.
15. Ibid., pp. 661, 674, 665.
16. Thoreau, *Walden*, p. 129.
17. Ibid., p. 329.
18. John H. White, Jr., "Railroads: Wood to Burn," in Brooke Hindle, ed.,

Material Culture in the Wooden Age (Tarrytown, N.Y.: Sleepy Hollow Press, 1981), pp. 199–201, 215.

19. Betty Flanders Thomson, *The Changing Face of New England* (New York: Macmillan, 1958), p. 31.

20. The most thorough history of American extinctions and extirpations is found in Peter Matthiessen, *Wildlife in America* (New York: Viking, 1959, rev. and updated ed., 1987).

21. John Muir, *The Story of My Boyhood and Youth* (Boston: Houghton Mifflin, 1913), p. 53.

22. Linnie Marsh Wolfe, ed., *John of the Mountains: The Unpublished Journals of John Muir* (Madison: University of Wisconsin Press, 1979), p. 8. Originally published by Houghton Mifflin, 1938.

23. Muir, *My First Summer in the Sierra* (Boston: Houghton Mifflin, 1979), p. 131.

24. Ibid.

25. Linnie Marsh Wolfe, ed., *John of the Mountains,* pp. 79–80.

26. Wolfe, *Son of the Wilderness: The Life of John Muir* (Madison: University of Wisconsin Press, 1978), p. 166. Originally published by Alfred A. Knopf in 1945.

27. Wolfe, ed., *John of the Mountains,* p. 95.

28. Thoreau, *The Maine Woods* (New York: Crowell, 1966), p. 83. See also Roderick Nash, *Wilderness and the American Mind,* 3rd ed. (New Haven: Yale University Press, 1982), p. 91.

29. William Frederic Badè, *The Life and Letters of John Muir* (Boston: Houghton Mifflin, 1923), vol. 1, p. 326.

30. Wolfe, *Son of the Wilderness,* p. 158.

31. Muir, "Wild Wool," *The Overland Monthly* 5 (April, 1875), p. 364.

32. Ibid.

33. Wolfe, ed., *John of the Mountains,* p. 138.

34. Muir, *The Mountains of California* (Garden City, N.Y.: Doubleday, 1961), p. 93. Originally published by Century, 1894.

35. Muir, *The Yosemite* (New York: Century, 1912), p. 262.

36. Wolfe, *Son of the Wilderness,* pp. 188–191.

37. Ibid., p. 344.

38. Thoreau, *Walden,* p. 138.

39. John Burroughs, *Accepting the Universe: Essays in Naturalism* (Boston: Houghton Mifflin, 1920), p. 304.

40. William Sloane Kennedy, *The Real John Burroughs* (New York: Funk & Wagnalls, 1924), p. 122.

41. Burroughs, *Accepting the Universe,* p. vii.

42. Clara Barrus, *The Life and Letters of John Burroughs* (Boston: Houghton Mifflin, 1925), vol. 2, p. 319.

43. Burroughs, *Notes on Walt Whitman, As Poet and Person,* 2nd ed. (New York: J. S. Redfield, 1871), p. 46. Originally published by American News Company, New York, 1867.

44. Burroughs, quoted in Clara Barrus, *The Life and Letters of John Burroughs,* vol. 1, p. 256.

45. Burroughs, *Accepting the Universe,* p. 146.
46. Burroughs, quoted in Clara Barrus, *The Life and Letters of John Burroughs,* vol. 2, p. 336.
47. Burroughs, *Ways of Nature,* in, *The Writings of John Burroughs* (Boston: Houghton Mifflin, 1905), vol. 14, p. 80.
48. Ibid., pp. 30–31.
49. Walter Harding and Carl Bode, eds., *The Correspondence of Henry David Thoreau* (New York: New York University Press, 1958), p. 489.
50. Wilson Flagg, *The Woods and By-Ways of New England* (Boston: James R. Osgood, 1872), p. vii.
51. Ibid., p. 80.
52. Ibid., pp. 111, 142.
53. Ibid., pp. 427, 433.
54. Flagg, *Studies in the Field and Forest* (Boston: Little, Brown, 1857), pp. 258–259.
55. Clarence E. Dutton, *Tertiary History of the Grand Cañon District* (Washington: U.S. Government, 1882), pp. 90, 56.
56. John Charles Van Dyke, *The Desert* (New York: Scribner's, 1901), p. 53.
57. Ibid., p. 129.
58. Ibid., p. ix.
59. Mary Austin, *Earth Horizon* (Boston: Houghton Mifflin, 1932), p. 198.
60. "I-Mary" came into conscious existence at age six:

It was a summer morning, and the child I was had walked down through the orchard and come out on the brow of a sloping hill where there were grass and a wind blowing and one tall tree reaching into infinite immensities of blueness. Quite suddenly after a moment of quietness there, earth and sky and windblown grass and the child in the midst of them came alive together with a pulsing light of consciousness. There was a wild foxglove at the child's feet and a bee dozing about it, and to this day [1931] I can recall the swift inclusive awareness of each for the whole — I in them and they in me and all of us enclosed in a warm lucent bubble of livingness.

See Mary Austin, *Experiences Facing Death* (London: Rider, 1931), pp. 24–25.
61. See Rae G. Ballard, "Mary Austin's *Earth Horizon:* The Imperfect Circle," unpublished dissertation, The Claremont Graduate School, 1977, for an analysis of Austin's preoccupation with pattern.
62. Lawrence Evers, "Mary Austin and the Spirit of the Land," in Mary Austin, *The Land of Journeys' Ending* (Tucson: University of Arizona Press, 1983), p. xviii.
63. Letter to D. T. MacDougal, 1922, quoted in Augusta Fink, *I-Mary* (Tucson: University of Arizona Press, 1983), p. 202.
64. On the influence of the Indians, see Mary Austin, *The American Rhythm* (New York: Harcourt, Brace, 1923), pp. 27–28, 39, and *Earth Horizon,* p. 289. The aid given by Lummis is covered in Fink, *I-Mary,* pp. 96–112.
65. Austin, *The Land of Little Rain* (Albuquerque: University of New Mexico Press, 1974), p. 11. Originally published by Houghton Mifflin, 1903.

66. Ibid., p. 25.
67. Austin, *The Land of Journeys' Ending*, pp. xxvii, 441–442.
68. Ibid., p. 40.

6. *Modern Developments*

1. John Hay, *In Defense of Nature* (Boston: Little, Brown, 1969), p. 120.
2. Hay, *The Undiscovered Country* (New York: Norton, 1981), p. 15.
3. Aldo Leopold, *A Sand County Almanac* (New York: Oxford University Press, 1949), p. 130.
4. Susan L. Flader, *Thinking Like a Mountain: Aldo Leopold and the Evolution of an Ecological Attitude Toward Deer, Wolves, and Forests* (Columbia: University of Missouri Press, 1974), pp. 60–61, 79–80.
5. Ibid., p. 153.
6. Leopold, *A Sand County Almanac*, pp. 224–225.
7. Joseph Wood Krutch, *The Modern Temper* (New York: Harcourt, Brace, 1929), p. 249.
8. Ibid.
9. Krutch, *The Voice of the Desert* (New York: William Sloane, 1954), p. 218.
10. Krutch, "If You Don't Mind My Saying So," *The American Scholar* 39 (Spring, 1970), p. 204.
11. Paul Brooks, *Speaking for Nature*, p. 281.
12. Rachel Carson, *Silent Spring* (Boston: Houghton Mifflin, 1962), p. 56.
13. Ibid., p. 162.
14. Henry Beston, *The Outermost House* (New York: Ballantine, 1971), p. 8. Originally published by Doubleday, 1928.
15. Ibid., p. 19.
16. Ibid., p. 169.
17. Ibid., p. 174.
18. Edward Abbey, *Desert Solitaire* (New York: McGraw-Hill, 1968), p. 135.
19. Ibid., p. xiii.
20. Ibid., p. xiv.
21. Ibid., p. 51.
22. Jan Wojcik, "The American Wisdom Literature of Farming," in *Agriculture and Human Values* 1 (Fall, 1984), p. 30.
23. Liberty Hyde Bailey, *The Country-Life Movement* (New York: Macmillan, 1911), p. 20.
24. Bailey, *The Holy Earth* (New York: Christian Rural Fellowship, 1943), pp. 21, 23. Originally published by Macmillan, 1915.
25. Loren C. Owings, *Environmental Values, 1860–1972: A Guide to Information Sources* (Detroit: Gale, 1976), p. 243.
26. Wendell Berry, *The Long-Legged House* (New York: Harcourt, Brace & World, 1969), p. 149.
27. Berry, *A Continuous Harmony* (New York: Harcourt Brace Jovanovich, 1972), p. 45.

28. Berry, *The Unsettling of America* (New York: Avon, 1978), p. 21. Originally published by Sierra Club, 1977.

29. Berry, *The Gift of Good Land* (Berkeley: North Point, 1981), p. 210.

30. Edward Hoagland, *Notes from the Century Before: A Journal from British Columbia* (New York: Random House, 1969), p. 13.

31. Ibid., pp. 40–41.

32. Ibid., p. 205.

33. Ibid., p. 271.

34. Ibid., p. 272.

35. Barry Lopez, *Arctic Dreams* (New York: Scribner's, 1986), p. xxiv.

36. Lopez, in "Barry Lopez," *Antaeus* 57 (Autumn, 1986), p. 297.

Index